United States Strategic Bombers 1945-2012

Edited by
Stuart Slade

Dedication

*This book is respectfully dedicated to the memory of
General Curtis Emerson LeMay*

Acknowledgements

This book draws heavily on the archives of the United States Air Force, which produced the now-declassified Standard Aircraft Characteristics sheet that provides the source for most of the content. These documents have been electronically cleaned to remove the effects of their age, including dirt and other stains plus pencil notations made over the years, but are otherwise unchanged. The efforts of Wally Abdel-Wahab and Melanie Bodetti, the librarians at Defense Lion Publications, were also a key factor in the production of this book. Ms. Abdel-Wahab and Ms. Bodetti maintain a filing system that includes articles published in more than 200 magazines that cover almost every defense-related subject imaginable. Finally, we would also like to acknowledge the contributions made by Donette Dolzall and the Copyedit team, who turned a rough-and-ready manuscript into a polished professional product.

Copyright Notice

Copyright © 2012 Defense Lion Publications, 22 Commerce Road, Newtown, Connecticut 06470. ISBN 978-0-578-10525-3. This compilation may not be reproduced or transmitted in any form or by any means, electronic or mechanical including photocopying, recording or by any information and retrieval system without permission in writing from the publisher

Contents

Introduction	**5**
Chapter One: Boeing B-29 Superfortress	**7**
Characteristics Summary B-29	9
Standard Aircraft Characteristics B-29	11
Standard Aircraft Characteristics B-29A	17
Standard Aircraft Characteristics B-29B	23
Chapter Two: Consolidated B-36 Peacemaker	**29**
Characteristics Summary B-36A	33
Standard Aircraft Characteristics B-36A	35
Characteristics Summary B-36B	41
Standard Aircraft Characteristics B-36B	43
Characteristics Summary B-36D	51
Standard Aircraft Characteristics B-36D	53
Characteristics Summary B-36D(III) Featherweight	63
Standard Aircraft Characteristics B-36D(III) Featherweight	65
Standard Aircraft Characteristics B-36F/H	71
Standard Aircraft Characteristics B-36F/H Featherweight	78
Characteristics Summary B-36J	83
Standard Aircraft Characteristics B-36J	85
Characteristics Summary B-36J(III) Featherweight	91
Standard Aircraft Characteristics B-36J(III) Featherweight	93
Chapter Three: Boeing B-47 Stratojet	**101**
Characteristics Summary B-47A	103
Standard Aircraft Characteristics B-47A	105
Characteristics Summary B-47B	111
Standard Aircraft Characteristics B-47B	113
Characteristics Summary B-47E(II)	119
Standard Aircraft Characteristics B-47E(II)	121
Characteristics Summary B-47E(IV)	128
Standard Aircraft Characteristics B-47E(IV)	130
Chapter Four: Boeing B-50 Superfortress	**137**
Characteristics Summary B-50A	139
Standard Aircraft Characteristics B-50A	141
Characteristics Summary B-50B	148
Characteristics Summary B-50D	150
Standard Aircraft Characteristics B-50D	152
Chapter Five: Boeing B-52 Stratofortress	**159**
Characteristics Summary XB-52	163
Standard Aircraft Characteristics XB-52	165
Characteristics Summary RB-52B	171
Standard Aircraft Characteristics B-52B	173
Characteristics Summary RB-52C	179
Standard Aircraft Characteristics RB-52C	181
Characteristics Summary B-52D	188
Standard Aircraft Characteristics B-52D	190
Characteristics Summary B-52E	197
Standard Aircraft Characteristics B-52E	200
Characteristics Summary B-52F	207
Standard Aircraft Characteristics B-52F	210
Characteristics Summary B-52G	217
Standard Aircraft Characteristics B-52G	220
Standard Aircraft Characteristics B-52H	228
Chapter Six: Convair B-58 Hustler	**237**
Characteristics Summary B-58A	239
Standard Aircraft Characteristics B-58A	241
Chapter Seven: North American XB-70 Valkyrie	**251**
Characteristics Summary B-70B	255
Standard Aircraft Characteristics B-70B	257
Chapter Eight: General Dynamics FB-111A Aardvark	**263**
Characteristics Summary FB-111A	265
Standard Aircraft Characteristics FB-111A	267
Chapter Nine: Boeing B-1 Lancer	**277**
Characteristics Summary B-1A	280
Standard Aircraft Characteristics B-1A	283
Chapter Ten: Northrop B-2 Spirit	**291**
Characteristics Summary YB-35B	293
Standard Aircraft Characteristics YB-35B	295
Characteristics Summary B-49	301
Standard Aircraft Characteristics B-49	303
Chapter Eleven: Long Range Strike-B	**309**
In Conclusion	**313**
Appendix One: Cost Breakdown	**317**
Appendix Two: Sources	**319**

Introduction

Strategic bombing owed its birth to the deadlock on the Western Front in World War One. Faced with an apparently immovable line of fortifications that stretched from Switzerland to the North Sea, nations looked for a way by which those fortifications could be bypassed. There were only three options: go around them, go under them, or go over them. Going around them meant an amphibious invasion of a hostile coastline. That was tried at the Dardanelles, but that experience showed the available technology was not up to the task. In addition, it would not solve the basic problem of the Western Front. Railways could bring defending troops to the scene of a battle faster than the attacker could advance during that battle. That basic fact condemned any land battle to deadlock. Going under the defenses by digging tunnels worked, but it was painfully slow and the technique could never be more than a tactical tool. That left going over the defenses, a possibility raised by the pre-war development of aircraft.

Dirigible airships and airplanes proved effective at bombing and they offered the ability to strike directly at the enemy's homeland, where his munitions of war were made. As the significance of air power began to grow, a serious doctrine of air warfare began to emerge. Commanders started to distinguish between "strategic" air operations against targets deep in enemy territory that were directed against vital war-making industries, and civilian morale and "tactical" operations directed against ground forces and their ability to move quickly to the scene of a battle.

Developing the Doctrine

As a result of the important role air power had played in the First World War, the formulation of theories of strategic bombing gave new impetus to the arguments for an independent air force. Strategic, or long-range, bombardment was intended to destroy an enemy nation's industry and thus its war-making potential, and only an independent air force would have the free hand necessary to go about that task. A doctrine emerged that stressed the precision bombing of industrial targets by heavily armed, long-range bombers. Today, the concept of bombing industrial targets deep in enemy territory with the resulting civilian casualties is often viewed with abhorrence and sometimes even described as a war crime. Yet, at the time when the concept of strategic bombing was evolving, it was regarded as being very much the humane alternative to the prospect of another war in the trenches. World War One had lasted five years and been responsible for the deaths of around 10 million military personnel and around seven million civilians. One small London family lost five of its eight sons in the trenches and that kind of tragedy was by no means unusual. Surely, if the supply of munitions could be cut off by the destruction of the factories that produced them, the war would end before those terrible statistics could be repeated.

From the relatively tiny strategic air force and ill-developed doctrine possessed by the United States after the First World War would grow the world's most powerful air force. By 1939, the Air Corps was still relatively small with 20,000 men and 2,400 aircraft. By 1944, it had grown to a nearly autonomous Army Air Force with almost 2.4 million personnel and 80,000 aircraft. In the end, 12 air forces went overseas and served against the Germans and Japanese. The doctrine evolved as experience was gained and the aircraft were developed to execute the doctrine.

Yet, in the early days, the doctrine failed. The available aircraft could not drop their bomb loads accurately enough to hit individual factories, nor could they carry the loads needed to destroy those targets. To make matters worse, anti-bomber defenses proved able to inflict severe casualties on the attacking bomber formations. The British Royal Air Force Bomber Command recognized these problems and switched to night attacks that were intended to burn entire cities down, taking the factories with them. The British bomber crews got to be very good at doing just that.

Rise of Strategic Air Power

The United States stuck with its doctrine of precision bombing in daylight. The first element in the development of the U.S. strategic bomber force was a new bomber, the B-29. This was the first true strategic bomber that had the range and carrying capacity to strike directly at an enemy heartland over trans-oceanic ranges. Yet, even this new bomber could not overcome the basic problems of accuracy. In addition, analysis of bombing results was leading to another unpleasant realization. There was no such thing as a key industry whose destruction would mean the end to munitions production and thus the destruction of war-making capacity. As munitions plants were destroyed, non-military production capacity would be stripped to keep war production running. If munitions production was to be stopped, industry in general had to be destroyed. All of it. The destruction of war-making potential essentially meant the destruction of everything else as well.

The second factor in the emergence of the U.S. strategic bomber force was a man, Gen. Curtis E. LeMay. By 1945, he had gained a reputation as a consummate professional of unmatched analytical skills and supreme command ability. The key to his success was an ability to take an immensely complicated problem and split it down into its components, then finding simple solutions to those component difficulties. This was matched by a work ethic that impelled him to master the technical intricacies of the problems his command faced. He dealt with the initial accuracy and mission accomplishment problems of his B-29s the same way the Royal Air Force had done. He sent his aircraft in at night, loaded down with incendiaries. One by one, Japanese cities vanished in a holocaust of fire.

The third element of the growing power of strategic bombing was a weapon, the atomic bomb. In the early days, it had been assumed that a few 250-pound bombs would irreparably destroy a factory. This had proved wildly optimistic. By 1945 it was taking fleets of several hundred bombers carrying as much as 10 tons of bombs each to achieve this result. The sheer power of the atomic bomb finally meant that a single aircraft could destroy an industrial target with a single blow. This was demonstrated at Hiroshima and Nagasaki, with the lesson being reluctantly absorbed by the Japanese. The Japanese High Command had been quite happy to accept the possibility that millions of their own citizens would be killed if the losses meant sufficient American casualties to force a negotiated peace. The atomic bomb demonstrated that strategic bombing would allow the Americans to destroy Japan at minimal cost to themselves. The prospect of total destruction finally ensured that Japan surrendered and that a final invasion was unnecessary. This development saved literally millions of lives.

After the Second World War, the United States came to rely upon a strategy of deterrence using nuclear weapons. Accordingly, the U.S. gave highest priority to its long-range atomic bombing force now known as Strategic Air Command. Initially, this was equipped with B-29s that lacked the range needed for truly intercontinental bombing missions. This led to the development of air refueling as a method of extending the reach of the aircraft. Yet, the financial stringencies of the late 1940s meant that the atomic striking force was small and the number of nuclear weapons at its disposal was even smaller. As the force level slowly expanded, B-29s that had been placed in storage after the surrender of Japan were recovered and returned to service. A new and developed version of the B-29, known as the B-50, was designed as their replacement. These were supplemented by an immense new aircraft, the B-36, that offered truly intercontinental range. The B-36 had another secret, one that was carefully concealed for many years. Its huge wings made it very lightly loaded and it could fly at altitudes far above those achievable by defending fighters.

Strategic Air Power Dominant

Under the guidance of General LeMay, Strategic Air Command became the centerpiece of Air Force planning. Rising to a level of peacetime operational readiness unprecedented in American history, SAC and its strategic bombers became the ultimate expression of American firepower. This did not come easily. After World War Two, a combination of rapid demobilization and severe financial problems meant that the U.S. strategic bomber fleet declined very sharply in both numbers and operational readiness. Despite its high priority, very few of the remaining SAC units were truly ready for combat. Morale in the force was low and training standards were poor. Base and aircraft security standards were minimal. Upon inspecting a SAC hangar full of U.S. nuclear strategic bombers, General LeMay found a single Air Force sentry on duty, armed only with a ham sandwich.

The extent to which standards in SAC had declined was starkly revealed with the infamous 1948 Dayton Raid. Intended as a means of assessing the true operational readiness of SAC, General LeMay ordered a maximum-effort "attack" on Dayton, Ohio. He was shocked to see that not one bomber got its payload within two miles of the aiming points and the average error was up to five miles. In many cases, this would have meant that even atomic bombs would not have damaged their targets. Obviously, action was needed and needed very quickly.

LeMay reformed SAC, root and branch. His basic assumption was that a nuclear war would start with a massive attack on the United States and that there would be no time for the kind of prolonged buildup that had been available in World War Two. The United States would go to war with what it had and the force that it had would have to be ready for war at any and all times. He subjected his men to vigorous training and long hours of hard work, but fought for additional pay and better housing to make their demanding lives more tolerable. Before his arrival, much of the available training time had been wasted on "cross-training." This was an effort to ensure that all crew members on a bomber could function in any of the crew assignments. What it actually meant was that nobody performed their primary duty to an acceptable standard while their ability at secondary duties was negligible. To the great relief of all, General LeMay abolished cross-training and concentrated on promoting excellence at primary duties.

Above all, LeMay created and cultivated the notion that SAC and its strategic bombers were *the* elite force in the United States. Perfection was the only acceptable standard. Top-performing crews were given spot promotions, it being clearly understood that the promotions would be removed if they ceased to be top-performing. Those who did not meet the required standard were ruthlessly discarded. The rest of the Air Force quickly dubbed the term "SAC-rificed" to refer to indoctrinating personnel with the need for this ruthless pursuit of perfect performance goals.

The upgrades in training and operational standards were matched by new aircraft. The B-29 and B-50 (now classed as medium bombers) were replaced by jet-engined B-47s, while the B-36 was replaced by the B-52. The old idea of bombers shooting their way through the defenses that surrounded their targets was abandoned and stress was placed on the bombers flying higher and faster to evade the defenses. Electronic warfare antennas replaced gun turrets; electronics operators replaced gunners. The technical progression continued, changing the appearance and operational characteristics of the strategic bombers, but their function remained the same – to engage the enemy, kill him and break his things.

The bomber force went supersonic with the lovely, lethal but ultimately doomed B-58 Hustler. By this time, the future viability of the "high and fast" means of penetration was being challenged. It was suggested that future generations of anti-aircraft missiles would be able to bring down manned bombers no matter how high and fast they flew. The response was to adopt new techniques that involved flying the bombers at treetop height, effectively flying under the defenses rather than over them. Finally, the ultimate expression of the strategic bomber was realized with the B-70 Valkyrie, a bomber that would have combined the ability to cruise at Mach 3 with truly intercontinental range.

Eclipse of the Strategic Bomber

By the time the first prototypes of the B-70 were flying, proponents of ballistic missiles had succeeded in convincing the U.S. Department of Defense that they had rendered manned bombers obsolete and, in what many believe was the worst strategic blunder made by the United States in the 1960s, the B-70 Valkyrie was canceled. Ironically, the projected developments in surface-to-air missile technology that were used to discredit the Valkyrie have never been realized. Yet, despite this cancellation, the strategic bombers continued to soldier on, with the B-52s proving their value in conflict after conflict.

Attempts to introduce a new strategic bomber continued throughout the 1970s and beyond. The primarily tactical F-111 was modified with extended wings, increased range, and the ability to handle stand-off missiles, as the FB-111 and this aircraft replaced the B-58 in the medium bomber role. A new heavy bomber was developed as the B-1A, only to be canceled by President Jimmy Carter, then revived as the B-1B by President Ronald Reagan. An entirely new concept of heavy bomber was then developed as the B-2 Spirit. This relied for its protection on its ability to evade radar detection. Sheer cost meant that only a handful of B-2s were built, and the number of bombers in the U.S. inventory has continued to decline as attrition and old age take its toll. Yet, in the early years of the 21st century, the importance and value of the strategic bombers were such that another new bomber development program was launched. The tale of the strategic bomber is not yet over.

Boeing B-29 Superfortress

Boeing B-29 takeoff.
Source: U.S. Air Force

When The Boeing Company produced the B-29 Superfortress during the Second World War, it brought about a revolution in basic bomber design. The B-29 was the first production aircraft to make extensive use of remotely controlled defensive armament that used a centralized fire control system. It was the first production bomber with fully pressurized crew compartments. Above all, the B-29 was the aircraft that dropped atomic bombs on Hiroshima and Nagasaki and thus brought the war in the Pacific to an abrupt end.

The B-29 started its life as a further development of the XB-15 of 1934. The XB-15 was a large, four-engined mid-wing cantilever monoplane. The structure was generally similar to that of earlier Boeing monoplanes with the exception that the wing from the main spar aft was covered with fabric instead of metal. The XB-15 proved to be seriously underpowered. Because of its low performance as compared to later aircraft, the XB-15 was never ordered into production, and the prototype was the only example to be built.

The earliest designs of the bomber that became the B-29 differed from the XB-15 primarily in the relocation of the wing from a low- to a high-mounted position on the fuselage and by the installation of a nosewheel undercarriage. The degree to which the XB-15 had been seriously underpowered was addressed by the adoption of the 2,000-horsepower Wright R-3350 Duplex Cyclone 18-cylinder air-cooled radials. These engines did not yet exist, and their adoption for the new design set the precedent for the incorporation of advanced aviation technology that was to distinguish the B-29 program.

Design Evolution

By March 1939, the design had evolved considerably. The wingspan was extended to 120 feet in order to provide enough fuel to reach a range of 4,500 miles. A twin fin-and-rudder was to have been used to facilitate the installation of tail armament. Gross weight was up to 66,000 pounds and maximum bomb load was 7,830 pounds. This aircraft, known to Boeing as the Model 334, bore a startling relationship to a later German project, the Messerschmitt 264, and there have been suggestions that the German design was based on stolen Boeing documentation. This is very unlikely and the similarity between the two designs appears coincidental. Boeing built a mockup of the Model 334 with its own funds in December 1939. It envisioned wing loadings as high as 64 pounds per square foot, a 12-man crew, and the ability to carry 2,000 pounds of bombs over distances in excess of 5,000 miles.

The outbreak of war in Europe and the Japanese military campaign in China led Gen. Henry H. (Hap) Arnold, the acting head of the Army Air Corps, to establish a special committee to make recommendations for the long-term needs of the Army Air Corps. As result, the Army issued a requirement for a long-range bomber that called for a speed of 400 mph, a range of 5,333 miles, and a bomb load of 2,000 pounds delivered at the halfway point at that range. The official specification was revised in April to incorporate the lessons learned in early European wartime experience, and now included more defensive armament, armor, and self-sealing tanks.

The Boeing Company responded with the Model 345, envisioned as a pressurized aircraft powered by four Wright R-3350 engines and capable of carrying a ton of bombs over the stipulated 5,333 miles at a cruising speed of 290 mph. The maximum bomb load was to be 16,100 pounds. The maximum speed was estimated to be 382 mph at 25,000 feet. The weight was to be 97,700 pounds. A total of 14 service-test examples were ordered under the designation YB-29. This was followed by a production order for 250 B-29s. After Pearl Harbor, a further 250 B-29s were ordered, with a third order for a thousand more B-29s following in early 1942.

Into Production

The first XB-29 flew on September 21, 1942 at Boeing Field, Boeing's chief test pilot, Edmund T. "Eddie" Allen, being at the controls. Although the performance and handling qualities of the B-29 were found to be excellent, the early R-3350 engines were subject to chronic overheating and caught fire upon the slightest provocation. This resulted in the crash of the second prototype on February 18,

1943, when an inextinguishable engine fire burned through the main wing spars and caused the wing to buckle. The XB-29 crashed into the Frye Meat Packing Plant factory, killing Eddie Allen and everyone else aboard, plus 19 workers on the ground. Fortunately, most Frye employees were on their lunch break when the factory burst into flames.

Despite this crash, the first of 14 YB-29s left the production line at Wichita on April 15, 1943, flying for the first time on June 26, 1943. The aircraft were delivered to the first B-29 combat unit, the 58th (Very Heavy) Bombardment Wing. They were followed by the first production B-29s, which began to roll off the production lines at Boeing-Wichita in September 1943. The first B-29s appeared from the production lines at Bell-Atlanta (Marietta) in February 1944, while the first Martin-Omaha B-29 was delivered in mid-1944. Eventually, 2,513 B-29s were built – 1,620 by Boeing at its Wichita, Kansas, plant; 536 by Martin at its Omaha, Nebraska, plant; and 357 by Bell at its plant in Marietta, Georgia. The last B-29 was delivered by Boeing-Wichita in October 1945. Bell-Atlanta delivered its last B-29 in January 1945, when the plant shifted production to the B-29B. The last B-29 was delivered by Martin-Omaha in September 1945.

The B-29 was followed by the B-29A, built by Boeing at the Renton plant. The B-29A was essentially the same as the B-29, differing primarily in having a very short stub wing center-section that did not project beyond the fuselage sides. Each pair of engine nacelles was fitted to a separate short section of wing. The outer wing panels were attached at the same point on B-29s and B-29As alike. Contrary to many reports, this change did not give the B-29A an additional foot of wingspan as compared to the B-29. A total of 1,119 B-29As were built, with block numbers reaching -75. The 20mm cannon was removed from the tail turret beginning with production Block 20, and a pair of 0.50-inch guns was added to the top forward turret to provide additional protection against fighter attacks coming from the front.

The B-29B was a lightened version of the Superfortress built exclusively by Bell-Atlanta. It had all but the tail defensive armament removed, since experience had shown that by that stage in the war, the only significant enemy fighter attacks were coming from the rear. The tail gun was aimed and fired automatically by the new APG-15B radar fire control system that detected the approaching enemy plane and made all the necessary calculations. A total of 311 B-29Bs were built between January and September 1945.

All variants of the B-29 went through a number of changes during its war service. The forward dorsal turret armament was increased to four 0.50-inch machine guns to provide additional protection from frontal attacks. However, the 20mm cannon was ineffective and deleted from the tail position. In the initial B-29 models, fuel was carried in 14 outer-wing, 8 inner-wing, and 4 bomb bay tanks, giving a maximum capacity of 8,168 U.S. gallons. An early modification added four tanks in the wing center-section, bringing total fuel capacity to 9,438 U.S. gallons.

A Nuclear Mission

The most significant B-29 modification program during the wartime years was designated "Silverplate." This allowed the B-29 to carry nuclear weapons. It should be noted that "Silverplate" is often mistakenly used to describe all nuclear-capable B-29s. But the program undertaken in the post-war era to modify B-29s for nuclear missions was designated "Saddletree" and was a rather different exercise.

All the Silverplate aircraft were assigned to the 509th Composite Group, the unit that dropped atomic bombs on Hiroshima and Nagasaki. For several years post-war, the 509th was the only nuclear-capable unit in the United States Air Force. Limitations on funding meant that its Silverplate B-29s were produced in small batches, with numerous detail differences among the aircraft. The Silverplate modifications included replacing the two 12-foot bomb bays and the fuselage section between them and installing a single 33-foot bomb bay. New bomb suspensions and bracing were attached for both the Mk 1 gun-configuration nuclear device and the Model 1561 implosion device. Separate twin-release mechanisms were mounted in each bay, using modified glider tow-cable attach-and-release mechanisms. Motion picture camera mounts were installed in the rear bay to document the test drops. The aircraft also received Curtiss-Electric reversible-pitch propellers, and snap-action pneumatic actuators for the bomb bay doors. Weight reduction was accomplished by removal of all gun turrets and armor plating. A total of 65 Silverplate B-29s were produced, with the survivors being passed from the 509th Composite group to the 97th Bomb Wing when the former converted to the B-50D in the summer of 1949.

An additional 80 B-29s were converted to nuclear-capable configuration under the Saddletree program authorized by Air Materiel Command project DOM-595 in January 1948. This was part of a larger effort ordered by the U.S. Joint Chiefs of Staff for the modification of 225 B-29, B-50, and B-36 bombers to carry nuclear weapons. The project was intended to be completed by December 1948 and was known by the code name "Gem." Gem also included "winterization" of 36 B-29s to permit deployment to Arctic bases, and the modification of 36 others to give them air refueling capability

Other Variants

Because a large number of B-29s were available post-war, the type was converted to a variety of new roles. A total of 117 were converted into reconnaissance aircraft, initially under the designation F-13 but redesignated the RB-29 in 1947. A small number of these aircraft were equipped as electronic intelligence aircraft and used to monitor Soviet radar emissions. Several of these aircraft were shot down by Soviet air defenses. Others were converted to WB-29 weather reconnaissance aircraft that had the role of monitoring Soviet airspace for evidence of Russian nuclear tests.

The most important role of the modified B-29s was serving as tankers. Air-to-air refueling was considered a vital capability if the B-29s (now considered medium bombers) were to reach targets in Russia. After experimenting with the British-developed drogue system and the Boeing Flying Boom, the Air Force settled on the latter. The designation KB-29P was assigned to 116 B-29s that were converted to boom refueling tankers by Boeing in 1950-51. The first of these was delivered to SAC in March 1950. These aircraft were the last B-29s in USAF squadron service, being finally retired in early 1960.

Characteristics Summary

BOMBER · B-29

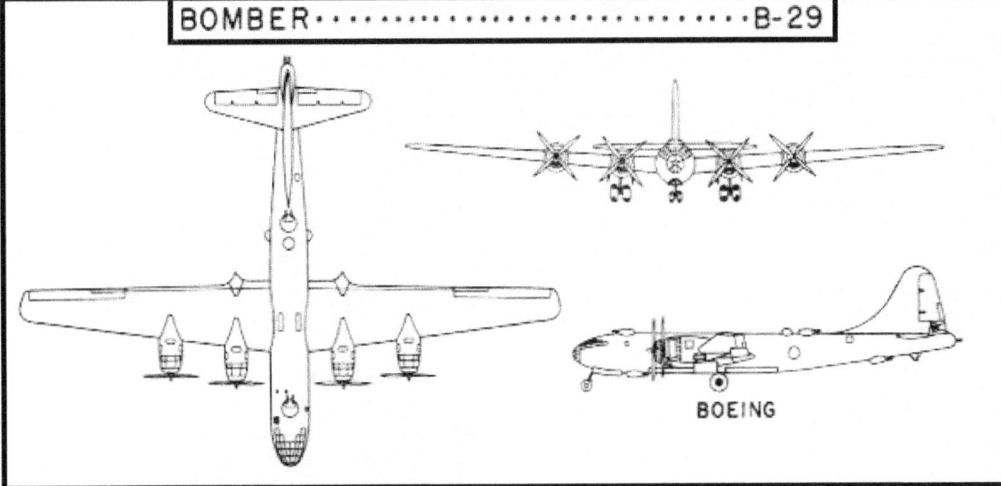

BOEING

Wing area .... 1720 sq ft   Length .... 99.0 ft

Span .... 141.2 ft   Height .... 27.8 ft

AVAILABILITY			PROCUREMENT			
Number available			Number to be delivered in fiscal years			
ACTIVE	RESERVE	TOTAL				

STATUS

SERVICE

1. First flight: September 1942 (XB-29)

2. First acceptance: September 1943

3. Production completed: June 1946

POWER PLANT

(4) R-3350-57, -57A Wright

	BHP	RPM	CRIT. ALT.
T.O:	2200	2800	
Max :	*2500	2800	31,400
Nor:	2000	2400	35,600

*Permitted by T.O. 01-20 EJA-92 dated 15 June 1945.

FEATURES

Crew: 11
Cabin Pressurization
Cabin Heating
Electronic Navigation
  Equipment
Bombing Radar
Max Fuel Capacity: 9548 gal

ARMAMENT

Turrets:	5
Guns:	(12) .50 cal
Ammunition:	6000 rds
Max Bomb Load:	(40) 500 lb
Max Bomb Size:	4000 lb

Characteristics Summary Basic Mission — B-29

```
|← ——————— 25,000 FT. ——————— 
|   ——————— 10,000 FT. ———————————
|← ——— COMBAT RADIUS = 1820 Nautical Miles ———→|
```

PERFORMANCE

COMBAT RADIUS	COMBAT RANGE	COMBAT SPEED
1820 naut. mi with 10,000 lb payload at 214 knots avg. in 17.4 hours.	**3390** naut. mi with 10,000 lb payload at 199 knots avg. in 17.2 hours.	**331** knots at 25,000 ft alt, max power
		MAXIMUM SPEED
		353 knots at 31,400 ft alt, max power

CLIMB	CEILING	TAKE-OFF
500 fpm sea level, take-off weight normal power	**23,800** ft 100 fpm, take-off weight normal power	ground run 4130 ft | ——— ft no assist | assisted
1730 fpm sea level, combat weight maximum power	**35,000** ft 500 fpm, combat weight maximum power	over 50 ft height 6100 ft | ——— ft no assist | assisted

LOAD	WEIGHTS	STALLING SPEED

Bombs: 10,000 lb
Ammunition:
6000 rds/.50 cal
 	
Fuel: 7866 gal
  protected 100 %
  droppable 11 %
  external 0 %
	Empty..... 71,500 lb
	Combat... 100,000 lb
	Take-off 140,000 lb
	limited by performance
		103 knots
		flaps down, take-off weight

		TIME TO CLIMB ———

NOTES

1. PERFORMANCE BASIS: NACA standard conditions no wind, single airplane;
   (a) Fuel consumption, increased 5 %, based on flight test data
   (b) Pilot's Handbook dated 13 January 1948

2. REVISION BASIS: Correct power plant data.

Standard Aircraft Characteristics

B-29 SUPERFORTRESS
Boeing

FOUR R-3350-79 or -81
WRIGHT

BY AUTHORITY OF
COMMANDING GENERAL
AIR MATERIEL COMMAND
U.S. AIR FORCE

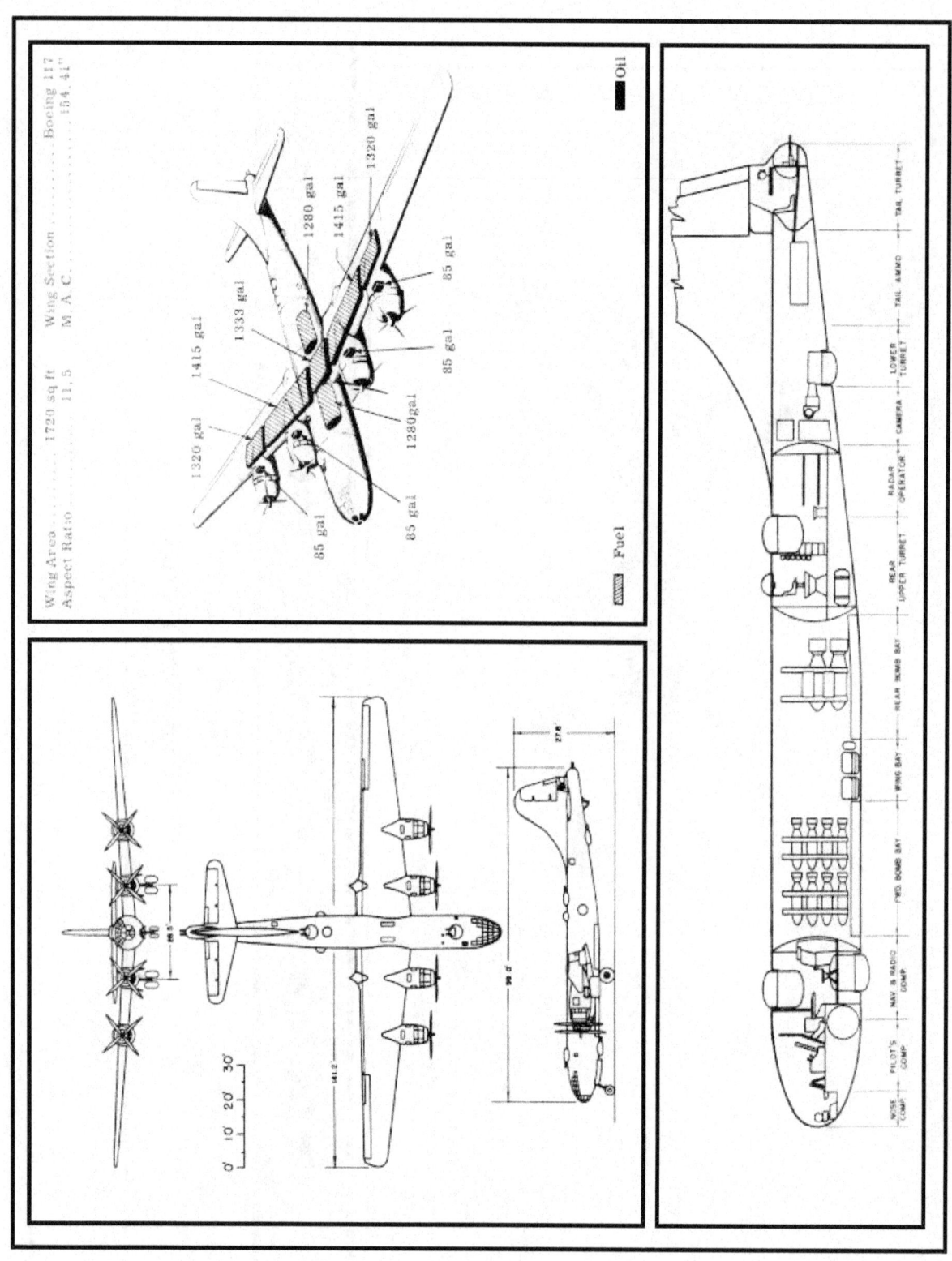

WEIGHTS

Loading	Lb	L.F.
Empty	74,500(A)	
Basic	74,050(A)	
Design	120,000	2.67
Combat	101,250	3.10
Max T.O.	†140,000	2.28
Max Land	†135,000	2.35

(A) Actual
° For Basic Mission
† Limited by performance
‡ Limited by strength

FUEL

Location	No. Tanks	Gal
Wg, outbd°	2	2640
Wg, inbd°	2	2830
Wg, ctr°	1	1333
Bomb bay	2	2560
	Total	9363
Spec.		MIL-F-5572
Grade		100/130

OIL

Cap. (gal)	340
Spec.	AN-0-8
Grade	S-7120-W-1100

ELECTRONICS

VHF Command	AN/ARC-3
Interphone	AN/AIC-2A
Liaison	AN/ARC-8
Radio Compass	AN/ARN-7
Marker Beacon	RC-193A
Homing Adapter	AN/ARR-1
Localizer	RC-103
Glide Path	AN/ARN-5A
Radio Altimeter	SCR-718C
Interrogator	SCR-729
Radar	AN/APQ-7 or AN/APQ-23A
Loran	AN/APN-9 or AN/APN-4
IFF	SCR-695
Raven	RCM

Mission and Description

The primary mission of the B-29 is the destruction of energy material and installations by aerial bombardment. It is provided with pressurized crew compartments and adequate heating and oxygen facilities for long range missions. Crew of 11 consists of pilots, co-pilot, flight engineer, navigator, radio operator, radar operator, bombardier and four gunners.

Direct current electrical power is supplied by six engine driven generators and one auxiliary power plant.

Early models are equipped with transfer type fuel systems while later models use the manifold type system.

Armament provided consists of five (5) turrets controlled by a central fire control system.

In later aircraft a formation stick was added to the C-1 auto-pilot to facilitate formation flying.

Development

Design initiated:	June 1940
First flight:	(XB-29) September 1942
First acceptance:	September 1943
Production completed:	June 1946

GUNS

No.	Cal	Rds ea	Location
4	.50	500	Fus. upr, fwd
2	.50	500	Fus. upr, aft
2	.50	500	Fus. lwr, fwd
2	.50	500	Fus. lwr, aft
2	.50	500	Tail, tur

POWER PLANT

No. & Model	(4) R-3350-79 or -81
Mfr	Wright
Engine Spec No.	9E-28266.5
Sup.	(Dual Turbo) B-11 or B-31
Red Gear Ratio	0.35
Prop. Mfr	Hamilton Std
Blade Design No.	6521A-6
Prop. Type	Hydromatic
No. Blades	4
Prop. Dia	16'-7"

ENGINE RATINGS

	BHP - RPM - ALT
T.O:	2200 - 2800
Mil:	2250 - 2600 - 2500
Nor:	2000 - 2400 - 4000

BOMBS

No.	Size	Type
4	4000	G.P.
8	2000	G.P.
12	1600	A.P.
12	1000	G.P.
40	500	G.P.

Max Bomb Load .... 20,000 lb

DIMENSIONS

Wing	
Span	141.2'
Incidence	4°
Dihedral	4°29'23"
Sweepback (LE)	7°01'26"
Length	93.0'
Height	27.8'
Tread	28.5'
Prop. Grd Clearance	1.3'

Loading and Performance - Typical Mission

CONDITIONS		BASIC MISSION I	MAX. BOMBS MISSION II	HIGH ALT MISSION III	TRAINING MISSION IV	FERRY RANGE V
TAKE-OFF WEIGHT	(lb)	140,000	140,000	140,000	120,000	138,278
Fuel at 6.0 lb/gal	(lb)	47,196	39,396	47,196	38,880	56,178
Military load (Bombs)	(lb)	10,000	20,000	10,000	None	None
Wing loading	(lb/sq ft)	81.4	81.4	81.4	70.6	80.4
Stall speed (power off)	(kn)	103	103	103	96	102
Take-off ground run at SL	(ft)	5230	5230	5230	3425	5050
Take-off to clear 50 ft	(ft)	7825	7825	7825	5660	7530
Rate-of-climb at SL	(fpm)	500	500	500	795	520
Time: SL to 10,000 ft	(min)	23.5	23.5	23.5	14.0	22.5
Time: SL to 20,000 ft	(min)	61.5	61.5	61.5	31.3	58.0
Service ceiling (100 fpm)	(ft)	23,950	23,950	23,950	35,650	25,000
Service ceiling (one engine out)	(ft)	19,400	19,400	19,400	30,750	20,650
COMBAT RANGE	(n. mi)	3445	2627	3095	3213	4493
Avg cruising speed	(kn)	198	202	223	190	191
Cruising altitude	(ft)	10,000	10,000	20,000	10,000	10,000
Total mission time	(hr)	17.54	13.15	14.94	17.07	23.65
COMBAT RADIUS	(n. mi)	1843	1466	1603	1640	—
Avg cruising speed	(kn)	215	216	238	211	—
Cruising altitude (s)	(ft)	10,000 & 25,000	10,000 & 25,000	20,000 & 30,000	10,000 & 25,000	—
Total mission time	(hr)	17.37	13.80	13.73	15.78	
COMBAT WEIGHT	(lb)	101,250	96,500	98,900	98,810	84,518
Combat altitude	(ft)	25,000	25,000	30,000	25,000	10,000
Combat speed	(kn)	331	333	348	332	293
Combat climb	(fpm)	1265	1410	1180	1340	2045
Combat ceiling (500 fpm)	(ft)	36,200	37,200	36,650	36,650	39,800
Service ceiling (100 fpm)	(ft)	39,600	40,600	40,100	40,100	43,200
Service ceiling (one engine out)	(ft)	34,700	36,100	35,450	35,450	39,150
Max rate-of-climb at SL	(fpm)	1625	1760	1690	1690	2160
Max speed at 10,000 ft	(kn)	347	348	348	348	353
LANDING WEIGHT	(lb)	83,564	82,574	83,564	83,064	84,518
Ground roll at SL	(ft)	2230	2210	2230	2220	2255
Total from 50 ft	(ft)	2960	2930	2960	2950	2985

NOTES
① Take-off power
② Max power
③ Normal power
④ Take-off and landing distances are obtainable at sea level using normal techniques. For airport planning, distances should be increased by appropriate factors to determine runway requirements.
○5 Detailed descriptions of the RADIUS & RANGE missions are given on page 6.
○6 For Radius Mission if Radius is "s-down."

CONDITIONS:
(a) Performance Basis: Flight test
(b) In computing Radius and Range, specific fuel consumptions have been increased 5% to allow for variations of fuel flow in service aircraft.
(c) Performance is based on powers shown on page 6.

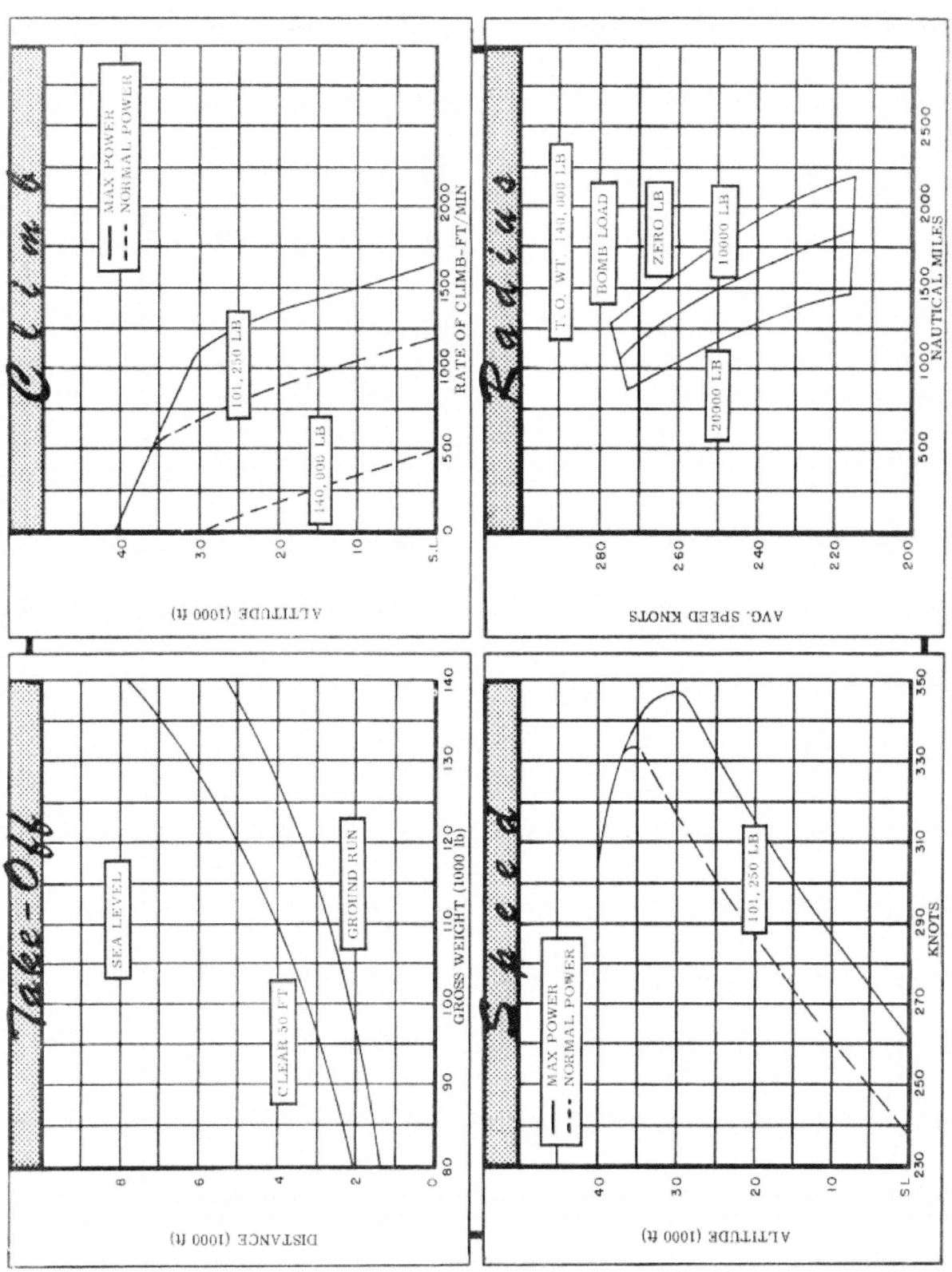

NOTES

FORMULA: RADIUS MISSIONS I, II & IV

Warm-up, take-off, climb on course to 10,000 ft at normal power, cruise at long range speeds to point where climb is made to arrive at 25,000 ft 30 minutes prior to bomb drop, cruise at long range speeds for 15 minutes, followed by 15 minutes normal power run into target, drop bombs and conduct 5 minutes normal power evasive action (no distance credit) and 10 minutes run out from target area at normal power, cruise back to base at long range speeds at 25,000 ft. Range free allowances include 10 minutes normal power at sea level for warm-up and take-off, 5 minutes normal power evasive action plus 5% of initial fuel for reserve.

FORMULA: RADIUS MISSION III

Same as I, II and IV except initial climb is to 20,000 ft and bombs are dropped at 30,000 ft.

FORMULA: RANGE MISSIONS I, II & IV

Warm-up, take-off, climb on course to 10,000 ft at normal power, cruise at long range speeds to point where climb is made to arrive at 25,000 ft 30 minutes prior to bomb drop, cruise at long range speeds for 30 minutes, to point where 90% of initial fuel has been used, drop bombs. Range free allowances include 10 minutes normal power at sea level for warm-up and take-off plus 10% of initial fuel for evasive action and landing reserve.

FORMULA: RANGE MISSION III

Same as Range Missions I, II and IV except initial climb is to 20,000 ft and bombs are dropped at 30,000 ft.

FORMULA: RANGE MISSION V

Warm-up, take-off, climb on course to 10,000 ft at normal power, cruise at long range speeds to point where 90% of initial fuel is used. Range free allowances include 10 minutes normal power at sea level for warm-up and take-off plus 10% of initial fuel for landing reserve.

GENERAL DATA:

(a) For detailed planning refer to Tech Order AN 01-20EJA-1.

(b) Engine ratings shown on page 3 are manufacturer's guaranteed ratings. Power values used for performance calculations are as follows:

	R-3350-79 or -81		
	BHP	RPM	CRIT ALT*
T.O:	2200	2800	
Max:	**2500	2800	31,400
Nor:	2000	2400	35,600

*With Turbo
**As established by AN 01-20EJ-92 dated 15 June 1945.

(c) The R-3350-79 and -81 are respectively the R-3350-57 and -57A engines modernized to increase engine strength and improve reliability.

(d) Bomb bay tanks are dropped when empty for all missions shown on page 4.

Standard Aircraft Characteristics

B-29A SUPERFORTRESS
Boeing

FOUR R-3350-57 or -57A
WRIGHT

BY AUTHORITY OF
COMMANDING GENERAL
AIR MATERIEL COMMAND
U.S. AIR FORCE

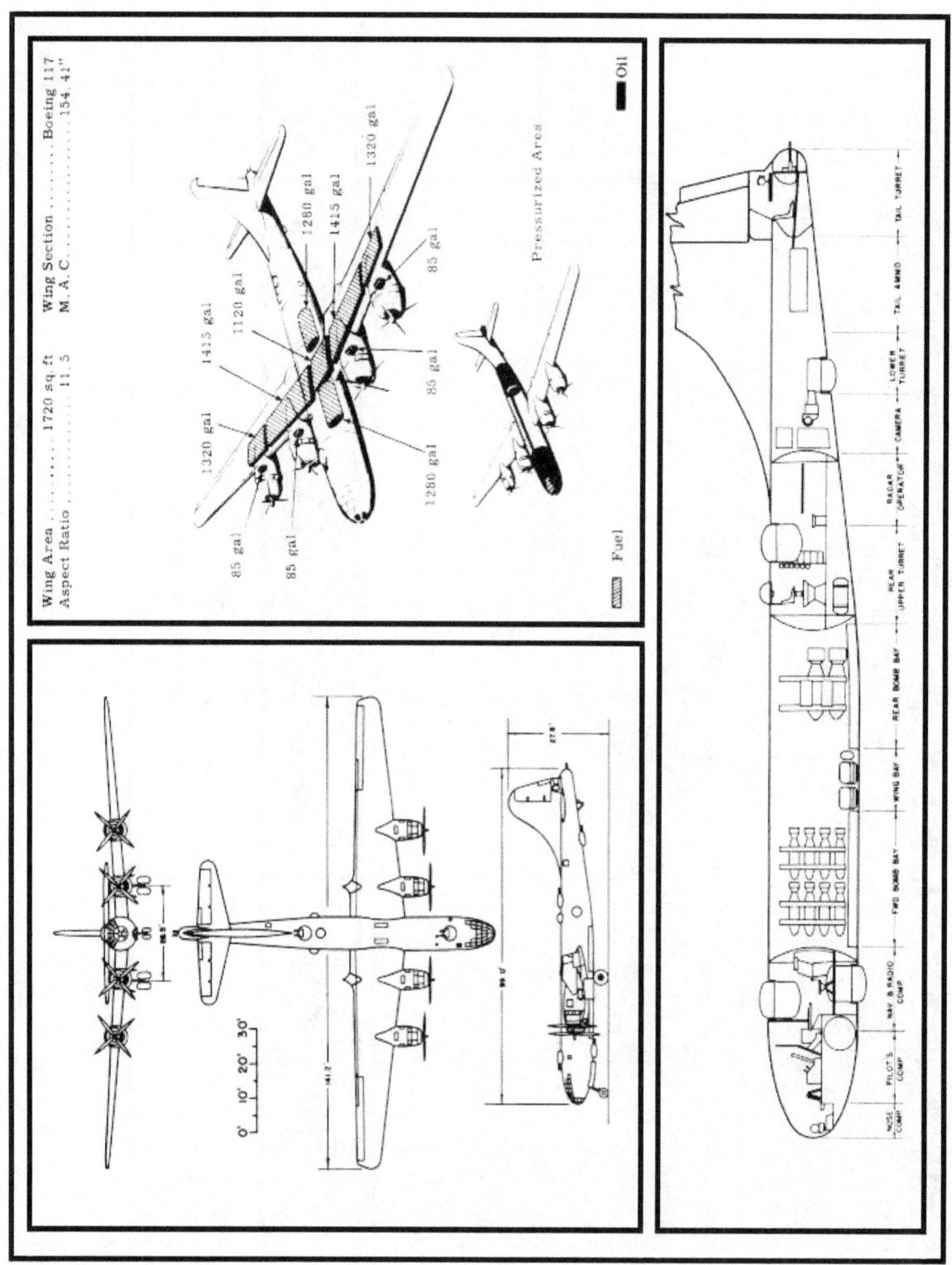

WEIGHTS

Loading	Lb.	
Empty	72,266(A)	2.67
Basic	74,560(A)	3.10
Design	120,000	2.28
Combat	101,472	2.35
Max T.O.	7140,000	
Max Land	9140,000	

(A) Actual
*For Basic Mission
† Limited by performance
‡ Limited by strength

FUEL

Location	No. Tanks	Cal
Wg. outbd*	2	2640
Wg. inbd*	2	2830
Wg. ctr*	1	1120
Bomb bay*	2	2560
	Total	9150

*s.s.

Grade 100/130

OIL

Cap. (gal) 340

Grade S-1120; W-1100

ELECTRONICS

VHF Command	AN/ARC-3
Interphone	AN/AIC-2A
Liaison	AN/ARC-8
Radio Compass	AN/ARN-7
Marker Beacon	RC-193A
Homing Adapter	AN/ARR-1
Localizer	RC-103
Glide Path	AN/ARN-5A
Radio Altimeter	SCR-718C
Interrogator	SCR-729
Radar	AN/APQ-7 or AN/APQ-23A
Loran	AN/APN-9 or AN/APN-4
Raven	RCM
IFF	SCR-695

Mission and Description

The primary mission of the B-29A is the destruction of enemy materiel and installations by actual bombardment.

It is provided with pressurized crew compartments and adequate heating and oxygen facilities on long range missions. The crew consists of pilot, co-pilot, bombardier, navigator, flight engineer, radio operator, four gunners and a radar operator.

Direct current electrical power is supplied by six (6) engine driven generators and one (1) auxiliary power plant.

Early models are equipped with transfer type fuel systems while later models use the manifold type system.

Armament provided consists of five (5) turrets controlled by a central fire control system.

In later aircraft a formation stick was added to the C-1 auto-pilot to facilitate formation flying.

The B-29A differs from the B-29 in the design of the wing center section resulting in a loss of 213 gallons of fuel in the center wing tank.

Development

First acceptance: .... January 1944
Production completed: .... June 1946

GUNS

No.	Cal	Rds ea	Location
4	.50	500	Fus. upr. fwd
2	.50	500	Fus. upr. aft
2	.50	500	Fus. lwr. fwd
2	.50	500	Fus. lwr. aft
2	.50	500	Tail. tur

BOMBS

No.	Size	Type
4	4000	G.P.
8	2000	G.P.
12	1600	A.P.
12	1000	G.P.
40	500	G.P.

Max Bomb Load .... 20,000 lb

POWER PLANT

No. & Model	(4) R-3350-7 or -57A
Mfr.	Wright
Engine Spec. No.	95-2826G-5
Sup. (Dual Turbo)	B-11 or B-31
Red. Gear Ratio	0.35
Prop. Mfr.	Hamilton Std
Blade Design No.	6521A-6
Prop. Type	Hydromatic
No. Blades	4
Prop Dia	16'7"

*Modernized

ENGINE RATINGS

	BHP	RPM	ALT	MIN
T.O.	2200	2800	S	5
Mil.	2200	2600	—	30
Nor.	2000	2400	—	Cont.

DIMENSIONS

Wing	
Span	141.2'
Incidence	4°
Dihedral	4°25'23"
Sweepback (LE)	7°1'26"
Length	99.0'
Height	27.8'
Tread	28.5'
Prop Grd Clearance	1.3'

Loading and Performance - Typical Mission

CONDITIONS			BASIC MISSION I	MAX. BOMBS MISSION II	HIGH ALT MISSION III	HIGH SPEED MISSION IV	FERRY RANGE V
TAKE-OFF WEIGHT		(lb)	140,000	140,000	140,000	140,000	137,610
Fuel at 6.0 lb/gal		(lb)	45,490	38,690	46,490	46,490	54,900
Military load (Bombs)		(lb)	10,000	20,000	10,000	10,000	None
Wing loading		(lb/sq ft)	81.4	81.4	81.4	81.4	80.0
Stall speed (power off)		(kn)	103	103	103	103	102
Take-off ground run at SL	④	(ft)	5230	5230	5230	5230	4980
Take-off to clear 50 ft	④	(ft)	7825	7825	7825	7825	7410
Rate-of-climb at SL		(fpm)	500	500	500	500	530
Time: SL to 10,000 ft	③	(min)	23.5	23.5	23.5	23.5	21.8
Time: SL to 20,000 ft	③	(min)	61.5	61.5	61.5	61.5	56.5
Service ceiling (100 fpm)	③	(ft)	23,950	23,950	23,950	23,950	25,500
Service ceiling (one engine out)	②	(ft)	19,400	19,400	19,400	19,400	21,100
COMBAT RANGE	⑤	(n. mi)	3321	2583	3925	1838	4593
Avg cruising speed		(kn)	199	204	223	259	191
Cruising altitude		(ft)	10,000	10,000	20,000	10,000	10,000
Total mission time		(hr)	16.88	12.85	13.71	7.37	23.10
COMBAT RADIUS	⑤	(n. mi)	1809	1428	1563	1036	---
Avg cruising speed		(kn)	216	215	239	275	---
Cruising altitude (s)		(ft)	10,000 & 25,000	10,000 & 25,000	20,000 & 30,000	10,000 & 25,000	---
Total mission time		(hr)	16.90	13.41	13.33	7.78	---
COMBAT WEIGHT	⑥	(lb)	101,472	96,900	99,330	103,806	85,000
Combat altitude		(ft)	25,000	25,000	30,000	25,000	10,000
Combat speed		(kn)	331	332	347	330	293
Combat climb		(fpm)	1260	1395	1165	1195	2025
Combat ceiling (500 fpm)	②	(ft)	36,150	37,100	36,550	35,650	39,700
Service ceiling (100 fpm)	③	(ft)	39,550	40,500	40,000	39,050	43,100
Service ceiling (one engine out)	②	(ft)	34,550	36,000	35,300	32,750	39,050
Max rate-of-climb at SL		(fpm)	1620	1745	1675	1555	2140
Max speed at 30,000 ft	②	(kn)	347	348	347	346	353
LANDING WEIGHT		(lb)	84,236	83,245	84,236	84,236	85,000
Ground roll at SL	④	(ft)	2250	2225	2250	2250	2260
Total from 50 ft	④	(ft)	2980	2950	2980	2980	3000

NOTES
① Take-off power
② Max power
③ Normal power
④ Take-off and landing distances are obtainable at sea level using normal technique. For airport planning, distances should be increased by appropriate factors to determine runway requirements.
⑤ Detailed descriptions of the RADIUS & RANGE missions are given on page 6.
⑥ For Radius Mission if Radius is shown.

CONDITIONS:
(a) Performance Basis: Flight test
(b) In computing Radius and Range, specific fuel consumptions have been increased 5% to allow for variations of fuel flow in service aircraft.
(c) Performance is based on powers shown on page 6.

20

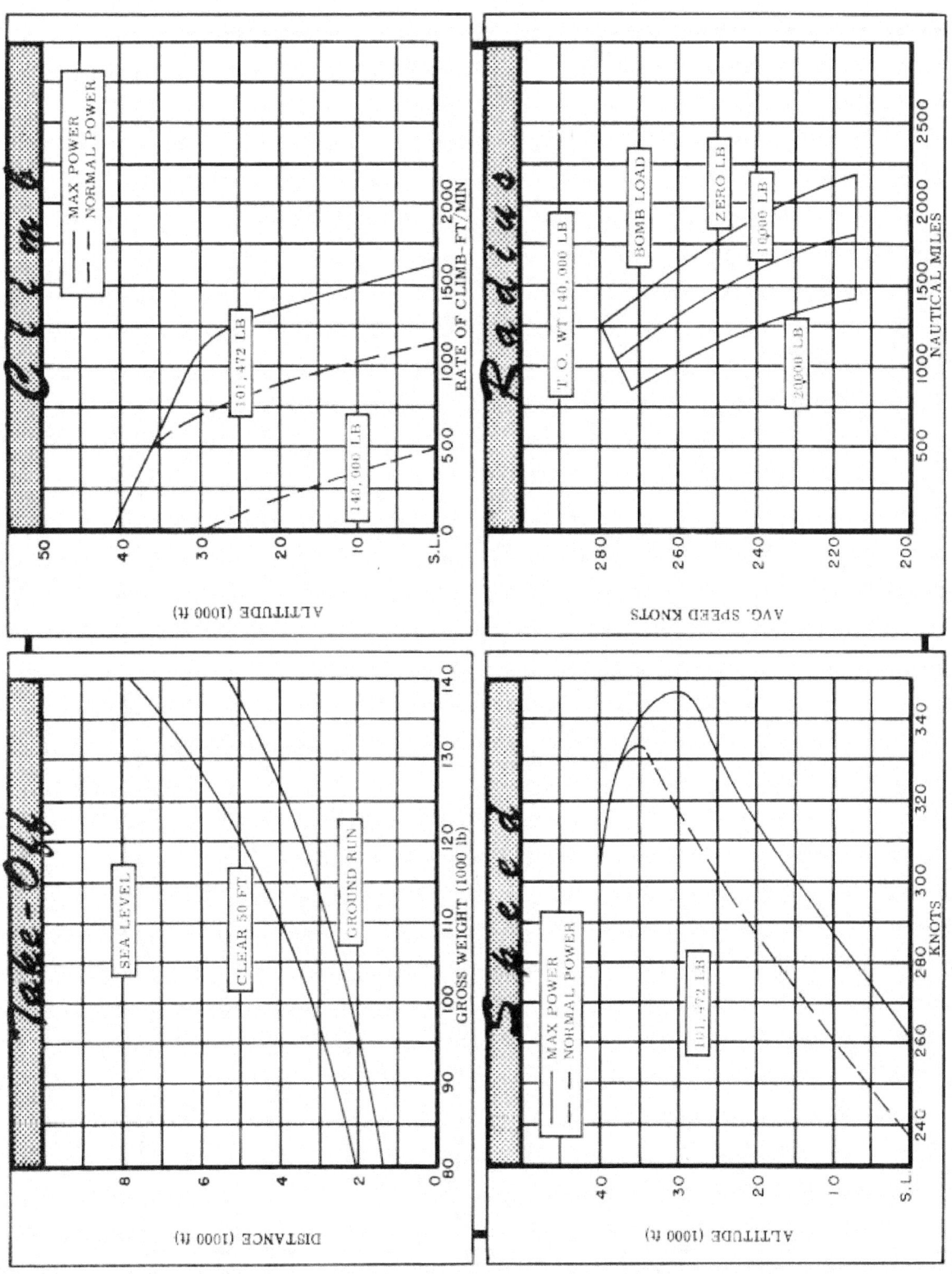

NOTES

FORMULA: RADIUS MISSIONS I & II

Warm-up, take-off, climb on course to 10,000 ft at normal power, cruise at long range speeds to point where climb is made to arrive at 25,000 ft 30 minutes prior to bomb drop, cruise at long range speeds for 15 minutes followed by 15 minutes normal power run into target, drop bombs and conduct 5 minutes normal power evasive action (no distance credit) and 10 minutes run out from target area at normal power, cruise back to base at long range speeds at 25,000 ft. Range free allowances include 10 minutes normal power at sea level for warm-up and take-off, 5 minutes normal power evasive action plus 5% of initial fuel for reserve.

FORMULA: RADIUS MISSION III

Same as Radius Mission I and II except initial climb is to 20,000 ft and bombs are dropped at 30,000 ft.

FORMULA: RADIUS MISSION IV

Same as Radius Mission I and II except cruising is done at normal power.

FORMULA: RANGE MISSIONS I & II

Warm-up, take-off, climb on course to 10,000 ft at normal power, cruise at long range speeds to point where climb is made to arrive at 25,000 ft 30 minutes prior to bomb drop, cruise at long range speeds for 30 minutes to point where 90% of initial fuel has been used, drop bombs. Range free allowances include 10 minutes normal power at sea level for warm-up and take-off plus 10% of initial fuel for evasive action and landing reserve.

FORMULA: RANGE MISSION III

Same as Range Missions I and II except initial climb is 20,000 ft and bombs are dropped at 30,000 ft.

FORMULA: RANGE MISSION IV

Same as Range Missions I and II except cruising is done at normal power.

FORMULA: RANGE MISSION V

Warm-up, take-off, climb on course to 10,000 ft at normal power, cruise at long range speeds to point where 90% of initial fuel is used. Range free allowances include 10 minutes normal power at sea level for warm up and take-off plus 10% of initial fuel for landing reserve

GENERAL DATA:

(a) For detailed planning refer to Tech Order AN 01-20EJA-1.

(b) Engine ratings shown on page 3 are manufacturer's guaranteed ratings. Power values used for performance calculations are as follows:

	R-3350 -57 or -57A		
	BHP	RPM	CRIT ALT*
T.O.	2200	2800	
Max.	**2500	2800	31,400
Nor.	2000	2400	35,600

*With Turbo
**As established by AN 01-20EJ-92 dated 15 June 1945.

(c) Bomb bay tanks are dropped when empty for all missions shown on page 4.

22

Standard Aircraft Characteristics

B-29B SUPERFORTRESS
Boeing

FOUR R3350-57, -57A WRIGHT

BY AUTHORITY OF
COMMANDING GENERAL
AIR MATERIEL COMMAND
U.S. AIR FORCE

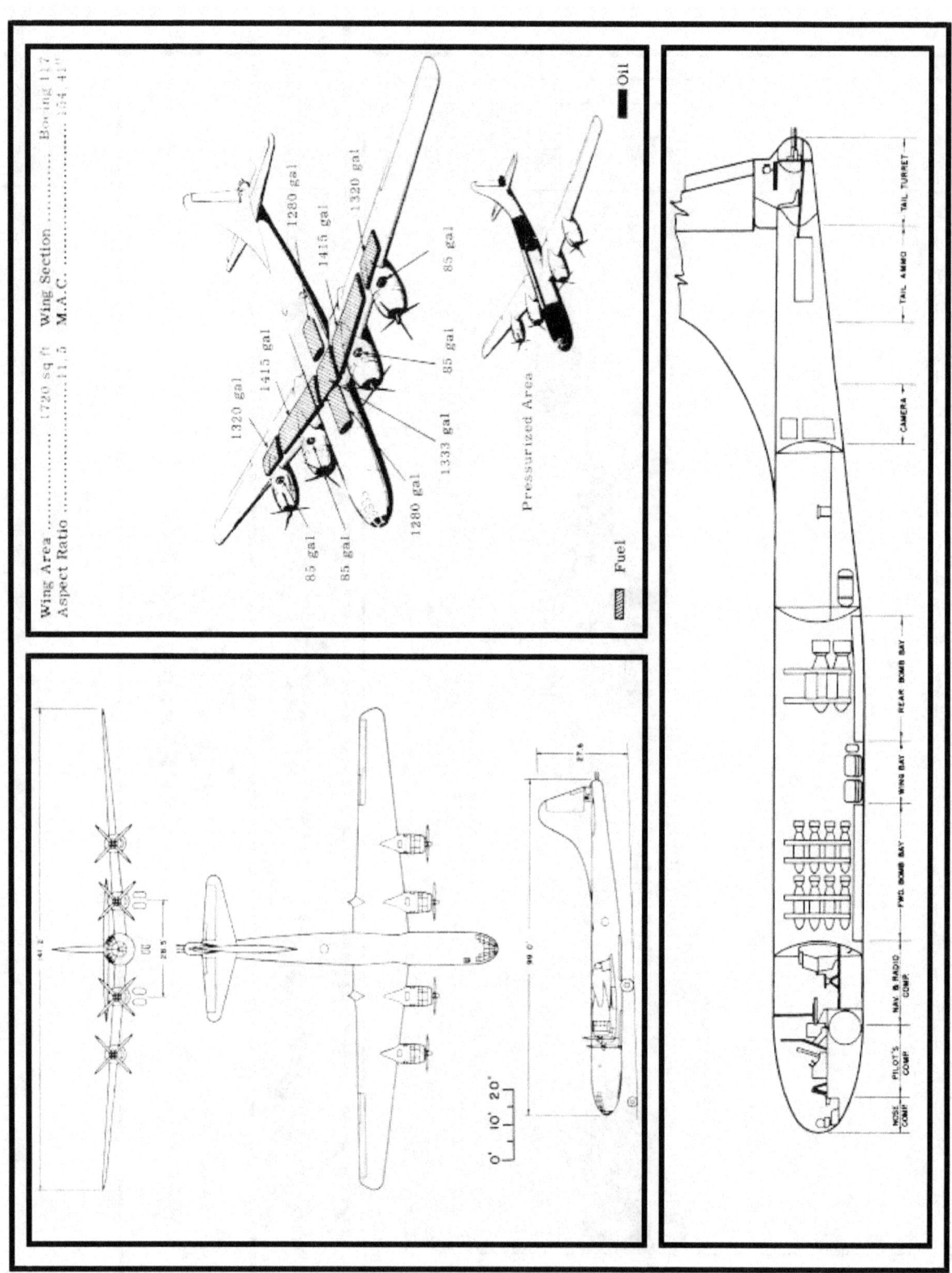

POWER PLANT

No. & Model	*(4)R-3350-57 or -57A
Mfr	Wright
Engine Spec No.	95-28266-5
Sup. (Dual Turbo)	B-11 or B-31
Red. Gear Ratio	0.35
Prop Mfr	Hamilton Std
Blade Design No.	6521A-6
Prop. Type	Hydromatic
No. Blades	4
Prop. Dia.	16'-7"

*Modernized

ENGINE RATINGS

BHP - RPM - ALT - MIN

T.O:	2200 - 2800 - S.L.
Mil	2200 - 2600 - Turbo - 30
Nor	2000 - 2400 - Turbo - Cont.

DIMENSIONS

Wing	
Span	141.2'
Incidence	4°
Dihedral	4°29'23"
Sweepback (LE)	7°1'26"
Length	99.0'
Height	27.8'
Tread	28.5'
Prop Grd Clearance	1.3'

Mission and Description

The primary mission of the B-29B is the destruction of enemy materiel and installations by aerial bombardment. It is a stripped version of the B-29 airplane incorporating the following:

A transfer type fuel system; a crew of ten (10), pilot, co-pilot, navigator, engineer, bombardier, radio operator, radar operator, left scanner, right scanner and tail gunner; radar operator's station in forward compartment; all turrets and accessories removed except tail turret housing three (3) .50 caliber guns and gunner; smooth closures for all turret and sight openings installed; incorporation of radar systems for navigation, bombing through overcast and night fighter protection in the tail.

Development

Some B-29B's were B-29's modified by AMC having only two tail guns, the majority were produced at Atlanta by Bell.

First acceptance from Bell	January 1945
Production completed	September 1945

BOMBS

No.	Size	Type
4	4000	G.P.
8	2000	G.P.
12	1600	A.P.
12	1000	G.P.
40	500	G.P.

Max Bomb Load ... 20,000 lb

GUNS

No.	Cal	Rds ea	Location
2	.50	500	Tail tur
1	.50	380	Tail tur

WEIGHTS

	Lb	L.F
Loading		
Empty	58,821(A)	
Basic	70,682(A)	
Design	120,000	2.67
Combat	*95,126	3.40
Max T.O.	†137,014	2.57
Max Land	‡135,000	2.35

(A) Actual
* For Basic Mission
† Limited by space
‡ Limited by strength

FUEL

Location	No. Tanks	Gal
Wg. outbd*	2	2640
Wg. inbd*	2	2830
Wg. ctr*	1	1333
Bomb bay*	2	2560
	Total	9363

*s.s.

Grade ... 100/130

OIL

Cap. (gal)	340
Grade	S-1120, W-1100

ELECTRONICS

VHF Command	AN/ARC-3
Interphone	AN/AIC-2A
Liaison	AN/ARC-8
Radio Compass	AN/ARN-7
Homing Adapter	RC-193A
Marker Beacon	AN/APN-2
Loran	RC-193
Localizer	AN/ARN-5A
Glide Path	SCR-718C
Radio Altimeter	SCR-695
IFF	SCR-729
Interrogator	AN/APQ-23A
Radar	RCM
Raven	
Gun Laying Radar	AN/APG-15B
Bomb.-Navigation Radar	AN/APQ-7

Loading and Performance - Typical Mission

CONDITIONS			BASIC MISSION I	MAXIMUM BOMBS II	BOMBS HIGH ALT. III	FERRY RANGE IV
TAKE-OFF WEIGHT	①	(lb)	135,744	136,464	135,744	135,024
Fuel at 8.4 lb/gal		(lb)	48,496	40,818	48,498	58,178
Military load (B-mbs)		(lb)	10,000	20,000	10,000	None
Wing loading		(lb/sq ft)	79.9	79.3	79.0	78.5
Stall speed (power off)		(kn)	102	102	102	102
Take-off ground run at SL	① ② ③ ④ ⑤	(ft)	4800	4860	4800	4725
Take-off to clear 50 ft		(ft)	7125	7225	7125	7025
Rate of climb at SL		(fpm)	618	602	618	625
Time SL to 10,000 ft		(min)	18.5	18.8	18.5	18.2
Time SL to 20,000 ft		(min)	43.5	45.0	43.5	43.0
Service ceiling (100 fpm)	②	(ft)	30,250	29,900	30,250	30,600
Service ceiling (one engine out)	②	(ft)	26,200	25,800	26,200	26,550
COMBAT RANGE		(n. mi)	3526	3076	3505	4939
Avg cruising speed		(kn)	191	195	207	185
Cruising altitude		(ft)	10,000	10,000	25,000	10,000
Total mission time		(hr)	20.73	15.94	13.27	26.83
COMBAT RADIUS	⑤	(n. mi)	2122	1725	1959	
Avg cruising speed		(kn)	208	210	235	
Cruising altitudes		(ft)	10,000 & 25,000	10,000 & 25,000	25,000 & 30,000	
Total mission time		(hr)	20.66	16.69	16.86	
COMBAT WEIGHT	⑤	(lb)	96,126	92,353	95,320	81,263
Combat altitude	②	(ft)	25,000	25,000	30,000	10,000
Combat speed	② ②	(kn)	344	345	360	308
Combat climb	② ②	(fpm)	1480	1610	1375	2210
Combat ceiling (500 fpm)	②	(ft)	38,000	38,750	38,200	41,450
Service ceiling (100 fpm)	③	(ft)	41,400	42,300	41,650	44,950
Service ceiling (one engine out)	③	(ft)	37,200	38,100	37,400	40,900
Max rate-of-climb at SL	②	(fpm)	1820	1925	1840	2330
Max speed at 30,000 ft	②	(kn)	360	361	360	368
LANDING WEIGHT		(lb)	78,071	77,687	78,071	81,263
Ground roll at SL	④	(ft)	2100	2090	2100	2180
Total from 50 ft	④	(ft)	2800	2790	2800	2900

NOTES
① Take-off power
② Max power
③ Normal power
④ Take-off and landing distances are obtainable at sea level using normal technique. For airport planning, distances should be increased by appropriate factors to determine runway requirements.
⑤ Detailed descriptions of the RADIUS & RANGE missions are given on page 6.
⑥ For Radius Mission if Radius if shown.

CONDITIONS:
(a) Performance Basis: Flight test
(b) In computing Radius and Range, specific fuel consumptions have been increased 5% to allow for variations of fuel flow in service aircraft.
(c) Performance is based on powers shown on page 6.

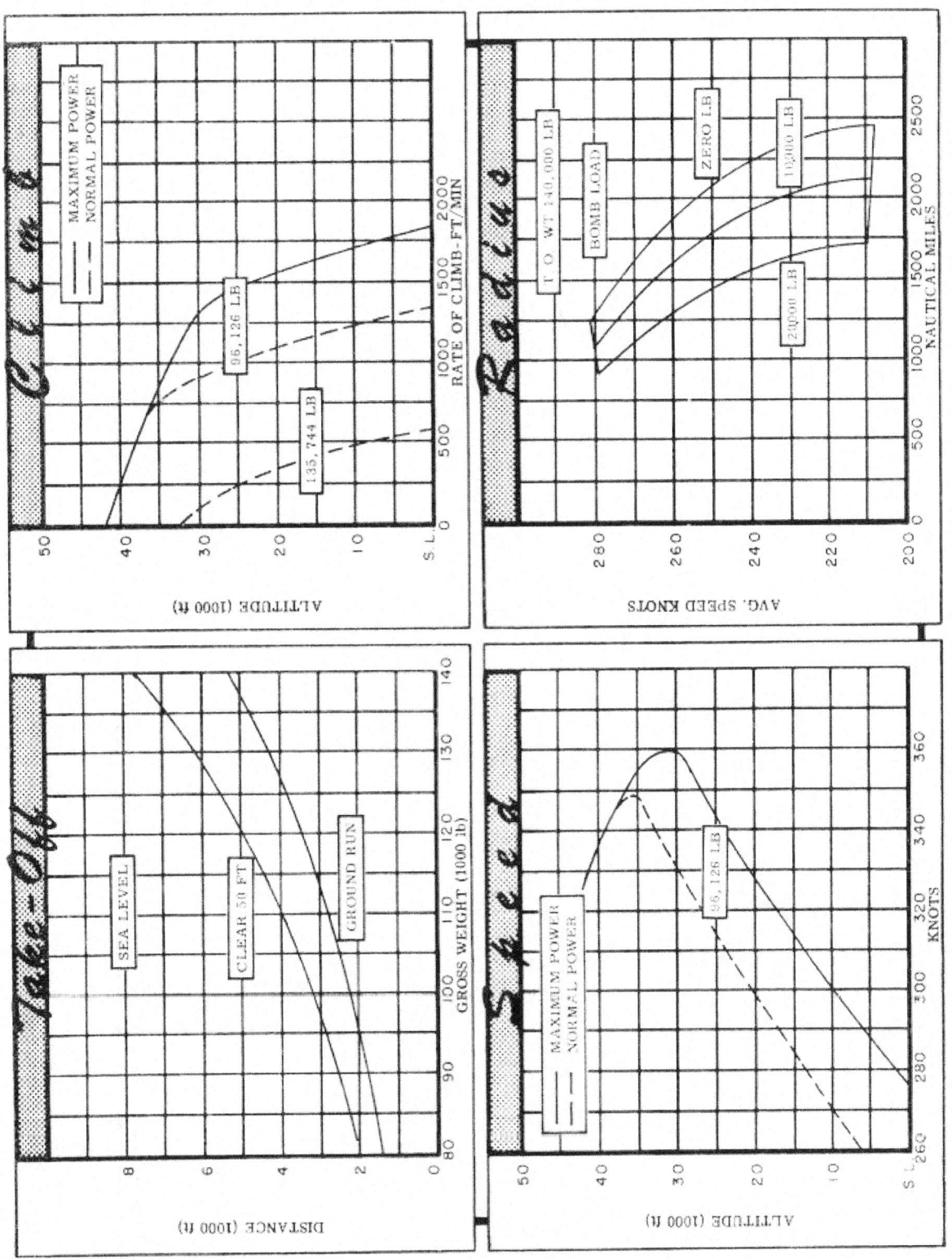

NOTES

FORMULA: RADIUS MISSION I & II

Warm-up, take-off, climb on course to 10,000 ft at normal power, cruise at long range speeds to point where climb is made to arrive at 25,000 ft 30 minutes prior to bomb drop, cruise at long range speeds for 15 minutes, followed by 15 minutes normal power run into target, drop bombs and conduct 5 minutes normal power evasive action (no distance credit), and 10 minutes run out from target area at normal power, cruise back to base at long range speeds at 25,000 ft. Range free allowances include 10 minutes normal power at sea level for warm-up and take-off, 5 minutes normal power evasive action plus 5% of initial fuel for reserve.

FORMULA: RADIUS MISSION III

Same as I and II except initial climb is to 25,000 ft and bombs are dropped at 30,000 ft.

FORMULA: RANGE MISSION I & II

Warm-up, take-off, climb on course to 10,000 ft at normal power, cruise at long range speeds to point where climb is made to arrive at 25,000 ft 30 minutes prior to bomb drop, cruise at long range speeds for 30 minutes to point where 90% of initial fuel has been used, drop bombs. Range free allowances include 10 minutes normal power at sea level for warm-up and take-off plus 10% of initial fuel for evasive action and landing reserve.

FORMULA: RANGE MISSION III

Same as Range Mission I & II except initial climb is to 25,000 ft and bombs are dropped at 25,000 ft.

FORMULA: RANGE MISSION IV

Warm-up, take-off, climb on course to 10,000 ft at normal power, cruise at long range speeds at 10,000 feet. Range free allowances include 10 minutes normal power warm-up and take-off, plus 10% initial fuel for landing reserve.

GENERAL DATA:

(a) For detailed planning refer to Tech Order AN 01-20EJA-1.

(b) Engine ratings shown on page 3 are manufacturer's guaranteed ratings. Power values used for performance calculations are as follows:

	R-3350-57 or -57A		
	BHP	RPM	CRIT ALT*
T.O.	2200	2800	
Max	*2500	2800	31,400
Nor.	2000	2400	35,600

*With Turbo

**As established by T.O. AN 01-20EF-42 dated 15 June 1944.

(c) Bomb bay tanks are dropped when empty for all missions shown on page 4.

The Convair B-36 Peacemaker

Convair B-36D.
Source: U.S. Air Force

One of the largest bombers ever built, the B-36 was the mainstay of the USAF's long-range strategic bombing deterrent during the late 1940s and early 1950s. Serving primarily as a strategic deterrent, the B-36 never saw any combat, although some aircraft were deployed to the Far East in 1953 as an overt threat to the Chinese should the armistice talks in Korea collapse. The B-36 was the last of the great piston-engined bombers and the last to be designed with a heavy battery of guns so that it could fight its way through enemy defenses.

AWPD-1

The B-36 owed its existence to the run of German victories in late 1939 and early 1940 that made it seem as if Britain might fall to a German invasion. In retrospect, this was never a serious possibility, but hindsight was not available in 1940 and it appeared possible that the USA would be deprived of any European allies in case of war. This would leave the nascent American bomber fleet without any forward bases from which to prosecute an attack on Germany. The war with Germany, something seen as being inevitable, would have to be carried out from bases in the United States itself. Consequently, the Air Corps felt that it would need a truly intercontinental bomber with the unprecedented ability to take off from bases inside the United States, fly to Germany, carry out its attacks, and then return. This concept gave rise to Air War Plans Division - Plan 1 (AWPD-1).

AWPD-1 was based on the theory of precision bombardment and called for identification, by scientific analysis, of those key links in the enemy's economy whose elimination would either cripple his capacity to wage war or else shatter his will to continue fighting. It drew upon years of doctrinal analysis and theoretical application of the principles of war, relying heavily on the concept that a nation's ability to pursue war depended on maintaining intact a closely knit and interdependent industrial fabric. Precision bombing, however, could destroy this fabric. By concentrating Allied bombing against objectives vital to the German war effort and the German people's livelihood, AWPD-1's planners aimed to accomplish the primary goal of any war – to defeat the enemy by breaking his will to fight. To accomplish this goal in the simplest and most efficient manner, Allied bombers were tasked with destroying the enemy's forces before they deployed into the field. AWPD-1's developers sought to destroy country's capability to fight by attacking it at the home front, and in doing so wreck the country's will to resist. These efforts contributed to shaping the general nature of Air Force thinking for years to come.

Executing AWPD-1 required a remarkable aircraft. On April 11, 1941, the U.S. Army Air Corps (USAAC), in an atmosphere of high secrecy, opened up a design competition for a bomber with a 450-mph top speed, a 275-mph cruising speed, a service ceiling of 45,000 feet, and a maximum range of 12,000 miles at 25,000 feet. It had to be able to carry a 10,000-pound bomb load a distance of 5,000 miles away and return, and had to be able to carry 72,000 pounds of bombs over a reduced range. It had to be able to take off and land on a 5,000-foot runway. Nothing like this aircraft had ever been built before.

In fact this plan was too ambitious, and it became apparent that the original performance specifications were unattainable. In order to accelerate the project, a conference of high-ranking U.S. Army Air Force (USAAF) officers met on August 19, 1941 and decided to scale down their requirements. The maximum range requirement was reduced to 10,000 miles and the effective combat radius requirement was cut to 4,000 miles with a 10,000-pound bomb load. The cruising speed was set at somewhere between 240 and 300 mph, and the service ceiling was to be 40,000 feet. On October 3, 1941, a review of preliminary data from Boeing, Consolidated Aircraft Corp, and Douglas decided that the Consolidated study was the most promising. This envisioned a bomber powered by six pusher engines mounted on huge wings joined to a circular-section fuselage.

Ironically, just as the design of the B-36 was being selected, the basic strategic situation was changing. The Battle of Britain had been fought and won. The defeat of the German Air Force eliminated any near-term possibility of an invasion. In fact, as more professional evaluations replaced the extreme pessimism of U.S. Ambassador to Great Britain Joseph Kennedy, who saw little prospect of the U.K. continuing with the war, it became apparent that a German invasion had never been a practical possibility. This meant that the Army Air Corps could, once again, rely on the availability of forward bases. This greatly reduced the value of the B-36 and made an alternative war plan based around the shorter-ranged B-29 plausible. This plan eventually emerged as AWPD-42. The basic principles of AWPD-42 guided U.S. aircraft procurement throughout World War Two, with the final order of battle in 1945 being almost exactly that proposed three years earlier. This suggests that had AWPD-1 been implemented, it would also have been completed as planned. This was, however, not to be.

No Longer a Priority

With AWPD-1 being abandoned, priorities assigned to the B-36 fell accordingly and the program took second or even third place to the production of the PBY flying boat and B-24 bomber. There was a brief resurgence in late 1941 when Japanese victories in the Pacific seemed to dictate the adoption of the very long-range B-36, but the turn of the tide in 1942 ended that brief period. Once again, the B-36 was consigned to a limbo in which development was very slow and outright cancellation seemed probable. The program was saved by a series of victories by the Japanese in the spring of 1943 that appeared to bring China near collapse. The USAAF was faced with the unpleasant prospect of the loss of bases in China, from where it planned to launch B-29 raids against Japan. It might turn out that the longer-ranged B-36 would be the only means of attacking the Japanese home islands if bases nearer Japan could not be secured. In order to induce contractors to pursue the B-36 with greater enthusiasm, Gen. Henry Arnold directed that orders be placed for 100 production examples. The Letter of Intent was signed by Convair on July 23. The new schedule called for the XB-36 prototype to be ready for flight by September 1944. The first production B-36 was due in August 1945, with the last to be delivered in October 1946.

By mid-1944, the capture of the Marianas has made available bases that allowed B-29s to attack the Japanese mainland. It was felt that a super long-range bomber was not now so urgently needed. Although the B-36 project would still continue, once again its priority was lowered and the program was barely ticking along. The contract for the 100 B-36s remained in effect, but no longer carried any priority rating. This situation remained until after the Japanese surrender, when the B-36 began to be viewed as a long-range nuclear weapons delivery vehicle capable of retaliating against an enemy without the need for forward bases. On August 6, 1945, General Arnold accepted the Air Staff's recommendation to keep the B-36 contract for 100 planes intact to provide four B-36 groups in the post-war USAAF.

Financial limitations in the late 1940s and labor strikes at Convair in October 1945 and February 1946 delayed the B-36 program by several months. The first XB-36 took off from Fort Worth, Texas, on its maiden flight on August 8, 1946, almost three years later than originally planned back in early 1941. It was the heaviest and largest landplane ever to fly up to that time. Flight tests showed that deficiencies existed with the wing flap actuating system, the engine cooling was poor, and turbulent airflow off the wings caused propeller vibration, which adversely affected the wing structure. Engine cooling was a problem, as it resulted in the inability of the XB-36 to maintain altitudes over 30,000 feet for any extended period of time. The range was too short and the speed was too low. These results caused pressure for the aircraft's cancellation to mount.

Production at Last

The initial production version was the B-36A, 22 of which were built. Nineteen of them were delivered to the 7th Bombardment Group (Heavy). The first delivery was made on June 26, 1948 and the last in February 1949. They were used exclusively for training and crew conversion. One of the B-36As made an extended flight of 33 hours 10 minutes, shuttling between Fort Worth and San Diego three times without stopping. It carried a 10,000-pound bomb load which was dropped midway from 25,000 feet on the Air Force Bombing Range at Wilcox, Arizona. The total distance flown was 6,922 miles. In May 1948, the same aircraft made a round trip of 8,062 miles lasting 33 hours 8 minutes. On June 30, 1948, a B-36A dropped 72,000 pounds of bombs during a test flight. In early 1950, Convair began converting the B-36As to the reconnaissance configuration. These were all redesignated RB-36E.

The first full-scale production version of the B-36 was the B-36B. This differed from the B-36A in having six 3,500-horsepower R-4360-41 Wasp Major engines with water injection. The extra 500 horsepower per engine allowed the B-36B to take off within a shorter runway distance and yielded slightly better performance. The B-36Bs were first assigned to the 7th Bombardment Group at Carswell AFB, the first aircraft arriving in November 1948. By the end of that year SAC had 35 B-36s in service on strength. Of the 73 B-36Bs built, 64 were converted to B-36D configuration with the addition of four General Electric J47-GE-19 turbojets paired in pods underneath the outer wings. They were redelivered with jets by February 1952

Installing Jets

The early B-36s equipped with only piston engines had proved to be underpowered, although the enormous wings meant the aircraft was lightly loaded. This suggested that the provision of additional engine power would bring about great improvements in performance. In October 1948, Convair proposed fitting two pairs of turbojets in pods underneath the outer wings. These turbojets would be used for takeoff and for short bursts of speed during the bombing run, and would have only a minimal effect on the range. These changes resulted in the B-36D. This featured two pairs of General Electric J47-GE-19 turbojets in pods underneath the outer wings to assist the six R-4360-41 engines. The jet engines increased the maximum speed to 435 mph and the ceiling to "more than 45,000 feet" (in fact, B-36Ds were soon performing routinely at 49,000 ft). In addition, they reduced the takeoff run by almost 2,000 feet. The pedestrian B-36 had suddenly become a star performer.

Several B-36Ds were stripped of all armament except the tail turret as lightweight, high-altitude aircraft. These planes were identified as Featherweight B-36Ds. The Featherweight program was carried out in three phases. Featherweight I included a general weight reduction effort in which all non-essential flying and crew comfort equipment was removed. It was followed by Featherweight II, which further reduced weight by removing non-essential capabilities such as provision for the defunct XF-85 Goblin fighter. The last stage of the Featherweight program was Featherweight Model III, which removed all the defensive armament, making it possible for the B-36 to reach altitudes in excess of 50,000 feet. This put the B-36 beyond the reach of contemporary defensive fighters and far above the reach of existing anti-aircraft guns.

Contemporary USAF documentation referred to the "unexpected ascendancy of the high-altitude, piston-engined bomber." When a captured MiG-15bis was tested against a Featherweight B-36D, the jet fighter was outclassed. It was wallowing on the edge of its performance envelope and any effort to fire its guns caused it to stall out. USAF F-86Fs fared no better. For a few brief years, the high-flying B-36s would be the Queen of the Skies. It was, of course, only a question of time before the increasing performance of interceptor fighters and the development of air-to-air guided missiles allowed the B-36s to be intercepted. Once that capability was achieved, the reign of the B-36 ended swiftly. For the last two years of its operational life, the B-36 was considered suitable only for night bombing missions.

The B-36D was followed by the B-36F, which differed in having more-powerful 3,800-horsepower Pratt & Whitney R-4360-53 engines. The B-36F also had improved radar and electronics countermeasures equipment, including the K-3A radar system and the APG-32 gun-laying radar. A chaff dispenser was installed to confuse enemy radar. A total of 34 B-36Fs were built, with the last being delivered in October 1952. A number of the new B-36Fs were modified as Featherweight aircraft during 1954.

The B-36H was the major production version of the B-36, with a total of 83 being built. The B-36H was very similar to the B-36F, but had a rearranged crew compartment and much improved electronics.

The B-36J was the final production version of the B-36. It was equipped with two additional fuel tanks, one on the outer panel of each wing, which increased the fuel load by 2,770 gallons, for a total fuel capacity of 36,396 gallons. It also had a much stronger landing gear, permitting a gross takeoff weight as high as 410,000 pounds. The last 14 B-36Js were manufactured as B-36J Featherweight IIIs. The crew was reduced to 13, and the blisters were replaced by flat windows. The reduction in weight enabled a service ceiling of 47,000 feet to be reached, although some missions were flown as high as 50,000 feet. These were the only aircraft to be built in Featherweight configuration. A total of 33 B-36Js were accepted, the last being delivered on August 14, 1954.

Strategic Reconnaissance Aircraft

Almost as many B-36s were built as strategic reconnaissance aircraft as were built as bombers. It had become apparent that the maps and charts of the Soviet Union that were available contained significant inaccuracies due to age, poor research and deliberate Soviet disinformation. The strategic reconnaissance aircraft had the task of locating the real position of the targets and relaying the information back to the bombers. In the early 1950s this was considered a vital mission, and the strategic reconnaissance groups had priority on available equipment.

There were four primary strategic reconnaissance versions of the B-36: the RB-36D, RB-36E, RB-36F and RB-36H. The RB-36 was outwardly identical to the standard B-36, but carried a crew of 22 rather than 15, the additional crew members being needed to operate and maintain the photographic reconnaissance equipment. The forward bomb bay in the bomber was replaced by a pressurized manned compartment equipped with 14 cameras. This compartment included a small darkroom where a photo technician could develop the film. The second bomb bay contained up to 80 T86 photo flash bombs, while the third bay could carry an extra 3,000-gallon droppable fuel tank or a nuclear weapon. The fourth bomb bay carried ferret electronic countermeasures (ECM) equipment. The defensive armament of sixteen 20mm cannon was retained, although some RB-36s were modified to the Featherweight III configuration. The extra fuel tanks increased the endurance to up to 50 hours.

The standard RB-36 carried up to 23 cameras, primarily K-17C, K-22A, K-38, and K-40 cameras. A special 240-foot focal length camera was tested on an ERB-36D. The long focal length was achieved by using a two-mirror reflection system. The camera was supposedly capable of resolving a golf ball at an altitude of 40,000 feet. The camera never became standard issue and, with the availability of new strategic reconnaissance systems, the RB-36 force was reassigned to bomber missions in 1956.

The FICON (FIghter CONveyor) project was an early 1950s attempt to extend the range of fighter and reconnaissance jets by having them operate as parasites from B-36 bombers. In January 1951, Convair converted an RB-36F as a platform for a modified F-84E Thunderjet. The modified aircraft was redesignated GRB-36F. The pair made up to 170 inflight launches and retrievals, including night operations. As a result, the USAF ordered 10 RB-36D aircraft modified to act as GRB-36D motherships. These aircraft saw limited service with the 99th Strategic Reconnaissance Wing carrying RF-84Ks of the 91st Strategic Reconnaissance Squadron. The aircraft operated for about a year before the system was quietly abandoned

Other Experimental Versions

As the new jet-engined B-47 and B-52 started to trickle into service, interest grew in using the B-36 as a mid-air refueling tanker that could refuel jet aircraft at higher altitudes and higher speeds relative to converted B-29 tankers. One B-36H was converted into a tanker in 1952, with the aircraft being tested with a B-47 receiver aircraft between May 1952 and January 1953. The modifications were modular and the aircraft could be converted back to its standard bomber configuration in only 12 hours. However, no other B-36 tanker conversions were carried out, allegedly because converted B-29s and B-50s, plus the new KC-97, were able to handle mid-air refueling much more economically. However, there is reason to believe that the light structure of the B-36 was already aging quickly and that the service life of tanker conversions would be uneconomically short.

The immense range of the B-36 opened the question of how the aircraft was to be escorted. As one possible solution to this range problem, the USAAF revived the parasite fighter idea of the early 1930s, and proposed that the long-range bombers carry their protective fighters inside their bomb bays. In March 1945, McDonnell Aircraft Corp submitted a proposal for the XP-85, an aircraft with an egg-shaped fuselage, a triple vertical tail, a tailplane with pronounced anhedral, and vertically folding swept-back wings. The engine was to be a 3,000-pound-thrust Westinghouse J34-WE-7 axial-flow turbojet with a nose intake and a straight-through exhaust. Since the XP-85 was to be launched and recovered from a retractable trapeze underneath its parent bomber, no conventional landing gear was fitted. A retractable hook was fitted to the fuselage in front of the cockpit. During recovery, the XP-85 would approach its parent bomber from underneath, and the hook would gently engage the trapeze. Once securely attached, the aircraft would be pulled up into the belly of the bomber.

The USAAF liked this proposed solution and specified that the 24th and subsequent B-36s should be capable of carrying one P-85 in addition to the usual bomb load. It was even planned that some B-36s would be modified so that they could carry three P-85 fighters and no bomb load. In any event, the idea was found impractical and was abandoned.

Stand-Off Missiles

The technology used to launch the RF-84K from the GRB-36F gave rise to another possibility. In 1952, Convair modified three B-36H aircraft to act as test platforms for the Bell GAM-63 Rascal rocket-powered air-to-surface guided missile. These aircraft were redesignated DB-36H, where the D stood for "Director." The GAM-63 was carried semi-recessed underneath the fuselage.

The GAM-63 missile was powered by a Bell-designed liquid-fueled rocket engine that developed a thrust of 4,000 pounds to give it a top speed of Mach 2.95. The missile could carry a 3,000-pound nuclear warhead up to 100 miles. By 1955 it was apparent that the B-36's in-service life was limited and that another aircraft would be more suited to carrying the Rascal missile. A plan for 11 other B-36s to be modified as Rascal carriers under the designation DB-36H was therefore abandoned.

Rascal was then assigned to the B-47 fleet and turned out to be a fairly accurate and effective missile, but with the rapidity of missile development in the 1950s, the concept rapidly became obsolete. The Rascal program was canceled on September 9, 1958.

Nuclear-Powered Aircraft

The basic theory of the ultra-long-range B-36 was taken to its logical conclusion with the idea of a nuclear-powered aircraft that would have endurance measured in days or even weeks rather than in hours. The possibility of building such an aircraft was carried out at Oak Ridge, Tennessee, in the late 1940s. It was known as NEPA (Nuclear Energy for the Propulsion of Aircraft) and was followed by another study by the Massachusetts Institute of Technology. This concluded that a nuclear-powered aircraft was feasible, but that it would take at least 15 years to develop.

In the envisioned nuclear propulsion system, air entered a compressor, where it would be heated by passing through the reactor and be exhausted through a jet nozzle. The engine would use an intermediate fluid to transfer the heat to the air rather than by passing the air through the reactor core itself. Before this engine could be built, it was essential to test the effects of nuclear reactor radiation on instruments, equipment, and airframe and to study shielding methods.

A B-36H that had been seriously damaged when a tornado struck Carswell AFB in 1952 was selected as the testbed. A prototype 1,000-kW nuclear reactor was mounted in the aft bomb bay. It did not power the aircraft, and its presence was purely to examine its effects on the airframe. The crew was housed entirely in a highly modified nose compartment shielded by lead and rubber, with a further 4-ton lead disc shield installed in the middle of the aircraft. The pilot and copilot were provided with a 1-foot-thick leaded-glass windshield. A closed-circuit television system enabled the crew to watch the reactor.

The aircraft made its first flight on September 17, 1955. All of the test flights were carried out over sparsely populated areas, and the reactor was not turned on until the plane was at a safe altitude. In mid-1956, the Air Force decided to cancel the WS-125A nuclear aircraft program. The NB-36H was decommissioned at Fort Worth in late 1957, having made 47 flights with the reactor on board. It was scrapped several months later, with the radioactive parts being buried.

Had the program continued, a nuclear-powered aircraft would have been built. There were proposals for a version of the B-36H (tentatively designated X-6) with a nuclear propulsion plant, but these never materialized.

B-36Fs In Flight
Source: U.S. Air Force photo

Characteristics Summary

BOMBER · · · · · · · · · · · · · · · B-36A

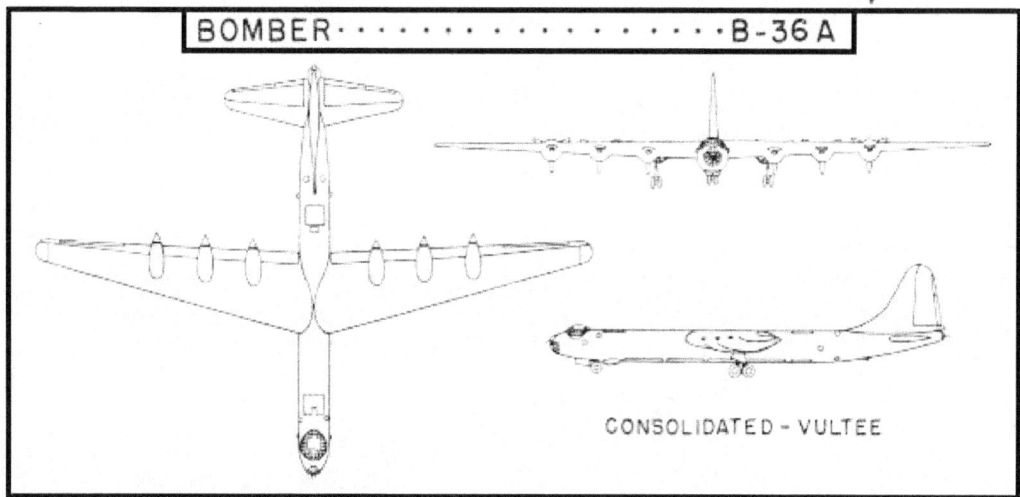

CONSOLIDATED - VULTEE

Wing area .... 4772 sq ft   Length .... 162.1 ft

Span .... 230.0 ft   Height .... 46.8 ft

AVAILABILITY			PROCUREMENT			
Number available			Number to be delivered in fiscal years			
ACTIVE	RESERVE	TOTAL				

STATUS

SERVICE

1. Design initiated: (XB-36) November 1941

2. First flight: (XB-36) 8 August 1946

3. First production: (B-36A) May 1947

4. Production completed: November 1948

POWER PLANT	FEATURES	ARMAMENT

(6) R-4360-25 Pratt-Whitney
 	
BHP - RPM - ALT.*
 	
T.O: 3000 - 2700 - S.L.
 	
Max: 3000 - 2700 - 34,000
 	
Nor: 2500 - 2550 - 37,000
 	
*Turbo critical
	Crew: 14
	Bombing-Navigation Radar
	Reverse Pitch Props
	Gun-Laying Radar & Loran
	Max. Design Fuel
	  Cap.: 27,010 gal (Wing tank-
	  age plus 2x3000 gal bomb
	  bay tanks)
	Can be field - modified to
	  carry 2 additional bomb bay
	  tanks permitting 33,010 gal
	  max fuel cap.
		Turrets: 8
		
		Guns: (16) 20mm
		
		Ammunition: 9200 rds
		
		Max Bomb Load: (72) 1000 lb
		
		Max Bomb Size: 4000 lb

Characteristics Summary Basic Mission B-36A

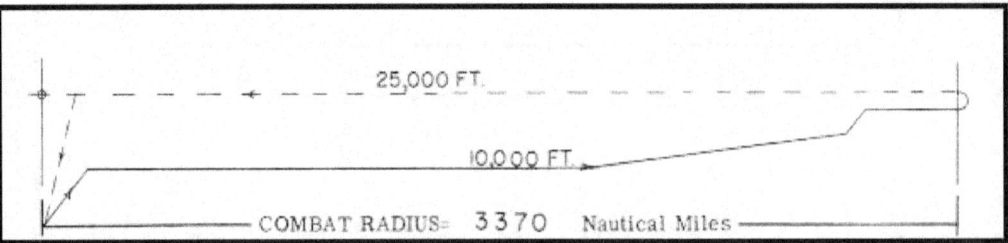

— COMBAT RADIUS = 3370 Nautical Miles —

PERFORMANCE

COMBAT RADIUS	COMBAT RANGE	COMBAT SPEED
3370 naut. mi with 10,000 lb payload at 189 knots avg. in 35.6 hours.	**6320** naut. mi with 10,000 lb payload at 181 knots avg. in 35.08 hours.	**290** knots at 25,000 ft alt, max power
		MAXIMUM SPEED
		300 knots at 31,600 ft alt, max power

CLIMB	CEILING	TAKE-OFF
502 fpm sea level, take-off weight normal power	**25,000** ft 100 fpm, take-off weight normal power	ground run **6000** ft | ——— ft no assist | assisted
1447 fpm sea level, combat weight maximum power	**35,800** ft 500 fpm, combat weight maximum power	over 50 ft height **8000** ft | ——— ft no assist | assisted

LOAD	WEIGHTS	STALLING SPEED

Bombs: 10,000 lb
Ammunition:
    9200 rds/20mm
 	
Fuel: 24,121 gal
  protected   61 %
  droppable   13 %
  external   0 %
	Empty..... 135,020 lb
	
	Combat... 212,800 lb
	
	Take-off 310,380 lb
	
	limited by space
		98 knots
		flaps down, take-off weight

		TIME TO CLIMB ———

NOTES

1. PERFORMANCE BASIS:
    (a) Estimated data based on preliminary flight test.
    (b) In computing Radius and Range, specific fuel consumptions have been increased 5% to allow for variation of fuel flow in service aircraft.

2. REVISION BASIS: To clarify fuel capacity data shown under "Features"

Standard Aircraft Characteristics

B-36A
Consolidated-Vultee

SIX R-4360-25
PRATT-WHITNEY

BY AUTHORITY OF
COMMANDING GENERAL
AIR MATERIEL COMMAND
U.S. AIR FORCE

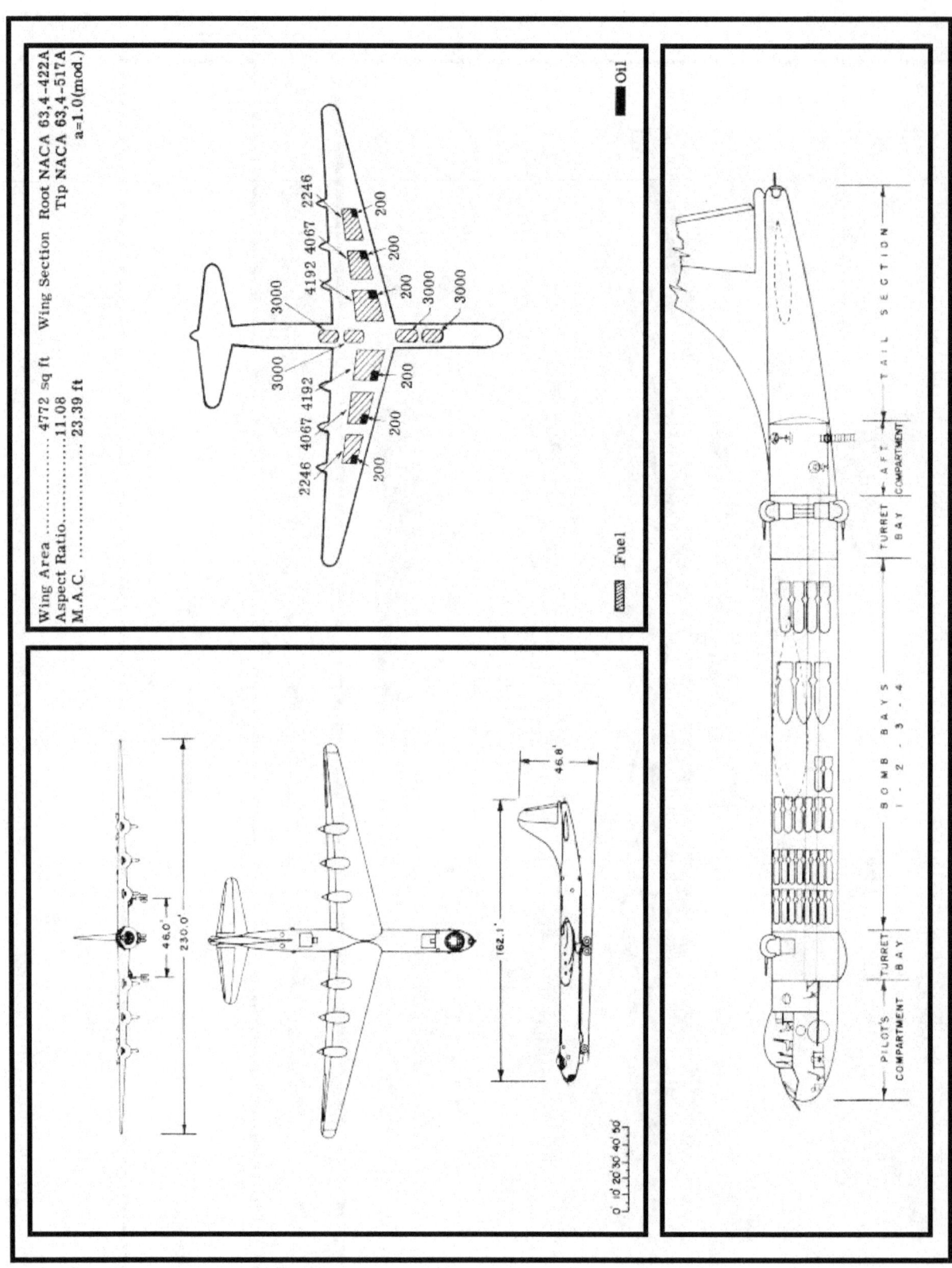

WEIGHTS

Loading	Gross	L.F.
Empty	135,020(A)	
Basic	142,842(E)	2.67
Design	278,000	
Combat*	212,800	
Max T.O.†	311,000	2.1
Max Land‡	311,000	2.1

*For basic mission
†Limited by performance
‡Limited by take-off weight
(A) Actual
(E) Estimated

FUEL

Location	Tanks	Gal.
Wings,outbd*	2	4492
Wings,inbd	2	8384
Wings ctr*	2	8134
Bomb bay*	†4	†12000
	Total	33,010

Spec. AN-F-48
Grade 100/130
*Self-sealing
†See page 6

OIL

Cap. (gal.)	1200
Spec.	AN-0-8
Grade	W-1100;S-1120

ELECTRONICS

VHF Command	AN/ARC-3
Range Recvr.	BC-453-B
Liaison	AN/ARC-11
Radio Compass	AN/ARN-7
Interphone	AN/AIC-2A
I.F.F.	SCR-695B
Blind Approach	RC-103A
Glide Path	AN/ARN-5A
Marker Beacon	RC-193
Bomb.-Nav.Radar	AN/APQ-23A
Loran	AN/APN-9
Gun Laying Radar	AN/APG-3

Mission and Description

The B-36A is a long range, high altitude, very heavy bombardment aircraft. The fuselage consists of a forward pressurized cabin, one non-pressurized turret bay, four non-pressurized bomb bays, aft pressurized cabin and the non-pressurized rear fuselage section.

Cabin heating; defrosting of blisters and enclosures, and propeller; wing and tail anti-icing are accomplished by heated air.

The defensive armament consists of eight remotely controlled turrets, six of which are retractable.

Engine-driven alternators supply 3 phase, 400 cycle AC power for the primary electrical system. DC electrical requirements are fulfilled from DC rectifiers. Hydraulic power is used for landing gear actuation, brakes, and nose wheel steering.

Development

Design Initiated (XB-36)	November 1941
First Flight: (XB-36)	August 1946
	May 1947
Production Completed:	November 1948

GUNS

No.	Size	Rds.ea.	Loc
2	20mm	400	Fus,nose
4	20mm	600	Fus,up, fwd
4	20mm	600	Fus,up,aft
4	20mm	600	Fus,lwr,aft
2	20mm	600	Fus,tail

BOMBS

No.	Size	Type
12	4000	G.P.
28	2000	G.P.
44	1600	A.P.
72	1000	G.P.
132	500	G.P.

Max Bomb Load: 72,000 lb.

POWER PLANT

No. & Model	(6) R-4360-25
Mfr	Pratt-Whitney
Superch	Dual Turbo
Red. Gear	0.381
Prop. Mfr	Curtiss
Prop Dia	19.0'
Prop Type	Electric
Blade Design	1129-8C6-24

ENGINE RATINGS

	BHP - RPM - Turbo
T.O:	3250 - 2700 - S.L.
Mil:	3000 - 2700 - 40,000
Nor:	2500 - 2550 - S.L.
	2500 - 2550 - 40,000

DIMENSIONS

Span	230.0'
Length	162.1'
Height	46.8'
Tread	46'
Prop Grd Clearance	4.46'

Loading and Performance - Typical Mission

CONDITIONS		BASIC		MAXBOMBS		HIGH ALT		MAX SPEED		FERRY
		RADIUS	RANGE	RADIUS	RANGE	RADIUS	RANGE	RADIUS	RANGE	RANGE
		I	II	III		IV		V		VI
TAKE-OFF WEIGHT	(lb)	310,380	310,380	311,000		310,380		310,380		311,000
Fuel/Oil	(gal)	24,121/965	24,121/965	14,434/577		24,121/965		24,121/965		26,745/1070
Military Load	(lb)	10,000	10,000	72,000		10,000		10,000		None
Total Ammunition	(rds/cal)	9200/20mm	9200/20mm	9200/20mm		9200/20mm		9200/20mm		None
Wing Loading	(lb/sq ft)	65.04	65.04	65.17		65.04		65.04		65.17
Stall Speed-(power off)	(kn)	98	98	98		98		98		98
TAKE-OFF DISTANCE SL ④										
Ground Run (no wind)	(ft)	6000	6000	6000		6000		6000		6000
To Clear 50 ft Obst	(ft)	8000	8000	8000		8000		8000		8000
CLIMB FROM SL										
Rate of Climb at SL ③	(fpm)	502	502	500		502		502		500
Time To 10,000 Feet ③	(min)	22.3	22.3	22.5		22.3		22.3		22.5
Time To 20,000 Feet ③	(min)	53.0	53.0	53.5		53.0		53.0		53.5
COMBAT RANGE or RADIUS	(n.mi)	3370	6320	1830		2485		1860		7934
Avg. Cruising Speed	(kn)	189	181	187		231		269		189
Total Mission Time	(hr)	35.6	35.08	19.57		21.52		13.83		42.17
Cruising Altitude	(ft)	⑤	⑤	⑤		⑤		⑤		⑤
COMBAT WEIGHT	(lb)	212,800	165,570	182,100		207,800		220,800		
Combat Altitude	(ft)	25,000	25,000	25,000		35,000		34,400		
SPEED										
Max Speed (combat alt) ②	(kn)	290	295	294		292		288		
Max Speed ②	(kn/alt)	300/31,600	310/33,000	307/32,400		302/31,800		293/31,400		
CLIMB										
Rate of Climb (combat alt) ②	(fpm)	1023	1617	1380		620		545		
Rate of Climb at SL ②	(fpm)	1447	2045	1810		1500		1367		
CEILING										
Combat Ceiling ②	(ft)	35,800	39,400	38,400		36,300		34,900		
Service Ceiling ③	(ft)	39,100	41,300	40,700		39,500		38,600		
LANDING WEIGHT SL	(lb)	158,080		153,850		158,080		158,080		153,200
Ground Roll ⑥	(ft)	1490		1450		1490		1490		1440
From 50'Obst ⑥	(ft)	2650		2600		2650		2650		2590

NOTES
① Take-off power
② Max power
③ Normal power
④ Take-off and landing distances are obtainable at sea level using normal technique. For airport planning add 25% to distances shown
⑤ Detailed descriptions of the RADIUS & RANGE missions are given on page 6.

CONDITIONS:
(a) Performance Basis: NACA standard conditions, no wind, single airplane
(b) Fuel consumption used in computing RADIUS & RANGE is based on manufacturer's estimates and flight tests increased 5%
(c) Performance based on powers listed on page 6.
(d) RADIUS & RANGE are based on operation where maximum continuous BMEP (178 psi) is maintained in all auto-rich power settings except as modified by propeller restrictions.

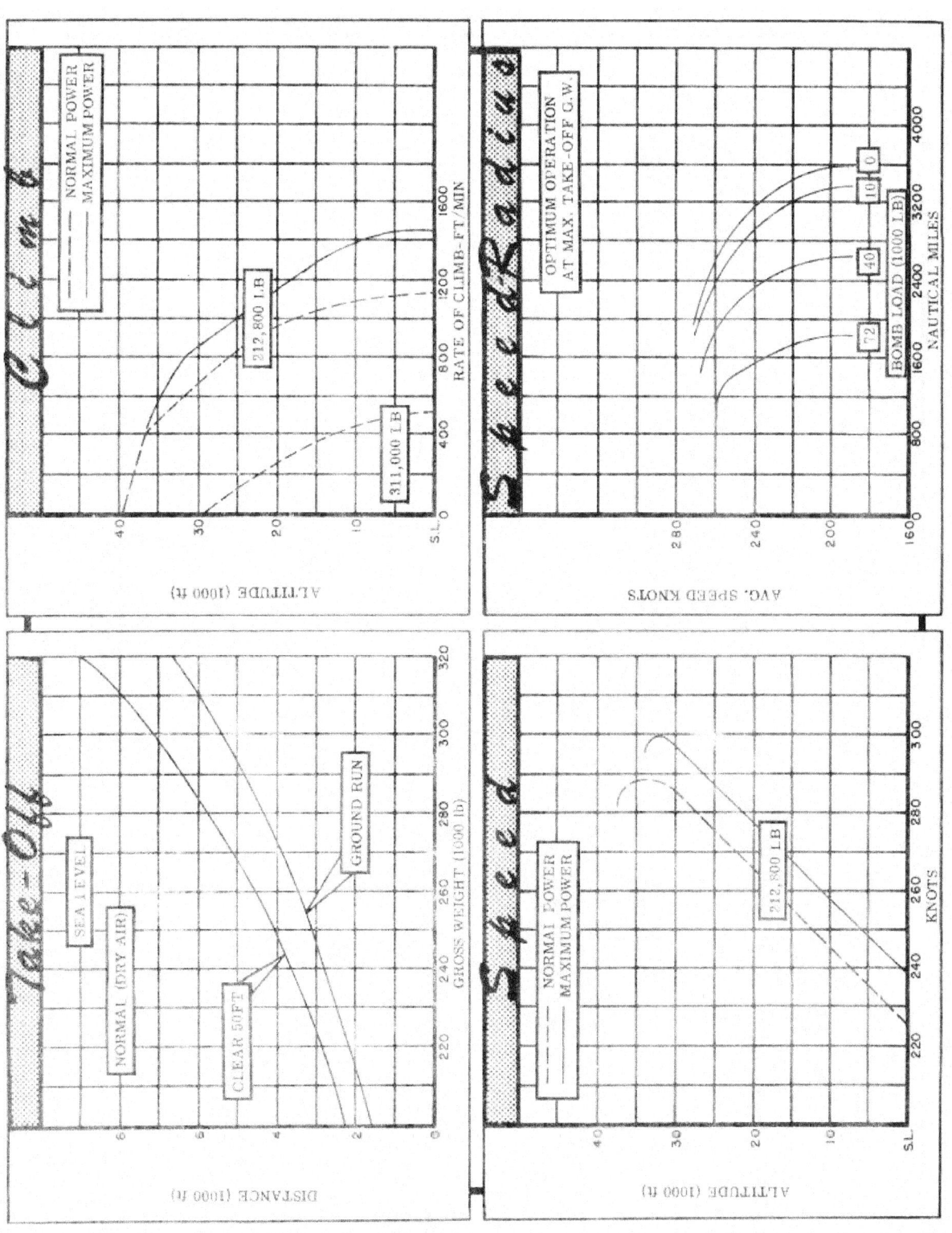

NOTES

RADIUS: MISSIONS I & III

Warm-up and take-off (allowing 10 min. normal rated power fuel consumption) and climb to 10,000 feet using normal rated power. Cruise at long range speeds at 10,000 feet to point where cruising climb is advantageous. Cruising climb is used to point where normal rated power climb is made to arrive at 25,000 feet thirty minutes prior to bomb drop. Long range speeds are flown for 15 minutes followed by a 15 minute normal rated power bomb run. Bombs are dropped and 5 minutes evasive action conducted (normal power, no distance credited); following evasive action a 10 minute normal rated power run out from the target area is made. Aircraft cruises toward base at long range speeds to point where cruising climb operation is entered to complete return to base. Endurance and landing reserve is 5% of the initial fuel loading.

RANGE: MISSIONS II & III

Warm-up and take-off (allowing 10 minutes normal rated power fuel consumption) and climb to 10,000 feet using normal rated power. At 10,000 feet the aircraft cruises at long range speeds to point where weight permits a gain by using a cruising climb. Cruising climb operation continues to point where a normal rated power climb is made to arrive at 25,000 feet 30 minutes prior to bomb drops. Aircraft cruises at long range speeds to point where 90% of initial fuel has been consumed; bombs are dropped. Endurance and landing reserve is 10% of initial fuel load.

RADIUS: MISSION IV

Allowances are the same as for missions I & II. Initial climb at normal rated power is to an altitude of 25,000 feet; climb is made to reach 40,000 feet 1000 nautical miles prior to target (instead of 30 min.). Following bomb drop aircraft cruises at long range speeds at 40,000 feet for 1000 miles; descent (no distance gained; no fuel used) is made to 35,000 feet from which point remainder of return flight is made in a cruising climb.

RADIUS: MISSION V

Allowances are the same as for missions I & II: initial climb at normal rated power is to 24,000 feet at which point a high speed cruising climb flight to a point 15 min. prior to bomb drop point is initiated. Bomb run, drop, and escape operations are as for mission I, after which the aircraft returns to base at high cruising speeds using a cruising climb technique.

RANGE: MISSION VI

Warm-up and take-off (allowing 10 minutes normal rated power fuel consumption) and climb to 10,000 feet using normal rated power. Cruise at long range speeds at 10,000 feet to point where weight permits cruising climb techniques to be advantageous; continue flight is cruising climb to point where 90% of initial fuel load has been consumed. Endurance and landing reserve is 10% of initial fuel load.

GENERAL DATA:

The B-36A may be field modified to carry a total of four bomb bay tanks; however the present weight restriction of 311,000 pounds limits usage to 5675 gallons of bomb bay fuel requiring two bomb bay tanks.

For detail planning refer to T.O. ANO1-5EUA-1.

In computing all radius and range missions the aircraft is flown at speeds corresponding to 99% maximum miles per pound. Where analysis indicates an improvement in miles per pound by using a cruising climb, this procedure has been utilized.

ENGINE RATINGS:

The power values used for performance calculations are as follows:

	R - 4360 - 25		
	BHP	RPM	ALT*
T.O:	3000	2700	S.L.
Max:	3000	2700	34,000
Nor:	2500	2550	37,000
*Turbo critical			

Characteristics Summary

BOMBER — B-36B

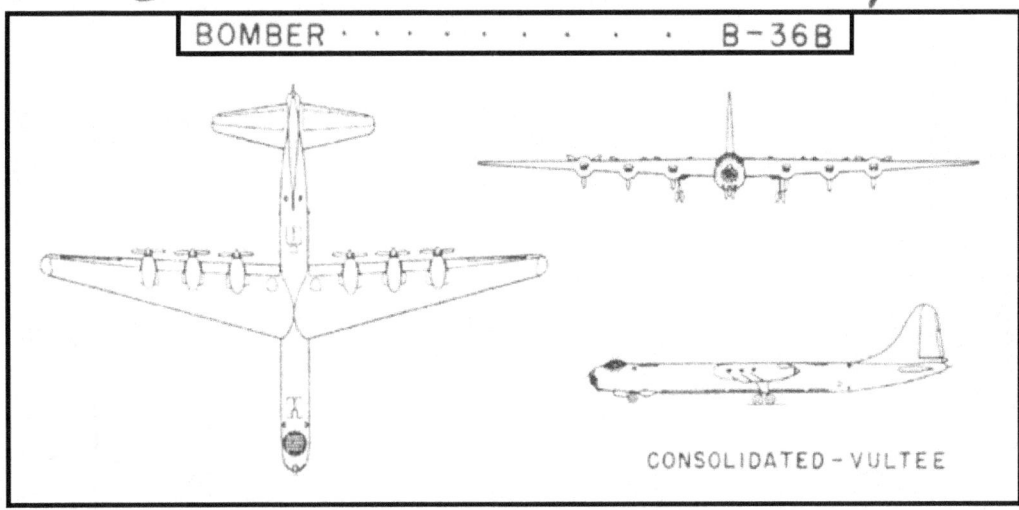

CONSOLIDATED-VULTEE

Wing area .... 4772 sq ft		Length .... 162.1 ft	
Span .... 230.0 ft		Height .... 46.8 ft	

AVAILABILITY			PROCUREMENT			
Number available			Number to be delivered in fiscal years			
ACTIVE	RESERVE	TOTAL				

STATUS

1. First flight: 8 Jul 48
2. First service use: Nov 48
3. Production completed: Sep 50

POWER PLANT

(6) R-4360-41
Pratt & Whitney
ENGINE RATINGS
BHP-RPM-ALT-MIN
T.O: *3500-2700-S.L.-5
  3250-2700-S.L.-5
Mil: *3500-2700-Turbo-30
  3250-2700-Turbo-30
Nor: 2650-2550-Turbo-Cont.

*Wet

FEATURES

Crew: 15
Cabin Pressurization
Thermal Anti-icing
Bomb-Navig.Radar, AN/ANQ-24
Gun-Laying Radar, AN/APG-3
Loran
Fuel Tank Purging
Max Fuel Cap: 33,010 gal

ARMAMENT

Turrets: 8
Guns: 16x20mm
Ammunition(tot): 9200 rds
Max Bomb Load: 2x43,000 lb
Max Bomb Size: 43,000 lb

Characteristics Summary Basic Mission · · · B-36B

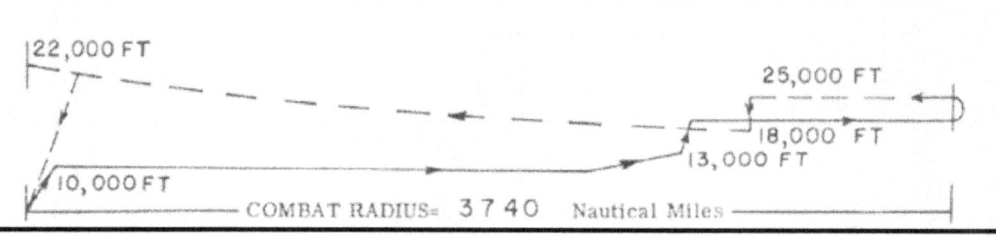

COMBAT RADIUS = 3740 Nautical Miles

PERFORMANCE

COMBAT RADIUS	COMBAT RANGE	COMBAT SPEED
3740 naut. mi with 10,000 lb payload at 177.5 knots avg. in 42.43 hours.	**7098** naut. mi with 10,000 lb payload at 176 knots avg. in 40.55 hours.	**308** knots at 25,000 ft alt, max power
		MAXIMUM SPEED
		331 knots at 34,500 ft alt, max power

CLIMB	CEILING	TAKE-OFF
500 fpm sea level, take-off weight normal power	**28,500** ft 100 fpm, take-off weight normal power	ground run 6030 ft — ft no assist · assisted
1510 fpm sea level, combat weight maximum power	**38,800** ft 500 fpm, combat weight maximum power	over 50 ft height 8520 ft — ft no assist · assisted

LOAD	WEIGHTS	STALLING SPEED

Bombs: 10,000 lb
Ammunition:
9200 rds/20mm
 	
Fuel: 26,217 gal
  protected 68 %
  droppable 20 %
  external 0 %
	Empty..... 140,640 lb
	Combat... 227,700 lb
	Take-off 328,000 lb
	
	limited by performance
		100.4 knots
		flaps down, take-off weight

		TIME TO CLIMB —

NOTES

1. PERFORMANCE BASIS:
   (a) Phase IV flight tests of No. 23, B-36B airplane.
   (b) Fuel density: 6.0 lb/gal
   (c) In computing Radius and Range, specific fuel consumptions have been increased 5% to allow for variation of fuel flow in service aircraft.
2. REVISION BASIS: To reflect performance data obtained from phase IV flight tests.

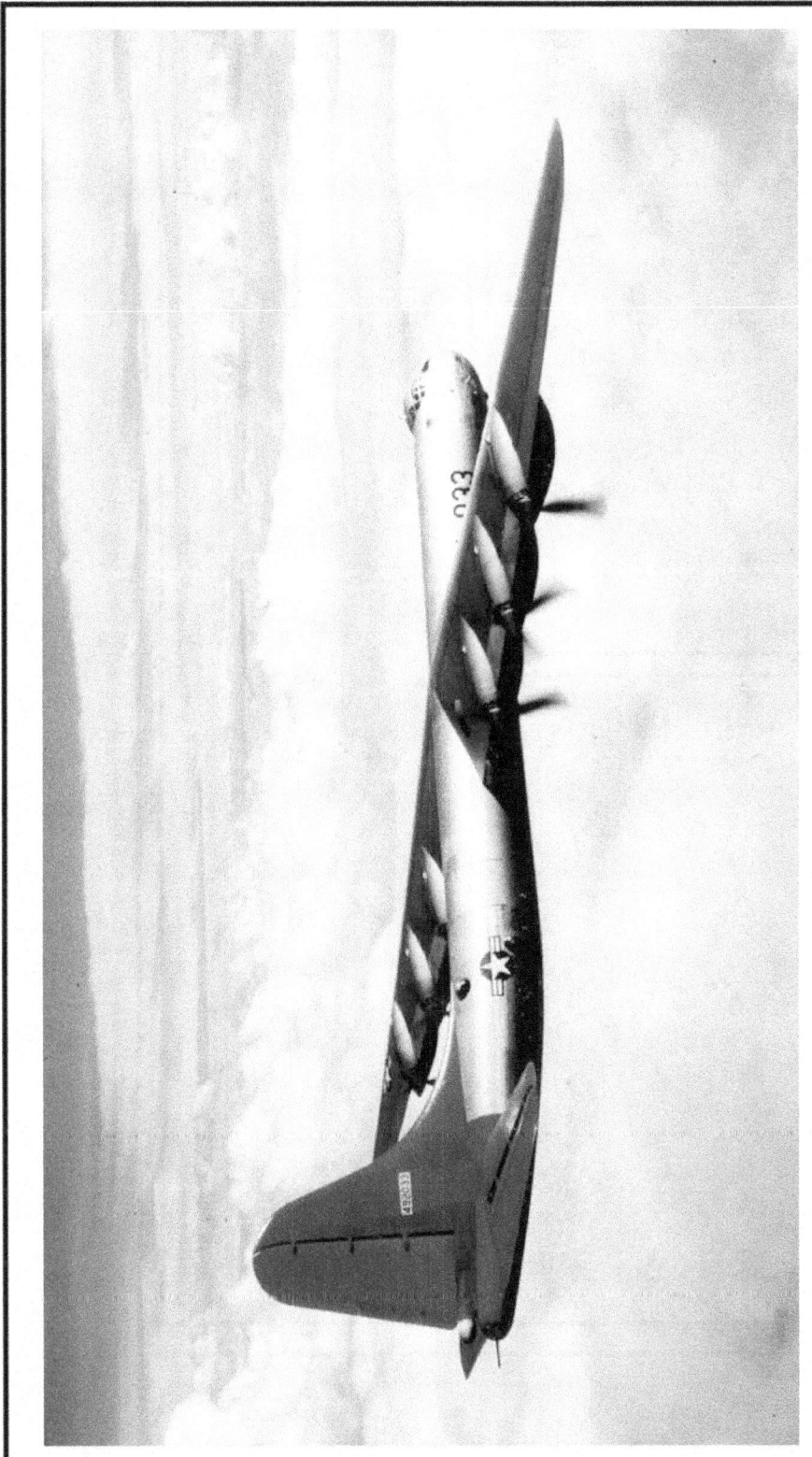

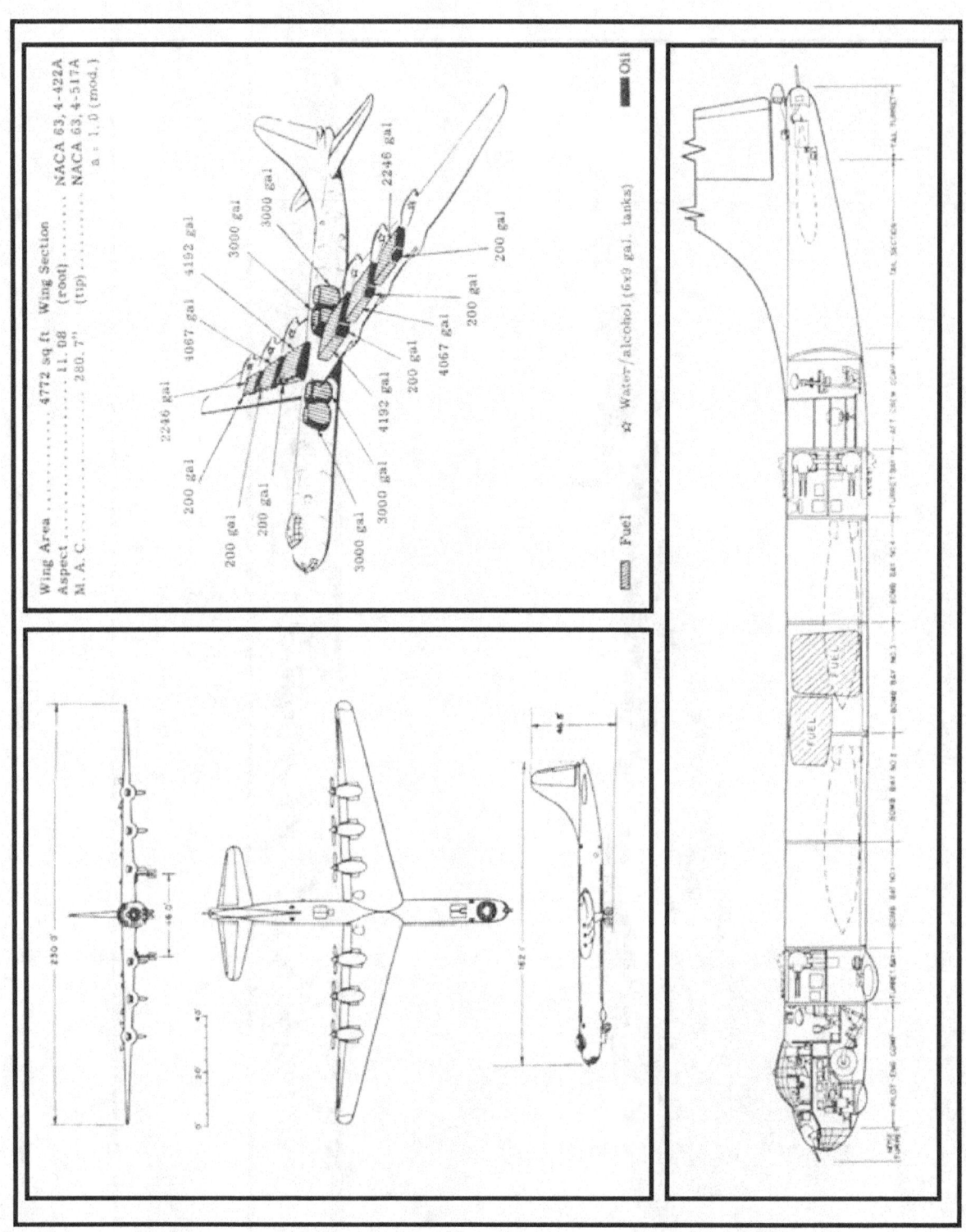

POWER PLANT

No. & Model	(6) R-4360-41
Mfr	Pratt-Whitney
Spec No.	A-7063-D
Sup. (turbo)	(2) BH-1
Turbo Mfr.	General Electric
Red. Gear Ratio	0.375
Prop. Mfr	Curtiss
Blade Design No.	1129-3C6-24
Prop. Type	CS, FF, Reverse
No. Blades	3
Prop. Dia.	19'-0"
Augmentation	Water/alcohol

ENGINE RATINGS

	BHP - RPM - ALT
T.O.	*3500 - 2700 - S.L.
	3250 - 2700 - S.L.
Mil	*3500 - 2700 - 500
Nor	2650 - 2550 - 5500
*Wet	

DIMENSIONS

Wing Span	230.0'
Incidence (root)	3°
(tip)	1°
Dihedral	2°
Sweepback (LE)	15°5'39"
Length	162.1'
Height	46.8'
Tread	46.0'
Prop. Grd Clearance	4.46'

Mission and Description

The B-36B is a long range, high altitude, very heavy bombardment type aircraft. The crew of 15 consists of the pilot, co-pilot, engineer, navigator, radar-bombardier, nose turret operator, radio operator, two upper forward gunners, two upper aft gunners, two lower aft gunners, APG-3 operator and auxiliary crew member. Crew compartments are pressurized, heated and ventilated. A pressurized tunnel permits crew movement between the forward and aft compartments. A low pressure oxygen system is provided. Portable oxygen units are utilized in case of emergency or for crew movement in nonpressurized parts of the airplane.

Cabin heating, defrosting of blisters and enclosures, and anti-icing of the propeller, wing and tail are accomplished by heated air.

The defensive armament consists of three remotely controlled retractable twin turrets, a nose turret and an APG-3 controlled tail turret. There are provisions in (18) B-36B aircraft for two remotely controlled VB-13 "Tarzon" bombs. Bombing-navigation is accomplished by APG-24 radar.

The CO_2 purging systems are provided; two for the wing tanks and one for the bomb bay tanks. Later aircraft have provisions for single-point refueling.

The Curtiss propeller incorporates a pitch changing mechanism which derives power from the propeller shaft through a hydraulically operated clutch. Final stages of feathering and initial stages of unfeathering are accomplished by an electric motor.

Major differences from the B-36A include change from R-4360-25 engines to -41 engines with fluid injection; provisions for larger bombs and additional equipment.

Development

First flight:	8 July 48
First service use:	Nov 48
Production completed:	Sep 50

WEIGHTS

Loading	Lb	L.F.
Empty	140,640(A)	
Basic	144,066(A)	
Design	278,000	2.45
Combat	*227,700(C)	
Max T.O.	†328,000	2.05
Max Land	†328,000	2.05

(A) Actual
(C) Calculated
* For Basic Mission
† Limited by performance (See page 7, Note "f")
‡ Limited by take-off weight

FUEL

Location	No. Tanks	Gal
Wg. outbd**	2	4492
Wg. inbd**	2	8384
Wg. ctr*	2	8134
Bomb Bay*	4	12,000
Self-sealing		33,010

**Partial self-sealing
† See page 7, General Data, note "b"
Grade: 115/145
Water/alcohol (gal): 54

OIL

Capacity (gal)	1200
Grade	W-1100; S-1120

GUNS

No.	Size	Rds ea	Location
2	20mm	400	Fus, nose
4	20mm	600	Fus, up, fwd
4	20mm	600	Fus, up, aft
4	20mm	600	Fus, lwr, aft
2	20mm	600	Fus, tail

BOMBS

No.	Size	Type
2	43,000	G.P.
3	22,000	D.P.
4	12,000	D.P.
12	4000	G.P.
28	2000	G.P.
44	1600	A.P.
72	1000	G.P.
132	500	G.P.

Max Bomb Load: 86,000 lb

ELECTRONICS

VHF Command	AN/ARC-3
Liaison	AN/ARC-8
Radio Compass	AN/ARN-7
Interphone	USAF Combat
IFF	SCR-695B
Glide Path	AN/ARN-5A or -5B
Bomb - Nav. Radar	AN/APQ-24
Blind Approach	RC-103A
Marker Beacon	RC-193A or B
Gun-Laying Radar	AN/APG-3
Range Receiver	BC-453B
Radar Altimeter	SCR-718
ECM See page 7, General Data, note "e"	

Loading and Performance - Typical Mission

CONDITIONS		BASIC MISSION	MAX BOMBS MISSION	40,000 FT 500 N.MI MISSION III	ALT ZONE 1000 N.MI MISSION IV	MAX SPEED MISSION V	FERRY RANGE MISSION VI
TAKE-OFF WEIGHT	(lb)	328,000	328,000	328,000	328,000	328,000	328,000
Fuel at 6.0 lb/gal(grade 115/145)	(lb)	157,304	82,831	157,304	157,304	157,304	165,775
Military load (Bombs)	(lb)	10,000	86,000	10,000	10,000	10,000	None
Wing loading	(lb/sq ft)	68.73	68.73	68.73	68.73	68.73	68.73
Stall speed(power off, land. config.) ①	(kn)	100.4	100.4	100.4	100.4	100.4	100.4
Take-off ground run at SL ①	(ft)	6030	6030	6030	6030	6030	6030
Take-off to clear 50 ft ①	(ft)	8520	8520	8520	8520	8520	8520
Rate of climb at SL ③	(fpm)	500	500	500	500	500	500
Time: SL to 10,000 ft ③	(min)	21.5	21.5	21.5	21.5	21.5	21.5
Time: SL to 20,000 ft ③	(min)	48.7	48.7	48.7	48.7	48.7	48.7
Service ceiling (100 fpm) ③	(ft)	28,500	28,500	28,500	28,500	28,500	28,500
Service ceiling (one engine out) ③	(ft)	29,100	29,100	29,100	29,100	29,100	29,100
COMBAT RANGE ④⑧	(n. mi.)	7098	2957	6668	5800	3438	7659
Average speed	(kn)	176	173	178/245	187/240	274	176
Initial cruising altitude	(ft)	10,000	10,000	10,000	10,000	32,400	10,000
Final cruising altitude	(ft)	25,000	25,000	40,000	40,000	40,000	21,800
Total mission time	(hr)	40.55	17.24	37.68	31.08	12.26	43.63
COMBAT RADIUS ④⑧	(n.mi.)	3740	1757	3500	3300	1875	—
Average speed	(kn)	177.5	180.5	186/266.5	198/263	288.5	—
Initial cruising altitude	(ft)	10,000	10,000	10,000	10,000	32,400	—
Bombing altitude ③	(ft)	25,000	25,000	40,000	40,000	39,300	—
Bomb run speed	(kn)	278	283	307	308.5	304	—
Final cruising altitude	(ft)	22,000	23,000	22,000	22,000	40,000	—
Total mission time	(hr)	42.43	19.70	37.87	33.57	13.24	—
COMBAT WEIGHT ⑤	(lb)	227,700	169,960	224,506	222,600	232,100	178,803
Combat altitude ②③	(ft)	25,000	25,000	40,000	40,000	39,300	25,000
Combat speed ②③	(kn)	308	312	314	314.5	307	313.5
Combat climb ②③ (fpm)		1110	1545	380	395	450	1700
Combat ceiling (500 fpm) ②③	(ft)	38,800	41,700	38,900	39,100	38,300	42,400
Service ceiling (100 fpm) ③	(ft)	42,500	43,500	42,600	42,650	42,350	44,100
Service ceiling (one engine out)③	(ft)	40,200	42,200	40,400	40,000	40,000	42,700
Max rate of climb at SL ②	(fpm)	1510	1920	1540	1555	1465	2070
Max speed at 34,500 ft ②	(kn)	331	338	332	332	330	340
LANDING WEIGHT ②	(lb)	168,561	163,310	168,561	168,561	168,561	178,807
Ground roll at SL ⑥	(ft)	2220	2130	2220	2220	2220	2400
Ground roll ⑦	(ft)	1700	1630	1700	1700	1700	1830
Total from 50 ft ⑥	(ft)	3320	3230	3330	3320	3320	3520
Total from 50 ft ⑦	(ft)	2800	2750	2800	2800	2800	2980

NOTES:
① Take-off power
② Max power
③ Normal power
④ Detailed descriptions of RADIUS & RANGE missions are given on page 6.
⑤ For IIadius Mission if radius is shown
⑥ Brakes only
⑦ Brakes plus 6 propellers at reverse thrust
⑧ Where two speeds are shown thus, 186/266.5 the first is the average for the entire mission and the second is the average in the combat zone.
⑨ Based on 3250 BHP at 2700 RPM

PERFORMANCE BASIS:
(a) Data source: Flight tests
(b) Performance is based on powers shown on page 7

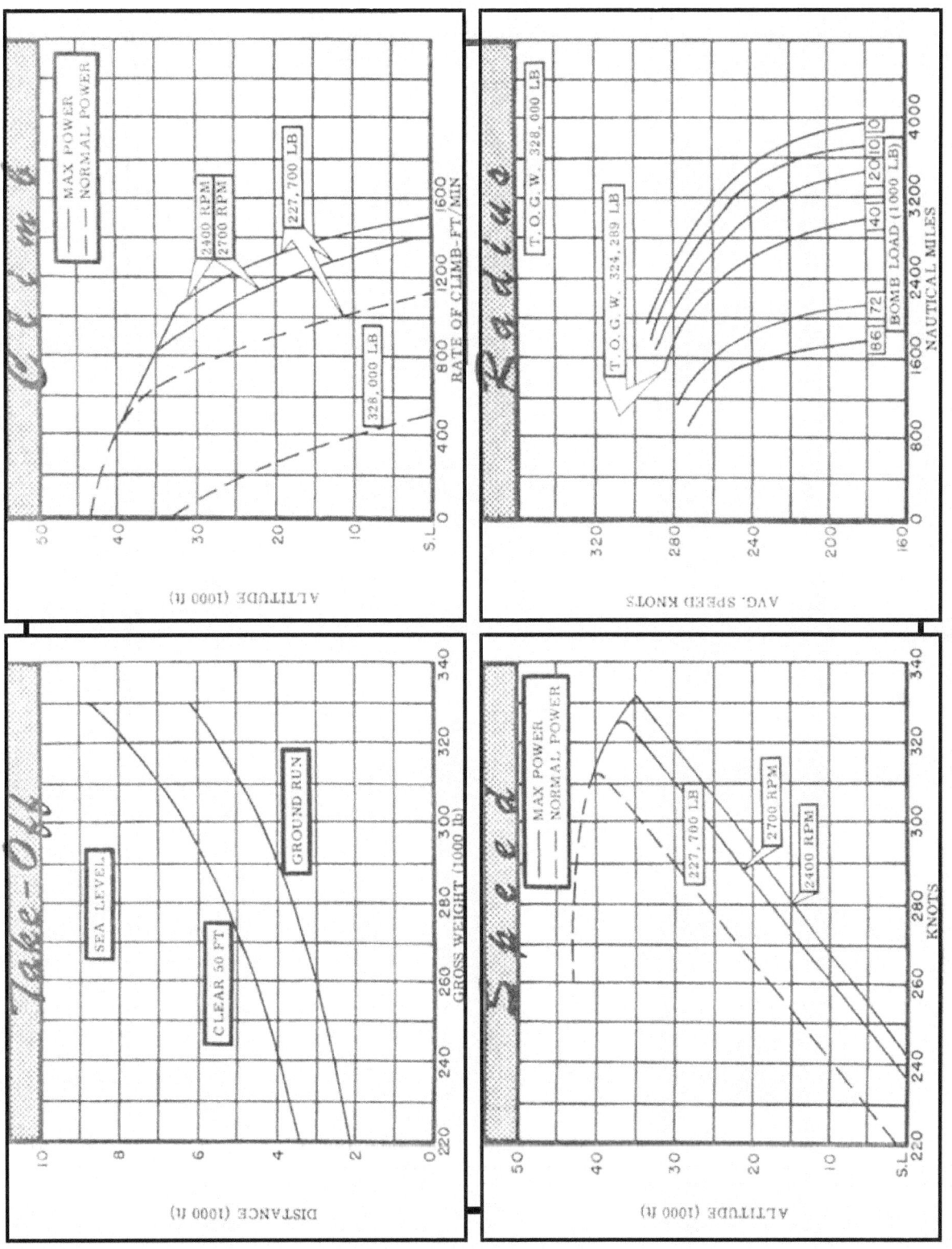

NOTES

FORMULA: RADIUS MISSION I

Start engines, warm-up, take-off, climb on course with normal power to 10,000 feet, cruise at long range speeds at altitudes for best range (10,000 feet minimum). Climb so as to arrive at 25,000 feet 30 minutes prior to target. Cruise long range speeds for 15 minutes, conduct 15 minute normal power bomb-run, drop bombs, conduct 5 minute evasive action plus 10 minutes escape at normal power. Return to base at altitudes for best range using long range cruise climb technique. Range free allowances include 10 minutes normal power fuel consumption for warm-up and take-off, 5 minutes evasive action at normal power fuel consumption and 5% initial fuel for landing and endurance reserve.

FORMULA: RANGE MISSION I

Same as outbound leg of Radius Mission I continued until 90% of initial fuel has been used and bombs are then dropped. Range free allowances include 10 minutes normal power fuel consumption for warm-up and take-off plus 10% of initial fuel for landing and endurance reserve.

FORMULA: RADIUS MISSION II

Same as Radius Mission I except for bomb load.

FORMULA: RANGE MISSION II

Same as Range Mission I except for bomb load.

FORMULA: RADIUS MISSION III & IV

Start engines, warm-up, take-off, climb on course with normal power to 10,000 feet, cruise at long range speeds at altitude for best range (10,000 feet minimum). Climb so as to arrive at 40,000 feet 500 (or 1000) nautical miles prior to target. Cruise long range speeds at 40,000 feet, conduct 15 minute normal power bomb-run, drop bombs, conduct 5 minute evasive action plus 10 minute escape at normal power. Cruise back 500 (or 1000) nautical miles from target at 40,000 feet at long range speeds. Return to base at altitudes for best range using cruise climb technique. Range free allowances include 10 minutes normal power fuel consumption for warm-up and take-off, 5 minutes evasive action at normal power fuel consumption and 5% initial fuel for landing and endurance reserve.

FORMULA: RANGE MISSION III & IV

Same as outbound leg of Radius Mission continued until 90% of fuel has been used. Range free allowances include 10 minutes normal power fuel consumption for warm-up and take-off plus 10% of initial fuel for landing and endurance reserve.

FORMULA: RADIUS MISSION V

Start engines, warm-up, take-off, climb on course to 32,400 feet using normal power, cruise to target at altitude and powers for best speed, conduct 15 minute normal power bomb run to target, drop bombs, conduct 5 minute evasive action and 10 minute escape from target at normal power. Return to base using cruising altitude (approx. 40,000 feet) and powers for best speed. Range free allowances include 10 minutes normal power fuel consumption for warm-up and take-off, 5 minutes evasive action at normal power fuel consumption plus 5% of initial fuel load for landing and endurance reserve.

FORMULA: RANGE MISSION V

Same as outbound leg of Radius Mission continued until 90% of fuel has been used. Range free allowances include 10 minutes normal power fuel consumption for warm-up and take-off plus 10% of initial fuel for landing and endurance reserve.

FORMULA: RANGE MISSION VI

Start engines, warm-up, take-off, climb on course with normal power to 10,000 feet, cruise at long range speeds at altitudes for best range (10,000 feet minimum) to point where 90% of initial fuel has been used. Range free allowances include 10 minutes normal power fuel consumption for warm-up and take-off plus 10% of initial fuel for landing and endurance reserve.

GENERAL DATA

(a) For detailed planning refer to Tech Order AN 01-5EUB-1.

(continued)

N O T E S

GENERAL DATA (continued)

(b) The B-36B may be field modified to carry a total of four bomb bay tanks; however, the present weight restriction of 328,000 pounds limits usage to 7393 gallons bomb bay fuel requiring three bomb bay tanks.

(c) For computing all radius and range missions the aircraft is flown at speeds corresponding to 99% of maximum miles per pounds at instantaneous gross weight and altitude. Where analysis indicates an improvement in miles per lb by using a cruising climb, the procedure has been utilized.

(d) Engine ratings shown on page 3 are guaranteed ratings. Power values used for performance calculations are as follows:

	R-4360-41		
	BHP	RPM	ALT**
T.O:	*3500	2700	S.L.
Max:	3250	2700	34,500
	†3250	2400	34,500
	2650	2550	39,300
Nor:	2650	2550	39,300

*Wet
†War emergency (Military power, 2400 rpm. high BMEP)
**With turbos

(e) ECM equipment consists of the following sets:

AN/APT-1, -4, -5A   AN/AHQ-8
AN/APR-4   AN/APA-38

(f) The following restriction is based on the strength of the landing gear: Max take-off gross weight equals 328,000 lb for B-36B aircraft with serial numbers 44-92068 thru -92070, 44-92076, 44,92082 thru -92087. All other B-36B's are limited to 278,000 lb gross weight for take-off except by special permission of AMC.

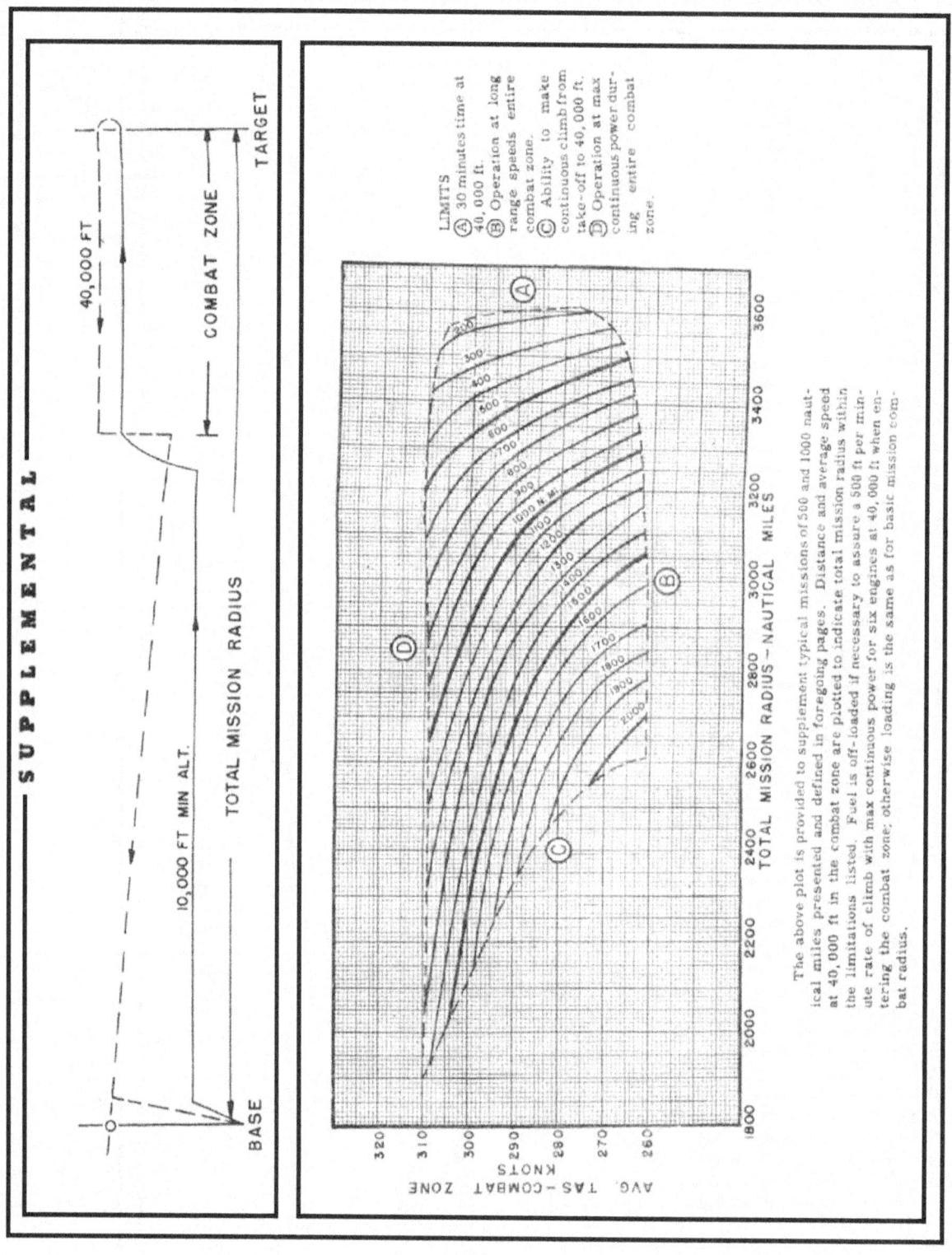

Characteristics Summary

BOMBER · · · · · · · · · · · · B-36D

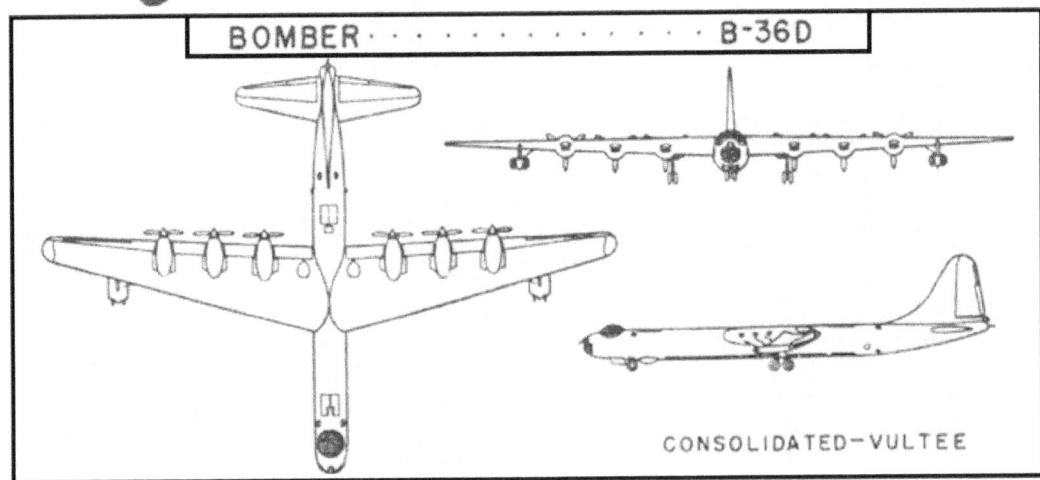

CONSOLIDATED-VULTEE

Wing area .... 4772 sq ft   Length .... 162.1 ft

Span .... 230.0 ft   Height .... 46.8 ft

AVAILABILITY

Number available

ACTIVE	RESERVE	TOTAL

PROCUREMENT

Number to be delivered in fiscal years

STATUS

1. Differs from B-36B by the addition of removable jet pods, new propeller blades and redesigned fuel system.
2. Design initiated: Jan 49
3. Prototype first flight: Mar 49
4. First Delivery: Aug 50
5. Production completed: Jun 51

Navy Equivalent: None

Mfr's Model: 36

POWER PLANT

(6) R-4360-41
Pratt and Whitney
ENGINE RATINGS
BHP-RPM-ALT-MIN
T.O: *3500-2700-Turbo-5
    3250-2700-Turbo-5
Mil: *3500-2700-Turbo-30
    3250-2700-Turbo-30
Nor: 2650-2550-Turbo-Cont.
*Wet

plus
(4) J47-GE-19
General Electric
S.L. Static LB-RPM-MIN
Max: 5200 - 7950 - 5
Mil: 5200 - 7950 - 30
Nor: 4730 - 7630 - Cont.

FEATURES

Crew: 15
Cabin Pressurization
Thermal Anti-icing
Gun-Laying Radar
Loran
Defensive ECM
Fuel Tank Purging
Removable Jet Pods
Max Fuel Cap: 33,626 gal

ARMAMENT

Turrets: 8

Guns: 16x20mm

Ammunition (tot.): 9200 rds

Max Bomb Load: 2x43,000 lb

Max Bomb Size: 43,000 lb

Characteristics Summary Basic Mission B-36D

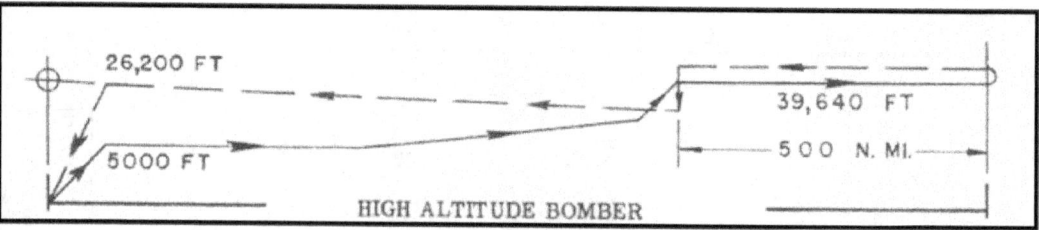

HIGH ALTITUDE BOMBER

PERFORMANCE

COMBAT RADIUS	FERRY RANGE	SPEED
3066 naut. mi with 10,000 lb payload at 193 knots avg. in 31.54 hours.	**7652** naut. mi with 30,716 gal fuel at 178.8 knots avg. in 42.79 hours at 356,854 lb T.O. wt.	COMBAT **351** knots at 39,640 ft alt, max power MAX **353** knots at 36,000 ft alt, max power BASIC **341** knots at 25,000 ft alt, max power

CLIMB	CEILING	TAKE-OFF
980 fpm sea level, take-off weight normal power	**33,100** ft 100 fpm, take-off weight normal power	ground run **4400** ft no assist —— ft assisted
2255 fpm sea level, combat weight maximum power	**40,700** ft 500 fpm, combat weight maximum power	over 50 ft height **5685** ft no assist —— ft assisted

LOAD	WEIGHTS	STALLING SPEED

Bombs: 10,000 lb
Ammunition: 9200rds/20mm
 	
Fuel: 29,995 gal
  protected 70.4 %
  droppable 0 %
  external 0 %
	Empty..... 161,371 lb
	Combat 250,300 lb
	Take-off 370,000 lb
	limited by structure
		106.8 knots
		power-off, landing configuration, take-off weight

		TIME TO CLIMB ——

NOTES

1. PERFORMANCE BASIS:
   (a) Flight Test (not substantiated by WADC)
   (b) For Combat Radius, J47 engines are used for take-off, all climbs, bomb run, evasive action and escape from target and all cruise above 30,000 feet.

2. REVISION BASIS: To reflect latest performance data.

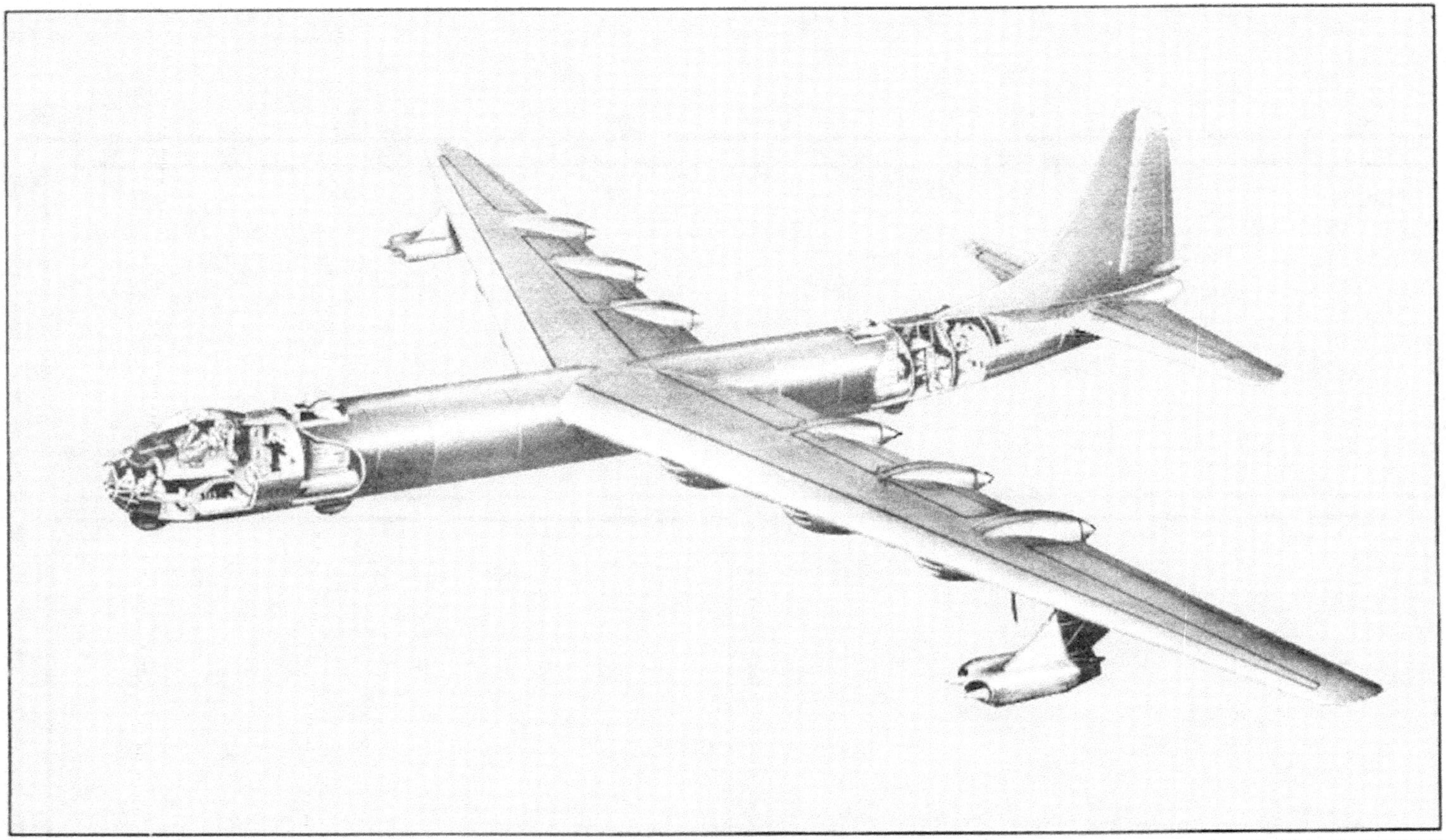

Standard Aircraft Characteristics

B-36D
Consolidated-Vultee

SIX R-4360-41
PRATT & WHITNEY
AND
FOUR J47-GE-19
GENERAL ELECTRIC

BY AUTHORITY OF
COMMANDING GENERAL
AIR MATERIEL COMMAND
U.S. AIR FORCE

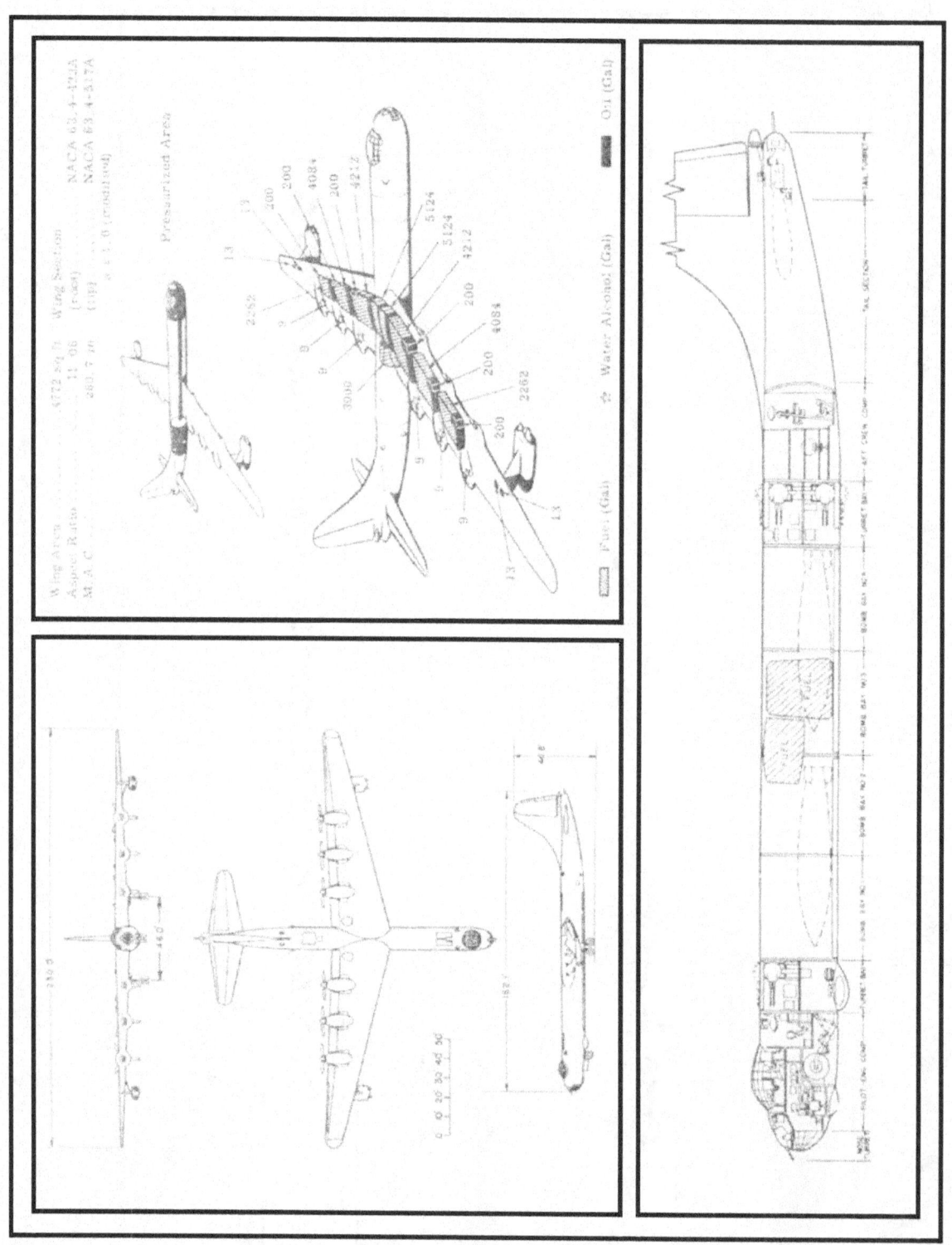

POWER PLANT

No. & Model	(6) R-4360-41
Mfr	Pratt & Whitney
Spec No.	A-7063-D
Turbo Mfr	General Electric
	(2) BH-1
Red. Gear Ratio	0.375
Prop. Mfr	Curtiss
Blade Design No.	1129-11C6-24
Prop. Type	CS, FF Reverse
No. Blades	3
Prop. Dia	9'-0"
Augmentation	Water/alcohol

	plus	
No. & Model		(4) J47-GE-19
Mfr		General Electric
Spec No.		E-589
Type		Axial
Length		143"
Diameter		39"
Weight (dry)		2475 lb

ENGINE RATINGS

	BHP - RPM - ALT - MIN
T.O.	*3500 - 2700 - Turbo - 5
	3250 - 2700 - Turbo - 5
Mil:	*3500 - 2700 - Turbo - 30
	3250 - 2700 - Turbo - 30
Nor:	2650 - 2550 - Turbo - Cont

*Wet plus

	LB - RPM - MIN
S. L. Static	
Max	5200 - 7950 - 5
Mil:	5200 - 7950 - 30
Nor:	4730 - 7630 - Cont

DIMENSIONS

Wing	
Span	230.0'
Incidence (root)	3°
(tip)	2°
Dihedral	2°
Sweepback (LE)	15°5'39"
Length	162.1'
Height	46.8'
Tread	46.0'
Prop. Grd Clearance	4.46'

Mission and Description

Navy Equivalent: None Mfr Model: 36

The B-36D is a long range, high altitude, very heavy bombardment type aircraft. The mission of the aircraft is the destruction by bombs of enemy ground and naval materiel objectives. The crew of 15 consists of the pilot, co-pilot, flight engineer, navigator, radar-bombardier, nose turret gunner, radio operator, two upper forward gunners, two upper aft gunners, two lower aft gunners, APG operator and auxiliary crew member. Crew compartments are pressurized, heated and ventilated. A pressurized tunnel permits crew movement between the forward and aft pressurized compartments. A low pressure oxygen system is provided. Portable oxygen units are utilized in case of emergency or for crew movement in non-pressurized parts of the aircraft.

Cabin heating, defrosting of blisters and enclosures and anti-icing of the propeller, wing and tail are accomplished by heated air. A bombing-navigational system with a vertical optical sight and radar equipment for blind for visual bombing and navigation is provided. This system allows for a single crew member to act as radar operator and bombardier. The defensive armament consists of three (3) remotely controlled, retractable twin turrets, a nose turret and an APG-controlled tail turret.

Three CO2 purging systems are provided, two for the wing tanks and one for the bomb bay tank. The aircraft has a single point refueling, manifold type fuel system.

The Curtiss propellers incorporate a pitch changing mechanism which derives power from the propeller shaft through a hydraulically-operated clutch. Final stages of feathering and initial stages of unfeathering are accomplished by an electric motor.

Development

Design initiated:	12 Jan 49
First flight prototype:	26 Mar 49
First delivery:	19 Aug 50
In current production	

BOMBS

No.	Size	Type
2	43,000	G.P.
3	22,000	D.P.
4	12,000	D.P.
12	4,000	G.P.
28	2,000	G.P.
44	1,600	A.P.
72	1,000	G.P.
132	500	G.P.

Max Bomb Load: 86,000 lb

WEIGHTS

Loading	Lb	L.F.
Empty	160,974(C)	
Basic	164,640(C)	
Design	357,500	2.08
Combat	†248,410	2.08
Max T.O.	†357,500	2.08
Max Land	†357,500	2.08

(C) Calculated
*For Basic Mission
† Limited by strength
For weights with pod removed see page 8, note (c)

FUEL

Location	No. Tanks	Gal
Wg. outbd*	2	4524
Wg. ctr*	2	8168
Wg. inbd*	2	8424
Center sec		10,248
Bomb bay**	1	3000
*Partial s.s.	Total	†34,364

**s.s.
Grade 115/145 Jet .52

OIL

		Recap
Capacity (gal)	S-1120:W-1200	1200
Grade	See page 8, note (u)	FLUID INJECTION
Eng Nac	6	54

GUNS

No.	Size	Rds ea	Location
2	20mm	400	Fus. nose
4	20mm	600	Fus. up, fwd
4	20mm	600	Fus. up, aft
4	20mm	600	Fus. lwr, aft
2	20mm	600	Fus. tail

ELECTRONICS

VHF Command	AN/ARC-3
Liaison	AN/ARC-8
Radio Compass	AN/ARN-7A
Marker Beacon	AN/ARN-12
I.F.F.	AN/APX-6
Blind Approach	RC-103D
Glide Path	AN/ARN-5B
Bombing-Nav. Radar	K-1, K-3 or K-3A
Loran	AN/APN-9A
Gun Laying Radar	AN/APG-3 or -32
Radio Range	BC-453B
Interphone	
Defensive ECM	USAF Combat

Loading and Performance — Typical Mission

B-360 PODS ATTACHED

CONDITIONS		BASIC MISSION I	MAX BOMBS II	40,000 FT ALT ZONE 500 N.MILES III	40,000 FT ALT ZONE 1000 N.MILES IV	MAX SPEED V	FERRY RANGE VI
TAKE-OFF WEIGHT	(lb)	357,500	357,500	357,500	357,500	357,500	357,500
Fuel at 6.0 lb/gal (grade 115/145)	(lb)	170,148	91,489	170,148	170,148	170,148	180,533
Military load (bombs)	(lb)	10,000	86,000	10,000	10,000	10,000	None
Wing loading	(lb/sq ft)	74.92	74.92	74.92	74.92	74.92	74.92
Stall speed (power off, landing configuration) ①	(ft)	105	105	105	105	105	105
Take-off ground run at SL ①	(ft)	4505	4505	4505	4505	4505	4505
Take-off to clear 50 ft ①	(ft)	5610	5610	5610	5610	5610	5610
Rate of climb at SL ③	(fpm)	1070	1070	1070	1070	1070	1070
Time SL to 10,000 ft ③	(min)	10.5	10.5	10.5	10.5	10.5	10.5
Time SL to 20,000 ft ③	(min)	23.7	23.7	23.7	23.7	23.7	23.7
Service ceiling (100 fpm) ④	(ft)	36,800	36,800	36,800	36,800	36,800	36,800
Service ceiling (one engine out) ②	(ft)	35,700	35,700	35,700	35,700	35,700	35,700
COMBAT RANGE ④⑦	(n. mi.)	6278	2675	6169	6030	2550	7175
Average speed	(kn)	182	176	185/254	185/253	321	484
Initial cruising altitude	(ft)	10,000	10,000	10,000	10,000	32,650	10,000
Final cruising altitude	(ft)	25,000	25,000	40,000	40,000	39,400	23,450
Total mission time	(hr)	34.77	15.28	33.47	32.55	8.11	39.17
COMBAT RADIUS ④⑦	(n. mi.)	3360	1485	3111	2870	1400	---
Average speed	(kn)	186	180	196/281	210/218	337	---
Initial cruising altitude	(ft)	10,000	10,000	10,000	10,000	32,630	---
Bombing altitude ③	(ft)	25,000	25,000	40,000	40,000	39,400	---
Bomb run speed	(kn)	343	329	351	353	332	---
Final cruising altitude	(ft)	25,200	25,000	25,200	25,200	39,400	---
Total mission time	(hr)	18.45	15.86	32.03	27.57	8.56	---
COMBAT WEIGHT ②	(lb)	248,410	213,200	244,800	242,200	256,700	195,021
Combat altitude ②	(ft)	25,000 ⑧	25,000	40,000	40,000	39,400	23,450 ⑧
Combat speed ②③	(kn)	344 ⑧	344 ⑧	364	364	363	325 ⑧
Combat climb ②	(fpm)	1720	3150	770	790	760	2500
Combat ceiling (500 fpm) ③	(ft)	41,850	43,900	42,050	42,200	41,350	44,350
Service ceiling (100 fpm) ③	(ft)	44,300	45,650	44,550	44,650	43,900	47,500
Service ceiling (one engine out) ②	(ft)	42,600	44,300	42,800	42,850	42,050	45,800
Max rate of climb at SL ③	(fpm)	2408	2887	2455	2485	2315	3292
Max speed at 34,300 ft ②	(kn)	373	378	374	374	372	380
LANDING WEIGHT ⑤	(lb)	185,859	184,585	185,859	185,859	185,859	185,921
Ground roll at SL ⑤⑥	(ft)	1750	1740	1750	1750	1750	1835
Total from 50 ft ⑥	(ft)	3025	3010	3025	3025	3025	3150

NOTES:
① Take-off power
② Max power
③ Normal power
④ Detailed descriptions of RADIUS and RANGE missions are given on page 8
⑤ For Radius Mission if radius is shown
⑥ Brakes only
⑦ When two speeds are shown thus 196/281, the first is the average for the entire mission and the second the average for the combat zone
⑧ Limited by propeller vibration

PERFORMANCE BASIS
(a) Data source: Preliminary flight test
(b) Performance is based on powers shown on page 8.

SUPPLEMENTAL
Loading and Performance — Typical Mission

B-36D PODS REMOVED

CONDITIONS		BASIC MISSION	MAX BOMBS	40,000 FT ALT ZONE 500 N MILES	40,000 FT ALT ZONE 1000 N MILES	MAX SPEED	FERRY RANGE
TAKE-OFF WEIGHT	(lb)	328,000	328,000	328,000	328,000	328,000	328,000
Fuel at 6.0 lb/gal (grade 115/145)	(lb)	155,151	77,134	155,151	155,151	155,151	165,536
Military load (bombs)	(lb)	10,000	86,000	10,000	10,000	10,000	None
Wing loading	(lb/sq ft)	68.73	68.73	68.73	68.73	68.73	68.73
Stall speed (power off, landing configuration) (1)	(kn)	101	101	101	101	101	101
Take-off ground run at SL (3)	(ft)	5000	6000	6000	6000	6000	6000
Take-off to clear 50 ft (3)	(ft)	8320	8320	8520	8520	8520	8520
Rate of climb at SL (3)	(fpm)	500	500	500	500	500	500
Time SL to 10,000 ft (3)	(min)	22.5	22.5	22.5	22.5	22.5	22.5
Time SL to 20,000 ft (3)	(min)	50.1	50.1	50.1	50.1	50.1	50.1
Service ceiling (100 fpm) (3)	(ft)	28,700	28,700	28,700	28,700	28,700	28,700
Service ceiling (one engine out) (2)	(ft)	29,120	29,120	29,120	29,120	29,120	29,120
COMBAT RANGE (4)	(n. mi.)	6690	2867	5810	5831	3282	7472
Average speed	(kn)	186	184	194/256	194/256	303	185
Initial cruising altitude	(ft)	10,000	10,000	10,000	10,000	34,250	10,000
Final cruising altitude	(ft)	25,000	25,000	40,000	40,000	39,400	26,800
Total mission time	(hr)	36.17	15.77	42.13	30.17	11.02	40.02
COMBAT RADIUS	(n. mi.)	3600	1564	3384	3150	1770	
Average speed	(kn)	188	189	195/270	207/267	286	
Initial cruising altitude	(ft)	10,000	10,000	10,000	10,000	34,250	
Bombing altitude	(ft)	25,000	25,000	40,000	40,000	39,400	
Bomb run speed	(kn)	277	266	308	310	305	
Final cruising altitude	(ft)	28,000	28,250	28,000	28,000	39,400	
Total mission time	(hr)	38.50	16.88	34.77	30.73	12.63	
COMBAT WEIGHT (5)	(lb)	229,950	193,900	226,650	223,700	235,800	179,018
Combat altitude	(ft)	25,000	25,000	40,000	40,000	39,400	26,800
Combat speed	(kn)	307	312	313	314	312	319
Combat climb	(fpm)	1060	1580	435	450	420	1900
Combat ceiling (500 fpm)	(ft)	38,950	41,300	39,200	39,400	38,450	42,300
Service ceiling (100 fpm)	(ft)	42,400	43,400	42,550	42,700	42,150	44,450
Service ceiling (one engine out)	(ft)	39,650	42,500	40,150	40,400	39,350	43,350
Max rate of climb at SL	(fpm)	1475	1863	1393	1335	1422	2061
Max speed at 34,600 ft	(kn)	330	338	331	332	329	340
LANDING WEIGHT (2)	(lb)	170,607	168,723	170,607	170,607	170,607	179,018
Ground roll at SL (6)	(ft)	1610	1590	1610	1610	1610	1690
Total from 50 ft (6)	(ft)	2830	2810	2830	2830	2830	2940

NOTES:
(1) Take-off power
(2) Max power
(3) Normal power
(4) Detailed descriptions of RADIUS and RANGE missions are given on page 8
(5) For Radius Mission if radius is shown, the second is the speed in the combat zone.
(6) Brakes only
(7) When two speeds are shown, thus 195/270, the first is the average for the entire mission

PERFORMANCE BASIS:
(a) Data source: Preliminary flight test
(b) Performance is based on powers shown on page 8.

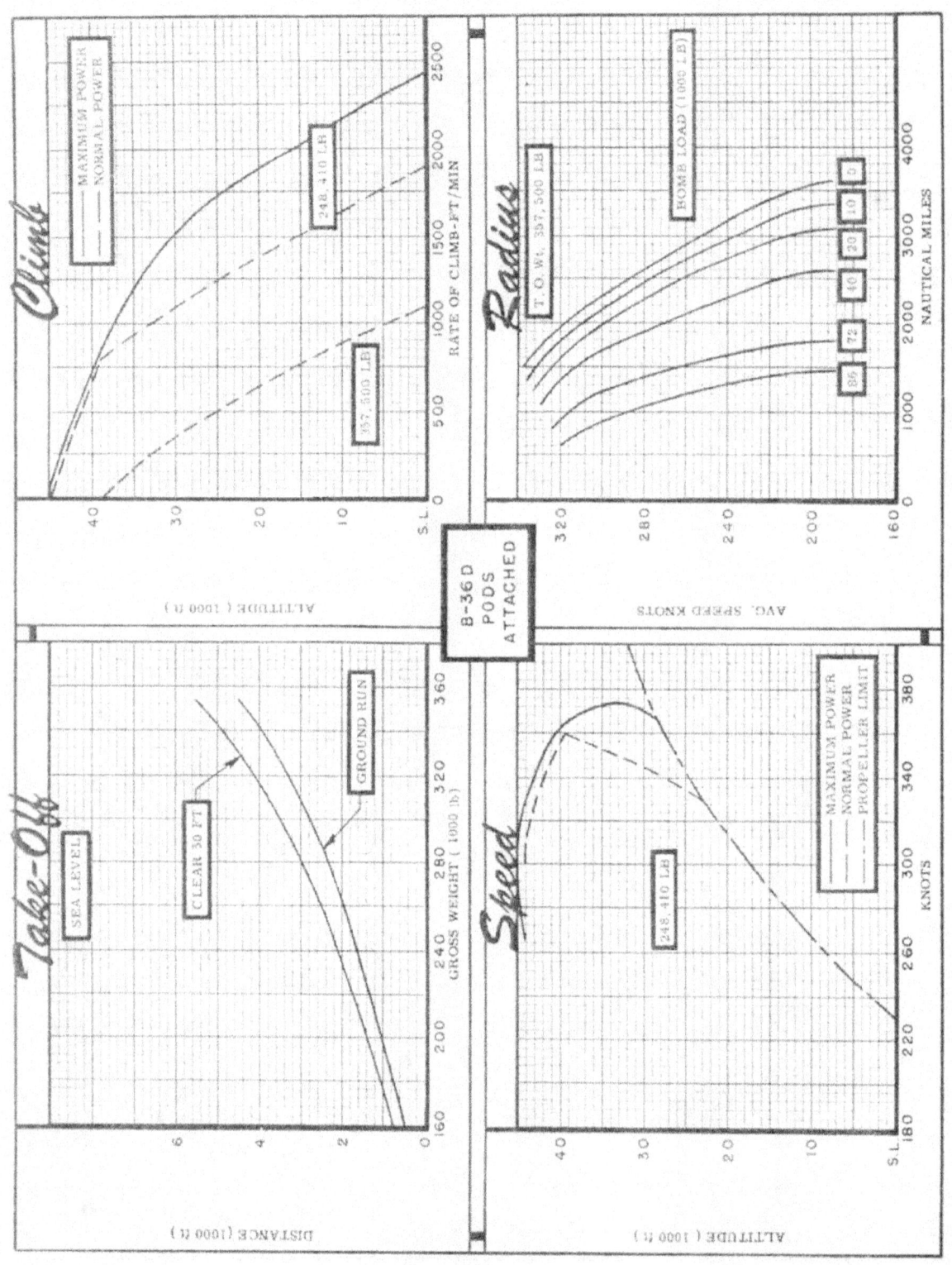

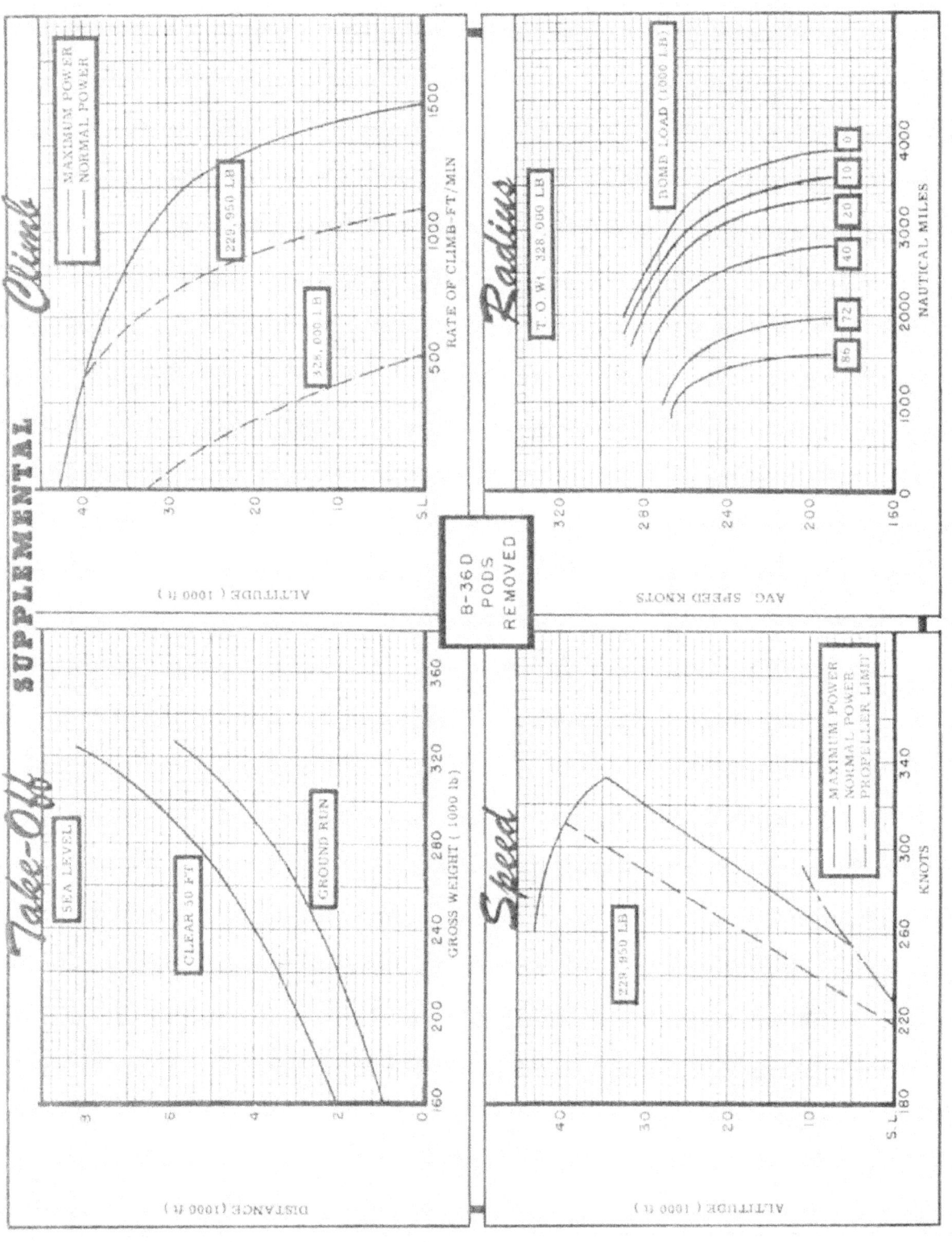

NOTES

FORMULA: RADIUS MISSIONS I & II

Start engines, warm-up, take-off and climb on course using normal power to 10,000 feet, cruise at long range speeds at altitudes for best range (10,000 feet minimum). Climb so as to arrive at 25,000 feet 30 minutes prior to target. Cruise at long range speeds for 15 minutes, conduct 15 minute bomb run at normal power, drop bombs, conduct 5 minutes evasive action and 10 minutes escape from target at normal power. Return to base at long range speeds, cruising at optimum altitude for mileage. Jet engines (if installed) are operating during take-off, climb and during normal power operation in target area. Range free allowances include 10 minutes normal power fuel consumption for R-4360-41 plus 5 minutes normal power fuel consumption for J47-GE-19 (if installed) for warm-up and take-off, 5 minutes normal power fuel consumption for R-4360-41 and J47-GE-19 (if installed) for evasive action, plus 5% of initial fuel load for landing and endurance reserve.

FORMULA: RADIUS MISSIONS III & IV

Start engines, warm-up, take-off and climb on course using normal power to 10,000 feet, cruise at long range speeds at 10,000 feet altitude. Climb so as to arrive at 40,000 feet 500 or 1000 nautical miles prior to target. Cruise at long range speeds at 40,000 feet followed by 15 minutes evasive action and 10 minutes escape from target at normal power. Cruise at long range speeds at 40,000 feet until 500 or 1000 nautical miles from target. Return to base at long range speeds and optimum altitude for mileage. Jet engines (if installed) are operative during take-off, all climbs, during normal power operation in target area and whenever operation gives better mileage-speed relationship than is obtainable with jet engines imperative. Range free allowances are the same as the Mission I & II.

FORMULA: RADIUS MISSION V

Start engines, warm-up and take-off, climb on course using normal power to altitude for optimum speed range operation (approx 32,000 feet), cruise toward target at altitude and powers for optimum speed-range. Conduct 15 minutes normal power bomb-run, drop bombs, conduct 5 minutes evasive action plus 10 minute escape from target at normal power, return to base at powers and altitude for best speed-range operation. Jet engines are operative (if installed) during take-off, climb, during normal power operation in target area and whenever operation gives better mileage-speed relationship than is obtainable with jet engines inoperative. Range free allowances are the same as for Radius Mission I & II.

FORMULA: RANGE MISSIONS I, II, III, IV & V

Same as outbound leg of radius missions continued until 90% of initial fuel load has been consumed. Range free allowances include 10 minutes normal power fuel consumption for R-4360-41 plus 5 minutes normal power fuel consumption for J47-GE-19 (if installed) for warm-up and take-off, plus 10% of initial fuel load for landing and endurance reserve.

FORMULA: RANGE MISSION VI

Start engines, warm-up, take-off and climb on course to 10,000 feet using normal power, cruise at long range speeds at altitude for best range (minimum 10,000 feet) until 90% of fuel has been consumed. Jet engines (if installed) are used for take-off and climb. Range free allowances are the same as Range Missions I through V.

GENERAL DATA

(a) Total fuel capacity is usable only for special loadings with equipment removed from the aircraft.

(b) Engine ratings shown on page 3 are manufacturers' guaranteed ratings. Power values used for performance calculations are as follows:

R-4360-41			J47-GE-19		
	BHP-RPM-ALT**	MIN		S.L. Static LB - RPM	MIN
T.O.	*3500-2700-S.L.	5	T.O.	5200-7950	5
Mil:	3250-2700-34,500-30		Max.	5200-7950	30
Max W.E.	3250-2400-34,500-15		Nor.	4750-7630	Cont
Nor.	2650-2550-39,300-Cont				
Nor.	2650-2550-39,300-Cont				

*Wet
**With turbos

(c) Weights with pods removed are as follows:

Loading	Lb
Empty	146,621
Combat	229,950
Take-off	328,000+

+Limited by performance.

SUPPLEMENTAL

COMBAT ZONE MISSIONS

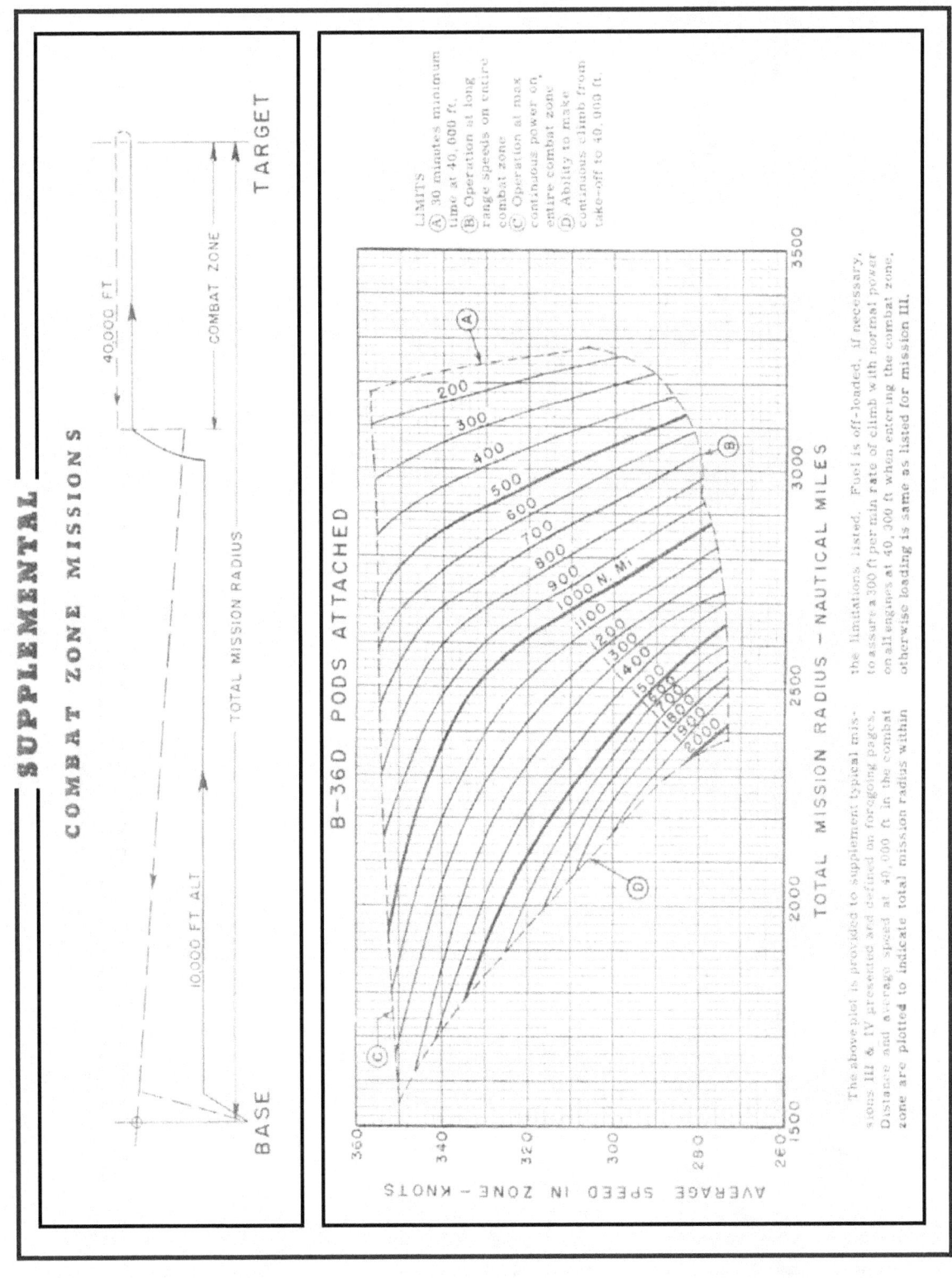

B-36D PODS ATTACHED

LIMITS
- Ⓐ 30 minutes minimum time at 40,000 ft.
- Ⓑ Operation at long range speeds on entire combat zone
- Ⓒ Operation at max continuous power on entire combat zone
- Ⓓ Ability to make continuous climb from take-off to 40,000 ft

The above plot is provided to supplement typical missions III & IV presented and defined on foregoing pages. Distance and average speed at 40,000 ft in the combat zone are plotted to indicate total mission radius within the limitations listed. Fuel is off-loaded, if necessary, to assure a 300 ft per min rate of climb with normal power on all engines at 40,000 ft when entering the combat zone, otherwise loading is same as listed for mission III.

SUPPLEMENTAL
COMBAT ZONE MISSIONS

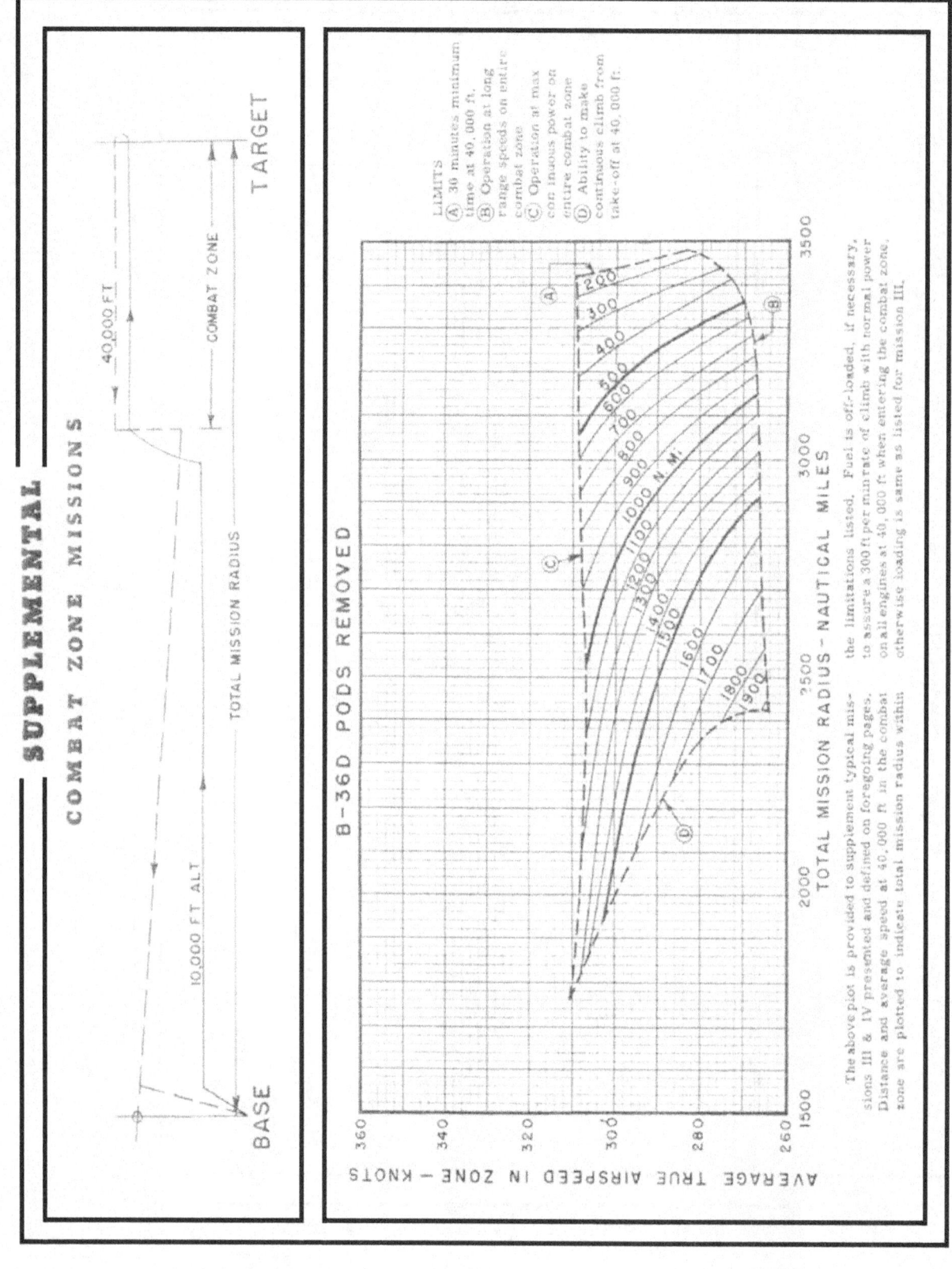

Characteristics Summary

BOMBER . . . . B-36D (III)

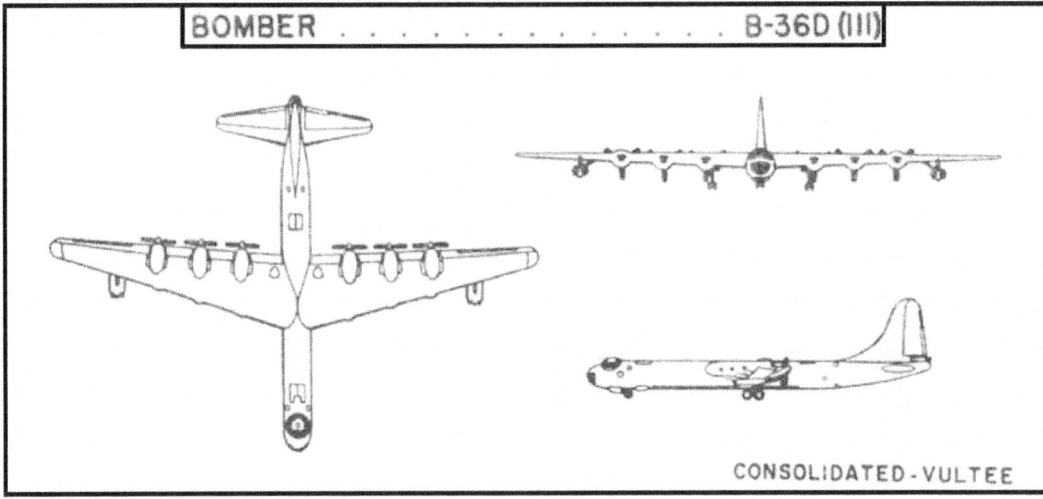

CONSOLIDATED-VULTEE

Wing Area. . . . . .4772 sq ft   Length. . . . . 162.1 ft

Span. . . . . .230.0 ft.   Height . . . . 46.8 ft

AVAILABILITY

Number available

ACTIVE	RESERVE	TOTAL

PROCUREMENT

Number to be delivered in fiscal years

STATUS

1. Contract Approved: Feb. 54
2. First Flight: June 54
3. First Delivery: June 54
4. Modification Completed: Dec. 54

Navy Equivalent: None

5. Major difference from the B-36D standard aircraft is the removal of all turrets except tail turret, self-sealing pads and fuel purging system; replacement of blisters by small flush windows.

Mfr's Model: 36

POWER PLANT

(6) R-4360-41
Pratt and Whitney
ENGINE RATINGS
BHP   RPM   ALT   MIN
T.O.:*3500 - 2700 - Turbo - 5
      3250 - 2700 - Turbo - 5
Mil: *3500 - 2700 - Turbo - 30
      3250 - 2700 - Turbo - 30
Nor: 2650 - 2550 - Turbo - Cont
*Wet

plus
(4) J47-GE-19
General Electric
S.L.Static   LB   RPM   MIN
Max: 5200 - 7950 - 5
Mil: 5200 - 7950 - 30
Nor: 4730 - 7630 - Cont

FEATURES

Crew. 13
Cabin Pressurization
Thermal Anti-Icing
Bombing-Navigational Radar
K-3A System
Chaff Dispenser AN/ALE-6
Gun-Laying Radar AN/APG-32 or AN/APG-32A
Loran
Defensive ECM
Single Point Fueling
Removable Jet Pods

Max Fuel Cap:. . .*33,626 gal

ARMAMENT

Turrets 1
Guns . ,2 x 20 mm (M-24A1)
Ammunition(tot) . . 1200 rds
BOMBS (max):
              Class (lb)   Load
WWII
(Box Fin):12 x 4000/72 x 1000
INTERIM
(Conical Fin):
              26 x 2000/129 x 500

NEW SERIES:
              6 x 3000/48 x 750

Characteristics Summary Basic Mission B-36D (III)

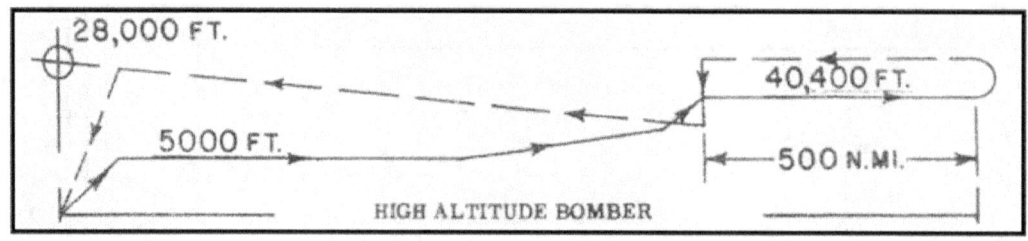

HIGH ALTITUDE BOMBER

PERFORMANCE

COMBAT RADIUS	FERRY RANGE	SPEED
3260 naut. mi with 11,408 lb payload at 192 knots avg. in 33.7 hours.	8200 Naut. Mi. with 32,957 gal fuel at 181 knots avg. in 45.5 hours at 370,000 lb T.O. wt.	COMBAT 359 knots at 40,400 ft alt, max power MAX 363 knots at 37,300 ft alt, max power BASIC 343 knots at 25,000 ft alt, max power

CLIMB	CEILING	TAKE-OFF
970 fpm sea level, take-off weight normal power	31,400 ft 100 fpm, take-off weight normal power	ground run 4400 ft no assist | ____ ft assisted
2330 fpm sea level, combat weight maximum power	41,300 ft 500 fpm, combat weight maximum power	over 50 ft height 5685 ft no assist | ____ ft assisted

LOAD	WEIGHTS	STALLING SPEED

Bombs: 10,000 lb
Chaff: 1408 lb
Ammunition: 1200 rds/20mm
Fuel: 30,991 gal
  protected (Part).. 0%
  droppable..... 0%
  external..... 0%
	Empty....... 161,264 lb
	Combat....... 244,400 lb
	Take-Off.... *370,000 lb
	*Limited by structure
		107 knots power-off, landing configuration, take-off weight

		TIME TO CLIMB

NOTES

1. Performance Basis:
    Calculations based on flight test of B-36D Aircraft with configuration adjustments.

2. Revision Basis:
    To reflect Featherweight Flight Test data and approved engineering changes.

Standard Aircraft Characteristics

B-36D-111

Consolidated-Vultee

SIX R-4360-41
PRATT & WHITNEY

FOUR J47-GE-19
GENERAL ELECTRIC

BY AUTHORITY OF
THE SECRETARY
OF THE AIR FORCE

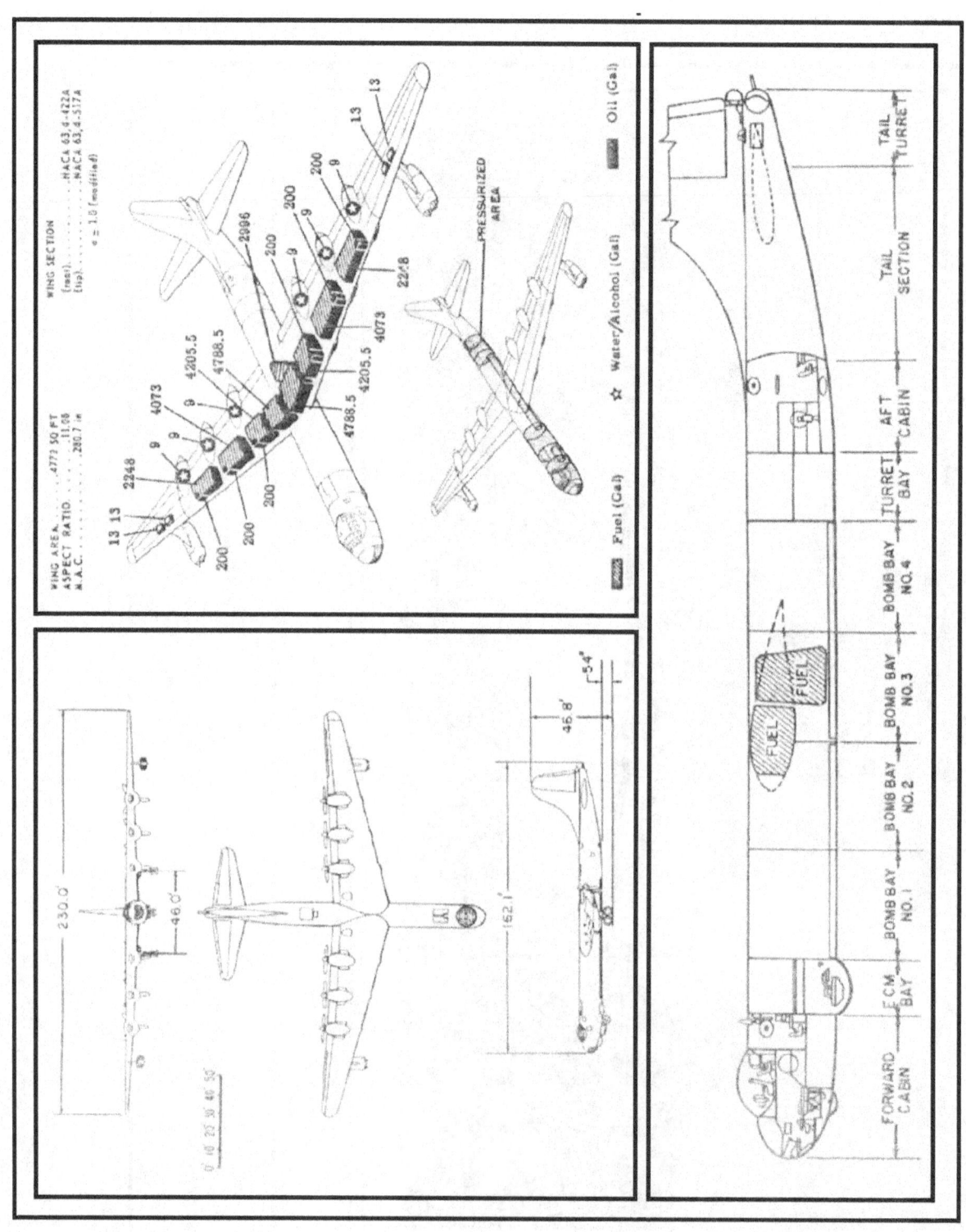

POWER PLANT

No. & Model	(6) R-4360-41
Mfr.	Pratt & Whitney
Engine Spec. No.	A-7063-E
Superch.	1 stg. 1 spd
Turbo Superch.	(2) BH-1
Turbo Mfr.	General Electric
Red. Gear Ratio	0.375
Prop Mfr	Curtiss
Blade Design No.	1129-17C6-24
Prop Type	CS, FF, Reverse
No. Blades	3
Prop Dia.	19'-0"
Augmentation	Water/alcohol

plus

No. & Model	(4) J47-GE-19
Mfr.	General Electric
Engine Spec No	E-569
Type	Axial
Length	144"
Diameter	39"
Weight (dry)	2495 lb
Tail Pipe	Fixed Area

ENGINE RATINGS

	BHP	RPM	ALT	MIN
T.O.:	*3500	2700	Turbo	5
	3250	2700	Turbo	5
Mil:	*3500	2700	Turbo	30
	3250	2700	Turbo	30
Nor:	2650	2550	Turbo	Cont

plus

	LB	RPM	MIN
S.L.Static			
Max:	5200	7950	5
Mil:	5200	7950	30
Nor:	4730	7630	Cont

DIMENSIONS

Wing	
Span	230.0'
Incidence (Root)	3°
(Tip)	1°
Dihedral	2°
Sweepback (LE)	15.5'
Length	162.1'
Height	46.8'
Tread	46.0'
Prop Grd Clearance	54"

Mission and Description

Mfr's. Model 35

Navy Equivalent: None

The principal mission of the B-36D-III is the destruction by bombs of strategic ground and naval materiel objectives.

The crew of 13 consists of aircraft commander, pilot, co-pilot, first engineer, second engineer, navigator, radar bombardier, observer, first radio operator, second radio operator, lower right and lower left scanners, and tail gunner.

Crew compartments are pressurized, heated and ventilated. Compartment heating; enclosure defrosting; wing and tail anti-icing are accomplished by heated air obtained from heat exchangers installed in the reciprocating engine exhaust system.

The defensive armament consists of a 20 mm gun tail turret, controlled by either AN/APG-32 or AN/APG-32A* radar.

The high lift devices are constant chord single slotted wing flaps extending from the fuselage to the outboard reciprocating engine nacelle. The flap system is composed of six flaps (three on each wing) which are mechanically and electrically synchronized in symmetrical pairs.

The major differences of the B-36D-III from the standard configuration are removal of: (1) all turrets except the tail turret; (2) self sealing pads; (3) fuel purging system; (4) crew comfort items; (5) gun sighting blisters; and (6) oxygen provisions from deleted crew stations.

* See note (d) page 6.

Development

Contract Approved	
First Flight	Feb 54
First Delivery	Jun 54
	Jun 54
Modification Completed	Dec 54

BOMBS

No.	Class (lb)	
	WW II (Box Fin)	
12		4000
28		2000
72		1000
132		500
	INTERIM (Conical Fin)	
26		2000
40		1000
129		500
	NEW SERIES	
6		3000
48		750

GUNS

No.	Type	Size	Rds Ea.	Loc.
2	M24A1	.20mm	600	Tail

WEIGHTS

	Lb	L.F.
Loading (A)	161,264	
Empty (A)	162,507	
Basic (A)		
Design	370,000	2.0
Combat	*244,400	
Max T.O.	†370,000	
Max Land	†357,500	2.0

(A) Actual   *For Basic Mission
† Limited By Structure

FUEL

Location	No. Tanks	Gal
Wg, outbd	2	4496
Wg, ctr.	2	8146
Wg, inbd	2	8411
Center sec.	2	9577
Bomb bay	1	2896
	Total	33,526
Grade		115/145
Specification		MIL-F-5572

OIL

Outboard (Jet)	4	(tot) 52
Wing (Recip)	6	1200
Grade (Jet)		1100
Specification (Recip)		MIL-L-6082A
(Jet)		MIL-L-6081A

WATER/ALCOHOL

Eng. Nacelle	6	(tot) 54

ELECTRONICS

UHF Command	AN/ARC-27
VHF Command	AN/ARC-3
Liaison	AN/ARC-21X
Radio Compass	AN/ARC-7A
Marker Beacon	RC-193A
IFF	AN/APX-6
Blind Approach	RC-103D
Glide Path	AN/ARN-5B
Bombing-Nav. Radar	K-3A
Loran	AN/APN-9
Gun-Laying Radar	†AN/APG-32
Radio Range	BC-453B
Interphone	USAF Combat
Defensive ECM	AN/APQ-31
Radar Set	
Chaff Dispenser	AN/ALE-6

*AN/ARN-12 Alternate Set
†See note (d) on page 6

Loading and Performance — Typical Mission

CONDITIONS		BASIC MISSION I	MAX BOMBS II	MAX ATTAIN. ALT III	HIGH SPEED IV	FERRY RANGE V
TAKE-OFF WEIGHT						
Fuel at 6 lb/gal (Grade 115/145)	(lb)	370,000	370,000	370,000	370,000	370,000
	(lb)	185,950	123,210	185,950	185,950	107,740
Payload (Bombs)	(lb)	10,000	72,000	10,000	10,000	None
Payload (Chaff)	(lb)	1408	1408	1408	1408	None
Wing Loading	(lb/sq ft)	77.5	77.5	77.5	77.5	77.5
Stall speed (power off)	(kn)	107	107	107	107	107
Take-off ground run at SL	(ft)	4400	4400	4400	4400	4400
Take-off to clear 50 ft	(ft)	5685	5685	5685	5685	5685
Rate of climb at SL	(fpm)	970	970	970	970	970
Rate of climb at SL (one eng. out)	(fpm)	1025	1025	1025	1025	1025
Time: SL to 10,000 ft	(min)	11	11	11	11	11
Time: SL to 20,000 ft	(min)	25	25	25	25	25
Service ceiling (100 fpm)	(ft)	33,400	33,400	33,400	33,400	33,400
Service ceiling (one eng. out)	(ft)	31,500	31,500	31,500	31,500	31,500
COMBAT RANGE	(n. mi)	3260	1885	3106	1495	8200
COMBAT RADIUS	(n. mi)	192	202	196	348	—
Average cruise speed	(kn)	359	—	—	—	181
Initial cruising altitude	(ft)	5000	5000	5000	29,300	5000
Target speed	(kn)	348	338	305	446	343
Target altitude	(ft)	40,400	36,800	44,900	36,600	28,000
Final cruising altitude	(ft)	28,000	28,400	28,000	41,300	28,000
Total mission time	(hr)	33.7	18.3	31.0	9.0	45.5
COMBAT WEIGHT	(lb)	244,400	213,660	242,000	254,700	183,100
Combat altitude	(ft)	40,400	36,800	44,900	38,600	28,000
Combat speed	(kn)	359	369	332	358	355
Combat climb	(fpm)	590	1250	170	680	2140
Combat ceiling (500 fpm)	(ft)	41,300	44,100	41,500	40,600	46,900
Service ceiling (100 fpm)	(ft)	45,600	48,000	45,700	44,400	49,800
Service ceiling (one eng. out)	(ft)	42,900	45,500	43,000	42,100	48,100
Max rate of climb at SL	(fpm)	2330	2760	2330	2195	3270
Max speed at optimum altitude	(kn/ft)	363/37,300	370/38,300	363/37,200	361/37,000	374/39,000
Basic speed at 25,000/35,000 ft	(kn)	343/362	347/367	343/362	342/360	350/370
LANDING WEIGHT	(lb)	182,900	160,480	182,900	182,900	183,100
Ground roll at SL	(ft)	1780	1760	1780	1780	1780
Ground roll (auxiliary brake)	(ft)	1580	1560	1580	1580	1580
Total from 50 ft	(ft)	3230	3210	3230	3230	3230
Total from 50 ft (auxiliary brake)	(ft)	3000	2980	3000	3000	3000

NOTES:
① Take-off power
② Max available power
③ Normal power
④ Detailed descriptions of Range and Radius missions given on page 6
⑤ Props reversed

PERFORMANCE BASIS:
(a) Data source: Calculated data based on flight test of B-36D Aircraft with configuration adjustments
(b) Performance is based on powers shown on page 6

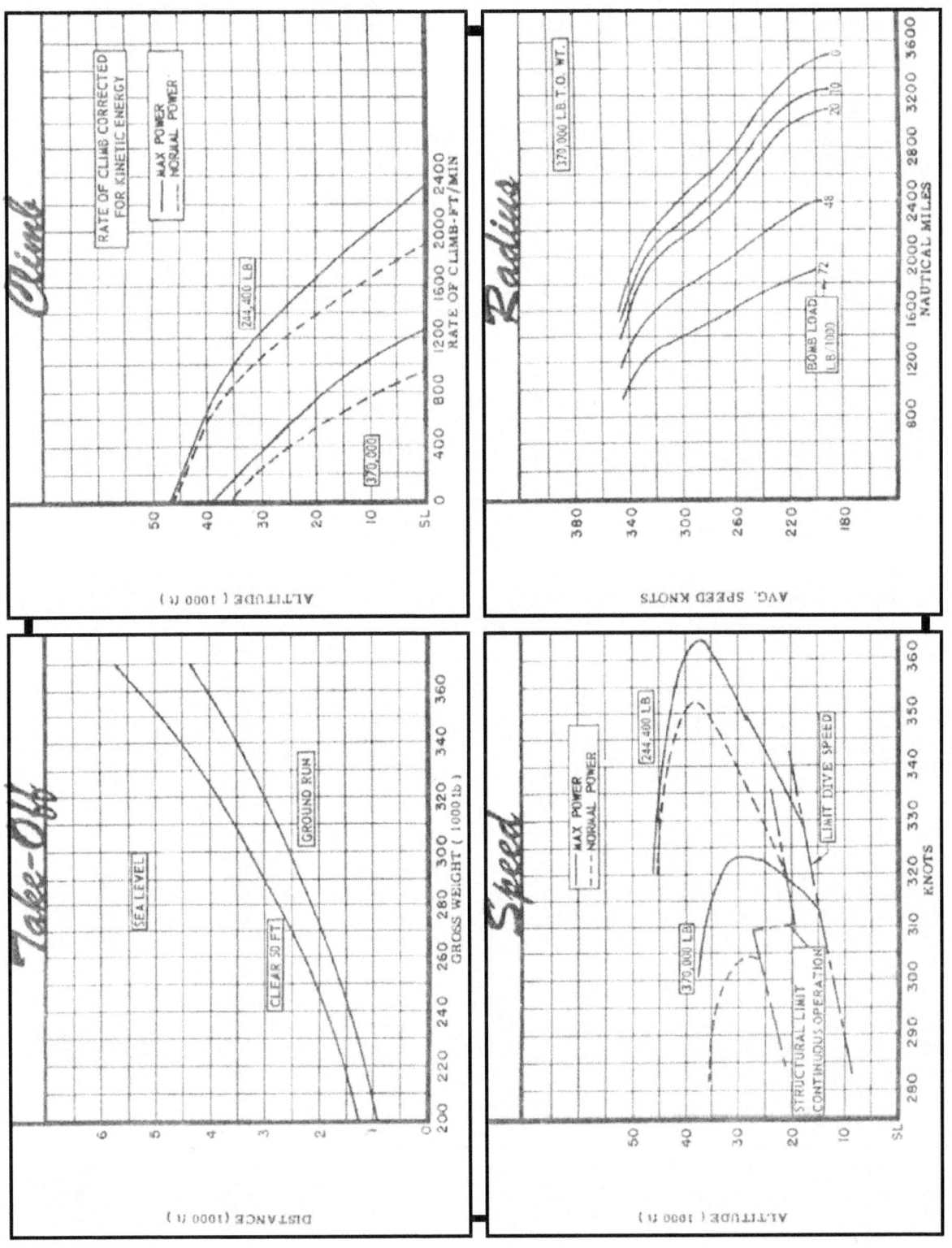

N O T E S

Formula: Radius Missions I & II

Warm-up, take-off and climb on course to 5000 feet at normal power, cruise out at long range speeds to point of cruise climb operation. Climb so as to arrive at cruise ceiling 500 nautical miles from target. Cruise at combat altitude with long range speeds until 15 minutes from target; conduct 10 engine normal power run in, drop bombs and chaff, conduct 2 minutes evasive action and 8 minutes escape from target at normal power. After leaving target area, cruise toward base using long range speeds at combat altitude until 500 nautical miles from target. Descend to optimum cruise altitude and cruise-climb to base. Range free allowances include 10 minutes normal power fuel consumption for reciprocating engines and 5 minutes normal power fuel consumption for jet engines for starting and take-off, 2 minutes normal power fuel consumption at combat altitude for evasive action, 30 minutes of fuel consumption at sea level for long range speeds (reciprocating engines only) plus 5% of initial fuel load for landing and endurance reserve.

Formula: Radius Mission III

Warm-up, take-off and climb on course to 5000 feet at normal power, cruise out at long range speeds to point where climb is made so as to arrive at maximum attainable altitude 500 nautical miles from target. Cruise on maximum attainable altitude flight path; 15 minutes from target conduct 10 engine normal power run in at altitude attained at start of run, drop bombs and chaff, conduct 2 minutes evasive action and 8 minutes escape from target at normal power. After leaving target area, cruise toward base using long range speeds at combat altitude until 500 nautical miles from target. Descend to optimum cruise altitude and cruise-climb to base. Range free allowances are the same as for Radius Mission I.

Formula: Radius Mission IV

Entire mission is conducted at normal power. Warm-up, take-off and climb on course to optimum altitude for high speed. Cruise at optimum altitude (or high speed to point where climb is made so as to arrive at cruise ceiling 500 nautical miles from target. Cruise to target at combat altitude, conduct run in, drop bombs and chaff, conduct 2 minutes evasive action, and 8 minutes escape from the target. After leaving target area, cruise toward base until 500 nautical miles from target; descend to optimum altitude for high speed and cruise-climb to base. If after bomb drop, optimum altitude for high speed is above combat altitude, climb is begun after 2 minutes evasive action. Range free allowances are the same as for Radius Mission I.

Formula: Range Mission V

Warm-up, take-off and climb on course to 5000 feet at normal power, cruise-climb at long range speeds until all usable fuel is consumed. Range free allowances are the same as for Radius Mission I except for omission of 2 minutes evasive action.

General Data:

(a) Total fuel capacity is usable only for special loadings with equipment removed from aircraft.
(b) Engine ratings shown on page 3 are manufacturer's guaranteed ratings. Power values for performance calculations are as follows:

(6) R4360-41					(4) J47-GE-19			
	BHP	RPM	ALT.	MIN		S.L.S.	LB	RPM	MIN
T.O.:	*3500	2700	S.L.	5	T.O.:	5010	7950	5
Max:	3250	2700	Up to 34,000 †	30	Max:	5010	7950	30
Nor:	2650	2550	Up to 39,000 †	Cont	Nor:	4700	7630	Cont

* Wet
† Turbosupercharger limitation

(c) For detailed planning refer to Technical Order 1B-36D(III)-1 and other applicable technical orders.
(d) AN/APG-32A Gun Laying Radar effective on aircraft USAF Serial No. 49-2647 thru 49-2654, 49-2656 and 49-2657. AN/APG-32 effective on aircraft USAF Serial No. 49-2655 and 49-2658 through 49-2668.

Performance Reference:

Convair Report FZA-36-330, dated 15 April 1955, "Performance Estimate for B-36D-III Aircraft Based on B-36D Phase IV Flight Tests and B-36F and H Featherweight Tests."

Revision Basis: To reflect Featherweight Flight Test (15 Apr 55) data and approved engineering changes.

Standard Aircraft Characteristics

B-36F
Consolidated-Vultee

SIX R-4360-53
PRATT & WHITNEY
FOUR J47-GE-19
GENERAL ELECTRIC

BY AUTHORITY OF
THE SECRETARY
OF THE AIR FORCE

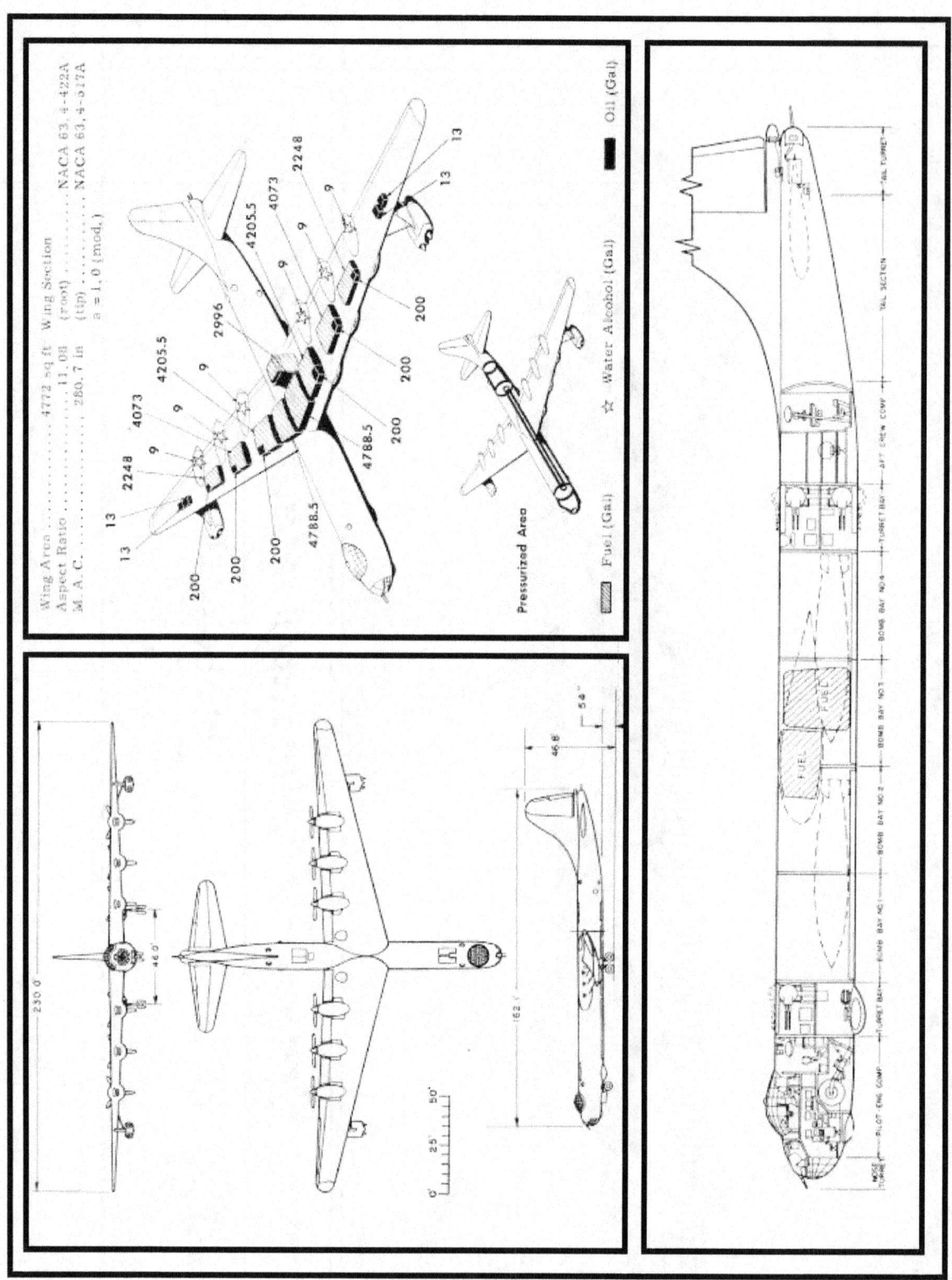

POWER PLANT

No. & Model	(6) R-4360-53
Mfr	Pratt & Whitney
Engine Spec. No.	A-7076-F
Superch.	1 stg.1 spd
Turbo Superch.	(2) BH-1
Turbo Mfr.	General Electric
Red. Gear Ratio	0.375
Prop. Mfr.	Curtiss
Blade Design No.	1129-17C6-24
Prop. Type	C.S. FF. Reverse
No. Blades	3
Prop. Dia.	19'0"
Augmentation	Water/Alcohol
	Plus

No. & Model	(4) J47-GE-19
Mfr.	General Electric
Engine Spec No.	E.589
Type	Axial
Length	144"
Diameter	39"
Weight (dry)	2495
Tail Pipe	Fixed Area

ENGINE RATINGS

	BHP - RPM - ALT - MIN
T.O:	*3800 - 2800 - S.L. - 5
Mil:	*3800 - 2800 - Turbo- 30
	3500 - 2800 - Turbo- 30
Nor:	2800 - 2600 - Turbo- Cont
	plus

S.L. Static	LB - RPM - MIN
Max:	5200 - 7950 - 5
Mil:	5200 - 7950 - 33
Nor:	4730 - 7630 - Cont

*Wet

DIMENSIONS

Wing	
Span	230.0'
Incidence (root)	3°
(tip)	2°
Dihedral	2°
Sweepback (LE)	5.5°
Length	152.1'
Height	46.8'
Tread	46.0'
Prop. Grd Clearance	34"

Mission and Description

Navy Equivalent: None   Mfr's Model: 36

The principal mission of the B-36F is the destruction by bombs of strategic ground and naval materiel objectives.

The crew of 15 consists of aircraft commander, pilot, co-pilot, first engineer, second engineer, navigator, radar-bombardier, observer, first radio operator, second radio operator, right upper aft gunner, left upper aft gunner, right lower aft gunner, left lower aft gunner, and tail gunner.

The copilot serves as left upper forward gunner and the second radio operator as right upper forward gunner. The first radio operator functions as ECM operator.

Crew compartments are pressurized, heated and ventilated and provided with an oxygen system for emergency use. Compartment heating, enclosure and blister de-frosting, and propeller, wing, and tail anti-icing are accomplished by heated air obtained from heat exchangers installed in the reciprocating engine exhaust system.

The K-3A Bombing-Navigation system with a vertical Y-3A optical sight and radar equipment for blind bombing and navigation is provided. This system allows a single crew member to act as radar operator and bombardier.

The defensive armament consists of eight 20mm gun turrets, six of which are retractable. The tail turret is controlled by AN/APG-32 radar.

Major difference of the B-36F from the B-36D is the installation of R-4360-53 engines in place of R-4360-41 engines.

Development

Prototype First Flight	Nov 50
First Delivery	Aug 51
Production Completed	Oct 51

BOMBS

No.	Class (lb)
	WW II (Box Fin)
12	4000
28	2000
72	1000
132	500
	INTERIM (Conical Fin)
22	2000
40	1000
129	500
	NEW SERIES
2	43,000
4	12,000
48	750
Max Bomb Load	86,000 lb

WEIGHTS

	lb	L.F.
Loading		
Empty	167,646 (A)	
Basic	172,302 (A)	
Design	370,000	2.0
Combat	¥254,300	
Max T.O.	¥370,000	2.0
Max Land	‡357,500	

(A) Actual
¥ For Basic Mission
† see note (e), page 7
‡ Limited by structure

FUEL

Location	No. Tanks	Gal
Wg. outbd*	2	4496
Wg. ctr*	2	8146
Wg. inbd	2	8411
Center sec	2	9577
Bomb bay	1	2996
	Total	33,626

Grade	115/145
Specification	MIL-F-5572

OIL

Outboard(Jet)	4	(tot) 32
Wing (Recip)	6	(tot) 1200
Grade (Recip)		1100
(Jet)		1005
Specification (Recip)	MIL-L-6082A	
(Jet)	MIL-L-6081A	

WATER/ALCOHOL

Eng Nacelle	6	(tot) 54

* Partial Self-Sealing
* Total capacity usable only for special loading when equipment has been removed from aircraft.

GUNS

No.	Type	Size	Rds ea	Location
2	M24A1	20mm	400	Fus,nose
4	M24A1	20mm	600	Fus,up,fwd
4	M24A1	20mm	600	Fus,up,aft
4	M24A1	20mm	600	Fus,lw,aft
2	M24A1	20mm	600	Fus,tail

ELECTRONICS

UHF Command	AN/ARC-27
VHF Command	AN/ARC-3
Liaison	AN/ARC-8
Radio Compass	AN/ARN-6
Marker Beacon	AN/ARN-12
IFF	AN/APX-6
Blind Approach	RC-103D or ARN-14
Glide Path	AN/ARN-5B
Bomb-Nav. Radar	K-3A
Gun Laying Radar	AN/APG-32
Range Rec'v'r	BC-453B
Interphone	
Defensive ECM	USAF Combat

Loading and Performance — Typical Mission

CONDITIONS		BASIC MISSION	MAX BOMBS	HIGH ALTITUDE	HIGH SPEED	FERRY RANGE
		I	II	III	IV	V
TAKE OFF WEIGHT	(lb)	370,000	370,000	370,000	370,000	369,578
Fuel at 6.0 lb/gal (grade 115/145)	(lb)	174,102	95,593	174,102	174,102	183,780
Payload (Bombs)	(lb)	10,000	86,000	10,000	10,000	None
Wing loading	(lb/sq ft)	77.5	77.5	77.5	77.5	77.4
Stall speed (power off)	(kn)	107	107	107	107	107
Take-off ground run at SL ①	(ft)	3990	3990	3990	3990	3990
Take-off to clear 50 ft ①	(ft)	5110	5110	5110	5110	5110
Rate of climb at SL ②	(fpm)	960	960	960	960	960
Rate of climb at SL (one eng. out) ②	(fpm)	970	970	970	970	970
Time: SL to 10,000 ft ②	(min)	12	12	12	12	12
Time: SL to 20,000 ft ②	(min)	26	26	26	26	26
Service ceiling (100 fpm) ②	(ft)	33,000	33,000	33,000	33,000	33,000
Service ceiling (one eng. out) ②	(ft)	30,350	30,350	30,350	30,350	30,350
COMBAT RANGE ④	(n. mi)					6727
COMBAT RADIUS ④	(n. mi)	2807	1167	2570	1326	
Average cruise speed ③	(kn)	204	223	225	346	190
Initial cruising altitude ③	(ft)	5000	5000	25,000	30,000	5000
Target speed	(kn)	349	336	352	349	349
Target altitude	(ft)	40,200	35,100	40,500	38,900	28,300
Final cruising altitude ③	(ft)	28,800	29,200	25,000	40,000	28,300
Total mission time	(hr)	26.7	10.1	22.2	8.0	35.4
COMBAT WEIGHT ②	(lb)	254,300	216,000	248,200	261,200	196,457
Combat altitude ②	(ft)	40,200	35,100	40,500	38,900	28,300
Combat speed ②	(kn)	360	370	361	359	358
Combat climb ②	(fpm)	570	1410	610	630	2020
Combat ceiling (500 fpm) ②	(ft)	40,900	43,900	41,300	40,400	45,700
Service ceiling (100 fpm) ②	(ft)	44,000	47,200	44,600	43,600	49,100
Service ceiling (one eng. out) ③	(ft)	41,400	44,300	41,600	40,800	46,300
Max rate of climb at SL ②	(fpm)	2110	2610	2180	2030	2940
Max speed at optimum altitude ②	(kn/ft)	363/37,100	373/38,300	365/37,400	361/36,400	375/39,100
Basic speed at 25,000 ft	(kn)	346	350	346	344	352
LANDING WEIGHT	(lb)	195,973	193,807	195,973	195,973	196,457
Ground roll at SL ③	(ft)	1890	1870	1890	1890	1900
Ground roll (auxiliary brake) ③	(ft)	1650	1630	1650	1650	1660
Total from 50 ft	(ft)	3340	3320	3340	3340	3350
Total from 50 ft (auxiliary brake)	(ft)	3110	3090	3110	3110	3120

NOTES:
① Take-off power
② Max power
③ Normal power
④ Detailed descriptions of Radius and Range missions given on page 7
⑤ Props reversed.

Performance Basis:
(a) Data source: Flight test
(b) Performance is based on powers shown on page 7.

SUPPLEMENTAL
Loading and Performance — Typical Mission

CONDITIONS		BASIC MISSION	MAX BOMBS	HIGH SPEED
TAKE-OFF WEIGHT	(lb)	VI 357,500	VII 357,500	VIII 357,500
Fuel at 6.0 lb/gal (grade 115/145)	(lb)	162,602	84,093	162,602
Payload (Bombs)	(lb)	10,000	86,000	10,000
Wing loading	(lb sq ft)	74.9	74.9	74.9
Stall speed (power off)	(kn)	105	105	105
Take-off ground run at SL	(ft)	3630	3630	3630
Take-off to clear 50 ft	(ft)	4640	4640	4640
Rate of climb at SL	(fpm)	1020	1020	1020
Rate of climb at SL (one eng. out)	(fpm)	1040	1040	1040
Time: SL to 10,000 ft	(min)	11	11	11
Time: SL to 20,000 ft	(min)	24	24	24
Service ceiling (100 fpm)	(ft)	34,800	34,800	34,800
Service ceiling (one eng. out)	(ft)	32,000	32,000	32,000
COMBAT RANGE	(n. mi)	2640		
COMBAT RADIUS	(n. mi)		965	1250
Average cruise speed	(kn)	205	235	348
Initial cruising altitude	(ft)	5000	5000	31,700
Target speed	(kn)	350	338	349
Target altitude	(ft)	40,500	35,800	39,500
Final cruising altitude	(ft)	28,800	29,300	40,000
Total mission time	(hr)	25.0	8.0	7.5
COMBAT WEIGHT	(lb)	250,300	212,000	257,000
Combat altitude	(ft)	40,500	35,800	39,500
Combat speed	(kn)	360	271	360
Combat climb	(fpm)	600	1420	610
Combat ceiling (500 fpm)	(ft)	41,100	44,300	40,600
Service ceiling (100 fpm)	(ft)	44,400	47,600	43,800
Service ceiling (one eng. out)	(ft)	41,700	44,700	41,300
Max rate of climb at SL	(fpm)	2160	2670	2090
Max speed at optimum altitude	(kn-ft)	364/37,400	373/38,500	363/37,200
Basic speed at 25,000 ft	(kn)	345	330	344
LANDING WEIGHT	(lb)	195,348	192,882	195,348
Ground roll at SL	(ft)	1900	1880	1990
Ground roll (auxiliary brake)	(ft)	1650	1640	1650
Total (from 50 ft)	(ft)	3340	3320	3340
Total from 50 ft (auxiliary brake)	(ft)	3120	3100	3120

NOTES:
① Take-off power
② Max power
③ Normal power
④ Detailed descriptions of Radius and Range missions given on page 7
⑤ Props reversed.

Performance Basis:
(a) Data source: Flight test
(b) Performance is based on powers shown on page 7.

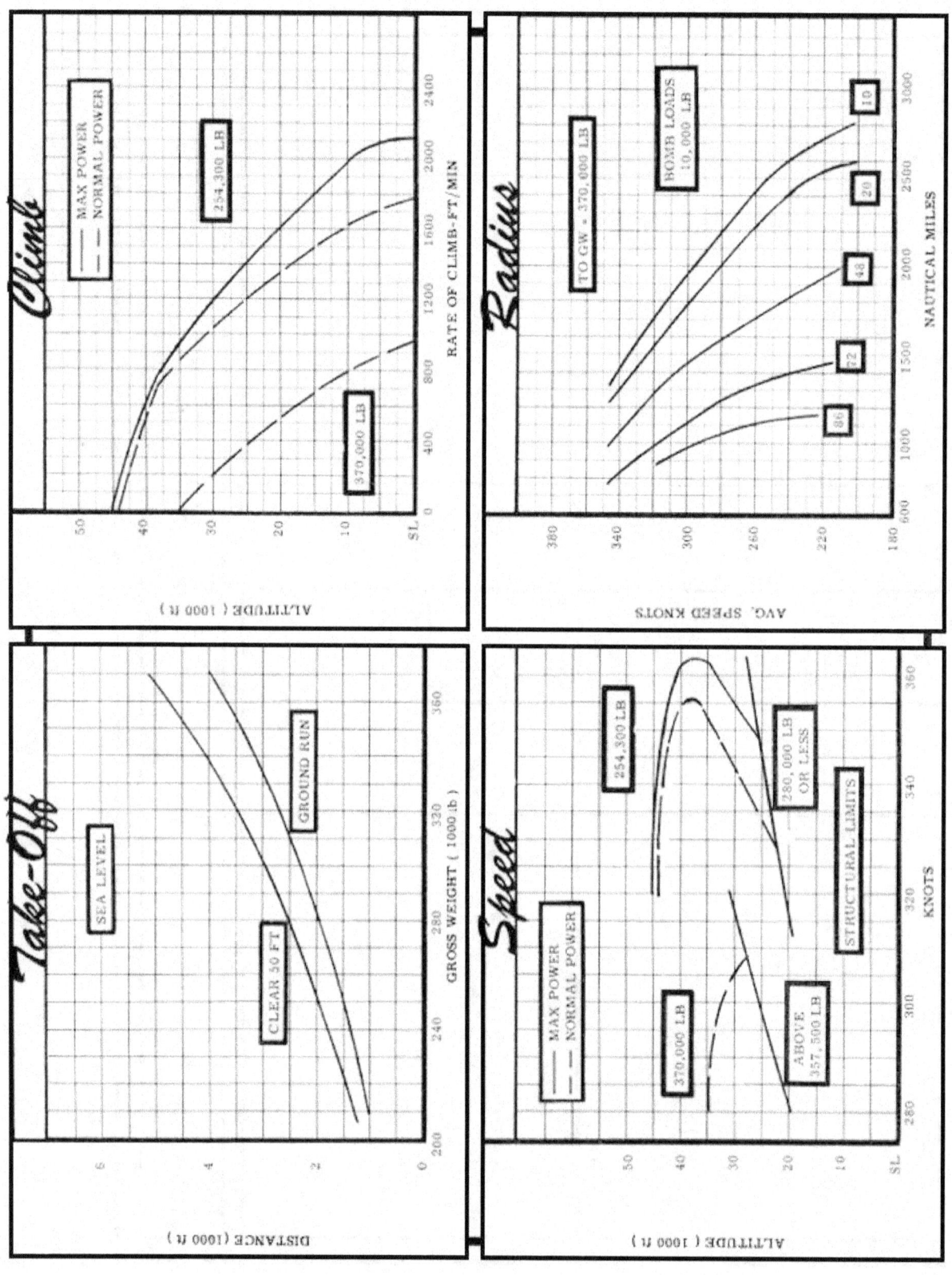

NOTES

FORMULA: RADIUS MISSIONS I, II, VI & VII

Warm-up, take-off and climb on course to 5000 ft at normal power, cruise out at long range speeds to point of cruise-climb operation. Begin climb to combat altitude, using long range climb powers, to arrive at cruise ceiling 500 nautical miles from target. Cruise at long range speeds at combat altitude, using best engine (reciprocating-jet) combinations, 15 minutes from target, conduct 10 engine normal power bomb run, drop bombs and chaff, and conduct 2 minutes evasive action and 8 minutes escape from target at normal power. After leaving target area, cruise back at long range speeds, using best engine combinations, until 500 nautical miles from target. Descend to optimum cruise altitude and cruise-climb back to base. Range free allowances include 10 minutes normal power fuel consumption for reciprocating engines and 5 minutes normal power fuel consumption for jet engines for starting and take-off, 2 minutes normal power fuel consumption at combat action, 30 minutes of fuel consumption for long range speeds at sea level (reciprocating engines only) plus 5% of initial fuel load for landing and endurance reserves.

FORMULA: RADIUS MISSION III

Warm-up, take-off and climb on course to 25,000 ft using long range climb powers; cruise out at long range speeds, using best engine combinations (reciprocating-jet) to point of climb. Climb, using long range climb powers, to combat altitude so as to arrive at this altitude 500 nautical miles from target. Conduct mission within 500 nautical mile zone the same as for Radius Missions I and II. Descend to 25,000 ft and cruise back to base at long range speeds, using best engine combinations. Range free allowances are the same as for Radius Missions I and II.

FORMULA: RADIUS MISSIONS IV & VIII

Entire mission is flown at normal power. Warm-up, take-off, and climb on course to cruising altitude. Cruise at optimum altitudes to combat altitude. Begin climb so as to arrive at this altitude 500 nautical miles from target. Cruise into target, drop bombs and chaff and conduct 2 minutes evasive action. Climb to best altitude for normal power cruise, Cruise-climb to base. Range free allowances are the same as for Radius Missions I and II.

FORMULA: FERRY RANGE MISSION V

Warm-up, take-off and climb on course to 5000 ft at normal power; cruise climb at long range speeds until all but reserve fuel is consumed. Range free allowances are the same as for Radius Missions I and II, except no fuel allowed for evasive action.

GENERAL DATA:

(a) All ceilings and rate of climb data are instantaneous values.

(b) Total fuel capacity is usable only for special loadings with equipment removed from the aircraft.

(c) Engine ratings shown on page 3 are manufacturer's guaranteed ratings. Power values used for performance calculations are as follows:

(6) R-4360-53				(4) J47-GE-19			
BHP	RPM	ALT	MIN		LB	RPM	MIN
T.O: *3800	2800	SL	5	T.O:	5010	7950	5
3500	2800	SL	5				
Max: 3500	2800	†Up to 35,000	30	Max:	5010	7950	30
Nor: 2800	2600	†Up to 35,000	Cont	Nor:	4700	7630	Cont

* Wet
† Turbo supercharger limitation

(d) For detailed planning refer to Technical Order 1B-36F-1 and other applicable technical orders.

(e) Take-off at 370,000 lb gross weight is authorized only for airplanes on which structural modifications to the main landing gear have been accomplished in accordance with ECP 1890B and ECP 1890L.

PERFORMANCE REFERENCE:

FZA-36-278 & FZA-36-276.

REVISION BASIS:

To reflect performance based on higher gross weights.

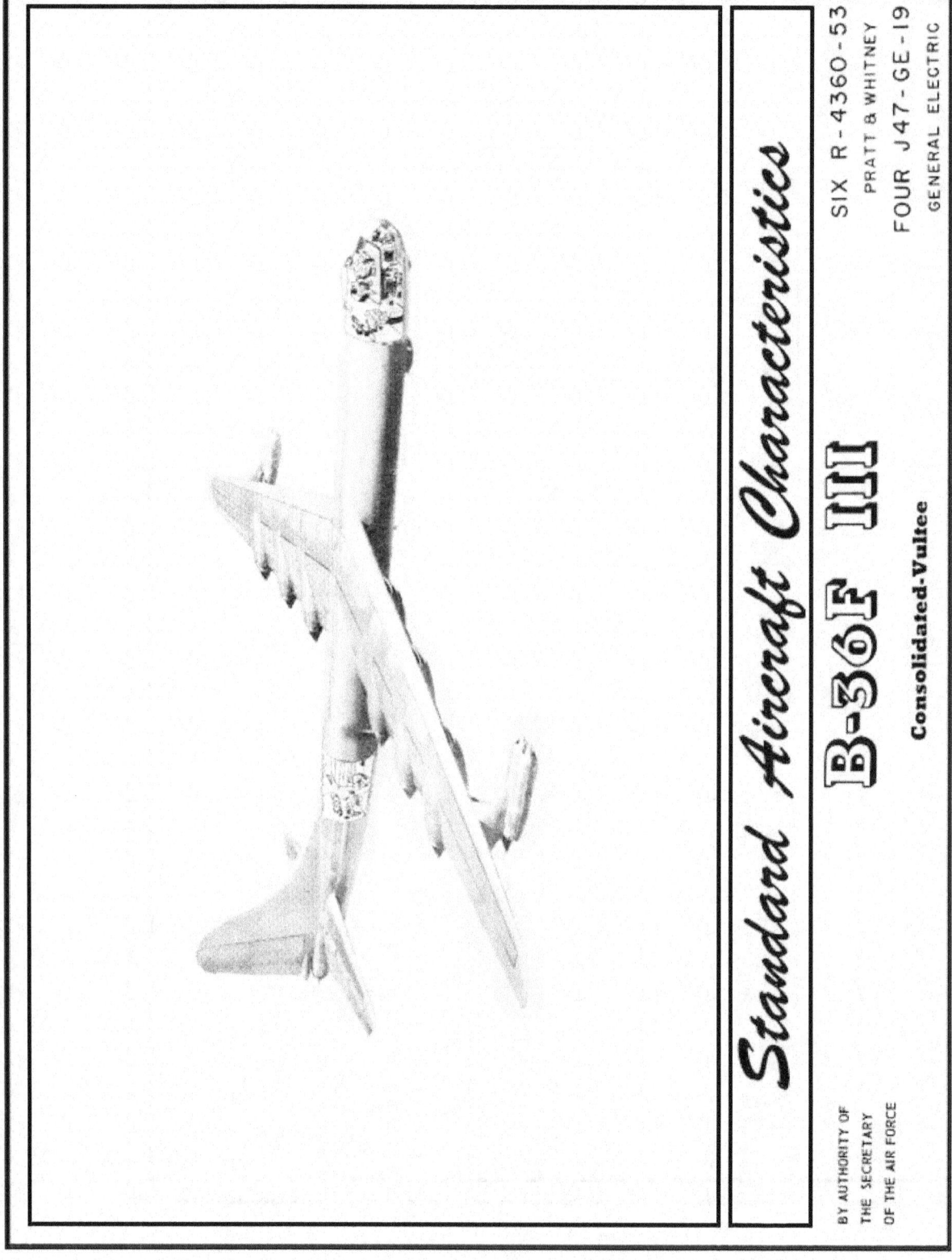

Standard Aircraft Characteristics

B-36F III

SIX R-4360-53 PRATT & WHITNEY
FOUR J47-GE-19 GENERAL ELECTRIC

Consolidated-Vultee

BY AUTHORITY OF
THE SECRETARY
OF THE AIR FORCE

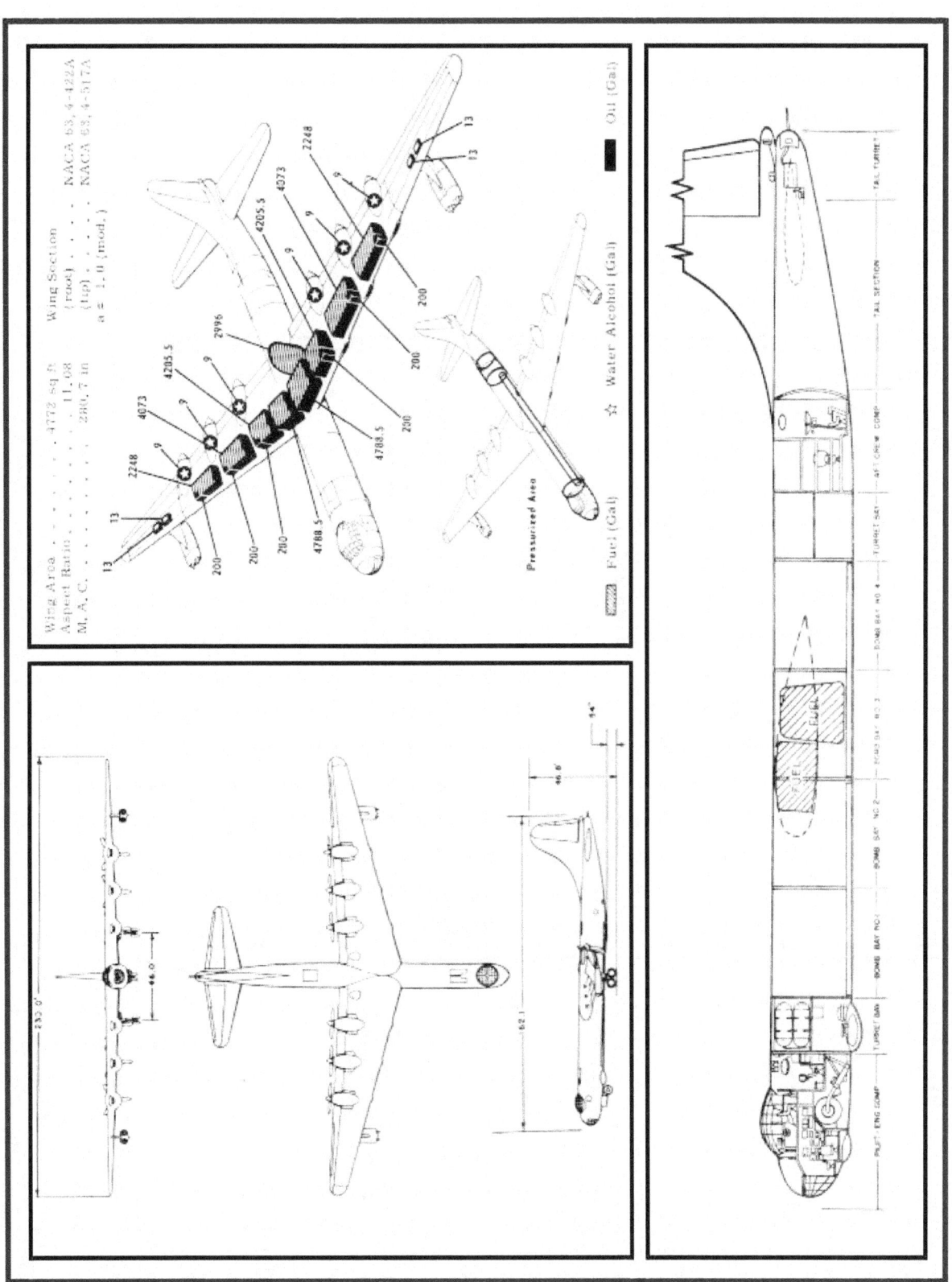

WEIGHTS

Loading	LB	L.F.
Empty	164,429 (C)	
Basic	166,081 (C)	
Design	370,000	2.0
Combat	+248,400	2.0
Max T.O.	+370,000	
Max Land	+357,500	

(C) Calculated
+ For Basic Mission
† Limited by structure

FUEL

Location	No. Tanks	Gal
Wg. outbd	2	436
Wg. ctr	2	846
Wg. inbd	2	841
Center sec	2	9577
Bomb Bay	1	2396
	Total	13,626

Grade.............115/145
Specification.......MIL-F-5572

OIL

Outboard (Jet).....4.......(tot) 32
Wing (Recip).......6.......(tot) 1200
Grade (Recip) 1100, (Jet)......1005
Specification (Recip) MIL-L-6082A
                (Jet) MIL-L-6081A

WATER/ALCOHOL

Eng Nacelle......6.......(tot) 54

ELECTRONICS

UHF Command............AN/ARC-27
VHF Command............AN/ARC-3
Liaison...............AN/ARC-8
Radio Compass.........AN/ARN-6
Marker Beacon.........AN/ARN-12
IFF...................AN/APX-6
Blind Approach..RC-103D or ARN-14
Glide Path............AN/ARN-5B
Bomb-Nav. Radar.........K-3A
Loran................AN/APN-9A
Gun Laying Radar.....AN/APG-32
Range Rec'r...........BC-453B
Interphone..........
Defensive ECM........USAF Combat
Chaff Dispenser......

Mission and Description

Navy Equivalent: None.   Mfr's Model: 36

The principal mission of the B-36F(III) is the destruction by bombs of strategic ground and naval material objectives.

The crew of 13 differs from that of the standard configuration in that the upper aft right and left gunners have been removed.

Crew compartments are heated and ventilated. Compartment heating, enclosure defrosting, wing and tail anti-icing are accomplished by heated air obtained from heat exchangers included in the reciprocating engine exhaust system. The oxygen system modification includes the removal of oxygen provisions from deleted crew stations.

The K-3A Bombing Navigation system with a vertical Y-3A optical sight and radar equipment for blind bombing and navigation is provided. This system allows a single crew member to serve as radar operator and bombardier.

The defensive armament consists of a 20mm gun tail turret, controlled by AN/APG-32 Radar.

The airplane has a single-point refueling, manifold type fuel system.

Development

Major differences of the B-36F(III) from the standard configuration are removal of all turrets except tail turret, self sealing pads, fuel purging system and crew comfort items; the replacement of blisters by small flush windows and the addition of dual automatic chaff dispensers.

Contract approved for modification of B-36F airplane to B-36F(III) Feb 54
First Delivery...May 54
Modification Completion Date..................................Dec 54

GUNS

No.	Type	Size	Rds on	Loc
2	M24A1	20mm	600	Fus. tail

BOMBS

No.	Class (lb)
WW II, Box Fins	
22	4000
28	2000
42	1600
72	1000
132	500
INTERIM (Conical Fin)	
4	12,000
1	10,000
22	2000
40	1000
128	500
NEW SERIES	
48	750

POWER PLANT

No. & Model.......(6) R-4360-53
Mfr................Pratt & Whitney
Engine Spec. No.......9-7870-F
Superch..............1.5t. 2spd
Turbo Superch...........(2) BH-1
Turbo Mfr.......General Electric
Red. Gear Ratio..........0.375
Prop. Mfr..............Curtiss
Blade Design No......1129-17C6-24
Prop Type........C.S, FF, Reverse
No. Blades..............3
Prop. Dia...............19'0"
Augmentation........Water/Alcohol

plus

No. & Model.......(4) J47-GE-19
Mfr..............General Electric
Engine Spec. No............E-339
Type.....................Axial
Length...................144"
Diameter.................39"
Weight (Dry).............2395
Tail Pipe.............Fixed Area

ENGINE RATINGS

	SHP	RPM	ALT	MIN
T.O.	*3800	2800	S.L.	5
Mil.	*3800	2800	Turbo	30
	2640	2800	Turbo	30
Nor.	2600	2600	Turbo	Cont

*Wet   plus

	LB	RPM	MIN
S.L. Static			
Max	5200	7950	5
Mil.	5390	7950	30
Nor.	4730	7550	Cont

DIMENSIONS

Wing
Span..................230'0"
Incidence (root).........3°
Dihedral..................2°
Sweepback (LE).........1°33'
Length................162'1"
Height................46'8"
Tread.................46'0"
Prop. Gnd. Clearance....34"

Loading and Performance — Typical Mission

CONDITIONS		BASIC MISSION I	MAX BOMBS II	MAX ALTITUDE III	HIGH SPEED IV	FERRY RANGE V
TAKE-OFF WEIGHT	(lb)	370,000	370,000	370,000	370,000	370,000
Fuel at 6.0 lb/gal (grade 115/145) ①	(lb)	184,430	120,690	183,430	183,430	185,220
Payload (Bombs) ②	(lb)	10,000	72,000	10,000	10,000	None
Payload (Crew) ②	(lb)	1408	1408	1408	1408	77.5
Wing loading	(lb/sq ft)	77.5	77.5	77.5	77.5	107
Stall speed (power off)	(kn)	107	107	107	107	3990
Take-off ground run at SL ③	(ft)	3990	3990	3990	3990	5110
Take-off to clear 50 ft ③	(ft)	5110	5110	5110	5110	970
Rate of climb at SL (one engine out) ③	(fpm)	970	970	970	970	980
Rate of climb at SL ③	(fpm)	980	980	980	980	11
Time SL to 10,000 ft	(min)	11	11	11	11	25
Time SL to 20,000 ft	(min)	25	25	25	25	34,000
Service ceiling (100 fpm)	(ft)	34,000	34,000	34,000	34,000	30,800
Service ceiling (one engine out)	(ft)	30,800	30,800	30,800	30,800	
COMBAT RANGE	(n. mi)					7600
COMBAT RADIUS ④	(n. mi)	3190	1745	2905	1420	
Average cruise speed	(kn)	212	220	213	356	205
Initial cruising altitude	(ft)	5000	5000	5000	32,300	5000
Target speed	(kn)	356	346	322	454	368
Target altitude	(ft)	40,200	37,100	45,100	38,700	34,700
Final cruising altitude	(ft)	34,600	34,900	34,600	38,500	34,700
TOTAL MISSION TIME	(hr)	29.7	15.7	26.7	8.3	37.1
Interception altitude	(ft)					
COMBAT WEIGHT	(lb)	248,400	216,500	245,200	258,900	186,500
Combat altitude	(ft)	40,200	37,100	45,100	38,700	34,700
Combat speed	(kn)	365	374	338	365	371
Combat climb	(fpm)	370	1100	175	595	1830
Combat ceiling (500 fpm)	(ft)	40,900	44,000	41,200	39,800	47,900
Combat ceiling (100 fpm)	(ft)	44,500	47,900	44,700	43,800	50,600
Service ceiling (one engine out)	(ft)	42,000	45,400	42,200	41,300	48,400
Max rate of climb at SL	(fpm)	2130	2545	2160	2025	3040
Max speed at optimum altitude	(fpm)	466/37,700	372/38,400	367/37,800	365/37,500	376/38,800
Basic speed at 25,000/35,000 ft ⑤		348/365	351/370	348/365	347/363	⑤ 354/374
LANDING WEIGHT	(lb)	185,540	183,900	185,540	185,640	186,520
Ground roll at SL	(ft)	1800	1790	1800	1800	1800
Ground roll (auxiliary brake) ⑥	(ft)	1580	1580	1580	1580	1580
Total from 50 ft ⑥	(ft)	3240	3240	3240	3240	3240
Total from 50 ft (auxiliary brake) ⑦	(ft)	3010	3010	3010	3010	3010

NOTES:
① Take-off power
② Max power
③ Normal power
④ Detailed descriptions of RADIUS and RANGE missions given on page 6
⑤ Brakes plus reversed props
⑥ Structural Limit for 25,000 ft alt.

PERFORMANCE BASIS:
(a) Data source: AF Phase IV Flight Test (substantiated by WADC)
(b) Performance is based on powers shown on page 6.

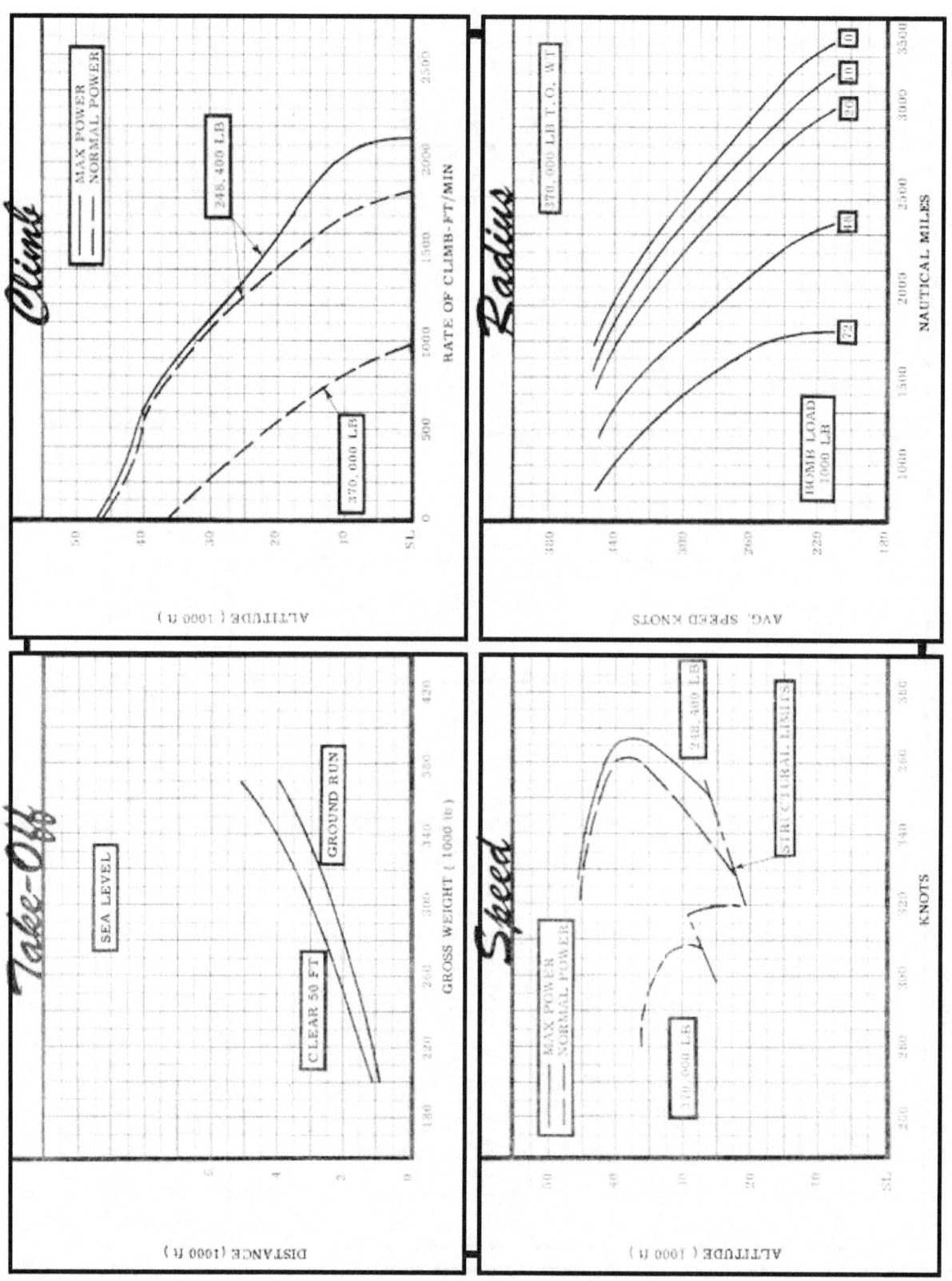

Characteristics Summary

BOMBER B-36J

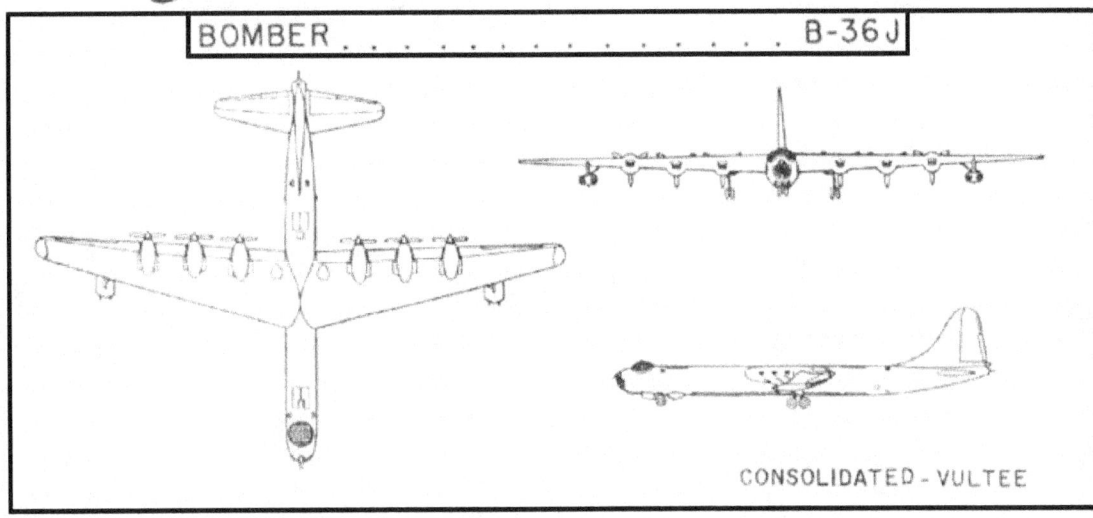

CONSOLIDATED - VULTEE

Wing Area	4772 sq ft	Length	162.1 ft
Span	230.0 ft	Height	46.8 ft

AVAILABILITY			PROCUREMENT			
Number available			Number to be delivered in fiscal years			
ACTIVE	RESERVE	TOTAL				

STATUS

1. First Flight Prototype: Jul 53
2. First Delivery: Oct 53
3. Production Completion Date: Jun 54 (est)
4. Major differences of the B-36J from the B-36H are the addition of outboard wing panel fuel tanks and strengthened landing gear to allow take-off gross weight of 410,000 lb.

Navy Equivalent: None　　　　　　　　　　　　　　　　　　　　　Mfr's Model- 36

POWER PLANT

(6) R-4360-53
Pratt & Whitney
ENGINE RATINGS

BHP - RPM - ALT - MIN
T.O.:*3800- 2800 - S.L. - 5
Mil: *3800- 2800 - Turbo - 30
　　　3500- 2800 - Turbo - 30
Nor: 2800- 2600 - Turbo - Cont

* Wet
plus
(4) J47-GE-19
General Electric
S.L.S.　LB - RPM - MIN
Max: 5200 - 7950 - 5
Mil:　5200 - 7950 - 30
Nor: 4730 - 7630 - Cont

FEATURES

Crew 15

Cabin Pressurization
Thermal Anti-icing
K-3A Bomb.-Nav. System
Chaff Dispenser
Loran
Defensive ECM
Fuel Tank Purging
AN/APG-41A Gun-Laying Radar
Single Point Fueling

Max Fuel Cap: ..*36,396 gal

*Includes bomb bay tank and outer wing panel tanks.

ARMAMENT

Turrets 8
Guns ... 16x20mm(M24A1)
Ammunition(tot).. 9200 rds

Bombs: (Max) Class　Load
WW II　　　　　　　(lb)
(Box Fin) . 12x4000/72x1000

Interim:
(Conical Fin)
　.... 22x2000/129x500
New Series:
　... *2x43,000/*2x43,000
Note:
*(2x43,000 lb) may be carried only when gross weight does not exceed 357,500 lb. For gross weights above 357,500 lb Max Bomb Load is (72x1000lb)

Characteristics Summary Basic Mission — B-36J

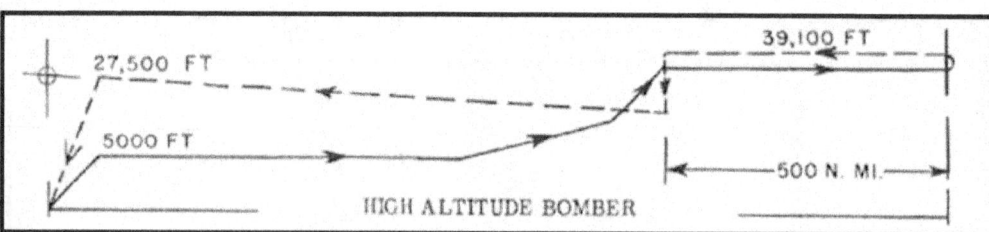

HIGH ALTITUDE BOMBER

PERFORMANCE

COMBAT RADIUS	FERRY RANGE	SPEED
2955 naut. mi with 11,408 lb payload at 198 knots avg. in 29.4 hours.	7144 naut. mi with 36,396 gal fuel at 188 knots avg. in 38.0 hours at 408,642 lb T.O. wt.	COMBAT 356 knots at 39,100 ft alt, max power MAX 357 knots at 36,400 ft alt, max power BASIC 340 knots at 25,000 ft alt, max power

CLIMB	CEILING	TAKE-OFF
720 fpm sea level, take-off weight normal power	27,400 ft 100 fpm, take-off weight normal power	ground run 5290 ft no assist | —— ft assisted
1920 fpm sea level, combat weight maximum power	39,900 ft 500 fpm, combat weight maximum power	over 50 ft height 6820 ft no assist | —— ft assisted

LOAD	WEIGHTS	STALLING SPEED
Bombs .... 10,000 lb Chaff .... 1408 lb Ammunition .... 9200 rds/20mm Fuel: 34,721 gal protected (part) 36.4% droppable 0% external 0%	Empty..... 171,035 lb Combat... 266,100 lb Take-off 410,000 lb limited by structure	113 knots power-off, landing configuration, take-off weight **TIME TO CLIMB**

NOTES

1. Performance Basis:
   (a) Flight test
   (b) Limited by capacity without removing equipment
2. Revision Basis: To reflect revised performance.

Standard Aircraft Characteristics

B-36J
Consolidated-Vultee

SIX R-4360-53
PRATT & WHITNEY

FOUR J47-GE-19
GENERAL ELECTRIC

BY AUTHORITY OF
THE SECRETARY
OF THE AIR FORCE

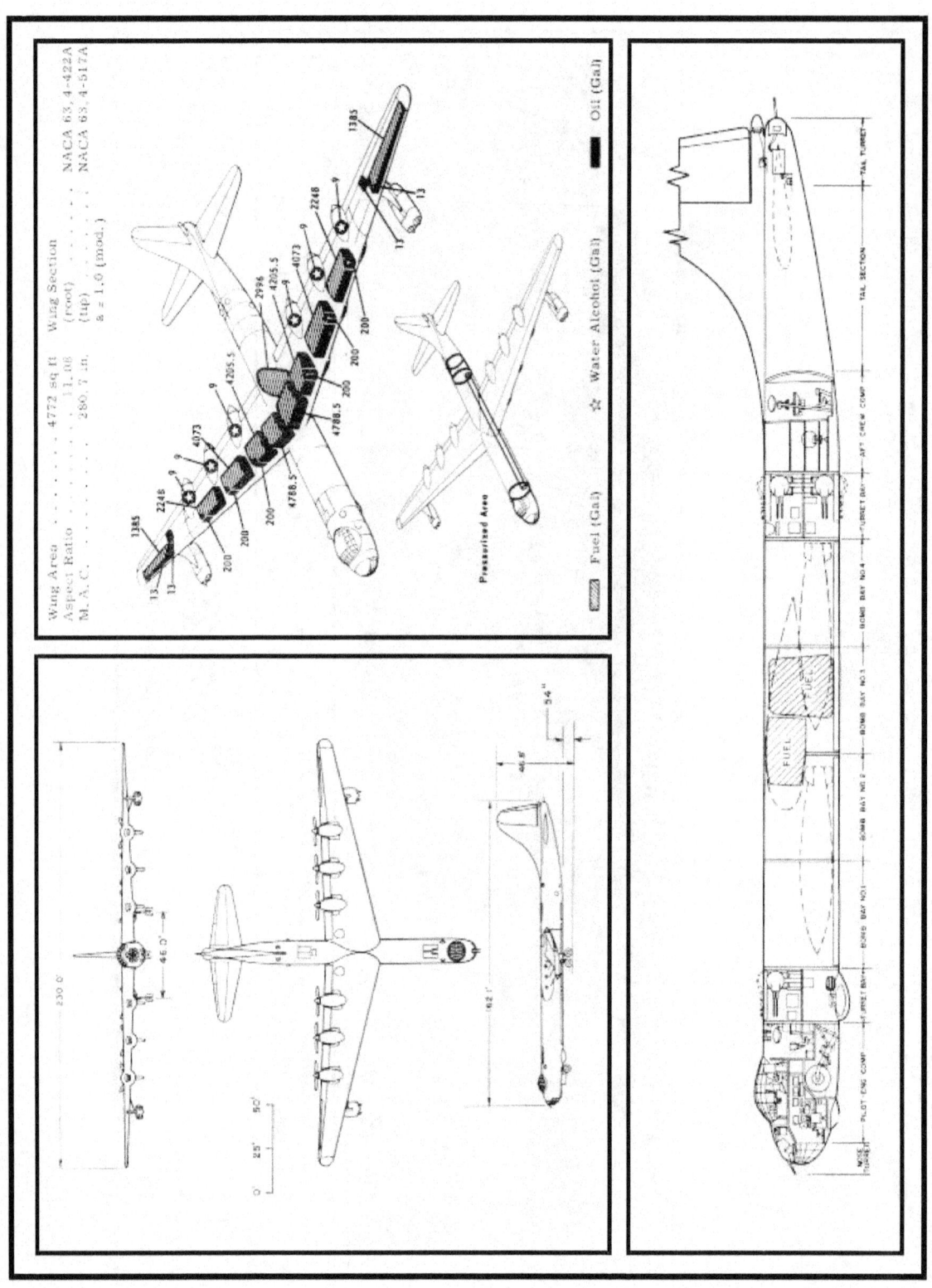

WEIGHTS

Loading	Lb	L.F.
Empty	171,035(C)	
Basic	176,670(C)	
Design	410,000	2.0
Combat	*286,100	
Max T.O.	†410,000	
Max Land.	‡357,500	2.0

(C) Calculated
* For Basic Mission
† Limited by strength (Landing gear and wings)
‡ Limited by strength (Landing gear)

FUEL

Location	No. Tanks	Gal
Wg. outer panel	2	2770
Wg. outbd *	2	4496
Wg. ctr *	2	8146
Wg. inbd	2	8411
Ctr sec (aux)	2	9577
Bomb bay	1	2996
	Total	36,396

Grade 115/145
Specification MIL-F-5572

OIL

		Gal
Outboard (Jet)		(tot) 52
Wing (Recip)	6	1200
Grade (Recip)		1100
(Jet)		1095
Specification (Recip): MIL-L-6082A		
(Jet): MIL-L-6081A		

WATER/ALCOHOL
Eng Nacelle 5 (tot) 54
* Partial Self-Sealing

ELECTRONICS

UHF Command	AN/ARC-27
VHF Command	AN/ARC-3
Liaison	AN/ARC-21x
Radio Compass	AN/ARN-6
Marker Beacon	AN/ARN-12
IFF	AN/APX-6
Omni-Range	AN/ARN-14
Glide Path	AN/ARN-18
Bomb.-Nav. Radar	K-3A
Loran	AN/APN-70
Gun-Laying Radar	AN/APG-41A
Interphone	AN/AIC-10
Defensive ECM	

Mission and Description

Mfr's Model 36
Navy Equivalent: None

The principal mission of the B-36J is the destruction by bombs of strategic ground and naval materiel objectives.

The crew of 15 consists of aircraft commander, pilot, co-pilot, first engineer, second engineer, navigator, radar-bombardier, observer, first radio operator, second radio operator, right upper aft gunner, left upper aft gunner, right lower aft gunner, left lower aft gunner, and tail gunner.

The co-pilot serves as right upper forward gunner and the second radio operator as left upper forward gunner. The first radio operator functions as ECM operator.

Crew compartments are pressurized, heated and ventilated and provided with an oxygen system for emergency use.

Compartment heating, enclosure and blister de-frosting, and propeller, wing, and tail anti-icing are accomplished by heated air obtained from heat exchangers installed in the reciprocating engine exhaust system.

The K-3A Bombing-Navigation system with a vertical Y-1A optical sight and radar equipment for blind bombing and navigation is provided. This system allows a single crew member to act as radar operator and bombardier.

The defensive armament consists of eight 20mm gun turrets, six of which are retractable. The tail turret is controlled by AN/APG-41A radar.

The airplane has a single-point fueling, manifold type fuel system.

Major differences of the B-36J from the B-36H are the addition of outer panel wing tanks and the strengthening of landing gear to allow take-off gross weight of 410,000 lb.

Development

First Flight Prototype	
First Delivery	Jul 53
Production Completion	Oct 53
	(est) Jun 54

GUNS

No.	Type	Size	Rds ea	Loc
2	M24A1	20mm	400	Fus. nose
4	M24A1	20mm	500	Fus. up, fw
4	M24A1	20mm	600	Fus. up, aft
4	M24A1	20mm	600	Fus. lw, aft
2	M24A1	20mm	600	Fus. tail

BOMBS

No.	Class (lb)
WW II (Box Fin)	
12	4000
28	2000
72	1000
132	500
INTERIM (Conical Fin)	
22	2000
40	1000
129	500
NEW SERIES	
2 *	43,000
4	12,000
48	750

* See note (f), page 6.

POWER PLANT

No. & Model	(6) R-4360-53
Mfr.	Pratt & Whitney
Engine Spec. No.	A-7074-F
Supeich	1 stg. 1 spd
Turbo Superch	(2) BH-1
Turbo Mfr	General Electric
Red. Gear Ratio	0.375
Prop. Mfr.	*Curtiss
Blade Design No.	129-17C8-24
Prop. Type	C.S., FF, Reverse
No. Blades	3
Prop. Dia	19'0"
Augmentation	Water/Alcohol

No. & Model	(4) J47-GE-19
Mfr.	General Electric
Engine Spec. No.	E-580
Type	Axial
Length	144"
Diameter	39"
Weight (dry)	2495
Tail Pipe	Fixed Area
*Alt. Blades: A.O. Smith, SP-36D

ENGINE RATINGS

	BHP	RPM	ALT	MIN
T.O.:	*3800	2800	S.L.	5
Mil:	*3800	2800	Turbo	30
Nor:	2800	2600	Turbo	Cont

	LB	RPM		MIN
S.L. Static				
Max:	5200	7950		5
Mil:	5200	7950		30
Nor:	4730	7630		Cont

*Wet

DIMENSIONS

Wing	
Span	230.0'
Incidence (root)	3°
(tip)	1°
Dihedral	2°
Sweepback (LE)	15°3'
Length	162.1'
Height	46.8'
Tread	46.0'
Prop. Grd Clearance	54"

Loading and Performance — Typical Mission

CONDITIONS		BASIC MISSION	T.O. LIMIT LOAD	HIGH ALTITUDE	HIGH SPEED	FERRY	MAX HEAVY BOMBS
		I	II	III	IV	V	VI
TAKE-OFF WEIGHT	(lb)	410,000	410,000	410,000	410,000	408,642	357,500
Fuel at 6.0 lb/gal (grade 115/145)	(lb)	208,326	145,627	208,326	208,326	218,376	79,127
Payload (Bombs)	(lb)	10,000	72,000	10,000	10,000	None	86,000
Payload (Chaff)	(lb)	1408	1408	1408	1408	None	1408
Wing loading	(lb/sq ft)	85.9	85.9	85.9	85.9	85.6	74.9
Stall speed (power off)	(kn)	113	113	113	113	113	105
Take-off ground run at SL ①	(ft)	5290	5290	5290	5290	5220	3530
Take-off to clear 50 ft ①	(ft)	6820	6820	6820	6820	6750	4640
Rate of climb at SL ②	(fpm)	720	720	720	720	720	990
Rate of climb at SL (one eng. out)	(fpm)	720	720	720	720	720	1000
Time: SL to 10,000 ft ③	(min)	15	15	15	15	14.9	11
Time: SL to 20,000 ft ④	(min)	35	35	35	35	34.8	24
Service ceiling (100 fpm) ⑤	(ft)	27,400	27,400	27,400	27,400	27,700	34,800
Service ceiling (one eng. out) ⑥	(ft)	25,000	25,000	25,000	25,000	25,000	32,000
COMBAT RANGE ①	(n. mi)					7144	
COMBAT RADIUS ④	(n. mi)	2950	1775	2660	1475		847
Average cruiser speed	(kn)	198	200	226	338	188	233
Initial cruising altitude	(ft)	5000	5000	25,000	25,000	5000	5000
Target speed	(kn)	344	325	346	339	328	332
Target altitude	(ft)	30,100	32,500	39,700	35,700	27,000	35,500
Final cruising altitude	(ft)	27,500	28,000	25,000	39,900	27,000	29,000
Total mission time	(hr)	28.4	17.4	23.5	9.2	38.0	7.8
COMBAT WEIGHT	(lb)	266,100	237,092	259,300	278,500	202,614	214,685
Combat altitude	(ft)	35,100	32,500	39,700	35,700	27,000	35,500
Combat speed	(kn)	396	364	337	355	352	368
Combat climb	(fpm)	569	1240	570	650	1910	1390
Combat ceiling (500 fpm)	(ft)	39,800	42,100	40,400	39,000	45,000	43,800
Service ceiling (100 fpm)	(ft)	43,600	45,700	43,600	42,200	48,900	48,800
Service ceiling (one eng. out)	(ft)	40,900	43,800	41,200	40,200	45,700	46,300
Max rate of climb at SL	(fpm)	1920	2270	1980	1820	2730	2560
Max speed at optimum altitude	(kn/ft)	357/36,400	366/37,000	359/36,600	355/36,000	372/38,500	371/38,060
Basic speed at 25,000 ft ②	(kn)	340	345	341	339	348	340
LANDING WEIGHT	(lb)	202,119	199,656	202,110	202,110	202,614	196,310
Ground run at SL	(ft)	1970	1940	1970	1970	1980	1910
Ground run (auxiliary brakes)	(ft)	1710	1680	1710	1710	1720	1660
Total from 50 ft	(ft)	3410	3380	3410	3410	3420	3360
Total from 50 ft (auxiliary brakes) ⑤	(ft)	3170	3140	3170	3170	3180	3120

NOTES:
① Take-off power
② Max power
③ Normal power
④ Detailed descriptions of Radius and Range missions given on page 6
⑤ All props reversed

Performance Basis:
(a) Data source: Flight Test
(b) Performance is based on powers shown on page 6

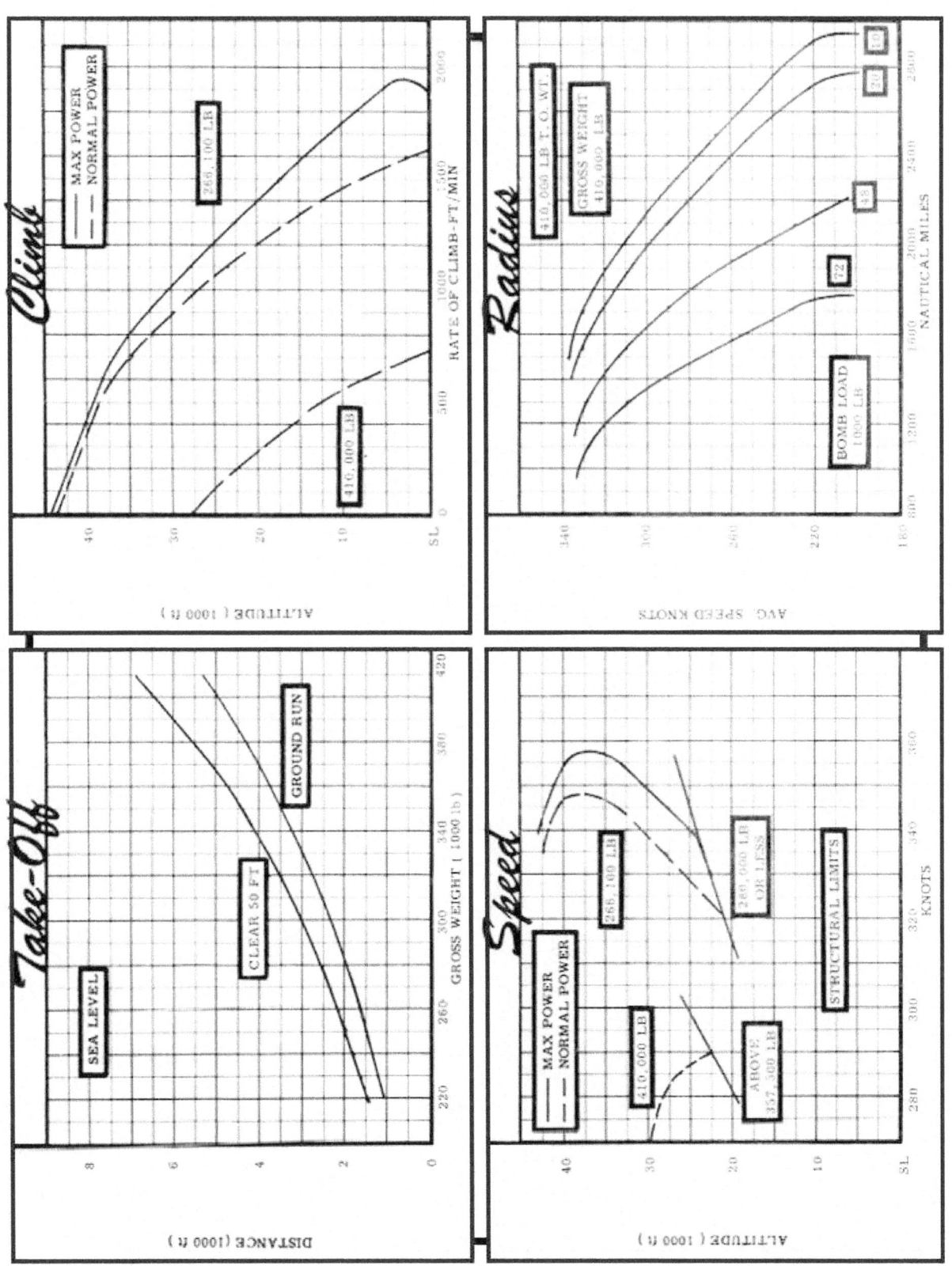

N O T E S

FORMULA: RADIUS MISSIONS I & II

Warm-up, take-off and climb on course to 5000 feet at normal power; cruise out at long range speeds to point of cruise-climb operation. Begin climb to combat altitude, using long range climb powers, to arrive at cruise ceiling 500 nautical miles from target. Cruise at long range speeds at combat altitude, using best engine (reciprocating-jet) combinations: 15 minutes from target, conduct 10 engine normal power bomb run, drop bombs and chaff and conduct 2 minutes evasive section and 8 minutes escape from target at normal power. After leaving target area, cruise back at long range speeds, using best engine combinations, until 500 nautical miles from target. Descend to optimum cruise altitude and cruise-climb back to base. Range free allowances include 10 minutes normal power fuel consumption for reciprocating engines and 5 minutes normal power fuel consumption for jet engines for starting and take-off, 2 minutes normal power fuel consumption at combat altitude for evasive action, 30 minutes of fuel consumption for long range speeds at sea level (reciprocating engines only) plus 5% of initial fuel load for landing and endurance reserves.

FORMULA: RADIUS MISSION III

Warm-up,' take-off and climb on course to 25,000 feet using long range climb powers; cruise out at long range speeds, using best engine combinations (reciprocating-jet) to point of climb. Climb, using long range climb powers, to combat altitude so as to arrive at this altitude 500 nautical miles from target. Conduct mission within 500 nautical mile zone the same as for Radius Missions I & II. Descend to 25,000 feet and cruise back to base at long range speeds, using best engine combinations. Range free allowances are the same as for Radius Missions I & II.

FORMULA: RADIUS MISSION IV

Entire mission is flown at normal power. Warm-up, take-off and climb on course to 25,000 feet. Cruise at optimum altitudes to combat altitude. Begin climb so as to arrive at this altitude 500 nautical miles from target. Cruise in to target, drop bombs and chaff and conduct 2 minutes evasive action. Climb to best altitude for normal power cruise. Cruise-climb to base. Range free allowances are the same as for Radius Missions I & II.

FORMULA: FERRY RANGE MISSION V

Warm-up, take-off and climb on course to 5000 feet at normal power; cruise climb at long range speeds until all but reserve fuel is consumed. Range free allowances are the same as for Radius Missions I & II, except no fuel allowed for evasive action.

GENERAL DATA:

(a) All ceilings and rate of climb data are instantaneous values.

(b) Total fuel capacity is usable only for special loadings with equipment removed from the aircraft.

(c) Engine ratings shown on page 3 are manufacturer's guaranteed ratings. Power values used for performance calculations are:

	(6) R-4360-53				(4) J47-GE-19		
	BHP	RPM	ALT	MIN		S.L.S.	LB	RPM	MIN
T.O:	*3800	2800	SL	5	T.O:	5010	7950	5
	3500	2800	SL	5				
Mil:	3800	2800	Up to **35,000	30	Max:	5010	7950	30
	3500	2600	Up to **35,000	30	Nor:	4700	7630	Cont
Nor:	2800	2600	Up to **35,000	Cont				

* Wet
** Turbo supercharger limitation

(d) For detailed planning refer to Technical Order 1B-36J-1, 1B-36F-1 and other applicable technical orders.

(e) Take-off at 370,000 lb gross weight is authorized only for airplanes with structural modifications (according to ECP-1890B and on all airplanes subsequent to No. 312 when incorporates the new design pivot shaft installed under ECP-1890C and 1890D).

(f) (2x43,000 lb) may be carried only when gross weight does not exceed 357,500 lb. For gross weights above 357,500 lb the Max Bomb Load is (72x1000 lb)

PERFORMANCE REFERENCE:

FZA-36-278 and contractor's extrapolated data.

REVISION BASIS: Initial Issue.

Characteristics Summary

| BOMBER | B-36J (III) |

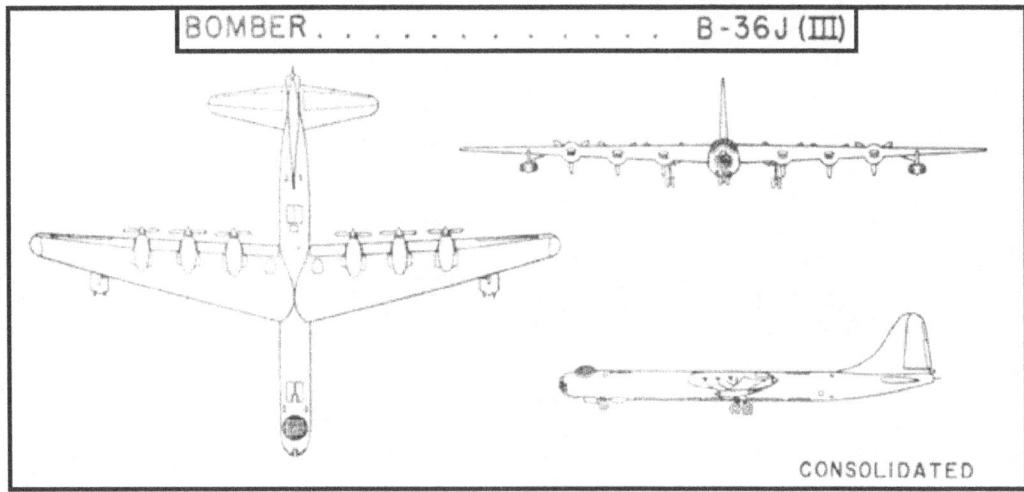

CONSOLIDATED

Wing Area . . . . 4772 sq ft   Length . . . . 162.1 ft

Span . . . . 230.0 ft   Height . . . . 46.8 ft

AVAILABILITY

Number available

ACTIVE	RESERVE	TOTAL

PROCUREMENT

Number to be delivered in fiscal years

STATUS

1. Major differences of the B-36J(III) from the standard configuration are removal of all turrets except tail turret, self-sealing pads, fuel purging system and crew comfort items; the replacement of blisters by small flush windows.
2. Contract approved for modification of B-36J to B-36J(III): Feb 54
3. First Delivery: Feb 54
4. Modification Completion Date: Jun 54

Navy Equivalent: None

Mfr's Model: 36

POWER PLANT

(6) R-4360-53
Pratt & Whitney

ENGINE RATINGS
BHP-RPM-ALT -MIN
T.O: *3800-2800 - SL -5
Mil: *3800-2800 - Turbo-30
  3500-2800 - Turbo-30
Nor: 2800-2600 - Turbo-Cont
*Wet

plus

(4) J47-GE-19
General Electric
S.L.S. LB - RPM - MIN
Max: 5200 - 7950 - 5
Mil: 5200 - 7950 - 30
Nor: 4730 - 7630 - Cont

FEATURES

Crew 13
Cabin Pressurization
Thermal Anti-Icing
Bombing-Navigation Radar K-3A System
Gun-Laying Radar AN/APG-41A
Chaff Dispenser
Loran
Single-Point Fueling
Defensive ECM

Max Fuel Cap:.. *36,396 gal
*Includes 2x1385 gal Wing Panel Fuel Tanks.
Note: Additional (2996 gal) bomb bay fuel tank necessary for missions other than Max Bomb Mission.

ARMAMENT

Turrets 1
Guns . . 2x20mm(M24-A1)
Ammunition (tot) . 1200 rds
BOMBS(max):
  Class(lb)   Load
WW II:
(Box Fin) 12x4000/72x1000
INTERIM:
(Conical Fin)
  22x2000/129x500
NEW SERIES:
  48x750/4x12,000

Characteristics Summary Basic Mission ... B-36J(III)

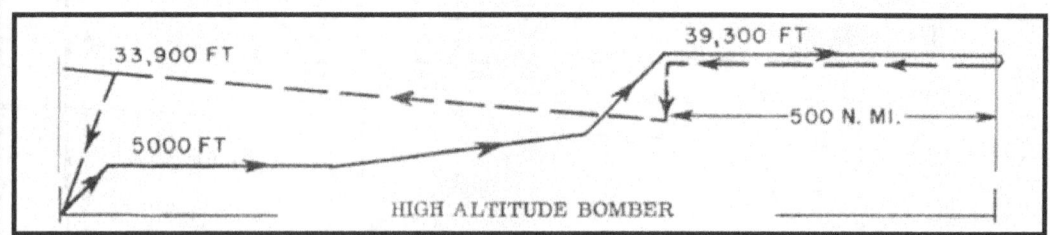

HIGH ALTITUDE BOMBER

PERFORMANCE

COMBAT RADIUS	FERRY RANGE	SPEED
3465 naut. mi with 11,408 lb payload at 197 knots avg. in 34.6 hours.	8200 naut. mi with 38,605 gal fuel at 188 knots avg. in 43.6 hours at 410,000 lb T.O. wt.	COMBAT 362 knots at 39,300 ft alt, max power MAX 363 knots at 37,500 ft alt, max power BASIC 346/362 knots at 25,000/35,000 ft alt, max power

CLIMB	CEILING	TAKE-OFF
780 fpm sea level, take-off weight normal power	28,500 ft 100 fpm, take-off weight normal power	ground run 5290 ft no assist | ——— ft assisted
1995 fpm sea level, combat weight maximum power	39,500 ft 500 fpm, combat weight maximum power	over 50 ft height 6820 ft no assist | ——— ft assisted

LOAD	WEIGHTS	STALLING SPEED
Bombs .... 10,000 lb Chaff .... 1408 lb Ammunition .... 1200 rds/20 mm Fuel: 36,640 gal protected 0 droppable 0 external 0	Empty..... 166,165 lb Combat... 262,500 lb Take-off 410,000 lb limited by structure	112 knots power-off, landing configuration, take-off weight **TIME TO CLIMB** ———

NOTES

1. Performance Basis:
   (a) AF Phase IV Flight Test (substantiated by WADC)

2. Revision Basis: To reflect latest performance due to weight change

Standard Aircraft Characteristics

B-36J III

Consolidated-Vultee

SIX R-4360-53
PRATT & WHITNEY

FOUR J47-GE-19
GENERAL ELECTRIC

BY AUTHORITY OF
THE SECRETARY
OF THE AIR FORCE

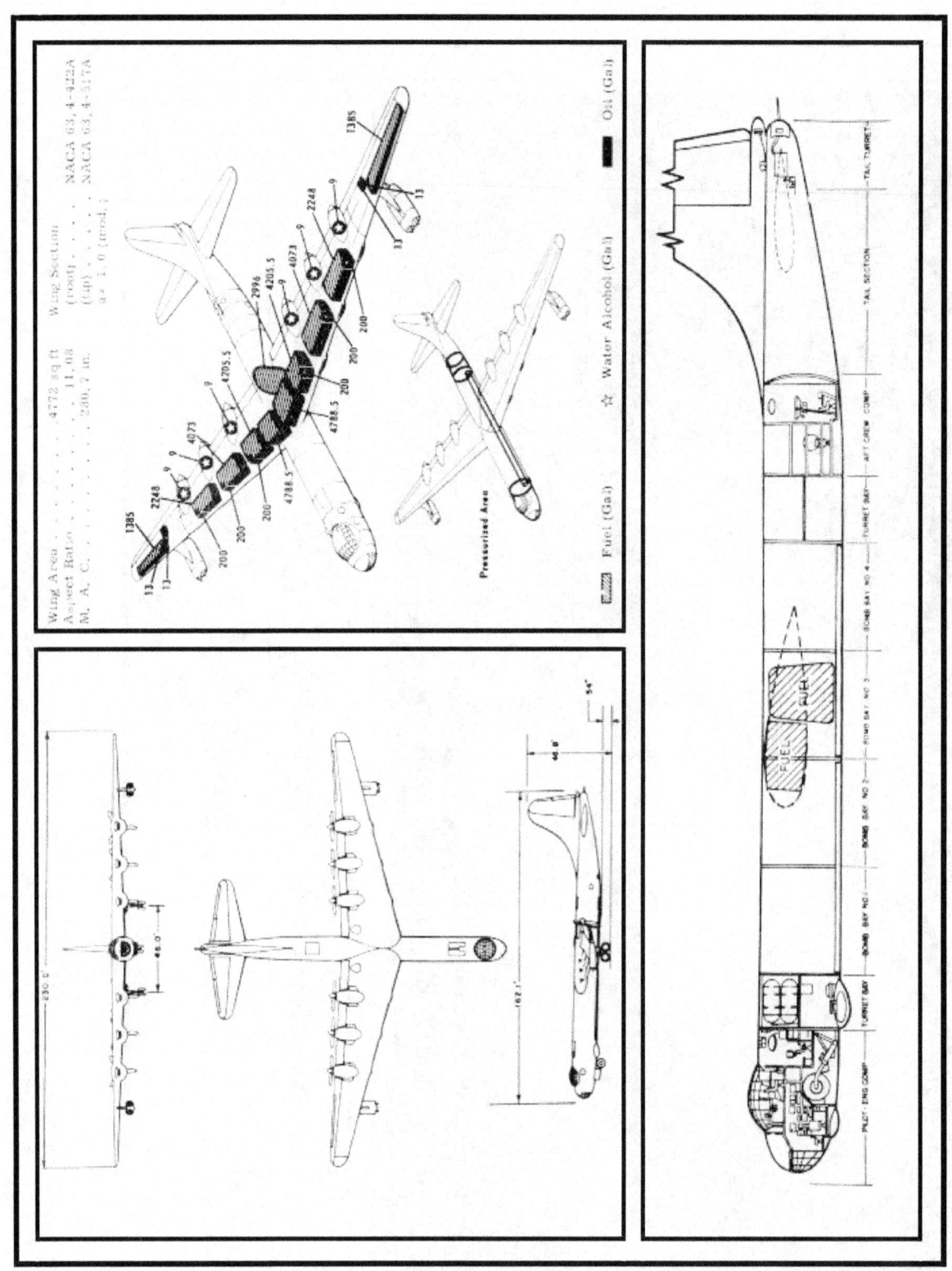

WEIGHTS

Loading	LB	L.F.
Empty	166,165 (C)	
Basic	167,813 (C)	
Design	410,000	2.0
Combat	*262,500	
Max T.O.	†410,000	2.0
Max Land	†357,500	

(C) Calculated
* For Basic Mission
† Limited by structure

FUEL

Location	No. Tanks	Gal
Wg, outer panel	2	2770
Wg, outbd	2	4496
Wg, ctr	2	8146
Wg, inbd	2	8411
Ctr sec (aux)	2	9577
Bomb bay	1	2996
	Total	*36,396
Grade		115/145
Specification		MIL-F-5572

Outboard (Jet) .... 4 (tot) 52
Wing (Recip) 6 1200
Grade (Recip) 1100
(Jet) 1005
Specification (Recip) .. MIL-L-6082A
(Jet) MIL-L-6081A

OIL
WATER/ALCOHOL
Eng Nacelle ...... 6 (tot) 54
*Additional (2996 gal) bomb bay fuel tank necessary for missions other than Max Bomb Mission.

ELECTRONICS

UHF Command	AN/ARC-27
VHF Command	AN/ARC-3
Liaison	AN/ARC-21
Radio Compass	AN/ARN-6
Marker Beacon	AN/ARN-12
IFF	AN/APX-6
Omni-Range	AN/ARN-14
Glide Path	AN/ARN-18
Bomb. Nav. Radar	K-3A
Loran	AN/APN-70
Gun Laying Radar	AN/APG-41A
Interphone	AN/AIC-10
Defensive ECM	
Chaff Dispenser	

Mission and Description

Navy Equivalent: None   Mfr's Model: 36

The principal mission of the B-36J(III) is the destruction by bombs of strategic ground and naval materiel objectives.

The crew of 13 differs from that of the standard configuration in that the upper aft right and left gunners have been removed. Compartment heating, enclosure defrosting, wing and tail anti-icing are accomplished by heated air obtained from heat exchangers installed in the reciprocating engine exhaust system. The oxygen system modification includes the removal of oxygen provisions from deleted crew stations.

The K-3A Bombing-Navigation system with a vertical Y-3A optical sight and radar equipment for blind bombing and navigation is provided. This system allows a single crew member to serve as radar operator and bombardier.

The defensive armament consists of a 20mm gun tail turret, controlled by AN/APG-41A Radar.

The airplane has a single-point refueling, manifold type fuel system.

Development

Major differences of the B-36J(III) from the standard configuration are removal of all turrets except tail turret, self-sealing pads, fuel purging system and crew comfort items; the replacement of blisters by small flush windows.

Contract approved for modification of B-36J(III) airplane to B-36J(III) .. Feb 54
First Delivery .... Feb 54
Modification Completion Date .... June 54

GUNS

No.	Type	Size	Rds ea	Loc
2	M24A1	20mm	600	Fus tail

BOMBS

No.	Class (lb)	
12		100
28		2000
45		1600
72		1000
132		500
	INTERIM (Conical Fin)	
4		12,000
22		10,000
40		1000
128		500
	NEW SERIES	
43		40

POWER PLANT

No. & Model	(6) R-1360-53
Mfr	Pratt & Whitney
Engine Spec. No.	A-7076-F
Supercharger	1 stg, 1 spd
Turbo Superch.	(2) BH-1
Red. Gear Ratio	0.375
Prop. Mfr.	Curtiss
Blade Design No.	1129-1C8-24
Prop Type	C.S., F.F., Reverse
No. Blades	3
Prop Dia	19'0"
Augmentation	Water/Alcohol
plus	
No. & Model	(4) J47-GE-19
Mfr	General Electric
Engine Spec. No.	E-389
Type	Axial
Length	144"
Diameter	39"
Weight (dry)	2425
Tail Pipe	Fixed Area
*Alternate Blades: A.O. Smith, SP-36J	

ENGINE RATINGS

	BHP	RPM	ALT	MIN
T.O.	3800	2800	SL	5
Mil	3800	2800	Turbo	30
	3500	2800	Turbo	30
Nor	2800	2600	Turbo	Cont
*Wet				

	LB	RPM		MIN
S.L. Static	5200	7950		5
Max	5200	7950		30
Mil				
Nor	4730	7630		Cont

DIMENSIONS

Wing	
Span	230'0"
Incidence (chord)	3°
(tip)	2°
Dihedral	15½'
Sweepback (LE)	122.1"
Length	
Height	46.8
Tread	
Eng. Grd. Clearance	54

Loading and Performance — Typical Mission

CONDITIONS		BASIC MISSION	MAX BOMBS II	MAX ALTITUDE III	HIGH SPEED IV	FERRY RANGE V
TAKE-OFF WEIGHT	(lb)	410,000	422,000	410,000	410,000	410,000
Fuel at 6.5 lb/gal (gross/115-145)	(lb)	259,440	157,300	247,840	259,840	231,640
Payload (Bombs)	(lb)	10,000	72,400	10,000	10,000	None
Payload (Chaff)	(lb)	1408	1408	1408	1408	None
Wing loading	(lb/sq ft)	85.9	85.9	85.9	85.9	85.9
Stall speed (power off)	(kn)	112	112	112	112	112
Take-off ground run at SL	(ft)	5290	5290	5290	5290	5290
Take-off to clear 50 ft	(ft)	6820	6820	6820	6820	6820
Rate of climb at SL	(fpm)	780	780	780	780	780
Rate of climb at SL (one engine out)	(fpm)	790	790	790	790	790
Time SL to 10,000 ft	(min)	14	14	14	14	14
Time SL to 20,000 ft	(min)	34	34	34	34	34
Service ceiling	(ft)	28,500	28,500	28,500	28,500	28,500
Service ceiling (one engine out)	(ft)	25,800	25,800	25,800	25,800	25,800
COMBAT RANGE	(n. mi)					8200
COMBAT RADIUS	(n. mi)	3465	2170	4225	1610	
Average cruise speed	(kn)	197	205	202	343	188
Initial cruising altitude	(ft)	5000	5000	5000	25,800	5000
Target speed	(kn)	352	348	324	346	346
Target altitude	(ft)	39,300	34,200	43,700	36,400	33,500
Final cruising altitude	(ft)	33,900	34,600	43,900	38,500	33,900
Total mission time	(hr)	34.6	20.9	31.5	10.0	43.6
TOTAL MISSION TIME	(hr)					
Interception altitude	(ft)					
COMBAT WEIGHT	(lb)	262,500	230,600	259,900	277,200	190,950
Combat altitude	(ft)	39,300	34,200	43,700	36,400	33,900
Combat speed	(kn)	362	363	358	359	372
Combat climb	(fpm)	545	1100	120	613	1500
Combat ceiling (500 fpm)	(ft)	39,500	42,600	39,700	37,600	47,200
Service ceiling (100 fpm)	(ft)	43,600	46,500	43,800	42,600	50,100
Max rate of climb at SL	(fpm)	41,800	43,600	43,200	40,200	47,900
Max speed at optimum altitude	(fpm)	1995	2360	2020	1865	2940
Basic speed at 25,000/35,000 ft	(kn/ft)	363/37,500	370/38,700	364/37,300	360/36,900	375/38,400
		346/362	350/368	346/363	344/359	354/373
LANDING WEIGHT	(lb)	190,750	187,590	190,750	190,750	190,350
Ground roll at SL	(ft)	1850	1820	1850	1850	1850
Ground roll (auxiliary brake)	(ft)	1640	1610	1640	1640	1640
Total from 50 ft	(ft)	3300	3270	3300	3300	3300
Total from 50 ft (auxiliary brake)	(ft)	3060	3040	3060	3060	3060

NOTES:
① Take-Off power
② Max power
③ Normal power
④ Detailed descriptions of RADIUS and RANGE missions given on page 6.
⑤ Brakes plus reversed props.
⑥ Structural limit for 25,000 ft. alt.

PERFORMANCE BASIS:
(a) Data source: Flight Test (Substantiated by WADC)
(b) Performance is based on powers shown on page 6.

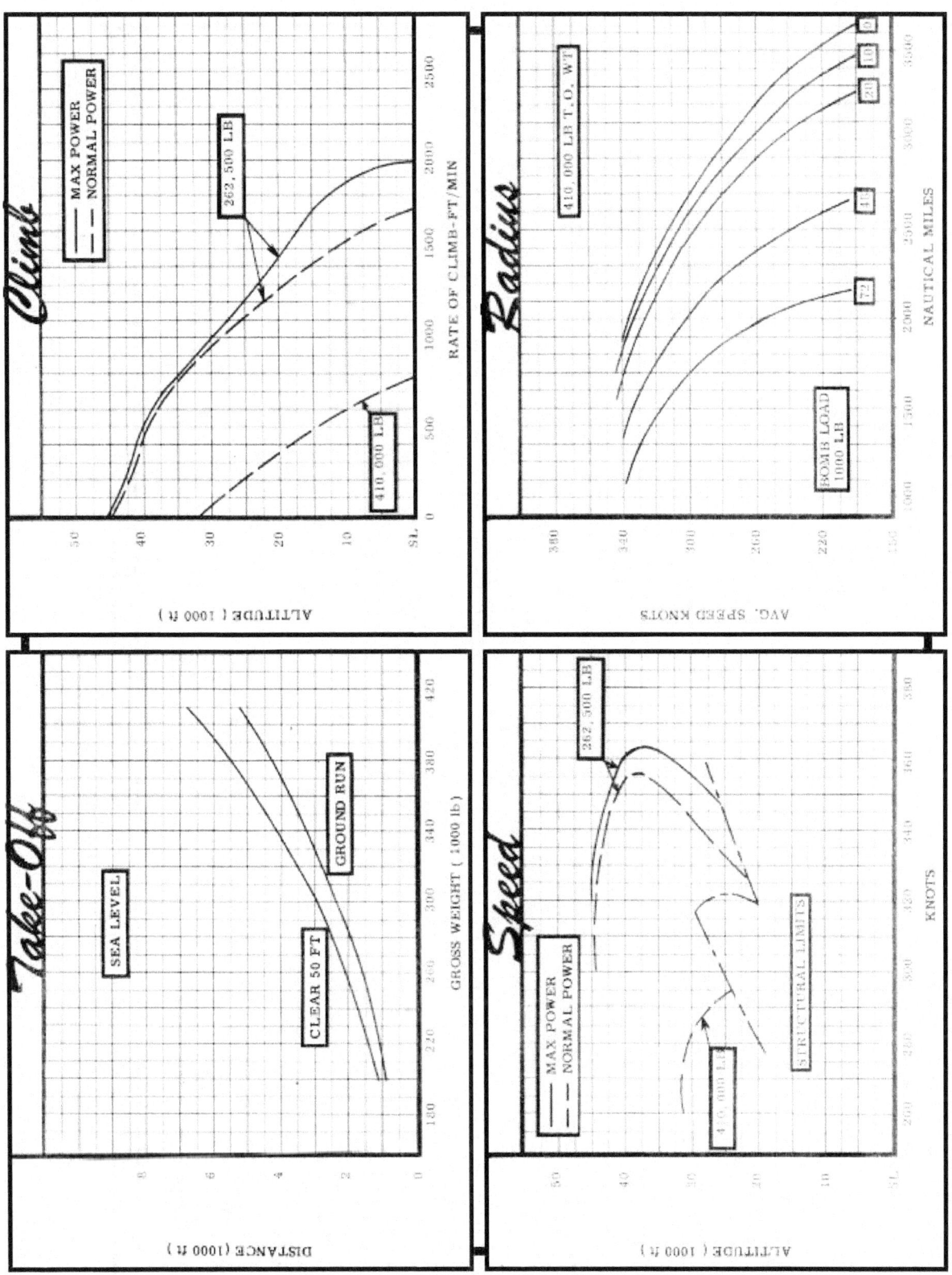

NOTES

FORMULA: RADIUS MISSIONS I & II

Warm-up, take-off and climb on course to 5000 ft at normal power; cruise out at long range speeds to point of cruise-climb operation. Begin climb to combat altitude, using long range climb powers, to arrive at cruise ceiling 500 nautical miles from target. Cruise at long range speeds at combat altitude, using best engine (reciprocating-jet) combinations, 15 minutes from target, conduct 10 engine normal power bomb run, drop bombs and chaff, and conduct 2 minutes evasive action and 8 minutes escape from target at normal power. After leaving target area, cruise back at long range speeds, using best engine combinations, until 500 nautical miles from target. Descend to optimum cruise altitude and cruise-climb back to base. Range free allowances include 10 minutes normal power fuel consumption for reciprocating engines and 5 minutes normal power fuel consumption for jet engines for starting and take-off, 2 minutes normal power fuel consumption at combat altitude for evasive action, 30 minutes of fuel consumption for long range speeds at sea level (reciprocating engines only) plus 5% of initial fuel load for landing and endurance reserve.

FORMULA: RADIUS MISSION III

Same profile and fuel reserves as for Radius Mission I with the following exceptions: Enter combat zone and cruise to within 15 minutes of target, maintaining maximum obtainable altitudes. Conduct (15 minute) 10 engine normal power bomb run, drop bombs and chaff and conduct 2 minutes evasive action and 8 minutes escape from target at normal power. Cruise toward base at target altitude, using best engine combination until 500 nautical miles from target. Descend to optimum cruise altitude and continue as in Radius Mission I.

FORMULA: RADIUS MISSION IV

Same profile and fuel reserves as for Radius Mission I with the following exceptions: Enter combat zone at maximum obtainable altitude, and cruise, using best engine combinations toward target at that altitude. Conduct the balance of the mission as in radius Mission III.

FORMULA: RADIUS MISSION IV

The entire mission is flown at normal power. Warm up, take off, and climb on course to 25,800 ft. Cruise at optimum altitudes to combat altitude, arriving 500 nautical miles from target. Cruise to target, drop bombs, and chaff and conduct 2 minutes evasive action, Climb to best altitude for normal power cruise. Cruise-climb to base. Range free allowances are the same as for Radius Mission I & II.

FORMULA: FERRY RANGE MISSION V

Warm-up, take-off and climb on course to 5000 ft at normal power; cruise-climb at long range speeds until all but reserve fuel is consumed. Range free allowances are the same as for Radius Missions I & II, except no fuel allowed for evasive action.

GENERAL DATA

(a) Engine ratings shown on page 3 are manufacturer's guaranteed ratings. Power values used for performance calculations are:

	(6) R-4360-53				(4) J47-GE-19		
	BHP	RPM	CRIT. ALT.	MIN	S.L.S.	LB	RPM	MIN
T.O.*| 3800	2800	SL	5	T.O.:	5910	7950	5
Max	3500	2800	Up to 35,000	30	Max:	5200	7950	30
Nor:	2800	2600	Up to 39,000	Cont	Nor:	4700	7630	Cont

*Wet Turbo supercharger limitation

(b) For detailed planning refer to Convair Report "FZA-36-119 "Performance Estimates for B36J (III)" dated 10 January 1955, Rev 31 May 1955.

(c) Take off at 370,000 lb cruise weight is authorized only for airplanes on which structural modifications to the landing gear have been accomplished in accordance with T.O. 1B-36-815 and T.O. 1B-36-889.

PERFORMANCE REFERENCE:

FZA-36-319 and applicable Technical Orders.

REVISION BASIS:

To reflect latest performance due to weight change.

98

SUPPLEMENTAL

HIGH ALTITUDE COMBAT ZONE CAPABILITIES

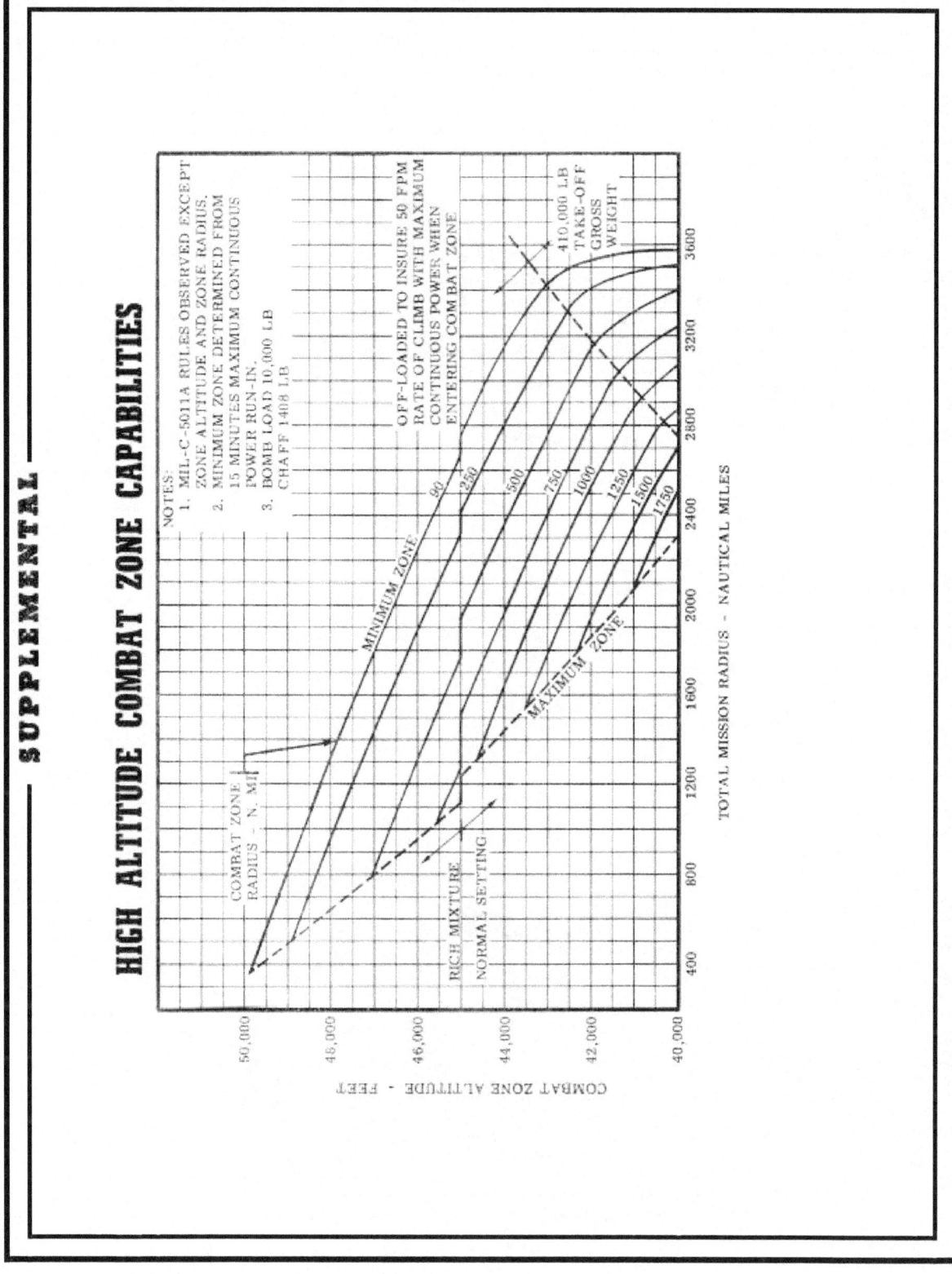

Convair GRB-36F in flight with Republic YRF-84F.
Source: U.S. Air Force

Convair NB-36H in flight. Note the radiation warning symbol on the tail.
Source: U.S. Air Force

The Boeing B-47 Stratojet

The first Boeing XB-47 built. Photo taken on Dec. 1, 1947, before its first flight.
Source: U.S. Air Force

The origin of the B-47 Stratojet can be traced back to the Second World War. In June 1943, the obvious advantages of jet engines for future aircraft led to an informal USAAF request for a fast photographic reconnaissance or medium bomber aircraft that would be capable of undertaking a wide range of missions. The responses to this requirement were favorable enough to turn a feasibility exercise into a formal requirement. The introduction of the German Arado Ar-234 bomber into service about this time emphasized the advantages that jet propulsion brought to bombing and reconnaissance missions.

On November 17, 1944, the USAAF issued a formal requirement for a jet-powered medium bomber with a maximum range of 3,500 miles, a combat radius of 1,000 miles, a service ceiling of 45,000 feet, and a maximum speed of 550 mph. The XB-47 was the third of four design proposals that were received by Army Air Force in response to this requirement. The other designs resulted in the North American XB-45, Convair XB-46, and Martin XB-48. These designs fell into two groups. The XB-45 and XB-46 were smaller four-engine tactical aircraft descended from the A-20/A-26 attack aircraft. The XB-47 and XB-48 were larger six-engine medium bombers that were successors to the B-25/B-26 medium bombers.

By the time this proposal had been presented, the Boeing XB-47 had already been changed greatly from its origins. It had actually pre-dated USAAF interest in a jet-engined medium bomber, having started life as a scaled-down version of the B-29 with four jet engines paired in two nacelles mounted underneath the wing. The aircraft still retained a close visual similarity to the B-29, but it featured a much thinner wing to increase the aircraft's speed. Wind tunnel testing showed that the proposed design was unsatisfactory, and it underwent a series of revisions that moved the engines from the wings to the fuselage. However, the design was soon to undergo a much more radical revision.

In the 1930s, German scientists had investigated the use of swept wings to improve the performance of high-speed aircraft. At the same time, the National Advisory Committee for Aeronautics (NACA) in the United States had carried out an independent investigation of the same phenomenon. Both sets of studies had come to the same conclusion: that the use of sweep angles as high as 45 degrees enhanced high-speed performance by delaying the formation of shock waves as the aircraft neared the speed of sound. However, because at that time there was no way enough power could be generated to drive an aircraft at the speeds in question, the issue seemed purely theoretical. In recent years it has become known that Russian design teams had investigated the same issue and come to the same conclusions.

Swept Wings Arrive

By 1944 it was apparent that jet engines would soon offer the power needed to push aircraft into the speed regions where swept wings would start to confer benefits. In this respect, the importance of German data is often overstated; the decision to apply swept-wing design concepts to the U.S. North American F-86 Sabre and the Russian MiG-15 was made before the German data was available. The significance of the capture of German data on swept wings was that it speeded the process of adopting swept-wing designs by providing independent confirmation of work carried out elsewhere. Boeing's adoption of swept wings for the B-47 was, however, the direct result of obtaining access to German data. Boeing's chief aerodynamicist, George Schairer, had accompanied the U.S. Army's Scientific Advisory Group in its inspections of German design facilities, and reported the details of German research on swept wings to Seattle. Boeing engineers immediately realized the significance of the data and stopped work on the straight-winged XB-47. Wind tunnel tests confirmed the essential validity of the German findings, and work began on a swept-winged version of the XB-47.

By this time, the idea of fuselage-mounted engines had fallen into disfavor since they presented a maintenance problem and constituted a fire hazard. The swept-wing XB-47 was revised to feature six jet engines, four paired in pylon-mounted inboard nacelles suspended underneath the inner wing and single units in pods attached to the wingtips. The design was further revised when the outboard engines were moved from the wingtips to pods underneath the outer wings 8 feet from the tip. The wingspan was increased to 116 feet. This was the final configuration for the prototype XB-47.

Work on the prototype XB-47 began in June 1946, with the aircraft being rolled out of the factory at Seattle on September 12, 1947. The XB-47 flew for the first time on December 17, 1947. Flight testing showed the aircraft to be 74 mph faster than the Martin XB-48. Even so, the performance of the XB-47 was less than anticipated. The aircraft's operational ceiling was 2,500 feet below that promised by Boeing, and 7,500 feet lower than that originally required by the USAAF. Its maximum speed was also slower than expected. These deficiencies were largely due to the use of J-35 engines in the first prototype. The second XB-47 was powered by J-47 engines that pushed its maximum speed past 600 mph.

While the B-36 heavy bomber program had been frequently threatened with cancellation due to its early problems and performance deficiencies, no such doubts seem ever to have been expressed about the B-47. Certainly the severe developmental problems experienced with the aircraft were the cause of grave concern in Strategic Air Command, but the sparkling performance of the new aircraft made any thought of terminating the program inconceivable. By now, the future structure of SAC would include both the heavy intercontinental bombers that could reach their targets from the United States and smaller medium bombers that would reach their targets by means of a combination of aerial refueling and forward bases. Almost by definition, the heavy bombers would be available in smaller numbers than desirable, so the medium bombers would be the maid-of-all-work required to undertake routine missions and day-to-day training. The medium bombers in question at that time were the B-29 and the B-50. Replacing them with the B-47 was SAC's highest priority in the early 1950s.

Into Service

Ten B-47As were ordered on October 28, 1948. These were explicitly considered to be test and training models and were not considered as being combat ready. The first of the B-47A aircraft flew on June 25, 1950 and entered service in May 1951 with the 306th Bombardment Wing. The early service experience with the B-47As revealed a whole slew of operational problems. They were critically underpowered, and had serious issues with their braking systems. These caused a number of dangerous incidents during aborted takeoffs and after gross weight landings on wet runways. It was these incidents that caused the development of braking parachutes for aircraft use.

While the B-47A was never considered to be more than a training and operational evaluation model, the B-47B was the first combat-ready version of the medium bomber. The major external difference between the B-47B and earlier versions was the replacement of the nose transparency with a solid metal nosecone containing a K-2 bombing navigation system. A total of 87 B-47Bs were ordered in November 1949. With the outbreak of the Korean War in 1950, the financial restrictions that had plagued USAF procurement in the late 1940s were lifted and the demand for B-47s increased dramatically. As a result, the B-47 program became the largest U.S. bomber production program since the end of the Second World War.

The B-47B was not considered to be a satisfactory aircraft. It was badly underpowered yet also seriously overweight. This made it unstable at high altitude and generally hard to maneuver. In fact, the flying characteristics of the B-47 were described as "horrible," with the aircraft introducing the term "coffin corner" to the aeronautical lexicon. At certain speed and altitude conditions, the stalling speed and critical Mach number were identical. This meant that pulling the nose back would stall the aircraft. Pushing the nose down would cause it to exceed its critical Mach number and it would break up. Under these conditions, the only way out was to hold the aircraft level and allow it to lose speed and altitude very slowly. Despite a growing reputation as a pilot-killer, plans were made for the acquisition of more Stratojets. A total of 1,760 B/RB-47s were ordered during 1952, but the order was later reduced and only 399 were delivered as B-47Bs, with the rest being delivered as B-47Es.

The deficiencies of the B-47B were so marked that a major rectification program designated "High Noon" was initiated. This effectively brought the B-47Bs up to the standards of the B-47E. The modifications featured the installation of ejector seats for all crew members, the deletion of the fixed JATO units in favor of a jettisonable 19- or 33-rocket assisted takeoff pack, provision for the delivery of thermonuclear bombs, addition of a reinforced landing gear that could handle higher takeoff weights, and the provision of an A-5 fire control system, an ARC-21 long-range radio, and better electronics countermeasures equipment. J47-GE-25 engines rated at 6,000 pounds thrust (7,200 with water injection) were installed. Later, 20mm cannon replaced the 0.50-inch machine guns in the tail turret.

Concern over the underpowered nature of the B-47 continued, with both the B-47C and B-47D being proposals for aircraft with four much more powerful engines replacing the six existing jets. Neither was adopted, and the main production version of the B-47 was the B-47E. This model consolidated all the lessons painfully learned with the B-47B. It standardized on six General Electric J47-GE-25 engines that offered 7,200 pounds of thrust with water injection. From an operational point of view, the most important feature of the B-47E was an inflight refueling receptacle for flying-boom mid-air refueling on the starboard side of the nose. Production ended with 1,341 B-47Es completed.

Phase Out

By December 1956, SAC had 27 combat-ready B-47 wings, with 1,204 combat-ready B-47 crews and 1,306 B-47 aircraft assigned. The emphasis in the B-47 groups was already shifting to low-altitude operations due to a perception that high-speed B-47s flying at low level would be less vulnerable to enemy countermeasures. SAC initially wanted 1,000 B-47s modified for low-level flying, a program that would demand fitting virtually the entire B-47 fleet with absolute altimeters, terrain-avoidance equipment, and Doppler radar. It quickly became apparent that a combination of cost and the structural damage caused by the stress of low-altitude flight would prevent this goal from being reached and the program was cut to 350 aircraft.

In March 1961, President John F. Kennedy directed that the phase-out of the B-47 be accelerated. However, this was delayed by the Berlin crisis of 1961-62. Once that passed, the B-47s were withdrawn from service and delivered to the storage facility at Davis-Monthan AFB. SAC's last two B-47s went to storage on February 11, 1966. The final epitaph on the B-47 was made by veteran Stratojet pilot Brig. Gen. Earl C. Peck in 1975. He remarked, "The B-47 was often admired, respected, cursed or even feared, but almost never loved."

Characteristics Summary

BOMBER — B-47A

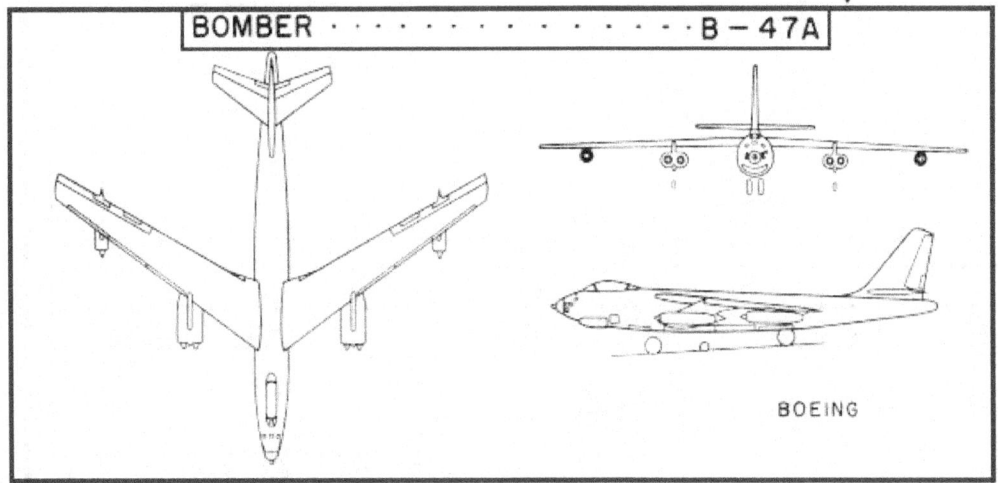

BOEING

Wing area .... 1428.0 sq ft   Length .... 106.7 ft

Span .... 116.0 ft   Height .... 27.9 ft

AVAILABILITY			PROCUREMENT			
Number available			Number to be delivered in fiscal years			
ACTIVE	RESERVE	TOTAL				

STATUS

1. Design initiated: December 1945 (XB-47)

2. First flight: December 1947 (XB-47)

3. First flight B-47A: April 1950

POWER PLANT

(6) Turbo-jet   J 47-GE-11
    General Electric

ENGINE RATINGS

S.L. Static	LB - RPM
T.O:	5200 - 7950
Mil:	5200 - 7950
Nor:	4730 - 7630

FEATURES

Crew: 3
Cabin Pressurization
Bycicle Landing Gear
Thermal Anti-icing
Bombing & Navigation Radar
Anti-skid Brakes
Braking Parachute
 ATO (prov.): 18 x 1000 lb thrust (15 seconds duration)
Max Fuel Capacity:
 9789 gal.

ARMAMENT

Space and structural provisions for a tail turret.

Max Bomb Load:
 (1) 22,000 lb

Max Bomb Size: 22,000 lb

Characteristics Summary Basic Mission · · · · B — 47A

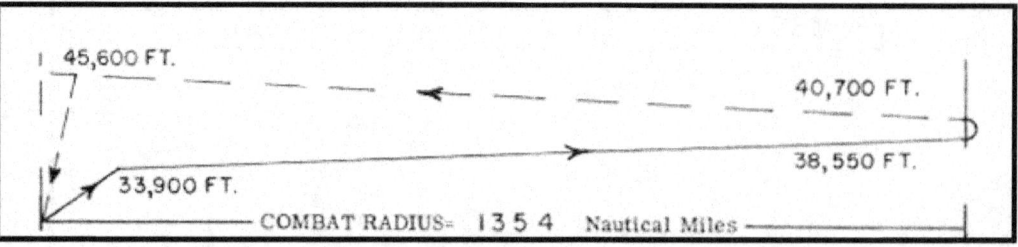

PERFORMANCE		
COMBAT RADIUS	**COMBAT RANGE**	**COMBAT SPEED**
1354 naut. mi with 10,000 lb payload at 422 knots avg. in 6.61 hours.	2648 naut. mi with 10,000 lb payload at 421 knots avg. in 6.38 hours.	490 knots at 35,000 ft alt, max power **MAXIMUM SPEED** 536 knots at 10,500 ft alt, max power
CLIMB	**CEILING**	**TAKE-OFF**
3100 fpm sea level, take-off weight normal power	35,500 ft 100 fpm, take-off weight normal power	ground run 5950 ft no assist | ft assisted
7000 fpm sea level, combat weight maximum power	43,800 ft 500 fpm, combat weight maximum power	over 50 ft height 6450 ft no assist | ft assisted
LOAD	**WEIGHTS**	**STALLING SPEED**
Bombs: 10,000 lb Ammunition: None Fuel: 9789 gal protected 100 % droppable 0 % external 0 %	Empty..... 73,149 lb Combat... 104,143 lb Take-off 150,500 lb limited by space	125 knots flaps down, take-off weight **TIME TO CLIMB** —

NOTES

1. PERFORMANCE BASIS:
   (a) Estimated data
   (b) In computing Radius and Range, specific fuel consumptions have been increased 5% to allow for variation of fuel flow in service aircraft.
2. Fuel density 6.7 lb/gal.
3. REVISION BASIS: To correct performance data to reflect long range cruise operation in lieu of max range cruise operation.

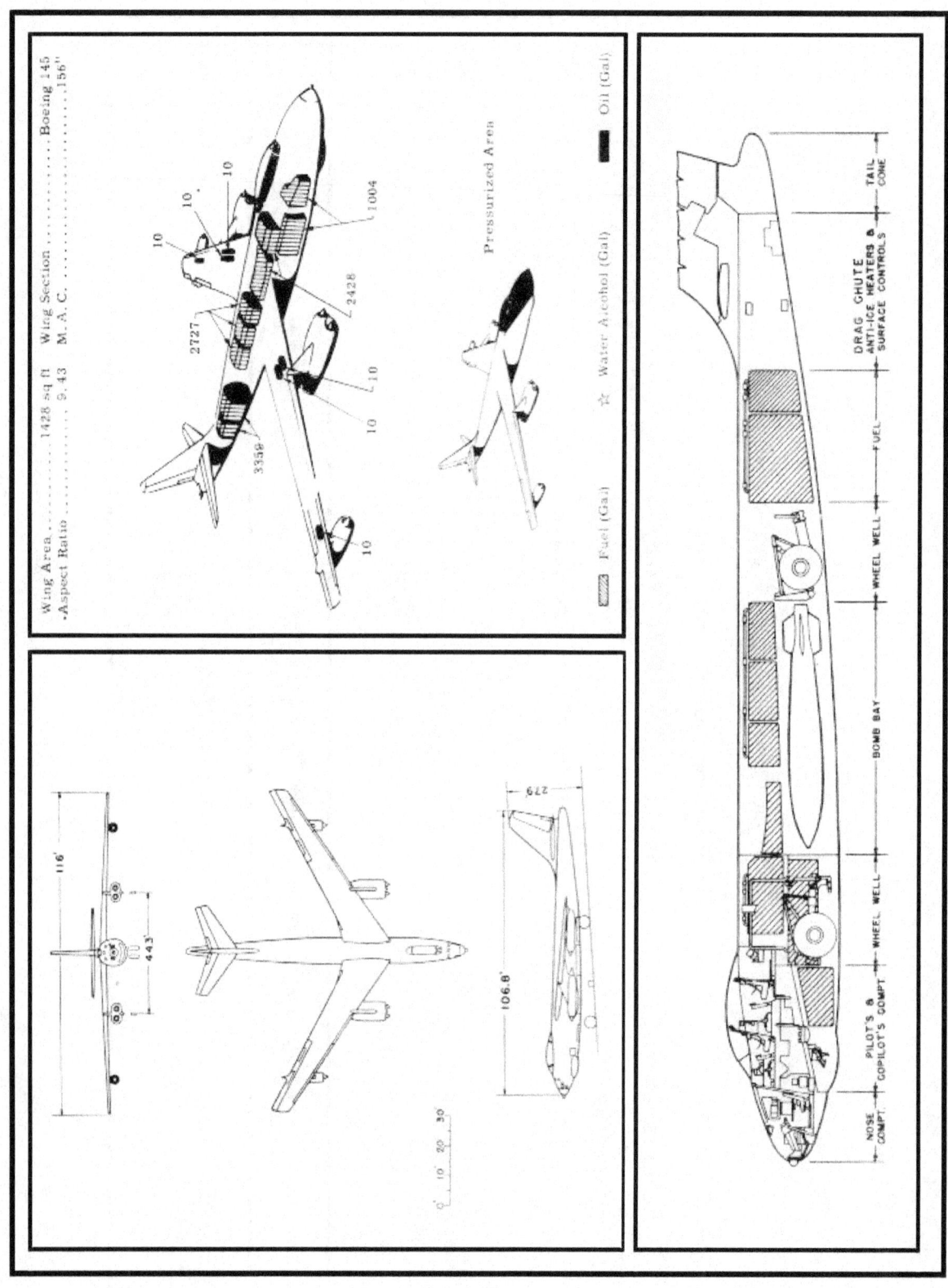

POWER PLANT

No. & Model	(6) J47-GE-11
Mfr	General Electric
Engine Spec. No.	E.583
Type	Axial Flow
Length	144"
Diameter	39"
Weight (dry)	2475 lb
	Provisions for:
	*ATO Units
No. & Model	(18) 14AS1000
Mfr	Aerojet
Weight (loaded)	203 lb ea.

*Serial No. 49-1901 does not have provisions for ATO

ENGINE RATINGS

S.L. Static	LB	RPM	MIN
Max:	5200	7950	5
Mil:	5200	7950	30
Nor:	4730	7630	Cont

*ATO Units Provisions

Thrust .... 18 x 1000 lb (14 seconds duration)

*Serial No. 49-1901 does not have provisions for ATO.

DIMENSIONS

Wing	
Span	116.0'
Incidence	2°45'
Dihedral	0°
Sweepback (LE)	36°37'
Length	106.8'
Height	27.9'
Tread	44.3'

Mission and Description

Navy Equivalent: None   Mfr's Model: 450-10-9

The B-47A is a high-speed, medium range swept-wing jet bomber whose tactical mission is the destruction by bombs of land or naval materiel objectives.

The normal crew consists of a pilot, co-pilot-gunner and a bombardier-navigator. The crew compartment, located in the forward part of the fuselage, is pressurized and has complete heating and ventilating facilities. Seat ejection is provided for the normal crew.

The electrically-operated, bicycle-type main landing gear consists of steerable dual-wheel front gear and dual-wheel rear gear. The outrigger landing gear consists of a single wheel retracting into the inboard nacelle. A K-2 Bombing-Navigational System is provided in four (4) of the 10 "A" airplanes.

There are provisions for solid rocket augmentation for take-off and a braking parachute is provided for decreasing landing roll distance. NESA glass windshield provided for pilot. Hydraulic boost provided for all three control surfaces. Anti-skid device for braking.

A type MH-7 automatic pilot is installed.

Development

Design initiated:	Dec 1945 (XB-47)
First flight:	Dec 1947 (XB-47)
First flight:	25 Jun 1950
Production completed:	Jun 1951

BOMBS

No.	Size	Type
1	10,000	Special
	Space and structural provisions	
1	22,000	G.P.
1	12,000	G.P.
2	4000	G.P.
9	2000	G.P.
16	1000	G.P.

Max Bomb Load .... 22,000 lb

WEIGHTS

Loading	Lb	L.F.
Empty	73,240(E)	
Basic	74,524(E)	
Operating	79,457	
Design	125,000	3.0
Combat	*106,060	
Max T.O.	†157,000	2.0
Max Land	‡157,000	

(E) Estimated
*For Basic Mission
†Limited by strength
‡Limited by max T.O.

FUEL

Location	No. Tanks	Gal.
Fus.main*	1	2428
Fus.ctr		2727
Fus.aft*		3359
Fus.aux*	1	1004
	Total	9518

*Self-sealing

Grade JP-3

OIL

Capacity (gal) 60
Grade 1005

ELECTRONICS

VHF Command	AN/ARC-3
Radio Compass	AN/ARN-6
Interphone	AAF Combat
Marker Beacon	RC-193A
Glide Path	*AN/ARN-5A
I.F.F.	*SCR-695B

*Space provisions only

GUNS

Space and provisions for tail turret mounting two (2) type M3 .50 cal machine guns.

Test installation of A-2 fire control system in aircraft Serial No. 1906.

Test installation of A-5 fire control in aircraft Serial No. 1908.

Loading and Performance — Typical Mission

CONDITIONS		MAX RANGE BASIC MISSION	HIGH ALT MISSION	FERRY RANGE
TAKE-OFF WEIGHT	(lb)	151,324	151,324	141,324
Fuel at 6.5 lb/gal (grade JP-3)	(lb)	61,867	61,867	61,867
Military load (Bombs)	(lb)	10,000	10,000	None
Wing loading	(lb/sq ft)	106	106	98.97
Stall speed (power off, landing configuration) (kn)		125	125	121
Take-off ground run at SL (ft) ③		6000	6000	5000
Take-off to clear 50 ft (ft) ③		7210	7210	6150
Rate of climb at SL (fpm) ③		3375	3375	3700
Time: SL to 20,000 ft (min) ③		7.9	7.9	7.2
Time: SL to 30,000 ft (min) ③		14.7	14.7	13.3
Service ceiling (100 fpm) (ft) ③		38,100	38,100	39,100
Service ceiling (one engine out) (ft) ②		35,500	35,500	37,300
COMBAT RANGE (n.mi.) ④		2634	2325	2856
Average speed (kn)		416	413	424
Initial cruising altitude (ft)		33,000	38,000	36,000
Final cruising altitude (ft)		43,000	46,000	45,000
Total mission time (hr)		6.21	5.49	6.73
COMBAT RADIUS (n.mi.) ④		1350	1200	—
Average speed (kn)		424	424	—
Initial cruising altitude (ft)		34,000	38,000	—
Bombing altitude (ft) ③		35,000	43,000	—
Bomb run speed (kn)		474 ⑦	458	—
Final cruising altitude (ft)		45,800	45,000	—
Total mission time (hr)		6.45	5.76	—
COMBAT WEIGHT (lb) ⑤		106,060	106,060	85,644
Combat altitude (ft)		35,000	43,000	45,000
Combat speed (kn) ②		474 ⑦	462	⑥
Combat climb (fpm) ②		2050	950	⑥
Combat ceiling (500 fpm) (ft) ②		44,300	44,300	⑥
Service ceiling (100 fpm) (ft) ②		46,200	46,000	⑥
Service ceiling (one engine out) (ft) ②		42,800	42,800	47,000
Max rate of climb at SL (fpm) ①		6200	6200	⑥
Max speed at 8800 ft ⑦		521	521	⑥
LANDING WEIGHT (lb)		85,644	85,644	85,644
Ground roll at SL (ft)		4610	4610	4610
Ground roll (auxiliary brake) (ft)		2600	2600	2600
Total from 50 ft (ft)		5730	5730	5730
Total from 50 ft (auxiliary brake) (ft)		3720	3720	3720

NOTES:
① Max power
② Military power
③ Normal power
④ Detailed descriptions of RADIUS and RANGE missions are given on page 6.
⑤ For Radius Mission if radius is shown
⑥ Data not available
⑦ Limited to Mach .815 by buffeting

PERFORMANCE BASIS:
(a) Data source: Flight test
(b) Performance is based on powers shown on page 6

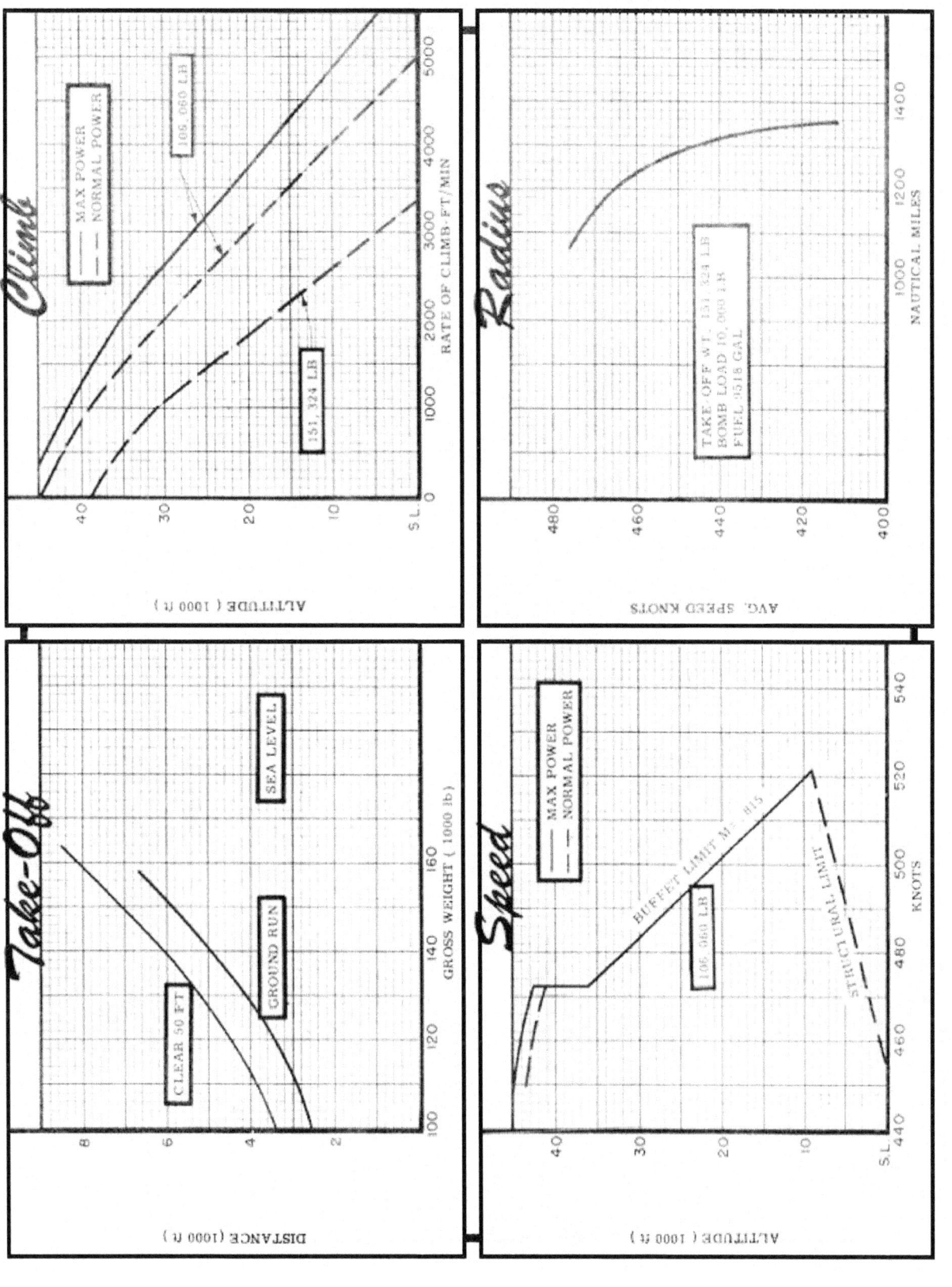

NOTES

FORMULA: RADIUS MISSION I

Take-off, climb on course to 33,900 ft at military power and maximum rate of climb cruise out at long range speeds increasing altitude at decreasing airplane weight, make 5 minute normal power bomb run to target, drop bombs, conduct normal power evasive action for 6 minutes, start cruise to home base at 40,700 ft altitude arriving over home base at 45,600 ft altitude. Range free allowances are: 5 minutes normal power fuel consumption for starting engines and take-off, plus 6 minutes normal power evasive action, plus 10% of initial fuel for reserve.

FORMULA: RANGE MISSION I

Same as outbound leg of the basic radius formula continued without dropping the bombs until 90% of the initial fuel has been used. Flight is terminated at 43,000 ft altitude leaving 10% of fuel reserve for combat, evasive action, landing reserve, or other considerations for which no distance is credited.

FORMULA: RADIUS MISSION II

Same as the basic radius formula except normal power cruise is used to give higher cruise altitude. Initial altitude for start of cruise out is 38,000 ft and final altitude over the home base is 45,000 ft. Range free allowances are the same as for the basic radius formula.

FORMULA: RANGE MISSION II

Same as outbound leg of radius mission II continued until 90% of initial fuel load has been used at terminal altitude of 46,000 ft. Range free allowances are 5 minutes normal power fuel consumption for starting engines and take-off plus 10% of initial fuel load for landing and endurance reserve.

GENERAL NOTES

(a) Times to climb do not include take-off time and time to accelerate to best climb speed.

(b) Engine ratings shown on page 3 are engine manufacturer's guaranteed ratings. Power values used in performance calculations are as follows:

S.L. Static	J47-GE-11		
	LB	RPM	MIN
Max:	5670	8030	5
Mil:	5610	8030	30
Nor:	4880	7450	Cont

(c) For detailed planning refer to T.O. AN 01-20ENA-1.

(d) Maximum take-off weight of 157,000 lb can be obtained with 22,000 lb bomb.

Characteristics Summary

BOMBER — B-47B

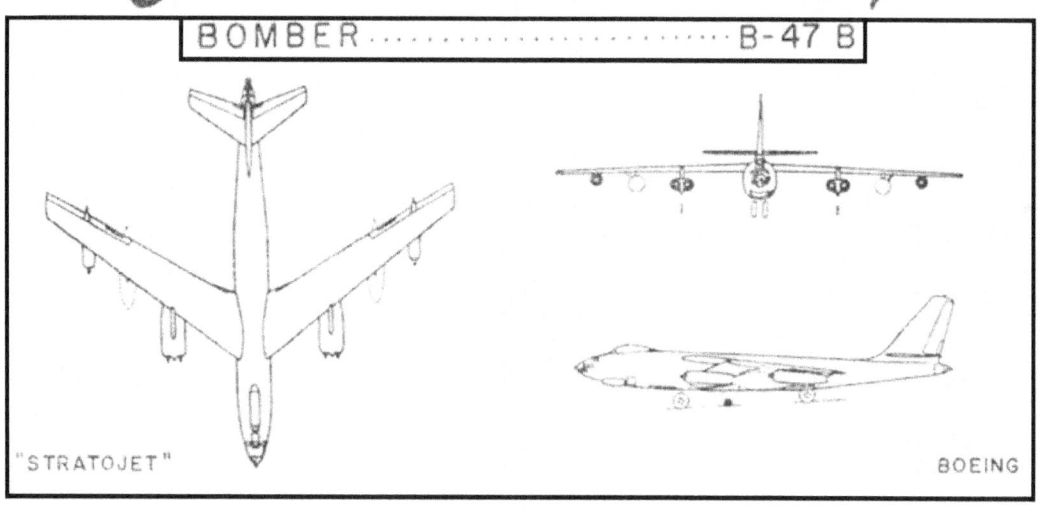

"STRATOJET" BOEING

Wing Area .... 1428 sq ft   Length .... 106.8 ft
Span .... 116.0 ft   Height .... 27.9 ft

AVAILABILITY

Number available

ACTIVE	RESERVE	TOTAL

PROCUREMENT

Number to be delivered in fiscal years

STATUS

1. Design initiated: Sep 48
2. First flight: 27 Feb 51
3. First acceptance: Mar 51
4. Production completion: Jun 53

Navy Equivalent: None

5. The 1st to 298th aircraft have -23 engines; -25 engines to be installed from the 298th aircraft on. B-47B aircraft with -25 engines assume Roman Numeral One (B-47B-I) configuration and are similar to B-47E-II configuration.

Mfr's Model: 450-67-27

POWER PLANT

(6) J47-GE-23
General Electric
ENGINE RATINGS
S.L.S.   LB - RPM - MIN
Max: 5910 - 7950 - 5
Mil: 5620 - 7800 - 30
Nor: 5270 - 7630 - Cont

ATO
Nr & Model...*†(33)14AS1000
Thrust (lb) 33,000
Duration (sec) 14
or
Nr & Model .. †(19)15KS1000
Thrust (lb) 19,000
Duration (sec) 15

† Manufactured by Aerojet

*See note c, Notes Block

FEATURES

Crew 3
Thermal anti-icing
Bombing-navigational radar
Anti-skid brakes
Braking parachute
Bail-out spoiler door
Internal fuel tank purging
(1)K-38 or alternates (vertical camera)
Single-point ground and air refueling provisions
B-4 fire control
K-4A bombing-nav. system

Max fuel capacity: 17,290 gal

ARMAMENT

Turrets: 1
Guns: ... 2x50 cal(M-3)
Ammunition:(tot) 1200 rds
BOMBS (Max)
   Class (lb)   Load
SHORT BOMB BAY
Interim: *3x2000 *13x500
New Series
          *7x750   *7x750
LONG BOMB BAY
WWII   2x4000   16x1000
Interim:
         *6x2000 *18x1000
          6x2000   8x1000
New Series
         *1x25,000 *21x750
          1x25,000   8x750

*Hi-Density Kit

Characteristics Summary Basic Mission — B-47 B

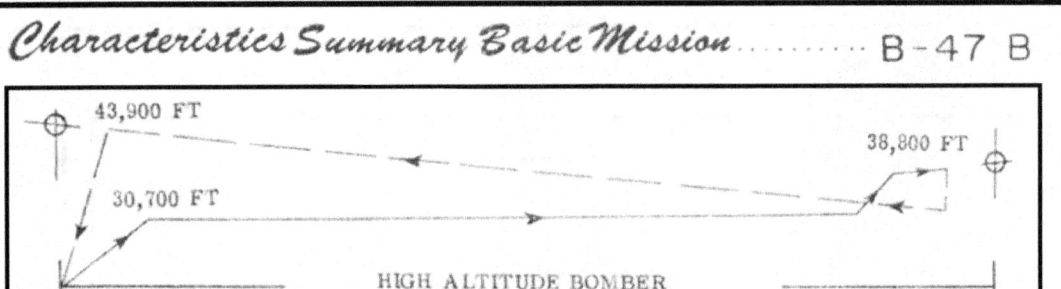

HIGH ALTITUDE BOMBER

PERFORMANCE

COMBAT RADIUS	FERRY RANGE	SPEED
1704 naut. mi with 10,000 lb payload at 433 knots avg. in 7.87 hours.	3861 naut. mi with 15,213 gal fuel at 432 knots avg. in 8.94 hours at 185,000* lb T.O. wt.	COMBAT 484 knots at 38,800 ft alt, max power ② MAX 528 knots at 16,300 ft alt, max power BASIC 491 knots at 35,000 ft alt, max power

CLIMB	CEILING	TAKE-OFF
2560 fpm sea level, take-off weight normal power	33,900 ft 100 fpm, take-off weight normal power	ground run 9100 ft no-assist / 7200 ft assisted
4775 fpm sea level, combat weight maximum power	40,800 ft 500 fpm, combat weight maximum power	over 50 ft height 10,650 ft no assist / 8650 ft assisted

LOAD	WEIGHTS	STALLING SPEED
Bombs: 10,000 lb Ammo: 1200 rds/50 cal Fuel: 13,900 gal protected 100 droppable 0 external 0	Empty..... 78,102 lb Combat... 122,650 lb Take-off 184,908* lb limited by space *Includes 1296 lb ATO charge	154 knots power-off, landing configuration, take-off weight
		TIME TO CLIMB

NOTES

1. Performance Basis:
   (a) Flight test data
   (b) Performance is shown for a B-47B aircraft not modified to the B-47B-I configuration. Performance of an aircraft that has been modified to Roman Numeral One configuration is similar to that presented for B-47E-II configuration.
   (c) Displacement rack must be used in carrying (19) 15KS1000 (Aerojet) ATO bottles or (30) 16NS1000 (Philips Petroleum) ATO bottles.
2. Placard Speed
3. Revision Basis:
   (a) To reflect changes in performance due to an increase in the in-flight gross weight; also change in security classification.

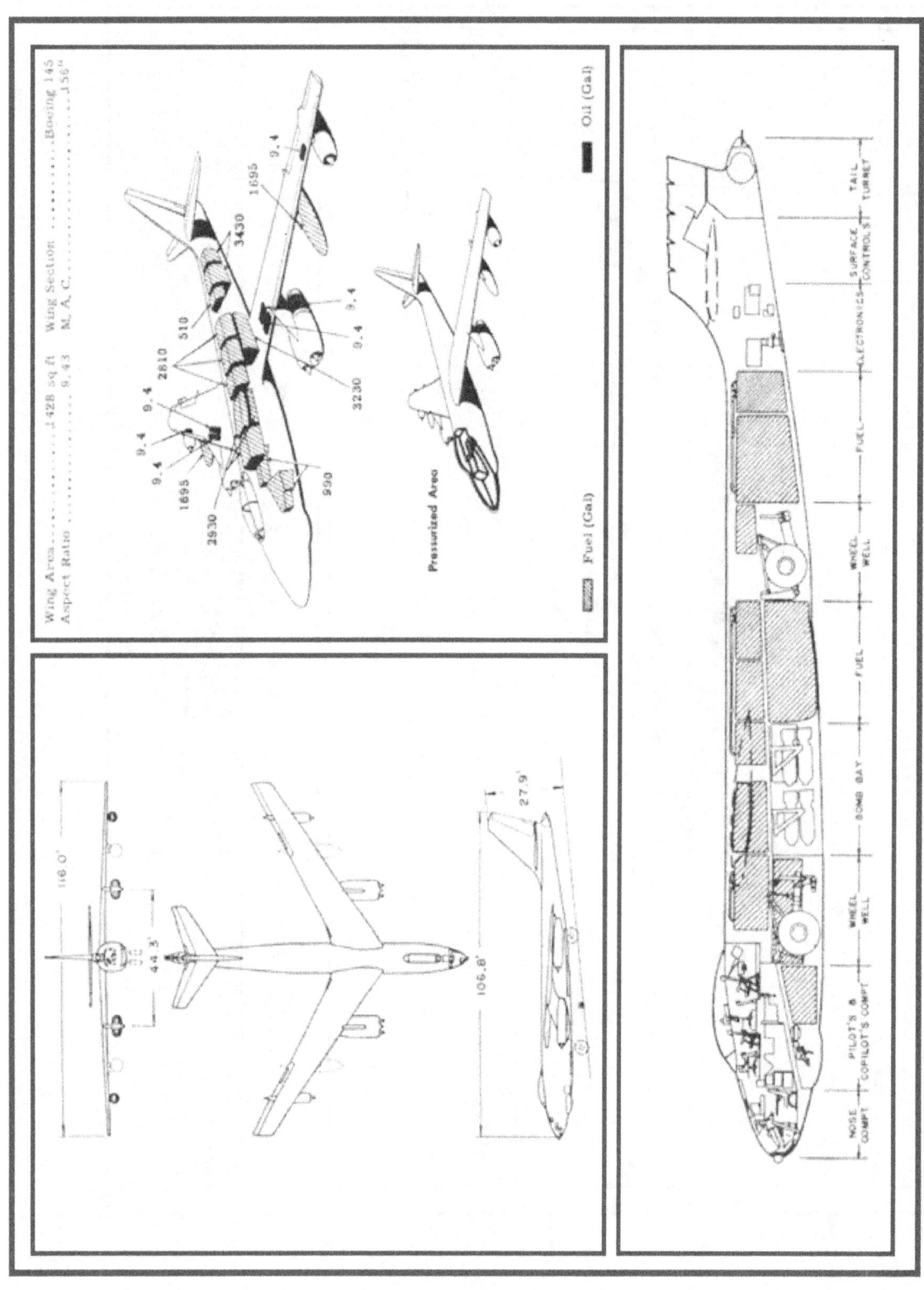

POWER PLANT

Nr & Model	(6) J47 GE-23
Mfr	General Electric
Engine Spec Nr	E-591b
Type	Axial
Length	145"
Diameter	39.5"
Weight (dry)	2512 lb
Tail Pipe	Fixed Area
Nr & Model	*(33)14AS1000 Aerojet
Mfr Weight (loaded)	209 lb ea
Nr & Mode	(19)15KS1000 Aerojet
Mfr Weight (loaded)	131 lb ea
See note (e) page 6	

ENGINE RATINGS

S L Static	LB	RPM	MIN
Max	5910	7950	5
Mil	5620	7800	30
Nor	5270	7630	Cont

ATO
Thrust(lb)		33,090
Duration (sec)		14
Thrust (lb) or		19,000
Duration (sec)		15

DIMENSIONS

Wing Span	116.0'
Incidence	2°45'
Dihedral	0°
Sweepback(L.E.)	36°27'
Length	106.8'
Height	27.9'
Tread(outrigger)	44.3'

Mission and Description

Navy Equivalent: None   Mfr's Model: 450-67-27

The principal mission of the B-47B is the destruction by bombs of land or naval materiel objectives.

The normal crew consists of pilot, co-pilot and observer. The observer's duties are navigation, bombing and operation of radar equipment. Features incorporated for improved crew comfort and efficiency include automatic heating, ventilation, pressurization, NESA glass de-icing for the pilot's windshield, rain repellant for windshield in lieu of windshield wipers and hydraulic boost on all control surfaces. A spoiler door is provided at the main entrance door to facilitate in-flight escape. The wing and empennage utilize thermal anti-icing. Single-point ground fueling and air-to-air refueling is provided.

A two-gun tail turret, controlled by radar sight at the co-pilots station, is installed. A B-4 fire control system is utilized. A rotatable seat allows the co-pilot to face aft while functioning as fire control operator.

Solid fuel rockets for assisted take-off, a braking parachute for deceleration on landing roll distance and an anti-skid device for braking are provided.

The bicycle type landing gear is electrically operated. There are provisions for a periscopic sextant and a bomb scoring device.

Development

Design initiated	Sep 48
First flight	Feb 51
First acceptance	Mar 51
Production completion	Jun 53

The 1st to 398th aircraft have -23 engines, the -25 engines will be installed from the 398th aircraft on. B-47B aircraft with -25 engines assume Roman Numeral One (B-47B-I) configuration and are similar to B-47E-II configuration.

BOMBS

See listings under Note "f", page 6.

GUNS

Nr	Size	Rds ea	Location
2	.50	600	Fuse. tail

CAMERAS

Vertical Station

Nr	Type	Lens
1	K-38	36"

or One of the following may be substituted:

1	K-38	24"	24"
1	K-17C	24"	12" 6"
1	K-22A	24"	12" 6"

Camera station is located in the lower aft portion of the fuselage aft of the bomb bay.

WEIGHTS

Loading	lb	L.F.
Empty	78,192(C)	
Basic	80,512(C)	
Design	125,000	3.0
Combat	#122,650	
Max T.O.	#185,000	2.0
Max In-Flt	#198,000	
	†221,000	2.0
Max Land	†180,000	

(C) Calculated
\# For Basic Mission
* Limited by strength of landing gear
† Without external tanks
†† With external tanks
Max T.O. weight includes ATO Charge

FUEL

Location	No. Tanks	Gal
Fwd. Main*	1	2940
Fwd. Main(Aux)	1	990
Center Main*	1	2810
Bomb Bay*	1	3230
Aft Main*	1	3490
Wing Droppable	2	3390
ATO Tank*	1	910
	Total	17,760
Grade		JP-4
Specification	MIL-F-5624A

OIL

Wing Panel	(ea) 35.4
Grade	1005
Specification	MIL-L-6081A

Self-Sealing except for 3 cells in forward main tank.

ELECTRONICS

VHF Command	AN/ARC-27
Omni-Direct. R.cvr	AN/ARN-14
Bombing-Nav. Radar	K-4A
Fire Control System	B-1-400
Radar Beacon	AN/APS-76
Interphone	USAF Combat
IFF	AN/APX-6
Glide Path R.cvr	AN/ARN-18
Radio Compass	AN/ARN-6A
ECM	AN/APT-5A
Marker Beacon	AN/ARN-12
Emergency Kryer	AN/ARA-26
Chaff Dispenser	AN/ALE-1
Warning Radar	AN/APS-54

Loading and Performance — Typical Mission

CONDITIONS			BASIC MISSION I	FERRY RANGE II
TAKE-OFF WEIGHT ⑤		(lb)	184,908	185,000
Fuel at 6.5 lb/gal (grade JP-4)		(lb)	90,350	98,882
Payload (Bombs)		(lb)	10,000	None
Wing loading		(lb/sq ft)	128	128
Stall speed (power off)		(kn)	154	154
Take-off ground run at SL	⑧①	(ft)	9100	9100
Take-off ground run with ATO	⑥①	(ft)	7200	7200
Take-off to clear 50 ft	⑧①	(ft)	10,650	10,650
Take-off to clear 50 ft with ATO	⑥①	(ft)	8650	8650
Rate of climb at SL		(fpm)	2560	2200
Rate of climb at SL (one engine out)	⑧②	(fpm)	2000	1640
Time: SL to 20,000 ft	③	(min)	9.8	10.6
Time: SL to 30,000 ft	③	(min)	19.6	23.0
Service ceiling (100 fpm)	⑧③	(ft)	33,900	31,950
Service ceiling (one engine out)	⑧②	(ft)	30,550	28,600
COMBAT RANGE	④	(n mi)		3861
COMBAT RADIUS	④	(n mi)	1704	
Average cruise speed		(kn)	433	432
Initial cruising altitude		(ft)	30,700	30,850
Target speed	③	(kn)	467	
Target altitude		(ft)	38,800	
Final cruising altitude		(ft)	43,900	43,600
Total mission time		(hr)	7.87	8.94
COMBAT WEIGHT		(lb)	122,650	92,290
Combat altitude	②	(ft)	38,800	43,800
Combat speed	②	(kn)	484	486
Combat climb	②	(fpm)	875	1025
Combat ceiling (500 fpm)	②	(ft)	40,800	46,650
Combat ceiling (100 fpm)	③	(ft)	42,100	47,950
Service ceiling (one engine out)	③	(ft)	39,300	45,200
Max rate of climb at SL		(fpm)	4775	6280
Max speed at optimum altitude	②⑨	(kn/ft)	528/16,300	528/16,300
Basic speed at 35,000 ft	②	(kn/ft)	491	496
LANDING WEIGHT		(lb)	91,850	92,290
Ground roll at SL		(ft)	4470	4500
Ground roll (auxiliary brake)	⑦	(ft)	2570	2600
Total from 50 ft		(ft)	5470	5500
Total from 50 ft (auxiliary brake)	⑦	(ft)	3570	3600

NOTES
① Take-off power
② Max power
③ Normal power
④ Detailed descriptions of RADIUS and RANGE missions given on page 6.
⑤ Includes 1296 lb ATO charge
⑥ With 18,000 lb ATO thrust
⑦ With 32 ft ribbon braking parachute
⑧ Values quoted are for take-off weight less ATO charge
⑨ Placard Speed

PERFORMANCE BASIS:
(a) Data source: Flight Test
(b) Performance is based on powers shown on page 6.

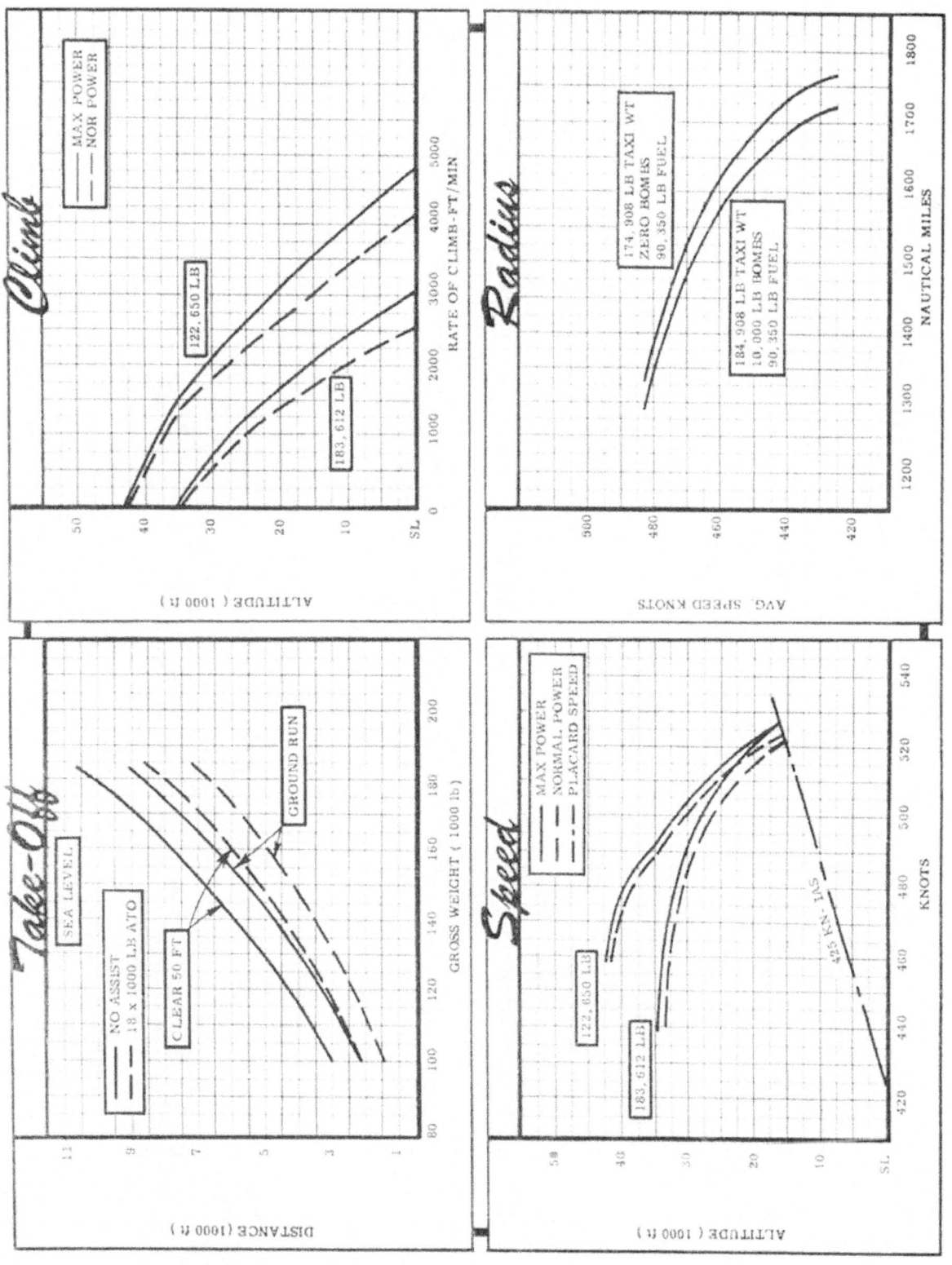

NOTES

FORMULA: RADIUS MISSION I

Take-off and climb on course to optimum cruise altitude at normal power. Cruise out at long range speeds increasing altitude with decreasing airplane weight. Climb so as to reach cruise ceiling fifteen (15) minutes from target. Run in to target at normal power, drop bombs, conduct two (2) minutes evasive action and eight (8) minutes escape from target at normal power. Cruise back to home base at long range speeds increasing altitude with decreasing airplane weight. Range free allowances include five (5) minutes normal power fuel consumption for starting engines and take-off, two (2) minutes normal power fuel consumption at combat altitude for evasive action and thirty (30) minutes of maximum endurance (four engines) fuel consumption at sea level plus 5% of initial fuel load for landing reserve.

FORMULA: RANGE MISSION II

Take-off and climb on course to optimum cruise altitude at normal power dropping external tanks when empty. Cruise out at long range speeds increasing altitude with decreasing airplane weight until all usable fuel is consumed.

Range free allowances include five (5) minutes normal power fuel consumption for starting engines and take-off and thirty (30) minutes of maximum endurance (four engines) fuel consumption at sea level plus 5% of initial fuel load for landing reserve.

GENERAL DATA:

(a) Engine ratings shown on page 3 are engine manufacturer's guaranteed ratings. Power values used for performance calculations are:

S.L. Static	(6) J47-GE-23		
	LB	RPM	MIN
T.O.	5790	7950	5
Max	5590	7800	30
Nor	5240	7630	Cont

(b) For detailed planning refer to Technical Order 1B-47E-1 and latest applicable technical orders.

(c) Maximum landing weight of 180,000 lb based on approximately 8 ft/sec ultimate rate of descent with 1G wing lift.

(d) Performance shown on page 4 is for a B-47B aircraft not modified to the B-47B-I configuration. Performance of an aircraft that has been modified to Roman Numeral One configuration is similar to that presented for B-47E-II configuration.

(e) (33) 14A61000 bottles can be carried with or without displacement rack, however the rack must be used in carrying (19) 15KS1000 bottles. (30) 16NS1000 M-15 ATO manufactured by Philips Petroleum, are also utilized with the displacement rack and gear.

(f) The following loadings reflect the capabilities of these configurations utilizing general purpose bombs:

SHORT BOMB BAY Hi-Density Kit		LONG BOMB BAY Hi-Density Kit		LONG BOMB BAY	
Nr	Class (lb)	Nr	Class (lb)	Nr	Class (lb)
WW II (Box Fin) Not Carried		WW II (Box Fin) Not Carried		WW II (Box Fin)	
				2	4000
				9	2000
				16	1000
				16	500
INTERIM (Conical Fin)		INTERIM (Conical Fin)		INTERIM (Conical Fin)	
3	2000	6	2000	6	2000
6	1000	18	1000	8	1000
13	500	28	500	8	500
NEW SERIES		NEW SERIES		NEW SERIES	
7	750	*1	25,000	*1	25,000
		1	12,000	8	750
		1	10,000		
		4	3000		
		21	750		

*A capability only. No Air Force Requirement.

PERFORMANCE REFERENCE:

Boeing Report WD-13365, dated 10 June 1955.

REVISION BASIS:

To reflect changes in performance due to an increase in the in-flight gross weight; also change in security classification.

Characteristics Summary

BOMBER . . . . B-47E II

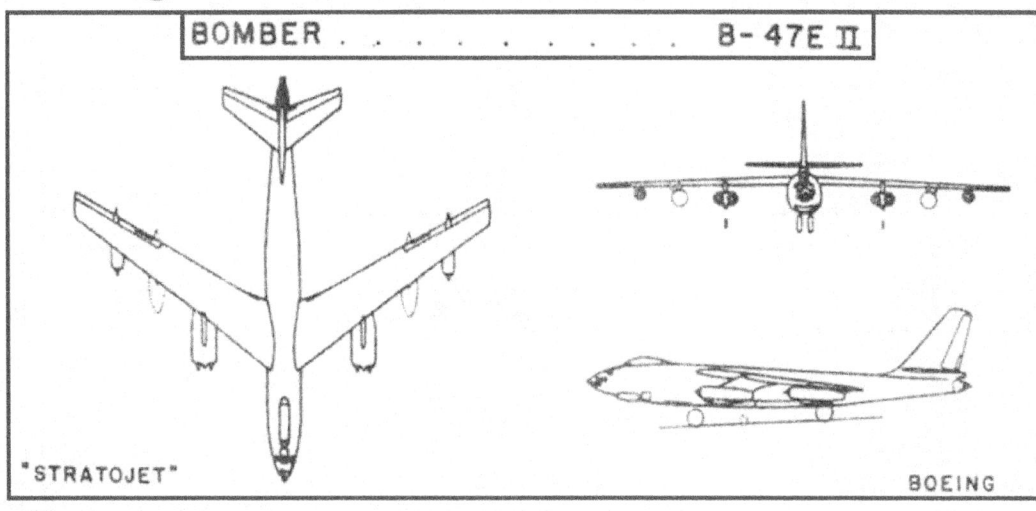

"STRATOJET" BOEING

Wing Area . . . . 1428 sq ft   Length . . . . 107.1 ft

Span . . . . 116.0 ft   Height . . . . 28.0 ft

AVAILABILITY

Number available

ACTIVE	RESERVE	TOTAL

PROCUREMENT

Number to be delivered in fiscal years

STATUS

1. Performance and Characteristics shown for the B-47E-II is representative of the Basic B-47E Airplane.
2. Engine change and landing gear modifications that have been made to B-47B-I aircraft closes the gap in the aircraft capability differential between the B-47B-I and the B-47E-II.

Navy Equivalent: None   Mfr's Model: 450-157-35

POWER PLANT

(6) J47-GE-25, -25A
General Electric
ENGINE RATINGS
S.L.S.   LB - RPM -   MIN
Max: *7200 - 7950 -   5
       5970 - 7950 -   5
Mil: 5670 - 7800 - 30
Nor: 5320 - 7630 - Cont
*wet
with water flow of 650 lb/min
ATO
Nr & Model *(M-15)(30)16NS1000
Thrust (lb) 30,000
Duration (sec) 16
       or
Nr & Model . . . . . . (19)15KS1000
Thrust (lb) 19,000
Duration (sec) 15
*see note (f) Notes block

FEATURES

Crew 3
Thermal anti-icing
MA-7A bombing navigation system
A-5 or MD-4 fire control system
Anti-skid brakes
Approach chute
Braking chute
Ejection seats
(1) K-38 or alternate vertical camera
Single-point and air refueling
External droppable ATO rack

Max fuel cap: *18,000 gal
*Includes wing drop tanks

ARMAMENT

Turrets: 1
Guns: . . . . 2 x 20mm (M24A1)
Ammunition: . . . . 700 rds(tot)
BOMBS: (Max)
        Class (lb)   Load
SHORT BOMB BAY
Interim: *3x2000   14x500
                       (M-123)
         †3x2000   3x2000

New   *7x 750   7x 750
Series: †4x 750   4x 750

*Hi-Density Kit †Lo-Density

119

Characteristics Summary Basic Mission . . . B-47 E II

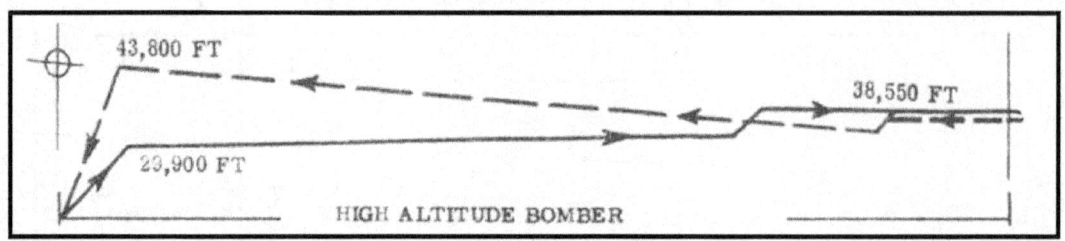

HIGH ALTITUDE BOMBER

PERFORMANCE

COMBAT RADIUS	FERRY RANGE	SPEED
1749 naut. mi with 10,845 lb payload at 433 knots avg. in 8.1 hours.	4035 naut. mi with 16,318 gal fuel at 433 knots avg. in 9.4 hours at 200,000 lb T.O. wt.	COMBAT 484 knots at 38,550 ft alt, max power MAX (e) 527 knots at 16,300 ft alt, max power BASIC 491 knots at 35,000 ft alt, max power

CLIMB	CEILING	TAKE-OFF
2430 fpm sea level, take-off weight normal power	33,100 ft 100 fpm, take-off weight normal power	ground run 7900 ft (c) no assist / 6200 ft (d) assisted
4660 fpm sea level, combat weight maximum power	40,500 ft 500 fpm, combat weight maximum power	over 50 ft height 9400 ft (c) no assist / 7600 ft (d) assisted

LOAD	WEIGHTS	STALLING SPEED
Bombs: 10,000 lb Chaff: 845 lb Ammunition: 700 rds/20mm Fuel: 14,610 gal protected 69.5 droppable 0 external 0	Empty..... 80,756 lb Combat... 124,875 lb Take-off 198,180 lb (b) limited by internal fuel capacity.	152.3 knots power-off, landing configuration, take-off weight
		TIME TO CLIMB

NOTES

1. Performance Basis:
   (a) Flight test data
   (b) Values quoted are for take-off weight less 3207 lb ATO and 5300 lb water-alcohol.
   (c) With medium flow water injection.
   (d) With medium flow water injection and (19) 15 KS1000 ATO bottles.
   (e) Placard speed
   (f) Displacement rack must be used in carrying (19) 15KS1000 (Aerojet) ATO bottles or (30) 16NS1000 (Phillips Petroleum) ATO bottles.

2. Revision Basis: Data coordinated by OCAMA.

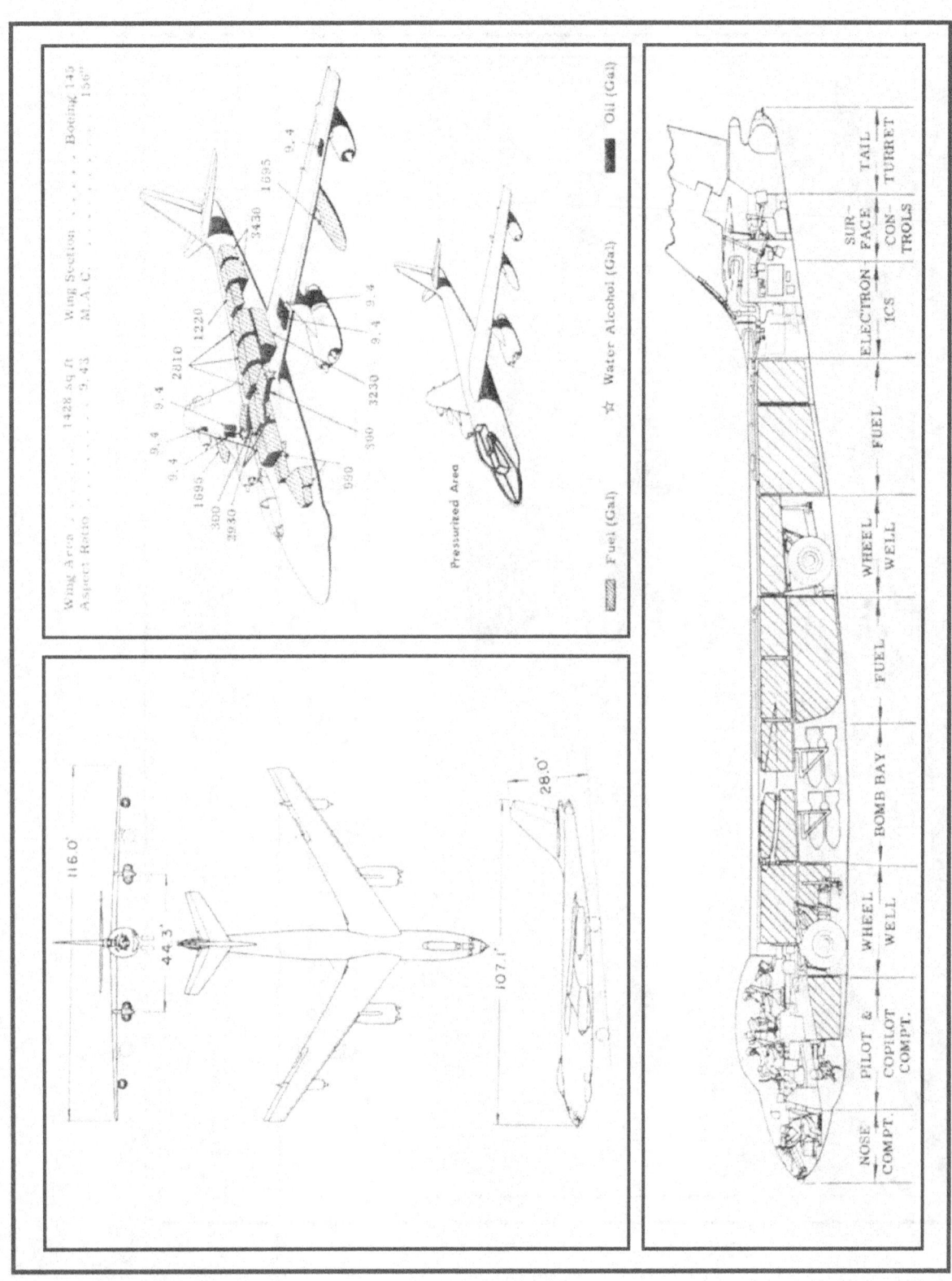

POWER PLANT

Nr & Model	(6)J47-GE-25, 25A
Mfr	General Electric
Engine Spec Nr	E-597A
Type	Axial Flow
Length	144"
Diameter	39.1"
Weight (dry)	2707 lb
Tail Pipe	Fixed Area
Augmentation	Water/Alcohol

ATO
Nr & Model (M'fr)	14HKS39000 Phillips Petroleum
Mfr	
Weight (loaded)	125.4 lb ea

Nr & Model	(15)14KS1000 Aerojet
Mfr	
Weight (loaded)	142 lb ea

*See note (d) page 6

ENGINE RATINGS

	S.L. Static	LB	RPM	MIN
Max:		7200	5	
Mil:		5970	7900	5
		5670	7800	30
Nor:		5420	7630	Cont

*wet
Water flow of 650 G/min

ATO
Thrust (lb)	39,000
Duration (sec)	15

Thrust (lb)	19,000
Duration (sec)	15

DIMENSIONS

Wing	116.9'
Span	
Incidence	2°45'
Dihedral	0°
Sweepback (LE)	36°37'
Length	107.1'
Height	28.0'
Tread (outrigger)	44.1'

WEIGHTS

	Lb
Landing	80,756(E)
Empty	
Basic	82,728(E)
Design	125,000
Combat	124,971
Max T.O.	200,000
Max Flight	221,000
Max Land	189,000

(E) Estimated
1 For Basic Mission
2 Limited by Strength
3 With external tanks

FUEL

Location	Nr. Tanks	Gal
Fwd. Main	1	2930
Fwd. Aux	1	990
Center Main	1	2810
Boml Bay		8250
Aft Main	1	1400
Wing, Drop		1390
Aft Tank	1	1220
	Total	18,090

Self-Sealing except for Tanks in forward bomb bay.

Grade: JP-4

OIL

Specification	MIL-O-6081A
Max Capacity	(gal) 15(?)
Grade	1010
Specification	MIL-L-6081A

WATER ALCOHOL
Wt: 1564 | 650

Mission and Description

Navy Equivalent: None   Mfr's Model: 450-157-51

The principal missions of the B-47E-II is that of strategic bombing at long range and high altitudes.

The aircraft has provisions for pilot, copilot, and observer. The aircraft has provisions for vacuum, heating, and operating of radar equipment. Full pressurization is incorporated for improved crew comfort and efficiency. An improved heating, ventilation, pressurization, NESA glass defrosting for the pilot's windshield, decreasing of windshield nose surface and adjust-ment of switches by rearranged cockpit of increased cockpit air conditioning. Crew comfort has been increased. Wings and empennage are also heated. Hydraulic boost on all control surfaces. Crew compartments are pressurized for daylight escape. There is an ejection seat for each crew member, new and used ejection seat are included.

The water alcohol injection system utilizes a total tank capacity of 600 gallons, which is located into an individual tooth of the tanks. Three such tanks are located in the inboard portion of the wing area on both sides. Solid propellant rockets are used for assisted take-off.

A new gas turbine starter is including. A radar dome is attached to the aircraft's ship fuselage to house the A-5 Fire Control System operation. Other features are; approach chute for increasing landing roll distance and an under-carriage braking device.

Development

Performance and Characteristics shown for the B-47E-II are representa-tive of the basic B-47E airplane.

Engine change and landing gear modifications that have been made to B-47B-II aircraft closes the gap in the aircraft capability differential be-tween the B-47B-I and the B-47E-II.

BOMBS

See Listings on Page 6, note c

GUNS

Nr	Type	Size	Rds/Gn	Loc
2	M24-1	20mm	350	Fuselage

CAMERAS

	Vertical Station	Lens
Nr	K-38	12"
	K-17	6"

One of the following may be substituted
	K-17	24"
	K-17C	24", 12", 6"
	K-22A	24", 12", 6"

Cameras shown is located in the lower aft portion of the fuselage aft of the bomb bay.

ELECTRONICS

VHF Command	AN/ARC-27
Omni-Direc. Recvr	AN/ARN-14
Bombing-Nav. Radar	MA-7A
Fire Control System	A-5 or MD-4
Radiation Equip	AN/APN-69
Interphone	AN/AIC-10
HF	AN/APX-6
Glide Path Recvr	AN/ARN-18
Radio Compass	AN/ARN-6
ECM	*AN/ALT-6
Marker Beacon	AN/ARN-12
Emergency Keyer	AN/ARA-26
Chaff Dispenser	AN/ALE-1
HF Liaison	AN/ARC-21
Warning Radar	AN/APS-54
D/F Group	AN/ARA-25
Gun Laying Radar	AN/APG-32

*See note (f) page 6

Loading and Performance — Typical Mission

CONDITIONS			BASIC MISSION	CRUISE CEILING	FERRY RANGE
TAKE-OFF WEIGHT ⑤		(lb)	96,120	95,180	200,000
Fuel at 6.5 lb/gal (grade JP-4)		(lb)	94,965	94,965	106,070
Payload (Bombs)		(lb)	10,000	10,000	
Payload (Chaff)		(lb)	845	345	
Wing loading		(lb/sq ft)	132.8	132.3	134.0
Stall speed (power off)		(kn)	152.3	152.3	152.9
Take-off ground run at SL		(ft)	7900	7900	8100
Take-off ground run with ATO	⑥⑩	(ft)	6200	6200	6400
Take-off to clear 50 ft		(ft)	9400	9400	9600
Take-off to clear 50 ft with ATO	⑥⑩	(ft)	7000	7000	7800
Rate of climb at SL		(fpm)	2130	2130	2160
Rate of climb at SL (one engine out) ⑥⑦		(fpm)	2170	2170	1750
Time: SL to 20,000 ft		(min)	10.5	10.5	11.6
Time: SL to 30,000 ft		(min)	20.7	20.7	25.8
Service ceiling (100 fpm)		(ft)	33,100	33,100	31,400
Service ceiling (one engine out) ⑥ ⑦		(ft)	30,400	30,400	28,800
COMBAT RANGE ④		(n mi)	—	—	4035
COMBAT RADIUS ④		(n mi)	1749	1507	
Average cruise speed		(kn)	433	467	433
Initial cruising altitude		(ft)	23,900	33,350	30,100
Target speed		(kn)	466	467	
Target altitude		(ft)	38,550	38,500	
Final cruising altitude		(ft)	43,800	47,000	43,700
Total mission time		(hr)	8.1	6.8	9.4
COMBAT WEIGHT		(lb)	124,675	125,295	93,156
Combat altitude		(ft)	38,550	38,500	43,700
Combat speed		(kn)	484	484	487
Combat climb		(fpm)	870	870	1050
Combat ceiling (500 fpm)		(ft)	40,500	40,450	46,500
Service ceiling (100 fpm)		(ft)	41,800	41,750	47,900
Service ceiling (one engine out) ⑥⑦		(ft)	40,000	39,950	46,100
Max rate of climb at SL		(fpm)	4660	4650	6150
Basic speed at 35,000 ft		(kn/ft)	527/16,300	527/16,300	528/16,400
		(kn)	491	491	496
LANDING WEIGHT		(lb)	92,600	92,600	93,156
Ground roll at SL		(ft)	4500	4500	4500
Ground roll (auxiliary brake) ⑪		(ft)	2600	2600	2600
Total from 50 ft		(ft)	5500	5500	5500
Total from 50 ft (auxiliary brake) ⑪		(ft)	3600	3600	3600

NOTES

① Take-off power
② Maximum power
③ Normal power
④ Detailed descriptions of RADIUS and RANGE missions given on page 6.
⑤ Includes 3297 lb ATO and 5309 lb water-alcohol.
⑥ 19 bottles ATO, medium flow water injection.
⑦ No ATO, medium flow water injection
⑧ Values quoted are for take-off weight less ATO and water-alcohol.
⑨ Placard speed
⑩ Brake chute deployed at touch-down

PERFORMANCE BASIS:
(a) Data source: Flight Test
(b) Performance is based on powers shown on page 6.

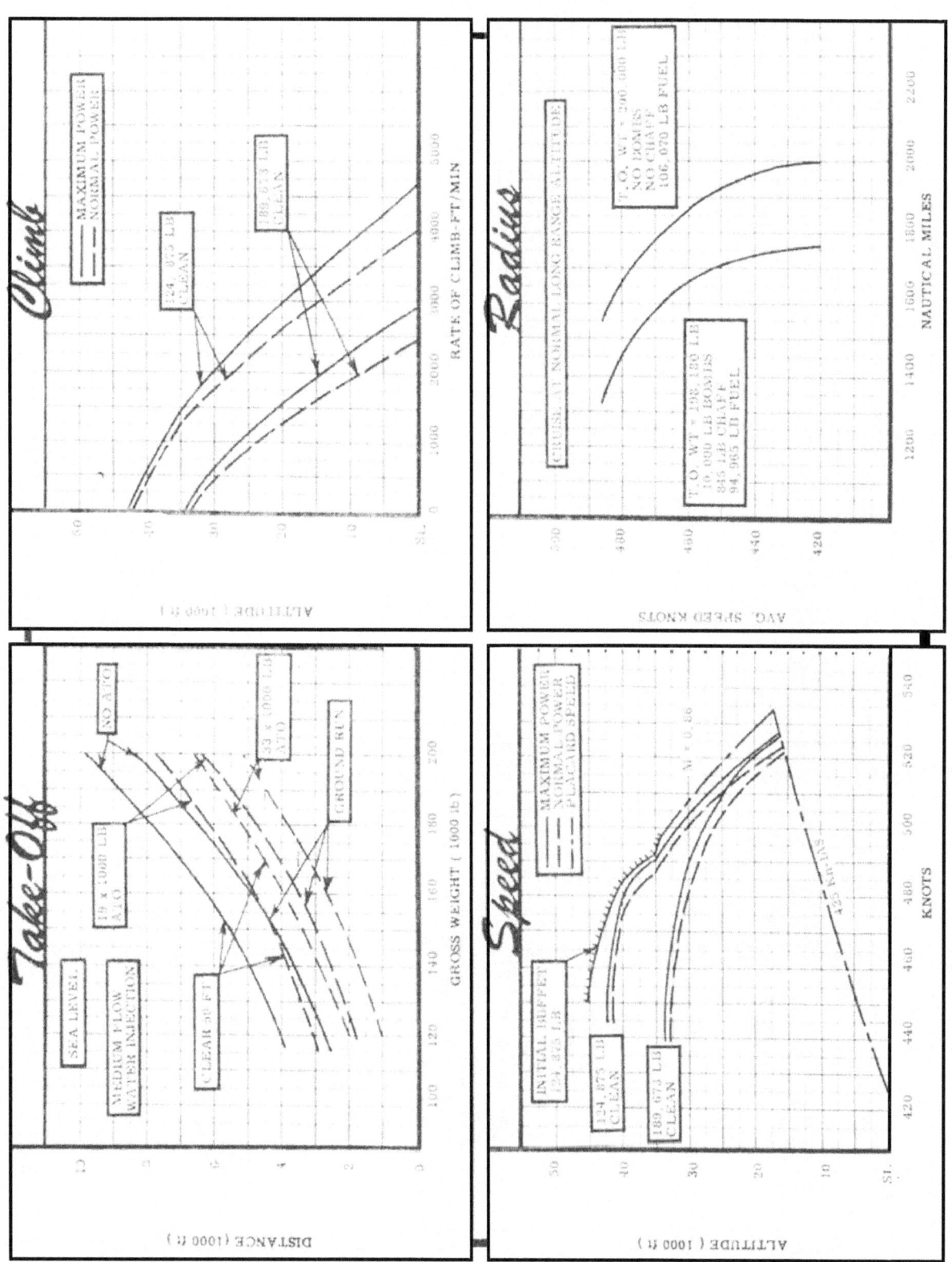

N O T E S

FORMULA: RADIUS MISSION I

Take-off and climb on course to optimum cruise altitude at normal power. Cruise out at long range speeds and altitudes. No external tanks are used for this mission. Climb to cruise ceiling and conduct a 15 minute level-flight bomb run at normal power. Drop bomb load and chaff and conduct 2 minutes evasive action and 8 minutes escape at normal power. Return to base at long range speeds and altitudes. Range-free allowances are fuel for 5 minutes at normal power at sea level for take-off allowances, 2 minutes at normal power at combat altitude for evasive action, and 30 minutes at maximum endurance airspeeds at sea level plus 5% of the initial fuel load for landing reserve.

FORMULA RADIUS MISSION II

Take-off and climbon course to cruise ceiling at military power. Cruise out at the cruise ceiling at normal power. No external tanks are used for this mission. Conduct a 15 minute level-flight bomb run, drop bomb load and chaff, and conduct 2 minutes evasive action at normal power. Climb back to cruise ceiling at military power and cruise back to base at the cruise ceiling at normal power. Range-free allowances are as stated for Radius Mission I.

FORMULA RADIUS MISSION III

Take-off and climb on course to optimum cruise altitude at normal power. Cruise out at long range speeds and altitudes, dropping external tanks when empty. Land at remote base with only reserve fuel remaining. Range-free allowances are fuel for 5 minutes at normal power at sea level for take-off allowance and fuel for 30 minutes at maximum endurance airspeeds at sea level plus 5% of the initial fuel load for landing reserve.

GENERAL DATA:

(a) Thrust values shown on page 3 are engine manufacturer's guaranteed ratings. Thrust values used in performance calculations are as follows:

S.L. STATIC	(6) J-47-GE-25 & -25A		
	LB	RPM	MIN
T.O.	7200*	7950	5
Max	5640	7800	30
Nor	5270	7630	Cont

* Medium flow water injection

(b) For detail planning refer to Technical Order 1B-47E-1 and latest applicable technical orders.

(c) The following loadings reflect the capabilities of the B-47E-II airplane utilizing general purpose bombs:

SHORT BOMB BAY Hi-Density Kit		SHORT BOMB BAY Lo-Density Kit	
No. ... Class (lb) WW II (Box Fin)		No. ... Class (lb) WW II (Box Fin) Not Carried	
INTERIM (Conical Fin)		INTERIM (Conical Fin)	
3	2000	3	2000
6	1000	4	1000
13	500 (T-127)	4	500 (T-127)
14	500 (M-123)	8	500 (M-123)
NEW SERIES		NEW SERIES	
6	750 Chem.	4	750 Chem.
	Cluster		Cluster
7	750	4	750

1. The Short Bomb Bay Hi-Density Kits are adaptable on all aircraft.
2. The Short Bomb Bay Lo-Density Kit can be utilized only in airplanes 617 thru 730; airplanes 1 thru 616 have provisions for this kit but must be modified to accept it.

(d) The displacement rack & gear must be utilized in carrying (19) 15KS1000 bottles or the (30) 16NS1000 M-15 ATO manufactured by Phillips Petroleum.

(e) When carrying the Basic Mission payload (10, 845 lb), full internal fuel load, and 5300 lb water-alcohol the 200,000 lb maximum taxi gross weight will be reached when the ATO weight is 5027 lb. For greater ATO loads it will be necessary to off-load fuel. This will decrease the radius performance as shown below:

[Graph: COMBAT RADIUS N.MI. vs ATO WEIGHT (including rack), LB — curves for 10,000 LB BOMB / 845 LB CHAFF / 5300 LB WATER ALCOHOL / NO EXTERNAL TANKS and 15KS1000 / 1AS1000 / 1AS1000]

(f) Various combinations of
TACAN AN/ARN-21
Rendezvous Equip. AN/ARN-76
ECM .... ALT-7, ALT-8 & QRC-49
HF Liaison ... AN/ARC-21 or AN/ARC-65
IFF .... APX-6A and APX-76

PERFORMANCE REFERENCE:

Boeing Report WD-13365, dated 10 June 1955 and WD-13360, dated 16 January 1956.

REVISION BASIS:

To reflect current characteristics and performance data.

SUPPLEMENTAL

The curves below present the radar performance of the B-45B-II airplane without air refueling. The graph on the left presents the fuel transfer requirements while the graph on the right shows the total mission radius as a function of the distance out to end of transfer.

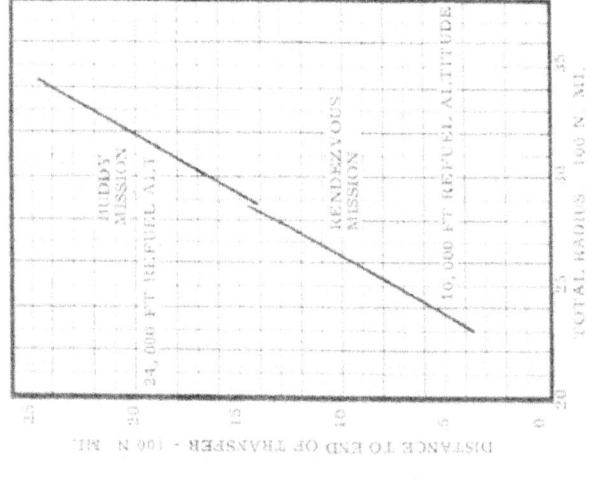

FORMULA — RENDEZVOUS MISSION

Take-off and climb on course to optimum cruise altitude at normal power. Cruise out at long range speeds and altitudes. Descend to 10,000 ft (no credit for distance or fuel consumed in descent). Rendezvous at maximum endurance airspeed for 30 minutes. Transfer fuel on course at 600 gpm at a true airspeed of 289 knots. After transfer climb on course to optimum cruise altitude at normal power. Remainder of mission is conducted to Basic Mission rules. External tanks are dropped when empty. Range-free allowances are as for Basic Mission except that landing allowance of 5% and 30 minutes max endurance is based on fuel load immediately after refuel and 5% of initial fuel load plus 30 minutes max endurance fuel flow at refuel altitudes for rendezvous.

FORMULA — BUDDY MISSION

Take-off and climb on course to optimum cruise altitude at normal power. Rendezvous for 10 minutes at maximum endurance airspeed. Cruise out with the tanker at long range speeds and altitudes. Descend to 24,000 feet altitude, transfer fuel on course at 900 gpm at a true airspeed of 340 knots. After transfer, climb on course to optimum cruise altitude. Remainder of mission is conducted to Basic Mission rules. External tanks are dropped when empty. Range-free allowances are as for the Basic Mission except that a 10 minute rendezvous is included and landing reserve is fuel for 30 minutes at maximum endurance airspeed at sea level plus 5% of the fuel load at the end of air refueling.

NOTE:

(a) Take-off weight is 200,000 lb.
(b) ATO load is 3207 lb (19) 15KS1050 bottles
(c) Water-alcohol load is 5300 lb.
(d) Refueled to capacity (213,268 lb) with external tanks.
(e) Bomb load is 10,000 lb, chaff load is 845 lb.

Characteristics Summary

BOMBER .... B-47E IV

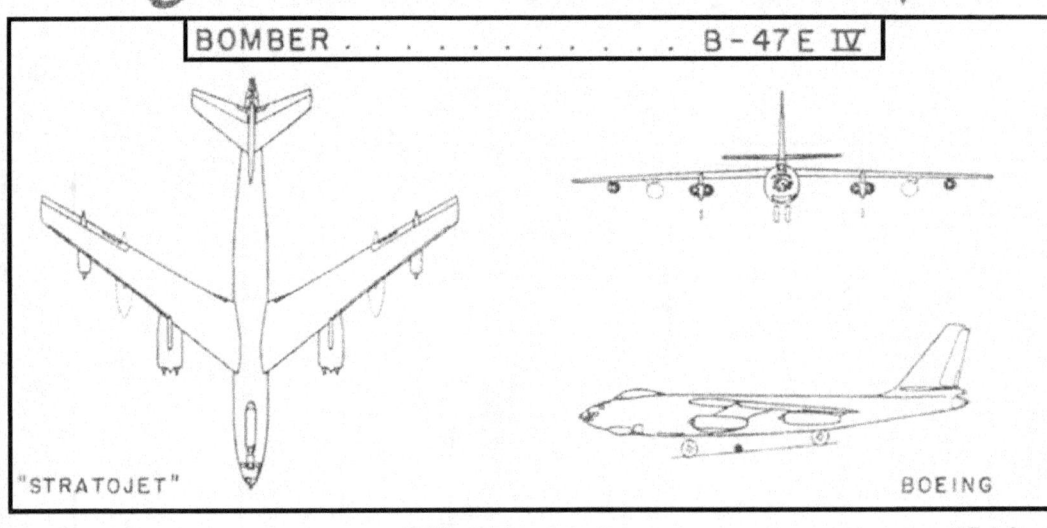

"STRATOJET"   BOEING

Wing Area .... 1428 sq ft   Length .... 107.1 ft
Span .... 116.0 ft   Height .... 28.0 ft

AVAILABILITY

Number available

ACTIVE	RESERVE	TOTAL

PROCUREMENT

Number to be delivered in fiscal years

STATUS

1. The B-47E-IV airplane differs from the Basic B-47E-II by the strengthening of the landing gear to permit heavier take-off weights.
2. Data is shown for the test articles (862nd B-47E). The modification is effective on the 862nd and subsequent aircraft.
3. Delivery date for first B-47E-IV: Feb 55

Navy Equivalent: None   Mfr's Model: 450-157-35

POWER PLANT

(6) J47-GE-25,-25A
General Electric
ENGINE RATINGS

S.L.S.   LB - RPM - MIN
Max(wet): *7200 - 7950 - 5
           5970 - 7950 - 5
Mil: 5670 - 7800 - 30
Nor: 5320 - 7630 - Cont
*With water flow of 650 lb/min

ATO
Nr & Model: .*†(33)14AS1000
Thrust (lb) 33,000
Duration (sec) 14
         or
Nr & Model: ..†(19)15KS1000
Thrust (lb) 19,000
Duration (sec) 15
   †Manufactured by Aerojet
  *See note (e), Notes block

FEATURES

Crew 3
Thermal anti-icing
MA-7A bombing-navigation system
A-5 fire control system
Anti-skid brakes
Approach chute
Braking chute
Ejection seats
Internal fuel tank purging
(1) K-38 or alternate vertical camera
Single-point and air refueling
External droppable ATO rack

Max fuel cap: *18,000 gal
  *Includes wing drop tanks and large ATO tank

ARMAMENT

Turrets: 1
Guns:.. 2 x 20mm (M24A1)
Ammunition: ..700 rds(tot)

BOMBS: (Max)
              Class (lb)   Load
SHORT BOMB BAY
Interim: *3x2000   14x 500
                   (M-123)
         † 3x2000   3x2000

New   *7x 750   7x 750
Series: † 4x 750   4x 750
LONG BOMB BAY
Interim: *6x 2000/18 x 1000
New
Series: *1x12,000/21 x 750
Special
Stores: 1x10,000/ 1x10,000
*Hi-Density Kit/†Lo-Density

128

Characteristics Summary Basic Mission — B-47E IV

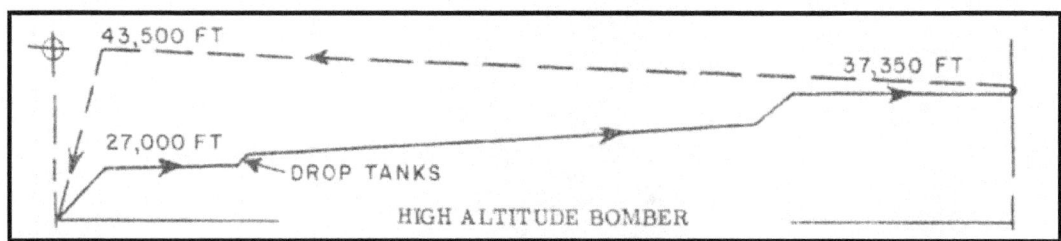

HIGH ALTITUDE BOMBER

PERFORMANCE

COMBAT RADIUS	FERRY RANGE	SPEED
2050 naut. mi with 10,845 lb payload at 435 knots avg. in 9.42 hours.	4340 naut. mi with 18,000 gal fuel at 434 knots avg. in 10.02 hours at 215,958 lb T.O. wt.	COMBAT 483[d] knots at 37,350 ft alt, **max** power MAX 528[d] knots at 16,300 ft alt, **max** power BASIC 490[d] knots at 35,000 ft alt, **max** power

CLIMB	CEILING	TAKE-OFF
1850 fpm sea level, take-off weight normal power	29,500 ft 100 fpm, take-off weight normal power	ground run 11,300 ft no assist | 7850 ft assisted [c]
850 fpm sea level, combat weight maximum power	39,300 ft 500 fpm, combat weight maximum power	over 50 ft height 12,000 ft no assist | 8800 ft assisted [c]

LOAD	WEIGHTS	STALLING SPEED

Bombs: 10,000 lb
Chaff: 845 lb
Ammunition: 700 rds/20mm
Fuel: 18,000 gal
  protected 56.5 %
  droppable 18.8 %
  external 18.8 %
	Empty..... 79,074 lb
	Combat... 133,030 lb (b)
	Take-off 225,958 lb
	limited by space
		166.1 knots power-off, landing configuration, take-off weight

		TIME TO CLIMB

NOTES

1. Performance Basis:
   - (a) Flight test data.
   - (b) Value quoted for take-off weight less 7109 lb ATO and 5300 lb water-alcohol.
   - (c) With 33 x 1000 lb thrust ATO bottles.
   - (d) Placard limit
   - (e) (33) 14AS1000 ATO bottles can be utilized with or without the displacement rack, however the displacement rack must be utilized in carrying max compliment of (19) 15KS1000. Rack is also utilized in carrying (30) 16NS1000 M-15 ATO. (Manufactured by Philips Petroleum).

2. Revision Basis: Data co-ordinated by OCAMA 25 Aug 59

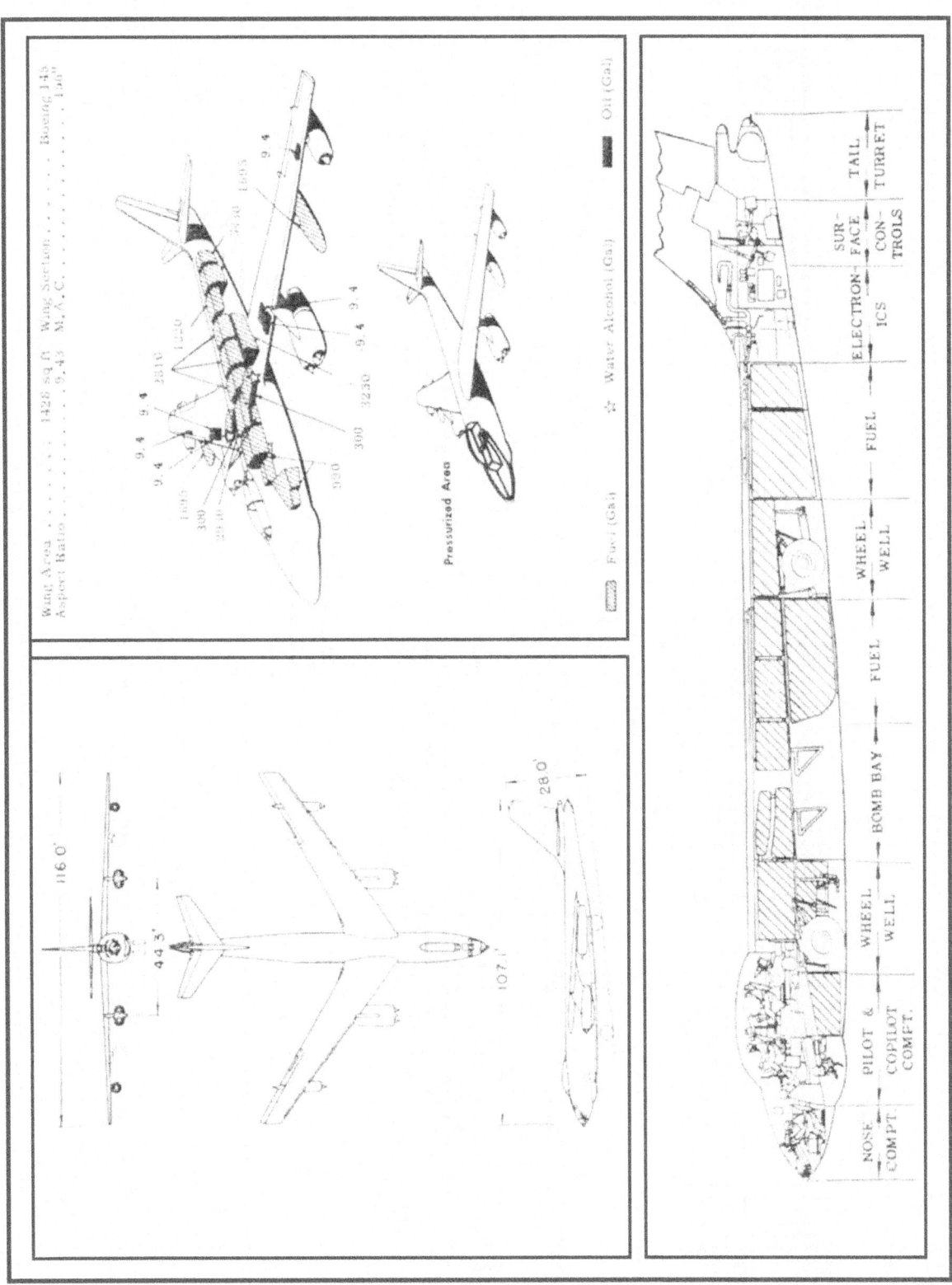

POWER PLANT

Nr & Model . . . . . . (6)J47-GE-25, 25A
Mfr . . . . General Electric
Engine Spec Nr E-397A
Type . . . . Axial Flow
Length . . . . 144"
Diameter . . . . 39.5"
Weight (dry) . . . . 2707 lb
Fuel Pipe . . . . Fixed Area
Augmentation ATO Water/Alcohol

Nr & Model (X) (4) . . (1)LN5U1000
Mfr . . . . Phillips Petroleum
Weight (loaded) . . . . . 276.4 lb ea
ATO

Nr & Model . . . . . . (1)10K51000
Mfr . . . . Aerojet
Weight (loaded) . . . . . 142 lb ea
*See note d on page 6

ENGINE RATINGS

S.L. Static	LB	RPM	MIN
Max	7200	7950	5
	3250	7950	5
Mil.	5670	7950	30
Nor	5320	7630	Cont
*Wet			

Water Flow of 650 lb/min
ATO
Thrust (lb) 20,000
Duration (sec) 16
or
Thrust (lb) 12,000
Duration (sec) 15

DIMENSIONS

Wing
Span . . . . 116.0'
Incidence . . . . 2°45'
Dihedral . . . . 0°
Sweepback (LE) . . . . . . 36°37'
Length . . . . 107.1'
Height . . . . 28.0'
Tread (outrigger) . . . . . . 44.3'

Mission and Description

Nav. Equipment: None   Mfr's Model: 450-157-35

The principal mission of the B-47E-IV is the destruction by bombs of land or naval material objectives.

The normal crew consists of pilot, co-pilot and observer. The observer's duties are navigation, bombing and operating of radar equipment. Features incorporated for improved crew comfort and efficiency are automatic heating, ventilation, pressurization, NESA glass de-icing for the pilot's windshield, de-frosting of windshield (crew windows and other transparent sections by recirculated warm air), thermal anti-icing for wings and empennage, and hydraulic boost on all control surfaces. Crew ejection seats are provided for in-flight escape. The pilot and co-pilot are ejected upward and the observer downward.

The water-alcohol injection system utilizes a total tank capacity of 600 gallons which is divided into six individual bladder-type tanks. Three each located on the inboard sections of the right and left wings. Solid propellant rockets are installed externally for assist take-off with a droppable rack.

A two-gun turret incorporating a radar computer at the co-pilot's station is installed. A versatile sea-level gunsight is used for the co-pilot functioning as the A-5 Fire Control System operator.

Other features are single-point and gas refueling, an approach chute to increase drag, drag chute for decreasing landing roll distance and an anti-skid braking device.

Development

The B-47E-IV airplane differs from the Basic B-47E-II by the strengthening of the landing gear to permit heavier take-off weights. Data is shown for the test article (80-2nd B-47E). The modification is effective on the 862nd and subsequent aircraft.

Delivery date of first B-47E-IV . . . . Feb 55

BOMBS

Nr	Class (lb)
1	Special Weapon

See listings on Page 6, note c.

GUNS

Nr	Type	Size	Rds ea	Loc
2	M24A1	20mm	350	Fus tail

CAMERAS

Nr	Type	Lens
1	Vertical Station	
	K-38	35"

One of the following may be substituted:
	K-37	12"
	K-38	24"
	K17C	24", 12", 6"
	K-22A	24", 12", 6"

Camera station is located in the lower aft portion of the fuselage aft of the bomb bay.

WEIGHTS

	lb	c.g.
Loading		
Empty	79,074 (P)	
Basic	81,044 (P)	
Design	125,000	3.0
Combat	131,050	
Max T.O.	7230,000	2.3
Max in-Flight	7221,000	
Max Land	7180,000	7.0

(P) Restricted:
For Basic Mission
1 Limited by strength
7 With external fuels

FUEL

Location	No. Tanks	Gal
Fwd Main	1	2530
Fwd Aux	1	990
Center Main	1	2810
Bomb Bay	1	1230
Aft Main	1	3430
Wing Drop	2	3390
AFT Tank		1320
	Total	18,000

Grade JP-4
Specification OIL MIL-F-5624A
Wing Panel . . . . 6 . . . (ea) 56.4
Grade 1005
Specification MIL-L-6081A
WATER ALCOHOL
Wg int 6 600
*Self sealing except for 2 cells in forward main tank

ELECTRONICS

UHF Command AN/ARC-27
Omni-Dir. Rcvr AN/ARN-14
Bombing-Nav. Radar MA-7A
Fire Control System . . . A-5 or Mb-4
Rendezvous Equip. . . AN/APN-69
AN/APX-7od or AN/APN-69
Interphone AN/AIC-10
IFF . . AN/APA-28 or AN/APX-6A
Glide Path Rec'vr AN/ARN-18
Radio Compass AN/ARN-6
ECM . . . . (2) AN/ALT-6
Marker Beacon AN/ARN-12
Emergency Keyer AN/ARA-26
Chaff Dispenser AN/ALE-1
continued on pg 6, note (e)

Loading and Performance — Typical Mission

CONDITIONS		BASIC MISSION	DESIGN BOMB LOAD	CRUISE CEILING	FERRY RANGE
TAKE-OFF WEIGHT	(lb)	225,958	230,000	225,958	215,113
Fuel at ⑥ lb/gal (Grade JP-4)	(lb)	117,408	115,030	117,000	117,000
Payload (bombs)	(lb)	10,000	18,000	10,000	None
Payload (Used)	(lb)				None
Wing loading	(lb/sq ft)	84.9	84.5	84.9	142.5
Stall speed (power off)	(kn)	149.6	152.4	145.5	162.1
Take-off ground run at SL	(ft)	10,400	10,900	10,400	9200
Take-off ground run with ATO	(ft)	7350	7700	7350	6350
Take-off to clear 50 ft	(ft)	12,000	12,950	12,000	10,750
Take-off to clear 50 ft with ATO	(ft)	8800	9200	8800	7750
Rate of climb at SL	(fpm)	1950	1900	1850	1950
Rate of climb at SL (one engine out)	(fpm)	1670	1610	1670	1720
Time SL to 20,000 ft	(min)	11.2	11.4	11.2	10.3
Time SL to Cruise Alt	(min)	16.4	19.6	22.4	18.8
Service ceiling (100 fpm)	(ft)	29,500	29,000	29,500	30,400
Service ceiling (one engine out)	(ft)	25,000	24,500	25,000	26,000
COMBAT RADIUS	(n. mi.)				4340
COMBAT RADIUS	(n. mi.)	434	446	475	
Average cruise speed	(kn)	475	476	475	434
Initial cruising altitude	(ft)	27,000	26,700	29,000	28,350
Target speed	(kn)	466	466		
Large altitude	(ft)	37,350	36,550	37,300	
Final cruising altitude	(ft)	43,500	43,550	40,750	41,500
Total mission time	(hr)	8.42	8.94	7.49	10.02
COMBAT WEIGHT	(lb)	185,030	186,485	185,330	93,990
Combat altitude	(ft)	37,350	36,550	37,300	47,500
Combat speed	(kn)	483	488	483	486
Combat climb	(fpm)	850	1050	850	1000
Combat ceiling (500 fpm)	(ft)	39,300	39,600	39,250	46,500
Service ceiling (100 fpm)	(ft)	40,500	40,500	40,250	47,100
Service ceiling (one engine out)	(ft)	38,500	38,100	38,500	46,000
Max rate of climb at SL	(fpm)	4450	4450	4350	6150
Max speed at SL	(kn)	528	531	528	523
Max speed at 16,300 ft	(kn)	490	491	490	494
LANDING WEIGHT	(lb)	93,990	93,785	93,990	93,940
Ground roll at SL	(ft)	4600	4600	4600	4600
Ground roll (auxiliary brake)	(ft)	2600	2600	2600	2600
Total from 50 ft	(ft)	5500	5500	5500	5500
Total from 50 ft (auxiliary brake)	(ft)	3500	3500	3500	3500

NOTES:
① Take-off power
② Maximum power
③ Normal power
④ Detailed descriptions of RADII's and RANGE missions given on page 6.
⑤ Volume limited, includes ATO and water alcohol.
⑥ 33 bottles ATO, medium flow water injection (see note (d), page 6)
⑦ No ATO, medium flow water injection
⑧ Values quoted are for T.O. weight less 7100 lb ATO and 5500 lb water and alcohol.
⑨ Placard speed.
⑩ Brake chute deployed at touchdown

PERFORMANCE BASIS
(a) Data Source: Flight test
(b) Performance is based on power shown on page 6.

Climb

Rate of Climb - FT/MIN vs Altitude (1000 ft)

- Max Power
- Normal Power
- 133,030 LB CLEAN
- 213,540 LB EXT. TANKS

Radius

Avg. Speed Knots vs Nautical Miles

- NO BOMB LOAD, NO CHAFF, T.O. GW 215,113 LB, 117,000 LB FUEL
- 10,000 LB BOMB, 845 LB CHAFF, T.O. GW 225,958 LB, 117,000 LB FUEL

Take-Off

Distance (1000 ft) vs Gross Weight (1000 lb)

- MEDIUM FLOW WATER INJECTION NO ATO
- MEDIUM FLOW WATER INJECTION 3×1000 LB ATO
- SEA LEVEL
- CLEAR 50 FT
- GROUND RUN

Speed

Altitude (1000 ft) vs Knots

- Max Power
- Normal Power
- Placard Speed
- $M = 0.86$
- (425 KN IAS)
- INITIAL BUFFET 133,030 LB
- 133,030 LB CLEAN
- 213,540 LB EXT. TANK

NOTES

FORMULA: RADIUS MISSIONs I & II

Take-off and climb on course to initial cruising altitude. Cruise out at long range speeds and altitudes, dropping external tanks when empty. Climb to cruise ceiling and conduct a 15 minute level-flight bomb run at normal rated thrust. Drop bomb load and chaff and conduct 2 minutes evasive action and 8 minutes escape at normal rated thrust. Return to base at long range speeds and altitudes. Range-free allowances are fuel for 5 minutes at normal rated thrust at sea level for take-off allowance, 2 minutes at normal rated thrust at combat altitude for evasive action, and 30 minutes at maximum endurance airspeeds at sea level plus 5% of initial fuel load for landing reserve.

FORMULA: RADIUS MISSION III

Take-off and climb on course to initial cruising altitude. Cruise out at normal rated thrust at cruise ceiling, dropping external tanks when empty. Conduct a 15 minute level flight bomb run, drop bomb load and chaff, and conduct 2 minutes evasive action at normal rated thrust. Return to base at normal rated thrust at cruise ceiling. Range-free allowances are as specified for Radius Missions I and II.

FORMULA: RANGE MISSION IV

Take-off and climb on course to initial cruising altitude. Cruise out at long range speeds and altitudes, dropping external tanks when empty. Land at remote base with only reserve fuel remaining. Range-free allowances are fuel for 5 minutes at normal rated thrust at sea level for take-off allowance and 30 minutes at maximum endurance airspeeds at sea level plus 5% of initial fuel load for landing reserve.

GENERAL DATA

(a) Thrust values shown on page 8 are engine manufacturer's guaranteed ratings. Thrust values used in performance calculations are as follows:

S.L.Static	(5) J47-GE-25 & -25A		
	LB	RPM	MIN
T.O.	7200	7950	5
Max	5640	7800	30
Nor	5270	7630	Cont

(b) For detail planning, refer to Technical Order 1B-47-E-1 and latest applicable technical orders.

(c) The following loadings reflect the capabilities of the B-47E IV (Heavyweight) airplane utilizing general purpose bombs:

SHORT BOMB BAY Hi-Density Kit		SHORT BOMB BAY Lo-Density Kit	
No. .... Class (lb)		No. .... Class (lb)	
WW II (Box Fin) Not Carried		WW II (Box Fin) Not Carried	
INTERIM (Conical Fin)		INTERIM (Conical Fin)	
3 2000		3 2000	
6 1000		4 1000	
13 .... 500 (T-127)		4 .... 500 (T-127)	
14 .... 500 (M-128)		8 .... 500 (M-128)	
NEW SERIES		NEW SERIES	
6 .... 750 Chem. Cluster		4 .... 750 Chem. Cluster	
7 750		4 750	

1. The Short Bomb Bay Hi-Density Kit is are otherwise on all aircraft.
2. The Short Bomb Bay Lo-Density Kit can be utilized only in airplanes 617 thru 750, airplanes 1 thru 616 may provisions for this kit but must be modified to accept it.

(d) The displacement rack must be utilized in carrying maximum complement of (4)Mk4/Mk5000 or the (3)Mk-NS3000 Wt.15 bottles ATO (Manufactured by Phillips Petroleum).

(e) Electronics combined from page 8
HF Liaison AN/ARC-21 AN/ARC-6
Warning Radar AN/APS-54
DF Group AN/ARA-25
Gun Laying Radar AN/APG-32
ECM (2) Various combinations of AN/ALT-6 AN/ALT-6A AN/ALT-7 and AN/ALT-6
TACAN AN/ARN-21

PERFORMANCE REFERENCE

Boeing Report D-13194 B-47 Performance Substantiation Manual
B-47E (-25 engines), B-47E and RB-47E dated 5 Jan 1954.

REVISION BASIS

To reflect current characteristics and performance data.

Boeing B-47E Stratojet
Source: U.S. Air Force

Boeing B-47A refueled by Boeing KC-97
Source: U.S. Air Force

Boeing B-50 Superfortress

Boeing B-50As In Formation.
Source: U.S. Air Force

The Boeing B-29 Superfortress was recognized as being underpowered at a very early point in its service career. Operating against targets in Japan from bases in the Marianas put great stress on the R-3350 engines and resulted in the loss of many aircraft. To remedy this situation, Pratt & Whitney offered to adapt a B-29 for its more powerful R-4360 engines. In April 1944, one B-29A was delivered to Pratt & Whitney so that the feasibility of the conversion could be assessed. The aircraft was readily recognizable by the new engine installation, with the oil cooler intake situated toward the rear of the nacelle.

The new aircraft was designated the XB-44 and showed considerably improved takeoff and climbing characteristics. However, by this time, many of the initial problems with the R-3350 had been resolved and stripping the B-29s of their defensive guns for low-level night incendiary raids on Japanese cities had reduced the strain on those engines. It was decided that the advantages offered by the XB-44 were not enough to justify disrupting the production of B-29s, and the aircraft remained a prototype.

Entering the Nuclear Age

This decision was changed by the introduction of nuclear weapons. For all its performance advances over earlier bombers, the B-29 was only just marginally capable of delivering an atomic bomb safely. At that time the Mark 1 atomic bomb had a yield of 12 kilotons and the Model 1561 yielded 20 kilotons. The new Mark 3 and Mark 4 devices coming soon would have yields in the 30- to 50-kiloton bracket, and that increase would eliminate the B-29's margin of safety. Suddenly, the re-engined B-29 looked a lot more attractive.

The first step in the design of a version of the existing B-29 optimized for the delivery of nuclear weapons was a complete revision of the basic B-29 airframe to take full advantage of the extra power offered by the Pratt & Whitney R-4360 engine. The traditional 24 ST aluminum structure of the B-29 was replaced by the newer 75 ST, which resulted in a wing that was 16 percent stronger than the wing of the B-29, and 600 pounds lighter. Other features included hydraulic rudder boost and nose wheel steering, enlarged flaps, a faster-acting undercarriage retracting mechanism, and the provision of reversible-pitch propellers that allowed the use of engine power as an aid to braking on short or wet runways. The most obvious visual change was a new, taller tail unit.

Funding Games

Originally, this aircraft was designated the B-29D. By the time the rework of the design had been completed, only 25 percent commonality existed between the B-29A and the B-29D. Accordingly, the designation of the latter was changed to B-50A in December 1945. This had the added benefit of making the aircraft appear to be a completely new design. Gaining funding for a new B-29 variant at a time when literally thousands of existing B-29s were being mothballed was highly questionable, but funding for production of a new type was much easier to justify. The timing of the designation change also meant that the interim B-50 had a later number than the B-47 that would replace it.

Seventy nine B-50As were ordered in 1946. The first B-50A flew on June 25, 1947. The last -A model was delivered in 1949 and the Strategic Air Command used these aircraft into the mid-1950s. About two-thirds of the B-50As were retrofitted with in-flight refueling equipment for receiving fuel from tanker aircraft. A B-50A named

Lucky Lady II was one of the modified aircraft so equipped, and it used the capability to become the first aircraft to fly around the world nonstop.

Strategic Reconnaissance

The B-50A was replaced on the production lines by the B-50B. The primary difference between the two was an increase in the gross weight from 168,480 pounds to 170,400 pounds and the installation of a new type of lightweight fuel cell. This was not entirely an advantage since the new cells leaked badly. To make matters worse, fuel tank overflows, leaking fuel check valves, failures of the engine turbo-chargers, generator defects, and other problems continued to plague the B-50. In any event, no B-50B aircraft would serve as a bomber. The RB-29s then used for strategic reconnaissance were deficient in range, operating altitude and speed (in 1952, two RB-29s were shot down by Russian fighters over the Sea of Japan). In addition to their obsolescence, the RB-29s were simply worn out. Accordingly, the entire B-50B production run (less one aircraft that was retained by Boeing for experimental work) was converted to RB-50B configuration. One RB-50 would be shot down in July 1953 and another in September 1956. In the former case, the RB-50 got a MiG-17 with its tail guns before being lost. The RB-50s served until they were replaced by RB-47s.

The next version of the B-50 was supposed to be the B-50C. This would have been powered by four new R-4360-43 turbo-compound engines that would have required a wider wingspan and a longer fuselage and would have been more than 50,000 pounds heavier than the existing B-50A. Accordingly, the B-50C was redesignated the B-54. General LeMay vigorously opposed development of the B-54 since it offered only limited advantages over the B-50. It came nowhere close to the capabilities of the B-36. In the stringent financial restrictions of the time, there seemed little point in developing the B-54, and General LeMay argued for the cancellation of the B-54 in favor of more B-36s. After balancing all factors involved, the Board of Senior Officers agreed with General LeMay and added that production of the B-47 Stratojet should be accelerated. The board's recommendations were approved by Secretary Stuart Symington and Gen. Hoyt Vandenberg in April 1949, and the B-54 project was formally canceled. The partially built YB-50C was also canceled and scrapped.

The Last Superfortress

The next (and final production) version of the B-50 was the B-50D. Changes included the addition of two 700-gallon fuel tanks mounted on outboard wing pylons, and a redesigned nose compartment "greenhouse" with an improved bomb sight window. Most of the D models were fitted with in-flight refueling receptacles as well. A total of 222 B-50D aircraft were built, the last being delivered in December 1950. The type was in service for only a short period of time, with withdrawal starting in late 1953 and being completed by October 1955. The retired B-50Ds were then converted for other roles such as KB-50 aerial refueling tankers, WB-50 weather reconnaissance aircraft, and TB-50 trainers. These modified aircraft remained in USAF service for another 10 years. A few KB-50s survived long enough to take part in the early stages of the Vietnam War. They flew out of Thai bases to refuel jet fighters that were running low on fuel while still over enemy territory. One KB-50 was lost while serving in this role, its wreckage being photographed by the North Vietnamese and identified as a B-52.

The B-50 spent most of its life in relative obscurity. It was overshadowed by the wartime service of its B-29 predecessor and its own service career was brief and undistinguished. In an era dominated by the B-36, B-47 and B-52, the B-50 was close to being an anachronism. Yet, the B-50 was an important step forward in Strategic Air Command's development. It introduced aerial refueling as a means of getting smaller bombers to their targets deep in hostile territory. While its service as a bomber was indeed brief, it provided a sound and reliable airframe for a variety of essential supporting duties that freed up more modern aircraft for combat roles.

Boeing KB-50J
Source: U.S. Air Force

Characteristics Summary

BOMBER · B-50A

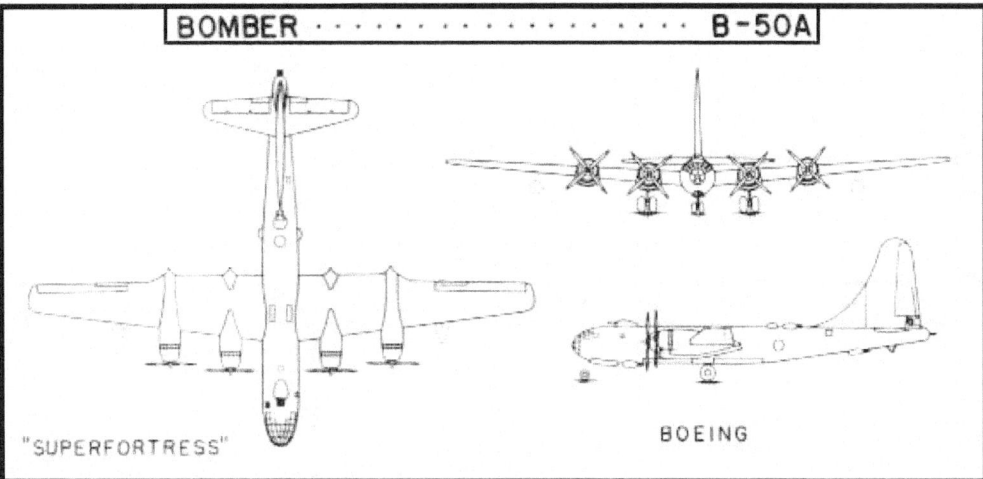

"SUPERFORTRESS" BOEING

Wing area................. 1720 sq ft	Length................. 99.0 ft
	Height................. 32.7 ft
Span................. 141.2 ft	(fin folded)................. 20.6 ft

AVAILABILITY

Number available

ACTIVE	RESERVE	TOTAL

PROCUREMENT

Number to be delivered in fiscal years

STATUS

1. First flight: Jun 47
2. First acceptance: Oct 47
3. Production completed: Jan 49
4. Some B-50A's are equipped with hose type in-flight refueling system.

Navy Equivalent: None   Mfr's Model: 345-2-1

POWER PLANT

(4) R-4360-35
Pratt & Whitney
ENGINE RATINGS

BHP-RPM-ALT MIN

T.O:*3500-2700- S.L.- 5
     3250-2700- S.L.- 5

Mil: *3500-2700-Turbo- 30
      3250-2700-Turbo- 30

Nor: 2650-2550-Turbo-Cont

*Wet

FEATURES

Crew: 11

Cabin Pressurization

Thermal Anti-icing

Bombing-Navigation Radar

Folding Fin and Rudder

Reverse Pitch Props

Formation Sticks

ECM Equipment

Max Fuel Cap: 10,772 gal

ARMAMENT

Turrets: 5

Guns: 13x.50 cal

Ammunition (tot): 6380 rds

Max Bomb Load:
  Internal: 40 x 500 lb
  External: 2 x 4000 lb

Max Bomb Size: 4000 lb

Characteristics Summary Basic Mission B-50A

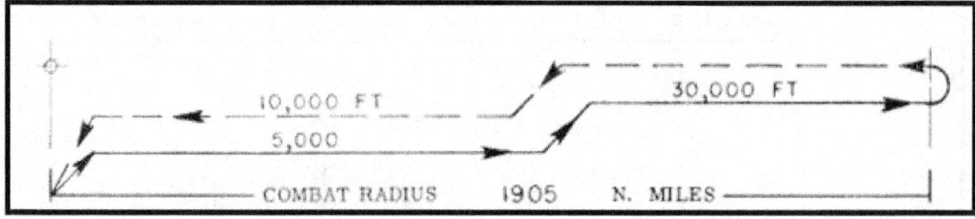

COMBAT RADIUS 1905 N. MILES

PERFORMANCE		
COMBAT RADIUS	**FERRY RANGE**	**S P E E D**
1905 naut. mi with 10,000 lb payload at 212 knots avg. in 17.70 hours.	4545 naut. mi with 10,772 gal fuel at 187 knots avg. in 23.96 hours at 158,480 lb T.O. wt.	COMBAT 340 knots at 30,000 ft alt, max power MAX 340 knots at 30,000 ft alt, max power BASIC 333 knots at 25,000 ft alt, max power
C L I M B	**C E I L I N G**	**TAKE - OFF**
675 fpm sea level, take-off weight normal power	26,550 ft 100 fpm, take-off weight normal power	ground run 5940 ft | —— ft no assist | assisted
2260 fpm sea level, combat weight maximum power	36,000 ft 500 fpm, combat weight maximum power	over 50 ft height 7425 ft | —— ft no assist | assisted
L O A D	**W E I G H T S**	**STALLING SPEED**

Bombs: 10,000 lb
Ammunition: 6380 rds/.50 cal
Fuel: 10,772 gal
  protected 87 %
  droppable 13 %
  external 13 %
	Empty..... 81,050 lb
	Combat... 120,500 lb
	Take - off 168,480 lb
	limited by space
		118 knots
		flaps down, take-off weight
		TIME TO CLIMB
		——

N O T E S

1. Performance Basis:
   (a) Flight test

2. Revision Basis: To conform to MIL-C-5011A Specification

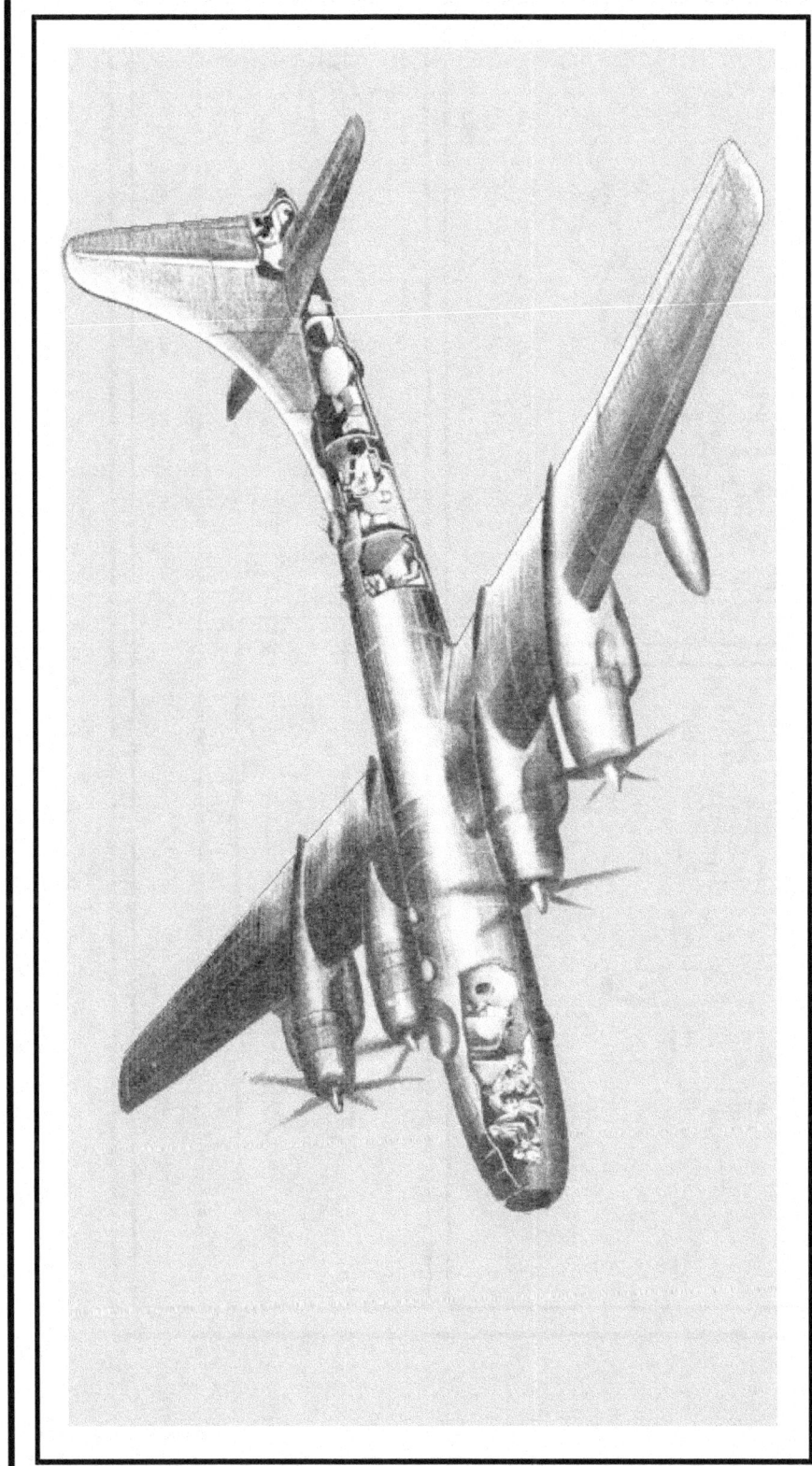

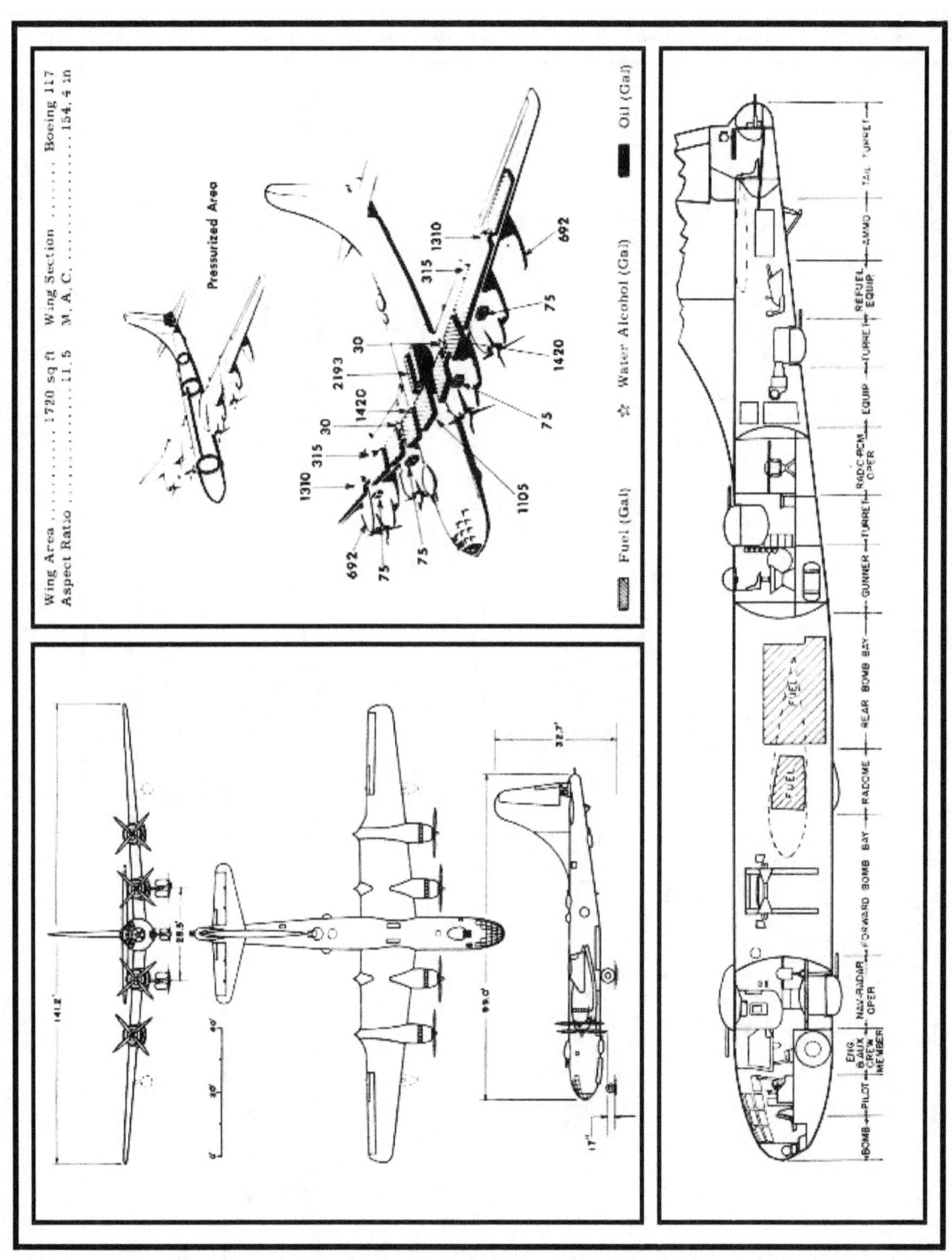

POWER PLANT

No. & Model	(4) R-4360-35
Mfr.	Pratt & Whitney
Engine Spec No.	A-7051-F
Superch.	1 stg. 1 spd
Turbo Superch.	(1) CH-7-B1
Turbo Mfr.	General Electric
Red. Gear Ratio	0.375
Prop. Mfr.	Curtiss
Blade Design No.	(see page 6, note)
Prop. Type	CS, FF, Reverse
No. Blades	4
Prop. Dia.	16'-8"
Augmentation	Water/Alcohol

ENGINE RATINGS

	BHP - RPM - ALT - MIN
T.O.	*3500 - 2700 - S.L. - 5
	3250 - 2700 - S.L. - 5
Mil.	*3500 - 2700 - Turbo - 30
	3250 - 2700 - Turbo - 30
Nor.	2650 - 2550 - Turbo-Cont.

*Wet

DIMENSIONS

Wing	
Span	141.2'
Incidence (root)	
Dihedral	4°20'
Sweepback (LE)	7°
Length	99.0'
Height	32.7'
Tread	29.6'
Height (fin block)	28.5'
Prop. Grd. Clearance	.17'

Mission and Description

Navy Equivalent: None   Mfr's Model: 345-2-1

The principal mission of the B-50A is the destruction by bombs of land and naval materiel objectives.

The normal crew consists of the pilot, co-pilot, engineer, navigator-bombardier, bombardier-navigator-radar operator, radio-radar operator, ECM operator, left side gunner, right side gunner, top gunner, tail gunner and extra crew member.

Cabin heating, ventilation and pressurization are incorporated for increased crew comfort on high altitude, long range missions.

The defensive armament consists of thirteen .50 caliber machine guns housed in five electrically-operated turrets which are remotely controlled from the sighting stations.

Some B-50A's are equipped with hose-type in-flight refueling system.

Development

First flight:	Jun 1947
First acceptance:	Oct 1947
Production completed:	Jan 1949

BOMBS

No.	Lb	Type
4	4000(int.)	G.P.
2	4000(ext.)	G.P.
8	2000	G.P.
12	1600	A.P.
12	1000	G.P.
40	500	G.P.

Max Bomb Load:
Internal 20,000 lb
External 8,000 lb

GUNS

No.	Size	Rds. ea.	Location
4	.50	500	Up. fwd
2	.50	500	Lwr. fwd
2	.50	500	Up. aft
2	.50	500	Lwr. aft
2	.50	500	Tur. tail
1	.50	380	Tur. tail

WEIGHTS

	Lb	L.F.
Loading		
Empty	81,050(C)	
Basic	85,155(A)	
Design	120,000	2.67
Combat	*120,500	
Max T.O (overload)	*168,480	
Max T.O (normal)	*158,250	
Max Land	*160,000	

(C) Calculated
(A) Actual
* For Basic Mission
* Limited by space
* Limited by performance
* Limited by structure
(See page 6 note a)

FUEL

	Gal.
Location No. Tanks	
Wgs. outbd. 2	2620
Wgs. inbd* 2	2840
Wg. ctr*	1105
Nac. skate* 2	630
Aft. bomb bay* 1	2193
Wgs. ext. 2 Total	1384
	10,772
Grade	115/145
Specification	MIL-F-5572

OIL

Nacelles 4	(to) 300
Grade	*1100,S-1120
Specification	MIL-O-6082
WATER/ALCOHOL	
Wg. inbd. 2	(to) 60

* Self-sealing

ELECTRONICS

VHF Command	AN/ARC-3
Liaison	AN/ARC-8
Interphone	AN/AIC-2A
Range Rcvr.	BC-453-E
Radio Compass	AN/ARN-7
Marker Beacon	BC-1278
IFF	SCR-695B
Localizer	RC-103A
Radar Gun Sight	AN/APG-15B
Auto Bomb	AN/ARA-5 & -10A
Glide Path	AN/ARN-5A
Loran	AN/APN-9 or -9A
Radio Alt	SCR-718C
Radar	AN/APQ-23A
Radio Set	AN/APN-68
Pulse Doppler	AN/APN-2B
ECM	AN/APA-52
(See page 6, note 6)	

Loading and Performance — Typical Mission

CONDITIONS		BASIC MISSION I	MAX BOMB II	HIGH ALTITUDE III	NORMAL WEIGHT IV	FERRY RANGE V
TAKE-OFF WEIGHT	(lb)	166,480	164,212	168,480	158,250	158,480
Fuel at 6.0 lb/gal (grade 115/145)	(lb)	64,632	51,474	64,632	54,400	64,612
Payload (Bombs)	(lb)	10,000	20,000	10,000	10,000	None
Wing loading	(lb/sq ft)	98.0	95.3	98.0	92.0	92.2
Stall speed (power off)	(kn)	116	116	116	114	114
Take-off ground run at SL ①	(ft)	5940	5496	5940	4960	4960
Take-off to clear 50 ft ①	(ft)	7425	6870	7425	6200	6200
Rate of climb at SL ①	(fpm)	675	730	675	820	815
Rate of climb at SL (one engine out) ②	(fpm)	520	590	520	665	655
Time: SL to 10,000 ft ③	(min)	16.0	14.0	16.0	13.0	13.0
Time: SL to 20,000 ft ③	(min)	38.0	33.0	38.0	39.0	39.0
Service ceiling (100 fpm) ③	(ft)	26,550	28,250	26,550	30,200	30,150
Service ceiling (one engine out) ③	(ft)	⑤	⑤	⑤	⑤	⑤
COMBAT RANGE ④	(n. mi.)					
COMBAT RADIUS ④	(n. mi.)	1905	1474	1675	1600	4545
Average speed	(kn)	212	215	282	212	187
Initial cruising altitude	(ft)	5000	5000	25,000	5000	5000
Target speed	(kn)	318	316	320	328	
Target altitude	(ft)	30,000	30,000	30,000	30,000	
Final cruising altitude	(ft)	10,000	10,000	30,000	10,000	5000
Total mission time	(hr)	17.70	14.56	12.86	14.84	23.96
COMBAT WEIGHT	(lb)	129,596	113,412	118,480	116,390	97,864
Combat altitude ②	(ft)	30,000	30,000	30,000	30,000	5000
Combat speed ②	(kn)	344	343	345	347	288
Combat climb ②	(fpm)	1520	1720	1380	1640	2960
Combat ceiling (500 fpm) ②	(ft)	36,000	36,800	36,200	36,400	38,800
Service ceiling (100 fpm) ③	(ft)	37,300	36,550	37,700	38,050	40,550
Service ceiling (one engine out) ③	(ft)	31,700	35,100	32,400	33,400	
Max rate of climb at SL ②	(fpm)	2260	2465	2305	2370	2973
Max speed at optimum altitude ②	(kn/ft)	344/30,000	348/30,000	345/30,000	347/30,000	352/30,000
Basic speed at 25,000 ft	(kn)	337	336	336	341	341
LANDING WEIGHT	(lb)	97,884	95,102	97,884	97,419	97,464
Ground roll at SL	(ft)	1715	1670	1715	1705	1715
Total from 50 ft	(ft)	3100	3050	3100	3085	3100

NOTES:
① T.O. power
② Max power
③ Normal power
④ Detailed descriptions of RADIUS and RANGE missions given on page 6
⑤ No data

PERFORMANCE BASIS:
(a) Data source: Flight test
(b) Performance is based on powers shown on page 6

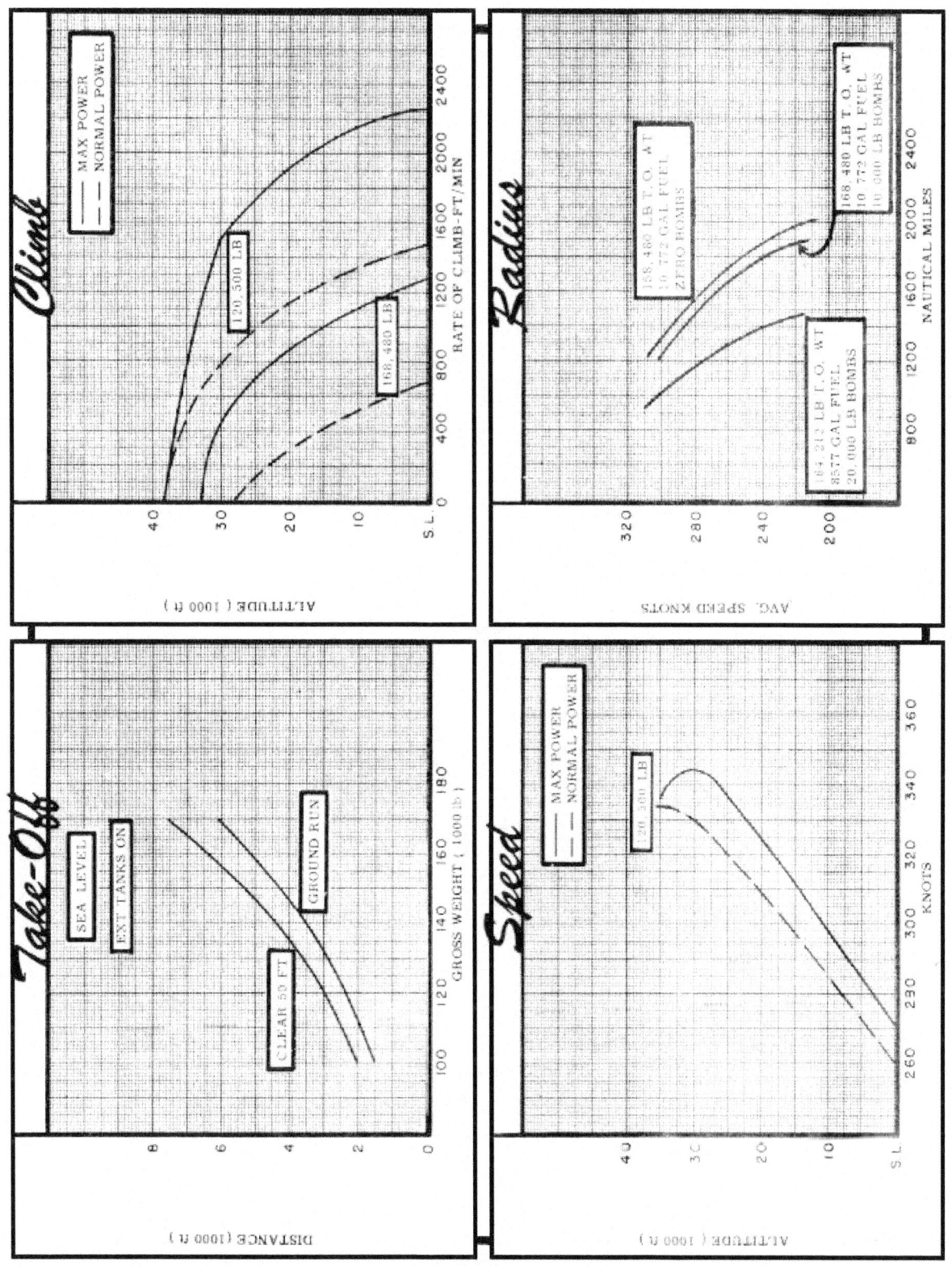

NOTES

FORMULA: RADIUS MISSIONS I, II & IV

Warm-up, take-off, climb on course to 5000 ft at normal power, cruise at long range speeds at altitude for best range but not less than 5000 ft. climb on course to reach cruising ceiling 500 nautical miles from target, cruise in level flight to target, conduct 15 minutes normal power bomb run drop bomb when carried, conduct 2 minutes evasive action at combat (no distance credit) and an eight minute run out from target area with normal power, cruise at long range speeds at combat altitude for 500 nautical miles, cruise back to base at long range speeds at not less than 5000 ft for best range. Range free allowances include 5 minutes normal power fuel consumption for warm-up and take-off, 2 minutes normal power evasive action, 5% initial fuel load for landing and endurance reserve plus fuel for 30 minutes maximum endurance at sea level.

FORMULA: RADIUS MISSION III

Same as Radius Mission I except initial climb is to 25,000 ft.

FORMULA: RANGE MISSION V

Warm-up, take-off, climb on course to 5000 ft at normal power, cruise at long range speeds at altitude for best range but not less than 5000 ft. Range free allowances include 5 minutes normal power fuel consumption for warm-up and take-off, 5% initial fuel load for landing reserve, plus 30 minutes fuel for long range speeds at sea level.

GENERAL DATA:

(a) This airplane makes good a flight and take-off limit load factor of 2 at a gross weight of 173,000 lb, although the landing gear and supporting structure does not meet the ground handling requirements of ANC-2ass these requirements were set up subsequent to the design of this airplane. The B-50B specification maximum weight is 164,500 lb which is the present recommended maximum due to limited side load strength of main and nose gears and supporting structure which might become critical in short-ed take-off.

(b) Engine ratings shown on page 3 are guaranteed values. Power values used in performance calculations are as follows:

(4) R-4360-35

	BHP	RPM	ALT
T.O:	*3500	2700	S.L.
MAX:	*3500	2700	15,000**
NOR:	*3250	2700	30,500**
	2650	2550	30,000**

* Wet
** Level flight critical altitude

(c) For detailed planning refer to Tech Order AN 01-20ELA-1.

(d) Installation provisions for ECM equipment include the following sets:

AN/APT-1   AN/APR-4
AN/APT-4   AN/ARQ-8

(e) B-50A airplanes equipped with C644S-B116 and B120 propellers utilize 1052-7C4-30 blades. B-50A airplanes equipped with C644S-A44 propellers utilize 1016-4C4-18 blades.

SUPPLEMENTAL
Loading and Performance - Typical Mission

CONDITIONS		BASIC MISSION
TAKE-OFF WEIGHT	(lb)	168,480
Fuel at 6.0 lb/gal (grade 115/145) (lb)		64,632
Military load (Bombs) (lb)		10,000
Wing loading (lb/sq ft)		98.0
Stall speed (power off, land config.) (kn)		118
Take-off ground run at SL (ft)		4775
Take-off to clear 50 ft (ft)		8650
Rate of climb at SL (fpm)		685
Time SL to 10,000 ft (min)		16.0
Time SL to 20,000 ft (min)		38.0
Service ceiling (100 fpm) (ft)		26,550
COMBAT RANGE (n. mi.)		4089
Average speed (kn)		204
Initial cruising altitude (ft)		10,000
Final cruising altitude (ft)		25,000
Total mission time (hr)		20.17
COMBAT RADIUS (n. mi.)		2137
Average speed (kn)		223
Initial cruising altitude (ft)		10,000
Bombing altitude (ft)		25,000
Bomb run speed (kn)		317
Final cruising altitude (ft)		25,000
Total mission time (hr)		19.42
COMBAT WEIGHT (lb)		121,700
Combat altitude (ft)		25,000
Combat speed (kn)		334
Combat climb (fpm)		1665
Combat ceiling (500 fpm) (ft)		35,800
Service ceiling (100 fpm) (ft)		37,100
Service ceiling (one engine out) (ft)		31,500
Max rate of climb at SL (fpm)		2255
Max speed at 10,000 ft (kn)		339
LANDING WEIGHT (lb)		97,080
Ground roll at SL (ft)		1310
Total from 50 ft (ft)		2330

1. Military Specification MIL-C-5011A dated 5 November 1951 redefines the combat radius to ground rules coordinated by the major USAF Air Commands and the Bureau of Aeronautics, U. S. Navy. Although in most cases the mission radius is reduced, this was considered to be more realistic based on Mission Profiles and Allowances proven in actual operation.

2. The combat radius for MIL-C-5011A is different from that based on MIL-C-5011 in that:

   a. Run into and out from the target area for high altitude bomber is at higher altitudes rather than at a specified altitude. This altitude corresponds to the cruise ceiling at the start of the combat zone, 500 n. mi. prior to target for reciprocating aircraft.

   b. Reserves are changed from a constant percentage of initial fuel as in MIL-C-5011 to a value equal to 5% of initial fuel load plus fuel for a specified period of 30 minutes long range at sea level.

   c. Combat range values are not quoted in MIL-C-5011A.

3. Certain items of performance quoted for MIL-C-5011A are different from those based on MIL-C-5011 in that:

   a. Time to climb values consider the effects of weight reduction during ground operation and climb.

   b. Average cruising speed does not include time and distance in climbs or target operation at normal power.

   c. Combat altitude is the altitude at which the actual target run is conducted.

   d. Basic speed is the maximum level flight speed within all operating limitations at the combat weight and at a specified altitude. This basic speed is quoted as a means of direct comparison of aircraft of similar type.

NOTES
1. Take-off power
2. Max power
3. Normal power
4. For Radius Mission

PERFORMANCE BASIS:
(a) Data source: Flight Tests

Characteristics Summary

BOMBER — B-50B

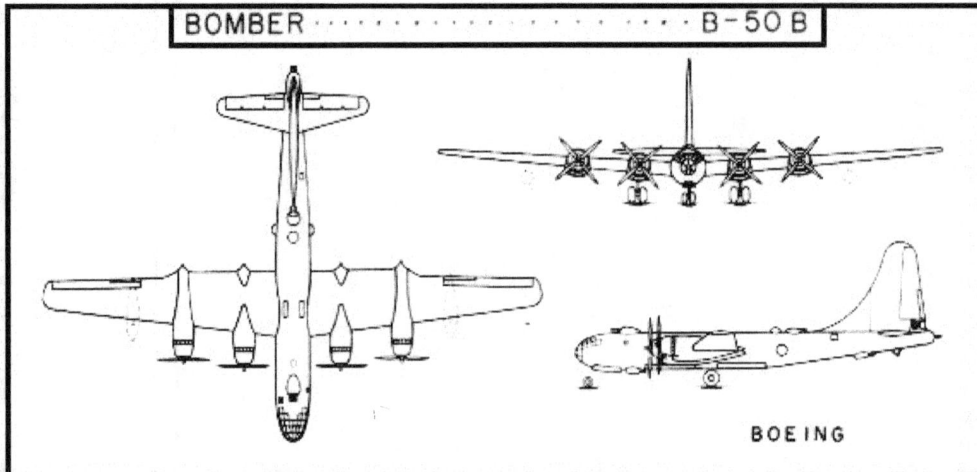

BOEING

Wing area .... 1720 sq ft   Length .... 99.0 ft

Span .... 141.2 ft   Height .... 32.7 ft

AVAILABILITY

Number available

ACTIVE	RESERVE	TOTAL

PROCUREMENT

Number to be delivered in fiscal years

STATUS

1. Original order to modify all B-50B's to RB-50B's has been changed. Sixteen (16) B-50B's will be retained.
2. First acceptance: December 1948
3. Production completed: May 1949

POWER PLANT

(4) R-4360-35 Pratt-Whitney

ENGINE RATINGS

BHP - RPM - ALT
T.O: *3500 - 2700 - S.L.
Mil: *3500 - 2700 - 500
     3250 - 2700 - 500
Nor: 2650 - 2550 - 5500

*Wet

FEATURES

Crew: 11
Cabin Pressurization
Thermal Anti-icing
Bombing - Navigation Radar
Folding Fin and Rudder
Reverse Pitch Props
Max Fuel Capacity:
              11,564 gal.

ARMAMENT

Turrets: 5
Guns: 13x.50 cal
Ammunition (tot.): 6380 rds
Max Bomb Load:
  Internal: 40x500 lb
  External: 2x4000 lb
Max Bomb Size: 4000 lb

Characteristics Summary Basic Mission · · · · · B-50B

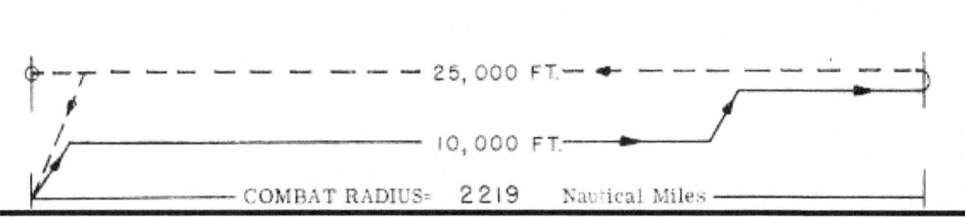

— 25,000 FT. —
— 10,000 FT. —
— COMBAT RADIUS = 2219 Nautical Miles —

PERFORMANCE

COMBAT RADIUS	COMBAT RANGE	COMBAT SPEED
2219 naut. mi	**4075** naut. mi	**346** knots at 25,000 ft alt, max power
with 10,000 lb payload	with 10,000 lb payload	**MAXIMUM SPEED**
at 237 knots avg.	at 218 knots avg.	**354** knots at 33,000 ft alt, max power
in 18.98 hours.	in 18.88 hours.	

CLIMB	CEILING	TAKE-OFF
580 fpm sea level, take-off weight normal power	**20,300** ft 100 fpm, take-off weight normal power	ground run 5230 ft no assist | —— ft assisted
1970 fpm sea level, combat weight maximum power	**34,100** ft 500 fpm, combat weight maximum power	over 50 ft height 7300 ft no assist | —— ft assisted

LOAD	WEIGHTS	STALLING SPEED

Bombs: 10,000 lb
Ammunition:
6380 rds/.50 cal
 	
Fuel: 11,564 gal
  protected 68 %
  droppable 31 %
  external 12 %
	Empty..... 78,980 lb
	Combat... 119,340 lb
	Take-off 170,757 lb
	limited by space
		106 knots flaps down, take-off weight

		TIME TO CLIMB ——

NOTES

1. PERFORMANCE BASIS:
   (a) Estimated data
   (b) Fuel density: 6.0 lb/gal
   (c) In computing Radius and Range, specific fuel consumptions have been increased 5% to allow for variation of fuel flow in service aircraft.

2. REVISION BASIS: Re-issue; see STATUS note 1.

Characteristics Summary

BOMBER · · · · · · · · · · · · · · · · · · · B-50D

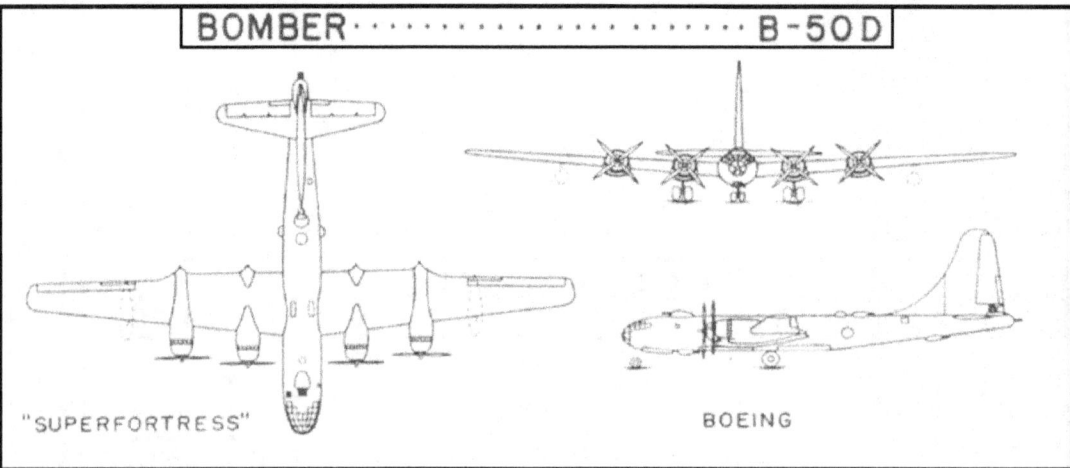

"SUPERFORTRESS"　　　　　　　　　　BOEING

Wing area.................... 1720 sq ft　　Length............................. 99.0 ft
　　　　　　　　　　　　　　　　　　　　Height............................. 32.7 ft
Span............................. 141.2 ft　　(fin folded)........................ 20.6 ft

AVAILABILITY			PROCUREMENT			
Number available			Number to be delivered in fiscal years			
ACTIVE	RESERVE	TOTAL				

STATUS

1. First flight: May 1949
2. First acceptance: May 1949

POWER PLANT

(4) R-4360-35
Pratt & Whitney

ENGINE RATINGS

```
           BHP - RPM
T.O:     *3500 - 2700
          3250 - 2700
Mil:     *3500 - 2700
Nor:      2600 - 2550
```

*Wet

FEATURES

Crew:　　　　　　　　　11
Cabin Pressurization
Thermal Anti-icing
Bombing-Navigation Radar
Folding Fin and Rudder
Reverse Pitch Props.
ECM Equipment
Max Fuel Cap:　　11,685 gal

ARMAMENT

Turrets:　　　　　　　　5

Guns:　　　　　　13x.50 cal

Ammunition: (tot.)　6380 rds

Max Bomb Load:
　Internal:　　　40x500 lb
　External:　　　2x4000 lb

Max Bomb Size:　　4000 lb

Characteristics Summary Basic Mission B-50D

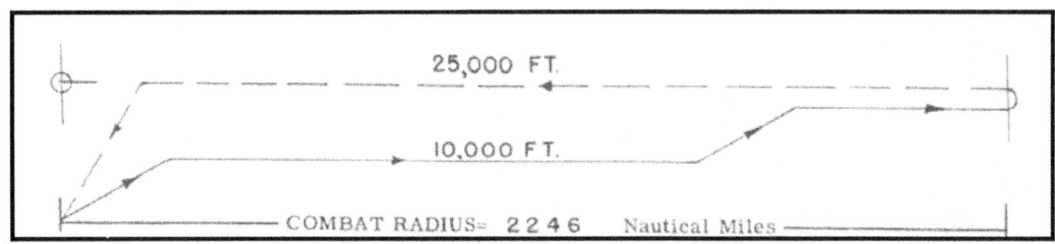

COMBAT RADIUS = 2246 Nautical Miles

PERFORMANCE

COMBAT RADIUS	COMBAT RANGE	COMBAT SPEED
2246 naut. mi with 10,000 lb payload at 225 knots avg. in 20.22 hours.	**4258** naut. mi with 10,000 lb payload at 206 knots avg. in 20.80 hours.	**330** knots at 25,000 ft alt, max power
		MAXIMUM SPEED
		335 knots at 30,500 ft alt, max power

CLIMB	CEILING	TAKE-OFF
623 fpm sea level, take-off weight normal power	**24,000** ft 100 fpm, take-off weight normal power	ground run **5050** ft no assist | ——— ft assisted
2165 fpm sea level, combat weight maximum power	**35,500** ft 500 fpm, combat weight maximum power	over 50 ft height **7050** ft no assist | ——— ft assisted

LOAD	WEIGHTS	STALLING SPEED
Bombs: 10,000 lb Ammunition: 6380 rds/.50 cal Fuel: 11,602 gal protected 89 % droppable 11 % external 11 %	Empty..... 80,609 lb Combat... 123,100 lb Take-off 173,000 lb limited by strength	**119** knots flaps down, take-off weight
		TIME TO CLIMB ———

NOTES

1. PERFORMANCE BASIS:
   (a) Flight test
   (b) Fuel density: 6.0 lb/gal
2. REVISION BASIS: To reflect flight test data

Standard Aircraft Characteristics

B-50D SUPERFORTRESS
Boeing

FOUR R-4360-35
PRATT & WHITNEY

BY AUTHORITY OF
THE SECRETARY
OF THE AIR FORCE

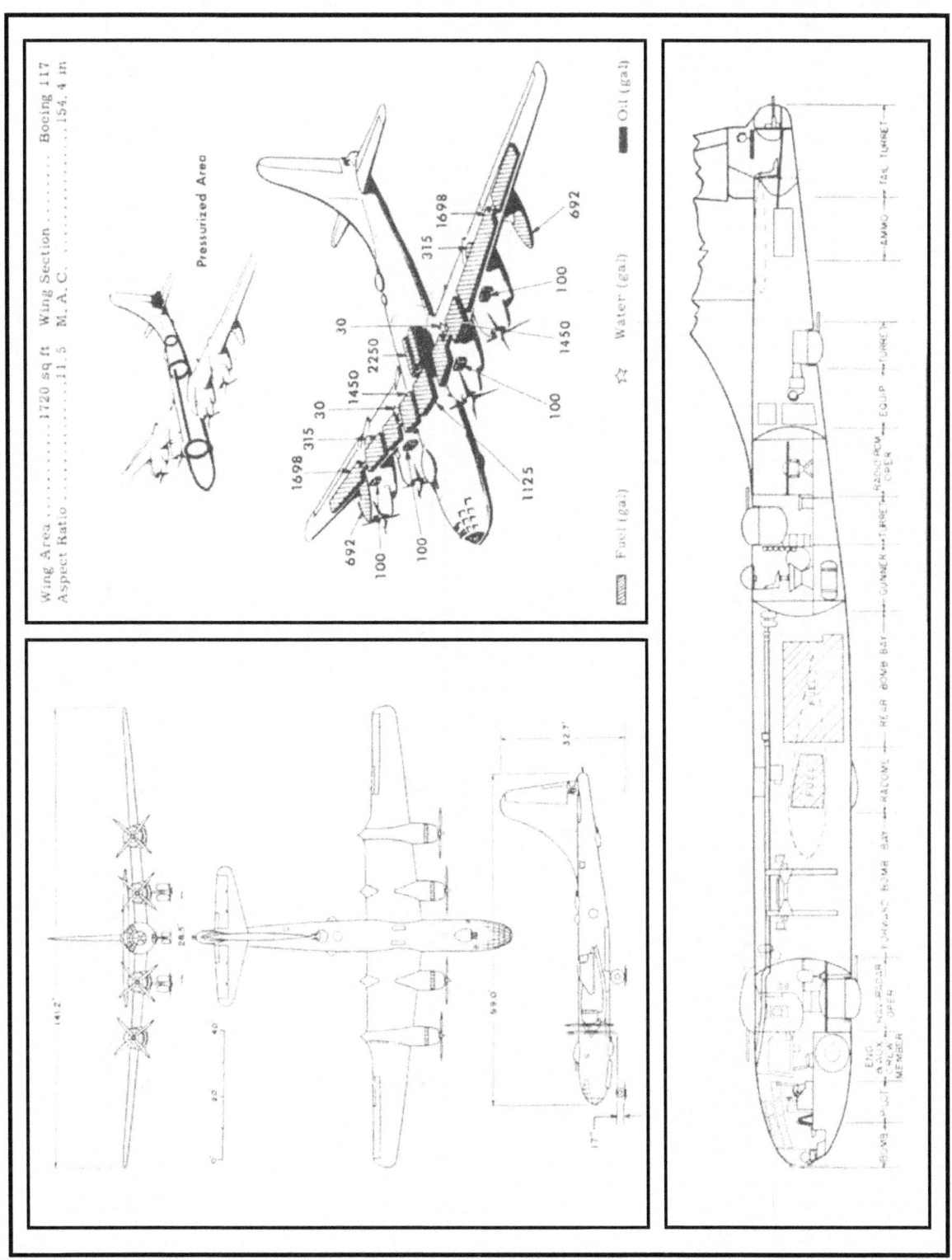

POWER PLANT

No. & Model	(4)R-4360-35
Mfr	Pratt & Whitney
Engine Spec. No.	A-7051-F
Superch	1 stg, 1 spd
Turbo Superch	(1)CH-7-B1
Turbo Mfr	General Electric
Red. Gear Ratio	0.375
Prop Mfr	Curtiss
Blade Design No.	1052-20C4-30
Prop Type	C5.FF Reverse
No. Blades	4
Prop Dia	16'8"
Augmentation	Water/Alcohol

ENGINE RATINGS

	BHP - RPM - ALT - MIN
T.O.	*3500 - 2700 - S.L. - 5
	3250 - 2700 - S.L. - 5
Mil.	*3500 - 2700 - Turbo - 30
	3250 - 2700 - Turbo - 30
Nor.	2650 - 2550 - Turbo-Cont

* Wet

DIMENSIONS

Wing	
Span	141.2'
Incidence (root)	4°
Dihedral	4°29'
Sweepback (LE)	7°9'
Length	99.0'
Height	39.0'
Height (fin folded)	20.6'
Tread	28.5'
Prop. Grd Clearance	17"

Mission and Description

Navy Equivalent: None Mfr's Model: 345-9-6

The principal mission of the B-50D is the destruction by bombs of land or naval materiel objectives.

The normal crew consists of the pilot, co-pilot, engineer, radio-ECM operator, left side gunner, right side gunner, top gunner and tail gunner.

Cabin heating, ventilation and pressurization are incorporated for increased crew comfort on high altitude, long range missions.

The defensive armament consists of thirteen .50 caliber machine guns housed in five electrically-operated turrets which are remotely controlled from the sighting stations.

Development

The B-50D is similar to the B-50A except for boom in-flight refueling equipment, increased fuel capacity, crew of 10 in lieu of 11, deletion of tail skid and other minor differences.

First flight	May 49
First acceptance	May 49
Production completed	Dec 50

BOMBS

No.	Lb	Type
4	4000 (int.)	G.P.
2	4000 (ext.)	G.P.
8	2000	G.P.
12	1600	A.P.
12	1000	G.P.
40	500	G.P.

Max Bomb Load:
Internal 20,000 lb
External 8000 lb

GUNS

No.	Size	Rds. ea	Location
4	50	500	Up. fwd
2	50	500	Lwr. fwd
2	50	500	Up. aft
2	50	500	Lwr. aft
2	50	500	Tur. tail
1	50	380	Tur. tail

WEIGHTS

Loading	Lb	L.F.
Empty	80,609(C)	
Basic	84,714(A)	
Design	120,000	2.67
Combat	*121,850	
Max T.O.(overload)‡	173,000	2.00
Max T.O.(normal)#	158,250	
Max Land	#160,000	

(A) Actual
(C) Calculated
* For Basic Mission
+ Limited by strength
‡ Limited by performance
# Limited by landing gear strength (See page 6, note g)

FUEL

Location	No. Tanks	Gal
Wgs. outbd*	2	3396
Wgs. mbd*	2	2900
Wg. ctr*	1	1125
Nac. skate *	4	630
Aft. bomb bay	1	2250
Wgs. ext	2	1384
	Total	11,685
Grade		115/145
Specification		MIL-F-5572

OIL

Nacelles	4	(tot) 400
Grade		W-1100,S-1120
Specification		MIL-O-6082

WATER/ALCOHOL
Wgs. inbd 2 (tot) 60
* Self sealing

ELECTRONICS

Glide Path	AN/ARN-5A
VHF Command	AN/ARC-3
Interphone	USAF Combat
Range Recvr	BC-453E
Liaison	AN/ARC-8
Radio Compass	AN/ARN-7
Marker Beacon	RC-193A
IFF	AN/APX-6
Localizer	RC-103A
Special Radar	AN/APQ-24
Loran Radar	AN/APN-9 or 9A
Auto Bomb	AN/ARW-10A
Radio Altimeter	SCR-718C
ECM (See page 6, note d)	
Radar	AN/APN-68
Radio Set	AN/APN-2B

Loading and Performance — Typical Mission

CONDITIONS		BASIC MISSION	MAX BOMB	HIGH ALTITUDE	NORMAL WEIGHT	FERRY RANGE
			II	III	IV	V
TAKE OFF WEIGHT	(lb)	173,000	169,642	173,000	158,250	163,519
Fuel at 6.0 lb/gal (grade 115/145)	(lb)	69,615	56,634	69,615	54,865	70,134
Payload (Bombs)	(lb)	10,000	20,000	10,000	10,000	None
Wing loading	(lb/sq ft)	109.5	92.6	109.5	92.0	95.1
Stall speed (power off)	(kn)	119	118	119	114	115
Take-off ground run at SL	(ft)	6420	6040	6420	4960	5440
Take-off to clear 50 ft	(ft)	8025	7550	8025	6200	6300
Rate of climb at SL	(fpm)	620	660	620	805	735
Rate of climb at SL (one engine out)	(fpm)	520	550	520	675	625
Time: SL to 10,000 ft	(min)	18	16	18	13	14
Time: SL to 20,000 ft	(min)	43	39	43	30	34
Service ceiling (100 fpm)	(ft)	24,000	25,550	24,000	29,900	28,150
Service ceiling (one engine out)	(ft)	⑤	⑤	⑤	⑤	⑤
COMBAT RANGE	(n. mi.)					5006
COMBAT RADIUS	(n. mi.)	2022	1625	1840	1660	
Average speed	(kn)	212	215	260	211	185
Initial cruising altitude	(ft)	5000	5000	25,000	5000	5000
Target speed	(kn)	320	317	425	326	
Final cruising altitude	(ft)	30,000	30,000	30,000	30,000	5000
Total mission time	(hr)	19.53	15.05	13.95	15.89	25.54
COMBAT WEIGHT	(lb)	121,850	115,700	119,990	116,050	97,700
Combat altitude	(ft)	30,000	30,000	30,000	30,000	5000
Combat speed	(kn)	343	346	344	345	279
Combat climb	(fpm)	1865	1630	1515	1620	2915
Combat ceiling (500 fpm)	(ft)	35,650	36,415	36,900	36,400	38,700
Service ceiling (100 fpm)	(ft)	36,900	38,000	37,250	37,950	40,430
Service ceiling (one engine out)	(ft)	31,600	34,400	32,400	34,350	41,600
Max rate of climb at SL	(fpm)	2200	2135	2240	2350	2875
Max speed at optimum altitude	(kn)	343	346	344	345	354
Basic speed at 25,000 ft	(kn)	337	340	338	340	344
LANDING WEIGHT	(lb)	97,675	96,640	97,675	96,935	97,700
Ground roll at SL	(ft)	1710	1685	1710	1690	1710
Total from 50 ft	(ft)	3065	3060	3065	3070	3090

NOTES:
① T.O. power
② Max power
③ Normal power
④ Detailed descriptions of RADIUS and RANGE missions given on page 6
⑤ No data

PERFORMANCE BASIS:
(a) Data Source: Flight test
(b) Performance is based on powers shown on page 6

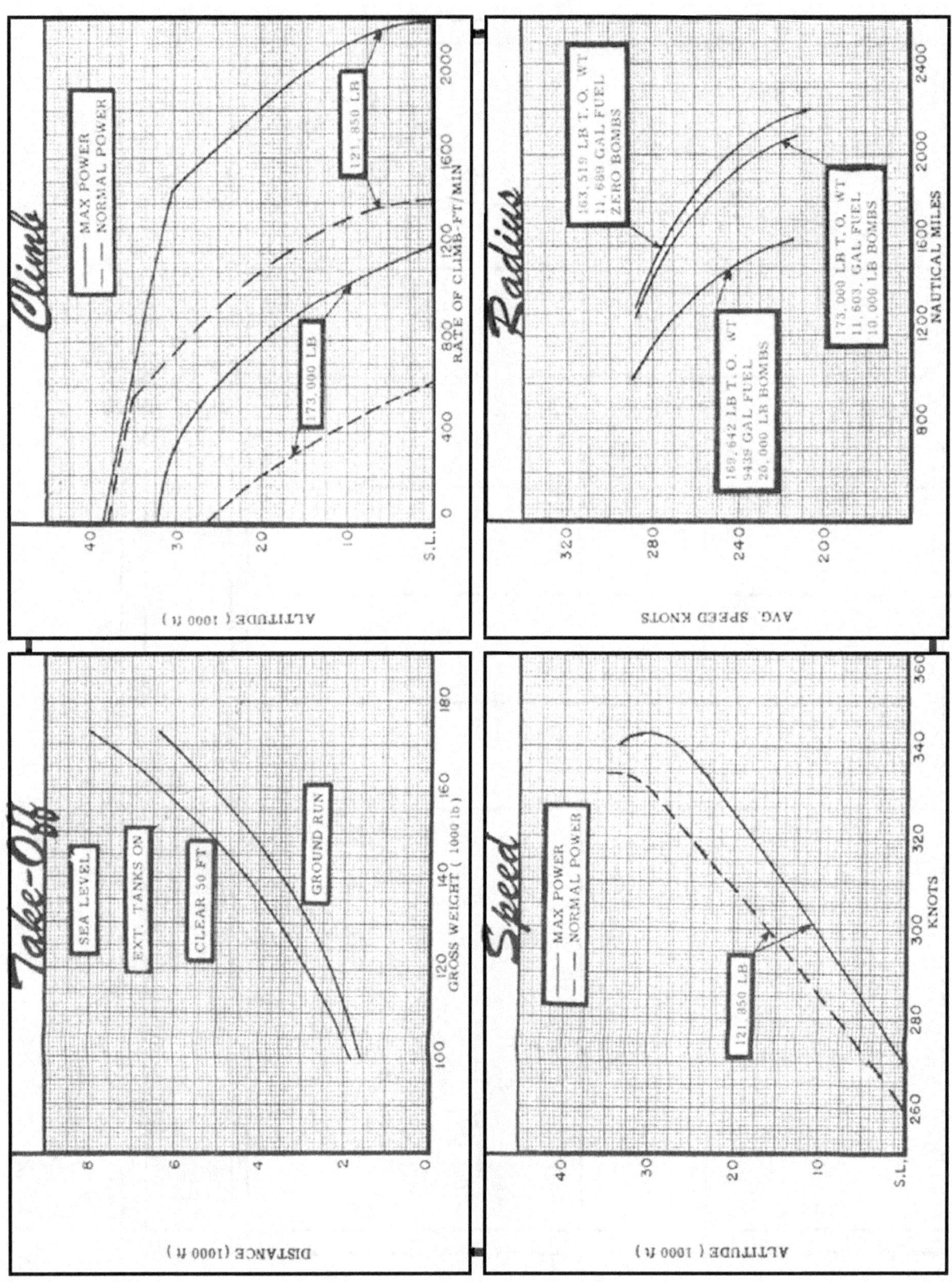

N O T E S

GENERAL DATA:

(a) This airplane makes good a flight and take-off limit load factor of 2 at a gross weight of 173,000 lb although the landing gear and supporting structure does not meet the ground handling requirements of ANC-2a as these requirements were set up subsequent to the design of this airplane. The B-50B specification maximum weight is 164,500 lb which is the present recommended maximum due to limited side load strength of main and nose gears and supporting structure which might become critical in aborted take-off.

(b) Engine ratings shown on page 3 are guaranteed values. Power values used in performance calculations are as follows:

(4) R-4360-35

	BHP	RPM	ALT
T.O.	*3500	2700	S.L.
MAX.	*3500	2700	15,000**
	*3250	2700	30,500**
NOR.	2650	2550	30,000**

* Wet
** Level flight critical altitude

(c) For detailed planning refer to Tech Order AN 01-20ELA-1.

(d) Installation provisions for ECM equipment include the following sets:

AN/APT-1   AN/APR-4
AN/APT-4   AN/AHQ-8
AN/APT-5A

FORMULA - RADIUS MISSIONS I, II & IV

Warm-up, take-off, climb on course to 5000 ft at normal power, cruise at long range speeds at altitude for best range but not less than 5000 ft. climb on course to reach cruising ceiling 300 nautical miles from target, cruise in level flight to target, conduct 15 minutes normal power bomb run (no distance credit) and an eight minute run out from target area with normal power, cruise at long range speeds at combat altitude for 300 nautical miles, cruise back to base at long range speeds at not less than 5000 ft for best range. Range free allowances include 5 minutes normal power fuel consumption for warm-up and take-off, 2 minutes normal power evasive action, 5% initial fuel load for landing and endurance reserve plus fuel for 30 minutes maximum endurance at sea level.

FORMULA - RADIUS MISSION III

Same as Radius Mission I except initial climb is to 25,000 ft.

FORMULA - RANGE MISSION V

Warm-up, take-off, climb on course to 5000 ft at normal power, cruise at long range speeds at altitude for best range but not less than 5000 ft. Range free allowances include 5 minutes normal power fuel consumption for warm-up and take-off, 5% initial fuel load for landing reserve, plus 30 minutes fuel for long range speeds at sea level.

SUPPLEMENTAL
Loading and Performance - Typical Mission

CONDITIONS			BASIC MISSION
TAKE-OFF WEIGHT	(lb)		173,000
Fuel at 6.0 lb/gal (grade 115/145)	(lb)		69,615
Military load (Bombs)	(lb)		10,000
Wing loading	(lb/sq ft)		100.5
Stall speed (power off, land. config.)	(kn)	①	119
Take-off ground run at SL	(ft)	③③③③	5050
Take-off to clear 50 ft	(ft)		7050
Rate of climb at SL	(fpm)		623
Time: SL to 10,000 ft	(min)		18.0
Time: SL to 20,000 ft	(min)		43.0
Service ceiling (100 fpm)	(ft)	③	24,000
COMBAT RANGE	(n. mi.)		4258
Average speed	(kn)		206
Initial cruising altitude	(ft)		10,000
Final cruising altitude	(ft)		25,000
Total mission time	(hr)		20.20
COMBAT RADIUS	(n. mi.)		2246
Average speed	(kn)		225
Initial cruising altitude	(ft)		10,000
Bombing altitude	(ft)		25,000
Bomb run speed	(kn)	⑤	313
Final cruising altitude	(ft)		25,000
Total mission time	(hr)		20.22
COMBAT WEIGHT	(lb)	④	123,100
Combat altitude	(ft)	②	25,000
Combat speed	(kn)	②	330
Combat climb	(fpm)	②	1610
Combat ceiling (500 fpm)	(ft)	③	35,500
Service ceiling (100 fpm)	(ft)	③	36,700
Service ceiling (one engine out)	(ft)	①	30,600
Max rate of climb at SL	(fpm)	②	2165
Max speed at 30,500 ft	(kn)		335
LANDING WEIGHT	(lb)		96,866
Ground roll at SL	(ft)		1300
Total from 50 ft	(ft)		2370

1. Military Specification MIL-C-5011A dated 5 November 1951 redefines the combat radius to ground rules coordinated by the major USAF Air Commands and the Bureau of Aeronautics, U. S. Navy. Although in most cases the mission radius is reduced, this was considered to be more realistic based on Mission Profiles and Allowances proven in actual operation.

2. The combat radius for MIL-C-5011A is different from that based on MIL-C-5011 in that:

   a. Run into and out from the target area for high altitude bomber is at higher altitudes rather than at a specified altitude. This altitude corresponds to the cruise ceiling at the start of the combat zone, 500 n. mi. prior to target for reciprocating aircraft.

   b. Reserves are changed from a constant percentage of initial fuel as in MIL-C-5011 to a value equal to 5% of initial fuel load plus fuel for a specified period of 30 minutes long range at sea level.

   c. Combat range values are not quoted in MIL-C-5011A.

3. Certain items of performance quoted for MIL-C-5011A are different from those based on MIL-C-5011 in that:

   a. Time to climb values consider the effects of weight reduction during ground operation and climb.

   b. Average cruising speed does not include time and distance in climbs or target operation at normal power.

   c. Combat altitude is the altitude at which the actual target run is conducted.

   d. Basic speed is the maximum level flight speed within all operating limitations at the combat weight and at a specified altitude. This basic speed is quoted as a means of direct comparison of aircraft of similar type.

NOTES
① Take-off power
② Max power
③ Normal power
④ For Radius Mission

PERFORMANCE BASIS:
(a) Data source: Flight Tests

Boeing B-52 Stratofortress

Boeing B-52D-1-BW in flight.
Source: U.S. Air Force

Despite the phenomenal range and carrying capacity of the B-36, it was essentially a product of the design art available in the late 1930s. Indeed, in many respects it employed earlier technology than the B-29 and B-50. For all its virtues, the B-36 could only be an interim aircraft that would provide an intercontinental capability until an aircraft that reflected wartime experience and the greatly advanced state of design art was available. That aircraft would become the B-52. More than 60 years after the prototype B-52 first flew, the aircraft is still the backbone of the U.S. strategic bomber fleet, and is now painted an overall low-visibility gray. Those who face the B-52 in air defense exercises are still warned to "never underestimate the Gray Lady."

The Boeing XB-52 was conceived in June 1945 in response to an examination by the Air Materiel Command of the characteristics required of a new generation of post-war bombers. The huge cost of seizing forward bases for B-29 operations against Japan had appalled U.S. strategists and resulted in a general consensus that reliance on such bases should be minimized. In essence, this meant that the 1942 decision to move from AWPD-1 to AWPD-42 was reversed and that any requirements for a post-war long-range strategic bomber would include the ability to carry out its mission without relying on advanced or intermediate bases controlled by other countries.

The B-36 Replacement

As Air Materiel Command continued its deliberations, a specification for a second-generation intercontinental bomber to replace the Convair B-36 began to hold center stage. This called for a bomber with an operating radius of 5,000 miles and a cruising speed of 300 mph at 34,000 feet. The aircraft was to be capable of a maximum speed of 450 mph. This requirement showed the influence of both the B-29 and the B-36 in that it included a heavy defensive armament based around an unspecified number of turrets for 20mm cannon. On the other hand, the influence of nuclear weapons was already evident, with the bomb load being specified as 10,000 pounds; in other words, a single nuclear weapon.

In February 1946, a Request for Proposals was issued to the aviation industry based on the characteristics laid down the previous November. Boeing, Glenn L Martin Company and Consolidated-Vultee Aircraft Corp all responded with preliminary design and cost data. The Boeing design was regarded as having the most promise and was selected for further development.

The original Boeing design was essentially an enlarged, six-engined B-29 using Wright XT35 Typhoon turboprop engines, each offering 5,500 shaft horsepower and driving six-bladed propellers. Jet engines had been briefly considered but rejected because their demand for fuel precluded achieving the range requirement. The aircraft envisioned was huge. Its wingspan was 221 feet, only slightly smaller than the B-36's, with a total wing area of 3,250 square feet. The proposed aircraft had the same overall length as the B-36 and featured a similar circular-section fuselage. It is hard to see this XB-52 as being anything other than a turboprop-powered B-36 with most of its huge bomb capacity replaced by fuel. Even so, Boeing was awarded a contract to produce a mock-up of its proposed design and perform the preliminary engineering work.

Performance Inadequate

Dissatisfaction with the Boeing concept started to develop very early despite its selection in the 1946 competition. It was too large and expensive for an aircraft that offered few performance advantages over the B-36. The real problem was that it had very little growth potential and would never be much more than it was at the time. Boeing tried to reduce size and cost by going to a four-turboprop design, but the losses in performance were far greater than could be justified by the savings in cost. Gen. Curtis LeMay, then Deputy Chief of Air Staff for Research and Development, was adamant that the aircraft in its revised form was not good enough. General LeMay believed that in order to be a viable heavy bomber, the B-52 needed a higher cruising speed and longer range.

In fact, at this point Boeing was at a dead end. The aircraft the company had designed simply could not achieve the performance levels demanded. A radical rethink was needed if the entire B-52 program was to avoid cancellation. Boeing designers produced a new design with a sharply tapered wing that showed 20 degrees of sweepback. The aircraft was still powered by four XT-35 turboprops. A major change was the adoption of a centerline landing gear underneath the fuselage similar to that fitted to the B-47, plus a set of outrigger wheels that retracted into the outer engine nacelles. The speed of the aircraft was creeping up at last and now reached an estimated 445 mph.

Unfortunately, this improvement had come too late. Aircraft performance had increased significantly in the two years that had passed since the original specification was laid down, and the levels of performance demanded then were no longer adequate. A Heavy Bombardment Committee had been established to explore alternative specifications. The committee came to the conclusion that speed and altitude were the most crucial elements for a bomber to evade enemy defenses and deliver an atomic bomb to a target. This conclusion led to a new set of criteria that specified a range of 8,000 miles and a cruising speed of 550 mph. These new requirements were officially issued in December 1947. As an interim stage, the cruising speed requirement was lowered to only 500 mph. That didn't change the fact that the proposed B-52 was still 50 mph short of even the interim target. Once again, the B-52 was on the verge of cancellation.

Boeing responded by producing a new design in which the turboprops drove coaxial propellers. Every possible way of saving weight was exploited, and the overall size of the aircraft was reduced. By the time they had finished, the Boeing engineers had produced a design with a maximum speed estimated at 500 mph at 41,000 feet. Much more impressively, its maximum range was 11,635 miles. Although they had no means of knowing it at the time, their rivals at the Tupolev Design Bureau were putting the finishing touches on a very similar design that would become the famous Tu-95 "Bear."

Jets Replace Turboprops

The extremely long range of the design was the key to the final step in the design process. The Air Force had always been interested in jet power for long-range bombers, but the high fuel consumption of the jets then available had ruled them out. However, the fuel capacity of the Boeing design was so great that it was thought it might be able to provide the necessary range when coupled with a new generation of more fuel-efficient engines. When the Boeing engineers arrived to present the latest iteration of their turboprop-powered bomber, they were given a weekend to produce a jet-powered version. The resulting design had eight J57 engines in the podded arrangement first used on the B-47. The angle of wing sweep was increased to 35 degrees and the wing area was increased by 1,400 square feet to 4,000 square feet. Estimated maximum speed was 565 mph at 46,500 feet, and combat radius with a 10,000-pound bomb load was estimated at 3,550 miles.

Only one more change remained to be made before construction of prototypes would start. It seemed quite likely that early versions of the J57 would not offer the fuel economy specified and that the B-52 would fall short of range requirements as a result. General LeMay, now the commander of Strategic Air Command, was thoroughly convinced of the virtues of the B-52. He asserted that the answer to the range problem lay in engine development and that it was unnecessary to accept inferior performance in either speed or range. Boeing provided an insurance policy by inserting a 22-foot plug in the fuselage for additional fuel.

After a final series of analysis of alternatives, the decision to build the prototypes was made. The first of these was ready in late 1951, by which time the decision to commit to mass production had already been made. The XB-52 had a crew of five, with the pilot and copilot seated in tandem under a B-47- style canopy. General LeMay did not favor this arrangement and preferred side-by-side cockpit seating, since this allowed more room for flight instrumentation and permitted the copilot to be a better assistant to the pilot. In August 1951 it was decided that the Air Force would adopt the side-by-side arrangement for production B-52s. Only two prototype aircraft, the XB-52 and YB-52, would retain the tandem seating.

Ground testing of the first prototype continued until a hydraulic system failure caused extensive damage to the wing trailing edges. The aircraft was rolled back into the Boeing plant for repair. As a result, the XB-52 did not become airborne until nearly a year later, and it was the second prototype, the YB-52, that was actually the first to get airborne – on April 15, 1952.

Initial Production

The initial production contract for the B-52 was awarded in February 1951. This called for the procurement of 13 B-52As to act as pre-production service test and evaluation aircraft. The B-52A differed from the X/YB-52 in having the completely redesigned forward fuselage demanded by General LeMay. The B-47-style bubble canopy and tandem seating arrangement for pilot and copilot were replaced by a side-by-side arrangement. In order to accommodate a more capable avionics suite and an extra crew member, the forward fuselage was lengthened by 21 inches. This meant that the B-52 now had a crew of six. The B-52A was capable of carrying an external tank on each outboard wing, although the tanks were rarely mounted. The aircraft was also fitted with an in-flight refueling system capable of receiving fuel from tankers fitted with the boom-type system.

In any event, the order was reduced from 13 aircraft to three in June 1952. The other 10 were reprogrammed as B-52Bs. The first B-52A was rolled out in March 1954 and made its first flight five months later. After service testing was completed, the three B-52A aircraft were used to test improvements planned for later B-52 models.

The outward appearance of the B-52B was identical to that of the B-52A. The primary difference was that the B-52B featured a fully operational bombing/navigation system, while the RB-52B variant was equipped with enhanced reconnaissance equipment. This consisted of a two-man pressurized capsule installed in the bomb bay which could perform electronic countermeasures or photographic reconnaissance work. The pod could be installed in about four hours.

A total of 50 B-52Bs were built, with 23 being pure bomber B-52Bs and 27 being dual-capable reconnaissance/bomber RB-52Bs. In fact, the difference between the two subtypes was nominal and, without its pod installed, the RB-52B was fully strike-capable.

The 50 B-52Bs were followed by another small production batch of 35 B-52C aircraft. These differed from the B-25B in that the 1,000-gallon underwing fuel tanks of the B-52A and B were replaced by 3,000-gallon tanks. This increased the total fuel capacity to 41,700 U.S. gallons. The B-52C was capable of carrying the multimission reconnaissance-observation pod designed for the RB-52B, but the aircraft retained its bomber designation.

The B-52Cs were followed by the first large-scale production model of the B-52, the B-52D. Production of this variant totaled 170 aircraft, delivered between June 1956 and November 1957. The B-52D was almost identical to the B-52C, with the only differences being the adoption of the MD-9 fire control system and elimination of the reconnaissance capability, the B-52D being built exclusively for the long-range bombing role.

The nature of the bombing mission was about to undergo a profound change just as the B-52Ds started to enter service. During the late 1950s, there was a worldwide perception that the rapid development of surface-to-air missiles would render manned combat aircraft obsolete. In Great Britain this led to the infamous 1957 defense review headed by Duncan Sandys that effectively put an end to the development of advanced combat aircraft in favor of missiles. In the United States, it appeared as if the growing capability of Soviet air defenses would make high-altitude operations with the B-52 increasingly hazardous in the future.

In response to this developing threat, SAC made a policy decision switch to low-altitude operations. Skimming in at altitudes of less than 500 feet would make the B-52 much harder to detect and engage. In addition, the basic limitations of Soviet radar and missile technology seemed to make the Soviet defenses far less reliable when engaging low-flying targets. As a result of this switch in operational concepts, it was decided that all B-52s except the early B-52Bs would now have to be capable of penetrating enemy defenses at low altitude. This involved modifying the B-52Ds with terrain-following radar, an improved bombing/navigation system, and Doppler radar, and with provision for carrying the AGM-28 Hound Dog cruise missile. What had appeared to be a relatively simple conversion rapidly became complex and costly.

As experience with low-level missions accumulated, it became apparent that the stress on the airframe was much greater than anticipated. Preventing catastrophic failures initially required strengthening the fuselage bulkhead and aileron bay, and reinforcing boost pump panels and wing foot splice plates. These changes were followed by additional repairs to upper wing splices inboard of the inner engine pods, reinforcement of the lower wing panels supporting both the inner and outer engine pods, and modifications to the upper-wing-surface fuel probe access doors and the lower portion of the fuselage bulkhead.

The Vietnam War

As the U.S. involvement in the Vietnam War steadily grew, the Air Force decided to convert most of its B-52Ds to conventional warfare capability for service in Southeast Asia. Numerous B-52Fs had already seen some service in Vietnam, and their ability to unload large tonnages of bombs in support of ground operations had become a valued tactical option. The plan was to use the older B-52D to build on this capability. The primary requirement was to carry a significantly larger load of conventional bombs than the B-52F could manage. This led to the Big Belly project that increased the internal bomb capacity to a maximum of 84 500-pound or 42 750-pound bombs. This was an internal change achieved by changing the arrangement of the bomb bay shackles. In addition, another 24 500-pound or 750-pound bombs could be carried on the underwing racks originally designed to carry Hound Dog cruise missiles. These were fitted with I-beam rack adapters and a pair of multiple ejection racks, bringing the maximum payload to 60,000 pounds of bombs. One cannot help but wonder if those planning this modification program found themselves missing the B-36 with its cavernous bomb bay and huge load-carrying capability.

As the intensity of the air war over Vietnam picked up, the B-52Ds were given a major electronic warfare upgrade. The passive warning part of this outfit included an ALR-18 automated set-on receiving set, an ALR-20 panoramic receiver set, and an APR-25 radar homing and warning system. The active jamming suite included four ALT-6B or ALT-22 continuous wave jamming transmitters, two ALT-16 barrage-jamming systems, and two ALT-32H and one ALT-32L high- and low-band jamming sets. Finally, the aircraft were equipped with six ALE-20 flare dispensers and eight ALE-24 chaff dispensers. Ironically, this was a far superior fit than was provided to the aircraft tasked with penetrating Soviet air defenses.

In 1972, after seven years of operations, the B-52s were turned loose against North Vietnam. A full-scale aerial assault on North Vietnam air bases, missile sites, oil storage facilities, ammunition dumps and railroad networks commenced. For the first time, targets in and around Hanoi and Haiphong would be attacked by the B-52s. Unfortunately, strict rules of engagement were enforced to lessen the risk of hitting civilian areas. These included prohibiting B-52s from maneuvering to evade SAMs or fighters once they had passed the initial point and were approaching the bomb release point. The B-52s had to fly on the same routes, at the same speed, and at the same altitudes. Inevitably the initial losses were heavy, with three B-52s being lost on the first night and no fewer than six on the second night. Yet, as the bombing offensive continued, cracks started to appear in the defenses. By the end of the bombing campaign, several hundred SAMs had been fired at B-52s, shooting down a total of nine B-52Ds and six B-52Gs. Onboard ECM equipment provided growing protection, with the North Vietnamese eventually resorting to firing their missiles in unguided salvoes. The overall loss rate of the B-52s was 2 percent when facing what was undoubtedly the most heavily defended target in the world. All the B-52s lost were shot down by SAMs, and none by fighters or anti-aircraft artillery (AAA). Five MiGs were claimed by B-52 tail gunners, but only two of them were actually confirmed.

Continuing Development

The B-52D was replaced on the production lines by the B-52E. This differed from the D model primarily in having the modifications for the low-altitude mission incorporated from scratch rather than installed as retrofits. A more sophisticated bombing and navigation suite, the ASQ-38, was fitted to the B-52E and to subsequent B-52 models. A total of 100 B-52Es were built. They were followed by 89 B-52Fs that differed only in having 11,200-pound-thrust J57-P-43W, -P-43WA, or -P-43WB turbojets.

The primary next model of the B-52 represented the first major redesign of the aircraft since the adoption of side-by-side seating with the B-52A. Design work on the B-52G started in June 1956 when the Convair B-58 Hustler program was suffering grave difficulties. The institution of an insurance policy was a sensible precaution aimed at preventing technical obsolescence of the strategic bomber force in the 1960s.

The primary objective of the redesign was to improve performance by reducing weight. Much had been learned about the aerodynamics of large structures since the basic design of the B-52 had been completed, and this was leveraged to produce the new design. Different materials were used in the construction of the airframe, and the wing structure was extensively redesigned. The rubber bladder-type tanks in the wings were removed and a new wing incorporating integrated fuel tanks was adopted. This meant the B-52G could carry 48,030 gallons of fuel, as opposed to the 41,553 gallons of the B-52F. The new wing also discarded use of ailerons and the B-52G depended on its spoilers for lateral control. The jettisonable 3,000-gallon underwing auxiliary fuel tanks were replaced by smaller, fixed 700-gallon tanks. These were rarely used to carry fuel, but their presence helped prevent wing flutter. They were also used to carry the crew's personal baggage.

In the fuselage, the tail gunner was moved from his position in the extreme rear of the aircraft to a new location beside the electronic warfare officer. The tail itself was dramatically changed, being reduced in height by 8 feet, but its chord widened to provide similar area. With extensive changes to the wings, fuselage and tail all being made, the B-52G was effectively a new aircraft. It is rumored that the aircraft was to have been the B-74, a designation that is officially unassigned, but was changed to B-52 because a modification of an existing aircraft would be easier to fund than a new design. This has never been confirmed, but the possibility would be an interesting reversal of the B-29/B-50 situation. Be that as it may, the B-52G was the most produced version of the B-52G, with 193 being delivered.

In the years that followed its service introduction, the improvements that had been instituted with the B-52G were shown to have a decided negative side. The earliest to be noted was that the elimination of the ailerons, acting in conjunction with the shorter rudder, increased the tendency of the aircraft to Dutch roll. The elimination of the ailerons meant that when a turn was initiated, the rising of the spoilers would induce a slight buffet and cause pitch-up. This made aerial refueling more difficult and increased fatigue when flying the aircraft.

Experience in Vietnam exposed further flaws. The integral fuel tanks and lighter structure made the B-52G suffer more severely from battle damage than the older B-52D had, and several G models were lost to damage that a D model would probably have survived. The elimination of the tail gunner's position was also a disadvantage, since it was found that the tail gunner sitting right aft had been an invaluable look-out for SAMs.

The B-52G was replaced on the production lines by the final variant of the family, the B-52H. In this variant, the water-injected J57 turbojet engines of the G model were replaced by Pratt & Whitney TF33-P-3 turbofans, and a 20mm M-61 Gatling gun was installed in the rear turret, replacing the four 0.5-inch machine guns previously mounted there. The new engines are much more economical than the old J57s, and have an improved combat radius with a 10,000-pound bomb load – from the 3,550 nautical miles of the J57s to 4,176 nautical miles. A total of 102 B-52H aircraft were built. The last B-52H was delivered to the 4136th Strategic Wing at Minot AFB on October 26, 1962, bringing production of the B-52 to an end.

Withdrawal from Service

The first proposals for withdrawing B-52s from service came in 1965, when Defense Secretary Robert Strange McNamara announced a phase-out program that could see the B-52Bs and B-52Cs retired along with all B-58 Hustlers and several subsequent B-52 models. The phased-out bombers were to be replaced by General Dynamics FB-111s. By this time, the B-52Bs and Cs were operating primarily as trainers and hacks, so their loss was not of major concern. The escalating demands of the Vietnam War and the diversion of B-52Ds to that theater meant that the retirement of the B-52Ds in question took longer than expected, and most of them remained flying until the type was withdrawn. The B-52Ds were to have been retired by 1971, but because they could carry much larger conventional bomb loads than other versions of the B-52, they were considered too valuable to lose. The B-52Ds remained in service much longer than expected, and the last of the type were retired in 1982-83. By that time, the B-52Es and B-52Fs had already been retired, the E models leaving service in 1969-70 and the F model in 1977-78.

Thus, by the mid-1980s, the B-52 fleet consisted only of the surviving B-52Gs and B-52Hs. Retirement of the B-52G began in the late 1980s, but the outbreak of the 1990-91 Gulf War put a temporary end to the process. The capability of the B-52 was demonstrated on February 16, 1991. That day, seven B-52Gs armed with 39 AGM-86C conventionally armed cruise missiles took off from Barksdale AFB. They refueled in mid-air twice before launching 35 of their air-launched cruise missiles (ALCMs) against targets in central and southern Iraq. The missiles struck their targets nearly simultaneously, scoring 33 hits and two misses. The B-52Gs then returned to Barksdale after having been in the air for 35 hours. Until very recently, this was the longest-ranging combat mission in the history of aerial warfare.

When the Gulf War ended, the decommissioning of the B-52G fleet was resumed. By the end of 1993, there were only a couple of dozen B-52Gs still flying. The last B-52G was retired in the spring of 1994. As of April 2011, 94 of the original 102 B-52H aircraft were still operational within the U.S. Air Force (85 Air Force and 9 Air Force Reserve). Some projections have these aircraft remaining in service until 2045. After all, *never* underestimate the Gray Lady.

The Gray Lady. Boeing B-52H-140-BW
Source: U.S. Air Force

Characteristics Summary

BOMBER — XB-52

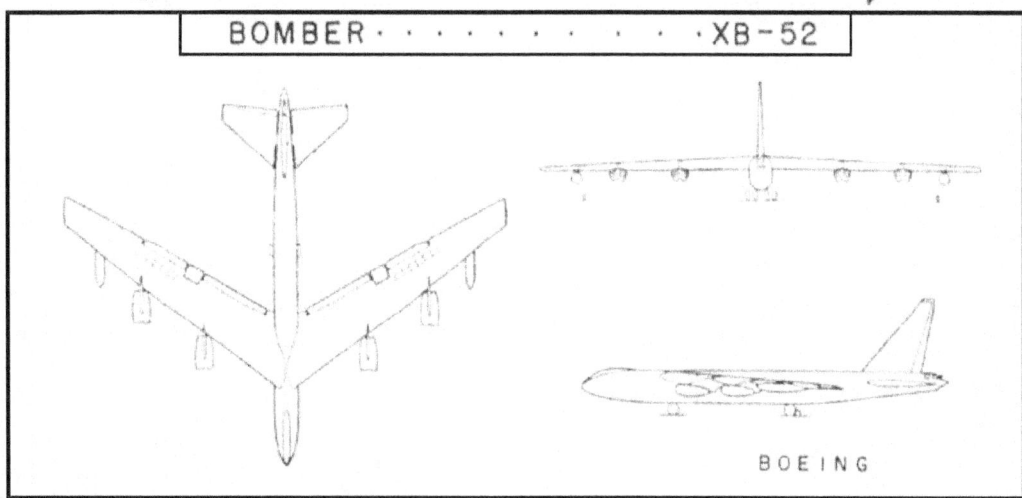

BOEING

Wing area .... 4000 sq ft   Length .... 152.7 ft

Span .... 185.0 ft   Height .... 48.25 ft

STATUS

The XB-52 passed through 4 preliminary design stages before the present configuration was decided upon as follows:

Date	Boeing Model No.	Gross Wt.(lb)	Power Plant
28 Jun 1946	462	360,000	(6) T35-1
7 Jan 1947	464-22	480,000	(4) T35-3
8 Dec 1947	464-35	280,000	(4) T35-5
27 Oct 1948	464-49	330,000	(8) YJ57-P-3
29 Mar 1950	464-67	390,000	(8) XJ57-P-1
6 Oct 1950	464-67	390,000 (W/O ATO)	(8) J57-P-(?)

Currrent development is as follows:

Present Design Initiated: .... 27 Oct 1948
Mock-up Inspection: .... 26 Apr 1949
Engine Nacelle Mock-up Inspection: .... 14 Jun 1950
First Flight (1st article): .... Oct 1951 (est)
First Flight (2nd article): .... Dec 1951 (est)

POWER PLANT

The first and second aircraft will be powered with (8) YJ57-P-3 engines (8700 lb max thrust/SLS). These engines will subsequently be modified to give the following thrust ratings: MAX and MILITARY, 9250 lb (with variable area nozzle) and 9000 lb (with fixed area nozzle); NORMAL, 8700 lb. These ratings were used for performance shown in this chart, however, the model designation for this model designation for this modified engine is undetermined. Further plans call for the addition of water injection and overspeed to increase take-off thrust. Consideration of future addition of a short type take-off afterburner is dependent upon effect on fuel specifics.

Liquid ATO used for performance is 39,000 lb thrust for 60 seconds. This will be reduced to 20,000 lb ATO when water injection becomes available.

FEATURES

Crew: 5
Auto. Cabin Pressurization
E-4 (mod.) Auto-Pilot
Bomb-Navig. Radar, K1A
Fire Control System, A3
Quadricycle Landing Gear
Vertical Camera Station
Deceleration Parachute
Aerodynamic Spoilers (air brake)
ATO (liquid): 30,000# thrust
Max Fuel Cap: 38,270 gal
 (incl. fuel for ATO)

ARMAMENT

Turrets: 1
Guns: 2x.50 cal
Ammunition (tot.):   1200 rds
Max Bomb Load: *25,000 lb
Max Bomb Size: *25,000 lb
*Space provisions only

Characteristics Summary Basic Mission · · · · XB-52

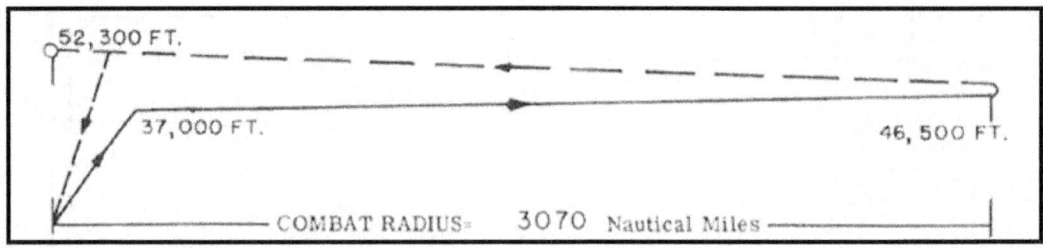

COMBAT RADIUS = 3070 Nautical Miles

PERFORMANCE

COMBAT RADIUS	COMBAT RANGE	COMBAT SPEED
3070 naut. mi with 10,000 lb payload at 451 knots avg. in 13.6 hours.	**6095** naut. mi with 10,000 lb payload at 454 knots avg. in 13.4 hours.	**516** knots at 35,000 ft alt, max power
		MAXIMUM SPEED
		531 knots at 20,000 ft alt, max power
CLIMB	**CEILING**	**TAKE-OFF**
2400 fpm sea level, take-off weight normal power	**39,500** ft 100 fpm, take-off weight normal power	ground run 7820 ft 4720 ft (e) no assist assisted
4550 fpm sea level, combat weight maximum power	**46,500** ft 500 fpm, combat weight maximum power	over 50 ft height 9700 ft 6220 ft (e) no assist assisted
LOAD	**WEIGHTS**	**STALLING SPEED**

Bombs: 10,000 lb
Ammo: 1200 rds/.50 cal
 	
Fuel: 36,540 gal
  protected 70 %
  droppable 5 %
  external 5 %
	Empty..... 155,200 lb
	Combat... 256,800 lb
	Take-off 390,000 lb
	limited by strength
		127 knots
		flaps down, take-off weight

		TIME TO CLIMB
		—

NOTES

1. PERFORMANCE BASIS:
   (a) Estimated data
   (b) Fuel density: 6.0 lb/gal
   (c) In computing Radius and Range, specific fuel consumptions have been increased 5% to allow for variation of fuel flow in service aircraft.
   (d) Performance based on max thrust of 9250 lb (variable area nozzle) and normal of 8700 lb (fixed area).
   (e) With 30,000 lb thrust ATO (liquid), 60 sec. duration
2. REVISION BASIS: Reissue

Standard Aircraft Characteristics

XB-52

Boeing

EIGHT J57-P-( )
PRATT & WHITNEY

BY AUTHORITY OF
COMMANDING GENERAL
AIR MATERIEL COMMAND
U. S. AIR FORCE

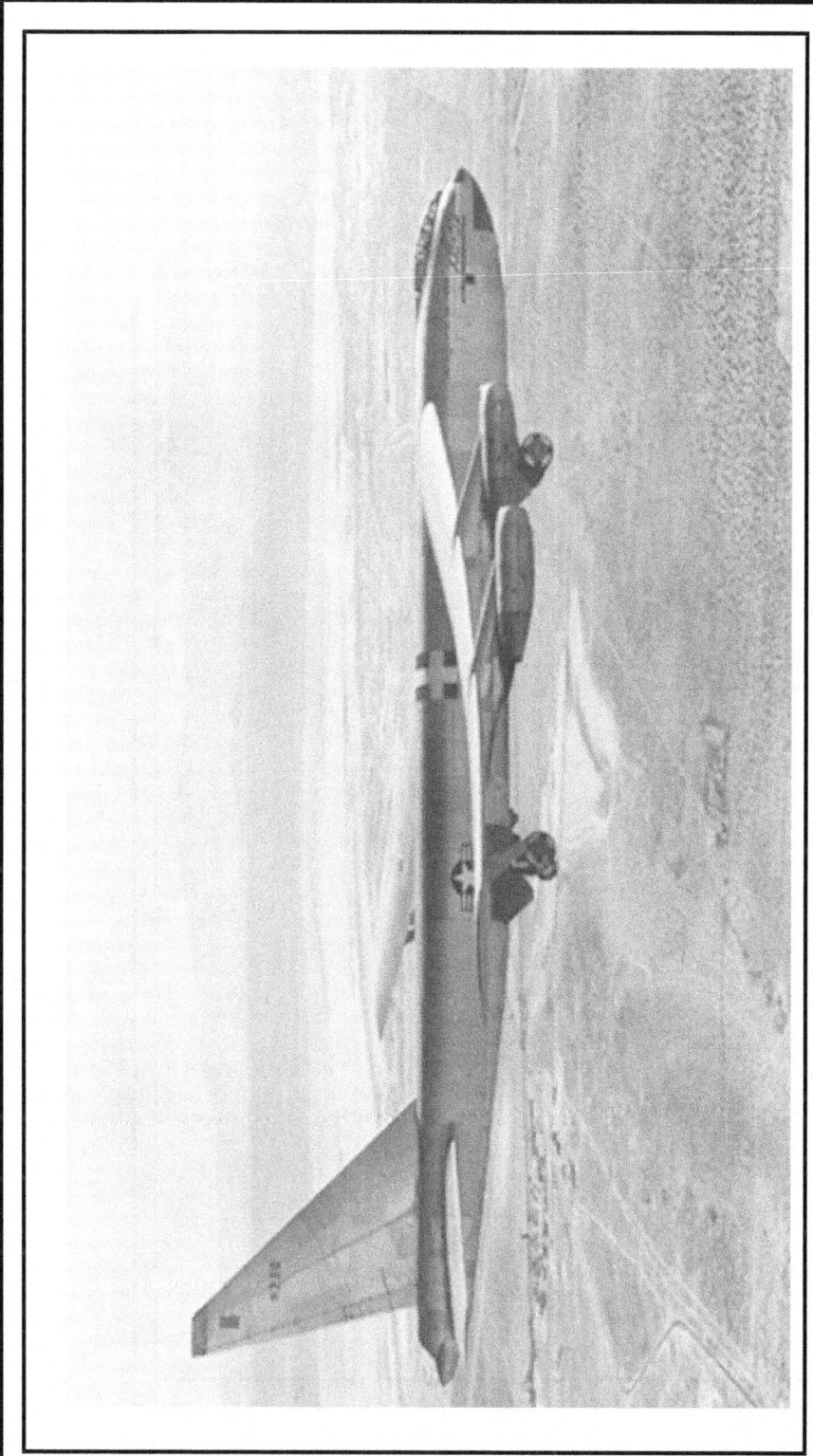

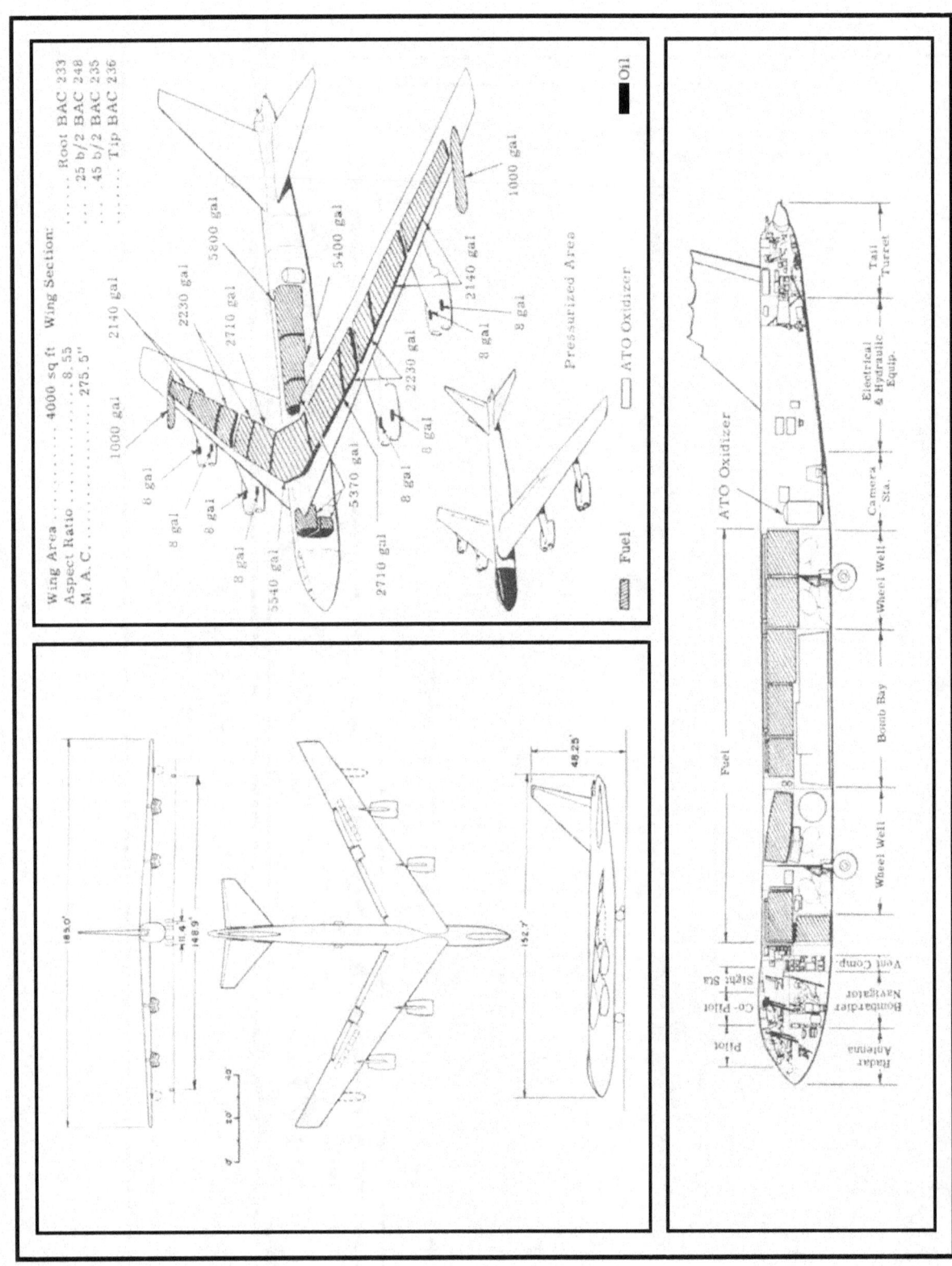

WEIGHTS

Loading	Lb	L.F.
Empty	155,200(E)	
Basic	156,700(E)	
Design	390,000	
Combat	*256,800	
Max T.O.	†390,000	2.0
Max Land	270,000	

(E) Estimated
* For Basic Mission
† Limited by strength (W/O expendable weight of liquid ATO)

FUEL

Location	No. Tanks	Gal
Wg*	4	9880
Wg	3	9820
Fus*	3	16,570
Wg. drop	2	2000**
*Self-sealing	Total	38,270**

**Includes ATO fuel

Grade......... JP-3 or 100/130

OIL

Capacity (gal)......... 64
Grade......... 1010

ELECTRONICS

UHF Command	AN/ARC-27
Liaison	AN/ARC-25A
Interphone	USAF Combat
Bombing-Navig. Radar	K-1A
Loran	AN/APN-9A
IFF	AN/APX-6
Fire Control System	A-3
Glide Path	AN/ARN-5B
Omni-Direct. Recvr	AN/ARN-14
ECM	*AN/APQ-27
Radar Beacon	*AN/APN-12

*Space provisions only

Mission and Description

The XB-52 is a long range, high altitude, high speed, heavy bomber designed for the destruction of surface targets.

The normal crew of five(5) consists of: Pilot, Co-Pilot-Flight Engineer; (2) Bombardier-Navigator-Weaponiers, Gunner-Radio Operator.

This aircraft resembles the B-47 and is equipped with a quadricycle main gear and wing-tip protecting gear. Automatic cabin pressurization and conditioning is provided for all operations. A liquid oxygen system is provided for crew use. The tail contains provisions for liquid rocket assisted take-off and a deceleration parachute. Control throughout the speed range from limit dive speed to landing speed is obtained by using spoilers, ailerons, and flaps on the wing, a moveable horizontal stabilizer, and conventional tail surfaces. The spoilers may also be used as airbrakes permitting descent from 55,000 feet to sea level at end of mission in approximately three minutes with gear down.

Development

The XB-52 passed through 4 preliminary design stages before the present configuration was decided upon as shown in the following table:

Date	Boeing Model No.	Gross Wt. (lb)	Power Plant
28 Jun 1946	462	360,000	(6) T35-1
7 Jan 1947	464-22	480,000	(4) T35-3
8 Dec 1947	464-35	280,000	(4) T35-5
27 Oct 1948	464-40	330,000	(8) YJ57-P-3
29 Mar 1950	464-67	390,000	(8) XJ57-P-1
6 Oct 1950	464-67	390,000 (W/O ATO)	(8) J57-P-(?)

Current development is as follows:

Present Design Initiated:	27 Oct 1948
Mock-up Inspection:	26 Apr 1949
Engine Nacelle Mock-up Inspection:	14 Jun 1950
First Flight (1st article):	Oct 1951 (est)
First Flight (2nd article):	Dec 1951 (est)

POWER PLANT

The first and second aircraft will be powered with (8) YJ57-P-3 engines (8700 lb max thrust/SLS). These engines will subsequently be modified to give the following thrust ratings: MAX and MILITARY, 9250 lb (with variable area nozzle) and 9000 lb (with fixed area nozzle); NORMAL 8700 lb. These ratings were used for performance shown in this chart, however, the model designation for this modified engine is undetermined. Further plans call for the addition of water injection and overspeed to increase take-off thrust. Consideration of future addition of a short type take-off afterburner is dependent upon effect on fuel specifics.

Liquid ATO used for performance is 30,000 lb thrust for 60 seconds. This will be reduced to 20,000 lb thrust ATO when water injection becomes available.

BOMBS

No.	Size	Type
1	25,000"	T-28E2
1	22,000"	T-40
1	13,000"	VB-13
1	12,000"	W-109
8	2000	G.P.
12	1000	G.P.
16	500	G.P.

*Space provisions only

Note: Overall dimensions of the irregular shaped bomb bay are 6'x6'x27' (approx.)

GUNS

No.	Cal.	Rds.vs.	Location
2	.50	600	Tail tur.

CAMERAS

(alternate installations)

No.	Type	Lens
1	K-17C	6", 12" or 24"
1	K-22A	6", 12" or 24"
1	K-37	12"
1	K-38	24" or 36"

DIMENSIONS

Wing	
Span	185.0'
Incidence (root)	6°
Dihedral (Chord plane)	2°30'
Sweepback (L.E.)	36°54'
Length	152.7'
Height	48.25'
Tread (outrigger)	148.9'
Tread (main gear)	11.4'

Loading and Performance - Typical Mission

CONDITIONS			BASIC MISSION	6000 LB BOMB MISSION
TAKE-OFF WEIGHT	⑧	(lb)	390,000	390,000
Fuel at 6.0 lb/gal(grade 100/130)		(lb)	219,240	223,398
Military load (Bombs)		(lb)	10,000	6000
Wing loading		(lb/sq ft)	97.5	97.5
Stall speed(power off, land. config.)		(kn)	127.0	127.0
Take-off ground run at SL	① ⑥	(ft)	7820	7820
Take-off ground run with ATO	①	(ft)	4720	4720
Take-off to clear 50 ft	① ⑥	(ft)	9700	9700
Take-off to clear 50 ft with ATO	①	(ft)	6220	6220
Rate of climb at SL	②	(fpm)	2400	2400
Time: SL to 30,000 ft	②	(min)	17.5	17.5
Time: SL to 37,000 ft	②	(min)	26.0	26.0
Service ceiling (100 fpm)	②	(ft)	39,500	39,500
Service ceiling (one engine out)		(ft)	⑤	⑤
COMBAT RANGE	③	(n. mi.)	6095	6265
Average speed		(kn)	454	454
Initial cruising altitude		(ft)	37,000	37,000
Final cruising altitude		(ft)	51,100	50,900
Total mission time		(hr)	13.4	13.85
COMBAT RADIUS	③	(n. mi.)	3070	3140
Average speed		(kn)	451	452
Initial cruising altitude		(ft)	37,000	37,000
Bombing altitude		(ft)	46,500	46,500
Bomb run speed		(kn)	480	480
Final cruising altitude	③	(ft)	52,300	52,100
Total mission time		(hr)	13.6	13.9
COMBAT WEIGHT	④	(lb)	256,800	259,000
Combat altitude		(ft)	35,000	46,300
Combat speed	①	(kn)	516	491
Combat climb	①	(fpm)	2150	300
Combat ceiling (500 fpm)	①	(ft)	46,500	46,300
Service ceiling (one engine out)	①	(ft)	49,900	49,500
Max rate of climb at SL	①	(fpm)	4550	⑤ 4550
Max speed at 20,000 ft	①	(kn)	531	531
LANDING WEIGHT		(lb)	180,300	181,000
Ground roll at SL		(ft)	2100	2100
Ground roll (auxiliary brake)	⑦	(ft)	1550	1550
Total from 50 ft		(ft)	2900	2900
Total from 50 ft (auxiliary brake)	⑦	(ft)	2300	2300

NOTES:
① Max power
② Normal power
③ Detailed descriptions of RADIUS & RANGE missions are given on page 6.
④ For Radius Mission radius is shown
⑤ Data not available
⑥ With 30,000 lb thrust ATO(60 sec.)
⑦ With drag chute
⑧ Does not include expendable weight of liquid ATO amounting to approximately 15,000 lb of oxidizer and gas.

PERFORMANCE BASIS:
(a) Data source: Estimates
(b) Performance is based on powers shown on page 6.

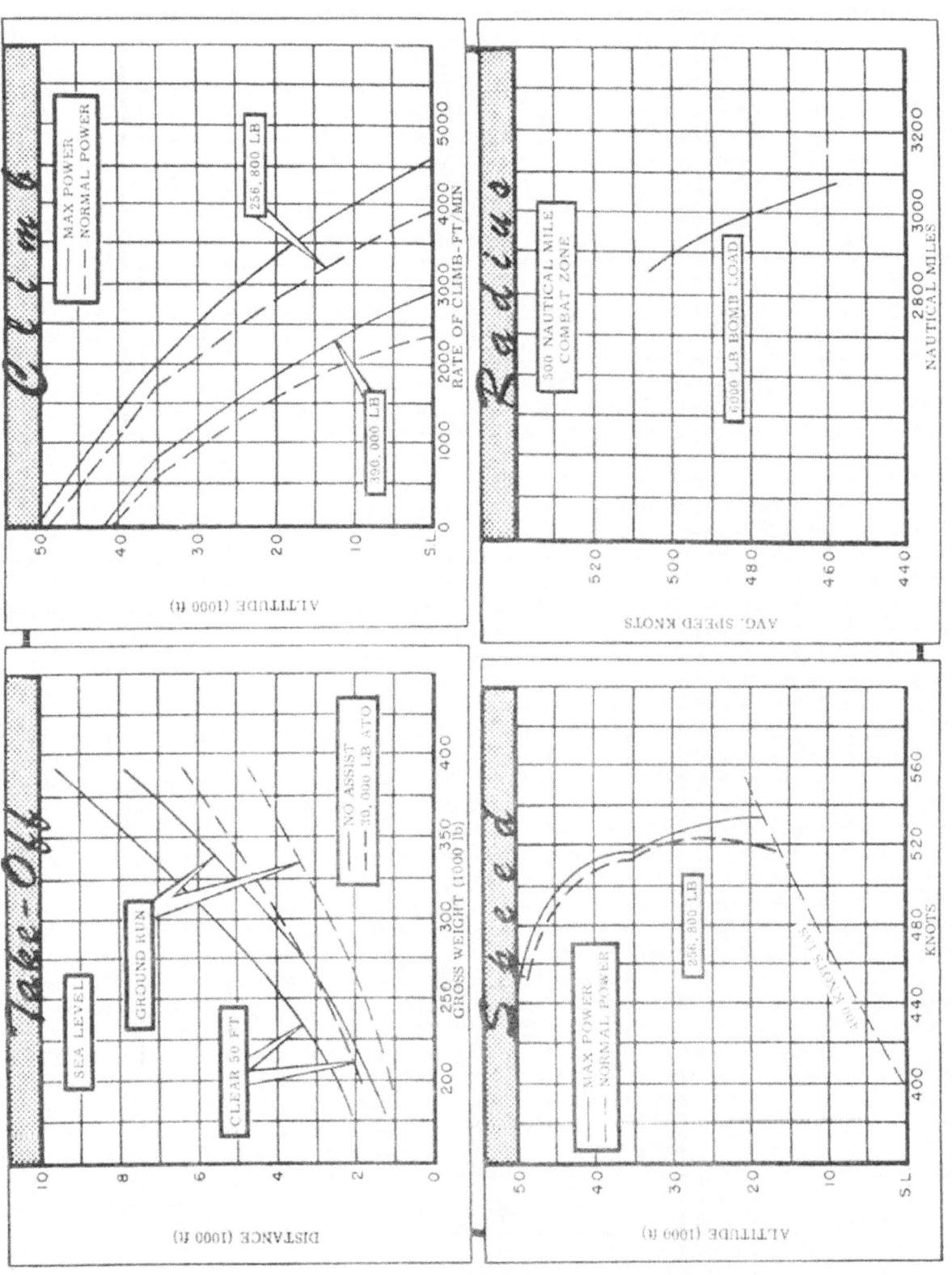

N O T E S

FORMULA: RADIUS MISSION I

Take-off, climb on course to 37,000 ft. altitude at aircraft speed for maximum rate of climb, cruise out at long range speeds increasing altitude with decreasing aircraft weight, make normal power bomb-run to target, conduct 6 minute normal power bomb-run, drop bombs, conduct normal power evasive action for 6 minutes, start cruise to home base at 46,500 ft. alt. arriving over home base at 52,300 ft. altitude. Range free allowances are: 5 minutes normal power fuel consumption for starting engines and take-off, plus 6 minutes normal power evasive action, plus 10% of initial fuel for reserve.

FORMULA: RANGE MISSION I

Same as outbound leg of the Basic Radius formula continued without dropping the bombs until 90% of the initial fuel has been used at 51,100 ft. alt., leaving 10% fuel reserve for combat, evasive action, landing reserve, or other considerations for which no distance credit is allowed.

FORMULA: RADIUS MISSION II

Same as the Basic Radius formula except 10,000 lb bomb is replaced by 6,000 lb bomb and additional fuel. Altitude at end of mission is 52,100 ft.

FORMULA: RANGE MISSION II

Same as Basic Range formula except 10,000 lb bomb is replaced with 6,000 lb bomb and additional fuel. Altitude at the end of the mission of 50,900 ft.

GENERAL DATA

(a) Data is based on estimates.

(b) Power values used in performance calculations are as follows:

S. L. Static	(8) J57-P-( )	
	LB	RPM
Max:	*9250	—
Nor:	8600	—
*With variable area nozzle		

Characteristics Summary

RECONNAISSANCE RB-52B

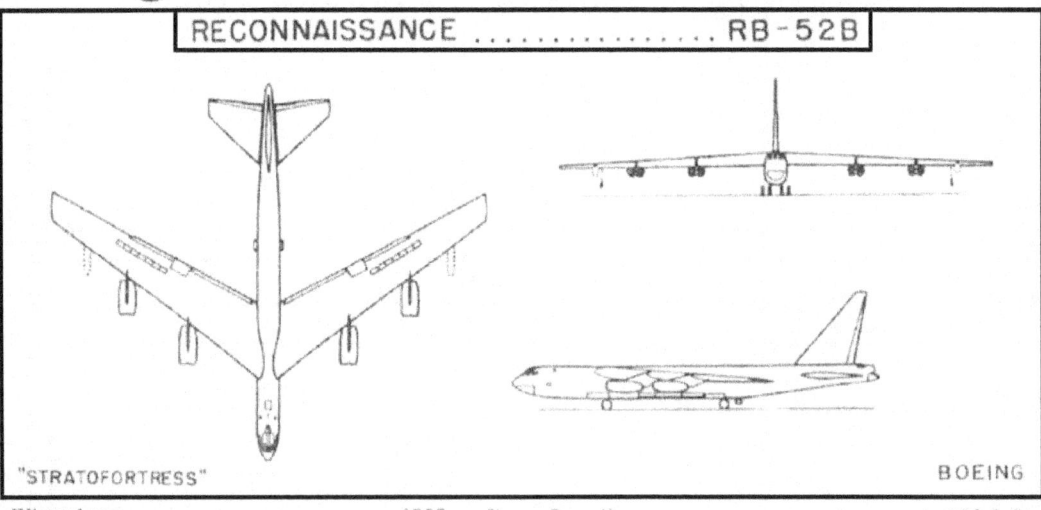

"STRATOFORTRESS"   BOEING

Wing Area .... 4000 sq ft	Length .... 156.5 ft
Span .... 185.0 ft	Height .... 48.3 ft

AVAILABILITY

Number available

ACTIVE	RESERVE	TOTAL

PROCUREMENT

Number to be delivered in fiscal years

STATUS

1. Design Initiated: Apr 52
2. First Flight: Dec 54 (est)
3. First Acceptance: Dec 54 (est)
4. The RB-52B (Reconnaissance Version) becomes an RB-52B (Bomber Version) when the capsule containing photographic, weather and electronic equipment is removed from the bomb bay.

Navy Equivalent: None   Mfr's Model: 464-201-1

POWER PLANT

(8) J57-P-1W
Pratt & Whitney
ENGINE RATINGS

S.L.S.   LB **RPM   MIN
Max: *11,100-6300 /9950-5
Mil: 9500-5950/9950-30
Nor: 8250-5700/9720 Cont

*Wet
**First figure represents low pressure spool, second figure represents high pressure spool.

ATO
No. & Model (4) 45KS5000
Mfr .... Aerojet
Thrust .... 4 x 5000
Duration (sec)............45

FEATURES

Crew: 8

Cabin Pressurization
Heating & Cooling
Deceleration Chute
Quadricycle Landing Gear
Interchangeable
  Reconnaissance Capsule
Vertical Camera Station
Steerable Landing Gear
K-3A Bombing - Nav. System
A-3A Fire Control System
Thermal Anti-icing

Max Fuel Capacity: 37,385 gal

ARMAMENT

Turret 1

Guns .... 4 x .50 cal (M-3)

Ammunition (tot).... 2400 rds

Max Flash Bombs:
            24 x M 120

Characteristics Summary Basic Mission RB-52B

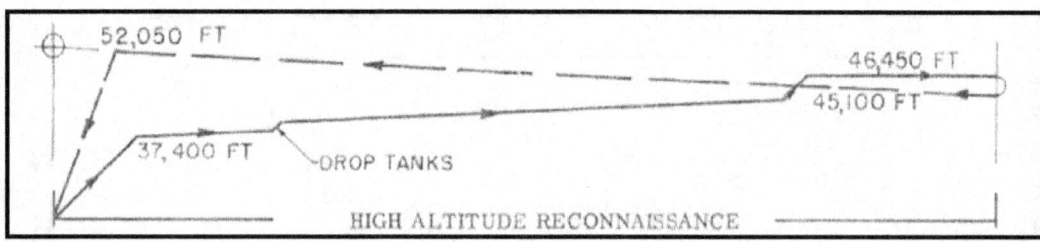

HIGH ALTITUDE RECONNAISSANCE

PERFORMANCE

COMBAT RADIUS	FERRY RANGE	SPEED
3095 naut. mi with 3700 lb payload at 457 knots avg. in 13.58 hours.	6235 naut. mi with 33,105 gal fuel at 457 knots avg. in 13.70 hours at 390,000 lb T.O. wt.	COMBAT 492 knots at 46,450 ft alt, max power MAX 542 knots at 19,500 ft alt, max power BASIC 517 knots at 35,000 ft alt, max power

CLIMB	CEILING	TAKE-OFF
2320 fpm sea level, take-off weight normal power	40,400 ft 100 fpm, take-off weight normal power	ground run 6040 ft no assist | 4600 ft assisted
4780 fpm sea level, combat weight maximum power	47,050 ft 500 fpm, combat weight maximum power	over 50 ft height 7700 ft no assist | 6100 ft assisted

LOAD	WEIGHTS	STALLING SPEED
Flash Bombs: 3700 lb Ammo: 2400rds -50cal Fuel: 32,536 gal protected 70 % droppable 6 % external 6 %	Empty..... 167,424 lb Combat... 264,610 lb Take-off 390,000 lb limited by structure (Does not include weight of ATO units)	127 knots power-off, landing configuration, take-off weight **TIME TO CLIMB**

NOTES

1. Performance Basis:
   (a) Preliminary flight test

2. Revision Basis: To reflect change in security classification.

Standard Aircraft Characteristics

B-52B STRATOFORTRESS
Boeing

EIGHT J57-P-19W, 29W, or 29WA
PRATT & WHITNEY

BY AUTHORITY OF
THE SECRETARY
OF THE AIR FORCE

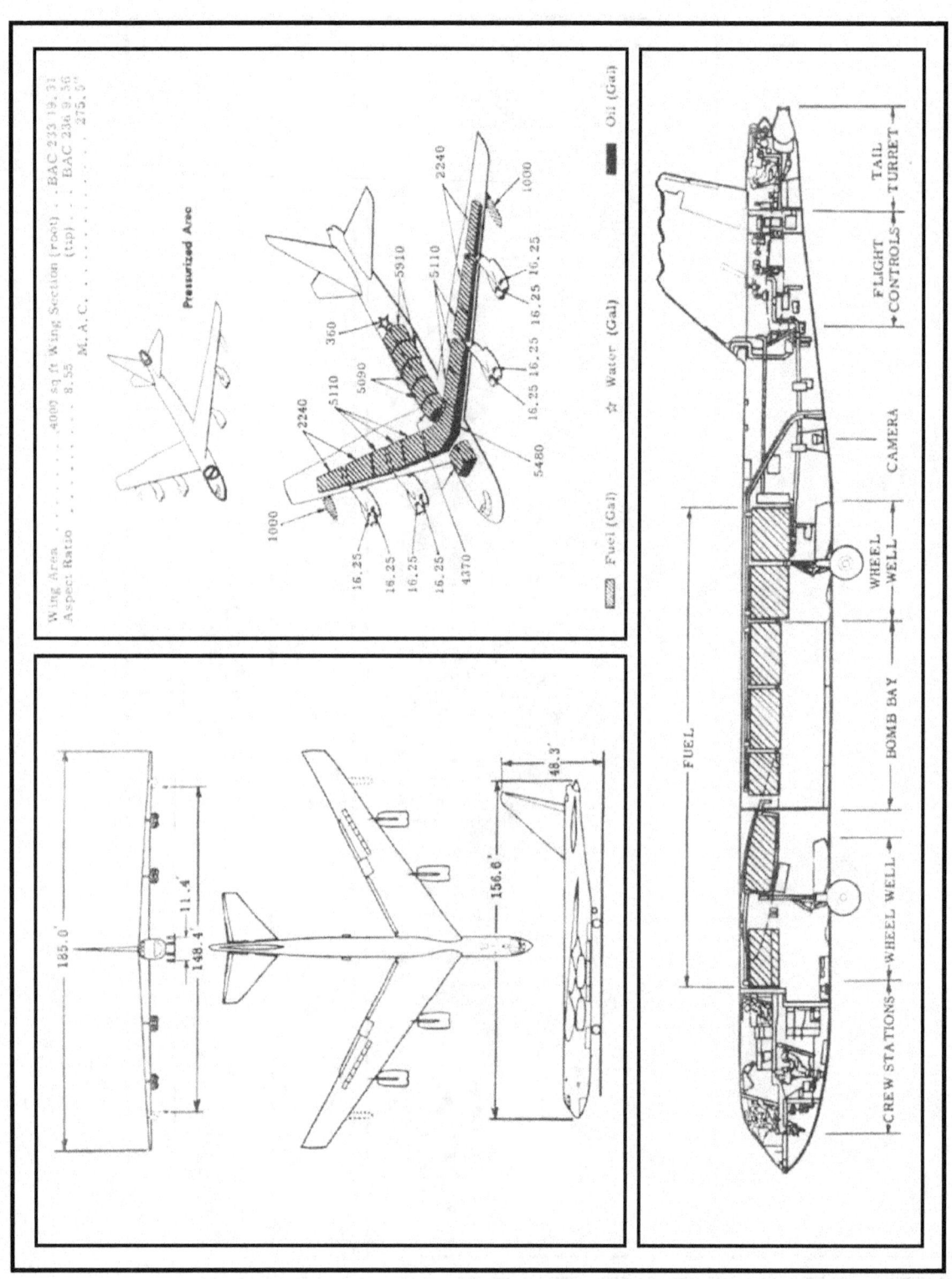

POWER PLANT

Nr & Model	(8)J57-P-19W
	or -29W -29WA
Mfr	Pratt & Whitney
Engine Spec No.	1649G
Type	Axial
Length	157.7"
Diameter	40.5"
Weight (dry)	J57-P-19W 2970 lb
Tail Pipe	Fixed Area
Augmentation	Water

Note: At present there are no requirements for ATO.

*J57-P-29W, 29WA . . . . 4150 lb

ENGINE RATINGS

S.L.Static LH - **RPM - MIN	
Max	*12,100 - 6450/9900 - 5
Mil	10,500 - 6150/9900 - 30
Nor	9000 - 5900/9650 - Cont

* Wet
** First figure represents low pressure spool; second figure represents high pressure spool

*J57-P-29W engine, Max T.O. rating 11,500 lb

DIMENSIONS

Wing	
Span	185.0'
Dihedral (chord plane)	2°30'
Incidence (root)	6°
Sweepback (LE)	36°54'
Length	156.6'
Height	48.3'
Height (t.e. folded)	20.8'
Tread (outrigger)	148.4'
(main gear)	11.4'

Mission and Description

Navy Equivalent None   Mfr's Model 464-201-3

The principal mission of the B-52B aircraft is the destruction of surface objects.

The normal crew of six consists of pilot, co-pilot, (2) bombardier-navigators, ECM operator and tail gunner. Automatic cabin pressurization, heating and ventilation are provided for crew comfort during normal and combat operation.

Ejection seats for emergency escape are afforded the crew except for the tail gunner who bails out after jettisoning the tail section containing the gun turret.

Flight control, throughout the speed range from limit dive speed to landing speed, is accomplished by use of spoilers and ailerons on the wing, elevators on an all-movable horizontal tail, and a rudder on a fixed vertical tail surface. The spoilers also function as air brakes.

Air is bled off the engines for thermal anti-icing of the wings and tail surface leading edges.

Other features are single-point ground and air refueling, braking parachute for decreasing landing roll distance, and a crosswind landing gear to aid in cross-wind take-off and landing.

The B-52B has provisions for the installation of the reconnaissance capsule in the bomb bay.

Characteristics and performance are shown for B-52B's contained within A.F. Serial Nos. 53-377 thru 53-398 with -19W engines. B-52B's Serial Nos. 52-004 thru 53-376 have -1W engines. See note (d) page 6

Development

Design Initiated	Feb 51
First Flight	Dec 54
First delivery to SAC	Oct 55

BOMBS

Nr	Class (lb)
27	New Series
	(Family of Clusters) . . 1000
	Special Weapons
2	MK-21
1	MK-6
Max Bomb Load (f)	43,000 lb

Note: Structural provisions for 50,000 lb bomb; space and structural provisions for GAM-63

GUNS

Nr	Type	Size	Rds ea	Location
4	M-3	.50	600	Tail tur
	or			
2	M24A1	20mm	400	Tail tur

CAMERAS

Nr	Type	Lens
1	K-38	36"
	or	
1	K-17C	6"
	or	
1	K-22	6"
1	O-15A Radar Recording	

WEIGHTS

Loading	lb	L.F.
Empty	164,081(C)	
Basic	167,210(C)	
Design	†430,000	2.0
Combat	*272,000	2.5
Max T.O.	**420,000	2.0
Max In-Flt.	‡415,000	2.0
Max Land	270,000	

(C) Calculated
* For Basic Mission
** Excludes 3000 lb water
† Max taxi wt. 10,000 lb bomb
‡ Limited by structure

FUEL

Location	Nr Tanks	Gal
Wg. outbd	2	4480
Wg. ctr.	1	5480
Wg. intbd*	4	10,220
Fus. fwd*	2	4370
Fus. ctr*	1	5090
Fus. aft*	1	5910
Wg. drop	2	2000
	Total	37,550

Grade JP-4
Specification . . MIL-F-5624

OIL
Nacelle . . . . 8 . . (tot)130
Specification . . MIL-L-7808A

WATER
Fus. aft . . . 1 360
*Self-sealing

ELECTRONICS

UHF Command	AN/ARC-34
Liaison	AN/ARC-21X
IFF	AN/APX-25
Radar Beacon	AN/APN-76A
ECM Trans (2)	AN/APT-8
ECM Trans (1)	AN/APT-9
ECM Trans (2)	AN/ALT-7
ECM Recv'r (1)	AN/APR-14
Interphone	AN/AIC-10
Bombing Sys	K-A
Nav. Recv'r	AN/ARN-14
Fire Control Sys.	A-3A or MD-5
ECM Recv'r (1)	AN/APR-9

See page 6 for additional equipment

Loading and Performance — Typical Mission

CONDITIONS		BASIC MISSION I	DESIGN MISSION II	MAX BOMB MISSION III	FERRY RANGE IV
TAKE-OFF WEIGHT ⑦	(lb)	420,000	420,000	420,000	414,810 ⑧⑨
Fuel at 6.5 lb/gal (grade JP-4)	(lb)	239,265	240,665	205,440	244,075
Payload (Bombs) ⑩	(lb)	10,000	8600	43,000	None
Wing loading	(lb/sq ft)	103.8	103.8	103.8	103.7
Stall speed (power off) ⑪	(kn)	141	141	141	141
Take-off ground run at SL ⑧	(ft)	6600	6600	6600	6580
Take-off to clear 50 ft ⑧	(ft)	8680	8680	8680	8650
Rate of climb at SL	(fpm)	2520	2520	2520	2525
Rate of climb at SL (one engine out) ② ⑩	(fpm)	2750	2750	2750	2760
Time: SL to 20,000 ft ③	(min)	9.6	9.6	9.6	9.5
Time: SL to 30,000 ft ③ ⑩	(min)	15.9	15.9	15.9	15.6
Service ceiling (100 fpm)	(ft)	39,350	39,350	39,350	39,350
Service ceiling (one engine out) ② ⑩	(ft)	38,900	38,900	38,900	38,900
COMBAT RANGE ④	(n. mi)				6380
COMBAT RADIUS ④	(n. mi)	3070	3090	2580	
Average cruise speed	(kn)	453	453	453	453
Initial cruising altitude	(ft)	34,950	34,950	34,950	35,200
Target speed	(kn)	476	476	476	
Target altitude	(ft)	45,750	45,800	44,700	
Final cruising altitude	(ft)	51,000	51,000	51,000	51,000
Total mission time	(hr)	13.56	13.69	11.43	14.15
COMBAT WEIGHT	(lb)	272,000	272,700	254,900	186,400
Combat altitude	(ft)	45,750	45,800	44,700	51,000
Combat speed	(kn)	496	495	506	507
Combat climb	(fpm)	790	770	1250	1210
Combat ceiling (500 fpm) ② ③	(ft)	47,100	47,000	48,350	54,900
Service ceiling (100 fpm) ②	(ft)	47,700	47,650	48,950	55,700
Service ceiling (one engine out) ②	(ft)	46,050	46,000	47,300	53,750
Max rate of climb at SL ②	(fpm)	5550	5540	6000	8350
Max speed at optimum alt ② ⑤	(kn/ft)	551/20,300	551/20,360	552/20,400	553/20,500
Basic speed at 35,000 ft ②	(kn)	520	520	522	525
LANDING WEIGHT	(lb)	186,200	186,300	185,300	186,400
Ground roll at SL ⑪	(ft)	2230	2230	2210	2230
Ground roll (auxiliary brake) ⑥ ⑪	(ft)	2000	2000	1990	2000
Total from 50 ft ⑪	(ft)	4210	4220	4180	4230
Total from 50 ft (auxiliary brake) ⑥ ⑪	(ft)	4000	4010	3980	4020

NOTES

① Take-off power
② Military power
③ Normal power
④ Detailed descriptions of RADIUS and RANGE missions given on page 6.
⑤ Limited by structure
⑥ With drag chute
⑦ Excludes 3000 lb water
⑧ Limited by fuel capacity
⑨ Initial buffet, flaps down, S.L.
⑩ In-flight weight limited to 415,000 lb. Braking force limited to 40,000 lb.

PERFORMANCE BASIS:
(a) Data source-Flight tests
(b) Performance is based on powers shown on page 3.

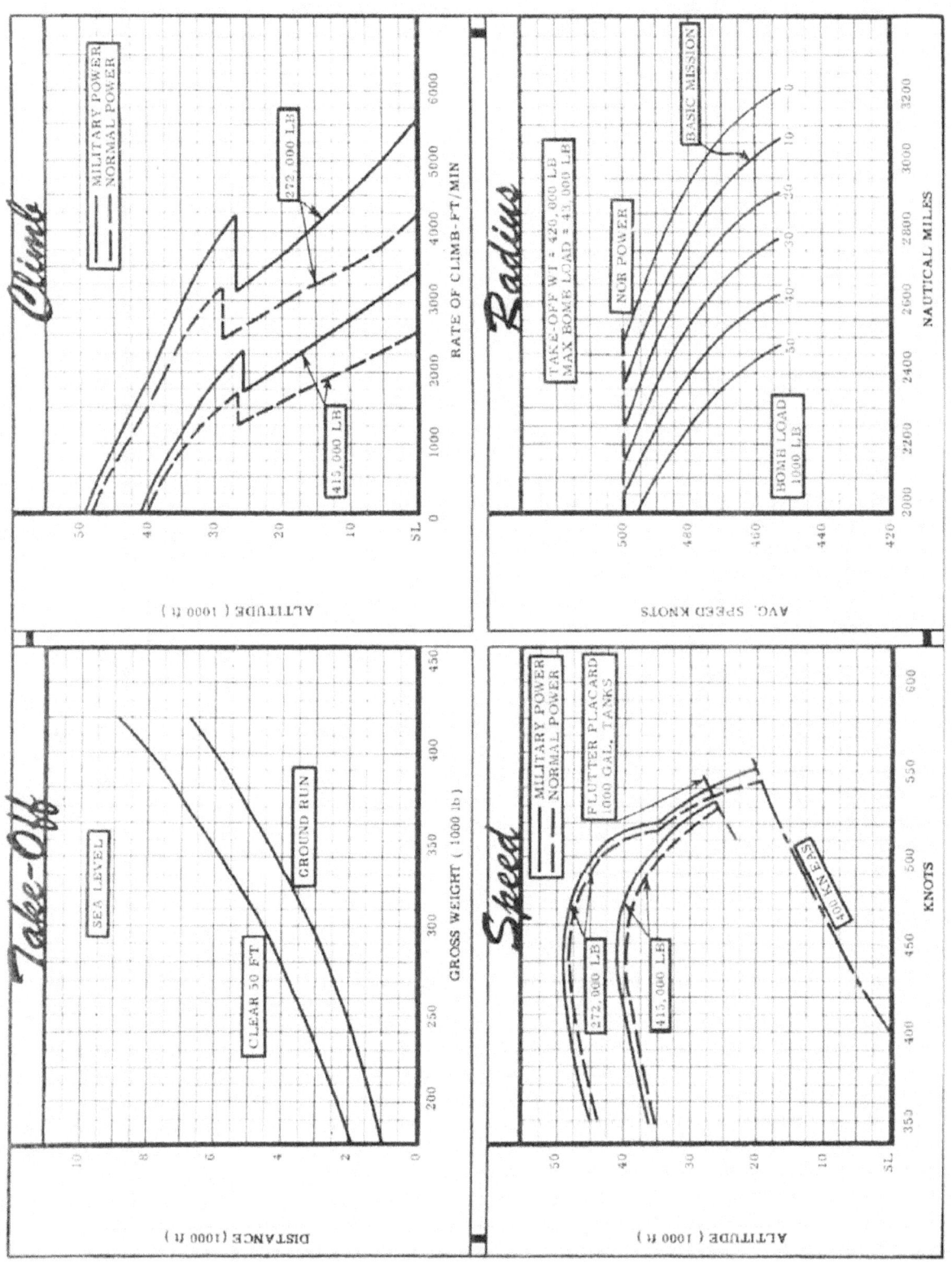

NOTES

FORMULA: RADIUS MISSIONS I, II & III

Take-off and climb on course to optimum cruise altitude at normal power. Cruise out at long range speed, increasing altitudes with decreasing weight; external tanks are dropped when empty. Climb so as to reach cruise ceiling 15 minutes from target. Run-in to target at normal power, drop bombs, conduct 2 minutes evasive action and 3 minutes escape at normal power. Cruise back to base at long range speed and optimum altitudes; as an alternate, a 45,000 foot ceiling may be maintained on the return leg with no radius penalty. Range-free allowances are fuel for 5 minutes at normal power for take-off allowance, fuel for 2 minutes at normal power for evasive action, and fuel for 30 minutes maximum endurance at sea level plus 5% of the initial fuel load for landing reserve.

FORMULA: RANGE MISSION IV

Take-off and climb on course to optimum cruise altitude at normal power. Cruise out at long range speed, increasing altitude with decreasing weight; external tanks are dropped when empty. Land at remote base with only reserve fuel remaining. Range-free allowances are fuel for 5 minutes at normal power for take-off allowance and fuel for 30 minutes maximum endurance at sea level plus 5% of the initial fuel load for landing reserve.

GENERAL DATA

(a) The landing reserve for the Basic Mission is equivalent to 750 nautical miles range at optimum speed and altitude.

(b) In-flight weight of 415,000 lb is pending approval by WADC.

(c) The following electronic equipment is supplemental to that shown under "Electronics" on page 3:

    Glide Path Receiver . . . . . (1) AN/ARN-18
    Marker Beacon . . . . (1) AN/ARN-12
    Early Warning . . . . (1) AN/APS-54
    Chaff Dispenser . . . . . . (1) AN/ALE-1

(d) O.W.E. increases approximately 2000 lb on B52 airplanes utilizing J57-P-29, -29WA engines resulting in a minor range decrease for a given T.O. weight.

PERFORMANCE REFERENCE

Boeing document D-15134B, "Substantiating Data Report - Models B-52B (J57-P-19W engines), B-52C and B-52D Standard Aircraft Characteristics Charts", dated 31 December 1956.

REVISION BASIS

To reflect change in security classification.

Characteristics Summary

| RECONNAISSANCE (BOMBER VERSION) .... RB-52C |

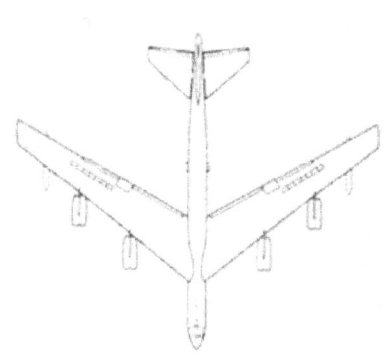

"STRATOFORTRESS" BOEING

Wing Area .... 4000 sq ft
Span .... 185.0 ft
Length .... 156.6 ft
Height (overall) .... 48.3 ft
Height (fin folded) .... 20.8 ft

AVAILABILITY

Number available

ACTIVE	RESERVE	TOTAL

PROCUREMENT

Number to be delivered in fiscal years

STATUS

1. Design Initiated: Dec 53
2. First Flight: Apr 56 (est)
3. First Acceptance: Apr 56 (est)
4. The RB-52C Bomber Version becomes a RB-52C when the capsule containing photographic, weather and electronic equipment is placed in the bomb bay.
5. Major differences from the RB-52B (Bomber Version) are the installation of J57-P-19W engines in place of J57-P-1W, & increase in fuel tank capacities.

Navy Equivalent: None

Mfr's Model: 464-201-6

POWER PLANT

(8) J57-P-19W
Pratt & Whitney
ENGINE RATINGS

S.L.S. LB - **RPM -MIN

Max: *12,100-6450/9900-5

Mil: 10,500-6150/9900-30

Nor: 9000-5900/9650-Cont

* Wet
** First figure represents low pressure spool; second figure represents high pressure spool.

Note: At present there are no requirements for ATO

FEATURES

Crew 6

Cabin Pressurization
Heating and Cooling
Thermal Anti-Icing
Braking Parachute
Quadricycle Landing Gear
Aerodynamic Spoilers (Airbrake)
Vertical Camera Station
Steerable Landing Gear
MA-6 Bombing-Nav. System
A-3A Fire Control System
Folding Fin

Max Fuel Cap: .. 42,110 gal

ARMAMENT

Turret 1
Guns .. 4 x .50 cal (M-3)
Ammunition (tot) . 2400 rds
BOMBS:
No.   Class (lb)
          New Series
27 (Family of Clusters) 1000
    Special Weapons
1 30,000
2 6000

Max Bomb Load:
.... 1 x 43,000 lb

Note: Structural provisions for 50,000 lb bomb; space and structural provisions for XB-63

Characteristics Summary Basic Mission — RB-52C
(BOMBER VERSION)

```
      51,950 FT                                    46,150 FT
         ↖                        ←
           34,750 FT
              ↘              ↙— DROP TANKS
                      HIGH ALTITUDE BOMBER
```

PERFORMANCE

COMBAT RADIUS	FERRY RANGE	SPEED
3625 naut. mi with 10,000 lb payload at 457 knots avg. in 15.93 hours.	**7260** (c) naut. mi with 42,110 gal fuel at 457 knots avg. in 15.93 hours at 447,500 lb T.O. wt.	COMBAT **489** knots at 46,150 ft alt, max power MAX **546** (b) knots at 20,000 ft alt, max power BASIC **518** knots at 35,000 ft alt, max power

CLIMB	CEILING	TAKE-OFF (d)
2240 fpm sea level, take-off weight normal power	**38,050** ft 100 fpm, take-off weight normal power	ground run 8350 ft no assist ——— ft assisted
5430 fpm sea level, combat weight maximum power	**47,350** ft 500 fpm, combat weight maximum power	over 50 ft height 10,650 ft no assist ——— ft assisted

LOAD	WEIGHTS	STALLING SPEED

Bombs .... 10,000 lb
Ammunition: 2400 rds/.50 cal
Fuel: 40,956 gal
  protected 63 %
  droppable 15 %
  external 15 %
	Empty..... 165,110 lb
	Combat... 279,900 lb
	Take-off 450,000 lb
	limited by structure
		136 knots
		power-off, landing configuration, take-off weight
		TIME TO CLIMB
		———

NOTES

1. Performance Basis:
   (a) Preliminary flight test of XB-52 and YB-52.
   (b) Limited by structure
   (c) Tanks carried all the way
   (d) Per design criteria the minimum take-off distances are: 7800 ft ground run and 10,050 ft over 50 ft obstacle.

2. Revision Basis: To reflect latest performance and characteristics data.

Standard Aircraft Characteristics

RB-52C
STRATOFORTRESS
Boeing

EIGHT J57-P-19W
PRATT & WHITNEY

BY AUTHORITY OF
THE SECRETARY
OF THE AIR FORCE

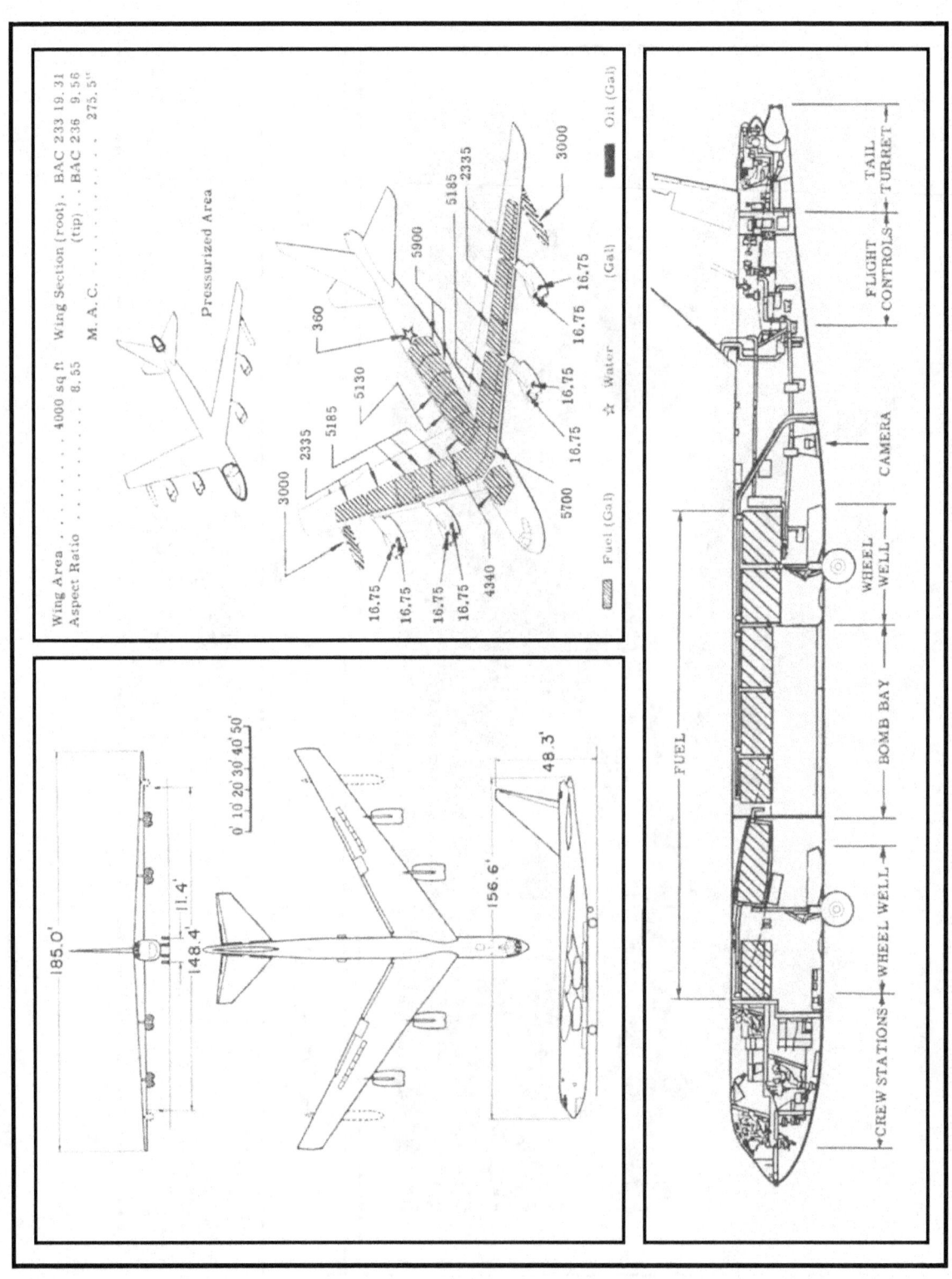

POWER PLANT

No. & Model	(8) J57-P-19W
Mfr	Pratt & Whitney
Engine Spec No.	A-1649D
Type	Axial
Length	157.7"
Diameter	40.5"
Weight (dry)	4035 lb
Tail Pipe	Fixed Area
Augmentation	Water

Note: At present there are no requirements for ATO

ENGINE RATINGS

S. L. Static LB - **RPM - MIN

Max*	*12,100-6450/9900-3
Mil	10,500-6150/9400-30
Nor	9000-5900/9650-Cont

*Wet

**First figure represents low pressure spool, second figure represents high pressure spool.

DIMENSIONS

Wing	
Span	185.0'
Dihedral (chord plane)	2°30'
Incidence (root)	8°
Sweepback (LE)	36°58'
Length	156.6'
Height (overall)	48.3'
Height (in folded)	20.8'
Tread (outrigger)	148.4'
Tread (main gear)	11.4'

Mission and Description

Navy Equivalent: None   Mfr's Model: 464-201-6

The principal mission of the RB-52C (Bomber Version) is the destruction of surface objects.

The normal crew of six consists of pilot, co-pilot, (2) bombardier-navigators, ECM operator and tail gunner.

Automatic cabin pressurization, heating and ventilation are provided for crew comfort during normal and combat operation.

Ejection seats for emergency escape are afforded the crew except for the tail gunner who bails out after jettisoning the tail section containing the gun turret.

Flight control, throughout the speed range from limit dive speed to landing speed is accomplished by use of spoilers, ailerons on the wing, elevators on an all-movable horizontal tail and a rudder on a fixed vertical tail surface. The spoilers also function as air brakes used in landing.

Thermal anti-icing of wing and tail surface leading edges is accomplished by air being bled off the engines.

Other features are single-point ground and aerial refueling, braking parachute for decreasing landing roll distance, and a steerable landing gear to aid in cross wind take-off and landing. The airplane utilizes the A-14 auto-pilot and the N-1 compass.

The RB-52C (Bomber Version) becomes a RB-52C when the capsule containing photographic equipment is placed in the bomb bay.

Major differences from the RB-52B (Bomber Version) are the installation of J57-P-19 engines in place of J57-P-19W engines and an increase in fuel tank capacities.

Development

Design Initiated	Dec 53
First Flight	(est) Apr 56
First Acceptance	(est) Apr 56

BOMBS

No.	Class (lb)	
	New Series	
27	(family of clusters)	1000
	Special Weapons	
1		30,000
2		8600
Max Bomb Load (1)		43,000

Note: Structural provisions for 30,000 lb bomb, space and structural provisions for XB-63

GUNS

No.	Type	Size	Rds ea	Loc
4	M-3	.50	600	Tail tur

CAMERAS

No.	Type	Lens
1	K-38	36"
1	K-22	6"
	or	
1	K-17C	6"
1	0-15 Radar Recording	

WEIGHTS

Loading	Lb	L.F.
Empty	165,110 (C)	
Basic	167,683	
Design	450,000	2.0
Combat	*279,900	2.4
Max T.O.	**450,000	2.0
Max Land	270,000	

(C) Calculated
* For Basic Mission
** Limited by structure, w/o ATO

FUEL

Location	No. Tanks	Gal
Wg. outbd	2	4670
Wg. ctr	4	5700
Wg. inbd*	4	10,370
Fus. fwd*	2	4340
Fus. ctr*	1	5130
Fus. aft*	2	5900
Wg. drop	2	6000
	Total	42,110

*Self-sealing
Grade ... JP-4
Specification ... MIL-F-5624A

OIL

Nacelle	8	(tot) 134
Grade		
Specification		MIL-L-7808A
WATER		
Fus. aft	1	360

ELECTRONICS

UHF Command Set	AN/ARC-34
Liaison	AN/ARC-21X
IFF	AN/APX-6
Radar Beacon	AN/APN-76A
ECM Trans (2)	AN/APT-6
ECM Trans (1)	AN/APT-9
ECM Trans (2)	AN/APT-16A
ECM Rec'v'r (1)	AN/APR-14
Interphone	AN/AIC-10
Bombing Sys	MA-6
Nav. Rec'v'r	AN/ARN-14
Fire Control Sys	A-3A
ECM Rec'v'r (1)	AN/ARR-9

see page 6 for additional equip.

Loading and Performance — Typical Mission

CONDITIONS		BASIC MISSION	DESIGN MISSION	MAX BOMB MISSION	FERRY RANGE
		I	II	III	IV
TAKE-OFF WEIGHT (lb)	①	450,000	450,000	430,000	447,500
Fuel at 6.5 lb/gal (grade JP-4) (lb)	①	266,215	267,615	232,905	273,715
Payload (Bombs) (lb)	③	10,000	8600	43,000	None
Wing loading (lb/sq ft)		112.5	112.5	112.5	111.9
Stall speed (power off) (kn)		136	136	136	136
Take-off ground run at SL (ft)	①	8350	8350	8350	8300
Take-off to clear 50 ft (ft)	①	10,650	10,650	10,550	10,600
Rate of climb at SL (fpm)		2240	2240	2240	2260
Rate of climb at SL (one eng. out) (fpm)		2450	2450	2450	2460
Time: SL to 20,000 ft (min)		11.1	11.1	11.1	11.0
Time: SL to 30,000 ft (min)		18.8	18.8	18.8	18.7
Service ceiling (100 fpm) (ft)		38,050	38,050	38,050	38,150
Service ceiling (one eng. out) (ft)		37,550	37,550	37,550	37,650
COMBAT RANGE (n. mi)					7260 ⑦
COMBAT RADIUS (n. mi)	④	3625	3645	3115	
Average cruise speed (kn)		457	457	457	457
Initial cruising altitude (ft)	③	34,750	34,750	34,750	34,850
Target speed (kn)		472	472	472	
Target altitude (ft)		46,200	46,200	45,050	
Final cruising altitude (ft)		51,950	51,950	52,000	51,550
Total mission time (hr)		15.93	16.03	13.68	15.93
COMBAT WEIGHT (lb)	②	279,900	280,750	262,450	191,900
Combat altitude (ft)	②	46,150	46,200	45,050	51,550
Combat speed (kn)	②	489	489	501	501
Combat climb (fpm)	②	700	680	1110	1010
Combat ceiling (500 fpm) (ft)	②	47,350	47,200	48,600	54,300
Service ceiling (100 fpm) (ft)	①	48,100	48,000	49,400	55,300
Max rate of climb (one eng. out) (fpm)	② ⑤	46,000	45,900	47,300	53,200
Max speed at 20,000 ft (fpm)		5430	5420	5850	7900
Basic speed at 35,000 ft (kn)		546	546	546	546
LANDING WEIGHT (lb)	②	518	518	519	521
Ground roll at SL (ft)		188,400	188,500	187,060	191,900
Ground roll (auxiliary brake) (ft)	⑥	2630	2630	2650	2670
Total from 50 ft (ft)		2260	2260	2250	2290
Total from 50 ft (auxiliary brake) (ft)	⑥	3430	3430	3400	3470
		3060	3060	3050	3090

NOTES:
① T.O. power
② Max power
③ Normal power
④ Detailed descriptions of Radius and Range missions are given on page 6
⑤ Limited by structure
⑥ With drag chute
⑦ Tanks carried all the way

Performance Basis:
(a) Data source: Flight tests on XB-52 and YB-52
(b) Performance based on data referenced on page 6.

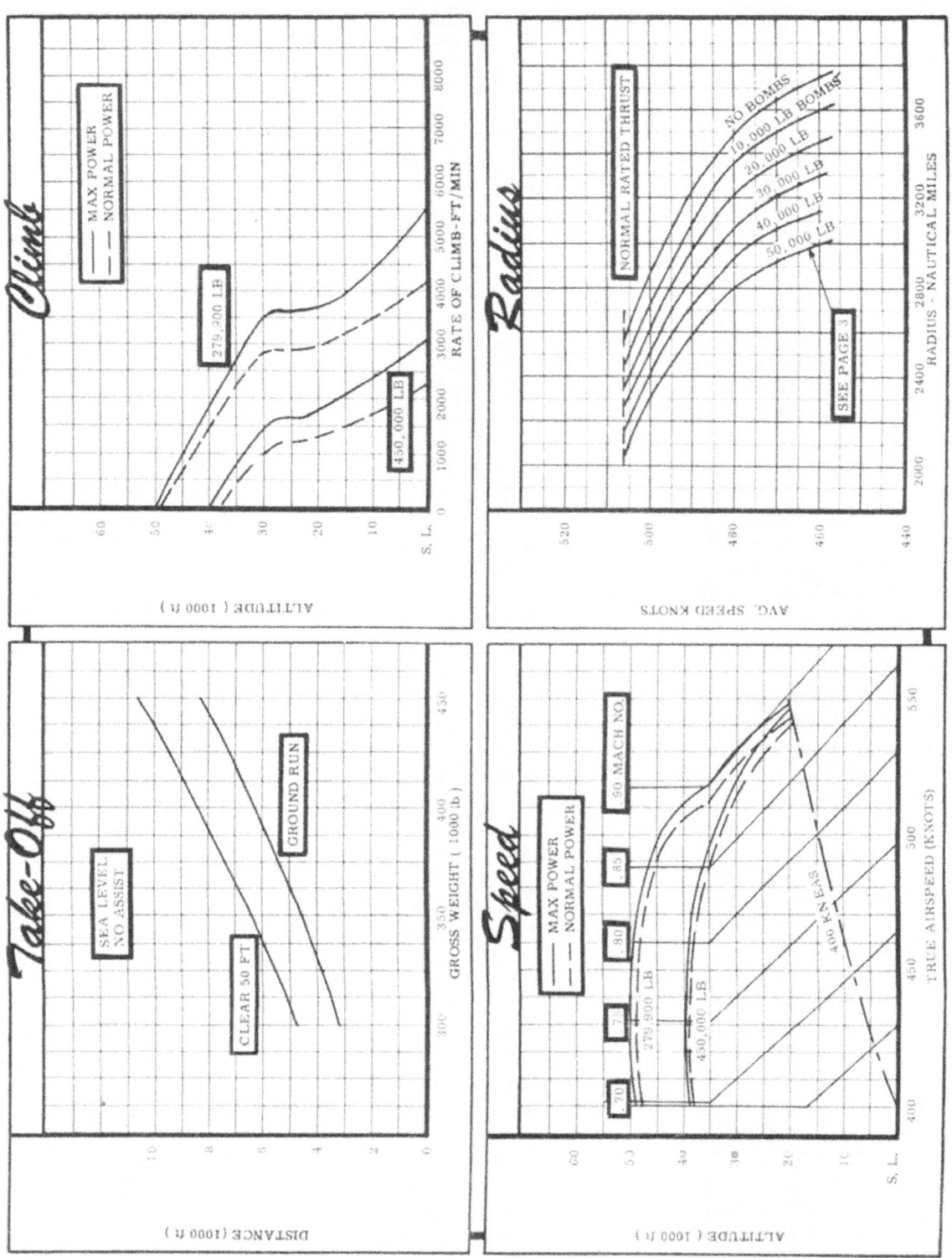

N O T E S

FORMULA: RADIUS MISSIONS I, II & III

Take-off and climb on course to optimum cruise altitude at normal power. Cruise out at long range speeds increasing altitude with decreasing airplane weight, external tanks are dropped, when empty. Climb so as to reach cruise ceiling fifteen (15) minutes from target. Run into target at normal power, drop bombs, conduct two (2) minutes evasive action and eight (8) minutes escape from target at normal power. Cruise back to home base at long range speeds increasing altitude with decreasing airplane weight. Range free allowances include five (5) minutes normal power fuel consumption for starting engines and take-off and two (2) minutes normal power fuel consumption at combat altitude for evasive action and thirty (30) minutes of maximum endurance (four engine) fuel consumption at sea level plus 5% of initial fuel load for landing reserve.

FORMULA: RANGE MISSION IV

Take-off and climb on course to optimum cruise altitude at normal power. Cruise out at long range speeds increasing altitude with decreasing airplane weight until all usable fuel is consumed. External tanks are carried to the end of the mission. Range free allowances include five (5) minutes normal power fuel consumption for starting engines and take-off and thirty (30) minutes of maximum endurance (four engines) fuel consumption at sea level plus 5% of initial fuel load for landing reserve.

GENERAL DATA:

(a) The prescribed fuel reserve for basic mission is equivalent to 910 nautical miles at best range conditions.

(b) Per design criteria the minimum take-off distances for 450,000 lb are as follows: 7800 ft ground run and 10,050 ft over 50 ft obstacle.

PERFORMANCE REFERENCE:

Boeing Document No. D-15134, subject "Substantiating Data Report - Model HB-52C Standard Aircraft Characteristics Charts", dated 25 May 1954.

REVISION BASIS:

To reflect latest performance and characteristics data.

The following Electronic equipment is supplemental to that shown under Electronics on Page 3:

Glide Path Receiver	(1)	AN/ARN-18
Direction Finder	(1)	AN/ARA-25
Marker Beacon	(1)	AN/ARN-12
Early Warning	(1)	AN/APS-54
Chaff	(2)	AN/ALE-1

SUPPLEMENTAL

Air Refueled Radius

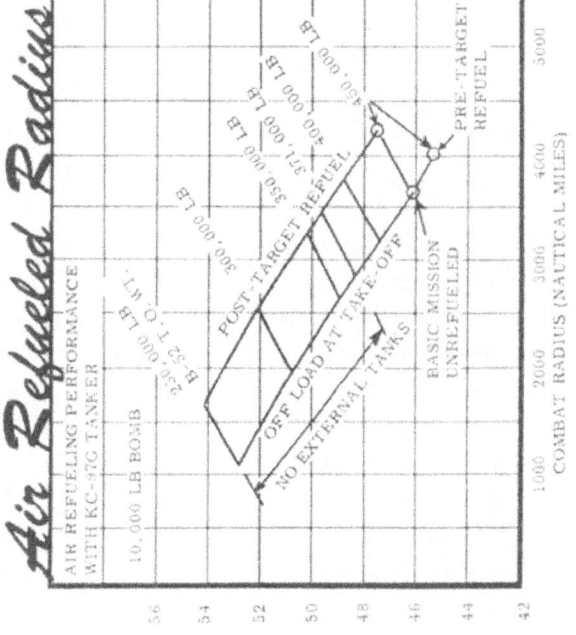

This chart shows alternate 10,000 pound bomb missions available by refueling either before bomb drop, after bomb drop, or by taking off at reduced weights. Aerial refueling with the KC-97G tanker is accomplished at 25,000 feet altitude with fuel allowance for rendezvous and transfer. No range credit is allowed for descent to 25,000 feet, climb back to cruise altitude is accounted for in range and fuel consumption.

Characteristics Summary

BOMBER	B-52D

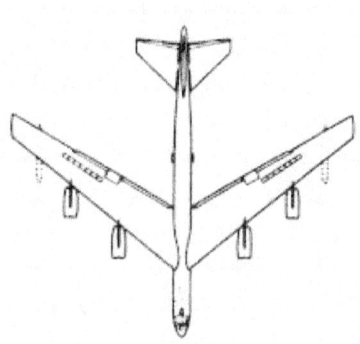
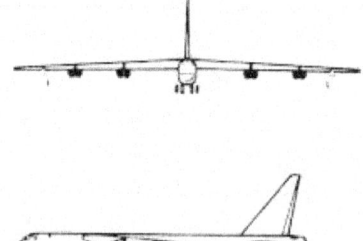

"STRATOFORTRESS"   BOEING

Wing Area .... 4000 sq ft   Length .... 156.6 ft
                                        Height (overall) .... 48.3 ft
Span .... 185.0 ft   Height (fin folded) .... 20.8 ft

AVAILABILITY

Number available

ACTIVE	RESERVE	TOTAL

PROCUREMENT

Number to be delivered in fiscal years

STATUS

1. The B-52D airplane is same as RB-52C except that it does not have the bomb bay (Capsule) convertibility to a reconnaissance characteristic.

2. Delivery: Five B-52D airplanes are scheduled for delivery ... Dec 56 (est)

Navy Equivalent: None   Mfr's Model: 464-201-6

POWER PLANT

(8) J57-P-19W
Pratt & Whitney
ENGINE RATINGS

S.L.S. LB - **RPM -MIN

Max: *12,100-6450/9900-5

Mil: 10,500-6150/9900-30

Nor: 9000-5900/9650-Cont

* Wet
** First figure represents low pressure spool; second figure represents high pressure spool.

Note: At present there are no requirements for ATO

FEATURES

Crew 6

Cabin Pressurization
Heating and Cooling
Thermal Anti-Icing
Braking Parachute
Quadricycle Landing Gear
Aerodynamic Spoilers (Air-brake)
Vertical Camera Station
Steerable Landing Gear
MA-6 Bombing-Nav. System
A-3A Fire Control System
Folding Fin

Max Fuel Cap: .. 42,110 gal

ARMAMENT

Turret 1
Guns .. 4 x .50 cal (M-3)
Ammunition (tot) . 2400 rds
BOMBS:
No.   Class (lb)
         New Series
27 (Family of Clusters) 1000
       Special Weapons
1 30,000
2 8600

Max Bomb Load:
.... 1 x 43,000 lb

Note: Structural provisions for 50,000 lb bomb; space and structural provisions for XB-63

Characteristics Summary Basic Mission — B-52D

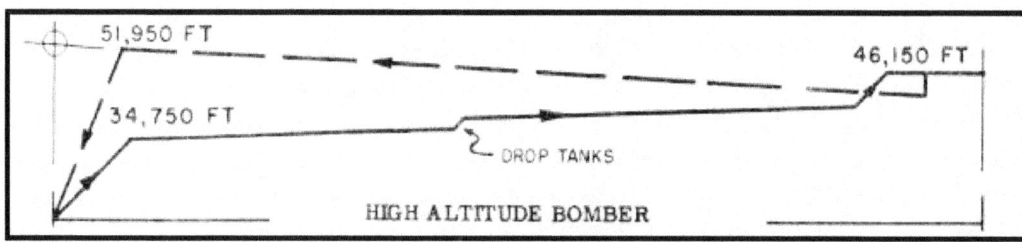

HIGH ALTITUDE BOMBER

PERFORMANCE

COMBAT RADIUS	FERRY RANGE	SPEED
3625 naut. mi with 10,000 lb payload at 457 knots avg. in 15.93 hours.	7260 (c) naut. mi with 42,110 gal fuel at 457 knots avg. in 15.93 hours at 447,500 lb T.O. wt.	COMBAT 489 knots at 46,150 ft alt, max power MAX 546 (b) knots at 20,000 ft alt, max power BASIC 518 knots at 35,000 ft alt, max power

CLIMB	CEILING	TAKE-OFF (d)
2240 fpm sea level, take-off weight normal power	38,050 ft 100 fpm, take-off weight normal power	ground run 8350 ft no assist | ――― ft assisted
5430 fpm sea level, combat weight maximum power	47,350 ft 500 fpm, combat weight maximum power	over 50 ft height 10,650 ft no assist | ――― ft assisted

LOAD	WEIGHTS	STALLING SPEED

Bombs .... 10,000 lb
Ammunition: 2400 rds/.50 cal
Fuel: 40,956 gal
  protected 63
  droppable 15
  external 15
	Empty..... 165,110 lb
	Combat... 279,900 lb
	Take-off 450,000 lb
	limited by structure
		136 knots power-off, landing configuration, take-off weight

		TIME TO CLIMB

NOTES

1. Performance Basis:
   - (a) Preliminary flight test of XB-52 and YB-52.
   - (b) Limited by structure
   - (c) Tanks carried all the way
   - (d) Per design criteria the minimum take-off distances are: 7800 ft ground run and 10,000 ft over 50 ft obstacle.

Revision Basis: To reflect latest performance and characteristics data.

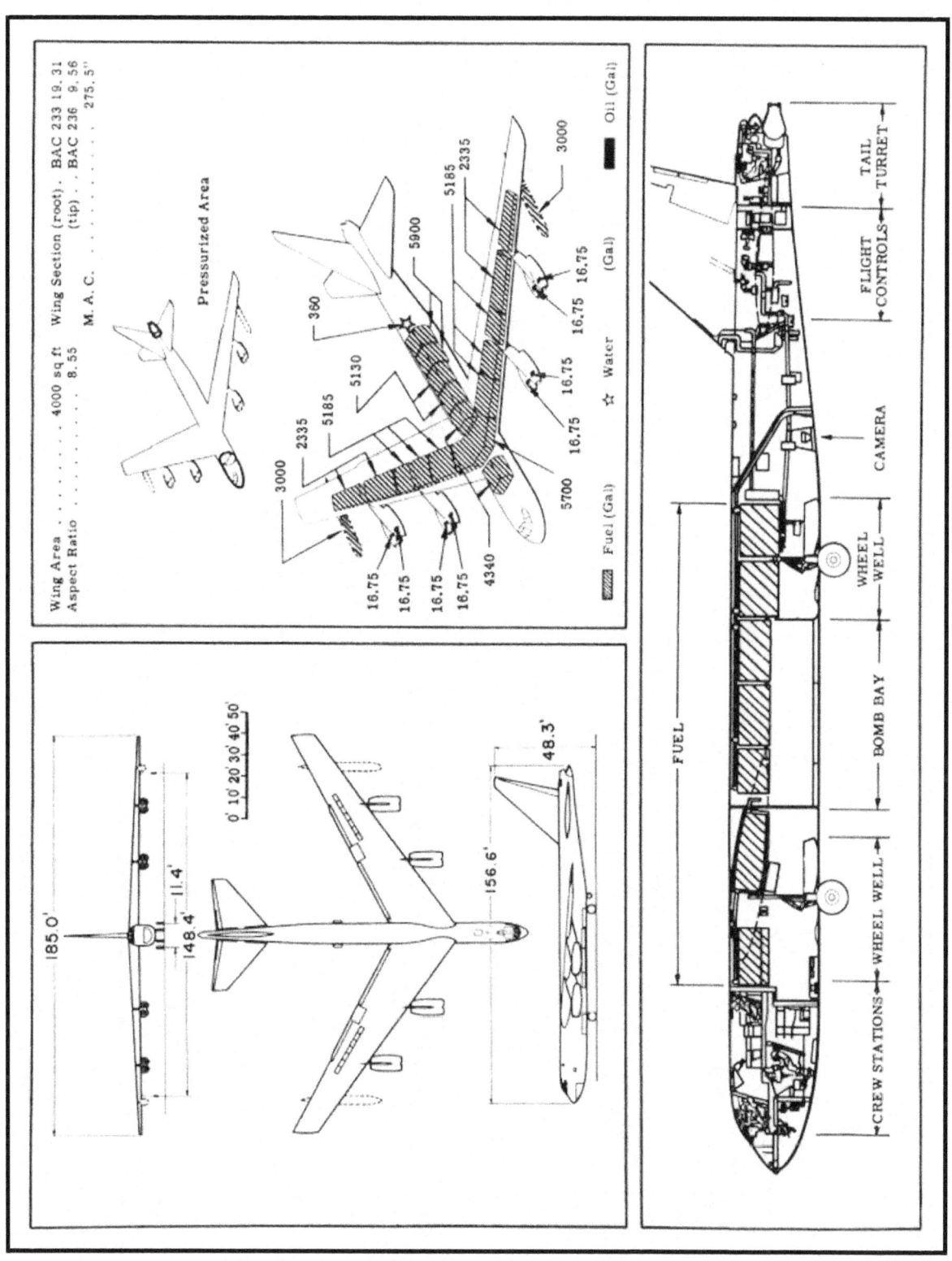

POWER PLANT

No. & Model	(8) J57-P-19W
Mfr	Pratt & Whitney
Engine Spec No.	A-1649D
Type	Axial
Length	157.7"
Diameter	40.5"
Weight (dry)	4035 lb
Tail Pipe	Fixed Area
Augmentation	Water

Note: At present there are no requirements for ATO

ENGINE RATINGS

S.L.Static LB-**RPM -MIN	
Max:	*12,100-6450/9900-3
Mil:	10,500-6150/9300-30
Nor:	9000-5900/9650-Cont

*Wet

**First figure represents low pressure spool; second figure represents high pressure spool.

DIMENSIONS

Wing	
Span	185.0'
Dihedral (chord plane)	2°30'
Incidence (root)	6°
Sweepback (LE)	36°58'
Length	156.6'
Height (overall)	48.3'
Height (fin folded)	20.8'
Tread (outrigger)	148.4'
Tread (main gear)	11.4'

Mission and Description

Navy Equivalent: None Mfr's Model: 464-201-6

The principal mission of the B-52D is the destruction of surface objects. The normal crew of six consists of pilot, co-pilot, (2) bombardier-navigators, ECM operator and tail gunner.

Automatic cabin pressurization, heating and ventilation are provided for crew comfort during normal and combat operation.

Ejection seats for emergency escape are afforded the crew except for the tail gunner who bails out after jettisoning the tail section containing the gun turret.

Flight control, throughout the speed range from limit dive speed to landing speed is accomplished by use of spoilers, ailerons on the wing, elevators on an all-movable horizontal tail and a rudder on a fixed vertical tail surface. The spoilers also function as air brakes used in landing.

Thermal anti-icing of wing and tail surface leading edges is accomplished by air being bled off the engines.

Other features are single-point ground and aerial refueling, braking parachute for decreasing landing roll distance, and a steerable landing gear to aid in cross wind take-off and landing. The airplane utilizes the A-14 auto-pilot and the N-1 compass.

The RB-52C (Bomber Version) becomes a RB-52C when the capsule containing photographic equipment is placed in the bomb bay.

Major differences from the RB-52B (Bomber Version) are the installation of J57-P-19W engines in place of J57-P-1W engines and an increase in fuel tank capacities.

Development

The B-52D airplane is same as RB-52C (Bomber Version) except that it does not have the bomb bay (Capsule) convertibility to a reconnaissance characteristic.

Delivery: Five B-52D airplanes are scheduled for delivery Dec 56 (est)

BOMBS

No.	Class (lb)
	New Series
27	(family of clusters) 1000
	Special Weapons
1	30,000
2	8600
Max Bomb Load (1)	43,000

Note: Structural provisions for 50,000 lb bomb; space and structural provisions for XB-63

GUNS

No.	Type	Size	Rds ea	Loc
4	M-3	.50	600	Tail tur

CAMERAS

No.	Type	Lens
1	K-38	36"
1	K-22	6"
	or	
1	K-17C	6"
1	0-15 Radar Recording	

WEIGHTS

	Lb	L.F.
Loading	165,110 (C)	
Empty	167,683	
Basic	450,000	
Design		2.0
Combat	*279,300	2.4
Max T.O.	**450,000	2.4
Max Land	270,000	2.0

(C) Calculated
* For Basic Mission
** Limited by structure; w/o ATO

FUEL

Location	No. Tanks	Gal
Wg, outbd	2	4670
Wg, ctr	1	5700
Wg, inbd*	4	10,370
Fus, fwd*	2	4340
Fus, ctr*	1	5130
Fus, aft*	1	5900
Wg, drop	2	6000
* Self-Sealing	Total	42,110
Grade		JP-4
Specification		MIL-F-5624A

OIL

Nacelle	8	(tot) 134
Grade		MIL-L-7808A
Specification		

WATER

Fus, aft	1	350

ELECTRONICS

UHF Command Set	AN/ARC-34
Liaison	AN/ARC-21X
IFF	AN/APX-6
Radar Beacon	AN/APN-76A
ECM Trans (2)	AN/APT-6
ECM Trans (1)	AN/APT-9
ECM Trans (2)	AN/APR-16A
ECM Recv'r (1)	AN/APR-14
Interphone	AN/AIC-10
Bombing Sys	MA-6
Nav. Recv'r	AN/ARN-14
Fire Control Sys	A-3A
ECM Recv'r (1)	AN/ARR-9

see page 6 for additional equip.

Loading and Performance — Typical Mission

CONDITIONS		BASIC MISSION	DESIGN MISSION	MAX BOMB MISSION	FERRY RANGE
		I	II	III	IV
TAKE-OFF WEIGHT	(lb)	450,000	450,000	450,000	447,500
Fuel at 6.5 lb/gal (grade JP-4)	(lb)	266,215	267,615	232,905	273,715
Payload (Bombs)	(lb)	10,000	8600	43,000	None
Wing loading	(lb/sq ft)	112.5	112.5	112.5	111.9
Stall speed (power off)	(kn)	136	136	136	136
Take-off ground run at SL ①	(ft)	8350	8350	8350	8300
Take-off to clear 50 ft ①	(ft)	10,650	10,650	10,650	10,600
Rate of climb at SL ③	(fpm)	2240	2240	2240	2260
Rate of climb at SL (one eng. out) ②	(fpm)	2450	2450	2450	2460
Time: SL to 20,000 ft ③	(min)	11.1	11.1	11.1	11.0
Time: SL to 30,000 ft ③	(min)	18.8	18.8	18.8	18.7
Service ceiling (100 fpm) ③	(ft)	38,050	38,050	38,050	38,150
Service ceiling (one eng. out) ②	(ft)	37,550	37,550	37,550	37,650
COMBAT RANGE ④	(n. mi)				7260 ⑦
COMBAT RADIUS ④	(n. mi)	3625	3645	3115	
Average cruise speed	(kn)	457	457	457	457
Initial cruising altitude ③	(ft)	34,750	34,750	34,750	34,850
Target speed	(kn)	472	472	472	
Target altitude	(ft)	46,150	46,200	45,050	
Final cruising altitude	(ft)	51,950	51,950	52,000	51,550
Total mission time	(hr)	15.93	16.03	13.68	15.93
COMBAT WEIGHT	(lb)	279,900	280,750	262,450	191,900
Combat altitude ②	(ft)	46,150	46,200	45,050	51,550
Combat speed ②	(kn)	489	489	501	501
Combat climb ②	(fpm)	700	690	1110	1010
Combat ceiling (500 fpm) ②	(ft)	47,350	47,200	48,600	54,300
Service ceiling (100 fpm) ③	(ft)	48,100	48,000	49,400	55,300
Service ceiling (one eng. out) ②	(ft)	46,000	45,900	47,300	53,200
Max rate of climb at SL ②	(fpm)	5430	5420	5850	7900
Max speed at 20,000 ft ② ⑤	(kn)	546	546	546	546
Basic speed at 35,000 ft ②	(kn)	518	518	519	521
LANDING WEIGHT	(lb)	188,400	188,500	187,050	191,900
Ground roll at SL	(ft)	2630	2630	2600	2670
Ground roll (auxiliary brake) ⑥	(ft)	2260	2260	2250	2290
Total from 50 ft	(ft)	3430	3430	3400	3470
Total from 50 ft (auxiliary brake) ⑥	(ft)	3060	3060	3050	3090

NOTES
① T.O. power
② Max power
③ Normal power
④ Detailed descriptions of Radius and Range missions are given on page 6
⑤ Limited by structure
⑥ With drag chute
⑦ Tanks carried all the way

Performance Basis:
(a) Data source: Flight tests on XB-52 and YB-52
(b) Performance based on data referenced on page 6.

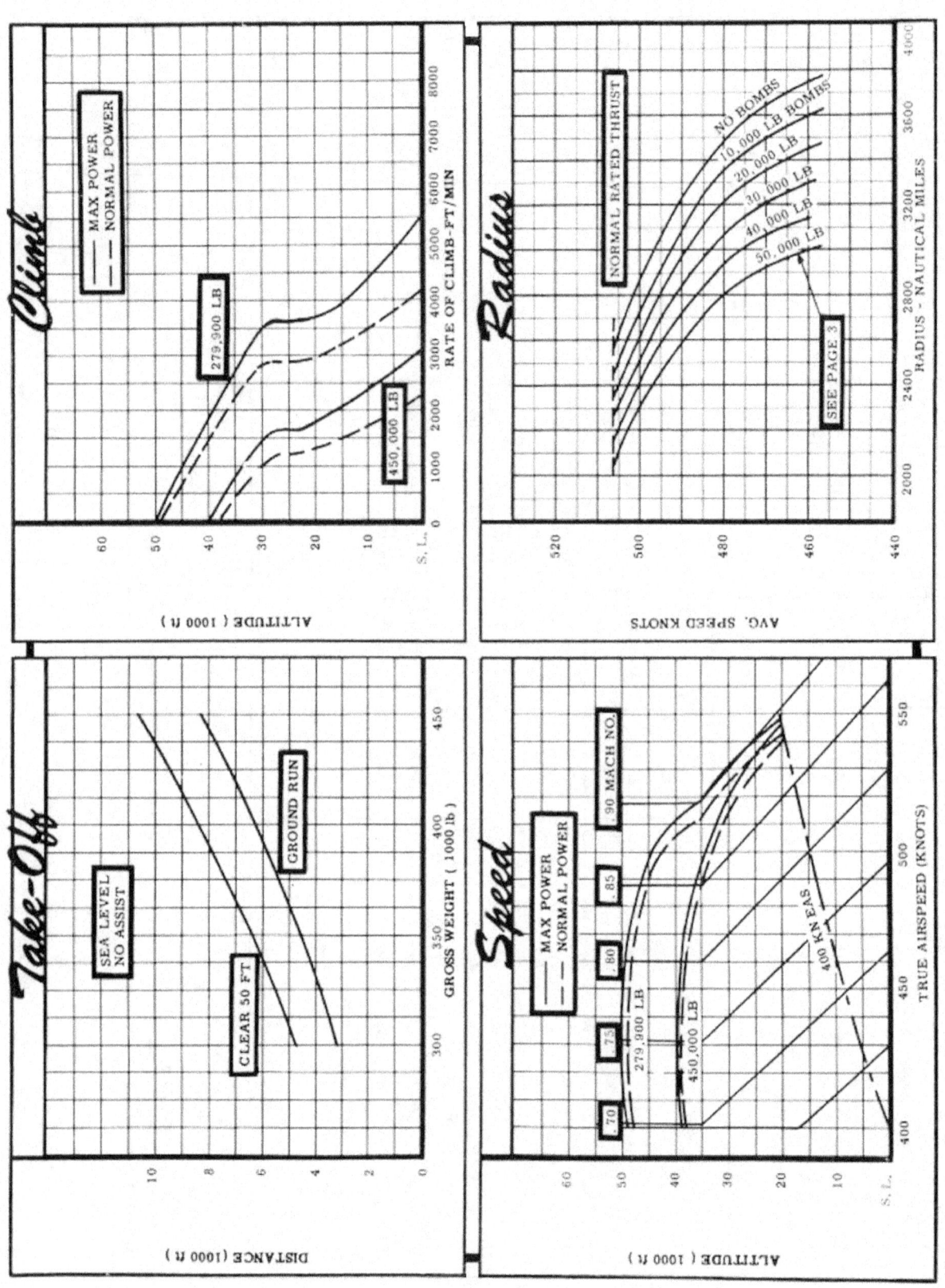

N O T E S

FORMULA: RADIUS MISSIONS I, II & III

Take-off and climb on course to optimum cruise altitude at normal power. Cruise out at long range speeds increasing altitude with decreasing airplane weight, external tanks are dropped, when empty. Climb so as to reach cruise ceiling fifteen (15) minutes from target. Run into target at normal power, drop bombs, conduct two (2) minutes evasive action and eight (8) minutes escape from target at normal power. Cruise back to home base at long range speeds increasing altitude with decreasing airplane weight. Range free allowances include five (5) minutes normal power fuel consumption for starting engines and take-off and two (2) minutes normal power fuel consumption at combat altitude for evasive action and thirty (30) minutes of maximum endurance (four engine) fuel consumption at sea level plus 5% of initial fuel load for landing reserve.

FORMULA: RANGE MISSION IV

Take-off and climb on course to optimum cruise altitude at normal power. Cruise out at long range speeds increasing altitude with decreasing airplane weight until all usable fuel is consumed. External tanks are carried to the end of the mission. Range free allowances include five (5) minutes normal power fuel consumption for starting engines and take-off and thirty (30) minutes of maximum endurance (four engines) fuel consumption at sea level plus 5% of initial fuel load for landing reserve.

GENERAL DATA:

(a) The prescribed fuel reserve for basic mission is equivalent to 910 nautical miles at best range conditions.

(b) Per design criteria the minimum take-off distances for 450,000 lb are as follows: 7800 ft ground run and 10,050 ft over 50 ft obstacle.

PERFORMANCE REFERENCE:

Boeing Document No. D-15134, subject "Substantiating Data Report - Model RB-52C Standard Aircraft Characteristics Charts", dated 25 May 1954.

REVISION BASIS:

To reflect latest performance and characteristics data.

The following Electronic equipment is supplemental to that shown under Electronics on Page 3:

Glide Path Receiver	(1)	AN/ARN-18
Direction Finder	(1)	AN/ARA-25
Marker Beacon	(1)	AN/ARN-12
Early Warning	(1)	AN/APS-54
Chaff	(2)	AN/ALE-1

SUPPLEMENTAL
Air Refueled Radius

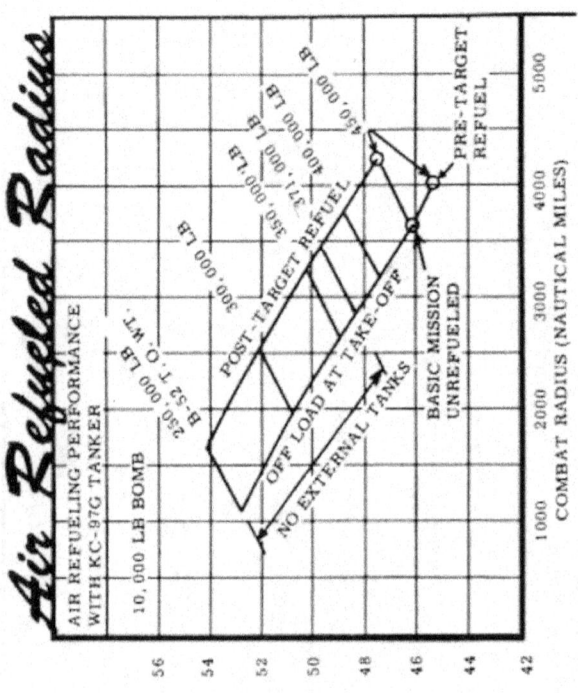

This chart shows alternate 10,000 pound bomb missions available by refueling either before bomb drop, after bomb drop, or by taking off at reduced weights. Aerial refueling with the KC-97G Tanker is accomplished at 25,000 feet altitude with fuel allowance for rendezvous and transfer. No range credit is allowed for descent to 25,000 feet, climb back to cruise altitude is accounted for in range and fuel consumption.

Characteristics Summary

BOMBER — B-52E

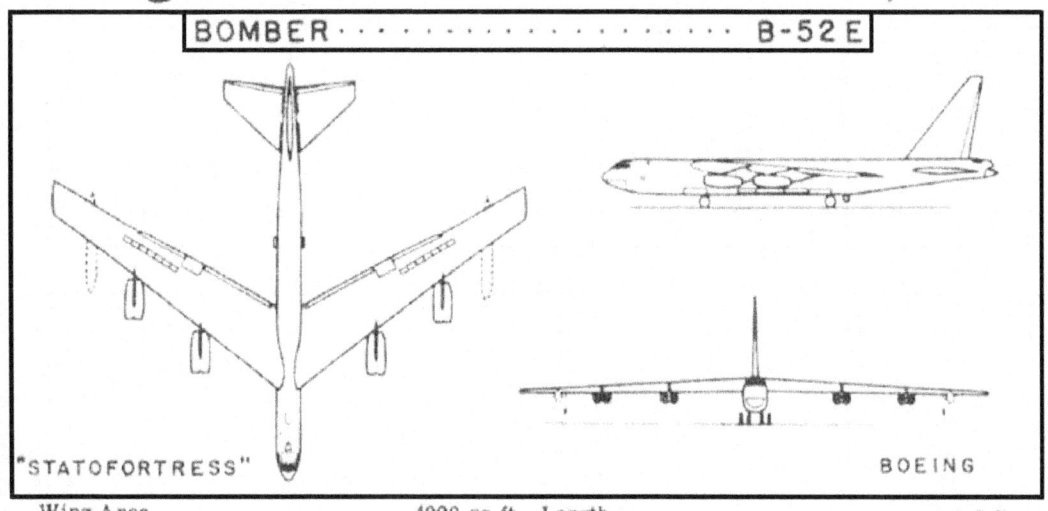

"STRATOFORTRESS" — BOEING

Wing Area .... 4000 sq ft Length .... 156.5 ft
Span .... 185.0 ft   Height (overall) .... 48.3 ft
                                     Height (fin folded) .... 21.5 ft

AVAILABILITY

Number available

ACTIVE	RESERVE	TOTAL

PROCUREMENT

Number to be delivered in fiscal years

STATUS

1. Design initiated: May 53
2. First flight: Nov 57
3. First delivery to SAC: Dec 57
4. The B-52E airplane is similar to the B-52D except for change in bombing-navigational system. The B-52E utilizes the AN/ASB-4A system.

Navy Equivalent: None   Mfr's Model: 464-259

POWER PLANT

(8) J57-P-19W or 29WA
Pratt & Whitney
ENGINE RATINGS

S.L.S   LB - **RPM -MIN
Max: *12,100-6450/9000-5
Mil: 10,500-6150/9900-30
Nor: 9000-5900/9650-
                     Cont

* Wet
** First figure represents low pressure spool; second figure represents high pressure spool.

FEATURES

Crew 6
Cabin pressurization, heating and cooling
Thermal Anti-icing
Braking parachute
Quadricycle landing gear
Aerodynamic spoilers (air-brake)
Strike camera station
AN/ASB-4 bombing-navig system
MD-9 fire control system
Folding fin
Pneumatic driven alternator & hydraulic packs
Liquid oxygen system
Crosswind landing gear

Max fuel cap: 41,553 gal

ARMAMENT

Turret 1
Guns ... 4 x .50 cal (M-3)
Ammunition (tot) .. 2400 rds
BOMBS:
Nr   Class (lb)
         New Series
27 (Family of Clusters) . 1000
         Special Weapons
MK-28 .... MK-53
MK-41 .... MK-57

Note: Structural provisions for 50,000 lb bomb; airplane will carry 4 ADM-20 and 2 AGM-28 missiles

Characteristics Summary Basic Mission — B-52E

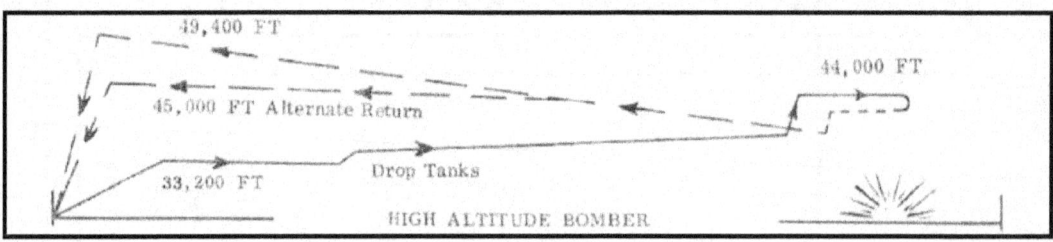

HIGH ALTITUDE BOMBER

PERFORMANCE

COMBAT RADIUS	FERRY RANGE	SPEED
3027 naut. mi with 10,000 lb payload at 453 knots avg. in 13.45 hours	6410 naut. mi with 41,024 gal fuel at 453 knots avg. in 14.17 hours at 450,000 lb T.O. wt.	COMBAT 496 knots at 44,000 ft alt, max power MAX 551 (c) knots at 20,200 ft alt, max power BASIC 520 knots at 35,000 ft alt, max power

CLIMB	CEILING	TAKE-OFF
2225 fpm sea level, take-off weight normal power	37,550 ft 100 fpm, combat weight normal power	ground run 8000 ft no assist
5125 fpm sea level, combat weight military power	45,800 ft 500 fpm, combat weight military power	over 50 ft height 10,300 ft no assist

LOAD	WEIGHTS	STALLING SPEED
Bombs: 10,000 lb Ammunition: 2400 rds/.50 cal Fuel: 39,287 gal protected 61.6 % droppable 14.4 % external 14.4 %	Empty..... 174,782 lb Combat.... 292,460 lb (b) Take-off 450,000 lb limited by structure	147 knots, initial buffet power-off, landing configuration, take-off weight
		TIME TO CLIMB 21.5 min to cruise altitude of 33,200 ft

NOTES

1. Performance Basis:
   (a) Data Source: Flight tests
   (b) Excludes 2500 lb water
   (c) Limited by structure
   (d) O.W.E. increases approximately 2000 lb on B-52 airplanes utilizing the J57-P-29WA engines resulting in a minor range decrease for a given T.O. weight.
2. Performance Reference: Boeing Document D-1513B "Substantiating Data Report - Models B-52B (-19W engines), B-52C and B-52D Standart Aircraft Characteristics Charts", 14 May 1957.
3. Revision Basis: To show change in Armament block, Page 1.

June 68.

Characteristics Summary Basic Mission B-52E

SUPPLEMENTAL

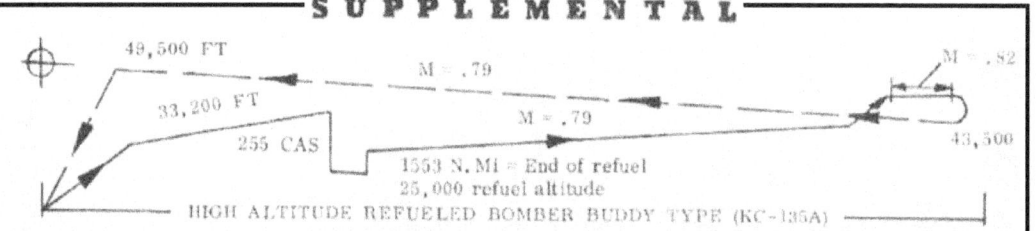

HIGH ALTITUDE REFUELED BOMBER BUDDY TYPE (KC-135A)

PERFORMANCE

COMBAT RADIUS	FERRY RANGE	SPEED	
3925 naut. mi with 10,000 lb payload at 453 knots avg. in 17.43 hours.	--- naut. mi with --- gal fuel at --- knots avg. in --- hours at --- lb T.O. wt.	COMBAT 43,500	486 knots at ft alt, mil power (c)
		MAX 20,200	551 knots at ft alt, max power
		BASIC 35,000	518 knots at ft alt, mil power

CLIMB	CEILING	TAKE-OFF
2225 fpm sea level, take-off weight normal power	37,550 ft 100 fpm, take-off weight normal power	ground run 8000 ft no assist
4575 fpm sea level, combat weight military power	43,900 ft 500 fpm, combat weight military power	over 50 ft height 10,300 ft no assist

LOAD	WEIGHTS	STALLING SPEED
Bombs: 10,000 lb Ammunition: 2400 rds/.50 cal Fuel: 39,288 gal protected 61.6 % droppable 14.4 % external 14.4 %	Empty..... 174,782 lb Combat ... 329,860 lb (b) Take-off 450,000 lb limited by structure	147 knots, initial buffet power-off, landing config- uration, take-off weight
		TIME TO CLIMB
		21.5 min to cruise altitude of 33,200 ft.

NOTES

1. Performance Basis:
   (a) Data Source: Flight Tests
   (b) Excludes 2500 lb water
   (c) Limited by structure
   (d) O.W.E. increases approximately 2000 lb on B-52 airplanes utilizing the J57-P-29WA engines resulting in a minor range decrease for a given T.O. Weight.

2. Revision Basis: To show change to Armament block, Page 1.

June 68.

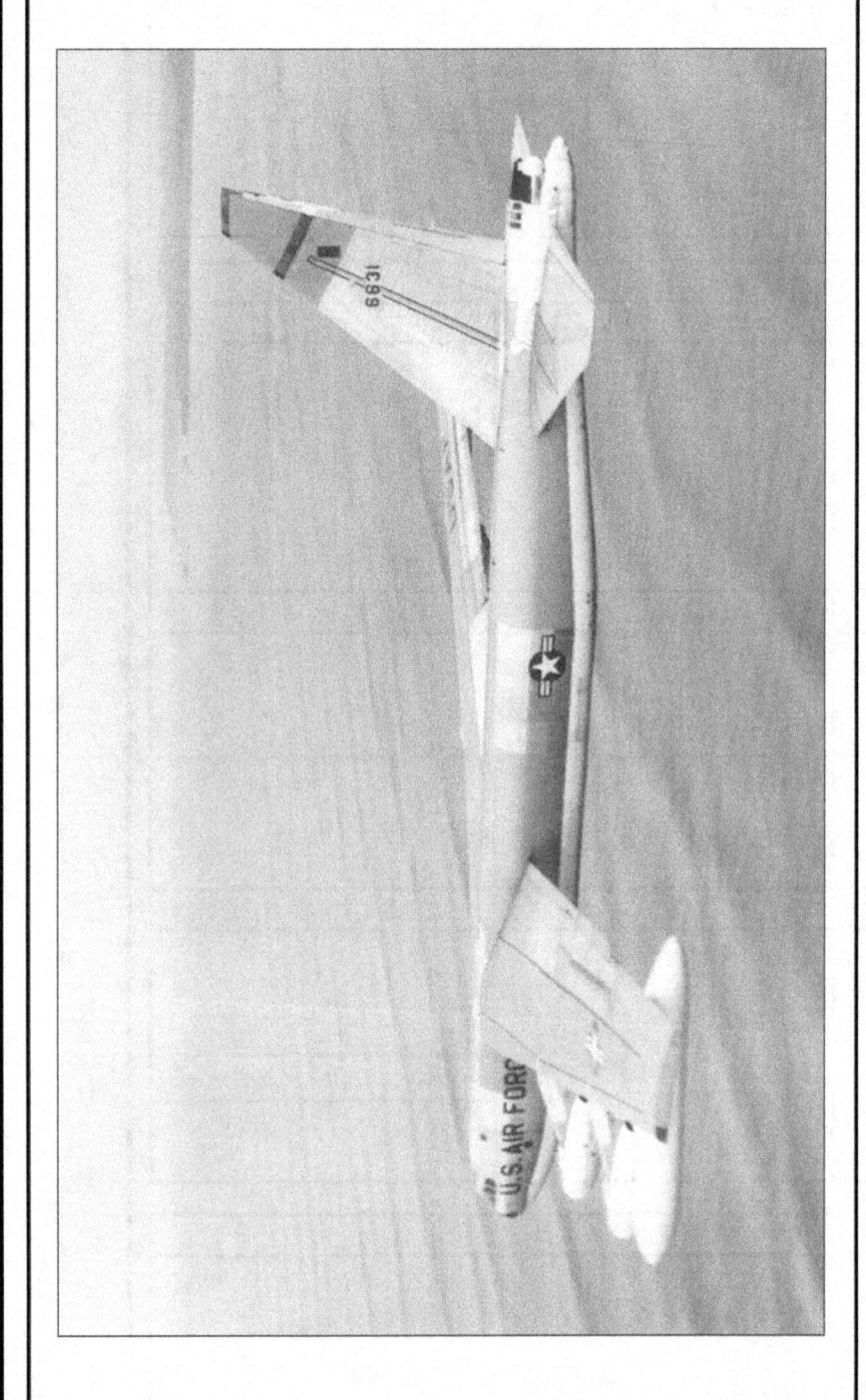

Standard Aircraft Characteristics

B-52E
STRATOFORTRESS
Boeing

EIGHT J57-P-19W, or -29WA
PRATT & WHITNEY

BY AUTHORITY OF
THE SECRETARY
OF THE AIR FORCE

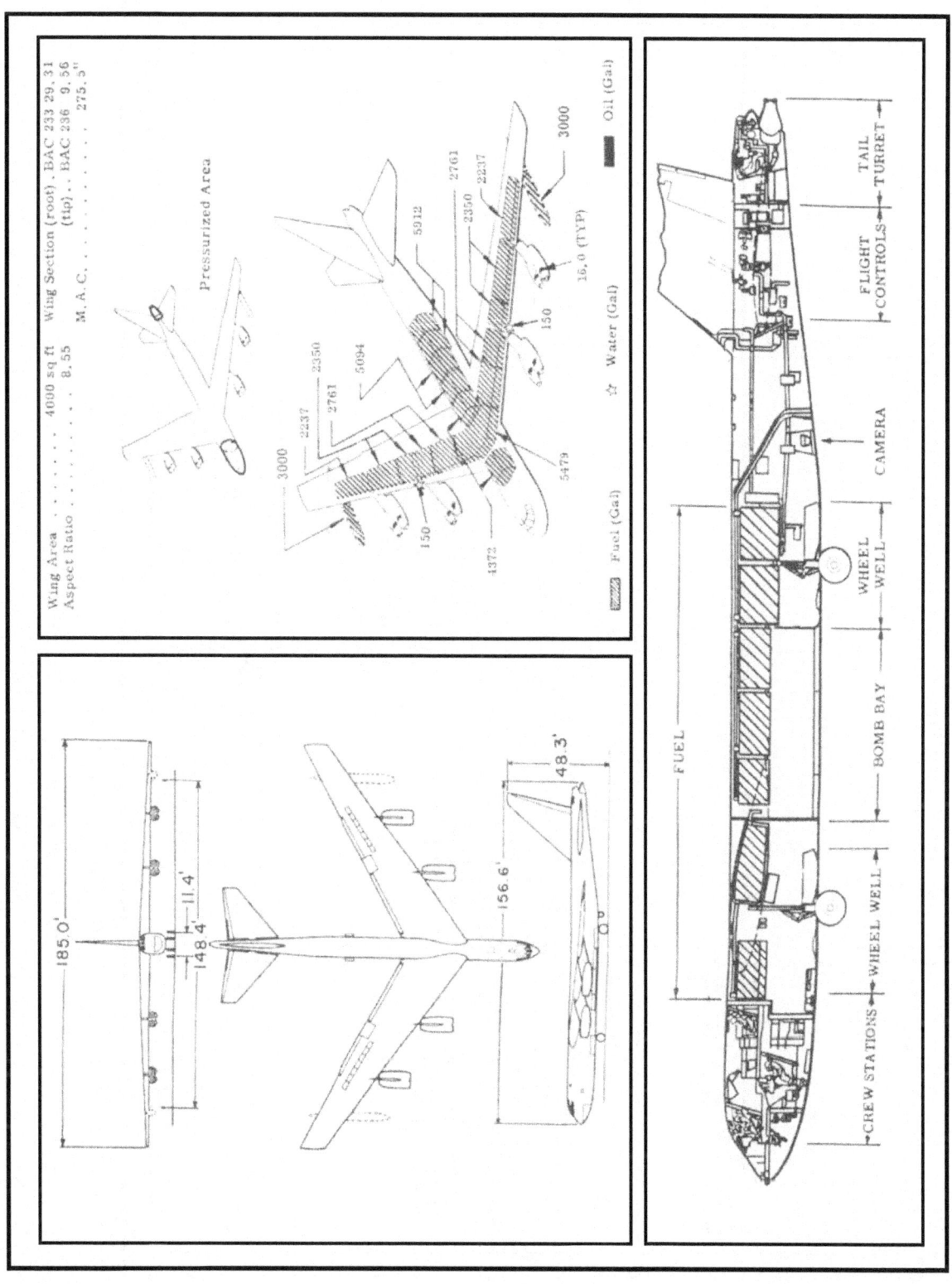

WEIGHTS

Loading	lb	L.F.
Empty	174,782 (C)	
Basic	175,124 (C)	
Design	460,000	2.0
Combat	*292,460	2.4
Max T.O.	**450,000	2.0
Max In-Flt	450,000	2.0
Max Land	***450,000	

(C) Calculated
* For Basic Mission
** Excludes 2500 lb water
*** For contact sinking speed of 6 ft/sec Max taxi wt, 2500 lb water Limited by structure

FUEL

Location	Nr Tanks	Gal
Wg, outbd	2	4474
Wg, ctr	1	5479
Wg, mains	4	10,222
Fus, fwd	2	4372
Fus, ctr	1	5094
Fus, aft	1	5912
Wg, drop	2	6060
	Total	41,553
Grade		JP-4
Specification		MIL-T-5624

OIL

Nacelle	8	128
Specification		MIL-L-007808F
WATER		
Wg, L.E.	2	300

ELECTRONICS

UHF Command	(2) AN/ARC-34
Liaison	AN/ARC-65X
IFF	AN/APX-25
Radar Beacon	AN/APN-69
ECM Trans	(3) AN/ALT-6B
ECM Receiver (1)	AN/APR-9
Interphone	AN/AIC-10A
Bombing Sys	AN/ASQ-38
Nav Recv'r	AN/ARN-14
Fire Control Sys	MD-9

See page 6 for additional equipment.

Mission and Description

Navy Equivalent: None   Mfr's Model: 464-259

The principal mission of the B-52E aircraft is the destruction of surface objects. The normal crew of six consists of pilot, co-pilot, navigator, bomb navigator, ECM operator and tail gunner.

Automatic cabin pressurization, heating and ventilation are provided for crew comfort during normal and combat operation.

Ejection seats for emergency escape are afforded the crew except for the tail gunner who bails out after jettisoning the tail section containing the gun turret.

Flight control, throughout the speed range from limit dive speed to landing speed is accomplished by use of spoilers and ailerons on the wing; elevators on an all-movable horizontal tail; and a rudder on a fixed vertical tail surface. The spoilers also function as air brakes used in landing.

Air is bled off the engines for thermal anti-icing of the wing and tail surface leading edges.

Other features are single-point ground and air refueling, braking parachute for decreasing landing roll distance, and a cross wind landing gear to aid in crosswind take-off and landing and a liquid oxygen system. The airplane utilizes the A/A24G-11 Auto Flight Control and the N-1 Compass.

The B-52E differs from the B-52D by the installation of the AN/ASQ-38 Bombing Navigational System in place of the AN/ASB-4s.

Development

Design Initiated	May 53
First flight	Nov 57
First delivery to SAC	Dec 57

GUNS

Nr	Type	Size	Rds ea	Loc
4	M-3	.50	600	Tail, tur

CAMERAS

Nr	Type	Lens
1	K-38	36"
1	K-22	6"
	or	
1	K-17D	6"
1	O-15 Radar Recording	

BOMBS

Nr		Class (lb)
27	New Series (Family of Clusters)	1000
	Special Weapons	
MK28		MK53
MK41		MK57

Note: Structural provisions for 50,000 lb bomb; airplane will carry 1 ADM-20 & 2 AGM-28 missiles.

POWER PLANT

Nr & Model	(8) J57-P-19W or -29WA
Mfr	Pratt & Whitney
Engine Spec Nr	A-1649G
Type	Axial
Length	157.7"
Diameter	40.5"
Weight (dry) (J57-P-19W)	*3970 lb
Tail Pipe	Fixed Area
Augmentation	Water

*J57-P-29WA engine . . . . 4150 lb

ENGINE RATINGS

	LB	**RPM	MIN
S.L. Static			
Max:	*12,100	6450/9900	5
Mil:	10,500	6150/9900	30
Nor:	9000	5900/9650	Cont

*Wet
**First figure represents low pressure spool; second figure represents high pressure spool.

DIMENSIONS

Wing	
Span	185.0'
Dihedral (chord plane)	2°30'
Incidence (root)	6°
Sweepback (LE)	36°58'
Length	156.5'
Height (overall)	48.3'
Height (fin folded)	21.5'
Tread (outrigger)	148.4'
Tread (main gear)	11.4'

202

Loading and Performance — Typical Mission

CONDITIONS			BASIC MISSION I	DESIGN MISSION II	MAX BOMB MISSION III	FERRY RANGE IV
TAKE-OFF WEIGHT	(7)	(lb)	450,000	450,000	450,000	450,000
Fuel at 6.5 lb/gal (grade JP-4)		(lb)	254,770	256,170	221,770	266,658
Payload (Bombs)		(lb)	10,000	8600	43,000	None
Payload (Chaff Flares)		(lb)	1000/168	1000/168	1000/168	None
Wing loading		(lb/sq ft)	112.5	112.5	112.5	112.5
Stall speed (power off)	(8)	(kn)	147	147	147	147
Take-off ground run at SL	(10)(11)	(ft)	8000	8000	8000	8000
Take-off to clear 50 ft	(11)	(ft)	10,300	10,300	10,300	10,300
Rate of climb at SL	(12)	(fpm)	2225	2225	2225	2225
Rate of climb at SL (one engine out)	(12)	(fpm)	2440	2440	2440	2440
Time: SL to 20,000 ft	(12)	(min)	10.8	10.8	10.8	10.8
Time: SL to 30,000 ft	(12)	(min)	18.0	18.0	18.0	18.0
Service ceiling (100 fpm)	(3)	(ft)	37,550	37,550	37,550	37,550
Service ceiling (one engine out)	(2)	(ft)	37,050	37,050	37,050	37,050
COMBAT RANGE	(4)	(n. mi.)				6410
COMBAT RADIUS	(1)	(n. mi.)	3027	3065	2655	
Average cruise speed		(kn)	453	453	453	453
Initial cruising altitude	(3)	(ft)	33,200	33,200	33,200	33,200
Target speed		(kn)	483	483	483	
Target altitude		(ft)	44,000	44,000	42,090	
Final cruising altitude		(ft)	49,500	49,400	49,700	49,900
Total mission time		(hr)	13.45	13.59	11.77	14.17
COMBAT WEIGHT		(lb)	292,460	292,450	277,950	299,913
Combat altitude	(2)(2)	(ft)	44,000	44,000	43,900	49,900
Combat speed	(3)	(kn)	496	496	505	504
Combat climb	(3)	(fpm)	750	750	1206	1210
Combat ceiling (500 fpm)	(12)(3)	(ft)	45,800	45,750	47,000	53,100
Service ceiling (100 fpm)	(12)(3)	(ft)	46,200	46,125	47,500	53,600
Max rate of climb at SL		(ft)	45,000	44,975	46,000	52,000
Max speed at optimum alt		(fps)	5325	5325	5380	5560
Basic speed at 35,000 ft	(5)	(kn)	551/20,200	551/20,200	551/20,200	551/20,560
		(kn/ft)	520	520	522	625
LANDING WEIGHT		(lb)	199,718	199,789	197,092	299,913
Ground roll at SL	(9)	(ft)	3175	3190	3170	3190
Ground roll (auxiliary brake)	(6)	(ft)	2880	2890	2875	2890
Total from 50 ft	(9)	(ft)	5400	5405	5390	5405
Total from 50 ft (auxiliary brake)	(9)	(ft)	4600	4610	4590	4610

NOTES:
1. Take-off power
2. Military power
3. Normal power
4. Detailed descriptions of RADIUS and RANGE missions given on page 6.
5. Limited by structure
6. With drag chute
7. Excludes 2500 lb water
8. Initial buffet, flaps down S. L.
9. Braking force limited to 40,000 lb

PERFORMANCE BASIS:
(a) Data source: Flight Test
(b) Performance is based on powers shown on page 3.

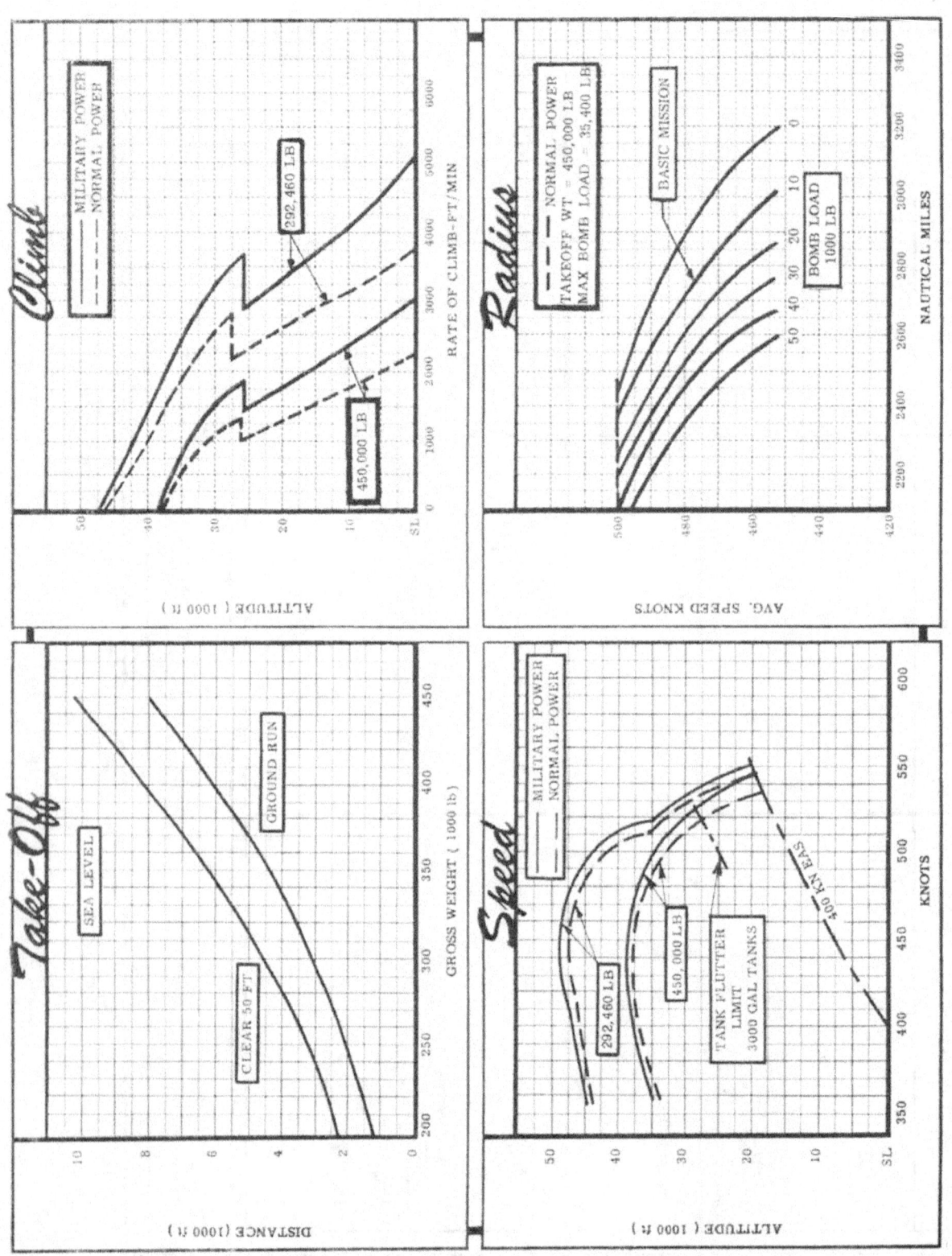

NOTES

FORMULA: RADIUS MISSIONS I, II & III

Take-off and climb on course to optimum cruise altitude at normal power. Cruise out at long range speed, increasing altitude with decreasing weight; external tanks are dropped when empty. Climb so as to reach cruise ceiling 15 minutes from target. Run in to target at normal power, drop bombs, conduct 2 minutes evasive action and 8 minutes escape at normal power. Cruise back to base at long range speed and optimum altitudes; as an alternate, a 45,000 foot ceiling may be maintained on the return leg with no radius penalty. Range-free allowances are fuel for 5 minutes at normal power for take-off, fuel for 2 minutes at normal power for evasive action, and fuel for 30 minutes maximum endurance at sea level plus 5% of the initial fuel load for landing reserve.

FORMULA: RANGE MISSION IV

Take-off and climb on course to optimum cruise altitude at normal power. Cruise out at long range speed, increasing altitude with decreasing weight; external tanks are dropped when empty. Land at a remote base with only reserve fuel remaining. Range-free allowances are fuel for 5 minutes at normal power for take-off, and fuel for 30 minutes maximum endurance at sea level plus 5% of the initial fuel load for landing reserve.

GENERAL DATA:

(a) The landing reserve for the Basic Mission is equivalent to 809 nautical miles range at optimum speed and altitude.

(b) The following electronic equipment is supplemental to that shown under "Electronics" on page 3:

Glide Path Receiver . . . . (1) AN/ARN-18 or AN/ARN-31
Marker Beacon . . . . (1) AN/ARN-32

"Electronics" cont'd

Early Warning . . . . (1) AN/APS-54
Chaff Dispenser . . . . (1) AN/ALE-1 or AN/ALE-27
UHF Dir. Finder AN/ARA-25
TACAN AN/ARN-21
RACON AN/APN-69
Doppler Radar AN/APN89A
Auto Astro Compass MD-1
True Heading Group N1-AJA-1
Rec'v'r System AN/APR-14
Flare Ejector . . . . (2) AN/ALE-20
ECM Trans . . . (4) AN/ALR-18
ECM Trans . . . (1) AN/ALT-13
ECM Trans . . . (1) AN/ALT-16
ECM Trans . . . (3) AN/ALT-15
Radar Altimeter AN/APN-150

(c) O. W. E. increases approximately 2000 lbs on B-52 airplanes utilizing the J57-P-29WA engines resulting in a range decrease for a given T. O. Weight.

PERFORMANCE REFERENCE:

Boeing document D-15134B, "Substantiation Data Report - Models B-52B (J57-P-19W engines), B-52C and B-52D Standard Aircraft Characteristics Charts", dated 14 May 1957.

REVISION BASIS:

To reflect current characteristic and performance data. Data re-coordinated by OCAMA.

(June 68)

MUNITIONS

TYPE	NR. LOADED	RACK CONFIGURATION	CLASS/ACTUAL WEIGHT (LBS)
CLUSTER RACKS			
M35 Cluster	27		750/690
M36 Cluster	27		750/900
M59 Semi-Armor-Piercing	27		1,000/1,140
M65 GP – Box Fin	15		1,000/1,104
M65 GP – Conical Fin	15		1,000/1,205
MK82 GP	27		500/531
M117 ④	27		750/823
M129A1 Photoflash	–		150/168
M124 Practice	27		250/264
M129/M129F1 Leaflet	27		750 1
MK36 Mine ③	18		1,000/1,110
MK50 Mine (unfinned) ② ③	27		500/544
MK52 Mine ② ③	18		1,000/1,194
MK53 Mine ③	27		500/378
SUU-24/A DISPENSER			
ADU-253 Cluster Bomb Adapter	72	1 SUU-24/A	136
ADU-253 Cluster Bomb Adapter	144	2 SUU-24/A	136
ADU-256 Cluster Bomb Adapter	72	1 SUU-24/A	168
ADU-256 Cluster Bomb Adapter	144	2 SUU-24/A	168
ADU-272 Cluster Bomb Adapter	72	1 SUU-24/A	185
ADU-272 Cluster Bomb Adapter	144	2 SUU-24/A	185
BLU-29/B Fire	48	1 SUU-24/A	165
BLU-29/B Fire	96	2 SUU-24/A	165
CLIP-IN (TWO)			
MK84 GP Bomb	8	All Stations	2,000/1,970
MK35 Mine	8	All Stations	2,000/2,013
MK39 Mine	8	All Stations	2,000/2,026
MK55 Mine	8	All Stations	2,000/2,120
MK56 Mine	4	Lower Stations	2,000/2,055

① Weights will depend on filler used.
② Low altitude only (400 – 3,000 feet above surface).
③ Rapid release not authorized.
④ M131 or MAU-103A/B fin.

Characteristics Summary

BOMBER B-52F

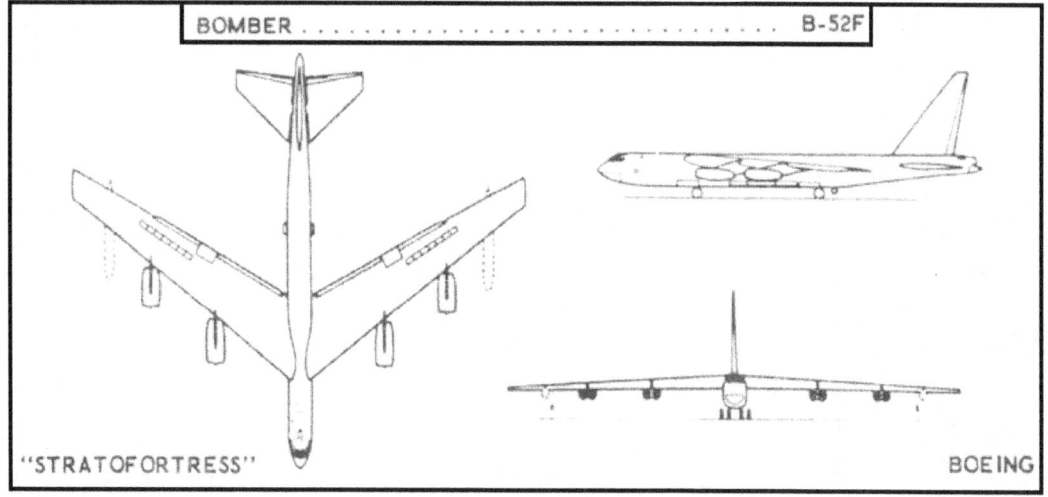

"STRATOFORTRESS"   BOEING

Wing Area .... 4000 sq ft	Length .... 156.5 ft
	Height (overall) ...... 48.3 ft
Span .... 185.0 ft	Height (fin folded) .... 21.5 ft

AVAILABILITY
Number available

TEST	INVENTORY	TOTAL

PROCUREMENT
Number to be delivered in fiscal years

STATUS

1. The B-52F airplane differs from the B-52C, D, E by the installation of the J57-P-43W engines in place of the J57-P-19W, 29W, and installation of engine driven alternators.
2. Modification of the wing structure, addition of new pods; improvement to water injection system are items necessary for incorporation of the J57-P-43W engines.
3. Program Initiated: .... Nov 54
4. First Flight: .... Mar 58
5. First Acceptance: .... May 58
6. Out of production: .... Dec 58

Navy Equivalent: None

Mfr's Model: 464-260

POWER PLANT

(8) J57-P-43W, WA or WB***
Pratt & Whitney
ENGINE RATINGS
SLS   LB - **RPM - MIN
Max: *13,750 - 6900/9650 -   5
Mil: 11,200 - 6100/9650 - 30
Nor: 9,500 - 6100/9350 - Cont

* Wet
** First figure represents low pressure spool; second figure represents high pressure spool.
*** Equipped with sound suppressors.

FEATURES

Crew 6
Cabin pressurization, heating and cooling
Braking parachute
Quadricycle landing gear
Aerodynamic spoilers (airbrake)
Strike camera station
ASB-4A high speed bombing radar
MD-9 fire control system
Folding fin
Crosswind steering
Engine driven alternators
Pneumatic driven hyd. packs
Anti-Skid Brakes
A/A42G-11 Auto. Flt. Control
Max fuel cap   41,553 gal

ARMAMENT

Turret 1
Guns .. 4 x .50 cal (M-3)
Ammunition (tot) 2400 rds
BOMBS.
No.
    New Series
27 (Family of Clusters)
       (1000 lb ea)
    Special Weapons
        MK-28
        MK-41
        MK-53
        MK-57

NOTE: Airplane will carry 4 ADM-20 & 2 AGM-28B Missiles
Max Bomb Load:(2)17,700 lb

Characteristics Summary Basic Mission B-52F

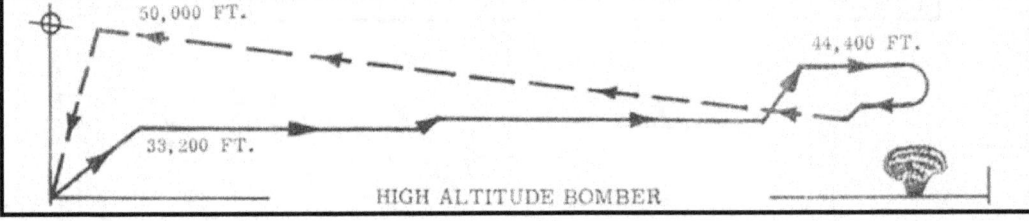

HIGH ALTITUDE BOMBER

PERFORMANCE

COMBAT RADIUS	FERRY RANGE	SPEED
3345 naut. mi with 10,000/1000/168 lb payload at 453 knots avg. in 14.03 hours.	6712 naut. mi with 41,406 gal fuel (b) at 453 knots avg. in 14.86 hours at 450,000 lb T.O. wt.	COMBAT 492 (TAS) knots at 44,400 ft alt, mil power MAX 553 (c) knots at 21,000 ft alt, mil power BASIC 521 knots at 35,000 ft alt, mil power
CLIMB	**CEILING**	**TAKE-OFF**
2300 fpm sea level, take-off weight normal power	37,800 ft 100 fpm, take-off weight normal power	ground run 7000 ft | Max Power
5600 fpm sea level, combat weight military power	46,000 ft 500 fpm, combat weight military power	over 50 ft height 9100 ft | Max Power
LOAD	**WEIGHTS**	**STALLING SPEED**
Bombs/Chaff: 10,000/1000/168 lb Ammunition 2400 rds/.50 cal Fuel: 39,669 gal protected 0 droppable 14.4 % external 14.4 % Density:(JP-4) lb/gal (6.5)	Empty..... 173,599 lb Combat... 291,570 lb (b) Take-off 450,000 lb limited by structure (inflight)	147 knots initial buffet power-off, landing con- figuration, take-off weight. **TIME TO CLIMB** 19.7 min to cruise altitude of 33,200 ft

NOTES

1. Performance Basis:
   (a) Data Source: Flight Test
   (b) Does not include 10,000 lb water
   (c) Limited by structure

2. Revision Basis: To indicate changes to engine designation and armament block.

June 68.

Characteristics Summary Basic Mission B-52F

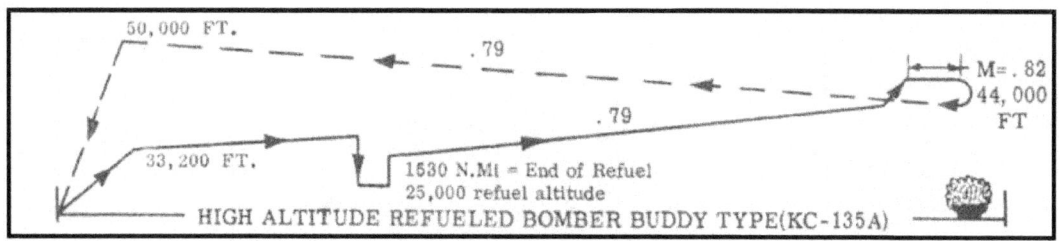

HIGH ALTITUDE REFUELED BOMBER BUDDY TYPE (KC-135A)

PERFORMANCE

COMBAT RADIUS	FERRY RANGE	SPEED
(d) 3978 naut. mi 10,000/400 lb payload at 453 knots avg. in 17.64 hours.	——— naut. mi with ——— gal fuel at ——— knots avg. in ——— hours at ——— lb T.O. wt.	(TAS) COMBAT 490 knots at 44,000 ft alt, max power (c) MAX 553 knots at 20,500 ft alt, max power BASIC 521 knots at 35,000 ft alt, max power

CLIMB	CEILING	TAKE-OFF
2300 fpm sea level, take-off weight normal power	37,800 ft 100 fpm, take-off weight normal power	ground run 7000 ft no assist / max power
4975 fpm sea level, combat weight military power	44,200 ft 500 fpm, combat weight military power	over 50 ft height 9100 ft no assist / max power

LOAD	WEIGHTS	STALLING SPEED
Bombo/Chaff: 10,000/400 lb Ammunition 2400 rds/.50 cal Fuel: 39,669 gal protected 0 % droppable 14.4 % external 14.4 % Density: JP-4 lb/gal (6.5)	Empty..... 173,599 lb Combat... 328,000 lb (b) Take-off 450,000 lb limited by structure	147 knots power-off, landing configuration, take-off weight
		TIME TO CLIMB 20.0 min to cruise altitude of 33,250 ft.

NOTES

1. Performance Basis:
   (a) Data Source: Flight Test
   (b) Does not include 10,000 lb water
   (c) Limited by structure
   (d) Surge valves closed; 3000 gal tanks on for refuel. Increase range by 2.4% when tanks are dropped after refuel.
2. Revision Basis: To indicate change to engine designation and armament block.

June 68.

Standard Aircraft Characteristics

B-52F
STRATOFORTRESS
Boeing

EIGHT J57-P-43W, WA, OR WB
PRATT & WHITNEY

BY AUTHORITY OF
THE SECRETARY
OF THE AIR FORCE

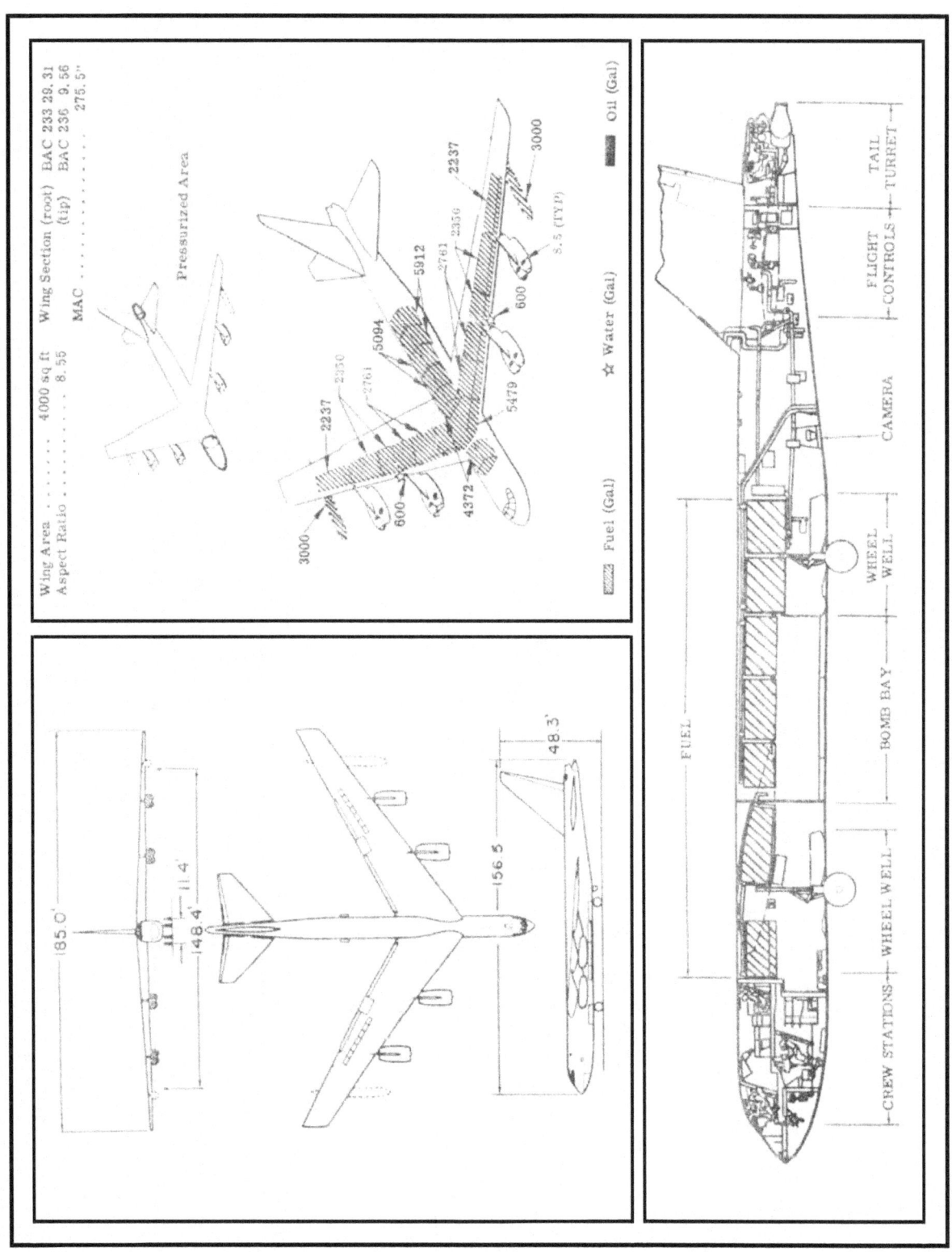

POWER PLANT

Nr & Model . . (8)	*J57-P-W, WA or WB
Mfr	Pratt & Whitney
Engine Spec Nr . . .	A1704E
Type	Axial
Length	167.3"
Diameter	38.9"
Weight (dry)	3870 lb
Tail Pipe	Fixed Area
Augmentation	Water

*Sound suppressors to be included in retrofit.

ENGINE RATINGS

	S.L.Static LB - **RPM - MIN
Max:	*13,750 - 6900/9650 - 5
Mil:	11,200 - 6400/9650 - 30
Nor:	9500 - 6100/9350 - Cont

* Wet
** First figure represents low pressure spool; second figure represents high pressure spool.

DIMENSIONS

Wing	
Span	185.0'
Dihedral (chord plane)	2°30'
Incidence (root) . . .	6°
Sweepback (LE)	36°58'
Length	156.5'
Height (overall) . . .	48.3'
Height (fin folded) .	21.5'
Tread (outrigger) . .	148.4'
Tread (main gear) . .	11.4'

WEIGHTS

	Lb	L.F.
Loading		
Empty	173,599 (C)	
Basic	176,104 (C)	
Design	460,000	2.0
Combat	*291,570	2.3
Max T.O. . . .	**450,000	2.0
Max In-Flight	450,000	2.0
Max Landing .	***450,000	---

(C) Calculated
* For Basic Mission
** Excludes 10,000 lb water
*** For contact sinking speed of 6 ft/sec
Max taxi wt. 10,000 lb water
Limited by structure

FUEL

Location	Nr Tanks	Gal
Wg, outbd	2	4474
Wg, ctr	1	5479
Wg, mains	4	10,222
Wg, fwd	2	4372
Fus, fwd	1	5094
Fus, ctr	1	5912
Fus, aft	2	6000
Wg, drop		
	Total	41,553

Grade		JP-4
Specification . . .		MIL-T-5624
	OIL	
Nacelle		(ea) 68
Specification . . .		MIL-L-007808F
	WATER	
Wg, L.E.		1200

ELECTRONICS

UHF Command (2)	AN/ARC-34
IFF	AN/APX-25
Radar Beacon	AN/APN-69
ECM Trans (3)	AN/ALT-6B
ECM Trans (3)	AN/ALT-13
ECM Receiver (1) . . .	AN/APR-9
ECM Receiver	AN/APR-14
Interphone	AN/AIC-10A
Bombing Nav Sys . . .	AN/ASQ-38
Nav Rec'r	AN/ARN-14
Fire Control Sys . . .	MD-9

Mission and Description

Navy Equivalent: None   Mfr's Model: 464-260

The principal mission of the B-52F aircraft is the destruction of surface objects.
The normal crew of six consists of pilot, co-pilot, navigator, bomb navigator, ECM operator and tail gunner.

Automatic cabin pressurization, heating and ventilation are provided for crew comfort during normal and combat operation.

Ejection seats for emergency escape are afforded the crew except for the tail gunner who bails out after jettisoning the tail section containing the gun turret.

Flight control, throughout the speed range from limit dive speed to landing speed is accomplished by use of spoilers and ailerons on the wing; elevators on an all-movable horizontal tail; and a rudder on a fixed vertical tail surface. The spoilers also function as air brakes used in landing.

Air is bled off the engines for thermal anti-icing of the wing and tail surface leading edges.

Other features are single-point ground and air refueling, braking parachute for decreasing landing roll distance, and a crosswind landing gear to aid in crosswind take-off and landing. The airplane utilizes the A/A42G-11 Auto Flight Control and the N-1 Compass.

Major differences of the B-52F from the B-52E are the installation of J57-P-W, WA, or WB engines in place of J57-P-19W engines and of engine driven alternators.

Development

Design Initiated:	
First Flight	Nov 54
First Acceptance	Mar 58
	May 58

BOMBS

Nr		Class (lb)
	New Series	
27	(Family of Clusters)	1000
24	(External)	750
	Special Weapons	
	MK-53	
	MK-28	
	MK-57	
	MK-41	

Note: Airplane will carry 4 AGM-20 & 2 AGM-28B missiles

GUNS

Nr	Type	Size	Rds ea	Loc
4	M-3	.50	600	Tail tur

CAMERAS

Nr	Type	Lens
1	K-38	36"
1	K-17C	6"
	or	
1	K-17D	6"
1	O-32 Radar Recording	

212

Loading and Performance — Typical Mission

CONDITIONS		BASIC MISSION I	DESIGN LOAD II	MAX BOMB LOAD III	FERRY RANGE IV	ALTERNATE LOAD V	MISSILE LOAD VI
TAKE-OFF WEIGHT ①	(lb)	450,000	450,000	450,000	450,000	450,000	450,000
Fuel at 6.5 lb/gal (grade JP-4)	(lb)	257,251	258,651	237,851	269,139	249,651	225,235
Payload (Bombs/Missiles)	(lb)	10,000		35,400	None	17,700	17,700/21,316 ⑪
Payload 3 (Chaff, Flares)	(lb)	1000/168	1000/168	1000/168	None	1000/168	1000/168
Wing loading	(lb/sq ft)	112.5	112.5	112.5	112.5	112.5	112.5
Stall speed (power off)	(kn)	147	147	147	147	147	147
Take-off ground run at SL	(ft)	7000	7000	7000	7000	7000	6100
Take-o T to clear 50 ft	(ft)	9100	9100	9100	9100	9100	9200
Rate of climb at SL	(fpm)	2300	2300	2300	2300	2300	2540
Rate of climb at SL (one engine out) ②	(fpm)	2660	2660	2660	2660	2660	2960
Time: SL to 20,000 ft	(min)	10.2	10.2	10.2	10.2	10.2	9.08
Time: SL to 30,000 ft	(min)	17.4	17.4	17.4	17.4	17.4	15.5
Service ceiling (100 fpm)	(ft)	37,800	37,800	37,800	37,800	37,800	38,500
Service ceiling (one engine out)	(ft)	37,500	37,500	37,500	37,500	37,500	38,200
COMBAT RANGE ④	(n. mi.)				6712		
COMBAT RADIUS ④	(n. mi.)	3163	3189	2862		3047	2536
Average cruise speed	(kn)	453	453	453		453	453
Initial cruising altitude	(ft)	33,200	33,200	33,200		33,200	33,200
Target speed ③	(kn)	484	484	484		484	484
Target altitude	(ft)	44,400	44,200	43,000		44,700	43,500
Final cruising altitude	(ft)	50,000	50,000	50,000		50,000	50,300
Total mission time	(hr)	14.03	14.4	12.66	14.86	13.5	10.76
COMBAT WEIGHT	(lb)	291,570	291,881	277,181	197,706	283,181	277,054
Combat altitude	(ft)	44,400	44,200	43,000	50,000	44,700	43,500
Combat speed	(kn)	492	492	500	504	496	500
Combat climb	(fpm)	825	839	1150	1300	900	1200
Combat ceiling (500 fpm)	(ft)	46,000	46,600	47,000	53,800	46,500	47,750
Service ceiling (100 fpm)	(ft)	46,700	46,700	47,600	54,500	47,400	49,000
Service ceiling (one engine out)	(ft)	45,300	45,730	46,100	52,800	46,000	48,000
Max rate of climb at SL	(fpm)	5600	5600	5750	5850	5800	5990
Basic speed at 35,000 alt	(kn)	553/21,000	553/21,000	554/21,000	555/21,000	553/21,000	559/21,000
	(kn/ft)	521	523	522	525	522	523
LANDING WEIGHT	(lb)	197,112	197,420	195,312	197,706	196,727	195,511
Ground roll at SL	(ft)	3125	3125	3075	3145	3075	3075
Ground roll (auxiliary brake)	(ft)	2200	2200	2180	2210	2190	2180
Total from 50 ft	(ft)	5545	5545	5495	5555	5505	5495
Total from 50 ft (auxiliary brake)	(ft)	4620	4620	4600	4630	4610	4600

NOTES

① Take-off power
② Military power
③ Normal power
④ Detailed descriptions of RADIUS and RANGE missions given on page 6
⑤ Limited by structure
⑥ With drag chute
⑦ Does not include 10,000 lb of water
⑧ Initial buffet, flaps down, S.L.
⑨ AGM-28's at take-off power
⑩ AGM-28's at maximum continuous power
⑪ 4 ADM-20's   4840 lb
    Droppable racks   590 lb
    2 AGM-28's   15,886
    Total   21,316 lb

PERFORMANCE BASIS:
(a) Data source: Flight test
(b) Performance is based on powers shown on page 3

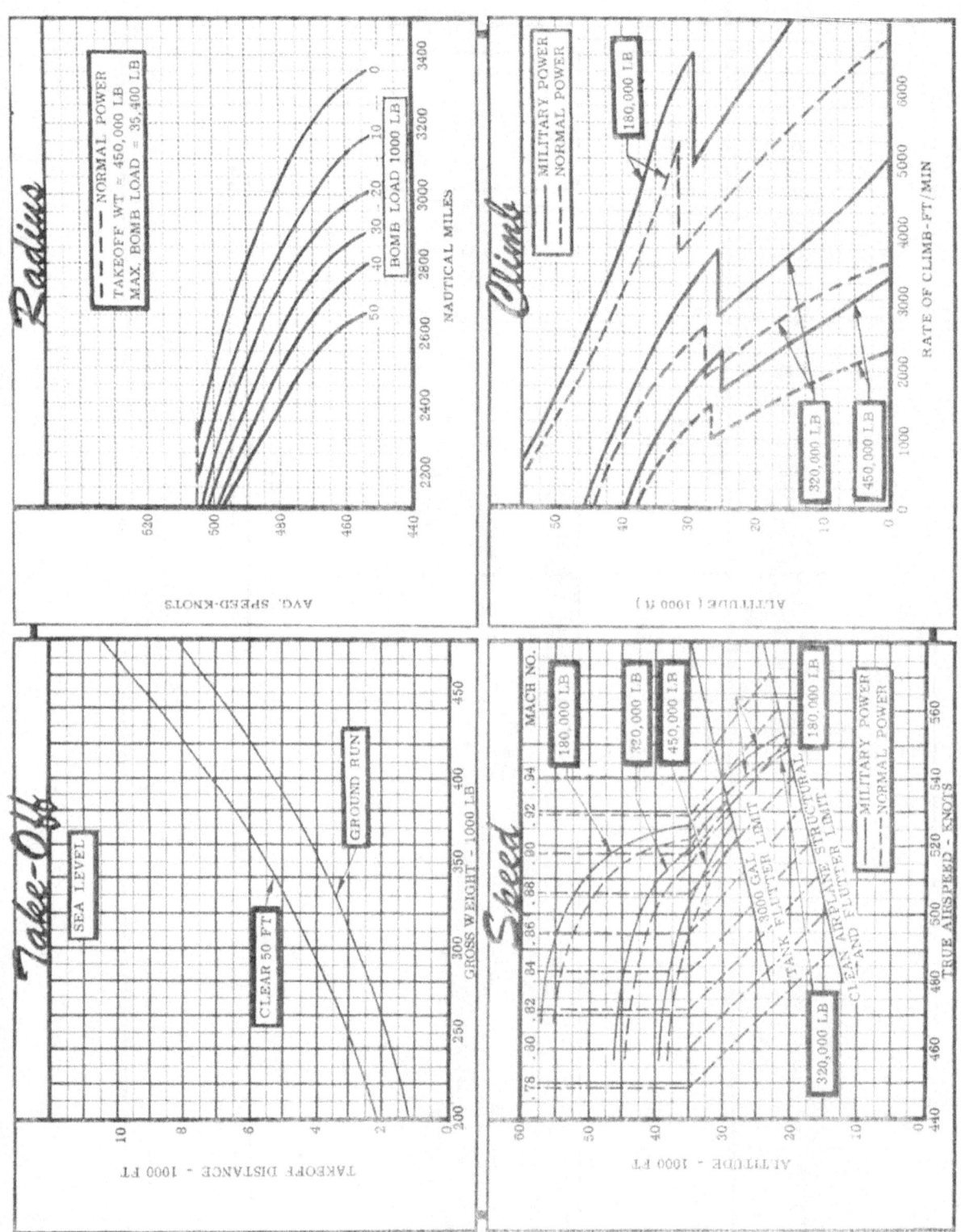

NOTES

FORMULA: BOMBER RADIUS MISSIONS I, II, III & V

Take off and climb on course to optimum cruise altitude at normal power. Cruise out at long range speed*, increasing altitude with decreasing weight; external tanks are dropped when empty. Climb so as to reach cruise ceiling 15 minutes from target. Run into target at normal power, drop bombs, conduct 2 minutes evasive action and 8 minutes escape at normal power. Cruise back to home base at long range speeds*, increasing altitude with decreasing airplane weight. Range free allowances include 5 minutes normal power fuel consumption for starting engines and takeoff, 2 minutes normal power fuel consumption at combat altitude for evasive action, and 30 minutes of maximum endurance (four engines) fuel consumption at sea level plus 5% of initial fuel for landing reserve.

FORMULA: BOMBER RANGE MISSION IV

Take off and climb on course to optimum cruise altitude at normal power. Cruise out at long range speed*, increasing altitude with decreasing weight until all fuel is consumed; external tanks are dropped when empty. Range free allowances include 5 minutes normal-power fuel consumption for starting engines and takeoff and 30 minutes of maximum endurance (four engines) fuel consumption at sea level plus 5% of initial fuel for landing reserve.

FORMULA: BOMBER RADIUS MISSION VI

Take off and climb on course to optimum cruise altitude at normal power (AGM-28's at maximum continuous power). Cruise out at long range speed*, increasing altitude with decreasing weight. Release AGM-28's and ADM-20's at their respective ranges from target. Climb so as to reach cruise ceiling 15 minutes from target. Run into target at normal power, drop bombs, conduct 2 minutes evasive action and 8 minutes escape at normal power. Cruise back to home base at long range speeds*, increasing altitude with decreasing airplane weight. Range free allowances include 5 minutes normal power fuel consumption for starting engines and takeoff, 2 minutes normal power fuel consumption at combat altitude for evasive action, and 30 minutes of maximum endurance (four engines) fuel consumption at sea level plus 5% of initial fuel for landing reserve.

*Long range speed is maximum speed for 99% maximum miles per pound of fuel.

GENERAL DATA:

(a) The prescribed fuel reserve for the basic mission is equivalent to the following reserve range at best range conditions:

B-52F Bomber .... 810 nautical miles

(b) Data based on engine surge bleed valves with T.O. 2J16-3-7-506 incorporated. For airplanes which do not have this T.O. incorporated, reduce mission radius and range numbers by 2%.

(c) The following electronic equipment is supplemental to that shown under "Electronics" on page 3.

Glide Path Receiver (1)	AN/ARN-31
Marker Beacon (1)	AN/ARN-32
Early Warning (1)	AN/APS-54
Chaff Dispenser (2)	AN/ALE-1 or AN/ALE-27
Direction Finder	AN/ARA-25
Liaison Radio	AN/ARC-65
ECM Trans (2)	AN/ALT-15H
ECM Trans (1)	AN/ALT-15L
ECM Trans (1)	AN/ALT-16
ECM Receiver (2)	AN/ALR-18
Automatic Astro Compass	MD-1
TRUE Heading Group	N1-AJA-1
Doppler RADAR	AN/APN-89A
TACAN	AN/ARN-21
Radar Altimeter	AN/APN-150

PERFORMANCE REFERENCE:

Boeing Document D2-1551, "Substantiating Data Report - Models B-52F J57-P-43WA engines), Standard Aircraft Characteristics Charts," revised Feb 65.

REVISION BASIS: To reflect current characteristics and performance data. Data recoordinated by OCAMA. (MMEAF)

MUNITIONS

TYPE	NR. LOADED	RACK CONFIGURATION	CLASS/ACTUAL WEIGHT (LBS)
\multicolumn{4}{c}{CLUSTER RACKS}			
M35 Cluster	27		750/690
M36 Cluster	27		750/900
M59 Semi-Armor-Piercing	27		1,000/1,140
M65 GP - Box Fin	15		1,000/1,104
M65 GP - Conical Fin	15		1,000/1,205
MK82 GP	27		500/531
M117 GP ⑤	27		750/823
M129A1 Photoflash	-		150/168
M124 Practice	27		250/264
M129/M129E1	27		750 1
MK36 Mine ③	18		1,000/1,110
MK50 Mine (unfinned) ② ③	27		500/544
MK52 Mine ② ③	18		1,000/1,190
MK53 Mine ③	27		500/378
\multicolumn{4}{c}{EXTERNAL MER}			
CBU-24B/B Cluster ④	24		750/830
MK81 GP	24		250/260
MK82 GP	24		500/531
MK82 Snakeye (high drag) GP ③	24		500/560
M117 GP ⑤	24		750/823
M117R (high drag) GP ③	24		750/880
M129E1 Leaflet	24		750 1
\multicolumn{4}{c}{SUU-24/A DISPENSER}			
ADU-253 Cluster Bomb Adapter	72	1 SUU-24/A	136
ADU-253 Cluster Bomb Adapter	144	2 SUU-24/A	136
ADU-256 Cluster Bomb Adapter	72	1 SUU-24/A	168
ADU-256 Cluster Bomb Adapter	144	2 SUU-24/A	168
ADU-272 Cluster Bomb Adapter	72	1 SUU-24/A	185
ADU-272 Cluster Bomb Adapter	144	2 SUU-24/A	185
BLU-29/B Fire	48	1 SUU-24/A	165
BLU-29/B Fire	96	2 SUU-24/A	165
\multicolumn{4}{c}{CLIP-IN (TWO)}			
MK84 GP Bomb	8	All Stations	2,000/1,970
MK25 Mine	8	All Stations	2,000/2,013
MK39 Mine	8	All Stations	2,000/2,025
MK55 Mine	8	All Stations	2,000/2,120
MK56 Mine	4	Lower Stations	2,000/2,055

Characteristics Summary

HEAVY BOMBER B-52G

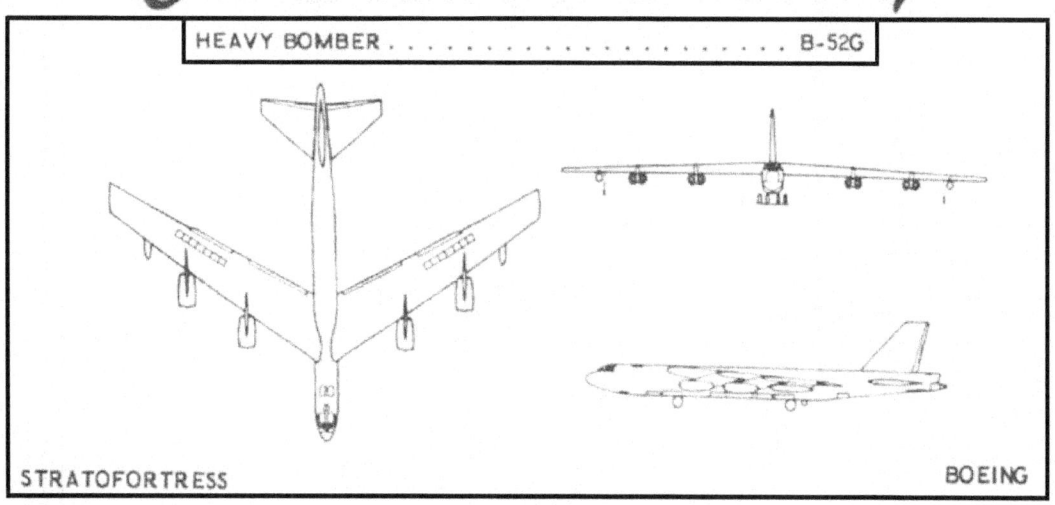

STRATOFORTRESS   BOEING

Wing Area . . . . 4000 sq ft.   Length . . . . 157.6 ft.
Span . . . . 185.0 ft. Height . . . . 40.7 ft.
                                                            Height (Fin folded) . . . . 21.5 ft.

AVAILABILITY

Number available		
TEST	INVENTORY	TOTAL

PROCUREMENT

Number to be delivered in fiscal years				
FY61				

STATUS

1. Major differences from the B-52F are: reduced span fin, deletion of ailerons, 700 gallon fixed external tanks, enlarged nose radomes, relocation of gunner, integral wing fuel tanks, reduced empty weight and increased max. gross weight.
2. Program Initiated: . . . . Jun 56
3. First Flight : . . . . Oct 58
4. First Acceptance . . . . Oct 58
5. Out of Production: . . . . Feb 61

Navy Equivalent: None   Mfr's Model: 464-253

POWER PLANT

(8) J57-P-43WB ***
Pratt & Whitney

ENGINE RATINGS
S.L.S. LB - **RPM - MIN
Max:*13,750 - 6800/9650 - 5
Mil: 11,200 - 6400/9650 - 30
Nor: 9,500 - 6100/9350 - Cont

* Wet
** First figure represents low pressure spool; second figure represents high pressure spool
*** Equipped with sound suppressors

Note: There are no requirements for ATO

FEATURES

Crew 6
Cabin pressurization, heating and cooling
ASB-9 Improved Hi Speed Bombing Radar
ASG-15 Fire control sys.
Quadricycle landing gear with cross-wing steering
Braking parachute
Aerodynamic spoilers (airbrakes)
Anti-skid brakes
Single-point ground and air refueling provisions
Liquid oxygen system
4 Engine driven 40 KVA alternators
6 Engine driven hyd. pumps
Folding fin.

Max fuel cap: 47,975 gal

ARMAMENT

Turret 1
Guns . . . . 4 x 50 cal
Ammunition . . (total) 2400 rds

BOMBS:
Nr.
27 (family of clusters)(1000 lb ea)
Special Weapons
  *MK 6
   MK 15
   MK 28
   MK 36
   MK 39
   MK 41

*1st 154 G's only
Note:
Airplane will carry 4 GAM-72 & 2 GAM-77 missiles or 4 GAM-87 missiles after retrofit.
Max Bomb Load: (2) 17,700 lb

Characteristics Summary Basic Mission — B-52G

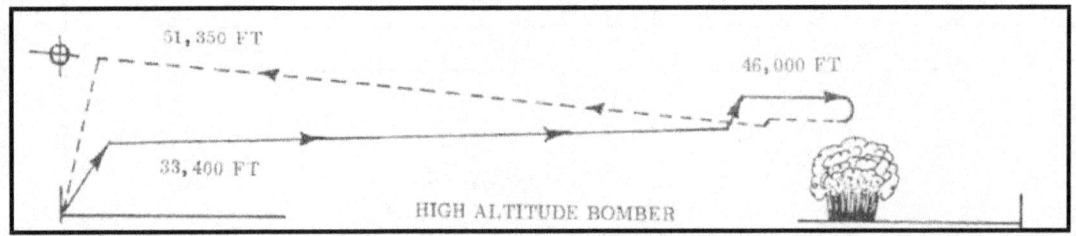

HIGH ALTITUDE BOMBER

PERFORMANCE (a)

COMBAT RADIUS	FERRY RANGE	SPEED
3460 naut. mi with 10,000/400/270 lb payload at 454 knots avg. in 15.30 hours.	**7270** naut. mi with 43,986 gal fuel at 454 knots avg. in 16.08 hours at (b)450,000 lb T.O. wt.	(TAS) COMBAT **495** knots at 46,000 ft alt, mil power MAX **553** (e) knots at 20,500 ft alt, mil power BASIC **521** knots at 35,000 ft alt, mil power

CLIMB	CEILING	TAKE-OFF
2425 fpm sea level, take-off weight normal power	**38,400** ft 100 fpm, take-off weight normal power	ground run **6750** ft
5850 fpm sea level, combat weight military power	**47,100** ft 500 fpm, combat weight military power	over 50 ft height **8800** ft

LOAD	WEIGHTS	STALLING SPEED

Bombs/Chaff/Flares:
10,000/400/270 lb
Ammunition 2400 rds./.50 cal.
 	
Fuel: 42,345 gal
  protected 0
  droppable 0
  external (c) 3.3
Density (JP-4) lb/gal (6.5)
	Empty..... 158,590 lb
	Combat... 281,390 lb
	Take-off (b) 450,000 lb
	limited by structure
	(inflight)
		147 knots
		power-off, landing configuration, take-off weight (d)

		TIME TO CLIMB **19.1** minutes to cruise altitude of 33,400 ft.

NOTES

1. Performance Basis:
    (a) Data Source: Flight test
    (b) Does not include 10,000 lb water
    (c) Based on 42,345 gallon load
    (d) Initial buffet
    (e) Limited by structure
2. Revision Basis: Data recoordinated.

SUPPLEMENTAL — B-52G
Characteristics Summary Basic Mission - ALTERNATE IN-FLIGHT

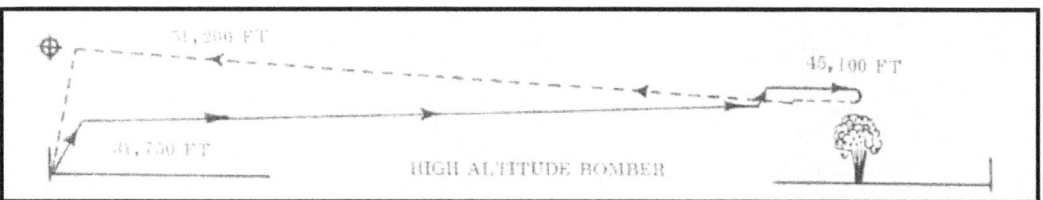

HIGH ALTITUDE BOMBER

PERFORMANCE (a)

COMBAT RADIUS	FERRY RANGE	SPEED (TAS)
3785 naut. mi with 10,000/400/270 lb payload at 454 knots avg. in 16.74 hours.	7735 naut. mi with 47,975 gal fuel at 454 knots avg. in 17.11 hours at (b) 475,928 lb T.O. wt.	COMBAT 494 knots at 45,100 ft alt, mil power MAX - 553 (c) knots at 20,500 ft alt, mil power BASIC 521 knots at 35,000 ft alt, mil power

CLIMB	CEILING	TAKE-OFF
2180 fpm sea level, take-off weight normal power	36,700 ft 100 fpm, take-off weight normal power	ground run 8100 ft
5560 fpm sea level, combat weight military power	46,150 ft 500 fpm, combat weight military power	over 50 ft height 10,350 ft

LOAD	WEIGHTS	STALLING SPEED
Bombs/Chaff/Flares: 10,000/400/270 lb Ammunition 2400 rds/.50 cal. Fuel: 47,975 gal protected 0 % droppable 0 % external 2.9 % Density (JP-4) lb/gal (6.5)	Empty..... 158,590 lb Combat... 294,650 lb Take-off (b) 486,598 lb limited by fuel capacity	153 knots power-off, landing config- uration, take-off weight (d)
		TIME TO CLIMB 20.1 minutes to cruise altitude of 31,750 ft.

NOTES

1. Performance Basis:
    (a) Data Source: Flight Test
    (b) Does not include 10,000 lb water
    (c) Limited by structure
    (d) Initial buffet

2. Revision Basis: Data recoordinated.

STANDARD AIRCRAFT CHARACTERISTICS

B-52G
STRATOFORTRESS
BOEING

EIGHT J57-P/F-43WB
PRATT & WHITNEY

BY AUTHORITY OF
THE SECRETARY
OF THE AIR FORCE

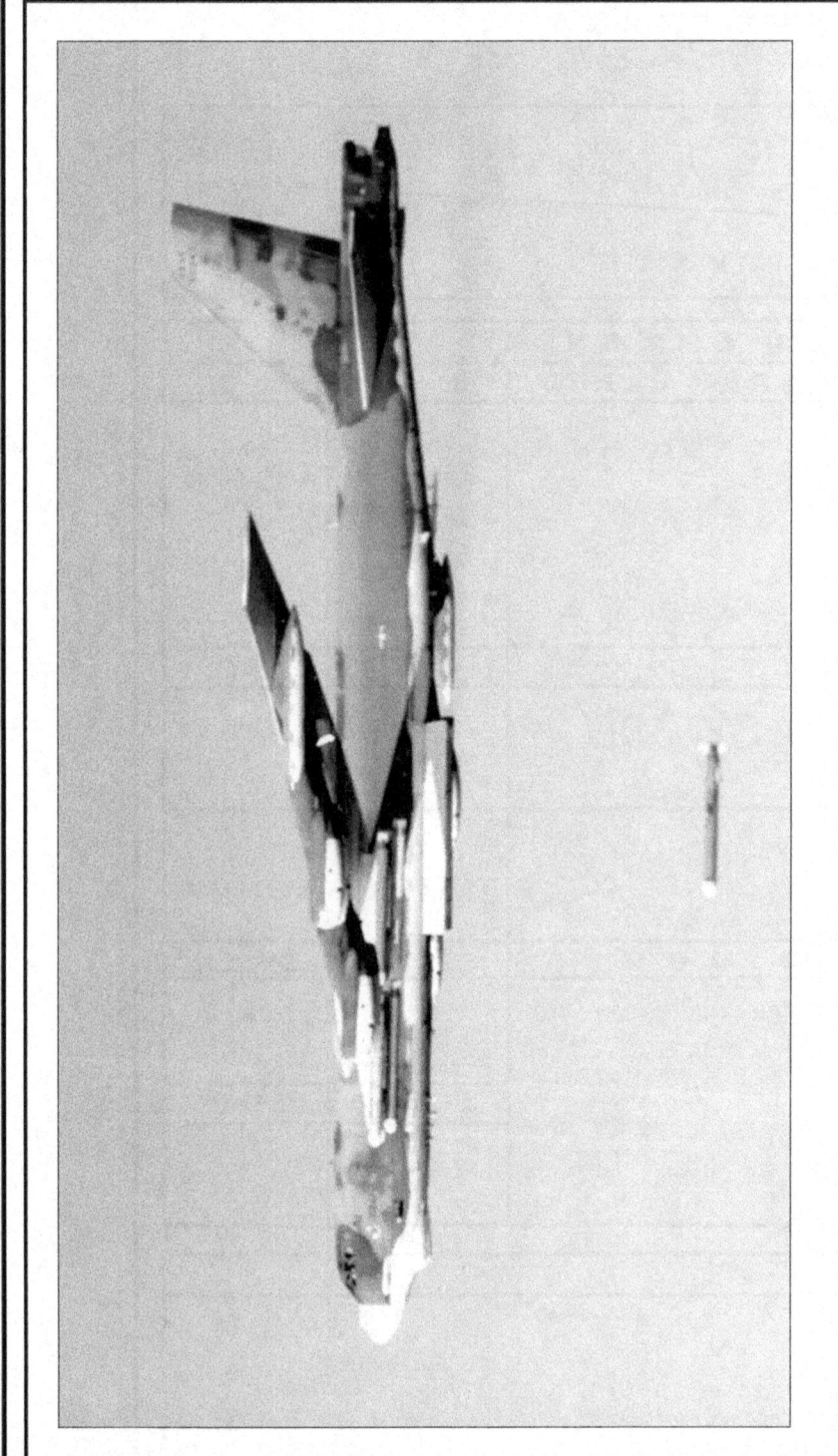

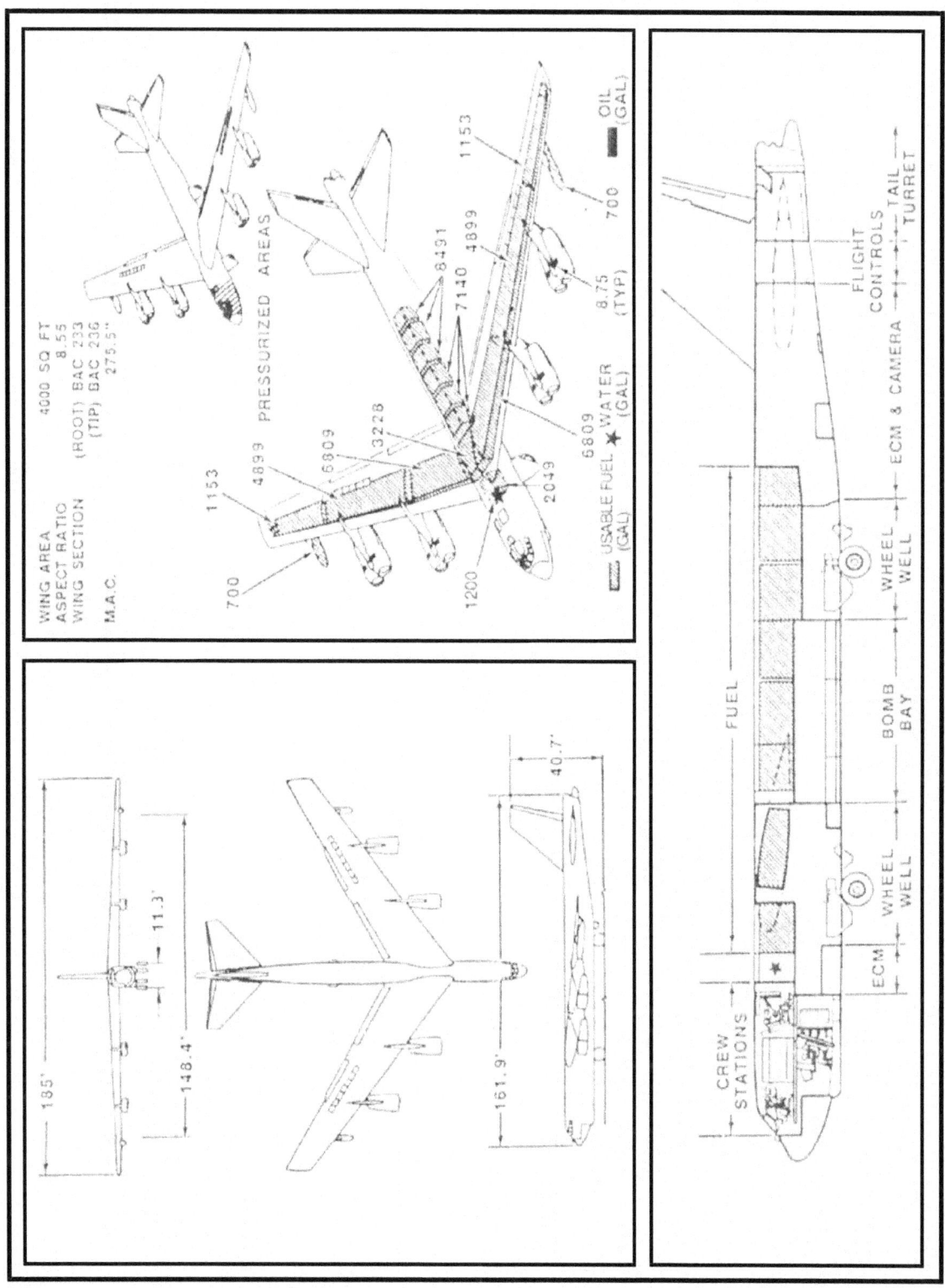

POWER PLANT

Nr & Model	(8) J57-P/F-43WB*
Mfr.	Pratt & Whitney
Eng. Spec. Nr	A1704-E
Type	Axial Flow, Gas Turbine
Length	167.3 in.
Diameter	38.9 in.
Weight (Dry)	3870 lb
Tail Pipe	Fixed Area
Augmentation	Water Injection

* Equipped with sound suppressors

ENGINE RATINGS

S.L. Status	LB	RPM*	MIN
Max.**	13,750	6900/9650	5
Mil	11,200	6400/9650	30
Nor	9500	6150/9350	Cont

* First figure represents low pressure spool, second figure represents high pressure spool
** With water injection (available for T.O. only)

FUEL

Location	Nr Tanks	Gal
Wing, Ext	2	1400
Wing, Outbd	2	2306
Wing, Mains	4	23,415
Wing, Ctr	1	3228
Fuselage, Fwd	1	2049
Fuselage, Ctr	3	7140
Fuselage, Aft		8491
Total		48,030

Grade: JP-4
Specification: MIL-T-36241

OIL

Nacelle	8	Total 70
Grade		Synthetic
Specification		MIL-L-7808J

WATER

Fuselage, Fwd	1	1200

MISSION AND DESCRIPTION

Mfr's Model: 464-253

The B-52G is an intercontinental heavy bombardment airplane capable of diverse missions including: reconnaissance, hard target penetration (high/low), tactical environment area denial, standoff ALCM launch (98 A/C), anti-ship/sea lane control (69 A/C), and combat crew trainer. The normal crew of six consists of pilot, copilot, navigator, radar navigator, ECM operator, and gunner.

Automatic cabin pressurization, heating, and ventilation are provided for crew comfort. Ejection seats for emergency escape are provided for all the crew. Flight control is accomplished by use of spoilers on the wing, elevators on the all-movable horizontal tail, and a rudder on the fixed vertical tail. The spoilers also function as airbrakes in descents and landing.

Other features are single point ground and air refueling, braking parachute for decreasing landing roll distance, steerable landing gear to aid in crosswind takeoff and landing, and a liquid oxygen system.

Development

Design Initiated	
First Flight	Jun 56
First Acceptance	Oct 58
Out of Production	Oct 58
	Mar 61

DIMENSION

Wing	
Span	185.0'
Dihedral (Chord Plane)	2.5°
Incidence (root)	6°
Sweepback (at 1/4 chord)	35°
Length (Overall)	161.9'
Height (Overall)	40.7'
Height (Fin Folded)	20'
Tread (Outrigger)	148.4'
Tread (Main Gear)	11.3'

ORDNANCE BOMBS, CONVENTIONAL

Nr Int/Ext	Class
27/24	500
27/24	750
12/18	1000
8/12	2000

BOMBS, NUCLEAR

Nr	Model
4	B-28 FI
4	B-28-0.1
4	B-43-0
1	B-43-1
4	B-53
4	B-61-0.1
4	B-61-7
4	B-83
	BDU-8/B (Practice)
4	BDU-38 (Practice)

WEIGHTS

Loading	Lb	L.F.
Empty	180,041	
Basic	183,250	
Design	*300,000	
Combat	**310,261	***2.0
Max Take-off	488,000	1.8
Max In-flight	+488,000	1.8
Max Loading	++450,000	

* Maximum Taxi Weight
** For Basic Mission
*** Maneuver Load Factor
+ Limited by Structure, Normal Procedures
++ For Contact Sinking Speed of 6 Ft./Sec.

CAMERAS

Nr	Type	Model	Lens
1	Bomb Nav	0-32	Radar Recording
1	Bomb Nav	KS-32A	
1	Video	RO-523/	
	Recorder	ASQ-175	
1	Strike	K-17C, D or	6"
1	Strike	K-38	36"
1	EVS	MX-9311/	
		AVQ-22	
1	FLIR	OR-118/AAQ-6	

ELECTRONICS

Navigation/Recognition Systems	
Radar Alt	AN/APN-150(V) or AN/APN-224
Transponder (IFF)	AN/APX-64(V)
Marker Beacon Radio	AN/ARN-32
Navigation Radio	AN/ARN-14
Glidepath Radio	AN/ARN-67 or AN/ARN-31
TACAN Radio Nav	AN/ARN-118(V)
Radio Beacon	AN/APN-59
Doppler Radar	AN/APN-218 or AN/APN-89A
Compass System	J-4
True Heading Computer	AN/AJA-1
Communication Systems	
Interphone System	AN/AIC-10A
UHF Command Radio	AN/ARC-164(V)
AFSATCOM	AN/ASC-19
Liaison	AN/ARC-190(V) or AN/ARC-58
UHF Line of Sight	AN/ARC-171
Electronic Warfare Systems	
Countermeasures System	AN/ALQ-117 or AN/ALQ-172(V)1
Countermeasures System	AN/ALQ-122/
Countermeasures Receiver	AN/ALR-20A
System	
Countermeasures Transmitting	AN/ALT-32H
System	AN/ALT-32L
Warning Receiver	AN/ALR-46(V)-4
Tail Warning System	AN/ALQ-153(V)-1
Power Management System	AN/ALQ-155
Blanking System	
Flare Ejector System	AN/ALE-20
Chaff Dispensing Set	AN/ALE-24
Other	
Offensive Avionics System Or	AN/ASQ-176
Weapon Control System	
Offensive	A/A42G-11
Automatic Flight Control System	Or AN/ASW-49
Heading-Vertical Ref. System	AN/AJN-8
Electro-Optical Viewing System	AN/ASQ-151
Fire Control System	AN/ASQ-15
Strategic Radar	AN/APQ-166

MISSILES

Nr Int/Ext	Model	Type
8/0	AGM-69	Short Range Attack Missile
0/12	AGM-86	Air Launched Cruise Missile
0/12	AGM-84	Harpoon

GUNS

Nr	Type	Size	Rds Ea.	Loc
4	M-3	50 cal	600	Tail Tur

B-52G LOADING AND PERFORMANCE – TYPICAL MISSION

CONDITIONS		NOTES	INTERNAL STORES, LIGHT PAYLOAD LOW MISSION I	INTERNAL STORES, LIGHT PAYLOAD HIGH MISSION II	INTERNAL STORES, HEAVY PAYLOAD LOW MISSION III	INTERNAL STORES, HEAVY PAYLOAD HIGH MISSION IV	INTERNAL & EXTERNAL STORES, HEAVY PAYLOAD LO MISSION V	FERRY MISSION VI
TAKE-OFF WEIGHT	(lb)	5,7	488,000	488,000	488,000	488,000	488,000	488,000
Fuel at 6.5 lb/gal (Grade JP-4)	(lb)		285,524	285,524	275,561	275,561	244,125	302,814
Payload (Bombs)	(lb)	9	14,337	14,337	24,300	24,300	50,676 (9)	–
Payload (Chaff/Flares/EVS water)	(lb)		720/336/113	720/336/113	720/336/113	720/336/113	720/336/113	–
Wing Loading	(lb/sq ft)		122	122	122	122	122	122
Stall Speed (power off)	(kn)	8	153	153	153	153	153	153
Take-off Ground run at S.L. (wet)	(ft)	1	8010	8010	8010	8010	8090	8010
Take-off to clear 50 ft (wet)	(ft)	1	10,220	10,220	10,220	10,220	10,320	10,220
Minimum Runway Required (wet)	(ft)	1	9590	9590	9590	9590	9680	9590
Take-off Ground run at S.L. (dry)	(ft)	2	11,200	11,200	11,200	11,200	11,370	11,200
Take-off to clear 50 ft. (dry)	(ft)	2	13,880	13,880	13,880	13,880	14,110	13,880
Minimum Runway Required (dry)	(ft)	2	13,600	13,600	13,600	13,600	13,840	13,600
Climb path angle (wet)(dry)	(%)	1/2	9.8/5.6	9.8/5.6	9.8/5.6	9.8/5.6	9.8/5.4	9.8/5.6
Climb path angle one engine out (wet)(dry)	(%)	1/2	6.4/3.3	6.4/3.3	6.4/3.3	6.4/3.3	6.1/3.3	6.4/3.3
Time: S.L. to 20,000 ft	(min)	3	12.0	12.0	12.0	12.0	14.6	12.0
Time: S.L. to 30,000 ft	(min)	3	21.1	21.1	21.1	21.1	29.4	21.1
Service ceiling (100 fpm)	(ft)	3	35,700	35,700	35,700	35,700	33,930	35,700
Service ceiling (one engine out)	(ft)	2	34,350	34,350	34,350	34,350	32,100	34,350
COMBAT RANGE	(n. mi)	4						6758
COMBAT RADIUS	(n. mi)	4	1890	3118	1772	2993	1077	
Average cruise speed	(kn)		460	459	460	459	461	459
Initial cruising altitude	(ft)		32,050	32,050	32,050	32,050	32,050	32,050
Final cruising altitude	(ft)		50,600	50,600	50,600	50,600	50,800	50,800
Total mission time	(hr)		9.2	13.6	8.7	13.1	5.7	14.8
Inflight refueled range	(n. mi)	10						8401
Inflight refueled radius	(n. mi)	10	2882	3964	2772	3848	2052	–
Inflight refueled mission time	(hr)	10	13.7	17.5	13.2	17.0	8.5	18.5
COMBAT WEIGHT	(lb)		310,261	297,758	306,265	293,032	296,394	190,186
Combat altitude	(ft)		S.L.	42,950	S.L.	42,650	S.L.	50,800
Combat climb	(fpm)	2	4987	754	5056	872	4795	879
Combat ceiling (500 fpm)	(ft)	2	43,600	44,400	43,850	44,700	43,060	53,095
Service ceiling (100 fpm)	(ft)	3	44,650	45,430	44,850	45,750	44,200	54,170
Service ceiling (one engine out)	(ft)	3	43,550	44,300	43,750	44,650	42,750	53,150
Max. rate of climb at S.L.	(fpm)	2	4987	5211	5056	5300	4795	8243
Max. speed at S.L.	(kn)	2,5	400	400	400	400	400	400
Max. speed/altitude	(kn/ft)	2,5	548/20,000	548/20,000	548/20,000	548/20,000	538/18,900	549/20,100
LANDING WEIGHT	(lb)		191,970	191,970	191,970	191,970	197,030	190,186
Stall Speed (power off)	(kn)	7	97	97	97	97	98	96
Ground RoB at S.L.	(ft)		3100	3100	3100	3100	3200	3100
Ground RoB (Auxiliary Brake)	(ft)	6	2300	2300	2300	2300	2400	2300
Total from 50 Ft	(ft)		5500	5500	5500	5500	5650	5500
Total from 50 Ft (auxiliary brake)	(ft)	6	4700	4700	4700	4700	4850	4700

NOTES

① Take-off Power
② Military Power
③ Normal Power
④ Detailed descriptions of range and radius missions are given on page 8
⑤ Limited by structure (load factor = 1.8)
⑥ With drag chute
⑦ 495,000 lb brake release gross weight. Assumes 2000 lb fuel and 5000 lb water consumed prior to liftoff
⑧ Initial buffet, flaps down, S.L.
⑨ M36 (int) 24,300 lb
   MK-55 (ext) 26,376 lb
   50,676 lb
⑩ Buddy refuel from KC-135A tanker flying radius mission

PERFORMANCE BASIS   Data Source: Flight Test

B-52G LOADING AND PERFORMANCE — NUCLEAR WEAPONS

CONDITIONS		NOTES	VII	VIII	IX	X	FERRY RANGE XI
TAKE-OFF WEIGHT							
Fuel at 6.5 lb/gal (Grade JP-4)	(lb)	5,7	488,000	488,000	488,000	488,000	488,000
Payload (Bombs)	(lb)		295,792	280,262	267,115	220,665	301,501
Payload (Chaff/Flares/EVS water)	(lb)	9	2850	17,780	27,064	64,552 (9)	—
Wing Loading	(lb/sq ft)		720/336/113	720/336/113	720/336/113	720/336/113	720/336/113
Stall Speed (power off)	(kn)		122.0	122.0	122.0	122.0	122.0
Take-off Ground run at S.L. (wet)	(ft)	8	153	153	153	153	153
Take-off to clear 50 ft (wet)	(ft)	1	8010	8010	8010	8070	8010
Minimum Runway Required (wet)	(ft)	1	10,220	10,220	10,220	10,300	10,220
Take-off Ground run at S.L. (dry)	(ft)	1	9590	9590	9590	9660	9590
Minimum Runway Required (dry)	(ft)	1	11,200	11,200	11,200	11,330	11,200
Take-off to clear 50 ft. (dry)	(ft)	1	13,880	13,880	13,880	14,060	13,880
Minimum Runway Required (dry)	(ft)	1	13,600	13,600	13,600	13,640	13,600
Climb path angle (wet)(dry)	(%)	1	9.8/5.6	9.8/5.6	9.8/5.6	9.6/5.4	9.8/5.6
Climb path angle one engine out (wet)(dry)		1	6.4/3.3	6.4/3.3	6.4/3.3	6.1/3.1	6.4/3.3
Time: S.L. to 20,000 ft	(min)	3	12.0	12.0	12.0	14.2	12.0
Time: S.L. to 30,000 ft	(min)	3	23.1	21.1	21.1	27.7	23.1
Service ceiling (100 fpm)	(ft)	3	35,700	35,700	35,700	34,270	35,700
Service ceiling (one engine out)	(ft)	2	34,350	34,350	34,350	32,450	34,350
COMBAT RANGE							
COMBAT RADIUS	(n.mi)	4	2011	1825	1665	1013	6714
Average cruise speed	(kn)	4	460	461	461	460	459
Initial cruising altitude	(ft)		32,060	32,060	32,060	32,630	32,060
Final cruising altitude	(ft)		50,450	50,380	49,960	48,970	50,640
Total mission time	(hr)		9.7	8.9	8.2	5.2	14.7
Inflight refueled range	(n.mi)	10					8358
Inflight refueled radius	(n.mi)	10	2993	2820	2666	1996	
Inflight refueled mission time	(hr)	10	14.1	13.4	12.7	9.6	18.4
COMBAT WEIGHT	(lb)		315,688	310,166	309,032	297,389	191,499
Combat altitude	(ft)		S.L.	S.L.	S.L.	S.L.	50,640
Combat climb	(fpm)		4894	4990	5008	4841	884
Combat ceiling (500 fpm)	(ft)	2	43,300	43,600	43,690	43,270	53,010
Service ceiling (100 fpm)	(ft)	2	44,300	44,640	44,710	44,370	54,040
Service ceiling (one engine out)	(ft)	2	43,160	43,480	43,590	42,950	52,980
Max rate of climb at S.L.	(fpm)	2	4894	4990	5008	4841	8187
Max. speed at S.L.	(kn)	2	400	400	400	400	400
Max. speed/altitude	(kn/ft)	2	548/20,000	548/20,000	548/20,000	542/19,350	549/20,000
LANDING WEIGHT	(lb)		193,179	193,789	197,652	206,614	191,499
Stall Speed (power off)	(kn)		97	97	98	100	96
Ground Roll at S.L.	(ft)		3150	3150	3200	3300	3100
Ground Roll (Auxiliary Brake)	(ft)	6	2300	2300	2400	2600	2300
Total from 50 Ft	(ft)		5575	5575	5650	5825	5500
Total from 50 Ft (auxiliary brake)	(ft)	6	4725	4725	4850	5125	4700

NOTES

① Take-off Power
② Military Power
③ Normal Power
④ Detailed descriptions of range and radius missions are given on page 8
⑤ Limited by structure (load factor = 1.8)
⑥ With drag chute
⑦ 435,000 lb brake release gross weight. Assumes 2000 lb fuel and 5000 lb water consumed prior to liftoff.
⑧ Initial buffet, flaps down, S.L.
⑨ B-28FI (int)   9360 lb
　 AGM-69A (int) 17,704 lb
　 AGM-85B (ext) 37,488 lb
　 64,552 lb
⑩ Buddy refuel from KC-135A tanker flying radius mission.

PERFORMANCE BASIS: Data Source: Flight Test

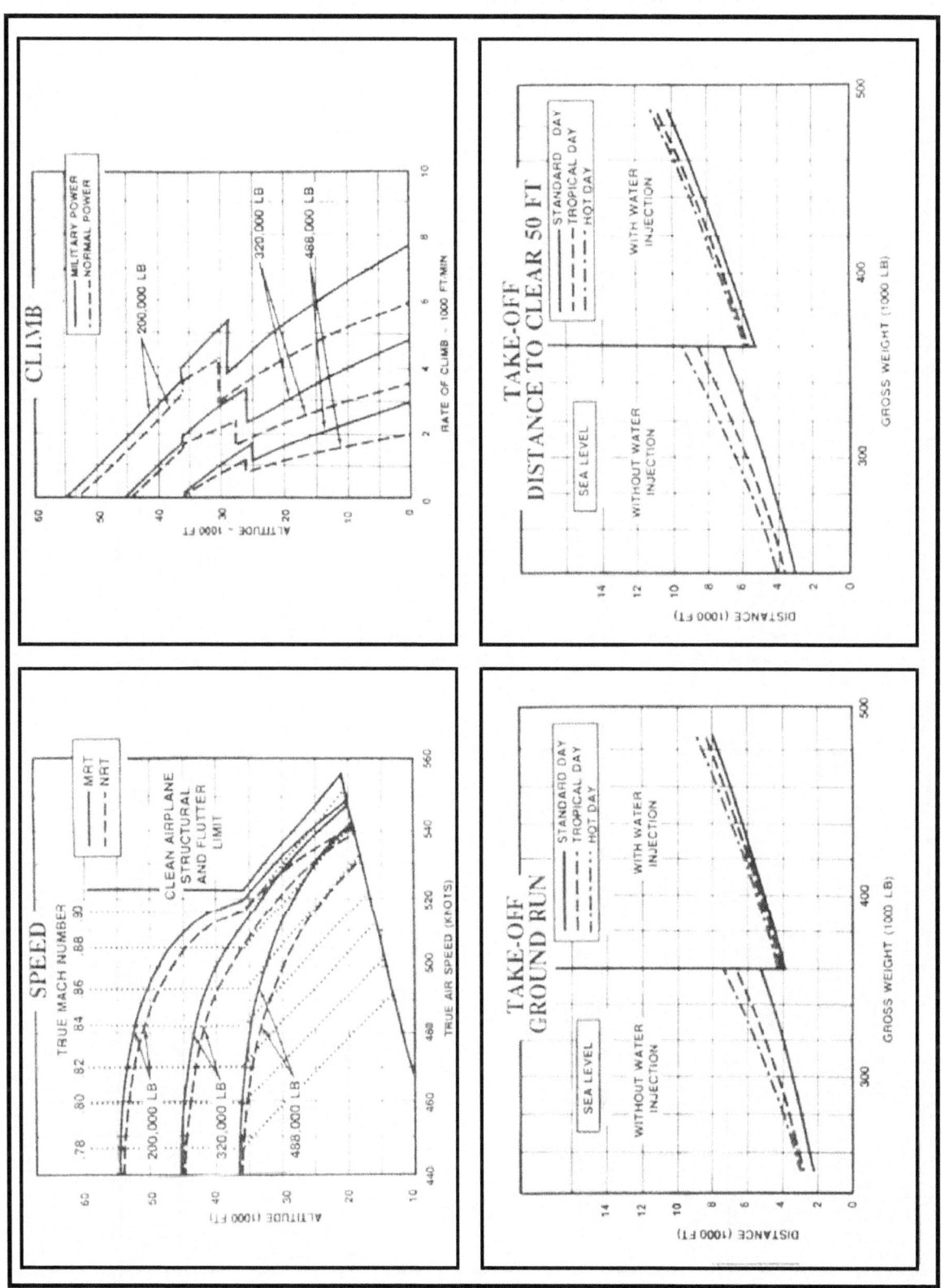

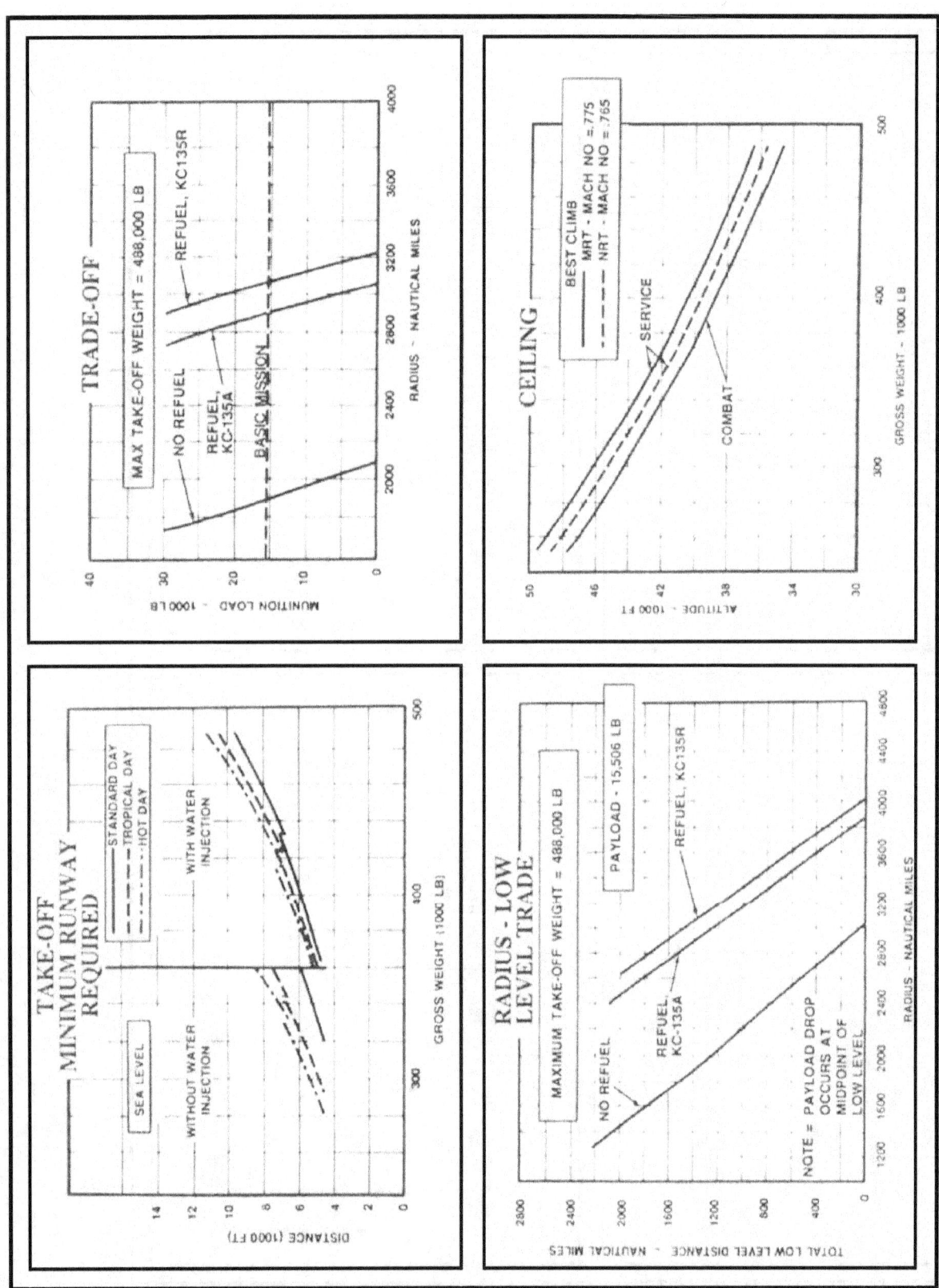

NOTES

FORMULA: BOMBER RADIUS MISSION I, III, V, VII, VIII & IX

Take-off and climb on course to optimum-cruise altitude at normal power. Cruise out at long range speed*, increasing altitude with decreasing weight. Descend to sea level 700 nautical miles (n.mi.) from target. Penetrate to target at 0.53 Mach number. Run into target at normal power and drop stores. Leave target and cruise at sea level and 0.53 Mach Number for a distance of 700 n.mi. Allow two minutes for evasive maneuvers. Cruise back to home base at long range speed*, increasing altitude with decreasing weight. Range-free allowances at normal power fuel consumption for starting engines and takeoff, two minutes at normal power for evasive maneuvers and 8000 pounds of fuel for landing reserve.

FORMULA: BOMBER RADIUS MISSION II & IV

Take-off and climb on course to optimum-cruise altitude at normal power. Cruise out at long range speed*, increasing altitude with decreasing weight. Climb to combat altitude 100 nautical miles (n.mi.) from target. Penetrate to target at combat altitude for 100 n.mi. at maximum speed with normal power and drop stores. Allow two minutes for evasive maneuvers. Leave target and cruise at combat altitude with normal power for 100 n.mi. Climb to cruise altitude with normal power. Cruise back to home base at long range speed*, increasing altitude with decreasing weight. Range-free allowances include five minutes at normal power fuel consumption for starting engines and takeoff, two minutes at normal power for evasive maneuvers and 8000 pounds of fuel for landing reserve.

FORMULA: BOMBER RANGE MISSION VI & XI

Take-off and climb on course to optimum-cruise altitude at normal power. Cruise out at long range speed*, increasing altitude with decreasing weight until all cruise fuel is consumed. Range-free allowances include five minutes at normal power fuel consumption for starting engines and takeoff and 8000 pounds of fuel for landing reserve.

FORMULA: BOMBER RADIUS MISSION X

Take-off and climb on course to optimum-cruise altitude at normal power. Cruise out at long range speed*, increasing altitude with decreasing weight. Descend to sea level 600 nautical miles (n.mi.) from target. Penetrate to target at 0.53 Mach number. Run into target at normal power and drop stores. Leave target and cruise at sea level and 0.53 Mach number for a distance of 600 nautical miles. Climb to cruise altitude with normal power. Cruise back to home base at long range speed*, increasing altitude with decreasing weight. Range-free allowances include five minutes at normal power fuel consumption for starting engines and takeoff, two minutes at normal power for evasive maneuvers and 8000 pounds of fuel for landing reserve.

REVISION BASIS:

To reflect current characteristics and performance data. To include missions showing aircraft carrying AGM-86B missiles.

PERFORMANCE REFERENCE:

Boeing Document D520-11174-1, "Substantiating Data Report – B-52G Standard Aircraft Characteristics Charts"

*Long range speed is maximum speed for 99% maximum miles per pound of fuel.

Standard Aircraft Characteristics

B-52H STRATOFORTRESS
Boeing

BY AUTHORITY OF
THE SECRETARY
OF THE AIR FORCE

EIGHT TF33-P-3
PRATT & WHITNEY

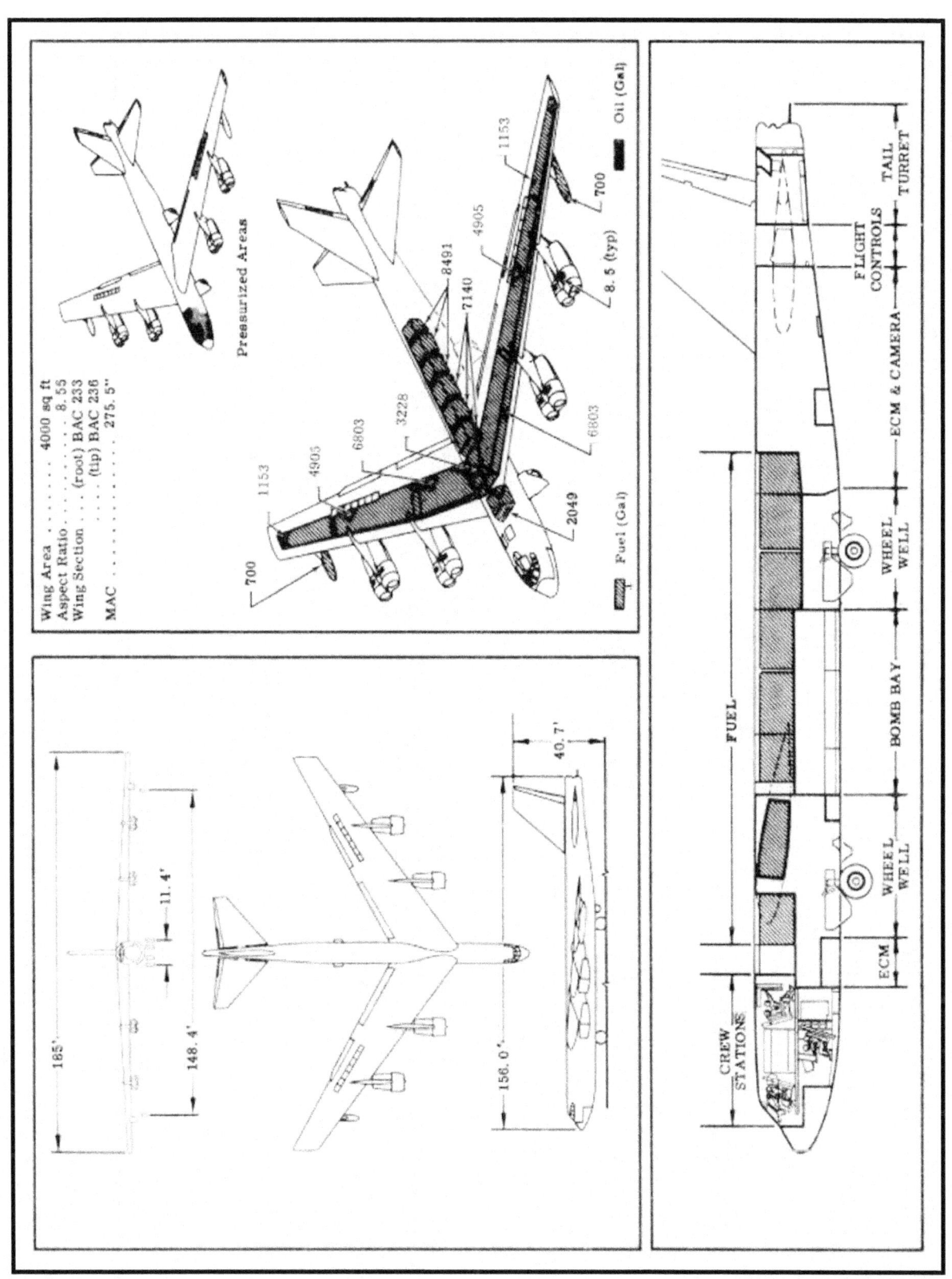

POWER PLANT

Nr & Model	(8)TF-33-P-3
Mfr	Pratt & Whitney
Engine Spec (15 Jul 60)	A1758D
Type	Axial
Length	136.32 in.
Diameter	52.93 in.
Weight (Dry)	3900 lb.
Tailpipe	Fixed Area

Note: At present there are no requirements for ATO.

ENGINE RATINGS

	LB	**RPM	MIN
SL Static			
Max:	*17,000	6550/10,050	5
Mil:	16,500	6470/10,000	30
Nor:	14,500	6150/ 9750	Cont

**First figure represents low pressure spool; second figure represents high pressure spool.

*T.O. thrust at inlet temperature 59 to 100° F.

DIMENSIONS

Wing	
Span	185.0
Dihedral (chord plane)	2°30'
Incidence (root)	6°
Sweepback (L.E.)	36°58'
Length (overall)	156.0'
Height (overall)	40.7'
Height (fin folded)	21.5'
Tread (outrigger)	148.4'
Tread (main gear)	11.4'

Mission and Description

Navy Equivalent: None   Mfr's Model: 464-261

The principal mission of the B-52H is the destruction of surface objectives. The normal crew of six consists of pilot, copilot, two bombardier-navigators, ECM operator, and gunner.

Automatic cabin pressurization, heating, and ventilation are provided for crew comfort. Ejection seats for emergency escape are provided for all the crew. Flight control is accomplished by the use of spoilers on the wing, elevators on the all-movable horizontal tail, and a rudder on the fixed vertical tail. The spoilers also function as airbrakes in descents and landing.

Other features are single-point ground and air refueling, anti-skid brakes, braking parachute for decreasing landing roll distance, a steerable landing gear to aid in crosswind takeoff and landing, and a liquid oxygen system. Major differences from the B-52G include TF-33-P-3 turbofan engines, deletion of water injection system, 120 KVA alternators, Ni-CAD batteries, static transformer-rectifier (P.C. power supply), and AN/ASG-21 fire control system.

Development

Design initiated	Jan 59
First flight	Mar 61
First acceptance	Mar 61
Last assembly line production	Jun 62
Last production scheduled for acceptance	Sep 62
Out of production	Oct 62

BOMBS

No.	Class (lb)
27 (family of clusters)	1,000 (max.)
	MK-15
	MK-28
	MK-36
	MK-39
	MK-41

Note: Airplane will carry 4 GAM-72 and 2 GAM-77 missiles.

Last 18 a/c will have forward firing rocket launchers.

GUNS

No.	Type	Size	Rds Ea	Loc
1	M-61	20mm	1242	Tail tur

CAMERAS

No.	Type	Lens
1	KS-32A	Radar Recording

WEIGHTS

	Lb
Loading	169,822
Empty	172,222
Basic	
Design	*500,000
Combat	**281,995 2.3
Max. Takeoff	***488,000 1.8
Design Inflight	≠450,000 2.0
Alternate Inflight	≠488,000 1.8
Design (Normal)	
Landing	270,000

*Maximum Taxi Weight
**For Basic Mission
***Alternate In-Flight Performance
≠Limited by Structure

FUEL

Location	No. Tanks	Gal.
		2306
Wing, Outbd	2	23,416
Wing, Inbd	4	
Wing, Ctr	1	3228
Fus, Fwd	1	2049
Fus, Ctr	3	7,140
Fus, Aft	3	8,491
Wing, Ext	2	1,400
	Total	48,030

Grade JP-4
Specification MIL-F-5624A

OIL

Nacelle	8 Total 68
Grade	Synthetic
Specification	MIL-L-7808C

ELECTRONICS

Command Radio Set	AN/ARC-34A
Aux UHF Radio	AN/ARC-34A
Liaison Radio	AN/ARC-58
Interphone	AN/AIC-18
Omni-Range Receiver	AN/ARN-14
Glide Path Receiver	AN/ARN-67
Marker Beacon Rec	AN/ARN-32
IFF Air to Ground	AN/APX-25A
Radar Beacon	AN/APN-69
Flare Dispenser	Boeing Spec
Bomb Nav System	10-30063
Auto Astrocompass	AN/ASB-9A
	MD-1

See page 8 for additional equip.

Loading and Performance — Typical Mission

CONDITIONS			BASIC MISSION I	DESIGN LOAD II	MAX. BOMB LOAD - III	FERRY RANGE IV	ALTERNATE LOAD V	MISSILE LOAD VI
TAKE-OFF WEIGHT	⑤ ⑦	(lb)	450,000	450,000	450,000	450,000	450,000	450,000
Fuel at 6.5 lb/gal (Grade JP-4)		(lb)	268,589	260,889	242,411	279,819	269,989	229,800 ⑪
Payload (Bombs)		(lb)	10,000	17,700	35,400	0	8600	17,700
Payload (Chaff)		(lb)	960	960	960	0	960	960
Payload (Flares)		(lb)	270	270	270		270	270
Payload (Missiles)		(lb)						25,736 ⑪
Wing loading		(lb/sq ft)	112.5	112.5	112.5	112.5	112.5	112.5
Stall speed (power off)	⑧	(kn)	147	147	147	147	147	147
Take-off ground run at S. L.	①-①	(ft)	6160	6160	6160	6160	6160	5370 ⑨
Take-off to clear 50 ft	①	(ft)	8120	8120	8120	8120	8120	7250 ⑨
Rate of climb at S. L.	②	(fpm)	3450	3450	3450	3450	3450	3570 ⑩
Rate of climb S. L. (one engine out)	②	(fpm)	3410	3410	3410	3410	3410	3540 ⑩
Time: S. L. to 20,000 ft	③	(min)	7.1	7.1	7.1	7.1	7.1	6.8 ⑩
Time: S. L. to 30,000 ft	③	(min)	12.5	12.5	12.5	12.5	12.5	12.0 ⑩
Service ceiling (100 fpm)	③	(ft)	39,050	39,050	39,050	39,050	39,050	39,300 ⑩
Service ceiling (one engine out)	②	(ft)	38,000	38,000	38,000	38,000	38,000	38,300 ⑩
COMBAT RANGE	④	(n mi)				8441		
COMBAT RADIUS	④	(n mi)	3890	3765	3470		3910	3105
Average cruise speed		(kn)	456	456	456	456	456	456
Initial cruising altitude		(ft)	33,600	33,600	33,600	33,600	33,600	33,600
Target speed	③	(kn)	472	472	472		472	470
Target altitude		(ft)	46,450	46,450	45,850		46,450	47,000
Final cruising altitude		(ft)	50,650	50,700	50,720	50,600	50,650	50,300
Total mission time		(hr)	17.2	16.7	15.4	18.0	17.3	13.7
COMBAT WEIGHT		(lb)	289,006	284,906	276,330	194,392	289,751	273,585
Combat altitude		(ft)	46,650	46,450	45,850	50,600	46,700	47,000
Combat speed		(kn)	487	491	499	509	487	493
Combat climb		(fpm)	645	765	1045	1495	615	800
Combat ceiling (500 fpm)	②	(ft)	47,200	47,500	48,100	55,200	47,200	48,200
Service ceiling (100 fpm)	①-②	(ft)	47,800	48,100	48,700	55,550	47,800	48,750
Service ceiling (one engine out)	②	(ft)	46,250	46,550	47,100	53,800	46,200	47,200
Max rate of climb at S. L.	②	(fpm)	6990	7100	7400	10,530	6970	7290
Basic speed at optimum altitude	② ⑤	(kn/ft)	555/(20,700)	555/(20,700)	555/(20,700)	555/(20,700)	555/(20,700)	553/(20,500)
Basic speed at 35,000 ft	②	(kn)	193,819	193,426	193,277	194,392	193,891	197,408
LANDING WEIGHT	②	(lb)	524	524	524	528	524	521
Ground roll at S. L.		(ft)	2370	2370	2370	2390	2370	2420
Ground roll (auxiliary brake)	⑥	(ft)	2170	2170	2170	2190	2170	2210
Total from 50 ft		(ft)	4480	4480	4480	4490	4480	4540
Total from 50 ft (auxiliary brake)	⑥	(ft)	4270	4270	4270	4280	4270	4330

NOTES

① Take-off Power
② Military Power
③ Normal Power
④ Detailed descriptions of radius and range missions are given on page 8
⑤ Limited by structure (load factor = 2.0)
⑥ With drag chute
⑦ Does not include fuel for 5 min at NRT (5130 lb)
⑧ Initial buffet, flaps down, S. L.
⑨ GAM-77's at take-off power
⑩ GAM-77's at maximum continuous power
⑪ 4 GAM-72's   4840 lb
   Droppable racks   590 lb
   2 GAM-77A's   20,306 lb
   Total   25,736 lb

PERFORMANCE BASIS: Estimated and substantiated by flight test of prototype B-52H airplane

Loading and Performance — Typical Mission

CONDITIONS		BASIC MISSION I (5)	DESIGN LOAD II	MAX. BOMB LOAD - III (5)	FERRY RANGE IV (12)	ALTERNATE LOAD V (5)	MISSILE LOAD VI (5)
TAKE-OFF WEIGHT (7)	(lb)	488,000	488,000	488,000	462,376	488,000	488,000
Fuel at 6.5 lb/gal (Grade JP-4)	(lb)	306,589	298,889	280,411	312,195	307,989	267,800
Payload (Bombs) (1)	(lb)	10,060	17,700	35,400	0	8600	17,700
Payload (Chaff) (3)	(lb)	960	960	960	0	960	960
Payload (Flares) (3)	(lb)	270	270	270	0	270	270
Payload (Missiles) (3)	(lb)						25,736 (11)
Wing loading	(lb/sq ft)	122	122	122	122	122	122
Stall speed (power off)	(kn)	153	153	153	153	153	153
Take-off ground run at S. L.	(ft)	7420	7420	7420	7220	7420	6480
Take-off to clear 50 ft	(ft)	9580	9580	9580	9340	9580	8500
Rate of climb at S. L.	(fpm)	3110	3110	3110	3160	3110	3220
Rate of climb at S. L. (one engine out) (2)	(fpm)	3070	3070	3070	3110	3070	3190
Time: S. L. to 20,000 ft (3)	(min)	8.0	8.0	8.0	7.8	8.0	7.6
Time: S. L. to 30,000 ft (3)	(min)	14.3	14.3	14.3	14.0	14.3	13.6
Service ceiling (100 ft/min) (3)	(ft)	37,400	37,400	37,400	37,600	37,400	37,600
Service ceiling (one engine out) (3)	(ft)	36,300	36,300	36,300	36,550	36,300	36,600
COMBAT RANGE (4)	(n mi)				8810		
COMBAT RADIUS (4)	(n mi)	4260	4145	3865		4285	3480
Average cruise speed	(kn)	456	456	456	456	456	456
Initial cruising altitude	(ft)	31,950	31,950	31,950	32,200	31,950	31,900
Target speed	(kn)	472	472	472		472	470
Target altitude	(ft)	45,800	45,550	45,000		45,850	46,150
Final cruising altitude	(ft)	50,450	50,500	50,500	50,450	50,450	50,100
Total mission time	(hr)	18.8	18.3	17.0	19.4	18.8	15.3
COMBAT WEIGHT	(lb)	302,973	298,923	290,340	196,045	303,716	287,015
Combat altitude	(ft)	45,800	45,550	45,000	50,450	45,850	46,150
Combat speed (2)	(kn)	486	490	499	509	485	491
Combat climb (2)	(fpm)	620	740	1015	1500	595	760
Combat ceiling (500 ft/min) (3)	(ft)	46,300	46,650	47,100	55,000	46,250	47,250
Service ceiling (100 ft/min) (3)	(ft)	46,900	47,150	47,700	55,350	46,850	47,800
Service ceiling (one engine out) (3)	(ft)	45,400	45,600	46,200	53,600	45,300	46,250
Max rate of climb at S. L. (2)	(fpm)	6640	6730	6960	10,450	6630	6920
Max speed at optimum altitude (2)	(kn/ft)	555/(20,700)	555/(20,700)	555/(20,700)	555/(20,800)	555/(20,700)	553/(20,500)
Basic speed at 35,000 ft	(kn)	523	523	523	528	523	521
LANDING WEIGHT	(lb)	195,758	195,365	195,216	196,045	195,829	199,347
Ground roll at S. L.	(ft)	2390	2390	2390	2400	2400	2440
Ground roll (auxiliary brake) (6)	(ft)	2180	2180	2180	2190	2190	2230
Total from 50 ft	(ft)	4510	4510	4510	4520	4520	4560
Total from 50 ft (auxiliary brake) (6)	(ft)	4290	4290	4290	4300	4300	4340

(1) Take-off power
(2) Military power
(3) Normal power
(4) Detailed descriptions of radius & range missions are given on page 8
(5) Limited by structure (load factor = 1.8)
(6) With drag chute
(7) Does not include fuel for 5 min at NRT (5130 lb)
(8) Initial buffet, flaps down, S. L.
(9) GAM-77's at take-off power
(10) GAM-77's at maximum continuous power
(11) 4-GAM-72's   4840 lb
    Droppable racks   590 lb
    2 GAM-77A's   20,306 lb
                        25,736 lb
(12) Limited by fuel capacity

PERFORMANCE BASIS:
Estimated and substantiated by flight test of prototype B-52H airplane.

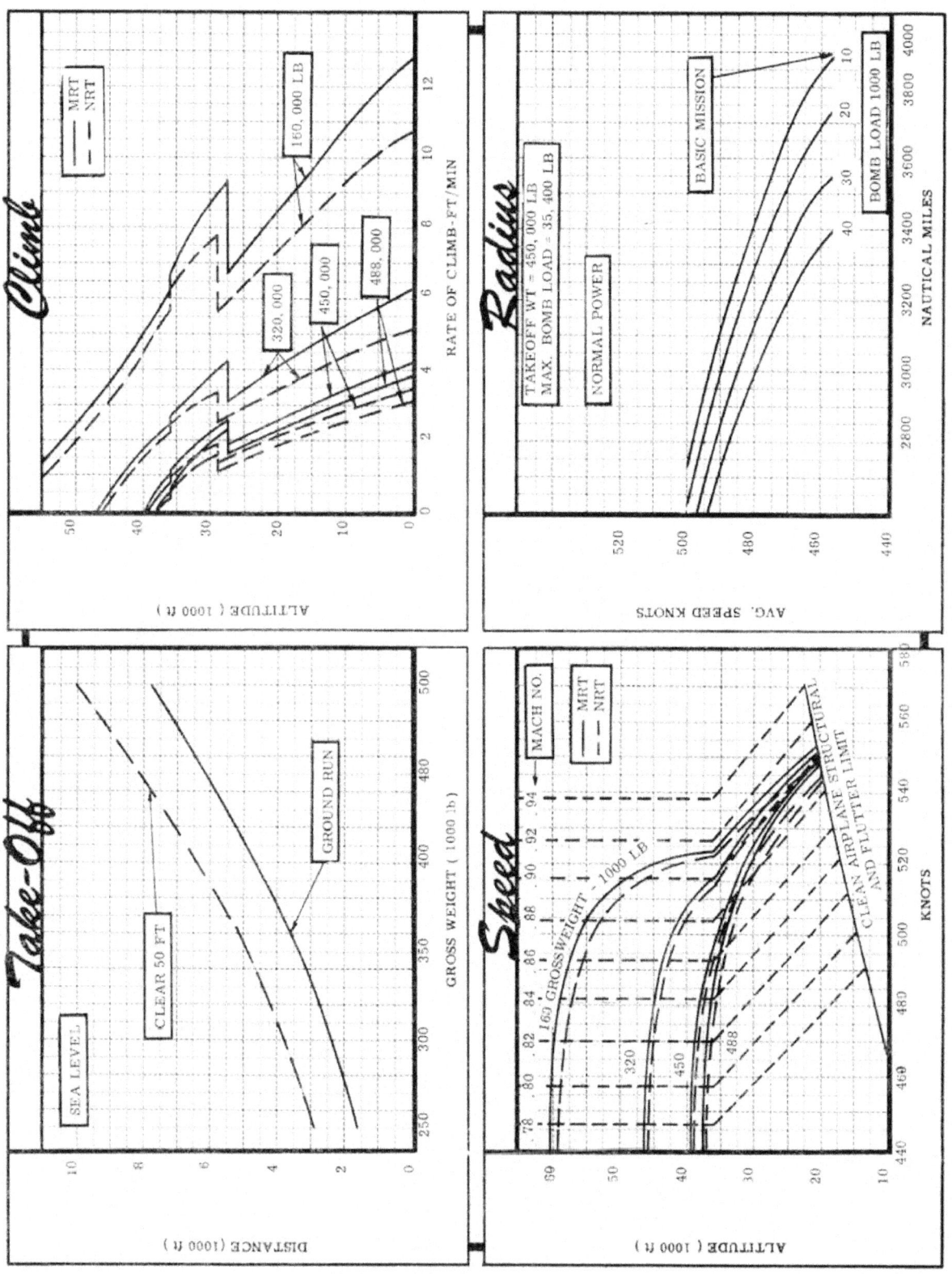

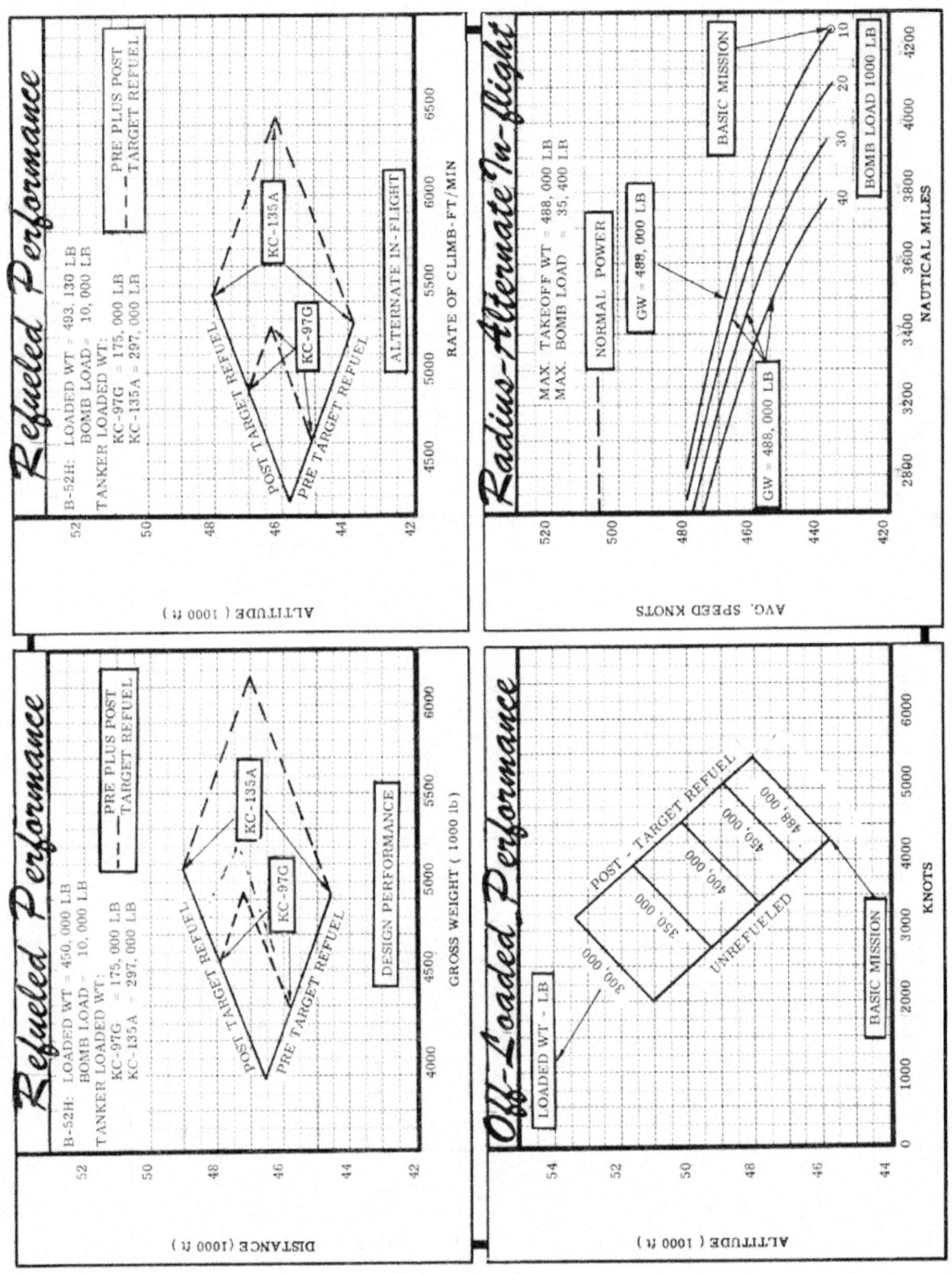

NOTES

GENERAL DATA:

(a) The prescribed fuel reserves for Basic Missions are equivalent to the following reserve ranges at 99% maximum range conditions:

B-52H Bomber	974 Nautical Miles
	1080 Nautical Miles (Alternate In-Flight)

(b) The following electronic equipment is supplemental to that shown under "Electronics" on Page 3:

True Hdg Comp Gr	AN/AJN-8
Grd Spd & Drift Angle Rdr	AN/APN-89
Fire Control System	AN/ASG-21
TACAN	AN/ARN-21
Chaff Dispenser (2)	Boeing Spec
ECM Receiver	AN/ALR-19
ECM Receiver (2)	AN/ALT-48
ECM Transmitter (3); (2) Hi; (1) Lo	AN/ALT-15
ECM Transmitter (2)	AN/ALT-16
ECM Transmitter (4)	AN/ALT-68
ECM Transmitter (6)	AN/ALT-13
(Complete Provisions only)	
VGH Sig Data Rec Set	A/24U-3
(Space Provisions only)	
IFF Air to Air	AN/APX-27B
IFF Air to Air Interrogator Fwd Coverage	
IFF Air to Air Interrogator Aft Coverage	

PERFORMANCE REFERENCE:

Boeing Document D3-3211, "Substantiating Data Report - Model B-52H" TF33-P-3 engines.

REVISION BASIS:

To reflect increase in empty weight and resulting performance changes due to ECP 1050 incorporation.

FORMULA: BOMBER RADIUS MISSIONS I, II, III, & V

Take off and climb on course to optimum cruise altitude at normal power. Cruise out at long range speed*, increasing altitude with decreasing weight. Climb so as to reach cruise ceiling 15 minutes from target. Run into target at normal power, drop bombs, conduct 2 minutes evasive action, and 8 minutes escape at normal power. Cruise back to home base at long range speeds*, increasing altitude with decreasing airplane weight. Range-free allowances include 5 minutes normal power fuel consumption for starting engines and takeoff, 2 minutes normal power fuel consumption at combat altitude for evasive action, and 30 minutes of maximum endurance (four engines) fuel consumption at sea level plus 5% of initial fuel for landing reserve.

FORMULA: BOMBER RANGE MISSION IV

Take off and climb on course to optimum cruise altitude at normal power. Cruise out at long range speeds*, increasing altitude with decreasing weight until all fuel is consumed. Range-free allowances include 5 minutes normal power fuel consumption for starting engines and takeoff, and 30 minutes of maximum endurance (four engines) fuel consumption at sea level plus 5% of initial fuel for landing reserve.

FORMULA: BOMBER RADIUS MISSION VI

Take off and climb on course to optimum cruise altitude at normal power (GAM-77's at maximum continuous power). Cruise out at long range speed*. Release GAM-77's and GAM-72's their respective ranges from bomb target. Climb so as to reach cruise ceiling 15 minutes from target. Run into target at normal power, drop bombs, conduct 2 minutes evasive action, and 8 minutes escape at normal power. Cruise back to home base at long range speeds*, increasing altitude with decreasing airplane weight. Range-free allowances include 5 minutes normal power fuel consumption for starting engines and takeoff, 2 minutes normal power fuel consumption at combat altitude for evasive action, and 30 minutes of maximum endurance (four engines) fuel consumption at sea level plus 5% of initial fuel for landing reserve.

*Long range speed is maximum speed for 99% maximum miles per pound of fuel.

One of the "Big Belly" B-52Ds releasing its 60,000-pound bomb load of bombs on enemy targets in Vietnam. It could carry up to 84 500-pound bombs or 42 750-pound bombs internally and 24 750-pound bombs externally on racks under the wings.
Source: U.S. Air Force photo

Convair B-58 Hustler

Convair XB-58 Hustler in flight
Source: U.S. Air Force

The origin of the B-58 can be traced back to May 1947, when Gen. Curtis LeMay wrote to Air Materiel Command requesting that conceptual work begin on a new jet-powered medium bomber that would be ready for service by the late 1950s. His specifications for the new aircraft included a combat radius of 2,500 miles, a cruising speed of at least 500 mph, and a gross weight of 170,000 pounds. It was proposed that the development of such an aircraft would follow the development of the B-52. This has led to a misconception that the aircraft was intended as a B-52 replacement. This was never the case; the new aircraft was always defined as a medium bomber and was intended as a replacement for the B-47.

In response to this letter, the War Department issued a requirement for a new medium bomber, designated the XB-55, to the aviation industry. The aircraft was to weigh less than 200,000 pounds, have a 2,000-mile radius, and be able to carry a 10,000-pound bomb load. Boeing submitted a response to this requirement that won official favor, but its proposal offered few major advances over the B-47 and, with production of the Stratojet accelerating, it seemed illogical to produce two different yet similar aircraft. Accordingly, the XB-55 program was terminated.

Meanwhile, the Consolidated-Vultee group had been exploring technical options for a new medium bomber. By June 1948, the company had evaluated more than 10,000 different combinations of wing areas, aspect ratios, thickness and sweep powered by both turbojets and turboprops. This had led the group to adopt a delta wing design. In passing, it should be noted that it is often asserted the adoption of the delta was the result of work carried out in Nazi Germany by Dr. Alexander M. Lippisch. In fact, the decision was made using data obtained from the National Advisory Committee for Aeronautics (NACA) that had independently explored many of the advantages of delta wings during the Second World War. The chief value of the captured German reports on delta-winged aircraft was that they confirmed the NACA findings and thus saved time.

Into Supersonics

The initial Consolidated proposal was for a small, delta-winged aircraft that would be carried most of the way to its target by a B-36. The aircraft would be flown by a two-man crew and would itself be divided into two components. An expendable pod would contain the bomb load, radar, and three expendable engines and their fuel. The other component would contain a single engine, fuel and the crew. This configuration meant that while the launch weight was 100,000 pounds (in excess of the weight-lifting capacity of even the B-36), landing weight would be reduced to only 17,900 pounds. Consolidated believed that the service ceiling of the aircraft would be 48,500 feet and that the aircraft would achieve Mach 1.6. This combination of speed and altitude was believed to eliminate the need for defensive armament.

In response to a requirement for a multimission all-weather strategic reconnaissance bomber capable of carrying 10,000 pounds of bombs, Convair (Consolidated-Vultee had finally become officially named Convair; the name had been in unofficial use since 1943) took the earlier concept and reworked it with two afterburning jet engines while retaining the underbelly pod for the bomb load and additional fuel. The aircraft had to have a combat radius of 5,000 miles with a single outbound inflight refueling and be capable of supersonic performance at altitudes in excess of 50,000 feet. In a very modern touch, it was required that the dimensions of the aircraft be minimized in order to reduce its radar cross-section. Very optimistically, given this demanding specification, the Air Force was to begin production within five years. This bomber was designated the B-58.

In the new Convair design, its wing planform was changed to a 60-degree delta wing with the trailing edge swept forward by 10 degrees. The aircraft was to be powered by four General Electric J79 turbojet engines, with the two inboard units mounted on underwing pylons and the two outboard engines mounted on the wing upper surface. These engines were then moved to the wingtips and finally to pylons under the wings. However, the most important changes came from a discovery that the drag estimates of delta wings in both the original NACA and the later German data were seriously over-optimistic. The results of these errors had included serious performance deficiencies in the XF-92 fighter. The solution was the adoption of the "Area Rule" that equalized cross-sectional area along the length of the aircraft. To achieve this, the fuselage was narrowed substantially in the area of the wings.

A final set of changes saw a re-arrangement of the crew accommodation and a reduction in the size of the underbelly pod. This proved to be the final form of the XB-58. Throughout 1954 and 1955, there was substantial debate over whether the aircraft should actually be built. General LeMay memorably remarked that the aircraft was just what SAC needed if the U.S. ever envisioned going to war with Canada. Eventually, the prospect of a high-altitude, supersonic bomber was too attractive to ignore and the decision was made to order enough aircraft to equip a single wing by mid-1960.

Production and Trials

By July 1956, construction of the first B-58 was well under way. Despite the delays that had taken place before construction started, work proceeded quite rapidly. The prototype was completed in late August, and was formally rolled out of the factory on September 4, 1956. It flew for the first time in February 1957 and started a test program that culminated with a weapons drop on December 20, 1957. By that time, the prototype had demonstrated a maximum speed of Mach 2.11 at altitudes over 50,000 feet and maintained a speed of Mach 1.15 for 91 minutes.

These trials revealed a disturbing number of problems. Some were engine-related and would be resolved as the J79s reached maturity. Others were more fundamental. Perhaps the most frightening for the crews was a phenomenon known as "fuel stacking." This took place when the aircraft accelerated or decelerated. The root cause was fuel moving in the tanks and causing sudden, violent changes of trim. These could be manifested as pitch or bank anomalies that could be serious enough to cause loss of control. Excessive vibration caused fatigue failures in the rear fuselage. Finally, faults in the braking systems caused the tires to overheat and burst. The good news was that aerial refueling trials, essential if the B-58 was to meet its range requirements, went perfectly. By June 1960, the test program was largely complete. The Air Force initially planned to order 290 B-58As to equip five wings, the first of which was to be ready for operational service in November 1960. However, funding shortages reared their heads and the number was first reduced to 148 and then to 118.

The key to the B-58 remained its use of underbelly pods. The standard pod was the MB-1C that contained two fuel tanks and a single free-fall thermonuclear device. This was replaced by the TCP, a two-component pod that placed the fuel tanks in a separate structure from the nuclear device. That allowed the tanks to be dropped while retaining the weapon. The proposed MA-1C pod was rocket powered and would have served as a stand-off weapon. It was canceled early in its development. Two reconnaissance pods were also proposed: the MC-1 that was dedicated to photo-reconnaissance duties and the MD-1 that would have been used for electronic reconnaissance. These pods were responsible for the RB-58A designation, which was never actually used. This use of interchangeable pods to suit a basic airframe for different missions is another example of how far ahead of its time the B-58 was.

The Conventional Role

The first of two B-58-equipped combat wings finally achieved combat-ready status in August 1962. By then, it was starting to outgrow its original role as a nuclear strike aircraft and experiments were conducted using the B-58 as a conventional bomber. In the Bullseye Project, experiments were conducted using B-58s as lead ships and pathfinders for Republic F-105Ds and McDonnell F-4C/Ds The concept was to use a B-58 as the lead ship, with four F-4s or F-105s in formation with it. The bomb run would be conducted by the B-58 and all stores would be released on its command. The B-58 was selected because of its speed capability and maneuverability, as it could not only stay with the two fighters, but it could also go faster, was more stable, and could turn inside either the F-4 or the F-105. It also provided an excellent radar system. One B-58 was even painted in Southeast Asia camouflage for these trials. The Bullseye Project was a complete success. Detection was minimal, with mutual electronic countermeasures (ECM) proving extremely successful. As a result, deployment of B-58s to Vietnam was seriously considered. It was rejected owing to the perceived political damage that would result if a B-58 was lost in action.

A follow-on to the B-58A was proposed as the B-58B. This would have had upgraded J79-GE-9 engines and a fuselage stretch to provide additional fuel capacity. The aircraft would also have had a much enhanced conventional weapons capability. A prototype B-58B was originally ordered, but the program was canceled before it was built. The B-58B was followed by another abortive development, the B-58C. In this variant, the afterburning J79s would have been replaced by non-afterburning J58s. This would have given the aircraft the ability to cruise at Mach 2.5, with a maximum speed of Mach 2.8. By the time the proposal was received, interest in the medium bomber was waning quickly.

Withdrawn from Service

The B-58 didn't last long in service. The decision to withdraw it was made in 1965 and the type started to be withdrawn from service by 1969. The official reasons were its cost, both as a procurement item and as a maintenance burden, and its high accident rate. By 1969, 26 of the 116 B-58s had crashed and several more had been damaged beyond economic repair. The B-58 was also doomed by its timing. It was unreservedly a high-altitude, high-speed bomber completely unsuited to the emerging doctrine of low-altitude penetration. In the low-altitude role, it was no faster than the B-52. The B-58 was also penalized for its short range compared with the B-52. By 1975, all the B-58s other than those assigned to museums had been scrapped. Ironically, the low-altitude penetration concept that had doomed the Hustler was already coming into question by the time the last aircraft were scrapped.

The final verdict on the B-58 is that it was probably just a little ahead of its time. It had spectacular performance but it obtained that by having difficult flying characteristics and using immature technologies that were hard to maintain. A few years later, technology developments would have produced a more flexible and forgiving aircraft.

Characteristics Summary

BOMBER (NON-REFUELED) B/RB-58A

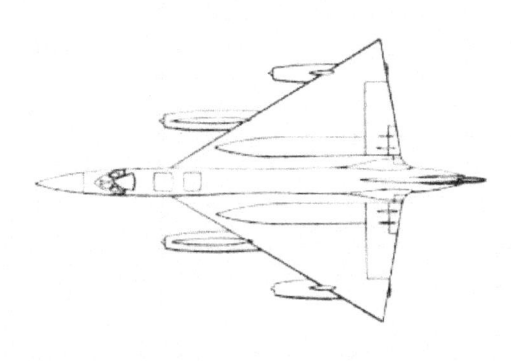
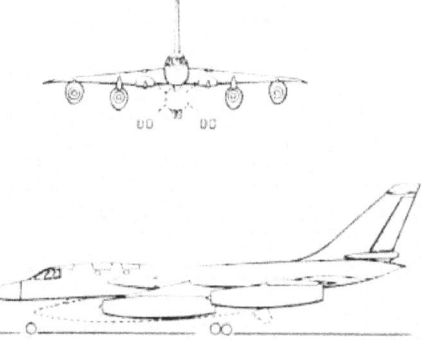

HUSTLER   CONVAIR

Wing area . . . . 1542.5 sq. ft.   Length . . . . 96.8 ft.
Span . . . . 56.8 ft.   Height . . . . 31.4 ft.

AVAILABILITY			PROCUREMENT			
Number available			Number to be delivered in fiscal years			
ACTIVE	RESERVE	TOTAL				

STATUS

1. Design Initiated: Feb. 51
2. First Flight: 11 Nov. 56

Navy Equivalent: None   Mfr's Model: 4

POWER PLANT

(4) J79-GE-5A

General Electric

S.L.S.   LB - RPM - MIN

Max: *15,600 - 7460 -

Mil: 10,000 - 7460 -

Nor: 9700 - 7460 - Cont

*With Afterburner

FEATURES

Crew. 3

Air Conditioning
Ejection Seats
Automatic Pilot
Power Operated Controls
Braking Parachute
Provisions for Single-Point Ground and Air Refueling
Chaff Dispenser
Defensive ECM
Rendezvous Equipment
Pod Concept

Max. Fuel Cap...15,369 gal

ARMAMENT

Turrets 1
Guns . . . 1 x 20mm (M-61)
Ammunition: (tot) . . . . . .
. . . . 580-1040 rds
Warhead*
Designation . . . .
. . . . Class C W-39-Mod I
Weight . . . . 6230 lb

*In Free Fall Bomb Pod

Characteristics Summary Basic Mission .. B/RB-58A

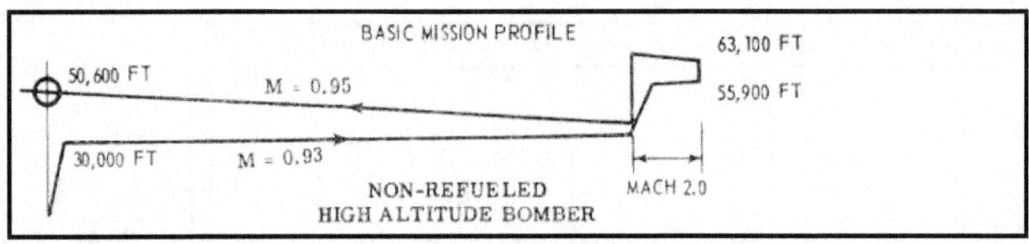

BASIC MISSION PROFILE
NON-REFUELED HIGH ALTITUDE BOMBER

PERFORMANCE

COMBAT RADIUS
2250 n.mi
with 200 n.mi radius
at Mach 2.0
in 7.9 hours.

FERRY RANGE
5634 n.mi
in 10.58 hours.

CLIMB
14,780 fpm
sea level, take-off weight
maximum power

CEILING
63,600 ft
500 fpm, combat weight
maximum power

LOAD
Warhead .. Class C (6230 lb)
Ammunition .580 rds/20 mm
Fuel .... 14,810 gal

WEIGHTS
Empty .... 51,061 lb
Combat ...... 85,500 lb
Take-off .... 158,000 lb

TAKE-OFF
ground run
5870 ft no assist | --- ft assisted
over 50 ft height
9030 ft no assist | --- ft assisted

SPEED
CRUISE **544** knots
average for cruise
COMBAT **1147** knots at 63,100 ft alt
MAX **1147** knots at 64,000 ft alt (b)

Radius
COMBAT ZONE MACH NO. = 2.0
(Plot of Combat Zone Radius - N. Miles vs. Total Mission Radius - N. Miles)

NOTES

1. Performance Basis:
   (a) Contractor's estimated data
   (b) High speeds restricted by engine and airframe structural limits
   (c) Mission performance is for B-58 delivering a free fall bomb pod

2. Revision Basis: To reflect current model designation and changes to Power Plant and Armament blocks.

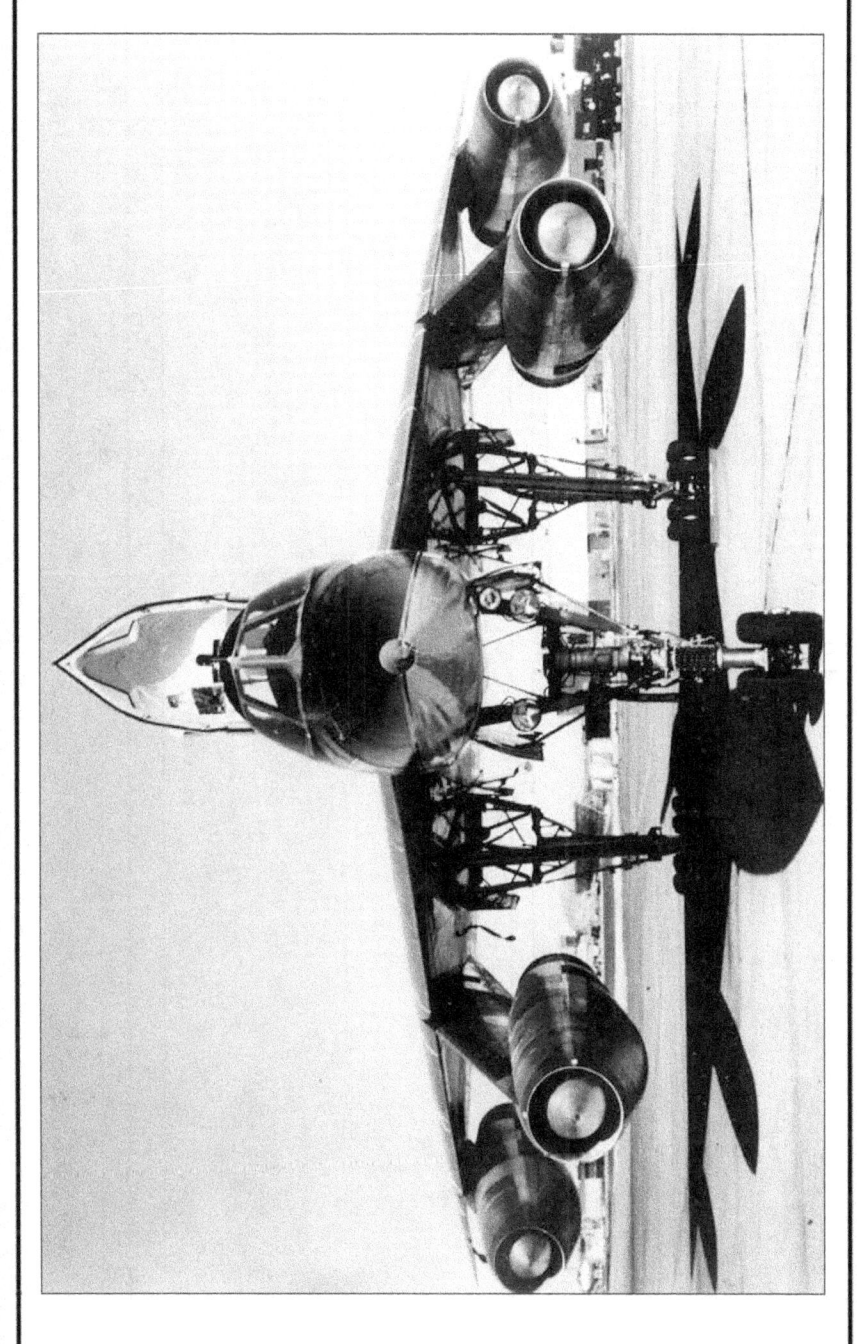

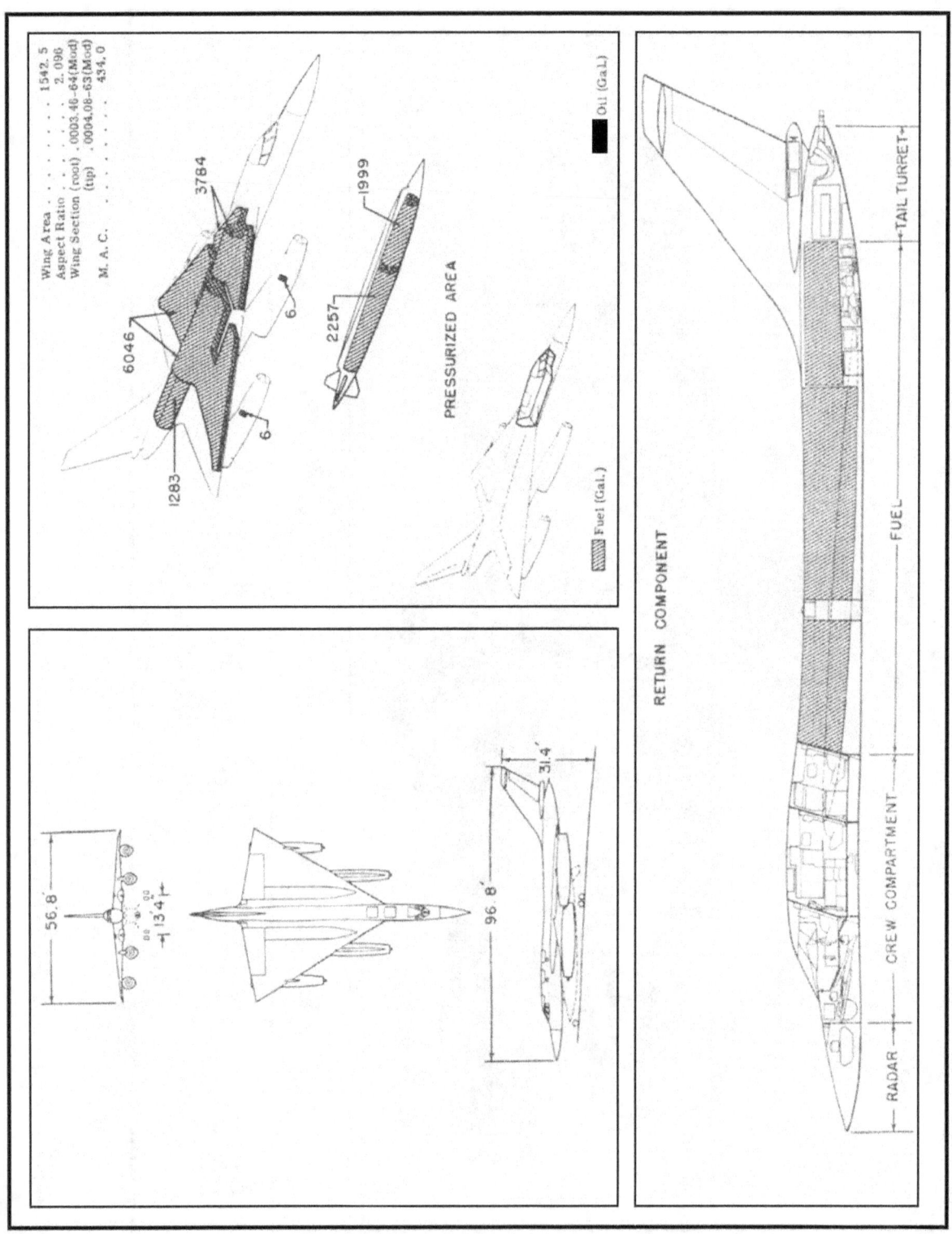

Mission and Description

Navy Equivalent: None   **Mfr's. Model: 4**

The principal mission of the B/RB-58A is to deliver a warhead in a free fall bomb pod, over a distant target, while traveling at supersonic speed, and the performance of electronic reconnaissance missions.

The crew consists of pilot, navigator-bombardier and a defense systems operator. The entire crew compartment is air conditioned; each crew station is equipped with an ejection seat.

Special features are the tailless design with a "delta" wing planform and the droppable pod housing the warhead and fuel for the outbound portion of the flight.

Other features include automatic pilot, power operated controls, braking parachute, and provisions for single-point ground and air refueling.

Development

Design Initiated . . . . 17 Feb. 51
First Flight . . . . .11 Nov. 56

WEIGHTS

Loading	Basic Airplane Lb. L.F.	With MB-1C Pod Lb. L.F.
Empty	51,061(c)	53,581(c)
Basic	51,501(c)	54,021(c)
Design	158,000 2.00	158,000 2.00
Combat	*107,250 3.00	
Max T.O.	*90,000 3.00	*158,000 2.00
Max Inflight	*125,147 2.00	**158,000 2.00
Max Land	#95,000 1.33	#95,000 1.33

(c) Calculated *For Basic Mission z Limited by space #Limited by gear strength **Refueled z Limited by c.g.

FUEL

Location	Basic Airplane No. Tanks Gal.	With MB-1C Pod No. Tanks Gal.
Fus/Wg, Fwd	1 3784	1 3784
Fus/Wg, Aft	1 6046	1 6046
Fus, Tail	1 1283	1 1283
Pod, Fwd. (drop)		1 1999
Pod, Aft (drop)		1 2257
Total	11,113	15,369

Grade JP-4
Specification MIL-F-5624B

OIL

Narelle . . . . No. Tanks Gal.
. . . . 4 24
Grade . . . . Synthetic
Specification MIL-L-7808

ELECTRONICS

Navigation-Bombing System . . . .
Defensive ECM System . . . .
Radar Warning System . . . .
Active Defense System MD-7
Civil Navigation Aids System ARN-50
UHF Communications System ARC-57
Interphone . . . Integral Part of ARC-57
Long Range Communication Set ARC-68
Air-to-Ground IFF System APX-47
Air-to-Air IFF System APX-48
Station Keeping-Rendezvous Equip. . . . . .
Indirect Bomb Damage Assessment . . . . . .
Inflight Printer . . . .

NOTE: Air Force Model Designations do not apply

POWER PLANT

No. & Model	(4)J79-GE-5
Mfr	General Electric
Engine Spec No.	E714C
Type	Axial
Length	202.0"
Diameter	35.2"
Weight (Dry)	3570 lb
Tail Pipe	Auto. Var. Area
Augmentation	Afterburner

ENGINE RATINGS

	LB	RPM	Min
S.L. Static			
Max:	*15,600	7460	
Mil:	10,000	7460	
Nor:	9700	7460	cont.

* With Afterburner

WARHEAD

Model W-39
Designation . . . . Class C
Weight . . . . 6230 lbs

GUNS

No.	Type	Size	Rds. ea.	Location
1	M-61	20mm	580	Tail, tur

Note: Capacity for 1040 rds.

DIMENSIONS

Wing
Span . . . . 56.8'
Incidence . . . . 3°0'
Dihedral (Outbd. of Sta. 56.5) . . . 3°14'
Sweepback . . . . 60°0'
Length . . . . 96.8'
Height . . . . 31.4'
Tread . . . . 13.3'

Loading and Performance - Typical Mission

CONDITIONS REFUELED MISSION		I BASIC MISSION	II MAXIMUM RADIUS	III 500 N. MI. COMBAT ZONE @ M = 2.0	IV FERRY RANGE
TAKE-OFF WEIGHT	(lb)	158,000	158,000	158,000	155,329
Fuel at 6.5 lb/gal (JP-4)	(lb)	96,338	96,338	96,338	99,807
Payload (Warhead)	(lb)	6230	6230	6230	None
Take-off ground run at SL	(ft)	5870	5870	5870	5650
Take-off to clear 50 ft	(ft)	9030	9030	9030	8700
Rate of climb at SL ①	(fpm)	14,780	14,780	14,780	15,100
Rate of climb at SL (one engine out) ①	(fpm)	9250	9250	9250	9450
REFUELED WEIGHT	(lb)	158,000	158,000	158,000	155,329
Transferred fuel	(lb)	64,100	64,100	64,100	64,000
Refuel radius	(n. mi)	2500	2500	2500	2500
Wing loading	(lb/sq ft)	102.3	102.3	102.3	100.7
Service ceiling (100 fpm) ①	(ft)	47,900	47,900	47,900	48,300
Service ceiling (one engine out) ①	(ft)	38,300	38,300	38,300	38,700
COMBAT RANGE	(ft)				8416
COMBAT RADIUS	(n. mi)	3910	4225	3200	
Combat zone radius	(n. mi)	100	--	500	--
Combat zone speed ②	(kn)	1147	--	1147	--
Target altitude	(ft)	52,700	38,800	53,000	--
Target speed ③	(kn)	1147	552	1147	--
Average cruise speed outside combat zone	(kn)	544	539	544	533
Initial cruise altitude	(ft)	30,000	30,000	30,000	30,000
Final cruise altitude	(ft)	50,350	50,150	50,700	49,500
Total mission time	(hr)	14.7	16.18	11.3	16.28
COMBAT WEIGHT	(lb)	107,250	111,030	105,050	62,150
Combat Altitude ②	(ft)	58,500	42,700	58,850	49,500
Combat speed ①	(kn)	1147	1147	1147	1147
Combat climb ①	(fpm)	1,000	15,600	1,000	17,800
Combat ceiling (500 fpm) ①	(ft)	59,000	58,300	59,350	66,400
Service ceiling (100 fpm) ①	(ft)	59,400	58,700	59,750	67,000
Service ceiling (one engine out) ①	(ft)	48,750	48,000	49,250	58,600
Maximum rate of climb at SL ①	(fpm)	38,000	36,600	38,300	64,000
Maximum speed at service ceiling ①		1147	1147	1147	1147
Basic speed at 35,000 ft ②	(kn)	1131	1131	1131	1131
LANDING WEIGHT	(lb)	58,800	59,400	57,900	62,150
Ground roll at SL	(ft)	2700	2730	2660	2845
Ground roll (parachute)	(ft)	2055	2080	2010	2200
Total distance from 50 ft	(ft)	5060	5100	5015	5225
Total distance from 50 ft (parachute)	(ft)	4415	4450	4365	4580

NOTES ① Max. Power
② High speeds restricted by engine and airframe structural limit
③ Data based on airplane carrying Free Fall Bomb Pod (MB-1C) with W-39 Warhead.

PERFORMANCE BASIS:
(a) Data source: Contractor's estimated data

Loading and Performance – Typical Mission

CONDITIONS NON-REFUELED MISSION		V BASIC MISSION	VI MAXIMUM RADIUS	VII 500 N. MI. COMBAT ZONE @ M = 2.0	VIII FERRY RANGE
TAKE-OFF WEIGHT	(lb)	158,000	158,000	158,000	155,329
Fuel at 6.5 lb/gal (JP-4)	(lb)	96,338	96,338	96,338	99,897
Payload (Warhead)	(lb)	6230	6230	6230	None
Wing loading	(lb/sq ft)	102.3	102.3	102.3	100.7
Take-off ground run at S.L.	(ft)	5870	5870	5870	5650
Take-off to clear 50 ft	(ft)	9030	9030	9030	8700
Rate of climb at SL	(fpm)	14,780	14,760	14,780	15,100
Rate of climb at SL (one engine out)	(fpm)	9250	9250	9250	9450
Time SL to 20,000 ft	(min)	6.9	6.9	6.9	6.7
Time SL to 30,000 ft	(min)	13.7	13.7	13.7	13.5
Service ceiling (100 fpm)	(ft)	47,900	47,900	47,900	48,300
Service ceiling (one engine out)	(ft)	38,300	38,300	38,300	38,700
COMBAT RANGE	(n.mi)	--	--	--	5634
COMBAT RADIUS	(n.mi)	2250	2720	1690	--
Combat zone radius	(n.mi)	200	--	500	--
Combat zone speed	(kn)	1147	--	1147	--
Target Altitude	(ft)	55,900	43,200	56,100	--
Target speed	(kn)	1147	552	1147	--
Average cruise speed outside combat zone	(kn)	544	539	544	533
Initial cruise altitude	(ft)	30,000	30,000	30,000	30,000
Final cruise altitude	(ft)	50,600	50,300	50,900	49,700
Total mission time	(hr)	7.9	10.13	5.24	10.58
COMBAT WEIGHT	(lb)	85,500	89,000	84,450	61,900
Combat altitude	(ft)	63,100	48,000	63,500	49,700
Combat speed	(kn)	1147	1147	1147	1147
Combat climb	(fpm)	1000	15,600	1000	18,000
Combat ceiling (500 fpm)	(ft)	63,600	63,000	64,000	66,600
Service ceiling (100 fpm)	(ft)	64,000	63,400	64,400	67,200
Service ceiling (one engine out)	(ft)	53,600	52,900	53,900	58,200
Maximum rate of climb at SL	(fpm)	47,800	45,800	48,200	64,200
Maximum speed at service ceiling	(kn)	1147	1147	1147	1147
Basic speed at 35,000 ft	(kn)	1131	1131	1131	1131
LANDING WEIGHT	(lb)	58,200	59,000	57,500	61,900
Ground roll at SL	(ft)	2680	2710	2645	2825
Ground roll (parachute)	(ft)	2020	2060	1990	2185
Total distance from 50 ft	(ft)	5040	5075	5000	5205
Total distance from 50 ft (parachute)	(ft)	4380	4425	4345	4565

NOTES: ① Max power ② Military Power ③ High speeds restricted by engine and airframe structural limit ④ Data based on airplane carrying Free Fall Bomb Pod (MB-1C) with W-39 Warhead.

PERFORMANCE BASIS:
(a) Data source: Contractor's Estimated Data

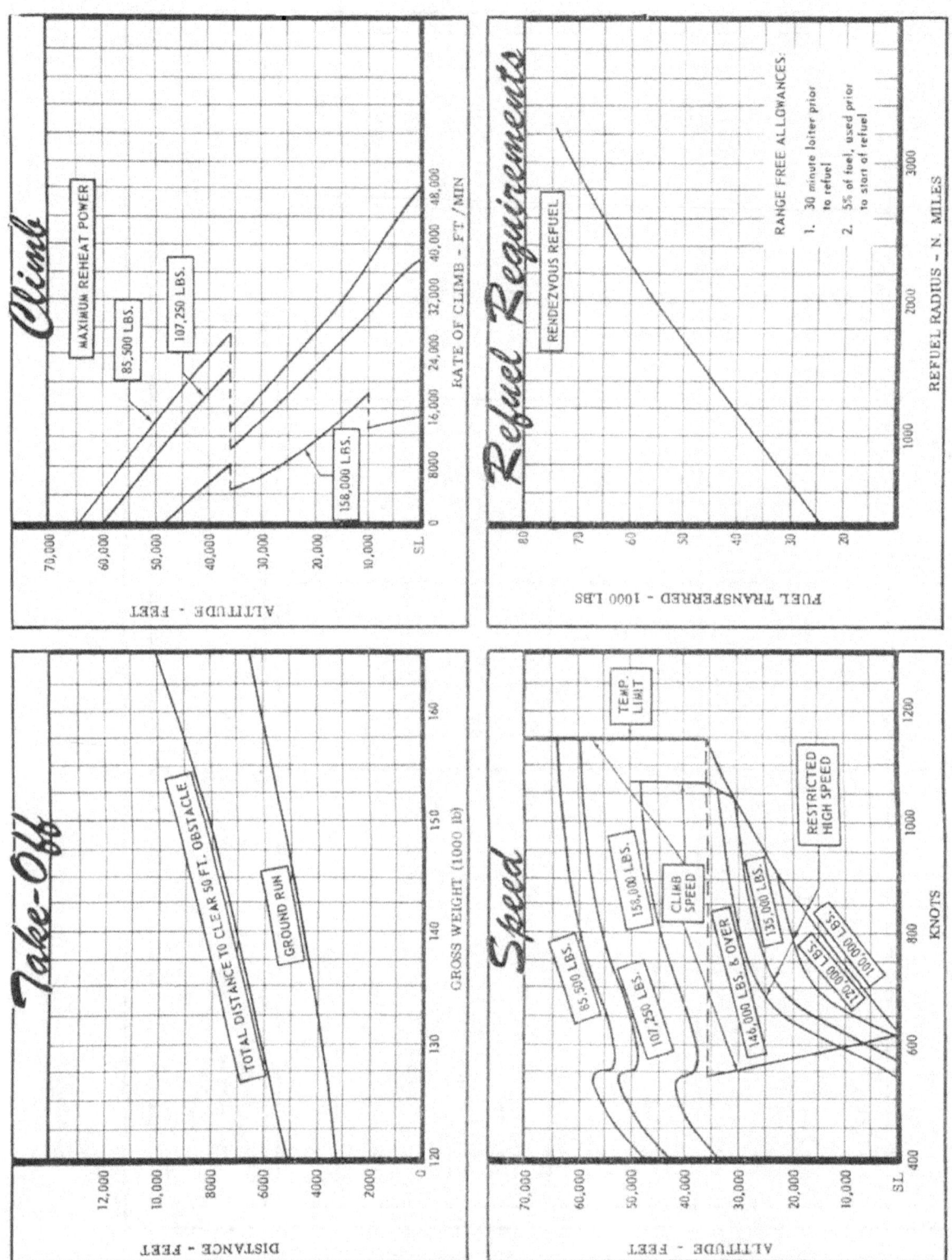

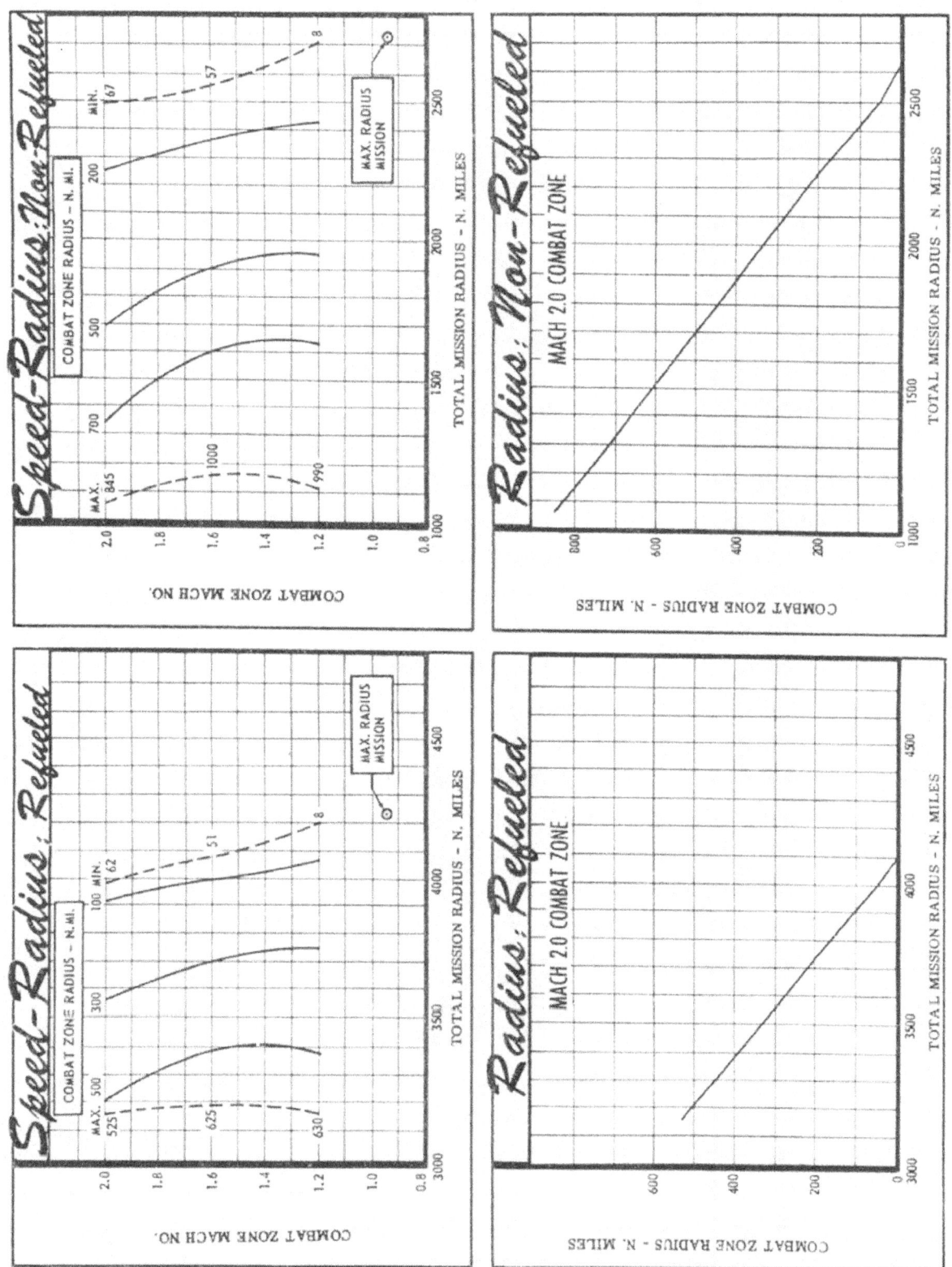

Notes

TYPICAL MISSION PROFILE

DESCRIPTION OF TYPICAL MISSIONS

Refueled Missions

Radius and range data shown on the Typical Missions pages are based on refueling the B-58 2500 nautical miles from the takeoff base. (2500 n.mi. is the maximum refuel radius permitted by Military Characteristics in meeting the radius requirement; it is not related to any tanker capability.) Data are based on the aircraft taking off, climbing on course with Military power, then cruising at long range speeds and altitudes to point of hookup for refueling. Range free allowances include: (a) 30 minutes for rendezvous, and (b) additional fuel equal to 5% of fuel burned prior to hookup. Refueling is conducted at an altitude of 30,000 feet and at a Mach number of 0.8.

Formula: Radius Mission I

After refueling, accelerate with maximum power to the speed for maximum range, cruise at maximum range speeds and altitudes until initiating the maximum power acceleration and climb to supersonic zone. The supersonic zone radius is 100 nautical miles and consists of flying in at Mach 2.0, dropping pod, and flying out the same distance at Mach 2.0. Cruise back to base is made at the Mach number and altitudes for maximum range. Range free allowance includes: 5 minutes of normal power and 1 minute of maximum power fuel consumption for warm-up and take-off, 30-minute cruise on maximum range flight path for refueling rendezvous; 5% of fuel burned prior to refuel, and a reserve fuel allowance sufficient to fly 8% of the creditable mission range plus that amount of fuel required for one GCA go-around (80 n.mi. at sea level).

Formula: Radius Mission II

After refueling, accelerate with maximum power to the speed for maximum range, cruise at maximum range speeds and altitudes, then climb on course with maximum power so as to reach cruise ceiling 15 minutes prior to pod drop. Conduct a bomb run of 15 minutes with normal rated power, drop pod, conduct 2 minutes of evasive action and 8 minutes of escape from target at normal rated power; then cruise back to base at optimum Mach number and altitudes for maximum range. Range free allowance includes: five minutes of normal power and one minute of maximum power fuel consumption for warm-up and take-off, 30-minute cruise on maximum range flight path for refueling rendezvous plus 5% of fuel burned prior to refuel, two minutes of evasive action at normal power, and a reserve fuel allowance sufficient to fly 8% of the creditable mission range plus that amount of fuel required for one GCA go-around (80 n.mi. at sea level).

Formula: Radius Mission III

Same as Radius Mission I except that the supersonic zone radius is 500 nautical miles.

Formula: Range Mission IV

After refueling, accelerate with maximum power to the speed for maximum range, cruise at maximum range speeds and altitudes until the fuel allotted for the mission has been consumed. The range free allowance is the same as for the Radius Mission I.

Non-Refueled Missions

Formula: Radius Mission V

Takeoff, climb on course with Military power to the altitude for maximum range, cruise at maximum range speeds and altitudes until the maximum power acceleration and climb to supersonic zone is initiated. The supersonic zone radius is 200 nautical miles and consists of flying in at Mach 2.0, dropping pod, and flying out the same distance at Mach 2.0. Cruise back to base is made at the Mach number and altitudes for maximum range. Range free allowance includes 5 minutes of normal power and 1 minute of maximum power fuel consumption for warm-up and take-off and a reserve fuel allowance sufficient to fly 8% of the creditable mission range plus that amount of fuel required for one GCA go-around (80 n.mi. at sea level).

Formula: Radius Mission VI

Takeoff, climb on course with Military power to the altitude for maximum range, cruise at speeds and altitudes for maximum range, and then climb on course with maximum power in order to reach cruise ceiling 15 minutes prior to pod drop. Conduct a bomb run of 15 minutes with normal rated power, drop pod, conduct 2-minute evasive action, and 8-minute escape from target at normal rated power; then cruise back to base at the Mach number and altitudes for maximum range. Range free allowance includes five minutes of normal power and one minute of maximum power fuel consumption for warm-up and take-off, the two minutes of evasive action at normal power, and a reserve fuel allowance sufficient to fly 8% of the creditable mission range plus that amount of fuel required for one GCA go-around (80 n.mi. at sea level).

Formula: Radius Mission VII

Same as Radius Mission V except that the supersonic zone radius is 500 nautical miles.

Formula: Range Mission VIII

Takeoff, climb on course with Military power to the altitude for maximum range, and cruise at maximum range speeds and altitudes until the fuel allotted for the mission has been consumed. The range free allowance is the same as for Radius Mission V.

SUPPLEMENTAL DATA

The curves on page 10 complete the coverage of the mission performance capabilities of the B-58. The upper plot shows target coverage capabilities of the B-58 flying a Mach 2.0 zone at altitude; the lower plot shows target coverage for the B-58 flying a sea level zone.

Three basic types of mission are depicted:

(1) non-refuel, radius missions with radius zones and with pre-target zones.

(2) refuel, radius missions with radius zones and with pre-target zones.

(3) refuel, 2000 n.mi. post-strike stage missions with pre-target zones.

For both the high altitude and the sea level missions, the plots show target distance vs. zone radius for missions with a radius zone and vs. zone range for missions with a pre-target zone.

Revision Basis:
To reflect current model designation and changes to Power Plant and Armament Blocks.

(15 NOV 58)

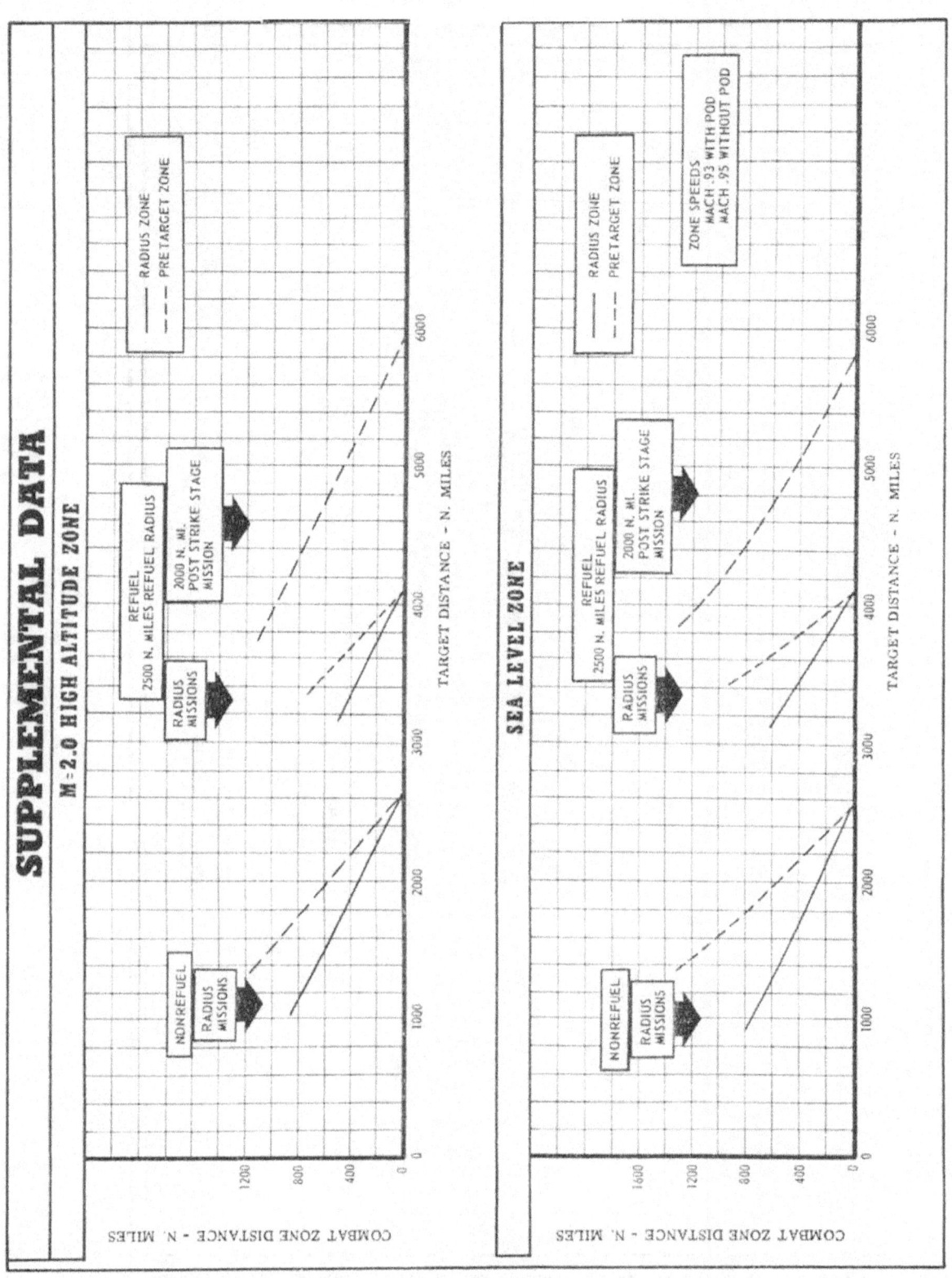

North American B-70 Valkyrie

North American XB-70 (AV-1) Valkyrie Taking Off
Source: U.S. Air Force

The B-70 program started in 1954 with consideration of a successor to the B-52. In its initial studies, the Air Force evaluated two approaches. One was for a nuclear-powered bomber capable of short bursts of supersonic speed, while the other called for a subsonic conventional bomber powered by chemical fuels. These studies gave rise to a requirement for an intercontinental manned bomber that would replace the B-52 beginning in 1965. The aircraft was to be capable of flying up to 1,000 miles at a speed greater than Mach 2 at altitudes greater than 60,000 feet. It was to be capable of carrying up to 20,000 pounds of nuclear weapons. The idea of a nuclear-powered aircraft was dropped at an early stage in the design process on grounds of cost and the potential risks in the event of an accident. Instead, the use of high-energy boron-based chemical fuels was envisioned.

Boeing and North American responded to this requirement, offering 700,000-pound aircraft. The Boeing team used a conventional swept-wing design. In contrast, North American selected an advanced canard-delta configuration. Neither design pleased the Air Force, which regarded both aircraft as being too large and expensive.

During this period, an interesting discovery was made. When measured in terms of miles traveled per gallon of fuel burned, aircraft flying in the Mach 3 bracket with engines optimized for that environment were significantly more economical than those flying at lower speeds. In other words, in that flight regime, the cruising speed of the aircraft was almost the same as its maximum speed. This was, to put it mildly, unexpected. What this meant was that an aircraft could use its fuel load more efficiently by running at Mach 3 throughout its flight plan than by cruising subsonic most of the way and then dashing in at high speed. Based on this discovery, the Air Force issued a requirement calling for a cruising speed of Mach 3.0 to 3.2, an over-target altitude of 70,000 to 75,000 feet, a range of up to 10,500 miles, and a gross weight not to exceed 490,000 pounds. The first operational wing of 30 B-70 aircraft was to be ready by late 1965.

The Bombers vs. Missiles Battle

Initially at least, the B-70 program was pursued with vigor. The development schedule was ambitious, calling for the first flight of the aircraft in December 1961. However, the impact of missile development on the program became apparent at an early stage. The first problems occurred as a result of the Navy developing the Polaris submarine-launched ballistic missile (SLBM). The establishment of a fleet of nuclear-powered ballistic missile submarines (SSBNs) was extremely costly, and caused a significant squeeze on the defense budget during late 1958 and early 1959.

Also at this time, the Atlas and Titan long-range ballistic missiles were finally reaching the point in their development where serious testing could begin. The supporters of ballistic missiles believed that intercontinental ballistic missiles would provide a more cost-effective deterrent than a new fleet of bombers. The opinion within SAC, strongly championed by Gen. Curtis LeMay, was that the missiles (both submarine-based and land-based) and bombers were complementary in character and provided different elements of the nuclear strike portfolio. The SAC believed that they should, therefore, be integrated into a single force. The general is reputed to have had a model of a U.S. Navy SSBN in his office with the famous SAC "Milky Way Band" painted around her bows to illustrate this philosophy. Nevertheless, conflict between the missile and bomber schools rose steadily to the point where President Dwight Eisenhower took a direct hand in the issue.

At a meeting on November 18, 1959, Gen. Thomas White claimed that the Soviets would "be able to hit the B-70 with rockets" and advocated the B-70 be "a bare minimum research and development program" at $200 million for fiscal year 1960. President Eisenhower suggested that the ICBM was "a cheaper, more effective way of doing the same thing" as the B-70 and said that he "saw no need for it." Eisenhower also said that the "B-70 will not be in production before a date 8 to 10 years from now" and said the B-70 was like "talking about bows and arrows at a time of gunpowder when we spoke of bombers in the missile age."

These statements are often used to suggest that the B-70 concept was obsolete before the aircraft even flew. In fact, the reality was rather different. General White was basing his opinion on an unrealistic extrapolation of defensive missile technology – in effect it was the same line of thought that resulted in the 1957 defense review by Britain's Duncan Sandys. The background was much the same in both countries: the newly developing missile industries vastly overstated what could be achieved using their technologies. In fact, anti-aircraft missiles of the performance and accuracy being projected for the near future in 1958 are still not available over 50 years later.

President Eisenhower's statements are also seriously misrepresented. An examination of National Security Council minutes shows that he was in the habit of making controversial or outlandish statements as a way of challenging a perceived dogma. His comments about the B-70 fall into this class; they were intended to provoke a detailed evaluation of the issues rather than express a fixed opinion. There was also a technical issue emerging at this time. The Department of Defense had concluded that the high-energy boron fuel program was too expensive and too risky, and canceled it outright. There was a danger that the absence of the high-energy chemical fuels would seriously compromise the performance of the Valkyrie. Accordingly, it was decided that the B-70 program would be reoriented to produce only a single experimental prototype while these issues were investigated and their impact on future procurement clarified.

This investigation took 10 months and its effects were to completely vindicate the B-70 design. The technical issues with the chemical fuels proved to be inconsequential, since greatly improved conventional jet fuels such as JP-6 were now available and replaced the boron-based fuels without compromising performance. By August 1960 it was becoming apparent that the development of anti-aircraft missiles was much slower and more challenging than had been predicted. In fact, the threat of surface-based anti-aircraft missiles to an aircraft flying at the speed and altitude parameters of the B-70 was found to be relatively low. The speed of the Valkyrie was high enough to allow the aircraft to get inside the command decision times of a defense system, meaning the aircraft could penetrate such air defenses at minimal risk. So low was the threat, in fact, that a proposed Defensive Anti-Missile System (DAMS) intended for the B-70 offered too little improvement in the aircraft's survivability to make carrying its weight worthwhile. On the other hand, the advantages of the B-70 in terms of targeting flexibility, recall ability, reassignability, and speed of response were so impressive that the aircraft was fully justified.

Valkyrie Ascendant

Accordingly, the Eisenhower administration announced that the downsizing of the XB-70 program would be reversed, and that the B-70 Valkyrie would now be scheduled for production and service. Twelve B-70 prototypes were now called for in the development program. Work on the weapons, sensor and defensive subsystems that had been placed on hold was restarted. In fact, the performance of the B-70 against existing and future Soviet air defenses was so impressive that an RS-70 variant (RS for reconnaissance strike) was also introduced that would provide a reconnaissance defense suppression capability. It was planned that 60 RS-70s would be available by 1969 to supplement the bomber fleet.

Another issue raised during this debate was that of radar cross-section. It was claimed that the Valkyrie had a radar cross-section some 10 times greater than that of the B-52 and that this would enable the defenses it faced to gain a decisive advantage over it. Once again, this argument grossly oversimplified a complex situation. The RCS is different for each "look-angle" (i.e., direction from the threat radar). When graphed in polar coordinates, RCS appears as shown. The following illustration depicts actual data for the B-70. As can be seen, RCS varies widely from different directions, by almost four orders of magnitude for this design.

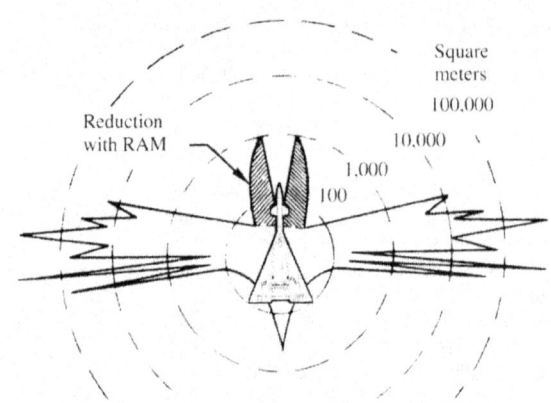

Radar Cross-Section of the B-70
Source: U.S. Air Force

Directions from which the RCS of an aircraft is very high are described as "spikes." These are typically perpendicular to the leading and trailing edges of the wing, perpendicular to the flat side of the aircraft, and directly off the nose and tail due to the inlets, nozzles, radome, and other features. For the B-70, huge spikes are evident to the sides perpendicular to the big flat sides of the nacelle. However, a B-70's cruising speed was well in excess of Mach 3 and it few at altitudes greater than 80,000 feet; therefore, intercepting a B-70 that was already flying past a defensive installation was impossible. The primary weakness in the B-70 RCS was that there were substantial spikes just off the nose, perpendicular to the leading edges of the canards, which had fairly low sweep. These would be eliminated on operational B-70s by the use of the radar-absorbing materials being developed for the A-12 and SR-71 Blackbird aircraft. This would have reduced the nose-on signature by several orders of magnitude to the point where it was smaller than the B-52's.

Change in Strategy

With the election of the Kennedy administration in 1960, a profound change in national strategy was introduced. Under President Eisenhower, U.S. strategy was based around two primary presumptions. The first of these was that nuclear warfare was so enormously destructive that it could not be survived. Because this was the case and since countries were run by rational people, the deliberate initiation of a nuclear war was simply inconceivable. All that had to be done to prevent such a war was to ensure that the nation that started one would not survive it, a posture that was called "deterrence." From this, it followed quite logically that since nobody was about to start a war they could not survive, the only way a war would start was as the unforeseen result of political and military blunders. Therefore, the primary national objective was to avoid making such blunders.

The second presumption was that the United States enormously outperformed its enemies in economic terms and that the margin by which it did so was steadily increasing. Thus, as long as there was no war, the supremacy of the United States would continue to increase until its enemies were so economically disadvantaged that they would no longer be a threat. All that was needed was to contain those enemies until that point was reached and to ensure that U.S. economic growth was maximized by reducing defense funding to a minimum. This policy was known as containment. The combination of deterrence and containment was the basis of 1950s U.S. strategy.

The key to this elegantly simple strategy was to avoid any catastrophic errors of judgment that would lead to a nuclear exchange. In Eisenhower's opinion, the primary danger area for such misjudgments was the Army (it should be remembered that Eisenhower had been an Army general and this outlook was, therefore, both firmly grounded in experience and counter to his service's interests). In this line of thinking, if a country had a large, powerful army, it would (on the principle that if one has a hammer, all problems start to look like nails) be tempted to use that army to solve problems. One day, this argument maintained, that would lead to a nuclear exchange. The only way to avoid that danger, therefore, would be to keep the army so weak that it did not provide the excuse to indulge in military adventurism.

This fitted in well with the need to reduce defense expenditure to a minimum. By the 1950s, armies had become mechanized and were becoming very expensive to run. Cutting the U.S. Army to a minimum served both aspects of strategic policy. Accordingly, the U.S. Army was, to its great institutional displeasure, cut back to a minimum. It was a tripwire, one that simply provided a potential aggressor with notice that a line existed beyond which nuclear destruction was imminent. This did not go down well with many senior defense authorities. Gen. Maxwell D. Taylor wrote a book entitled *The Uncertain Trumpet* that condemned the Eisenhower defense policy in no uncertain terms.

The Soviet Union under Premier Nikita Khrushchev was perfectly well aware of this strategy and knew it would work given time. Its response was to attempt to expand Soviet influence using proxy forces in the "Third World" (then defined as neither the U.S. nor the Soviet Union) and therefore expand Soviet military and economic power accordingly. This had been anticipated and under containment was accommodated by the creation of regional allies (U.S. proxies) who would confront the Soviet proxies. Since neither set of proxy forces were nuclear-armed or *directly* represented anybody who was, the confrontation carried no risk of escalation.

The new administration had read *The Uncertain Trumpet* and it had profoundly affected President Kennedy's thinking. He saw Soviet maneuvering in the Third World as a long-term potential threat to the United States that had to be countered. He was determined to re-create a large and powerful American army that would be used to directly confront Soviet proxy forces in the Third World regions. Creating this army would require massive amounts of funding that had to be found somewhere. Robert McNamara wasn't his first choice of defense secretary; two previous picks had refused the position. He was the one, however, who offered a way to carry out the new strategic policy by increasing "efficiency" in the Department of Defense.

To carry out the strategic policy of the Kennedy administration, it was necessary to find both financial resources to build the new army and human resources to act as a training cadre for it. The manpower was found by gutting ARADCOM (Army Air Defense Command) and transferring its personnel into the new armored and infantry formations. In the process, the nascent U.S. ballistic missile defense system was destroyed. Financial resources would be made available by standardization and by replacing the concept of strategic supremacy with sufficiency. At some point in this process, McNamara became aggressively and dogmatically opposed to the B-70 Valkyrie.

The Battle of the Studies

McNamara's primary weapon in achieving his desired results was the creation of theoretical studies that provided a numerical analysis of a problem leading to a statistically rational conclusion. He had introduced this technique into the management of the Ford Motor Company, where McNamara had been responsible for the design and introduction of the Edsel range of family cars. The idea of comprehensive studies evaluating a given problem was hardly new; an entire industry had grown up during the 1950s specializing in just such analyses. McNamara's innovation was his insistence that all the opinions and information used in such analyses be evaluated in numerical terms. Furthermore, he understood that the answers given by such studies were predetermined by the terms of reference of the study. Therefore, by carefully selecting the terms of reference and by managing the conversion of information into numerical terms, he could produce a study that gave him the answers he wanted. If by chance it did not, then the study would be rerun until it did.

This strategy had already been used by McNamara in a prolonged fight with the U.S. Navy over whether aircraft carriers should be nuclear or conventionally powered. The Navy had been very cautious in its approach to the adoption of nuclear power for both surface ships and submarines. While the Navy ordered the *Nautilus* and *Seawolf* successively in 1951 and 1952, it didn't order mass-produced nuclear submarines until the arrival of the four Skate class submarines in 1955, one year after *Nautilus* commissioned. The same policy applied to the surface fleet. After the order for the cruiser *Long Beach* in 1956 and then the frigate *Bainbridge* in 1958, there was no mass production of nuclear surface ships until those prototypes had been evaluated. Basically, the Navy was taking a "wait and see" approach to nuclear propulsion for each major class of warships, and actually did go on record as opposed to a second nuclear carrier until CVAN-65 had been evaluated thoroughly. That is why none of the proposed Enterprise and Long Beach sister ships got laid down, even though they were bandied around in "dream books," and why CVA-66 was conventionally powered.

After the first experience with CVAN-65 showed the major advantages obtained by nuclear power, the Navy did an about face and strongly supported nuclear propulsion for all major combatant ships. This resulted in the "First Navy" study that was given to McNamara. It concluded that "nuclear propulsion does permit a significant increase in the beneficial military results for a given expenditure," and that CVA-67 and all other future major warships should be nuclear-powered. McNamara rejected the report and ordered another study to be done. The "Second Navy" study was quite detailed and focused on the life-cycle cost differential between oil- and nuclear-powered task forces. It concluded that there was only a 3 percent cost differential in favor of the oil-burning task force, and that the advantages of a nuclear task force were so great as to outweigh the slightly increased cost. This study concluded that "a nuclear CVAN-67 is designed to carry ammunition, aircraft fuel, and propulsion fuel for conventional escorts sufficient to deliver at least 60 percent more air strikes than a conventional CVA-67 before replenishing."

McNamara rejected this report as well and replaced it with one that assumed the conventionally powered carrier had 100 percent availability and absolutely perfect positioning of underway replenishment ships, keeping the oil-burning CV only four hours astern of the CVN after five days. The fact that operational experience had shown that sea conditions in the Atlantic were often so rough that underway replenishment wasn't possible was explicitly excluded. In practice, this led to the carriers burning aviation fuel in their boilers to make their destinations. The fact that the high sustained speed of the nuclear-powered carriers was a major defense against submarine attack was also excluded. With the advantages of nuclear power excluded, McNamara was able to claim that his studies "proved" conventionally powered carriers were more cost-effective.

The Attack on the Bombers

Another McNamara obsession was standardization and the reduction of the number of aircraft types in U.S. service. The most notorious example of this was the F-111 program. The U.S. Navy had a requirement for a carrier-based heavy interceptor that would break up Soviet naval aviation attacks with salvoes of long-range guided missiles. The U.S. Air Force had a requirement for a low-altitude tactical bomber capable of striking targets in the rear areas of a Soviet army invading Western Europe. McNamara decided that the same aircraft should fulfill both roles despite the fact that there were virtually no characteristics in common between them. He then added the role of a B-58 replacement (to produce the FB-111) and a land-based interceptor (to substitute for the proposed F-12) to the mix.

By this time, SAC was operating a B-47 fleet that was over a decade old, and had received so many modifications that a wide variety of subvariants existed. The B-52 was a capable system, but also was configured into a variety of subvariants that defeated the aim of standardization. The B-58 was short-ranged. So, in the interests of standardization, McNamara called for 345 B-52s (C-F models), and for the B-58s to be retired by 1971 and replaced by FB-111s. This would leave just 255 B-52G and H models in service, achieving much needed standardization and commonality. Congress had already appropriated money for 45 more B-52H models. In an ominous sign of what was to come, McNamara refused to release the funds.

The reasoning behind the attack on the bomber fleet actually had little to do with standardization. McNamara attempted to prove that the bomber fleet was irrelevant by producing one of his notorious studies that claimed to show that 75 percent of the USSR industrial base and 50 percent of the USSR's population would be destroyed by whatever programmed ICBMs in the U.S. survived a USSR first strike. Any manned bombers would arrive hours after such a missile strike and their megatonnage would only "bounce the rubble." This result had, of course, been achieved by simply ignoring the capabilities that the bombers brought to the table, grossly overstating the vulnerability of the bombers to air defenses, and greatly understating both the real cost of ballistic missiles and their vulnerability to interception. In effect, McNamara was reviving all the arguments that had been made in the 1959 evaluations of the B-70 program – arguments that were then discredited.

Looking back 40 years later, it is apparent that the arguments presented by McNamara were substantially bogus and that the real issue was financial. In order to free up funds for the greatly increased conventional forces, he imposed a new philosophy of nuclear "sufficiency" rather than nuclear "supremacy." Nuclear forces would be capped at a level that his analyses suggested would be sufficient to destroy the Soviet Union as a functional society. It was assumed that when the Soviets had built to the equivalent "sufficiency" level, they too would stop building strategic nuclear systems and the result would be "stability." Jumping ahead, the Soviet Union never gave up the idea of obtaining nuclear supremacy and regarded the U.S. "sufficiency" as a gift from the gods. It then went on to reach sufficiency and went right on building to the point where it had achieved strategic supremacy by the mid-1970s.

There was a subtle undercurrent to this doctrine. The concepts of "sufficiency" and "stability" were essentially predicated on the concept of "technological stability." This view essentially held that the maintenance of strategic stability was predicated on there being no radical change in weapons technology or capability. Here, almost certainly, lie the reasons for McNamara's virulent opposition to the B-70 Valkyrie, for this aircraft really was a radical breakthrough. In many ways it combined the advantages of both bombers and missiles. It could be recalled once launched, so it could be flown in times of tension to wait at fail-safe points. This was, after all, what was already being done with B-52s. However, from those fail-safe points, the B-70 could get to targets faster than missiles launched from North Dakota. It would be very hard to shoot down and it was already apparent that the advances in anti-aircraft missile technology predicted in 1957 were a long, long way from being achieved. It could find targets that were concealed or unidentified and refine target data as needed. In short, it was exactly the sort of radical change in capabilities that would discredit the defense posture being promoted by McNamara and the Kennedy administration. The B-70 had to be canceled, not because it was ineffective but because it was far too effective. Accordingly, the entire program was canceled and cut back to three aircraft that would be dedicated to high-speed research only.

This decision caused outrage. Congressional opposition to the cancellation led to a showdown in the Senate where McNamara's blustering, polemics, cherry-picked data and manipulated "studies" were no match for General LeMay's professionalism, astute grasp of technical details, and meticulous staffwork. After every claim made by McNamara had been refuted, the Senate Armed Services Committee voted by 31 to 5 to allocate $363.7 million to fund the production of 60 B-70 bombers, at a unit cost of $6.06 million.

McNamara ignored the Senate vote and refused to release the money allotted to the B-70 program. Only two XB-70s were built. The first, AV-1, was limited to Mach 2.8 due to airframe and engine factors, but the second, AV-2, was capable of cruising at Mach 3.1. Unfortunately, AV-2 was lost in a mid-air collision before its performance envelope could be explored. The third XB-70, AV-3, was canceled and scrapped before completion.

Characteristics Summary

| BOMBER (SUPERSONIC) | XB-70B Air Vehicle Nr 3 |

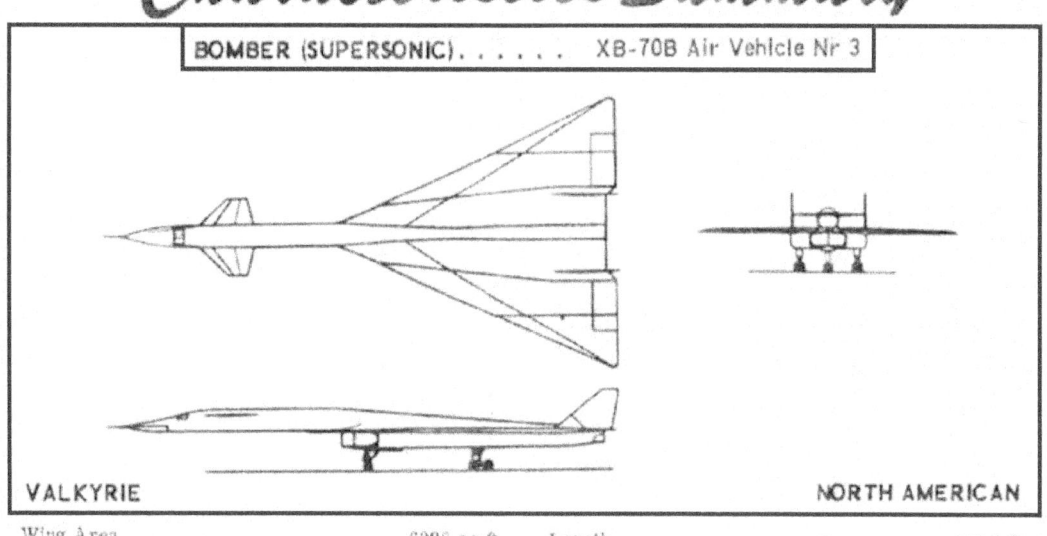

VALKYRIE   NORTH AMERICAN

Wing Area . . . . 6298 sq ft.   Length . . . . 185.8 ft.
Span . . . . 105.0 ft.   Height . . . . 30.7 ft.

AVAILABILITY

Number available

TEST	INVENTORY	TOTAL
		1

PROCUREMENT

Number to be delivered in fiscal years

FY 65			

STATUS

1. Design Initiated: . . . . Nov 55
2. Mock-up: . . . . Mar 59
3. First Flight . . . . Dec 64 (est)
4. Prototype air vehicles are to be used to obtain test data in the B-70 flight spectrum.

Navy Equivalent: None   Mfr's Model: NA-278

POWER PLANT

(6) YJ93-GE-3

General Electric

S.L.S.   LB -RPM -   MIN

Max: *28,000 - 6825 - Cont
Mil: 19,900 - 6825 - Cont
Nor: 17,700 - 6825 - Cont

*With afterburner

FEATURES

Crew 4
Canard
Airframe constructed from steel and titanium
Variable area inlet
Convergent-divergent exhaust nozzle
Folding wing tips
ILS AN/ARN-58
IFF radar AN/APX-46
UHF command . . . AN/ARC-50
Interphone AN/AIC-18
TACAN AN/ARN-65

Max fuel capacity: 46,745 gal
Grade JP-6

GUIDANCE

Bomb-Nav Sys . . . AN/ASQ-28
Frequency Diversity Radar with high resolution attachment
Stellar Inertial Platform
Doppler Radar
Main & Emergency Digital Computers
Operator's Console

SPECIAL STORES

BOMBS:
Nr.
1 . . . . Class A
2 . . . . Class B
2 . . . . Class C
6-8 . . . . Class D

Characteristics Summary Basic Mission. XB-70B Air Vehicle Nr 3

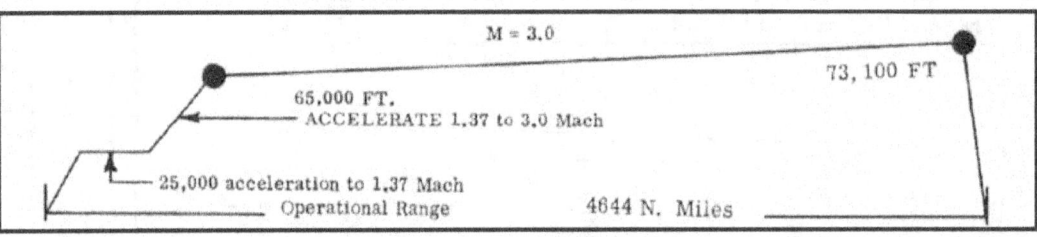

PERFORMANCE [1]

COMBAT RADIUS	OPER. RANGE	SPEED
NOT APPLICABLE	4644 naut. mi with 10,000 lb payload in 3.54 hours	CRUISE at max speed 1721 knots at 65,000-73,100 ft alt. min A/B |//
CLIMB	**CEILING**	**TAKE-OFF**
7260 fpm sea level, take-off weight military power	79,250 ft 100 fpm, 291,036 lb (3) maximum power	ground run 7900 ft no assist / ft assisted
33,100 fpm sea level, 291,036 lb (3) maximum power	79,000 ft 500 fpm, 291,036 lb (3) maximum power	over 50 ft height 11,290 ft no assist / ft assisted
LOAD	**WEIGHTS**	**MIN. SAFE SPEED**
10,000 lb Store Fuel: 45,869 gal protected 0 % droppable 0 % external 0 %	Empty..... 206,100 lb Combat .. 291,036 lb (3) Take - off 542,029 lb	163 knots T.O. wt. 109 knots Landing wt. with canard flaps down

NOTES

1. Performance Basis: Estimated data
2. Revision Basis: Recoordinated. XB-70A (Veh #3) changed to XB-70B.
3. 291,036 lb is the weight 1200 N. Mi. prior to mission completion.

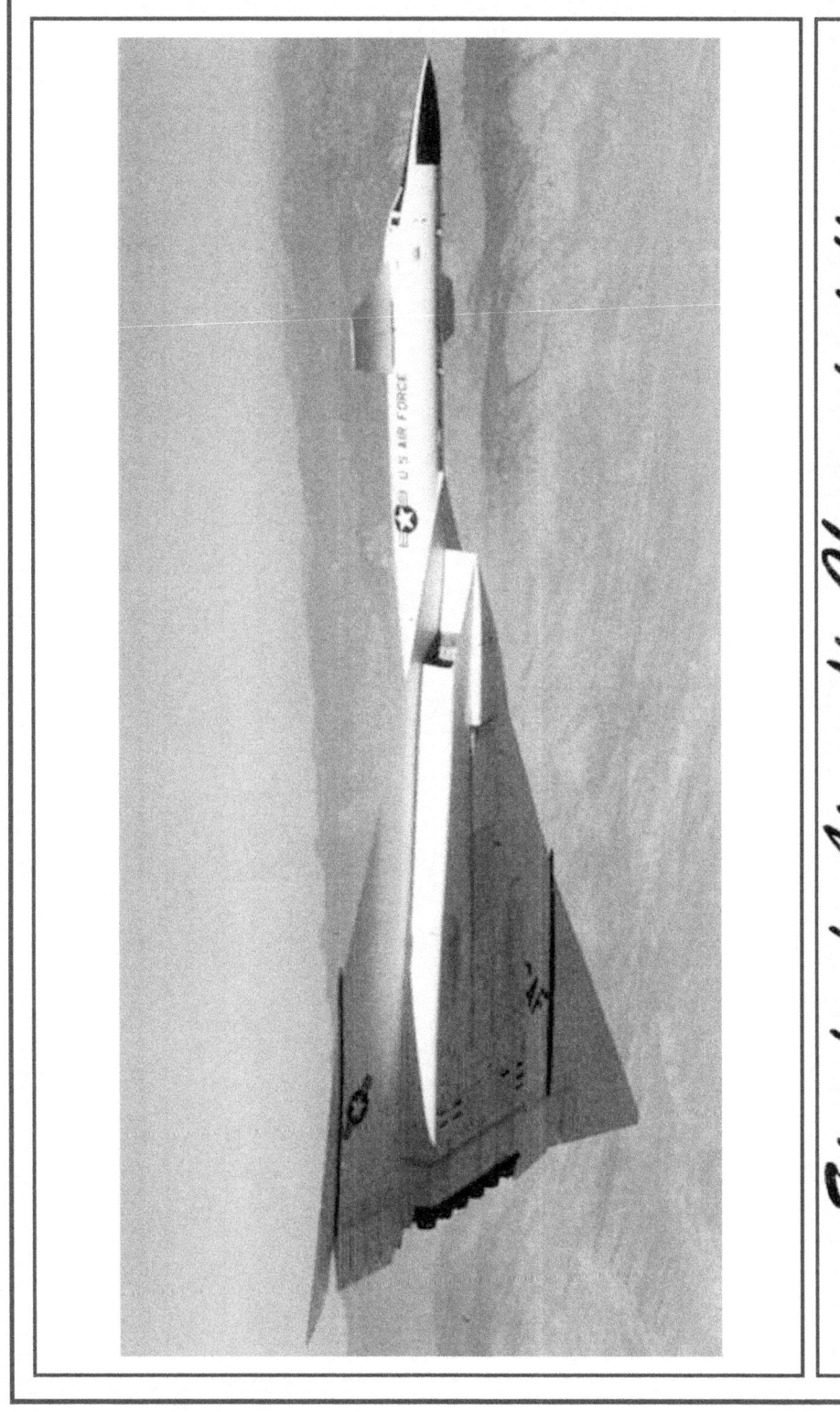

Standard Aircraft Characteristics

XB-70B
VALKYRIE
North American

SIX YJ93-GE-3
GENERAL ELECTRIC

BY AUTHORITY OF
THE SECRETARY
OF THE AIR FORCE

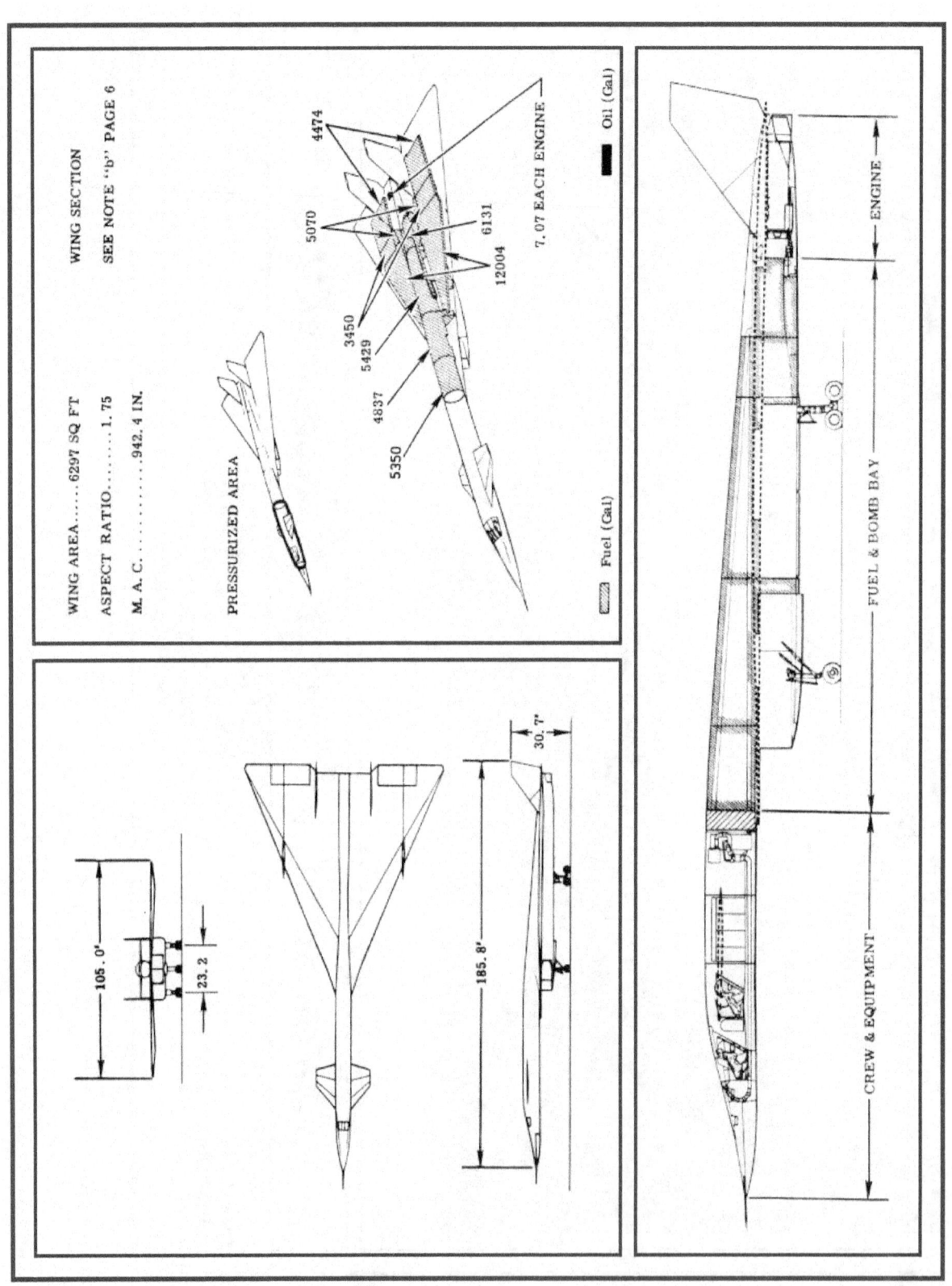

POWER PLANT

Nr and Model	(6)YJ93-GE-3
Mfr	General Electric
Engine Spec Nr	*E757F
Type	Axial Turbo Jet
Length	236.3"
Diameter	54.15"
Weight (dry)	*5220 Lb
Tail Pipe	Mech, Variable C/D
Augmentation	Afterburner

*As modified by ASD Letter ASNVPP dated Sep. 12 1962

WEIGHTS

Loading	Lb	L.F.
Empty	208,100 (E)	
Basic	209,030 (E)	
Design	534,792	2.0
Combat	*310,687	
Max T.O.	*542,029	2.0
Max in flt	534,792	
Max landing	*296,292	2.0

(E) Estimated
* For standard mission
** Limited by mission
+ Limited by structure

Mission and Description

Navy Equivalent: None   Mfr's Model: NA-278

The primary purpose of this Air Vehicle is to demonstrate the technical feasibility of the B-70 configuration and the functional operation of a prototype bombing-navigation system in a sustained Mach 3 high altitude environment.

Special features include selective placement of wing, body and inlet duct for obtaining high lift-to-drag ratios, a canard configuration, variable area inlet with mechanically controlled convergent-divergent nozzle, and airframe construction of steel and titanium. A bombing and navigation system is provided for release of test weapons and navigational demonstration.

The crew consists of a pilot, co-pilot, bombing-navigation operator, and flight observer.

ENGINE RATINGS

SLS	LB	-	RPM	-	MIN
Max	28,000	-	6825	-	Cont
Mil	19,900	-	6825	-	Cont
Nor	17,700	-	6825	-	Cont

FUEL

Location	Nr Tanks	Gal
Fuselage	5	26,817
Wing and duct	6	19,928
		46,745

Grade JP-6
Specification MIL-F-25656A

OIL

Fuselage	6	42.4
Specification		MIL-L-9236B

Development

Design initiated	Nov 55
Date of contract	Dec 57
Mock-up	Mar 59
First flight	(est) Dec 64

XB-70B designation replaces XB-70A(Air Vehicle Nr 3)

DIMENSIONS

Wing
Span	105.0'
Incidence (root)	0°
(tip)	-3.6°
Dihedral	0°
Sweepback (25% chord)	58.8°
Length	185.8'
Height	30.7'
Tread	25.2'

BOMBS

Nr		Weight
	Special Weapons*	
1	Class A	25,000
2	Class B	20,000

*Space provisions only

ELECTRONICS

Glide path-localizer marker beacon receivers, AN/ARN-58
IFF transponder, AN/APX-46
UHF command radio set, AN/ARC-50
Intercommunications set, AN/AIC-18
Tactical aid to navigation (TACAN), AN/ARN-65
Flight control system
Bomb nav subsystem, AN/ASQ-28

Loading and Performance — Typical Mission

CONDITIONS		STANDARD MISSION I	BASIC MISSION II	ALTERNATE BASIC MISSION III	FERRY MISSION IV
TAKEOFF WEIGHT	(lb)	537,899	542,029	537,899	537,899
Fuel at 6.7 lb/gal (grade JP-6)	(lb)	313,192	307,322 ⑥	313,192	313,192
Payload	(lb)	*	10,000 ⑥	*	none
Wing loading	(psf)	85.4	86.1	85.4	85.4
Minimum usable flying speed	(kn)	162.8	163.3	162.8	162.8
Takeoff speed	(kn)	206.7	207.5	206.7	206.7
Takeoff ground run at SL	(ft)	7770	7900	7770	7770
Takeoff to clear 50 ft ①	(ft)	11,110	11,290	11,110	11,110
Rate of climb at SL	(fpm)	7330 ②	7260 ②	7330 ②	7330 ②
Time: SL to 20,000 ft ③	(min)	3.55 ②	3.53 ②	3.50 ②	3.55 ②
Time: SL to acceleration altitude ③	(min)	5.38 ②	5.36 ②	5.25 ②	5.38 ②
Service ceiling (100 fpm)	(ft)	27,800 ②	27,600 ②	27,800 ②	27,800 ②
COMBAT RANGE ④	(n mi)	3972	4644	4890	3972
Recovery distance	(n mi)	1200	1200	1200	---
Average cruise speed (subsonic/supersonic)	(kn/kn)	---/1721	---/1721	---/1721	---/1721
Initial supersonic cruise altitude	(ft)	65,000	65,000	65,000	65,000
Final supersonic cruise altitude	(ft)	72,000	73,100	73,000	72,900
Refuel speed	(kn)	---	---	---	---
Total mission time	(hr)	2.46	3.54	3.69	2.46
COMBAT WEIGHT	(lb)	310,687	291,036	279,105	261,887
Combat altitude ①	(ft)	69,600	70,900	71,600	72,900
Combat speed	(kn)	1721	1721	1721	1721
Combat climb ①	(fpm)	14,000	14,100	14,100	13,900
Combat ceiling (500 fpm) ①	(ft)	77,800	79,000	79,800	81,050
Service ceiling (100 fpm) ①	(ft)	78,050	79,250	80,050	81,300
Max rate of climb at SL ①	(fpm)	31,100	33,100	34,400	36,600
Max speed at optimum altitude ①	(kn/ft)	1721/78,100	1721/80,100	1721/79,300	1721/81,350
Basic speed at 35,000 ft	(kn)	1089	1089	1089	1089
LANDING WEIGHT	(lb)	261,887	242,527	232,337	261,887
Ground roll at SL	(ft)	5920	5580	5370	5920
Ground roll (auxiliary brake) ⑤	(ft)	4110	3870	3720	4110
Total from 50 ft	(ft)	7610	7180	6930	7610
Total from 50 ft (auxiliary brake) ⑤	(ft)	5800	5470	5280	5800
Minimum usable flying speed	(kn)	113.6	109.4	107.0	113.6
Touchdown speed	(kn)	153.6	148.0	145.0	153.6

NOTES:
* Space provisions only
① Maximum power
② Military power
③ Allows for weight reduction during ground operation and climb
④ Detailed description of RANGE missions given on page 6
⑤ With drag chute

PERFORMANCE BASIS:
(a) Data source: Estimated
(b) Performance is based on powers shown on page 6
(c) Fuel flow data used in computing STANDARD and FERRY missions are increased 5%.

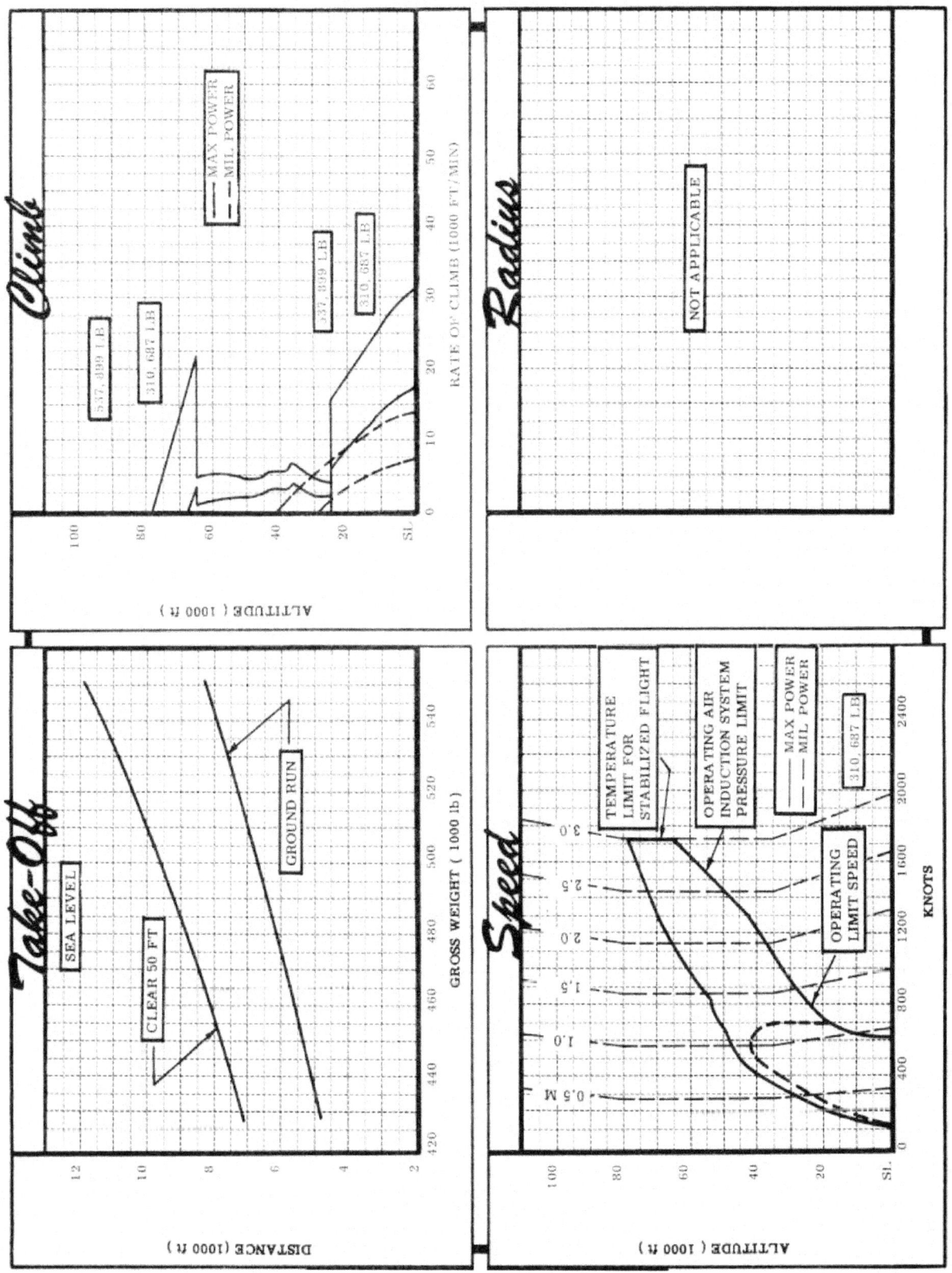

N O T E S

FORMULA: RANGE MISSION I AND IV

Take-off and accelerate to climb speed with maximum power, climb on course to 25,000 feet with military power, accelerate to Mach 1.37 at 25,000 feet, accelerated climb from 25,000 feet to Mach 3.0 cruise altitude, cruise at Mach 3.0. Range free allowances include 5 minutes normal power for starting engines, 1 minute maximum power for take-off and acceleration, and a fuel reserve equal to 30 minutes loiter at sea level at speeds for maximum endurance plus 5% of initial fuel.

FORMULA: RANGE MISSION II AND III

Alert concept take-off, accelerate to climb speed with maximum power, climb on course to 25,000 feet with military power, accelerate to Mach 1.37 at 25,000 feet, accelerated climb from 25,000 feet to Mach 3.0 cruise altitude, cruise out at Mach 3.0. Decelerate with military power, descend to 20,000 feet with idle power, loiter 16 minutes at 20,000 feet at speeds for maximum endurance, descend to sea level with idle power. Credit is taken for distance covered during deceleration and descent from Mach 3.0 cruise altitude to 20,000 feet. Range free allowances include alert concept take-off, 16 minutes loiter at 20,000 feet, descent from 20,000 feet to sea level and a fuel reserve equal to 1 minute military power plus 9 minutes loiter at sea level.

REVISION BASIS:

To reflect changes in weights of weight block.

GENERAL DATA:

(a) Engine ratings shown on page 3 are guaranteed values. Installed values used in performance calculations are as follows:

	(6) YJ93-GE-3	
SLS	LB	RPM
Max	24,277	6825
Mil	16,803	6825
Nor	15,599	6825

(b) Wing Section:

Root to W.S. 186 . . . . 2.0% . . . . 30-70 Hex (Mod)
W.S. 460 to W.S. 630 . . . . 2.5% . . . . 30-70 Hex (Mod)

Mean Camber (Leading Edge)

In the Airstream Direction
B.P. 0 . . . . 0.15°
B.P. 107 . . . . 4.40°
B.P. 153 . . . . 3.15°
B.P. 257 . . . . 2.33°
B.P. 367 – Tip . . . . 0.00°

General Dynamics FB-111 Aardvark

General Dynamics FB-111A loaded with four AGM-69 SRAMs.
Source: U.S. Air Force

The FB-111 owed its origin to a March 1958 Tactical Air Command need for a replacement for the F-100, F-101, and F-105 fighter-bombers that were currently in service. The initial TAC specification was extremely demanding and was technically impossible to achieve. It was replaced by a 1960 requirement for an attack aircraft capable of achieving a Mach 2.5 performance at high altitude and a low-level dash capability of Mach 1.2. It was to have a short and rough airfield performance, and was to be capable of operating out of airfields as short as 3,000 feet in length. It was to have a 1,000-pound internal payload (a nuclear weapon), plus a lifting payload between 15,000 and 30,000 pounds carried on external racks.

At the same time, the U.S. Navy had a requirement for a two-seat carrier-based fighter that would replace the McDonnell F-4 Phantom and the Vought F-8 Crusader. This aircraft was intended to loiter on patrol for up to six hours and engage inbound Soviet naval attack aircraft with AIM-54 long-range air-to-air missiles. Given this operational profile, supersonic speed was not essential.

Despite the fact that these two proposals had absolutely nothing in common and many of their characteristics were mutually exclusive, Defense Secretary Robert McNamara ordered that they be combined in a single aircraft. In addition, McNamara wanted the aircraft to be capable of being used by the Army and the Marine Corps as a close-support aircraft. The project came to be known as the Tactical Fighter Experimental, or TFX. After a highly controversial selection process that was tainted by accusations of corruption, McNamara announced that the General Dynamics proposal had been selected, apparently on grounds that the design offered greater potential for standardization.

The new aircraft was designated the F-111, with the F-111A being the Air Force version and the F-111B being the naval variant. Development was very challenging, with the aircraft suffering major weight problems and extreme difficulty with its engines. Eventually, the naval version was abandoned and replaced by the F-14 Tomcat. The Air Force persisted with its version despite additional design and production issues, and the aircraft eventually matured into an extremely effective strike bomber.

Strategic Bomber Version

Faced with the destruction of the B-70 Valkyrie program and the impending retirement of much of the SAC inventory of bombers, SAC needed a new aircraft to replace the older aircraft. The obvious answer, to restore the B-58 Hustler to production in its upgraded and improved B-58B version, was precluded on cost and political grounds. A new heavy bomber program, the Advanced Manned Strategic Aircraft (AMSA), had been started, but the extreme reluctance of McNamara to release funds for its development was leading to slow progress, and there was no indication of when or if a serviceable aircraft would be produced. Given McNamara's obsession with using derivatives of the F-111 for every requirement being presented, a strategic bomber development of the F-111 seemed the only practical alternative.

General Dynamics responded with a suggestion for a strategic version of the F-111A designated the FB-111A. This differed from the F-111A primarily in having the fuselage extended from 73 feet 5-1/2 inches to 75 feet 7 inches in order to accommodate the additional fuel required for strategic missions. The aircraft also adopted the longer wings originally developed for the abortive F-111B. The undercarriage and landing gear were strengthened to cope with the increased weight of the FB-111, and uprated engines, TF30-P-7s, were adopted. A more advanced avionics suite was specified that included an inertial navigation system, digital computers and advanced displays.

The primary weapon of the FB-111A was to be the Boeing-designed AGM-69A Short-Range Attack Missile (SRAM). The FB-111A could carry two SRAMs in the internal weapons bay along with two more on the inner underwing pylons. Typically, four 600-U.S.-gallon drop tanks were carried on the outermost underwing pylons. For longer-range missions, the SRAMS carried on the inner wing pylons could be replaced by 600-gallon drop tanks, bringing the total to six.

The Air Force wanted a total of 263 FB-111As that would equip a total of 14 squadrons by 1969. However, the technical problems associated with the baseline F-111s drove up costs and seriously delayed production. The cost issue forced a reduction in numbers to 126. When McNamara was finally removed as Secretary of Defense, the opportunity was taken to cancel the remaining order in favor of the more appropriate B-1 bomber, and FB-111 production ended with the 76th aircraft. These equipped two bomb wings, effectively making the FB-111 a one-for-one replacement for the B-58. These two wings were declared operational in 1972.

Service Career

Ironically, given its background and troubled technical history, the FB-111A proved a remarkably successful aircraft. In November 1970, the still-experimental FB-111A took top honors in bombing and navigation during SAC's competition at McCoy AFB in Florida. This was to be the start of a long run of successes in SAC bombing and navigation exercises. Despite this, it was still only a medium-range bomber that required extensive tanker support and relied on foreign bases for strategic missions. Also, the aircraft was cramped and had little in the way of space and weight margins to allow for future modifications and upgrades. Most importantly, it was impossible to expand its ECM capability to counter new threats or to enhance its offensive avionics by adding new-technology electronics. So, while the aircraft was top-of-the-line in the 1970s, it would fall steadily behind the curve and was distinctly dated 10 years later.

By the mid-1980s, the North American B-1B was arriving in service and the FB-111 was surplus to requirements. In addition, there were growing concerns over the safety of the SRAMs and their W69 nuclear warheads in the event of a fire. This caused the missiles to be removed from the inventory in 1990. A decision was made to convert the 34 lowest-time airframes to conventional bombers as the F-111G, with the balance of the survivors being retired. The F-111Gs served mostly as trainers, but 15 of them were purchased by the Royal Australian Air Force in 1993 to supplement that country's fleet of F-111A and F-111C aircraft. The Australian F-111Gs remained in service until 2007, when they were finally retired.

The basic shortcomings of the FB-111 related to its origins as a tactical strike aircraft. In an effort to produce a version more suited to the strategic role, General Dynamics offered the FB-111B in 1979. This had the General Electric F101 turbofan engines in place of the Pratt & Whitney TF30s. The fuselage was extended 88 feet 2-1/2 inches, and additional SRAMs were to be carried on underwing pylons. The General Dynamics proposal featured the production of 155 FB-111Bs by conversion of existing F-111Ds and FB-111As. The costs involved were found to be excessive and the proposal was abandoned. The basic concept continued to be explored, but the availability of the B-1B effectively eliminated the developed versions of the FB-111 from serious consideration.

General Dynamics FB-111A of the 380th SAW at Mather Air Force Base, Calif.
Source: U.S. Air Force

CHARACTERISTICS SUMMARY

BOMBER FB-111A

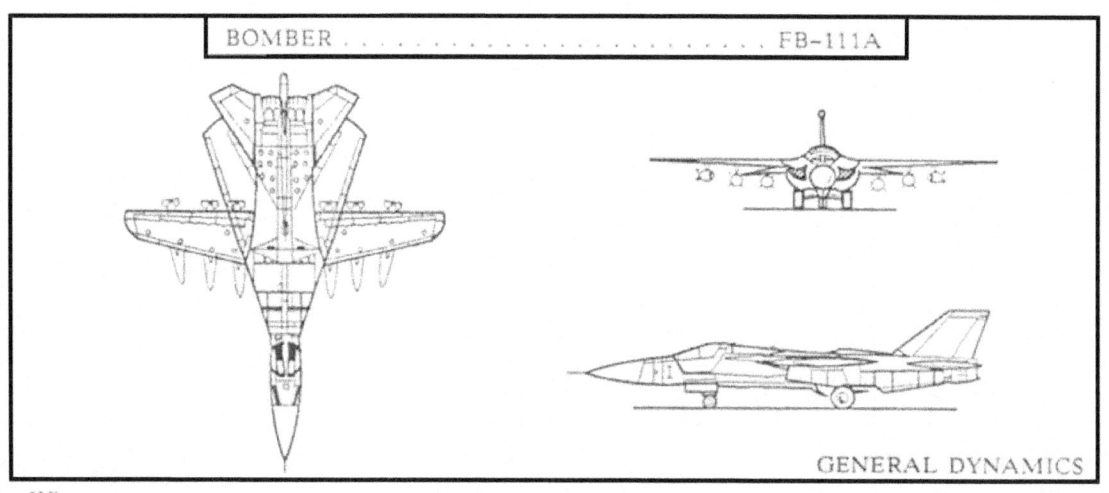

GENERAL DYNAMICS

Wing Area	550 sq ft	Length	73.47 ft
Span (extended)	70 ft	Height	17.04 ft

AVAILABILITY			PROCUREMENT			
Number available			Number to be delivered in fiscal year			
ACTIVE	RESERVE	TOTAL				

STATUS

1. Design initiated .... Aug 63
2. Contract approved .... Dec 66
3. Mock-up .... Nov 66
4. First flight .... July 67
5. First acceptance .... Sep 69
6. Total production aircraft contracted for 76
7. Production completed .... Apr 71

NAVY EQUIVALENT: NONE   MFG'S MODEL: 12

POWER PLANT

(2) TF30-P-107 Turbofan

(Pratt & Whitney)

ENGINES RATINGS

SLS	LB - RPM	-MIN
Max:	*20,350 -14,550	- 45
Int:	12,350 -14,400	- 45
Max Cont:	10,800 -14,150	- Cont

* With afterburner operating

FEATURES

Crew 2
ECM Equipment
Variable Sweep Wing
Integrated Crew Escape Module
Automatic Pilot
Automatic Terrain Following Radar
Precision Digital Bombing/
   Inertial Navigation System
Full Span Wing Leading and
   Trailing Edge High Lift
   Devices
Inflight Refueling
All Weather Day or Night
   Operating Capability
Intercontinental Range
Supersonic Capability: 1.1M
   @ SL to 2.2M @ Alt
Air Conditioning
Speed Brake
Tail Hook (Arresting)
Landing Gear Sod Field Capability
Fuel Capacity (Internal) ...... 5623 Gal

ARMAMENT

TYPE	NO.
Nuclear Air-to-Ground	
Missiles AGM-69A (SRAM)	6
Nuclear Bombs	
B-43, B-57, B-61	6 ea
Conventional Bombs:	
M-117, M-117D, M-117R	16
MK-82 and MK-82	
Snakeye (LD)	24
MK-82, MK82 Snakeye (LD)	24
MK-82 Snakeye (HD)	20
MK-84	4
MK-36	20
Dispensers	
CBU-24/49/52/58/71	20
MK-20	20

CHARACTERISTICS SUMMARY BASIC MISSION — FB-111A

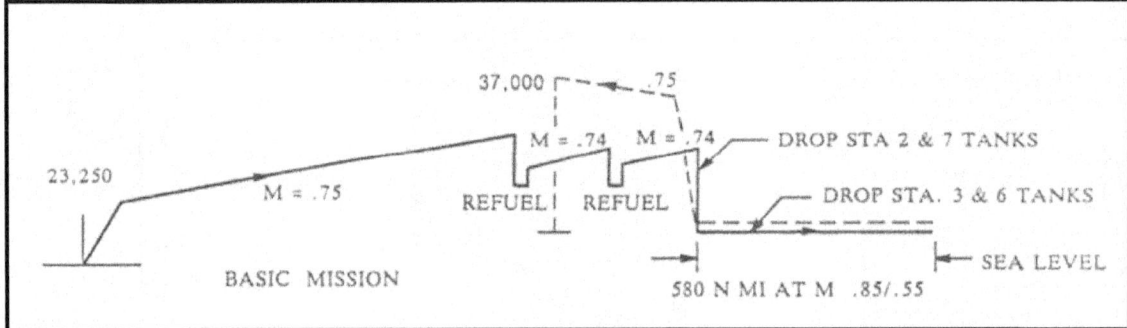

PERFORMANCE

COMBAT RADIUS	FERRY RANGE	SPEED
4435 naut mi with (4) AGM-69A + 4 tanks outbound (subsonic) at 455 kts avg; return (subsonic) at 430 kts avg with 585 naut mi SL combat zone radius and 5520 naut mi total mission distance in 12.45 hours	**4313** naut mi with 9233 gal fuel at 436 knots avg in 9.53 hours at 114,277 lb T.O. wt (6) 600 gal tanks dropped.	COMBAT **728** knots at zero ft alt, A/B power* MAX **1262** knots at 50,000 ft alt, A/B power** BASIC **1185** knots at 35,000 ft alt, A/B power* *V_H limit **Cont engine operation limit

CLIMB	CEILING	TAKE-OFF
2685 fpm sea level, takeoff weight intermediate power	**22,780** ft 100 fpm, take-off weight intermediate power	ground run **5350** ft no assist | ___ ft assisted
28,600 fpm sea level, combat weight maximum power, .95M 72.5° sweep	**51,750** ft 500 fpm, combat weight maximum power	over 50 ft height **6670** ft no assist | ___ ft assisted

LOAD	WEIGHTS	LANDING DIST.

Missiles (4) .... 8988 lb
Fuel transferred
  by tanker ..... 63,367 lb
Fuel: 7446 gal
  protected   0 %
  droppable   32.2 %
  external   32.2 %
	Empty .... 47,481 lb
	Combat .... 69,367 lb
	Take-off ...... 110,649 lb
		ground run **1720** ft | over 50 ft height **2730** ft
		
		Wt **3248** lb

NOTES

1. Performance Basis:
   (a) Contractors Data Based on flight test and wind tunnel results.
   (b) Convair Aerospace Division, Fort Worth Operation Reports:
   FZA-12-6021; FZA-12-6007; FZW-12-6037

2. Landing distance without thrust reverser or drag chute

Revision Basis: To update engine designation.

STANDARD AIRCRAFT CHARACTERISTICS

FB-111A
GENERAL DYNAMICS

BY AUTHORITY OF
THE SECRETARY
OF THE AIR FORCE

TWO TF30-P-107
PRATT & WHITNEY

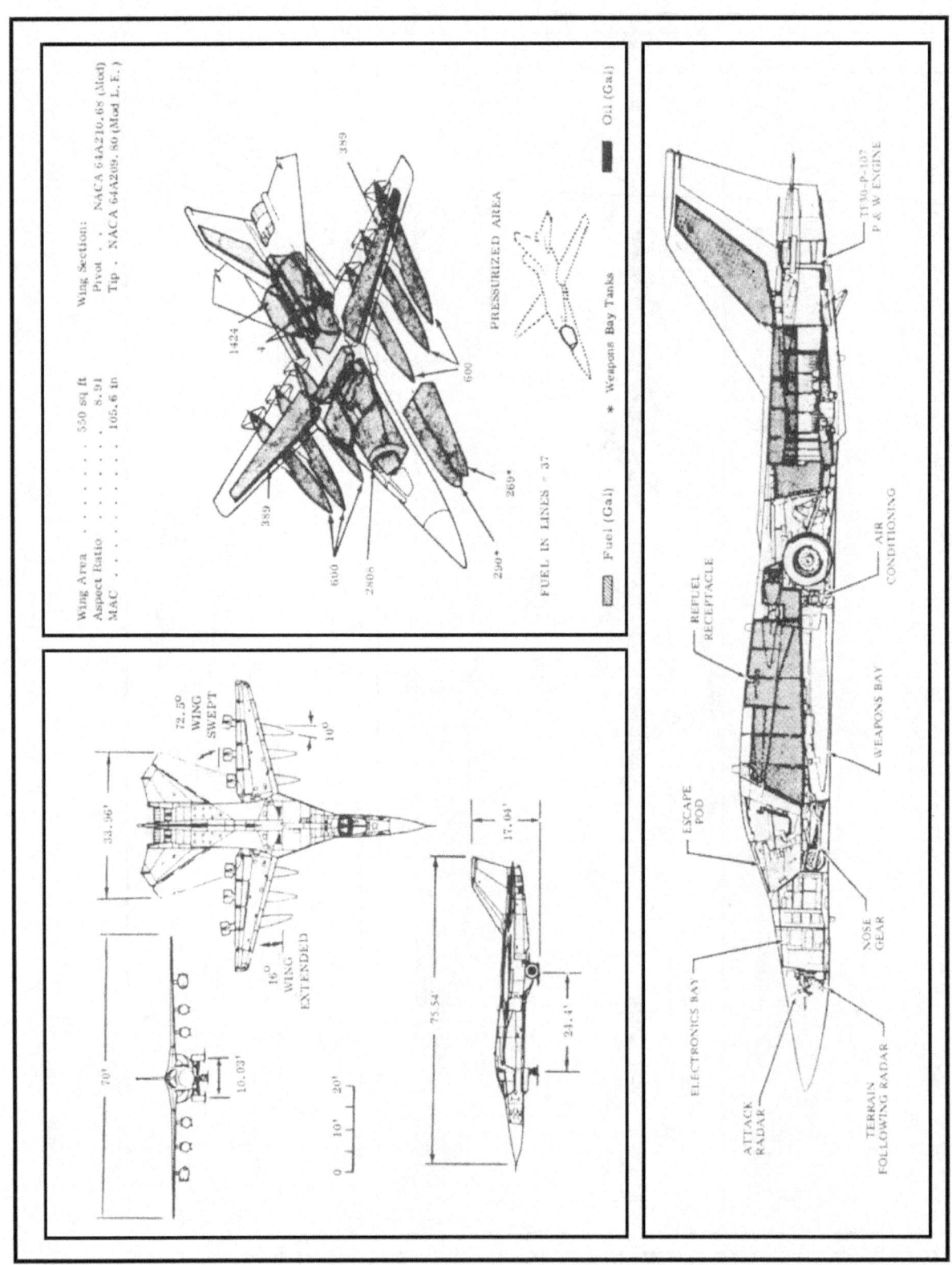

POWER PLANT

No. & Model	(2) TF30-P-107
Mfr	Pratt & Whitney
Eng Spec Nr	A-6118
Type	Twin Spool Turbofan
Length	241.4 in.
Diameter (compressor face)	38.12 in.
Weight (dry)	4121 lb
Nozzle	Variable Area, Blow-in Door Ejector
Augmentation	Afterburning

ENGINE RATINGS

S.L. Static	LB	- RPM(N_2) - MIN
Max:	*20,350	- 14,550 - 45
Intermed:	12,350	- 14,400 - 45
Max Cont	10,800	- 14,150 - Cont

* With afterburner operating

DIMENSIONS

Wing	
Span (extended)	70.0 ft
(swept)	33.96 ft
LE Sweep (extended)	16.0°
(swept)	72.5°
Incidence (16° sweep)	
(root)	1°
(tip)	-3°
Dihedral	1.0°
Length	75.54 ft
Height	17.04 ft
Tread	10.03 ft

WEIGHTS

Loading	Lb	L.F.
Empty	47,481	
Basic	49,558	
Design	109,890	3
Combat	67,876	3
Max T.O. (overload)	119,243	**2
Max T.O. (normal)	116,115	**2
Max Inflight	122,900*	2.68
Max Landing	109,000	**2

All Weights are Calculated
 For Basic Mission
 Limited by Performance
* Refueled
** Slats and Flaps Extended

FUEL

Location	No. Tanks	Gal
Wing	2	778
Fwd Fuselage	3	2808
Aft Fuselage	2	1424
Fuel Lines	–	37
Primary Weapon Bay	1	269
Secondary Weapon Bay	1	290
Ext Wing, drop	6	3600
	Total	9206

Grade	JP-4
Specification	MIL-T-5624

OIL

Fuselage	2	
	Total	8
Specification		MIL-L-7808

ELECTRONICS

UHF Communication	AN/ARC-164
HF Radio	AN/ARC-190
Interphone	AN/AIC-25
Air-to-Ground IFF	AN/APX-64V
TACAN	AN/ARN-118
ILAS	AN/ARN-58A
X-Band Transponder	AN/APX-78
Inertial Bomb Nav System	AN/AJN-16
GP Digital Computer	AN/AYK-18

(Continued on page 9)

MISSION AND DESCRIPTION

Navy Equivalent: None   Mfr's Model: 12

The principal mission of the FB-111A is that of a strategic bomber capable of delivering nuclear or conventional weapons against all known or anticipated enemy targets in any weather, day or night, anywhere in the world. The aircraft achieves this capability through its wide Mach-altitude flight envelope, large fuel capacity, versatile avionics systems, and multiple weapons loading capabilities. This wide flight envelope (Mach 1.1 at sea level to Mach 2.2 at altitude) is primarily attributable to the aircraft's inflight variable-sweep wings plus its turbofan afterburning engines. These design features provide maximum range at all speed/altitude combinations for either rapid global deployment or long-range combat. Mission success is enhanced by onboard penetration aids and the ability to accurately approach and attack targets in all weather conditions at high speeds and minimum terrain clearance.

The major structural features of the aircraft are large one-piece machined structural members and honeycomb bonded stress skin panels. The airplane's high-lift devices consist of full-span, double-slotted trailing edge flaps with Fowler motion, full-span variable camber leading edge slats and a rotating glove section. The forward main landing gear door serves as a speed brake when the landing gear is retracted.

The two crew members sit side-by-side in a pressurized compartment, which is completely separable to serve as an emergency escape module. This feature improves freedom of movement and comfort by precluding the necessity for a personal parachute and survival gear to be strapped to the crew member. The module is designed to permit safe escape throughout the flight envelope including zero altitude and zero speed. The Flight Control and Autopilot System, operated from the left or Aircraft Commander's station, is a power boosted system including triple redundant circuitry for the stability augmentation section and direct mechanical linkage with artificial feel from the pilot to the surface servo actuators. The Navigator/Bombardier's station on the right is the primary avionics systems control station but may also be quickly equipped with necessary flight controls to permit a right seat crew member to perform pilot functions.

Development

Contract Approved	Dec 66
First Flight (Prototype)	July 67
First Acceptance (Production)	Aug 68
Production Completion	Jun 71
Total Production Aircraft Contracted For	76

ARMAMENT

Conventional or nuclear armament can be carried in the enclosed weapons bay and/or externally on wing pylons. Additional fuel can be carried internally in weapons bay tanks and/or externally in pylon-mounted 600-gallon fuel tanks.

(See table on page 10)

LOADING AND PERFORMANCE – TYPICAL MISSION

CONDITIONS REFUELED MISSIONS		I BASIC MISSION LOADING AND PROFILE	II BASIC MISSION LOADING AND S.L. PROFILE	III BASIC MISSION LOADING AND SUPERSONIC PROFILE
TAKE-OFF WEIGHT	(lb)	110,123	110,123	110,123
Fuel at 6.5 lb/gal (grade JP-4)	(lb)	48,410 ⑦	48,410 ⑦	48,410 ⑦
Payload	(lb)	9098	9098	9098
Takeoff ground run at S.L. (flaps = 25°)	(ft)	5280	5280	5280
Takeoff to clear 50 ft. (flaps = 25°)	(ft)	6600.	6600	6600
Rate of climb at S.L.	(fpm)	2712	2712	2712
Rate of climb at S.L. (one engine out)	(fpm)	3504	3504	3504
Time: S.L. to 20,000 ft	(min)	14.45	14.45	14.45
Wing loading	(lb/sq ft)	200.2	200.2	200.2
Stall speed (power off, flaps = 25°)	(kt)	158.6	158.6	158.6
Service ceiling (100 fpm)	(ft)	23,260	23,260	23,260
Service ceiling (one engine out)	(ft)	26,787	26,787	26,787
REFUELED WEIGHT	(lb)	110,123	110,123	110,123
Transferred Fuel	(lb)	62,715	62,715	62,715
Refuel Distance	(n mi)	3460	3460	3460
COMBAT RANGE				
Total mission distance	(n mi)	5535	5236	5202
Combat distance	(n mi)	4455	4248	4602
Combat zone radius	(n mi)	580.	488	100
Dash speed	(kt)	562/364 ⑫	562/364 ⑫	1262
Target altitude	(ft)	S.L.	S.L.	47,700
Target speed	(kt)	562	562	1262
Average cruise speed	(kt)	441	424	442
Initial cruise altitude	(ft)	23,500	23,500	23,500
Final cruise altitude	(ft)	37,500	S.L.	37,500
Total mission time	(hr)	12.57	12.29	11.36
COMBAT WEIGHT	(lb)	69,376	72,500	61,300
Combat altitude	(ft)	S.L.	S.L.	50,000
Combat speed	(kt)	728	728	1262
Combat climb	(fpm)	20,928	19,760	6520
Combat ceiling (500 fpm)	(ft)	51,830	51,180	53,690
Service ceiling (100 fpm)	(ft)	52,050	51,380	53,910
Service ceiling (1 engine out)	(ft)	38,230	37,480	40,780
Maximum rate of climb at S.L.	(fpm)	28,660	27,320	32,750
Basic speed at 35,000 ft	(kt)	1262	1262	1262
LANDING WEIGHT	(lb)	1188	1188	1188
	(lb)	53,248	53,248	53,248
Ground roll at SL	(ft)	1720	1720	1720
Total distance from 50 ft	(ft)	2740	2740	2740

NOTES:
① Intermediate power
② Maximum power
③ Dry concrete runway
④ LE = 26°
⑤ LE = 72.5°
⑥ Flap deflection = 34°
⑦ (4) B-43 bombs
⑧ (24) M-117A1 bombs
⑨ Optimum mach number (long range cruise)
⑩ M = 2.2
⑪ Single engine cruise speed
⑫ Dash speed – in/out
⑬ Climb speed
⑭ Climb to cruise alt. = 17,500 ft
⑮ Combat weight = landing weight
⑯ V_H limit

PERFORMANCE BASIS:
(a) Data source - calculated data based on Category II flight tests.
(b) Performance based on power shown on page 7.

LOADING AND PERFORMANCE — TYPICAL MISSION

CONDITIONS REFUELED MISSIONS		IV ALTERNATE MISSION LOADING AND PROFILE	V ALTERNATE MISSION LOADING AND HIGH ALTITUDE PROFILE
TAKE-OFF WEIGHT	(lb)	108,650	108,650
Fuel at 6.5 lb/gal (grade JP-4)	(lb)	36,552	36,552
Payload	(lb)	22,170 ⑧	22,170 ⑧
Takeoff ground run at S.L. (flaps = 25°)	(ft)	5300	5300
Takeoff to clear 50 ft. (flaps = 25°)	(ft)	6620	6620
Rate of climb at S.L.	(fpm)	2310	2310
Rate of climb at S.L. (one engine out)	(fpm)	2690	2690
Time: S.L. to 20,000 ft	(min)	18.6 ⑭	18.6 ⑭
Wing loading	(lb/sq ft)	197.5	197.5
Stall speed (power off, flaps = 25°)	(kt)	160.6	160.6
Service ceiling (100 fpm)	(ft)	15,500	15,500
Service ceiling (one engine out)	(ft)	21,580	21,580
REFUELED WEIGHT	(lb)	108,650	108,650
Transferred Fuel	(lb)	52,045	52,045
Refuel Distance	(n mi)	2075	2075
COMBAT RANGE			
Total mission distance	(n mi)	4520	4920
Combat distance	(n mi)	2260	2460
Combat zone radius	(n mi)	185	–
Dash speed	(kt)	463/562 ⑫	–
Target altitude	(ft)	S.L.	18,000
Target speed	(kt)	463	433
Average cruise speed	(kt)	415	432
Initial cruise altitude	(ft)	17,400	17,400
Final cruise altitude	(ft)	37,600	37,600
Total mission time	(hr)	10.75	11.41
COMBAT WEIGHT	(lb)	78,750	77,300
Combat altitude	(ft)	S.L.	28,500
Combat speed	(kt)	728	1118
Combat climb	(fpm)	17,680	15,618
Combat ceiling (500 fpm)	(ft)	50,840	50,190
Service ceiling (100 fpm)	(ft)	51,100	50,390
Service ceiling (1 engine out)	(ft)	35,630	36,010
Maximum rate of climb at S.L.	(fpm)	24,920	25,440
Maximum speed at 50,000 ft	(kt)	1262	1262
Basic speed at 35,000 ft	(lb)	1188	1188
LANDING WEIGHT	(lb)	53,020	53,020
Ground roll at SL	(ft)	1700	1700
Total distance from 50 ft	(ft)	2720	2720

NOTES:
① Intermediate power
② Maximum power
③ Dry concrete runway
④ LE = 26°
⑤ LE = 72.5°
⑥ Flap deflection = 34°
⑦ (4) B-43 bombs
⑧ (24) M-117A1 bombs
⑨ Optimum mach number (long range cruise)
⑩ M = 2.2
⑪ Single engine cruise speed
⑫ Dash speed – in/out
⑬ Climb speed
⑭ Climb to cruise alt. = 17,500 ft
⑮ Combat weight = landing weight
⑯ V_H limit

PERFORMANCE BASIS:
(a) Data source - calculated data based on Category II flight tests.
(b) Performance based on power shown on page 7.

LOADING AND PERFORMANCE – TYPICAL MISSION

CONDITIONS NONREFUELED MISSIONS		VI RADIUS MISSION BASIC LOADING AND PROFILE	VII RADIUS MISSION ALTERNATE LOADING AND PROFILE	VIII RADIUS MISSION ALTERNATE LOADING AND HIGH ALTITUDE PROFILE	IX FERRY MISSION	X FERRY MISSION MAXIMUM EXTERNAL FUEL
TAKE-OFF WEIGHT	(lb)	110,123	108,650	108,650	85,990	114,468
Fuel at 6.5 lb/gal (grade JP-4)	(lb)	48,410	36,552	36,552	36,552	60,026
Payload	(lb)	9098 ⑦	22,170 ⑧	22,170 ⑧	–	–
Takeoff ground run at S.L. (flaps = 25°)	(ft)	5280	5300	5300	2930 ⑥	5900
Takeoff to clear 50 ft. (flaps = 25°)	(ft)	6600	6620	6620	3900 ⑥	7300
Rate of climb at S.L.	(fpm)	2712	1206	1206	5120	2658
Rate of climb at S.L. (one engine out)	(fpm)	3504	2004	2004	6150	2480
Time: S.L. to 20,000 ft	(min)	14.45	21.6	21.6	5.82	16.0
Wing loading	(lb/sq ft)	200.2	197.6	197.6	156.4	208.1
Stall speed (power off, flaps = 25°)	(kt)	158.6	160.6	160.6	130.5	159
Service ceiling (100 fpm)	(ft)	23,260	15,500	15,500	32,000	21,080
Service ceiling (one engine out)	(ft)	26,787	21,580	21,580	33,800	25,550
COMBAT RANGE						
Total mission distance	(n mi)	1614	1300	1890	3033	4313
Combat distance	(n mi)	805	650	945	3033	4313
Combat zone radius	(n mi)	622	200	–	–	–
Dash speed	(kt)	562/362 ⑫	463/562 ⑫	–	–	–
Target altitude	(ft)	S.L.	S.L.	22,200	–	–
Dash speed	(kt)	562	463	426	–	–
Target speed	(kt)	435	431	431	437	442
Average cruise speed	(kt)	23,300	17,400	17,400	27,600	22,800
Initial cruise altitude	(ft)	37,200	37,600	37,600	37,500	37,000
Final cruise altitude	(ft)	4.0	2.9	4.33	6.96	9.8
Total mission time	(hr)	67,876	63,930	62,100	52,516 ⑮	54,218 ⑮
COMBAT WEIGHT	(lb)	S.L.	S.L.	32,600	37,500	37,000
Combat altitude	(ft)	728	728	1160	–	–
Combat speed	(kt)	29,300	31,300	11,900	–	–
Combat climb	(fpm)	52,200	53,080	53,500	56,380	55,700
Combat ceiling (500 fpm)	(ft)	52,400	53,300	53,720	43,880	43,180
Service ceiling (100 fpm)	(ft)	38,720	39,960	40,450	33,800	32,750
Service ceiling (1 engine out)	(ft)	26,000	27,650	28,500		
Maximum rate of climb at S.L.	(fpm)	1262	1262	1262	1262	1262
Basic speed at 35,000 ft	(kt)	1185	1185	1185	1185	1185
LANDING WEIGHT	(lb)	53,248	53,020	53,020	52,516	54,218
Ground roll at SL	(ft)	1840	1830	1830	1820	1875
Total distance from 50 ft	(ft)	2920	2900	2900	2880	2950

NOTES:
- ① Intermediate power
- ② Maximum power
- ③ Dry concrete runway
- ④ LE = 26°
- ⑤ LE = 72.5°
- ⑥ Flap deflection = 34°
- ⑦ (4) B-43 bombs
- ⑧ (24) M-117A1 bombs
- ⑨ Optimum mach number (long range cruise)
- ⑩ M = 2.2
- ⑪ Single engine cruise speed
- ⑫ Dash speed – in/out
- ⑬ Climb speed
- ⑭ Climb to cruise alt. = 17,500 ft
- ⑮ Combat weight = landing weight
- ⑯ V_H limit

PERFORMANCE BASIS:
(a) Data source – calculated data based on Category II flight tests.
(b) Performance based on power shown on page 7.

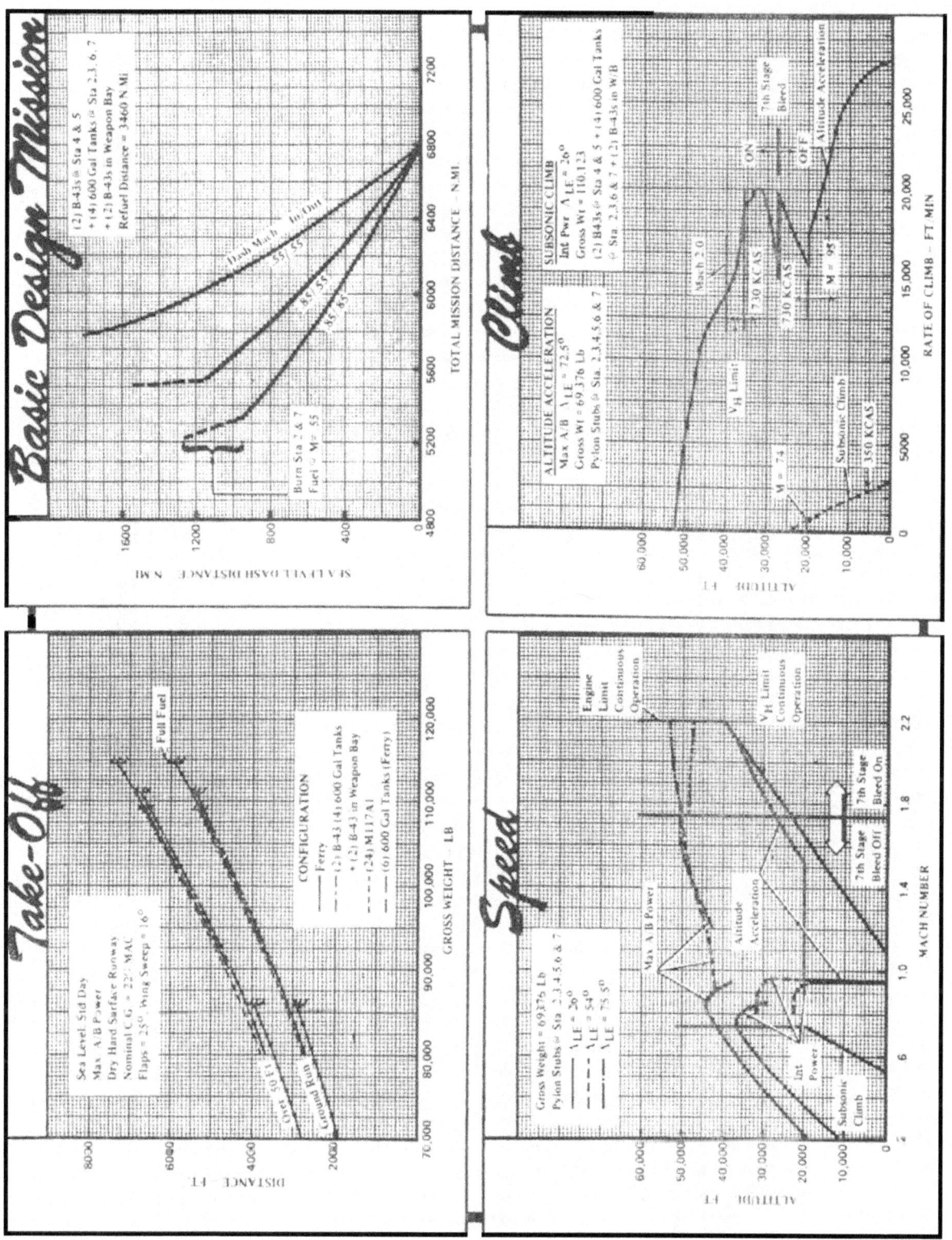

NOTES

REFUELED MISSIONS

Range data presented for the refueled missions consider refueling the FB-111A with a KC-135A having a minimum post-refuel stage of 1000 nautical miles. The mission segments prior to refuel include takeoff, climb on course with Military power and buddy cruise with the tanker at co-speed (but not co-altitude) to the point of hook-up for refueling. The refuel operation is then conducted at the best speed and altitude for the FB-111A calculated at its refueled weight utilizing Military power and considering the tanker downwash effects.

FORMULA: POST-COMBAT STAGE MISSION I

After refueling, cruise at maximum range speed and altitude until initiation of the sea level combat zone. The combat zone is initiated after the fuel in the inboard fixed pylon tanks has been expended and these tanks and pylons have been jettisoned. A radius sea level combat zone is then performed with the penetration at Mach .85 and the withdrawal at Mach .55. All weapons are released simultaneously at the mid-point of the zone. Upon completion of the combat zone a Military power climb on course to best cruise altitude and speed is conducted. Maximum range cruise is then maintained until the total distance from the end of the combat zone is 500 nautical miles. Range free fuel allowances include: 5 minutes of Normal power plus 1 minute of Maximum power fuel consumption at sea level static conditions for warm-up, takeoff and acceleration to climb speed; 5% of fuel burned during takeoff, climb and buddy cruise; and a fuel reserve equal to 5% of fuel onboard at the end of last refuel plus 20 minutes maximum endurance fuel consumption at sea level.

FORMULA: POST-COMBAT STAGE MISSION II

Same as Post-Combat Mission I except the inboard fixed pylon tank is consumed at Mach .55 and sea level immediately after refuel and the 500-nautical-mile post-combat stage is conducted at Mach .55 and sea level.

FORMULA: POST-COMBAT STAGE MISSION III

After refueling, cruise at maximum range speed and altitude until all external fuel has been consumed and the tanks and pylons jettisoned. Immediately thereafter, initiate a Maximum power acceleration to Mach 2.2 and 40,000 feet. A radius combat zone is conducted from this condition. It consists of a Mach 2.2 climb to best cruise altitude followed by a Mach 2.2 cruise to and from the target. All weapons are released simultaneously at the mid-point of the zone. Upon completion of the combat zone, a distance of 500 nautical miles at maximum range speed and altitude is flown. Range free fuel allowances are the same as Post-Combat Stage Mission I.

REFUELED MISSIONS (continued)

FORMULA: RADIUS MISSION IV

Refuel distance for this mission is limited to 2075 nautical miles. Immediately after refuel, a radius sea level combat zone is initiated which consists of a penetration at Mach .70 and a withdrawal at Mach .85. All weapons are released simultaneously at the midpoint of the zone. Upon completion of the combat zone, a Military power climb on course to best cruise altitude is performed. Maximum range cruise is then maintained for return to takeoff base. Range free fuel allowances are the same as Post-Combat Stage Mission I.

FORMULA: RADIUS MISSION V

Same as Radius Mission IV except the entire mission is flown at best cruise speed and altitude; i.e., there is no combat zone. All weapons are released simultaneously at the mid-point of the mission.

NONREFUELED MISSION

FORMULA: RADIUS MISSION VI

Takeoff, climb on course with intermediate power to altitude for best cruise and cruise at maximum range speed and altitude until initiating the combat zone. A sea level radius combat zone is performed such that the zone radius is equal to the zone radius of Post-Combat Stage Mission I. Penetration speed is Mach .85, withdrawal speed is Mach .55 and all weapons are released simultaneously at the mid-point of the zone. Upon completion of the combat zone, a Military power climb on course to best cruise altitude is performed. Maximum range cruise is then maintained for return to takeoff base. Range free fuel allowances include 5 minutes of Normal power plus 1 minute of Maximum power fuel consumption at sea level static conditions for warm-up, takeoff and acceleration to climb speed and a reserve fuel equal to 5% of fuel onboard at engine start plus 20 minutes maximum endurance fuel consumption at sea level.

FORMULA: RADIUS MISSION VII

Same as Radius Mission VI except the combat zone speeds and distances match those of Radius Mission IV.

FORMULA: RADIUS MISSION VIII

Same as Radius Mission VI except the entire mission is flown at best cruise speed and altitude; i.e., there is no combat zone. All weapons are released simultaneously at the mid-point of the mission.

(Continued on page 9)

N O T E S

FORMULA: RANGE MISSION IX

Takeoff, climb on course with intermediate power to altitude for best cruise and cruise at maximum range speed and altitude until the fuel allotted for the mission has been consumed. Range free fuel allowances are the same as Radius Mission VI.

FORMULA: RANGE MISSION X

Same as Range Mission IX. The external fuel tanks (and pylons) are jettisoned in pairs in an outboard-to-inboard sequence as they are emptied.

GENERAL NOTES

(a) Performance based on flight test and wind tunnel results (performance report reference: General Dynamic/Fort Worth Report FZA-12-6021, 20 August 1974.

(b) For all missions where external fuel is utilized, the external tanks (and pylons) are jettisoned prior to weapon release (if applicable) in symmetrical pairs as the fuel is consumed.

(c) Mission for maximum gear limit takeoff weight of 122,900 pounds has not been established for this report.

GENERAL NOTES (Continued)

(d) Engine ratings shown on page three are engine manufacturer's guaranteed ratings; comparable installed values used were:

Sea Level Static Thrust	Lbs
Maximum	16,116
Intermediate	10,116
Max Continuous	8843

(e) All performance data are based on a standard day atmosphere.

(f) REVISION BASIS: Update Electronics block; and miscellaneous other corrections on pages 1, 2, 3, and 9.

ELECTRONICS (Continued from page 3)

ODSS	AN/ASG-25
Attack Radar	AN/APQ-114
Radar Altimeter	AN/APN-232V
Terrain Following Radar Set	AN/APQ-171
Doppler Radar Set	AN/APN-218
Astrocompass	AN/ASQ-119
Countermeasures Set	AN/ALQ-137
Infrared Receiver Set	AN/AAR-34
CMDS	AN/ALE-28
RWR	AN/ALR-62(V)3

STORE LOADINGS

STORES	PYLON STATIONS			WEAPONS BAY		PYLON STATIONS			TOTAL
	2	3	4	RB	LB	5	6	7	
NUCLEAR BOMBS									
B-43		1	1	1	1	1	1		6
B-57		1	1	1	1	1	1		6
B-61		1	1	1	1	1	1		6
CONVENTIONAL BOMBS									
M-117, M117D, M117R		4	4			4	4		16
MK-82, MK-82 Snakeye (LD)		6	6			6	6		24
MK-82 Snakeye (HD)		6	4			4	6		20
MK-84		1	1			1	1		4
MK-36		6	4			4	6		20
MISSILES									
AGM-69A		1	1	1	1	1	1		6
DISPENSERS									
CBU-24/49/52/58/71		6	4			4	6		20
MK-20		6	4			4	6		20
EXTERNAL TANKS									
600 gallon	1	1	1			1	1	1	6

Boeing B-1 Lancer

B-1A in flight with wings extended (25-degree sweep position).
Source: U.S. Air Force

With the cancellation of the B-70 Valkyrie, the U.S. Air Force started to examine future manned bombers and their potential role in strategic policy. At the time, it was assumed that the long-range strategic missile would be the backbone of the strategic force, with manned long-range bombers being relegated to a secondary role. It was also believed that ability to fly through enemy airspace at extremely low altitudes was the key to survival in the face of sophisticated air defenses. The very high-speed requirement that had driven development of the B-70 was therefore discarded, and the new bomber would be subsonic.

Studies in Low Level

The first iteration in the new program was designated the Subsonic Low-Altitude Bomber (SLAB). This was a 500,000-pound fixed-wing aircraft with a total range of 11,000 nautical miles, with 4,300 of these miles being flown at low altitudes. This aircraft then evolved into a developed version designated the Extended Range Strike Aircraft (ERSA), which had a weight of 600,000 pounds and featured a variable sweep wing. Despite this feature and being a somewhat larger and heavier aircraft, ERSA was significantly shorter ranged than SLAB, being capable of a range of 8,750 nautical miles, with 2,500 of these miles being flown at altitudes as low as 500 feet. This suggests that the performance estimates that had been made for SLAB were already recognized as being over-optimistic. A third iteration of the same basic concept was designated Low-Altitude Manned Penetrator (LAMP). This traded a further proportion of the aircraft's range in favor of a heavier bomb load. LAMP was intended to have a 6,200-nautical-mile range, 2,000 miles being flown at low altitude.

The determined opposition of McNamara to manned bomber programs meant that all three of these studies were conceptual in nature and avoided the presentation of any actual proposal to the aviation companies. However, they did result in a body of basic knowledge of the demands presented by low-altitude decisions of this duration. This data was then used to construct a requirement for a new bomber designated the Advanced Manned Precision Strike System (AMPSS). In November 1963, Boeing, General Dynamics, and North American were issued Requests for Proposals for the AMPSS. This resulted in an immediate and negative reaction from McNamara, who kept tight control over funds being allocated to this project and ensured that, once again, only basic conceptual studies unrelated to any actual aircraft were carried out. Nevertheless, the AMPSS studies were sufficiently detailed to reveal that many of the conclusions drawn from the earlier work had been erroneous and that any aircraft based on them would be prohibitively costly.

These conclusions led to another re-examination of the projected aircraft and significant changes to the mission profile. The project was redesignated the Advanced Manned Strategic Aircraft (AMSA). This still envisioned an aircraft that was primarily intended for low-altitude penetration but now included high-altitude supersonic performance capability for transit to the target area. The AMSA was much smaller than its predecessors, weighing in at 375,000 pounds.

The range of the AMSA was set at 6,300 nautical miles, 2,000 of which would be flown at low altitude.

McNamara was, predictably, strongly opposed to the AMSA concept but was persuaded to release funds for preliminary work on the grounds that the studies involved would be of general benefit to the airframe, avionics and propulsion industries. Accordingly, AMSA contracts were awarded to Boeing, General Dynamics, and North American for airframe development, Curtiss-Wright, General Electric and Pratt & Whitney were awarded contracts for engine development, while IBM and Hughes Aircraft were assigned the development of new avionics systems.

Development At Last

Work continued to progress slowly, but by 1968, enough basic data had been gathered to issue advanced development contracts. The Joint Chiefs of Staff had recommended the immediate development of the AMSA, but McNamara vetoed the proposal. It was his last decision. McNamara was asked to resign by President Lyndon Johnson and left office on February 29, 1968. He was succeeded in office by Clark Clifford. Widely known and respected in Washington and knowledgeable on defense matters, Clifford commenced work undoing some of the damage done during the seven years McNamara had been in charge of the Department of Defense.

Part of this effort was related to the strategic aircraft programs. McNamara's obsession with forcing the selection of F-111 derivatives for every conceivable application was abruptly ended and, as a direct result, FB-111A procurement was terminated at 76 aircraft. In its place, the AMSA effort was fully funded. When Richard Nixon became president in January 1969, the new Secretary of Defense, Melvin Laird, reviewed Clark Clifford's decisions and confirmed the decision to reduce planned acquisition of FB-111s to 76, and recommended that the AMSA design studies be accelerated. AMSA was officially assigned the designation B-1A in April 1969. A production total of 240 B-1A aircraft were planned, with service entry scheduled for 1979.

Two factors had significantly impacted the program by this time. One was that North American Aviation had merged with Rockwell Standard Corporation to create North American Rockwell. In time this group became Rockwell International and the North American Aviation group disappeared. The other was that the low-altitude penetration doctrine that had dominated U.S. aviation strategy for almost two decades was coming under question. In Vietnam, it had become apparent that low-flying aircraft were vulnerable to even primitive air defenses. If enough people fired rifles at an area of sky the aircraft had to fly through, some of those bullets would hit something vital. The proliferation of man-portable anti-aircraft missiles added emphasis to this scenario. It appeared as if flying low over a defended area was becoming very hazardous. Flying higher eliminated most of these low-technology, man-portable threats. Above 15,000 feet they were inconsequential.

Added to this growing appreciation of the threats at low altitude were other lessons from Vietnam. Experience had shown that the key factors in evading a surface-to-air missile attack were warning and time. Given enough warning of a missile launch and enough time to jam the inbound missile, even the most sophisticated missiles could be evaded. A final factor in the equation was the introduction of precision-guided weapons. These meant that bombs dropped from medium or high altitude could be delivered as accurately as those dropped from low down.

Flying in at medium or high altitude restricted the weapons that could be fired at the inbound bombers to the largest and most sophisticated types. This greatly complicated issues for the defense. If the inbound aircraft were flying at high speed, the time available for the defenses to react was also greatly reduced. Now, the utter folly of the B-70 cancellation almost 15 years earlier was revealed. Its operational altitude was so high that only a tiny proportion of the defensive weapons available could reach it. Simple physics meant that the missiles that could reach the B-70 and have adequate energy to intercept it would be large, expensive and immobile. The speed of the B-70 meant that it could be through the area covered by a defensive system before the delays inherent in that system allowed it to react. The truth of this analysis was already being exposed by the SR-71 reconnaissance aircraft. This was already flying in some of the most heavily defended airspace in the world, yet no SR-71 ever came close to being intercepted – let alone destroyed or damaged. Yet the service-standard B-70 would have been faster and higher-flying than the SR-71.

It was too late to resurrect the B-70; the best that could be done was to give the new B-1A some approximation of the earlier aircraft's performance. The requirement for the new aircraft demanded a maximum speed of Mach 2.25 at high altitude but, significantly, the maximum speed requirement for low altitude was reduced from Mach 1.2 to Mach 0.85. The service ceiling was set at 62,000 feet, 25,000 feet less than the B-70 but enough to give a measure of immunity to anti-aircraft missiles.

Rise and Fall and Rise

The first B-1 flight aircraft was rolled out on October 26, 1974. It made its first flight a little less than a month later when it was shuttled over to Edwards AFB to begin its flight test program. This went surprisingly smoothly for a large, complex aircraft that contained a number of developmental systems. The aircraft successfully passed its Initial Operational Test & Evaluation in September 1976, with the Phase 1 flight test program completed later the same month. By the end of the year, the Air Force had decided that the B-1A met the requirements that had been laid down and was ready for production.

Unfortunately, once again disaster struck the U.S. strategic bomber fleet. For reasons that defy understanding or analysis, the new presidential administration of Jimmy Carter announced that plans to produce the B-1A would be canceled, and that the defense needs of the United States would be met by ICBMs, SLBMs, and a fleet of modernized B-52s armed with ALCMs. The official reason announced by the Carter administration was the rising costs of the B-1, yet the truth was, the cost increases in question were mostly due to inflation, which was running riot at that time. The claims that air-launched cruise missiles fired from other aircraft would offer superior capability were also false, since that combination lacked the merits of flexibility that distinguished the bombers. The most likely explanation was that the Soviet Union had demanded the cancellation of the B-1 as a price for agreeing to sign human rights agreements.

Fortunately, research and development flying by the four prototypes was allowed to continue at Edwards AFB. The ability of the aircraft to fly at Mach 2.2 was demonstrated in October 1978. This flight program came to an end on April 29, 1981, by which time the combined total of test hours flown by the prototypes had reached 1,895 hours. This background of experience was invaluable when President Ronald Reagan decided to restore the B-1 to production.

Enter the B-1B

The new B-1B was the result of a Rockwell design effort to produce a minimal-change version of the B-1A that could act as a cruise missile launch platform as well as a long-range strike bomber. The aircraft would be strengthened in order to raise the maximum takeoff weight from 395,000 to 477,000 pounds. Much of this extra weight was taken up by additional fuel, increasing range from 6,011 nautical miles to 7,455. The most significant change was the elimination of the Mach 2-plus dash capability by simplifying the engine inlets and overwing fairings. This reduced maximum speed to Mach 1.25 but made it possible to eliminate the variable geometry air intakes, making it possible to configure them for minimal radar cross-section. These changes, along with the use of radar-absorptive material covering critical areas of the surface, would, it was hoped, make it possible to build an aircraft with only a tenth of the radar cross-section of the B-1A. It was believed that with this level of signature reduction, the new B-1B would remain capable of penetrating Soviet air defenses without excessive losses up to the end of the century.

This sudden interest in reducing the radar cross-section of the B-1 reflected growing interest in what was popularly known as "stealth technology." This was widely believed to be some magical black art that would somehow make military equipment invisible. In reality, drastic reductions in radar cross-section were another approach to penetrating air defense systems in that they reduced to a minimum the time in which those systems had to react. The basic idea was the same as giving an aircraft very high speed. An air defense zone covered a given area. If an aircraft could cross that area faster than the system could react, then the air defense system would be ineffective. The high-speed approach was a brute force solution to this equation: the aircraft would simply blast through the defense zone. The answer to high-speed penetration was to increase the area covered by the air defense zone by using high-powered radars and longer-ranged surface-to-air missiles. There are, of course, technical limits on how fast aircraft can fly, how far radars can see, and how far surface-to-air missiles can reach. By the 1980s, all three limits appeared to have been reached.

Radar cross-section reduction was another and more sophisticated approach to the same issue. Instead of being used to blast through a large defended area at high speed, a small radar cross-section would be applied to greatly reduce the area covered by the air defense radars. This much smaller area could be crossed by a slower aircraft in the same amount of time that the larger area could be crossed by faster ones – or even in less time. Relatively limited reductions in cross-section area could confer significant benefits, and these had been exploited in the SR-71 and would have been used with the B-70. Using more advanced and much more expensive building techniques promised much greater reductions in radar cross-section, to the point where the aircraft using them were barely visible on radar even at short ranges. The problem was that the 1980s implementation of those techniques severely limited performance and had adverse impacts on handling characteristics.

An evaluation had shown that the B-1B was an effective aircraft that would fill the gap that had developed in the strategic U.S. posture until a new bomber that featured massive radar cross-section reduction, the B-2, was available. Accordingly, 100 B-1Bs and 132 B-2s were ordered.

The first B-1B was assembled largely by hand and incorporated several subassemblies of the No. 5 B-1A, which had been under construction when the B-1A program was canceled. This may explain reports that B-1A production was not restricted to the four aircraft officially listed but that at least one and possibly three additional aircraft had been built. The first production B-1B was delivered in September 1984. The second aircraft was delivered almost a year later. There was no official B-1B prototype as such, and the aircraft was declared ready for delivery to Strategic Air Command barely eight months after its first flight. The 100th and last aircraft was delivered on May 2, 1988

Service Problems

Despite the fact that the B-1B was developed on schedule and within budget, the aircraft quickly developed a sour operational reputation. Some of the complaints were the result of the aircraft being switched back from a high-altitude/high-speed penetration profile to a low-altitude penetration mission. Experience showed that it was difficult to fly a large, heavily loaded aircraft in terrain-following mode and have enough margin of safety to be able to fly around or over obstacles. The maneuvers required were costly in terms of fuel burn, and the aircraft could not achieve the ranges demanded. In addition, the airframe and engine modifications that had changed the B-1A to the B-1B posed unexpected integration problems. The large number of unique systems on the aircraft were also a major source of performance and maintenance problems. These particularly affected the aircrafts avionics and defensive electronics warfare systems. All of these problems were greatly exacerbated by the failure of later administrations to vote adequate maintenance and support funding for the B-1 fleet.

Recent History

The B-1Bs were all initially assigned to Strategic Air Command. With the collapse of the USSR and the end of the Cold War, all USAF bombers stood down from nuclear alert on September 27, 1991. Strategic Air Command stood down on June 1, 1992, and its bomber force was transferred to a new Air Combat Command created by the merger of SAC and TAC. This command was responsible for all USAF fighter, attack, reconnaissance, and combat rescue aircraft. This move was followed by the removal of the B-1B's nuclear capability in 1995 with the elimination of its nuclear arming and fuzing hardware

In order to solve the shortage of maintenance and support funding, the USAF reduced its active fleet of B-1Bs from 92 to 60 aircraft, with the first B-1B being retired in August 2002. The aircraft has since been continuously upgraded, with one major effort being the Conventional Mission Upgrade Program, which includes a number of weapons upgrade phases. Global Positioning System navigation and Joint Direct Attack Munitions capability have also been integrated into the B-1B. Most recently, Lightening laser designation and target acquisition systems have been installed.

The B-1B fleet has been prominent in supporting operations in Afghanistan and Iraq, where its ability to loiter over a battlefield for hours to provide instant precision-guided munitions support for troops on the ground has been a major tactical and operational advantage. During the first six months of Operation Enduring Freedom, eight B-1s dropped nearly 40 percent of the total tonnage delivered by coalition air forces. This included nearly 3,900 JDAMs, or 67 percent of the total. In Operation Iraqi Freedom, the aircraft flew less than 1 percent of the combat missions while delivering 43 percent of the JDAMs used.

Assuming the B-1B is given the necessary upgrades, the Air Force may keep the aircraft in service until approximately 2038. It is, however, expensive to maintain and operate. In June 2010, senior U.S. Air Force officials met to consider retiring the entire fleet to meet budget cut demands. Other proposals include a new B-1R that would effectively revert to the Mach 2.2 B-1A in a conventional-only configuration.

Note: *With the B-1A, the public availability of Characteristics Summary and Standard Aircraft Characteristics documentation ceases, as these documents for the B-1B and B-2 are considered to be classified information.*

Characteristics Summary

BOMBER B-1A

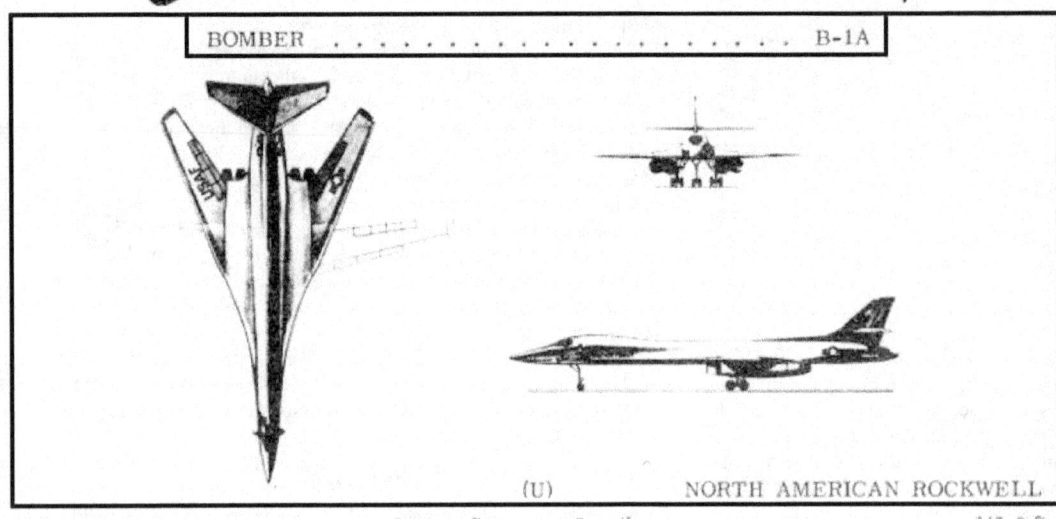

(U) NORTH AMERICAN ROCKWELL

Wing Area . . . . 1946 sq ft	Length . . . . 145.3 ft
Span (sweep angle 35°) . . . . . 136.7 ft	Height . . . . 33.6 ft
(sweep angle 67.5°) . . . . . 77.8 ft	

AVAILABILITY

Number available

ACTIVE	RESERVE	TOTAL

PROCUREMENT

Number to be delivered in fiscal years

STATUS

1. Date of Contract: Jun 70
2. First Flight: Dec 74

Navy Equivalent: None

(C) POWER PLANT

(4) F101-GE-100

General Electric

ENGINE RATINGS

S.L.S.   LB   - RPM - MIN

Max   *29,850 - † - Cont
Intermed: 16,150 - ‡ - Cont

* Afterburner
† HPR/LPR 14,820/8115
‡ HPR/LPR 14,850/8115

(C) FEATURES

Crew 4

Variable-Sweep Wing
Single slotted flaps
Leading-edge slats
External Compression Inlet
Spoilers
Power operated controls
Automatic pilot
Rotary Missile Launcher
Air Refueling Prov.
Crew compartment provides
  "shirt-sleeve" environment
Crew escape system consists
  of an ejectable module

(C) Max fuel capacity: 34,104 gal
(C)   Internal: 30,786 gal
(C)   Weapons Bay: 3318 gal

(U) ARMAMENT

MISSILES

Nr	Type
24 (int)	SRAM . . AGM-69A
8 (ext)	SRAM . . AGM-69A

BOMBS

Nr	Class	(lb)
30	M117 or M117R	750
84	MK82 or MK82 SN	500
24	MK84	2000
135	Bluff shape	500

ELECTRONICS

Specific Avionics equipment will be determined during RDT & E program.

Characteristics Summary Basic Mission — B-1A

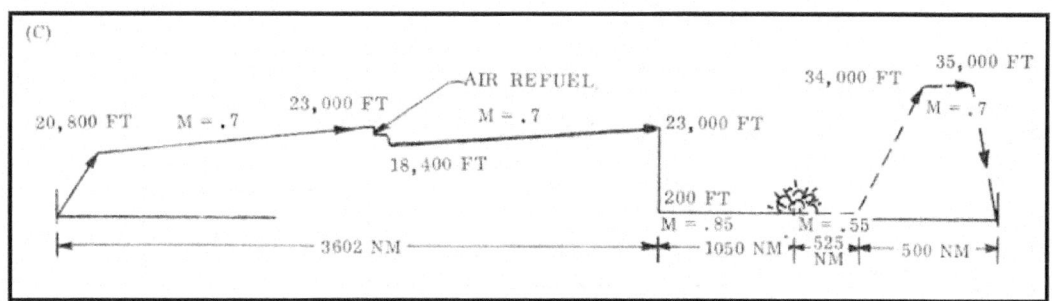

PERFORMANCE

COMBAT RADIUS	(C) FERRY RANGE	(C) S P E E D
(C) **5675** naut. mi with 50,000 lb payload at a penetration & target speed of .85 mach/562 knots in 12.7 hours.	**6242** naut. mi with 33,195 gal fuel at 417 knots avg. in 15.0 hours at 395,000 lb T.O. wt.	COMBAT .95 mach/628 knots at 200 ft alt, max thrust MAX 2.2 mach/1262 knots at 53,200 ft alt, max thrust BASIC 1.9 mach/1095 knots at 35,000 ft alt, max thrust
(C) **C L I M B**	(C) **C E I L I N G**	(C) **TAKE-OFF**
2600 fpm sea level, take-off weight intermediate thrust	**24,600** ft 100 fpm, take-off weight intermediate thrust	ground run **5840** ft | ——— ft no assist | assisted
22,600 fpm sea level, combat weight maximum thrust	**52,800** ft 500 fpm, combat weight maximum thrust	over 50 ft height **7500** ft | ——— ft no assist | assisted
(C) **L O A D**	(C) **W E I G H T S**	(C) **STALLING SPEED**
Weapons: . . . . . 50,000 lb Fuel (ramp): . . . 25,503 gal *(AAR): . . . 15,870 gal *Transferred in flight from Tanker aircraft.	Empty . . . . . . 173,000 lb Combat . . . . . . 229,700 lb *Ramp Weight . . . 395,000 lb Take-off . . . . 389,800 lb Max Inflight . . . . 422,000 lb * Limited by strength (landing gear)	**158** knots power-off, landing configuration, take-off weight
		(C) **TIME TO CLIMB**
		21 min, SL to initial cruise altitude (20,800 ft), T.O. wt, Intermediate thrust.

(U) NOTES

1. Performance Basis:
   (a) Estimated data
   (b) Wind tunnel data plus engine contractor's fuel flow data.

2. To reflect SPO Status data.

Characteristics Summary Basic Mission B-1A

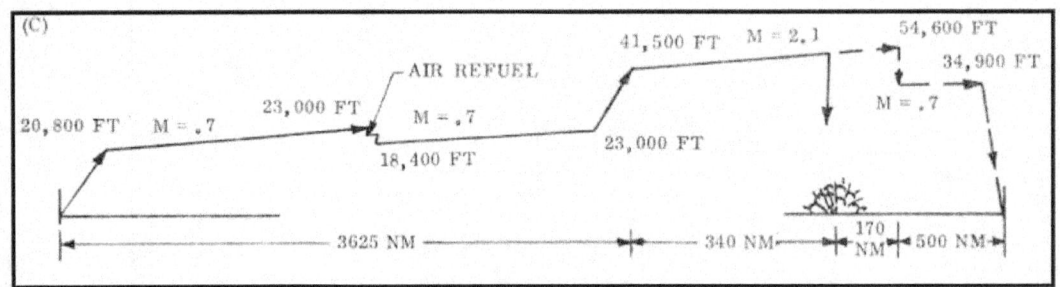

PERFORMANCE

COMBAT RADIUS	(C) FERRY RANGE	(C) S P E E D
(C) **4610** naut. mi with 25,000 lb payload at a penetration & target speed of 2.1 mach/1205 knots in 9.6 hours.	**6242** naut. mi with 33,195 gal fuel at 415 knots avg. in 15.0 hours at 395,000 lb T.O. wt.	COMBAT 2.1 mach/1205 knots at 53,000 ft alt, max thrust MAX 2.2 mach/1262 knots at 55,400 ft alt, max thrust BASIC 1.9 mach/1095 knots at 35,000 ft alt, max thrust
(C) **C L I M B**	(C) **CEILING**	(C) **TAKE-OFF**
2600 fpm sea level, take-off weight intermediate thrust **22,600** fpm sea level, combat weight maximum thrust	**24,600** ft 100 fpm, take-off weight intermediate thrust **52,800** ft 500 fpm, combat weight maximum thrust	ground run **5840** ft / ―― ft no assist / assisted over 50 ft height **7500** ft / ―― ft no assist / assisted
(C) **L O A D**	(C) **W E I G H T S**	(C) **STALLING SPEED**
Weapons . . . . . 25,000 lbs Fuel (ramp): . . . 29,349 gal *(AAR): . . . 15,870 gal *Transferred in flight from Tanker aircraft.	Empty . . . . . . 173,000 lb Combat . . . . . . 225,925 lb Ramp . . . . . . *395,000 lb Take-off . . . . . 389,800 lb Max Inflight . . . 411,526 lb *Limited by strength (landing gear)	**158** knots power-off, landing configuration, take-off weight (C) **TIME TO CLIMB** 21 min, SL to initial cruise altitude (20,800 ft), T.O. wt, intermediate thrust.

(U) N O T E S

1. Performance Basis:
   (a) Estimated data
   (b) Wind tunnel data plus engine contractor's fuel flow data.

2. To reflect SPO Status Data.

Standard Aircraft Characteristics

B-1A

ROCKWELL INTERNATIONAL

FOUR F101-GE-100
GENERAL ELECTRIC

BY AUTHORITY OF
THE SECRETARY
OF THE AIR FORCE

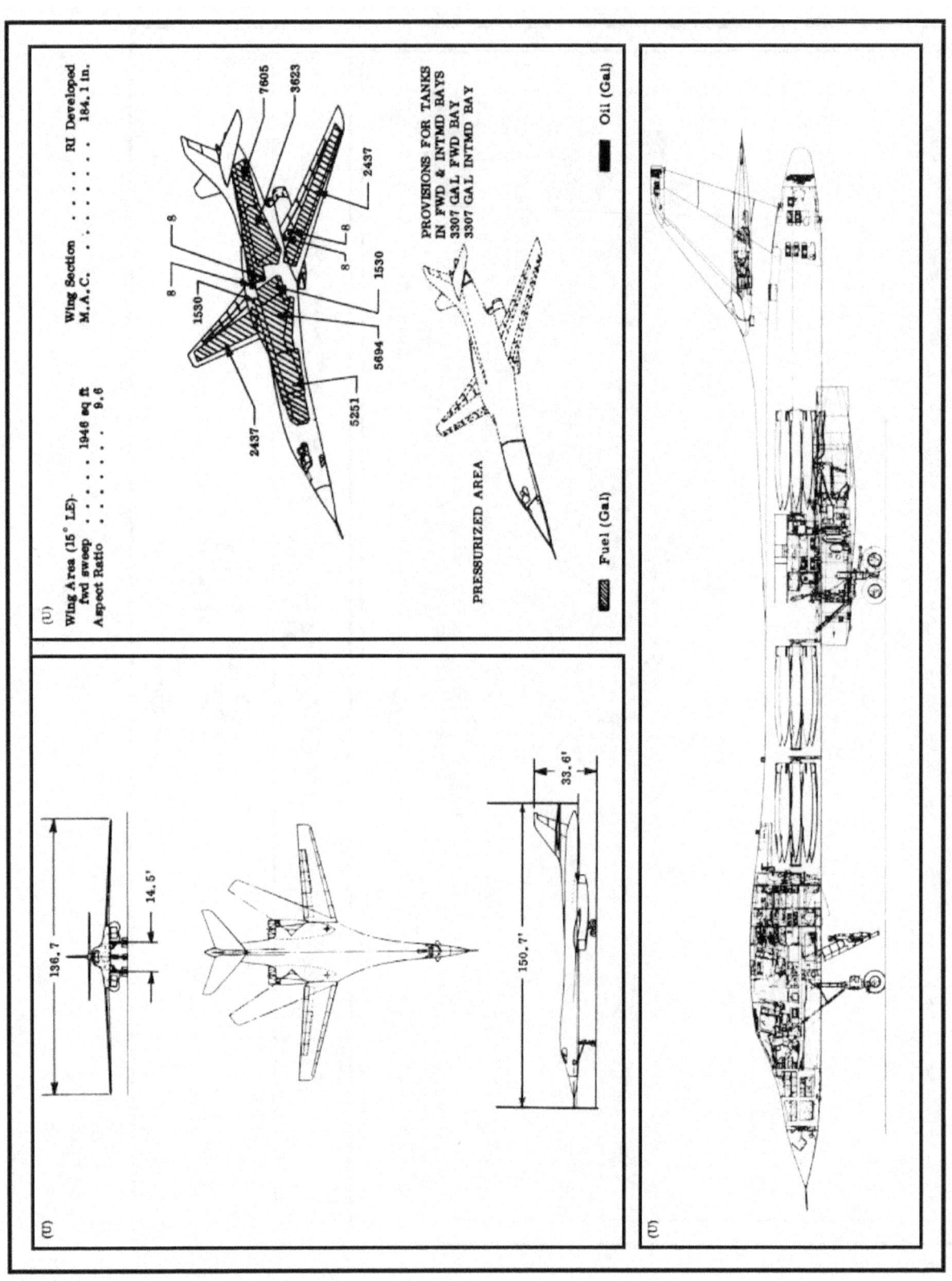

(U) POWER PLANT

Nr & Model	(4) F101-GE-100
Mfr	General Electric
Engine Spec Nr	CP45-B0002
Type	Axial Turbofan
Length	180.7"
Diameter	55.2"
Weight (Dry)	4165 lb
Tail Pipe	Auto, Variable Area
Augmentation	Afterburner

(U) ENGINE RATINGS

S.L.S.	LB - †RPM - MIN
Max:	*29,850 - 14,820/8115 - Cont
Intermed:	16,150 - 14,850/8115 - Cont

* Afterburner operating
† HP Rotor/LP Rotor

(U) DIMENSIONS

Wing
- *Span . . . 136.7'
- Incidence (Butt Line 163.5) . . . 2°
- (Tip) . . . 0° 0'
- †Dihedral . . . -1° 56'
- Sweepback (Variable) . . . 15° to 67 1/2°
- Length . . . 150.7'
- Height . . . 33.6'
- Tread . . . 14.5'

*Most fwd sweep position (15° 0')
†At 40% chord line

(U) Mission and Description

Navy Equivalent: None

The principal mission of the B-1 is to deliver a 50,000 pound payload at supersonic speed at sea level or a 25,000 pound payload at supersonic speed and high altitude to a distant target.

The crew consists of aircraft commander (pilot), co-pilot and two subsystems operators, one for offensive systems and the second for defensive systems.

The B-1 is a variable sweep low-wing, trailing-tail air vehicle with the blended wing-body concept, structural mode control vanes for low-level high speed penetration, external compression inlet and rotary missile launchers.

Other features include single-slotted flaps with a fowler action extension, leading-edge slats, rolling panel tail, spoilers, power-operated controls, automatic pilot and single-point ground and air refueling provisions.

The crew escape system consists of four ejection seats for emergency use by the crewmen. In addition, provisions are made for two instructors to bailout from the bottom of the crew compartment in case of emergency.

Development

Date of Contract	Jun 70
First Flight	Dec 74

(U) MISSILES

Nr	Type	Designation
24 (Internal)	SRAM	AGM-69A
8 (External)	SRAM	AGM-69A

(U) BOMBS

Nr	Type
84	MK-82 or MK-R2 (Snakeye)
30	M117 or M117R
30	SUU-30H/B
24	MK-84
24	B-61 or B-77
12	B-43
Max Bomb Load (Int)	75,000 lb

(U) WEIGHTS

Loading	Lb	L.F.
Empty	173,000 (E)	
Basic	176,423 (E)	
Combat	*229,709	3.0 (1)
Max Taxi	†395,000	
Max T.O.	389,800	1.88 (2)
Max In Flt	422,000	1.87 (3)
Max Land	‡346,500	2.86 (4)

(E) Estimated
* For Basic Mission
† Limited by gear strength
‡ 8 fps rate of sink
(1) Wg Sweep = 65°
(2) Wg Sweep = 15°
(3) Wg Sweep = 15° to 65°
(4) Wg Sweep = 65° to 67 1/2°

(U) FUEL

Location	Nr Tanks	Gal
Wing	2	4874
Fuselage	6	25,233
Max Internal	(Total)	30,107
Weapon bay	2	6614
	Total	36,721
Grade		JP-4
Specification		MIL-T-5624

OIL

Nacelles	4	32
Grade		Synthetic
Specification		MIL-L-7808

(C) ELECTRONICS

OFFENSIVE AND DEFENSIVE AVIONICS

A quick reaction and low altitude penetration capability is provided by the Offensive system using existing forward-looking (AN/AIQ-144), doppler (AN/APN-200), terrain following (AN/APN-146), and altitude (AN/APN-194) radar and dual inertial memory (AN/AJN-17) units which are adapted to operate with real-time digital control. These elements provide accurate navigation, free-fall weapon delivery, and SRAM launch. The Defensive system is tailored to only the major threats to low altitude penetration. It consists of radio frequency surveillance and electromagnetic countermeasures equipment, again adapted to operate with the digital control system. Mission and Traffic Control is provided by a standard complement of equipment:

UHF Radio	AN/ARC-109		ILS	AN/ARN-108
HF Radio	AN/ARC-123		Direction Finder	AN/ARA-50
Intercom	AN/AIC-27		IFF	AN/APX-64
TACAN	AN/ARN-91		Rescue Beacon	AN/PRC-90

Loading and Performance—Typical Mission

(C) CONDITIONS		I BASIC MISSION	II SUPERSONIC MISSION	III FERRY MISSION
TAKEOFF WEIGHT	(lb)	395,000	395,000	395,000
Fuel at 6.5 lb/gal (JP-4)	(lb)	165,769	190,769	215,769
Payload (Internal) ⑤	(lb)	50,000	25,000 ⑥	None
Wing loading	(lb/sq ft)	203	203	203
Stall speed (Power off)	(kn)	158	158	158
Takeoff ground run at SL	(ft)	5840	5840	5840
Takeoff to clear 50 ft	(ft)	7500	7500	7500
Rate of climb at SL	(fpm)	2600	2600	2600
Rate of climb at SL (one engine out)	(fpm)	5400	5400	5400
Time: SL to initial cruise alt.		21	21	21
Service ceiling (100 fpm)	(ft)	24,600	24,600	24,600
Service ceiling (one engine out) ⑤	(ft)	28,000	28,000	28,000
REFUELED WEIGHT	(lb)	422,000	422,000	----
Transferred fuel	(lb)	103,154	103,154	----
Wing loading	(lb)	217	217	----
Service ceiling (100 fpm) ② ⑤	(ft)	23,000	23,000	----
Service ceiling (one engine out)	(ft)	26,000	26,000	----
COMBAT RANGE ①	(n. mi)	5675	4610	6242
Penetration distance	(n. mi)	1375	510	----
Penetration speed	(M/km)	.85/562	2.1/1205	----
Target speed ④	(M/km)	.85/562	2.1/1205	----
Target altitude	(ft)	200	200	----
Average cruise speed outside penetration zone	(kn)	440	440	417
Initial cruising altitude	(ft)	20,800	20,800	20,800
Final cruising altitude	(ft)	35,000	34,900	35,000
Total mission time	(hr)	12.7	9.6	15.0
COMBAT WEIGHT	(lb)	229,709	225,925	195,196
Combat altitude	(ft)	200	53,000	35,000
Combat speed	(M/km)	.95/628	2.1/1205	2.1/1205
Combat climb	(fpm)	22,600	350	14,000
Combat ceiling (500 fpm)	(ft)	52,800	53,000	55,000
Service ceiling (100 fpm) ⑥	(ft)	35,000	53,500 ⑥	37,300 ⑥
Service ceiling (one engine out)	(ft)	30,000	31,000	33,000
Maximum rate of climb at SL ② ③	(fpm)	22,600	23,000	32,000
Maximum speed at optimum altitude ①	(M/km/ft)	2.2/1262/53,000	2.2/1262/53,200	2.2/1262/54,000
LANDING WEIGHT	(lb)	192,680	194,375	195,195
Ground roll at SL	(ft)	2630	2650	2680
Total from 50 ft	(ft)	3680	3700	3710

NOTES

① Maximum afterburner thrust
② Intermediate thrust
③ Detailed description of RANGE missions are given on page 7.
④ Cruise thrust
⑤ All one engine out ceilings are subsonic ceilings
⑥ 24 SRAM missiles
⑦ 12 SRAM missiles

PERFORMANCE BASIS:

(a) Data source: Wind tunnel data and engine contractor fuel flows.

(b) Performance is based on powers shown on page 3.

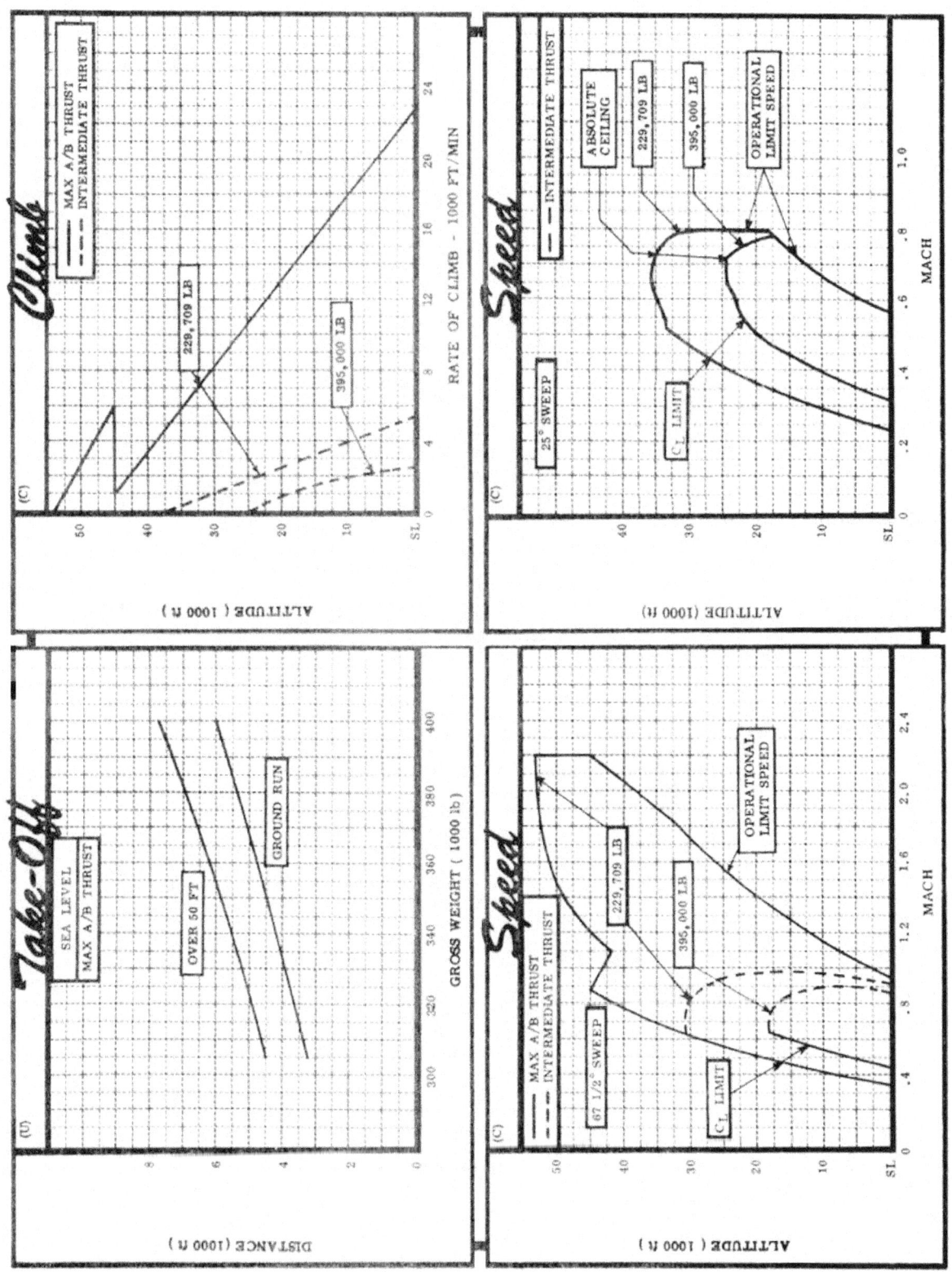

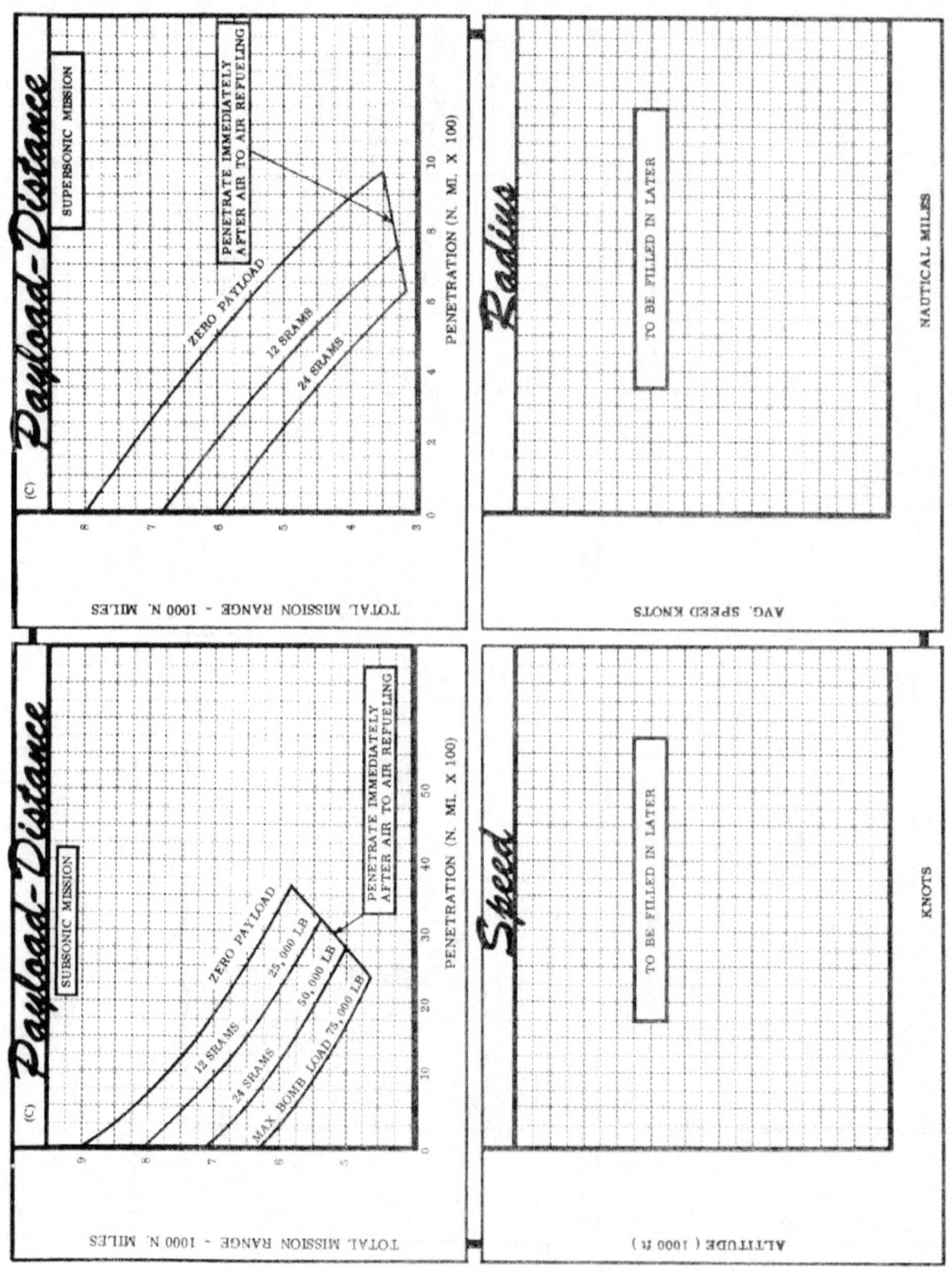

288

NOTES

FORMULA: RANGE MISSION I

Take-off and accelerate to climb speed with maximum afterburner thrust, climb on course with intermediate thrust to best cruise altitude. Buddy cruise at max range speed and best cruise altitude with a KC-135 tanker (301,600 lb start engine weight) to refuel point. Descend to refuel point. Hook-up and refuel on course to point where the KC-135 has a recovery distance of 1000 n. miles and the B-1 is refueled to max in-flight weight. Descend to best cruise altitude and cruise at max range speed and best cruise altitude to the 3600 n. mile total pre-penetration distance. Descend to 200 ft. accelerating to inbound dash speed (M = .85) (No distance credited or fuel used). Dash 1950 n. miles at 0.85 mach, extend electro-visual system pod last 16 minutes inbound, deliver 20,960 lb payload on target, withdraw 525 n. miles at 0.85 mach at 200 ft. Climb on course with intermediate thrust to best cruise altitude. Cruise at max range speed and best cruise altitude for a total recovery distance of 500 n. miles. Range free allowances include 5 minutes at intermediate thrust plus 1 minute at max afterburner thrust at sea level static for starting engines, taxi, take-off and acceleration to climb speed, 5% of fuel used prior to refuel for hook-up and contingency allowance and a landing reserve of 30 minutes at maximum endurance speed at sea level plus 5% of initial fuel load.

FORMULA: RANGE MISSION II

Take-off, initial climb, buddy cruise and refuel portions are same as for Range Mission I. After refuel, descend to best cruise altitude and cruise at max range speed and best cruise altitude. Climb and accelerate with maximum afterburner thrust to arrive at Mach 2.1 penetration speed and altitude at 3600 n. mile total pre-penetration distance. Cruise at best altitude at Mach 2.1 for 340 n. miles, deliver 25,000 lb payload on target, cruise at best altitude at Mach 2.1 for 170 n. miles. Descend to best cruise altitude, cruise at max range speed and best cruise altitude for a total recovery distance of 500 n. miles. Range free allowances include 5 minutes at intermediate thrust plus 1 minute at max afterburner thrust at sea level static for starting engines, taxi, take-off and acceleration to climb speed, 5% of fuel used for hook-up and contingency allowance and a landing reserve of 30 minutes at maximum endurance speed at sea level plus 5% of initial fuel load.

FORMULA: RANGE MISSION III (FERRY)

Take-off and accelerate to climb speed with maximum afterburner thrust, climb on course with intermediate thrust to best cruise altitude, cruise out at max range speed and best altitude until only landing reserve fuel remains. Range free allowances include 5 minutes at intermediate thrust plus 1 minute at max afterburner thrust at sea level static for starting engines, taxi, take-off and acceleration to climb speed and a landing reserve of 30 minutes at maximum endurance speed at sea level plus 5% of initial fuel load.

GENERAL NOTES:

(a) No distance credited or fuel used during descents.

PERFORMANCE REFERENCE:

Wind tunnel data plus engine contractor's fuel flow data.

REVISION BASIS:

Update security classification marking.

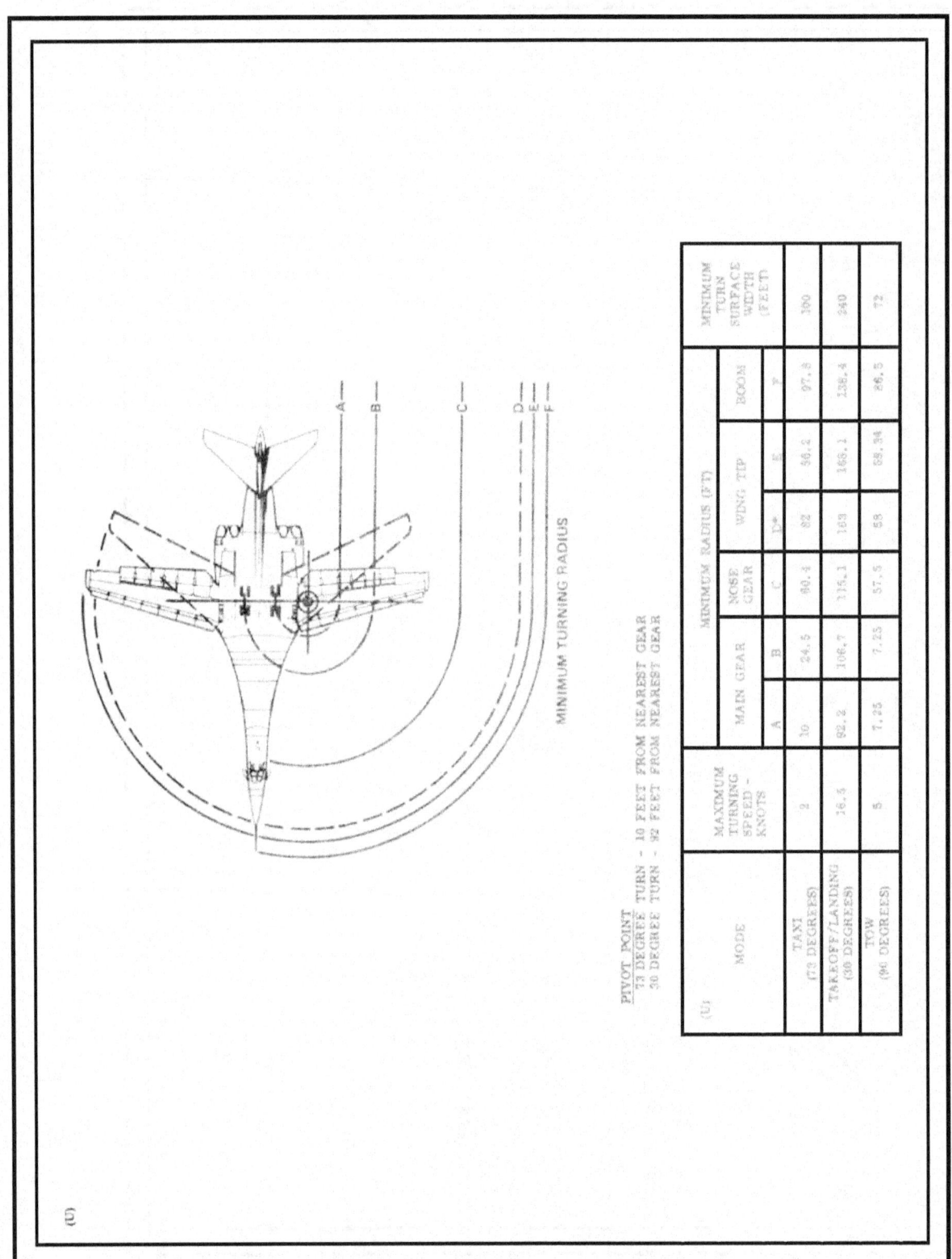

MINIMUM TURNING RADIUS

PIVOT POINT
73 DEGREE TURN - 10 FEET FROM NEAREST GEAR
30 DEGREE TURN - 92 FEET FROM NEAREST GEAR

(U) MODE	MAXIMUM TURNING SPEED - KNOTS	MINIMUM RADIUS (FT)							MINIMUM TURN SURFACE WIDTH (FEET)
		MAIN GEAR		NOSE GEAR	WING TIP		BOOM		
		A	B	C	D*	E	E*	F	
TAXI (73 DEGREES)	2	10	24.5	60.4	82	56.2		97.8	380
TAKEOFF/LANDING (30 DEGREES)	16.5	92.2	106.7	115.1	163	163.1		138.4	340
TOW (90 DEGREES)	5	7.25	7.25	57.5	58	58.34		86.5	72

Northrop B-2 Spirit

Northrop B-2A in flight.
Source: U.S. Air Force

In an odd way, the story of the Northrop B-2 Spirit takes the story of U.S. strategic bombers full circle. When the requirements that gave rise to the Boeing B-29 Superfortress and the Consolidated B-36 Peacemaker were circulated, the Northrop company offered a radical design that was based on Northrop's earlier work with flying wing designs. Northrop had pioneered this design concept in the decade before World War Two, but had never managed to generate any strong interest in the theory. However, the requirements of the new strategic bomber programs were so hard to achieve given the existing state-of-the-art that Northrop believed its radical flying wing design would be a contender.

First Step – The B-35

The basic rationale behind the adoption of a flying wing design was that the concept provided both low drag and high lift. This meant that, all other factors being equal, a flying wing design could carry any weight faster and farther than conventional aircraft. It was also hoped that a flying wing would be less complex to build than a conventional aircraft since it had no added tail or fuselage. Finally, a flying wing presented a smaller target when seen from fore or aft or from the side when engaged in either offensive or defensive operations. These claims seemed too good not to be investigated.

Northrop's proposal was designated the B-35, with an order for 13 YB-35 service test aircraft being placed in December 1942. A contract for 200 B-35s was formally issued on June 30, 1943. The first production B-35 was to be delivered by June 1945. The development contract also included the construction of four N9M flying wing test aircraft to train pilots in handling such aircraft and determine whether the general concept was feasible.

By early 1944, experience with the N9M had shown unexpected difficulties with the flying wing concept, while design and construction of the full-scale B-35 was proving much more difficult and expensive than had been anticipated. Intriguingly, it appears that the Horten brothers in Nazi Germany, who were also strong supporters of flying wing designs (albeit less advanced in concept than Northrop's products), were encountering similar problems. The B-35 was going to be significantly slower and shorter-ranged than originally anticipated, while the engineering difficulties looked set to delay the first flight until 1947. Accordingly, the June 1943 production contract was canceled. It was, however, decided to build the XB-35 and YB-35 aircraft in order to conduct detailed research on the characteristics of large, flying wing aircraft.

Flight testing of the YB-35s revealed major problems with the engine installation and gearing. In addition, the aircraft proved to be unstable and virtually impossible to hold straight and level during a bomb run. These problems proved largely insoluble and, in any case, the performance of the piston-engined YB-35 was already outdated. However, the installation of jet engines in the B-35 airframe seemed to offer a solution to the engine problems and a way of enhancing performance. Accordingly, a contract for the conversion of two of the YB-35 flying wings into jet configuration was issued. Initial plans called for replacing the four piston engines with four J-35s, with two more J-35s being slung under the wings in pods. This configuration was designated the YB-35B. However, this model was quickly deemed inadequate and replaced by a more extensive revision of the design. These aircraft were designated the XB-49.

Second Step – The B-49

The YB-49 was effectively a B-35 with its four piston engines removed and replaced by eight 4,000-pound-thrust Allison J35-A-5 turbojets mounted in banks of four on either side of the wing center-section. The first YB-49 flew for the first time on October 21, 1947 with the second aircraft following in January 1948. Flight testing showed that B-49 had less than half the range of the piston-engined B-35, and that the basic instability of the earlier aircraft had not been corrected. After just 20 test flights, the second YB-49 crashed, killing the pilot and all four crew members. The cause of the crash was never fully determined, but structural failure due to excess speed was the leading suspect.

Despite the crash, the Air Force found the speed and range of the YB-49 attractive enough to warrant continued development. However, there was already a basic problem with the Northrop design that would preclude its use as a bomber. The B-35 and B-49 both carried their bomb loads in eight individual bomb bays cut into the under-surface of the wing outboard of the main crew cabin. The British had already found this to be a very bad idea, but in the environment of the late 1940s, it was even more crippling than Bomber Command had surmised. The wing bomb cells were too small to carry an atomic bomb. Restructuring the wing to carry an atomic bomb would create so much drag that performance would be seriously degraded. If the B-49 was to be procured, it would have to be as a strategic reconnaissance aircraft. This was a viable role, so the Air Force continued with plans for the conversion of nine of the remaining 11 YB-35 airframes to RB-49 configuration with eight jet engines. In addition, orders were placed for 30 new RB-49s to be built as jet-powered aircraft.

Continued flight testing with the single remaining YB-49 was universally depressing. The aircraft was extremely unstable and difficult to fly. It was also completely unsuitable for use as a bomber since it could not hold a steady course or a constant airspeed and altitude. In addition, the aircraft displayed a continuous rocking motion and a persistent yaw. This combination of flight characteristics threw the bomb sights off and gave the YB-49 a much poorer average error rate than the B-39 and B-36 during bombing trials. These problems also limited the value of the aircraft in the reconnaissance role. Eventually, the YB-49 was determined to be excessively costly, hard to maintain, and difficult to fly, and it was determined that it couldn't do anything that existing aircraft in the inventory couldn't do better. The RB-49 would be much slower than the RB-47. And, the flying wings still couldn't carry atomic bombs. The B-49 was canceled, with cancellation of the YRB-49 following shortly afterward.

With the value of hindsight, it is possible to determine that the stability problems with the flying wing were insoluble given the limitations of 1940s technology. The Horten flying wings had the same problems, with the Ho.229 prototype crashing on its third flight. Making a flying wing design work required the use of fly-by-wire technology, which was only developed much later.

Third Time Lucky – The B-2

The B-2 program started life as the Advanced Technology Bomber (ATB). This program was another attempt to develop a new bomber for the U.S. Air Force that could replace both the B-52 and the recently canceled B-1A and, in addition, also replace the B-52. The approach to the task of penetrating Soviet airspace with a full load of nuclear weapons was radically new, though. Instead of blasting through the defenses at high speed and altitude or attempting to run in under the defense systems, the Advanced Technology Bomber would use an unparalleled level of signature reduction to avoid being seen at all. The technical challenges presented by this requirement were obviously enormous, and development of the B-2 promised to be extremely expensive. For this reason, for the ATB program aviation companies formed consortia to submit their bids.

Lockheed teamed with Rockwell to produce an aircraft designated Senior Peg. This was effectively a much enlarged version of the still-secret F-117. Northrop teamed with both Boeing and Ling-Temco-Vought and offered a proposal code-named Senior Ice. This revisited the B-49 program but applied modern computer-controlled flight systems to correct the instability problems and reshaped the entire aircraft to minimize radar cross-section. In October 1981, the Northrop proposal was selected as winner of the Advanced Technology Bomber competition.

While the new B-2 was a direct descendent of the B-49, it differed radically from the earlier aircraft. The design took the flying wing concept one stage further than the B-49 and dispensed completely with vertical rudders or fins. This alone was a major step toward drastic reductions in radar cross-section, The shape of the wing was defined by 12 mathematically straight lines in two groups of six exactly parallel lines. A thick supercritical wing section was adopted to accelerate air passing over the wing to supersonic speeds. The load-carrying problems that had ultimately killed the B-35 and B-49 were accommodated by making the center-section of the wing much thicker than the rest of the wing structure. This thickened area was essentially a very short fuselage that did not extend beyond the planform of the wings. It contained the cockpit, the weapons bays, and the electronics. The aircraft was powered by four engines, arranged in two pairs that were housed in another bulge in the wing surface. One bulge was on each side of the abbreviated fuselage.

The aim of reducing the visibility of the B-2 was achieved by covering the entire aircraft with a radar-absorbing material that eliminated radar reflections. Vulnerability to long- and short-range infrared detection and missile guidance systems was achieved by cooling the engine exhaust as quickly and efficiently as possible. The engine tail pipes are built into the top of the wing, with the primary nozzles well ahead of the trailing edge. The exhaust from the engines is fed into channels that are directed outward. These are fitted with flow mixers that blend the hot core exhaust stream with the cold boundary layer air. The dilution of the hot engine exhaust with cold air is accelerated by the wide and flat shape of the engine exhausts themselves.

The B-2 was rolled out in November 1988 and made its first flight in July 1989. The first production B-2As were delivered to the Air Force in December 1993, but by this time it was apparent that the number of aircraft built would be far less than the originally planned 132. A defense review chaired by Defense Secretary Richard Cheney reduced total planned B-2 production to 75, with production peaking at 12 aircraft per year in the mid-1990s. With the collapse of the USSR and the end of the Cold War, President George H.W. Bush decided that only 21 B-2As would be built, although the test aircraft would be brought up to operational standards. These 21 aircraft were issued to the 509th Bomb Wing. In March 1999, two B-2As from the 509th flew a 31-hour round-trip mission against targets in Kosovo. This mission also marked the first use of the GBU-29/30 JDAM in combat. Almost 60 years after launch of development of the flying wing, it had finally dropped a bomb in anger.

Note: *The Characteristics Summary and Standard Aircraft Characteristics documents for the B-2 are still considered to be classified information and are not available to the public. Historically, the original XB-35 had already been canceled when the Characteristics Summary and Standard Aircraft Characteristics documents were initiated, so there is no documentation available for the B-35 in its original configuration. However, Characteristics Summary and Standard Aircraft Characteristics documents for the YB-35B and B-49 are available, and these have been reproduced since they give insight into the performance of the flying wings as compared to conventional aircraft at a similar technology level.*

Characteristics Summary

BOMBER YB-35B

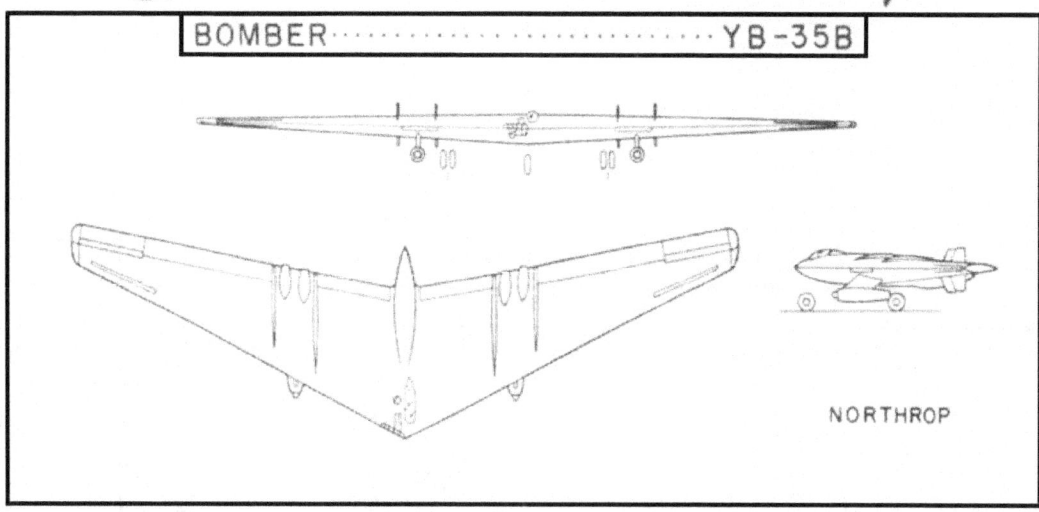

NORTHROP

Wing area .... 4000 sq ft
Span .... 172.0 ft
Length .... 53.1 ft
Height .... 20.1 ft

AVAILABILITY			PROCUREMENT			
Number available			Number to be delivered in fiscal years			
ACTIVE	RESERVE	TOTAL				

STATUS

SERVICE TEST

1. Construction completion of first airplane scheduled for December 1949 (estimated).
2. First flight: January 1950 (estimated)
3. First delivery: February 1950 (estimated)

POWER PLANT	FEATURES	ARMAMENT
(6) Turbo-jet J 35-A-19 Allison ENGINE RATINGS S.L. Static LB - RPM T.O: 4900 - 7800 Mil: 4900 - 7800 Nor: 4240 - 7400	Crew: 4 Cabin Pressurization and Cooling Max Fuel Capacity: 14,688 gal	NONE

Characteristics Summary Basic Mission — YB-35B

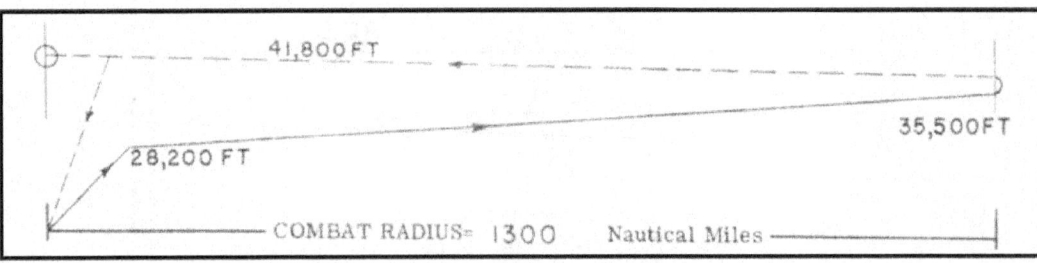

PERFORMANCE

COMBAT RADIUS	COMBAT RANGE	COMBAT SPEED
1300 naut. mi with 0 lb payload at 337 knots avg. in 7.9 hours.	2640 naut. mi with 0 lb payload at 337 knots avg. in 7.9 hours.	380 knots at 35,000 ft alt, max power
		MAXIMUM SPEED
		381 knots at 35,332 ft alt, max power

CLIMB	CEILING	TAKE-OFF
1500 fpm sea level, take-off weight normal power	30,200 ft 100 fpm, take-off weight normal power	ground run 4280 ft no assist ---- ft assisted
3050 fpm sea level, combat weight maximum power	36,200 ft 500 fpm, combat weight maximum power	over 50 ft height 5380 ft no assist ---- ft assisted

LOAD	WEIGHTS	STALLING SPEED

Bombs: None
Ammunition: None
 	
Fuel: 13,500 gal
  protected 37 %
  droppable 0 %
  external 0 %
	Empty..... 82,807 lb
	Combat... 125,715 lb
	Take-off *175,000 lb
	limited by strength
		88 knots
		flaps down, take-off weight

		TIME TO CLIMB ————

NOTES

1. PERFORMANCE BASIS: (a) Estimated data
   (b) In computing Radius & Range, specific fuel consumption has been increased 5% to allow for variation of fuel flow in service aircraft.
2. Fuel density 6.7 lb/gal.
3. YB-35 & A (recip. engines) modified as YB-35B to accommodate (6) turbo jets for use in exploration and development of flying wing type aircraft.
4. REVISION BASIS: Initial issue
   *Limited to 85% design gross weight pending static test.

Picture Shows XB-35

Standard Aircraft Characteristics

XB-35B
FLYING WING
Northrop

SIX J-35-A-19
ALLISON

BY AUTHORITY OF
COMMANDING GENERAL
AIR MATERIEL COMMAND
U.S. AIR FORCE

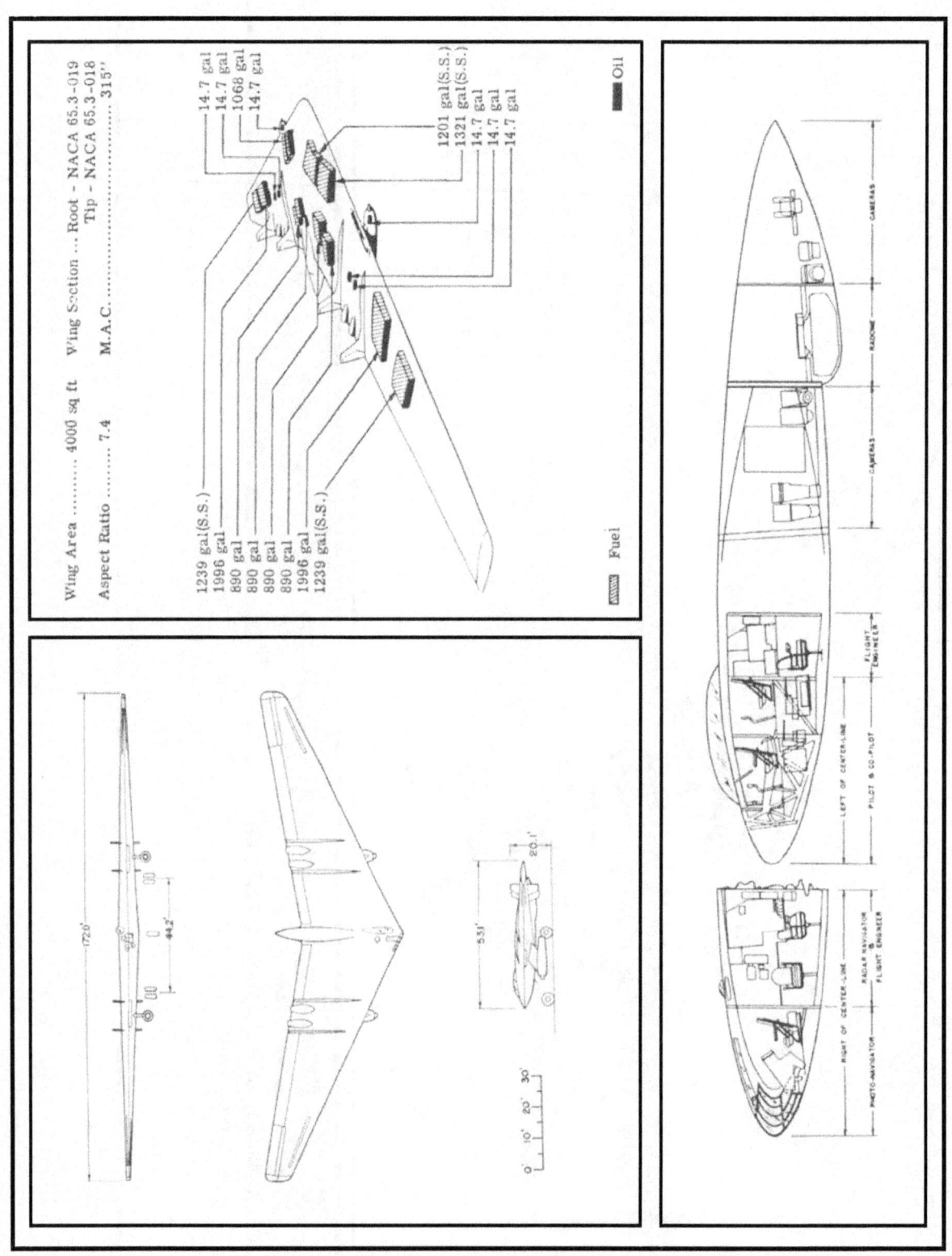

WEIGHTS

Loading	Lb	L.F.
Empty	82,807(E)	
Basic	82,882(E)	
Design	206,000	2.0
Combat	*125,715	
Max T.O.	†175,000	
Max Land	150,000	

(E) Estimated
*For basic mission
†Limited by strength to 85% design gross weight pending static tests.
‡Limited by strength.

FUEL

Location	No. Tanks	Gal.
Wings,outbd*	2	2478
Wings,center	2	3992
Wings,inbd	6	5696
Wings,inbd	2	2522
	Total	14,688
Spec.	AN-F-32,AN-F-48, AN-F-58	
Grade	JP-1,100/130,JP-3	

OIL
Capacity (gal) 88
Spec. AN-0-9
Grade 1010

ELECTRONICS

VHF Command AN/ARC-3
Liaison AN/ARC-8
Interphone .... USAF Combat
Radio Compass AN/ARN-7

Mission and Description

The mission of the YB-35B airplane is to further explore and develop the potentialities of flying wing type aircraft.

The crew consists of a pilot, co-pilot, flight engineer and navigator plus provisions for an observer.

The aircraft is a modification of the YB-35 and YB-35A aircraft (reciprocating engines) to accommodate six turbo jet type engines. The aircraft is of "pure" flying wing configuration using elevons—combination elevators and ailerons and split type wing tip drag rudders for control. Four vertical fins are installed replacing four propellers and associated shaft housing.

The crew compartment is pressurized to maintain an equivalent of 5000 feet altitude up to 28,000 feet and a constant differential pressure above 28,000 feet. Emergency oxygen system is provided, as are window defrosting, air conditioning, dust protection and sound proofing. The electrically-retractable landing gear is of the tricycle type with steerable nose wheel.

Development

Construction completion 1st airplane: ....
First flight: .... January 1950 (estimated)
First delivery: .... February 1950 (estimated)
                           December 1949 (estimated)

BOMBS
NO PROVISIONS

GUNS
NO PROVISIONS

POWER PLANT

No. & Model .... (6) J35-A-19
Mfr. .... Allison
Engine Spec. No. Allison No. 280
Type & Stages ... Axial Flow (11)
Length .... 138"
Diameter .... 37"
Weight (dry) .... 2210 lb

ENGINE RATINGS

S.L. Static	LB - RPM
T.O:	4900 - 7800
Mil:	4900 - 7800
Nor:	4240 - 7400

DIMENSIONS

Span .... 172.0'
Length .... 53.1'
Height .... 20.1'
Tread .... 44.2'

Loading and Performance - Typical Mission

CONDITIONS		BASIC RADIUS I	BASIC RANGE II	OVERLOAD RADIUS III	OVERLOAD RANGE IV	FERRY RANGE V
TAKE-OFF WEIGHT	(lb)	175,000	175,000	182,967	182,967	
Fuel & Oil	(gal)	13,500/88	13,500/88	14,688/88	14,688/88	
Military Load	(lb)	None	None	None	None	
Total Ammunition	(rds/cal)	None	None	None	None	
Wing Loading	(lb/sq ft)	43.8	43.8	45.7	45.7	
Stall Speed-(power off)	(kn)	88	88	90	90	
TAKE-OFF DISTANCE SL						
Ground Run (no wind) ①④	(ft)	4280	4280	5050	5050	
To Clear 50ft Obst ④	(ft)	5380	5380	6450	6450	
CLIMB FROM SL						
Rate Of Climb at SL ③	(fpm)	1500	1500	1420	1420	
Time To 26,650 Feet ③	(min)	24.6	24.6	22.8	22.8	SAME AS MISSION II
Time To 28,200 Feet ③	(min)					
Service Ceiling (100 f.p.m.) ③	(ft)	30,200	30,200	28,900	28,900	
COMBAT RANGE	(n.mi)		2640		2740	
COMBAT RADIUS ⑤	(n.mi)	1300		1365		
Avg. Cruising Speed	(kn)	337	337	339	338	
Total Mission Time	(hr)	7.9	7.9	8.2	8.2	
Cruising Altitude	(ft)	28,200	28,200	26,650	26,650	
		35,500	41,800	35,000	41,700	
COMBAT WEIGHT	(lb)	125,715	93,601	129,390	94,399	
Combat Altitude	(ft)	35,000	35,000	35,000	35,000	
SPEED						
Max Speed (combat alt) ②	(kn)	380	380	380	380	
Max Speed At 35,332 Ft ②	(kn)	381	381	381	381	
CLIMB						
Rate Of Climb (combat alt) ②	(fpm)	600	1190	550	1170	
Rate Of Climb At SL ②	(fpm)	3050	4270	2950	4230	
CEILING						
Combat Ceiling (500 fpm) ②	(ft)	36,200	42,400	35,500	42,250	
Service Ceiling (100 fpm) ②③	(ft)	41,500	47,500	40,800	47,400	
Service Ceiling (100 fpm) ③	(ft)	38,600	44,700	38,000	44,600	
LANDING WEIGHT SL	(lb)	93,601	93,601	94,399	94,399	
Ground Roll ④	(ft)	1090	1090	1200	1200	
From 50' Obst. ④	(ft)	2940	2940	2950	2950	

NOTES
① Take-off power
② Max power
③ Normal power
④ Take-off and landing distances are obtainable at sea level using normal technique. For airport planning add 25% to distances shown.
⑤ Detailed descriptions of the RADIUS & RANGE missions are given on page 6.

CONDITIONS:
Performance Basis: (a) Estimated data
(b) In computing Radius and Range, specific fuel consumption has been increased 5% to allow for variations of fuel flow in service aircraft.
(c) Performance is based on powers shown on page 3.

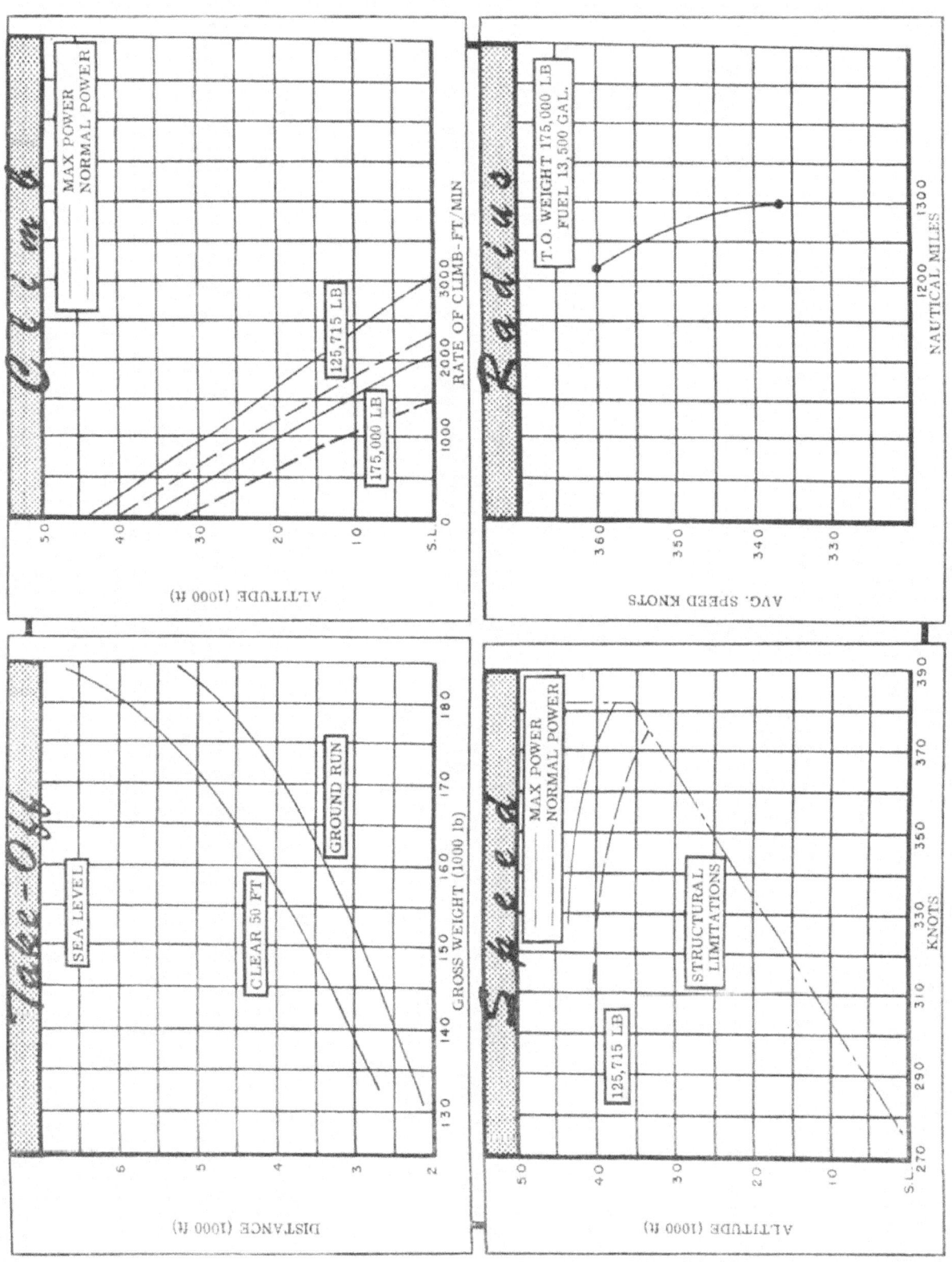

NOTES

FORMULA: RADIUS MISSION I

Warm-up, take-off and climb on course to 28,200 feet altitude at maximum power and maximum rate of climb, cruise out at long range speeds increasing altitude with decreasing airplane weight, make 6 minute normal power bomb run to target, conduct normal power evasive action for 6 minutes, start cruise to home base at 35,900 feet altitude arriving over home base at 41,800 feet altitude. Range free allowances are: 5 minutes normal power fuel consumption for starting engines and take-off, plus 6 minutes normal power evasive action, plus 10% of initial fuel for reserve.

FORMULA: RANGE MISSION II

Same as the outbound leg of the Basic Radius Formula continued until 90% of the initial fuel has been used at 41,800 feet altitude, leaving 10% fuel reserve for combat, evasive action, landing reserve or other considerations for which no distance credit is allowed.

FORMULA: RADIUS MISSION III

Same as the Basic Radius Formula; initial altitude for start of cruise out is 26,650 feet and final altitude over the home base is 41,700 feet. Range free allowances are the same as for the Basic Radius Formula.

FORMULA: RANGE MISSION IV

Same as the Basic Range Formula; initial altitude for start of cruise out is 26,650 feet and final altitude is 41,700 feet.

Characteristics Summary

BOMBER -- YB-49

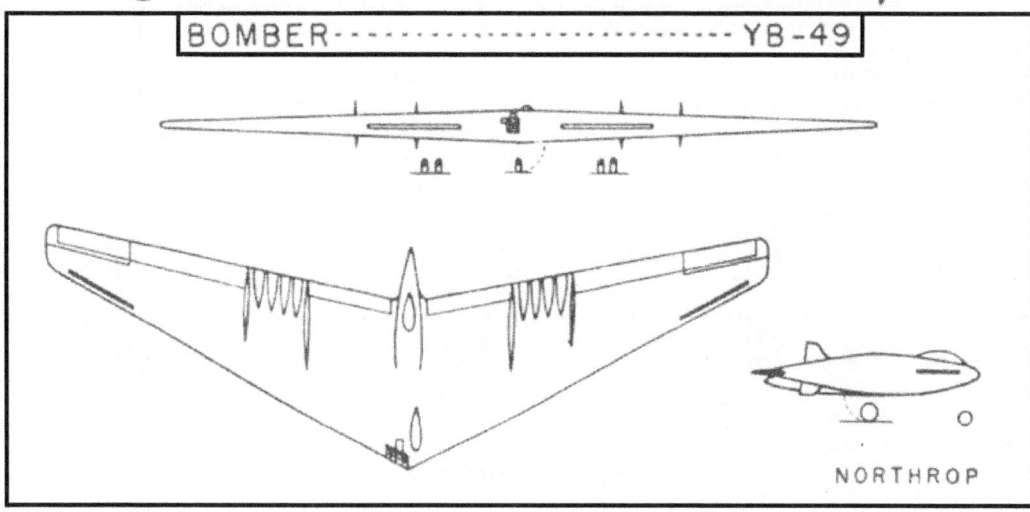

NORTHROP

Wing Area .... 4000 sq ft	Length .... 53.1 ft
Span .... 172.0 ft	Height .... 15.2 ft

AVAILABILITY

Number available

ACTIVE	RESERVE	TOTAL

PROCUREMENT

Number to be delivered in fiscal years

STATUS

SERVICE TEST

1. Authorization for conversion from YB-35's to YB-49's : June 1945
2. First Flight: October 1947
3. Two service test articles completed
4. First article acceptance: June 1948; Second article: May 1949

POWER PLANT

(8) J35-A-15
Allison

ENGINE RATINGS

S.L. Static	LB - RPM
Max:	3750 - 7700
Mil:	3750 - 7700
Nor:	3270 - 7400

FEATURES

Crew: 6

Pressurization

Cooling

Heating

Max Fuel Cap: 14,542 gal.

ARMAMENT

Turrets: None

Guns: None

Max Bomb Load: 10x1600 lb

Max Bomb Size: 4000 lb

Characteristics Summary Basic Mission — YB-49

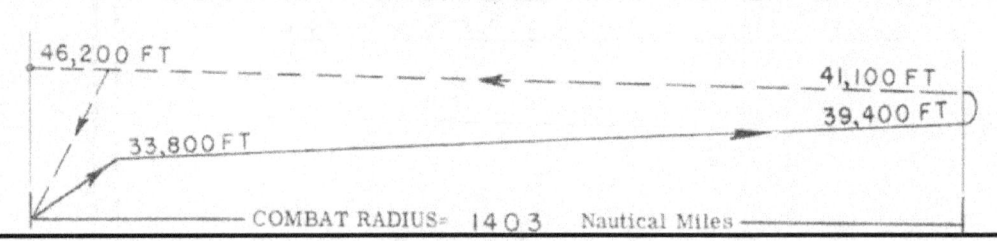

COMBAT RADIUS = 1403 Nautical Miles

PERFORMANCE

COMBAT RADIUS	COMBAT RANGE	COMBAT SPEED
1403 naut. mi with 10,000 lb payload at 365 knots avg. in 7.87 hours.	**2828** naut. mi with 10,000 lb payload at 365 knots avg. in 7.84 hours.	**403*** knots at 35,000 ft alt, max power
		MAXIMUM SPEED
		428* knots at 20,800 ft alt, max power

CLIMB	CEILING	TAKE-OFF
1780 fpm sea level, take-off weight normal power	**35,400** ft 100 fpm, take-off weight normal power	ground run 4850 ft no assist | — ft assisted
3785 fpm sea level, combat weight maximum power	**40,700** ft 500 fpm, combat weight maximum power	over 50 ft height 5850 ft no assist | — ft assisted

LOAD	WEIGHTS	STALLING SPEED

Bombs: 10,000 lb
 	
Fuel: 13,647 gal
  protected 37 %
  droppable 0 %
  external 0 %
	Empty..... 88,442 lb
	Combat... 133,569 lb
	Take-off 193,938 lb
	Limited by space
		90 knots
		flaps down, take-off weight

		TIME TO CLIMB
		—

NOTES

1. PERFORMANCE BASIS:
   (a) Calculated data based on manufacturer's flight test and wind tunnel data.
   (b) In computing Radius and Range, specific fuel consumptions have been increased 5% to allow for variation of fuel flow in service aircraft.
2. Fuel Density: 6.7 lb/gal.
3. REVISION BASIS: To reflect change in take-off weight
   *Mach number limitation

Standard Aircraft Characteristics

YB-49 FLYING WING

EIGHT J35-A-15 ALLISON

BY AUTHORITY OF
COMMANDING GENERAL
AIR MATERIEL COMMAND
U.S. AIR FORCE

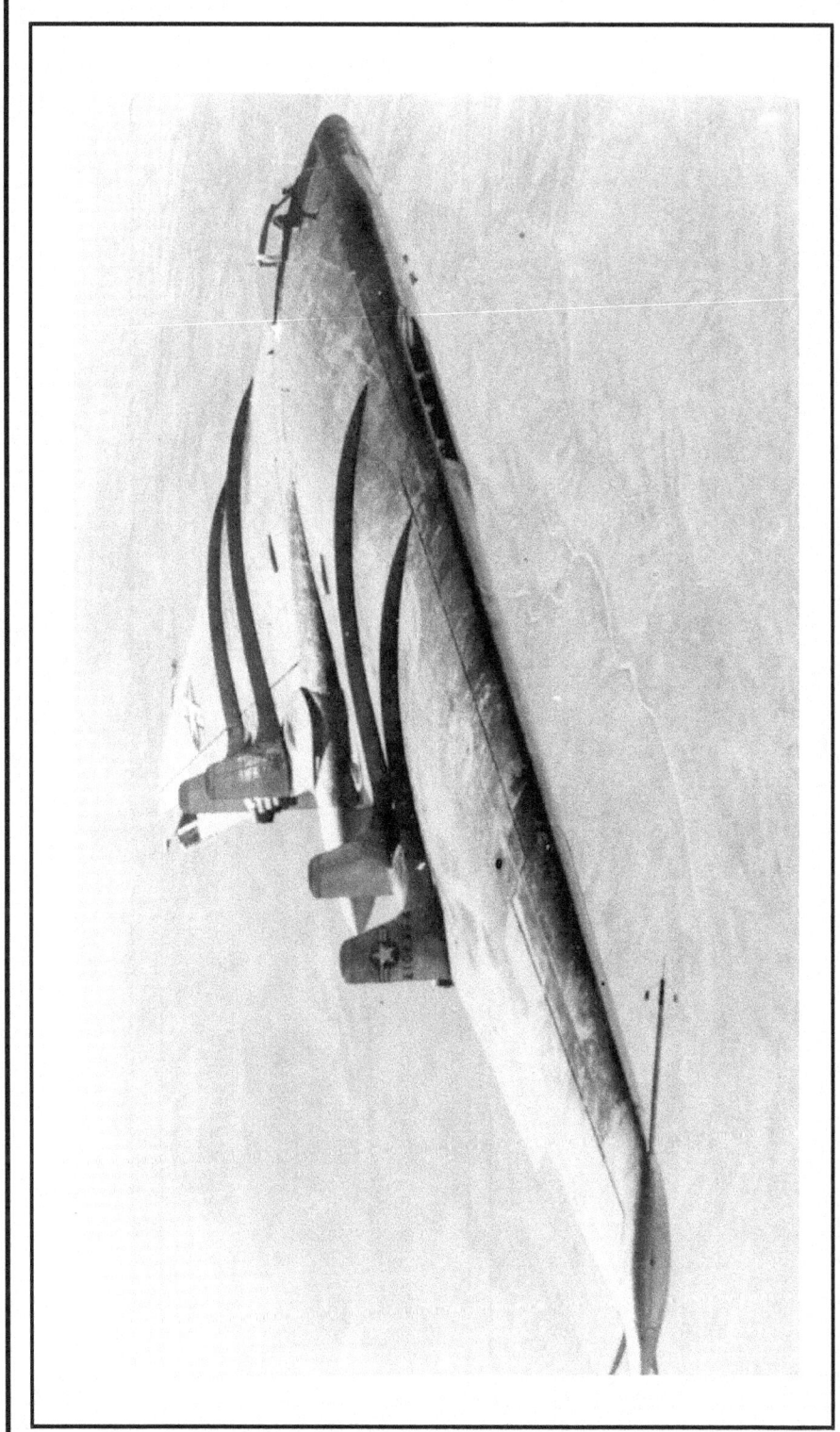

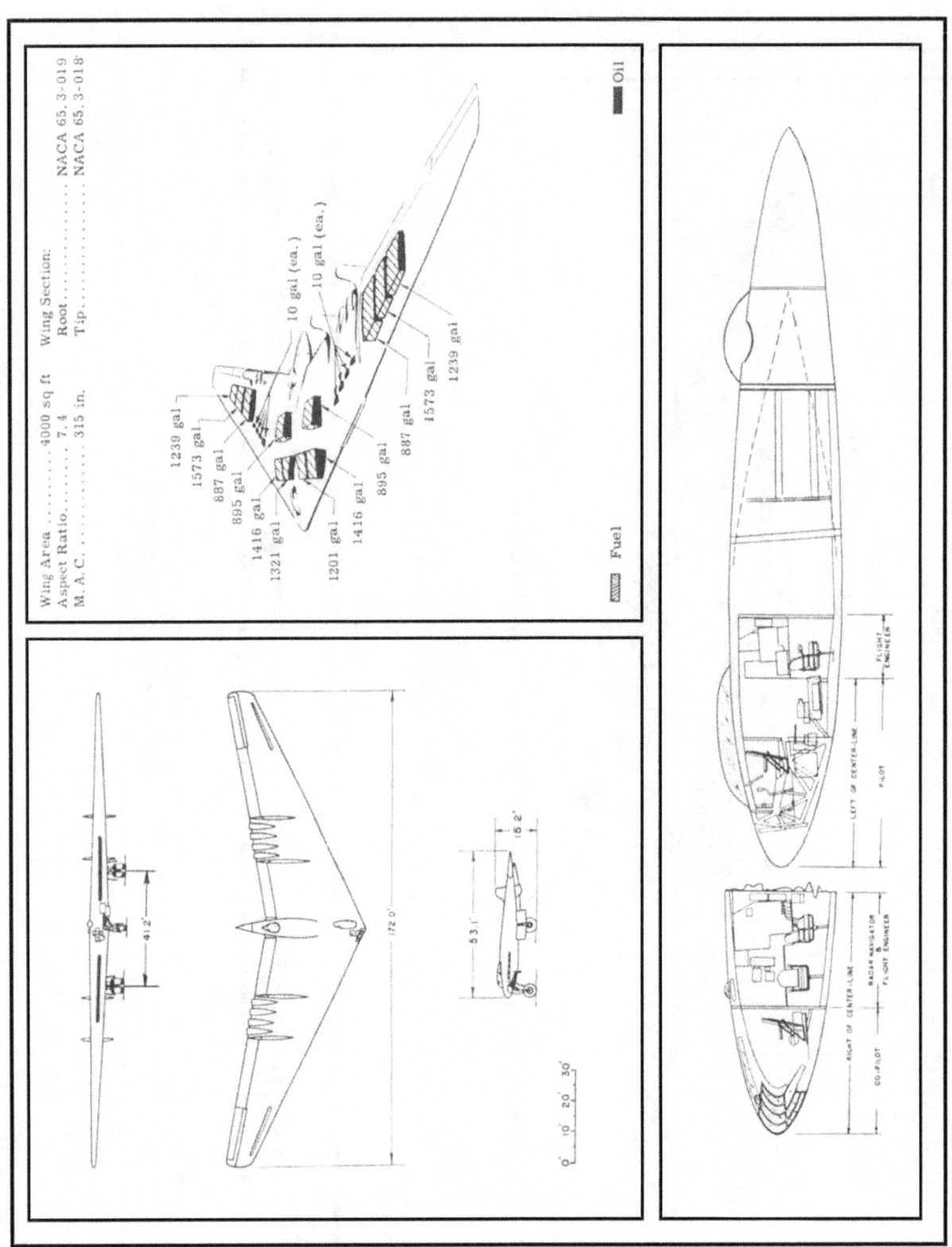

WEIGHTS

Loading	Lb	L.F.
Empty	88,442(A)	
Basic	90,173(A)	
Design	213,552	2.0
Combat	*133,569	
Max T.O.	†193,938	
Max Land.	146,550	

(A) Actual
* For basic mission
† Limited by space

FUEL

Location	No. Tanks	Gal
Main*	4	5000
Aux.	6	7752
Bomb bay	2	1790
*Self-sealing	Tot.	14,542
Spec.		AN-F-48
Grade		JP-1

OIL

Capacity (gal)		80
Spec.		AN-O-8
Grade		1010

ELECTRONICS

VHF Command	AN/ARC-3
Liaison	AN/ARC-8
Interphone	AN/AIC-2
Radio Compass	AN/ARN-7
Marker Beacon	RC-193
Localizer	RC-103
Glide Path	AN/ARN-5
IFF	SCR-695
Range Rcvr	SCR-274N

Mission and Description

The mission of the YB-49 is to further explore and develop the potentialities of "flying wing type" aircraft.

The crew consists of a pilot, co-pilot, navigator, bombardier, radio operator and engineer.

The aircraft is a modification of the YB-35 and YB-35A aircraft (reciprocating engines) to accommodate eight turbo jet type engines and is of "pure" flying wing configuration using elevons - combination elevators and ailerons - and split type wing tip drag rudders for control. Four vertical fins are installed to improve directional stability.

The electrically operated landing gear is of the tricycle type with steerable nose wheel.

Two auxiliary power units installed in bomb bays 3 and 6 provide AC power. Fuel tanks for the APU's are installed in bomb bay 5.

The crew compartment is pressurized to maintain an equivalent of 5000 ft altitude up to 28,000 feet and a constant differential pressure above 28,000 feet. Window defrosting, air conditioning, dust protection and sound proofing is provided.

Development

Authorization for conversion from YB-35's to YB-49: June 1945
First flight: October 1947
Two service articles completed
First article acceptance, June 1948; Second article: May 1949

GUNS

NO PROVISIONS

BOMBS

No.	Size	Type
2	4000	G.P.
5	2000	G.P.
10	1600	A.P.
10	1000	G.P.
30	500	G.P.
Max Bomb Load:	16,000 lb	

POWER PLANT

No. & Model	(8) J35-A-15
Mfr.	Allison
Engine Spec. No.	E-571
Type & Stages	Axial Flow (11)
Length	168"
Diameter	40"
Weight (dry)	2400 lb

ENGINE RATINGS

	LB - RPM
S. L. Static	
Max:	3750 - 7700
Mil:	3750 - 7700
Nor:	3270 - 7400

DIMENSIONS

Span	172.0'
Length	53.1'
Height	15.2'
Tread	41.2'

Loading and Performance – Typical Mission

CONDITIONS		BASIC MISSION I	MAX. BOMB MISSION II	FERRY RANGE III
TAKE-OFF WEIGHT	(lb)	193,938	193,539	190,284
Fuel at 6.7 lb/gal	(lb)	91,442	85,438	97,431
Military load (Bombs)	(lb)	10,000	16,000	None
Wing loading	(lb/sq ft)	48.5	48.4	47.6
Stall speed (power off)	(kn)	90	90	89
Take-off ground run at SL ①④	(ft)	4850	4780	4530
Take-off to clear 50 ft ①④	(ft)	5850	5775	5470
Rate-of-climb at SL ②	(fpm)	2480	2470	2530
Time: SL to 20,000 ft ②	(min)	11.9	11.8	11.4
Time: SL to 30,000 ft ②	(min)	22.0	21.8	21.0
Service ceiling (100 fpm) ②②	(ft)	37,400	37,500	37,900
COMBAT RANGE ⑤	(n. mi)	2828	2520	3105
Avg cruising speed	(kn)	365	364	365
Cruising altitude (s)	(ft)	33,800- 44,600	33,900- 43,700	34,500- 46,000
Total mission time	(hr)	7.84	7.00	8.59
COMBAT RADIUS ⑤	(n. mi)	1403	1322	
Avg cruising speed	(kn)	365	365	
Cruising altitude (s)	(ft)	33,800- 46,200	33,900- 46,400	
Total mission time	(hr)	7.87	7.42	
COMBAT WEIGHT ⑥	(lb)	133,569	129,870	102,596
Combat altitude ②⑦	(ft)	35,000	41,600	46,000
Combat speed ②⑦	(kn)	403	403	403
Combat climb ②⑦	(fpm)	1010	480	540
Combat ceiling (500 fpm) ②	(ft)	40,700	41,300	46,000
Service ceiling (100 fpm) ②	(ft)	45,200	45,700	49,700
Max rate-of-climb at SL ②	(fpm)	3785	3900	4980
Max speed at ___ ft ②⑦	(kn/alt)	428/	430/	433/
LANDING WEIGHT	(lb)	20,800	20,000	18,000
Ground roll at SL ④	(ft)	101,640	100,645	102,596
Total from 50 ft ④	(ft)	2000	1950	2025
		3875	3850	3920

NOTES
① Take-off power
② Max power
③ Normal power
④ Take-off and landing distances are obtainable at sea level using normal technique. For airport planning add 25% to distances shown.
⑤ Detailed descriptions of the RADIUS & RANGE missions are given on page 6.
⑥ Radius mission if radius is shown.
⑦ Mach number limitation

CONDITIONS
(a) Performance Basis: Calculated data based on manufacturer's flight test and wind tunnel test.
(b) In computing Radius and Range, specific fuel consumptions have been increased 5% to allow for variations of fuel flow in service aircraft
(c) Performance is based on powers shown on page 6.

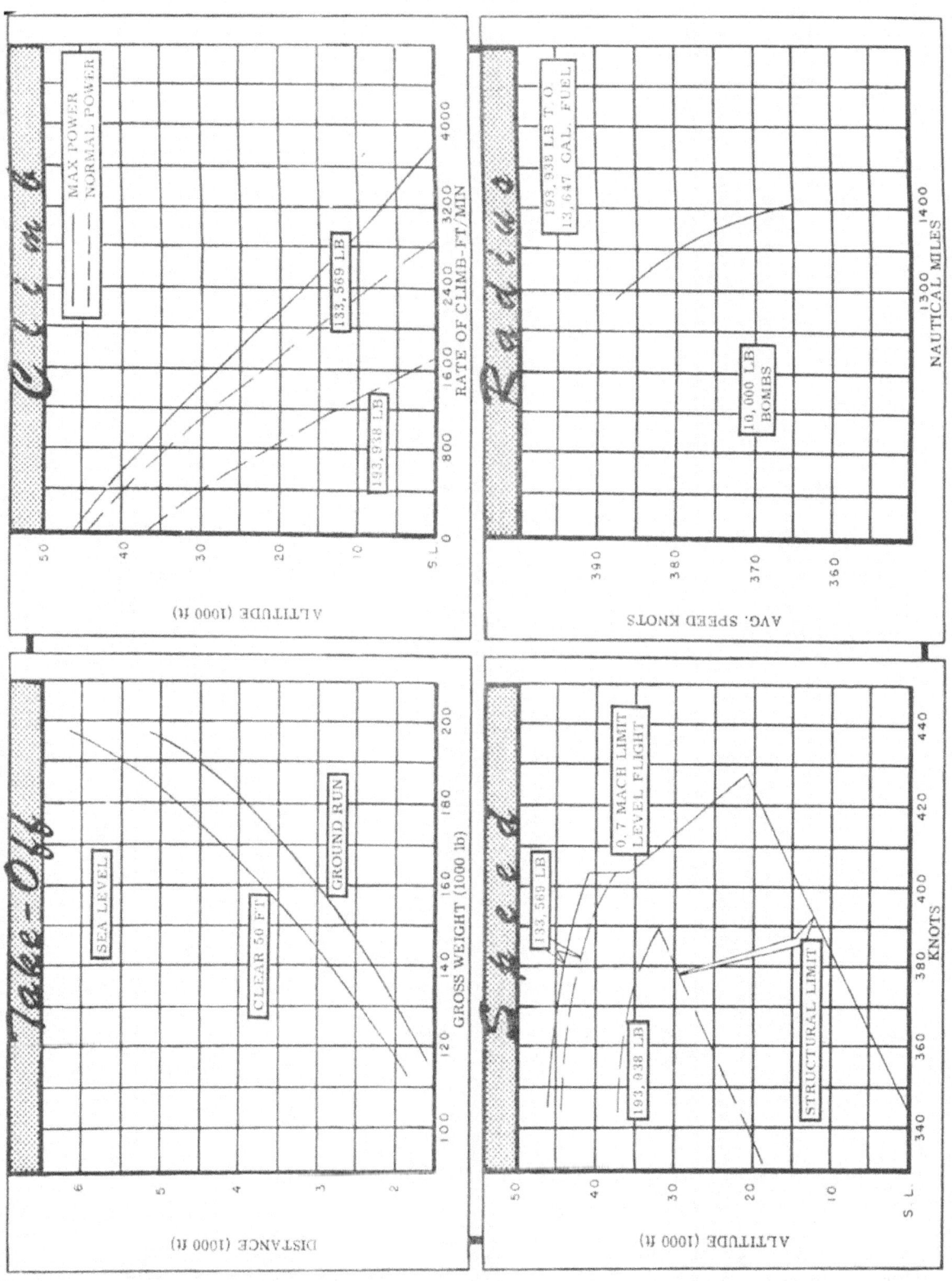

NOTES

FORMULA: RADIUS MISSION I

Warm-up, take-off and climb on course to 33,800 ft altitude at maximum power and maximum rate of climb, cruise out at long range speeds increasing altitude with decreasing airplane weight, make 6 minute normal power bomb-run to target, drop bombs, conduct normal power evasive action for 6 minutes, start cruise to home base at 41,100 ft altitude arriving over home base at 46,200 ft altitude. Range free allowances are: 5 minutes normal power fuel consumption for starting engines and take-off, plus 6 minutes normal power evasive action, plus 10% of initial fuel for landing and endurance reserve.

FORMULA: RANGE MISSION I

Same as the outbound leg of the Basic Radius formula continued until 90% of the initial fuel has been used at 44,600 ft altitude, leaving 10% fuel reserve for combat evasive action, landing reserve or other consideration for which no distance credit is allowed.

FORMULA: RADIUS MISSION II

Same as the Basic Radius formula, initial altitude for start of cruise out is 33,900 ft and final altitude over the home base is 46,400 ft. Range free allowances are the same as for the Basic Radius formula.

FORMULA: RANGE MISSION III

Same as the Basic Range formula, initial altitude for start of cruise out is 34,500 ft and final altitude is 46,000 ft. Range free allowances are the same as for the Basic Range formula.

GENERAL NOTES

(a) Airplane performance based on engine performance from G. E. Bulletin No. DF-81576, dated 26 May 1947.

(b) Engine ratings shown on page 3 are engine manufacturer's guaranteed ratings. Power values used in performance calculations are as follows:

J35-A-15	LB - RPM
S. L. Static	
T.O.	4000 - 7700
Max:	4000 - 7700
Nor:	3500 - 7400

308

Long-Range Strike-B

One Northrop-Grumman Proposal For LRS-B.
Source: U.S. Air Force

By the 1990s it appeared that the career of the strategic bomber was reaching its end. The B-1B was compromised by design changes halfway through its development and by being short-changed on spares and support funding. The B-2 Spirit had only been built in tiny numbers and its huge cost effectively prevented it from being anything more than a "silver bullet" tasked with specific and limited missions. Only the B-52H was reliable, available in significant numbers, and capable of a wide range of operations. Structural surveys showed that the Gray Lady would probably outlast both of her planned replacements, but once old age had taken its toll and the last B-52 stood down, there would be no replacement. Attrition was already steadily reducing the strategic bomber fleet, as by 2010, seven B-1s, one B-2, and four B-52Hs had crashed.

The declining numbers of the strategic bomber fleet and the reassignment of much of that fleet to non-nuclear missions had impacts across the operational spectrum. Once, the requirement had been for the bombers to reach their targets, destroy them, and return. If necessary, they would be air-refueled on their way in, but the intent was for them to drop their payloads, return, collect more weapons, and hit the targets missed or overlooked the first time around. In the 1950s it was already accepted that the missions of the medium bomber fleet would be essentially one-way, with the aircraft either recovering to foreign bases or making it to friendly territory before running out of fuel and being abandoned by their crews. In the 1960s the formulation of missions changed, with the criterion for range becoming distance to target plus an allowance for finding a friendly airbase or airborne tanker. However, the declining number of bombers in the 1980s and 1990s meant the survivors had to engage a larger number of targets (implying a much greater weight of weapons), and "find friendly territory" became "tanks dry over final target."

Renaissance?

The situation was, however, beginning to change. One factor was the development of precision-guided munitions that radically changed the bombing equations. For the first time, the range of bombs using laser or electro-optical guidance or being steered to GPS coordinates meant that targets could be taken out by very small numbers of conventional bombs. The equation changed from the number of aircraft sorties required to ensure destruction of a target to the number of targets a given aircraft could destroy in a mission. Suddenly, the heavy loads carried by the strategic bombers became very attractive. They offered the ability of destroying a large number of targets per mission. Another factor that became increasingly important as the world entered the 21st century was the range of the strategic bombers. With foreign bases becoming thin on the ground and beset by political restrictions, the ability to mount operations from bases within the United States became much more attractive. In effect, the world was returning to the realm of AWPD-1, where the United States had to plan on projecting power from its homeland.

A third factor that became significant was the realization that air defense systems were not as effective as had been believed and that they actually offered much less danger to air operations than had been assumed. A combination of precision-guided munitions, highly developed electronic warfare systems, and 40 years' experience in developing air defense suppression jeopardized the protection offered by conventional air defenses. It became apparent that while the initial battle against such systems might be hard-fought, that battle would be won by the attacking aircraft and would be over in a few days at most. Thereafter, the attacking air power would have a free hand to exploit the advantages offered by air supremacy. This recognition resulted in a division between the "first day" aircraft that would need to be capable of engaging and defeating the air defense systems and the "second day" aircraft that could operate safely in a much more benign environment.

Taken in combination, these developments opened a new mission profile to the strategic bombers. They could be deployed over a battlefield once the air defenses had been suppressed and be maintained on station for many hours. During that time, they could provide the troops on the ground with precision-guided munitions support with much reduced waiting time. This was a valuable and effective operational technique, and the strategic bombers started to see an increased mission tempo in response to the new requirements.

In March 1999, the U.S. Air Force presented a "bomber roadmap" to Congress that stated it would not need to replace the "large payload, long range and rapid response characteristics" of the existing bomber fleet until 2037, assuming that it was able to sustain the existing B-52H, B-1B and B-2A aircraft with upgrades to improve maintainability, deployability and survivability. The Air Force also estimated that the B-1B would start to reach the end of its service life in 2018 and the B-2A in 2028, while the B-52H would still be viable in 2044. In a strategic attack mission, the B-52Hs would be tasked with launching cruise missiles rather than performing penetration missions. Therefore, any development work would be concentrated on replacing the B-1B and the B-2A in the penetration role. However, it was believed the new bombers would not be required until 2037, and, thus, that there was no need to start work on a replacement until 2034. This estimate probably represented the nadir of the strategic bomber force.

In response to the terrorist attacks of September 11, 2001 that destroyed the World Trade Center towers in New York and damaged the Pentagon, the United States committed to combating the al-Qaeda organization that had carried out the atrocities. The initial response was to engage the base area of al-Qaeda and the country that was giving the group refuge – Taliban-ruled Afghanistan. The mode of attack adopted was to send Special Forces advisors to assist Afghan United Front resistance fighters opposing the Taliban and to provide air support for their operations. The immediate results of this response were some highly innovative tactical concepts. Cavalry charges returned to the operational portfolio, only this time with the horsemen being supported by helicopter gunships.

The air operations part of this war revealed some limitations in the use of precision-guided munitions. They proved not to be that useful when trying to take on dispersed targets such as irregular troops in defensive (or offensive) positions. Also, they weren't that impressive to onlookers. A 250-pound guided munition may have exploded at exactly the right time and in exactly the right place to destroy its target, but it didn't look that destructive, something that harmed the morale of the irregulars being supported. There was a need for a solution that could engage targets dispersed over a wide area and be obviously, spectacularly, destructive. The answer was the B-52H.

The heavy bombers made their appearance at the battle of Mazar-i-Sharif where they carpet-bombed the Taliban defenders, inflicting heavy casualties and driving the remainder of the defenders into headlong retreat. The intervention of the Gray Lady was decisive in both driving the enemy back and providing a morale boost to the United Front troops, who appreciated the obvious destructive power of the carpet bombing. The victory at Mazar-i-Sharif showed that the heavy bombers were back in the game and that the role they could play was strategically decisive.

Bomber 2018

The first sign of renewed interest in the construction of strategic bombers came from Europe. In January 2002, Noel Forgeard, chief executive of Airbus, said, "When one sees the importance of the B-52 in Afghanistan, it underlines the fact that Europe does not have such a weapon. We could make some effort of imagination to see if an Airbus platform could be used." While this was, and remained, conceptual, it represented a significant change from the mindset of a decade earlier when European thought had condemned the B-1B and B-2A as the products of an outdated perception.

In 2004, the U.S. Air Force revealed a plan to field an "interim" heavy bomber starting in 2015 rather than wait until 2035. However, the Air Force was unable to include a budget for the interim heavy bomber into its existing five-year plan, so the program start was deferred to 2008, with the service entry date becoming 2018. The new interim heavy bomber therefore became known as Bomber 2018 and was included in the 2006 Quadrennial Defense Review. Northrop Grumman was the first company to make public a response to this initiative, offering a bomber variant of the X-47B remotely piloted aircraft capable of delivering a 30,000-pound bomb load over a 6,000-nautical-mile range with a sustained cruise speed of Mach 2 to Mach 2.4.

This proposal proved to be excessively ambitious. By March 2007, the Air Force had refined its requirements to a manned, subsonic bomber that could lift a payload of 28,000 pounds over an unrefueled radius of 2,000 nautical miles. The aircraft was to feature low-observable technology to penetrate hostile air defenses and then loiter over hostile territory to search for concealed or relocated targets. Essentially this aircraft was a downsized B-2A and fitted into the gap between the F-15E and the B-2A. Much emphasis was placed on the need to exploit existing technologies in order to reduce cost and technical risk. In early 2008, Boeing and Lockheed Martin teamed up to compete with Northrop Grumman for the Bomber 2018 program, which was believed to envision the procurement of around 100 aircraft.

The rest of 2008 was filled with a debate over whether Bomber 2018 was possible, what its role would be, whether it was affordable and how the design tasks would be approached. No funding for the new aircraft was included within the FY09 budget request. However, by the end of the debate (in which the Air Force itself maintained a dignified silence), Bomber 2018 was listed among the Air Force's top five priorities.

In 2008 a Democrat-controlled government was elected, and, as the Air Force was well aware, such governments have a track record of scrapping whatever bomber program the Air Force has at the time. Sure enough, Defense Secretary Robert Gates announced that Bomber 2018 was being scrubbed from procurement plans and that all development efforts pertaining to the aircraft had been terminated. Accordingly, funding requested for Bomber 2018 in the FY10 budget was deleted.

Next Generation Bomber

Despite this setback, the Air Force continued to invest in its new long-range strike aircraft under the program title "Next Generation Bomber." The primary reason for the demise of Bomber 2018 had been the impending START talks with the Russians and uncertainty over what the outcome of those talks would be. The Russians were known to be particularly concerned over the capabilities of the American strategic bomber fleet and were demanding onerous restrictions upon it. That, to a perceptive administration, should have been a strong indicator as to where the Russians believed the primary danger to them resided. The point was not lost on the Air Force, which specifically included a nuclear penetration mission in the portfolio for the Next Generation Bomber.

The new effort was kept alive by means of a $140 million funding line on the FY10 unfunded priorities statement. In September 2009, faced with almost unanimous opposition from both the House and Senate, Gates reversed his position and endorsed efforts to develop the Next Generation Bomber. He quoted rising Chinese military power as a major driver toward development of the new aircraft, citing their "investments in cyber and anti-satellite warfare, anti-air and anti-ship weaponry and ballistic missiles that could threaten America's primary way to project power and help allies in the Pacific – in particular our forward air bases and carrier strike groups."

Although the design concepts being explored with the Next Generation Bomber remained classified, a few details were beginning to leak out. One indicator was the construction of a new hangar at the Groom Lake Air Force test flight center. This was much larger than previous installations and was screened from public view by a specially built berm. Another indicator was a sudden interest in very high-altitude flight. The Air Force did not regard the B-2A as being survivable in daylight because of the risk of visual detection by fighter aircraft. However, at altitudes of over 60,000 feet, an aircraft was much less likely to be spotted visually and was screened by the darkness of the sky above it. Another issue that indicated the way the Air Force was thinking was the development of very large munitions such as the 30,000-pound Massive Ordnance Penetrator intended to destroy hardened and deeply buried targets. Surely, observers thought, the new bomber would be able to carry such weapons.

About this time in development of the Next Generation Bomber came a demand for a new-generation reconnaissance aircraft that would combine an intelligence, surveillance and reconnaissance (ISR) function using the same airframe. In effect, the ISR aircraft would be a strategic reconnaissance partner to the bombers. This is, of course, a throwback to the older concept where the B-36 and B-47 were partnered by the RB-36 and RB-47. Conceptually, the Next Generation Bomber was beginning to look rather like the programs that had been in development 60 years earlier, although the technologies being considered were beyond anything aircraft designers of the late 1940s could have envisioned.

The FY11 budget proposals revealed that the Air Force planned to invest $1.7 billion in development of the Next Generation Bomber over the next five years. Of this, $200 million was contained within the FY11 budget. The project entry-to-service date for the Next Generation Bomber was left unspecified, but was estimated to be between 2022 and 2026. At this time, the partnership agreement between Lockheed Martin and Boeing for the Next Generation Bomber was terminated, with each company going its own way on the proposed program. The new bomber development program then started to gain traction at last, with the aircraft being described as a stealthy, nuclear-hardened and nuclear-capable aircraft capable of carrying at least 20,000 pounds of ordnance over an operational radius of 4,000 nautical miles.

Long Range Strike - B

With the new aircraft finalized, the Next Generation Bomber was redesignated Long Range Strike-B (the B presumably standing for bomber), or LRS-B. This program was strongly endorsed by Defense Secretary Gates. In an interesting shift of paradigms, LRS-B would primarily be a conventional strike aircraft, with nuclear strike as a secondary mission. As details of the project trickled out, it became known that the Air Force planned a fleet of 80 to 100 of the new aircraft, at an estimated cost of $550 million each. Intriguingly, allowing for inflation this is exactly what the B-1A cost before its cancellation. The design would use as much existing state-of-the-art equipment as possible and exploit the development work of the F-22 and F-35 programs. Much of the development work needed would be assigned to the Rapid Capabilities Office to speed service introduction and cut down on bureaucratic delays. This, it was hoped, would allow Initial Operational Capability to be achieved by the original date of 2018.

The FY13 budget allocated $292 million to the LRS-B development, with the planned total funding through 2017 being $6.3 billion. At this point, speculation was already beginning to suggest that the original planned total of 80 to 100 aircraft was being increased to 175-200. The reasoning behind this is that after the 100th aircraft, the unit cost starts to drop quickly as economy of scale cuts in. Also, it was suggested that proposals to make the new aircraft "optionally manned" had been dropped, since the value of having crewmen in the immediate loop far exceeded the small savings that would be achieved by excluding a crew. A new added objective was to provide a supersonic dash capability, provided this could be combined with the required level of signature reduction. Stealth capability is no longer a substitute for speed but complementary to it.

The effect of fast-tracking the LRS-B would be significant, but it is still hard to see how the projected Initial Operational Capability date of 2020 will be met. This would require a schedule resembling the following:

- 2014 - Complete design, and start assembly process
- 2016 - Deliver first aircraft for developmental testing
- 2017 - Operational Test & Evaluation
- 2018 - Begin deliveries to Training unit (four aircraft)
- 2019 - Begin deliveries to Operational Squadron
- 2020 - Eight aircraft in one Operational Bomb Squadron to achieve IOC

This is a very tight and ambitious time scale unless a significant part of this program already exists in hardware form. Back in 2007 it was revealed that Northrop Grumman had received as much as $3 billion in funding for an unidentified black program, which may have been related to the 2018 Bomber concept. If this connection is true, then it is quite likely that significant work has already been done on a basic stealthy airframe. If this is indeed the case, the 2020 date suddenly becomes much more plausible. It may well be that Northrop Grumman already has a near-perfected design that can go quickly to full development, flight testing and production.

It is also quite possible that the LRS-B is not a new aircraft at all but a logical, linear development of the existing B-2, much as the F/A-18E/F was a linear development of the F/A-18C/D. This does not, of course, preclude the argument presented in the previous paragraph. The B-2A is a child of 1980s technology and design art. It uses signature reduction techniques that are laborious, a maintenance liability and a major contributor to the B-2A's low overall availability. For example, panel joins and doors all need to have their joints covered with a special radar-absorptive tape that needs to be regularly peeled off and replaced if routine maintenance is to be performed. The radar-absorptive coating that covers the B-2A airframe is also a major maintenance burden. These features demand that B-2s be housed in special climate-controlled hangars that exist only at Whiteman AFB in Missouri, Diego Garcia in the Indian Ocean, and Guam. This limits deployment of the B-2 and the number of sorties that the aircraft can undertake.

In a developed derivative of the B-2, both products will be replaced by new coatings that are much easier to repair and/or replace, with the down-time needed to apply and cure the coatings decreasing from days to minutes.

Another major change has been the power of the computers used in designing the aircraft. The B-2 was designed in the earliest days of computational flight dynamics (CFD) before the complex airflow over an aircraft could be modeled in three dimensions. As a result, the design compromise between aerodynamics and signatures was weighted toward the simplest aircraft shapes. Now, more than 30 years later, computer calculating power and memory have increased to the point where much better signature management can be combined with shapes that offer higher efficiency and improved safety margins. This may also allow increased performance from flying wing design aircraft that have previously been limited in this regard.

These changes appear to make a less costly but better performing development of the basic B-2 concept plausible. This is especially the case if the tooling for B-2 production is still in storage. Apparently, the most recent U.S. military aircraft tooling to be destroyed was for the F/FB-111 in 2001, the KC-135 in 1995, and the B-52 in 1990. The tooling for all aircraft newer than the F/FB-111 except the F-4 is still stored, mostly at Davis Monthan AFB.

Further into the Future

While current efforts are concentrated on the LRS-B (which seems set to become the B-3), this aircraft is still only an interim bomber intended to maintain the strategic bomber fleet at acceptable numerical and readiness levels. The 2037 date for another new bomber that will be of a much more radical design is still in place. This aircraft will face a world where new technology weapons are likely to make much accepted wisdom about air operations highly questionable at best. For example, it is probable that directed energy weapons will have made their service debut by then. Sensor technologies will have improved dramatically, with multiple types of sensor being netted together so that the weaknesses of one will be offset by another. The constantly increasing speed and data-handling capacity of computer networks will also tend to reduce the command loop decision times. All of these factors will combine to make for a much more hazardous environment for aircraft.

Some of the effects of these developments are already becoming apparent. Defense against ballistic missiles was once considered to be a technologically challenging task that required the skills of the most scientifically advanced nations. In fact, this was an inaccurate assessment, and shooting down ballistic missiles was always much easier than opponents of such systems were prepared to admit. The problem was that the speed of the inbound missiles was such that reacting within the timeframe available pushed data networking to its limits. Now that this problem has been overcome by modern computer capabilities, the spread of anti-ballistic missile systems is worldwide. More than a dozen nations are actively working to develop or install such systems, and not all of them are friendly toward the United States.

Low-observable technology itself is coming under attack. The F-117 had a high degree of immunity against the higher-frequency radars used for target acquisition and fire control, but its ability to evade low-frequency long-range search radars was less well-developed. This led to the situation where radars designed during World War Two and immediately afterwards were dusted off, given a superficial revamp, and marketed as "anti-stealth radars," since their very low frequencies by modern standards gave them significant capability against F-117-style targets. The B-2A was a different design, optimized for maximum signature reduction against long-range, low-frequency surveillance radars. Its performance against high-frequency sets was not so good, this being accepted on the grounds that it could detect such sets and go around them.

Already, netting both types of radar together is being presented as one way of detecting the intrusion of stealthy aircraft into contested airspace. However, there is a more elegant way of resolving the problem. Most modern radars are software controlled and their emission characteristics can be manipulated within very wide boundaries. Furthermore, their data extraction and plotting capabilities are such that they can tease out even otherwise-inconsequential contacts from the mass of returns that they receive. Taken together, these developments place grave demands on the designers attempting future radar cross-section reductions.

The problem with low-observable technologies is that once they are countered, the aircraft using them have very little left in the way of evasive capability. The presumption is that by 2037, stealth technology will have seen the end of its reign and attention will have reverted to avoiding the defenses by flying higher than they can reach and faster than they can respond. This perception was reflected by one observer of the 2037 bomber, who remarked, "High and fast is the new stealth." One can imagine the ghosts of the B-70 design team nodding in agreement. It seems generally accepted that the 2037 bomber will be hypersonic, reaching at least Mach 6 and possibly twice that. It will exploit new engine technologies that will allow it to fly at altitudes of over 250,000 feet. Whether or not it will have a pilot is open to debate, with the proponents of having "a pilot in the loop" pitted against those promoting the advantages that allegedly accrue by adopting a pilotless configuration. It may well be that both will be successful and the piloted aircraft will be the command ship for a supporting group of unpiloted machines.

Both LRS-B and Bomber 2037 are "first day systems," intended to take on the best that the defenses can offer and win through. Yet, as we have seen, another mission has grown that does not require such capability. This "second day" mission requires long endurance so the aircraft can loiter over a relatively benign battlefield and deliver a heavy load of guided munitions to support the troops fighting on the ground below. This requirement is probably more relevant to the conflicts being fought today than the "first day" mission, yet is not addressed by either the LRS-B or Bomber 2037. There is a definite requirement for such a "bomb truck" that is not, as far as is known, being addressed.

It is an interesting thought that in 1937, the U.S. Army Air Corps was just introducing the first of its real strategic bombers. The B-17 lumbered along at 190 mph to carry a maximum of 9,600 pounds of bombs over a tactical radius of 800 miles. Bomber 2037 looks set to cruise to its target at speeds in excess of 4,000 mph, carrying 28,000 pounds of bombs over a tactical radius of 5,000 miles. The world has certainly changed.

In Conclusion. . . . .

What The Future May Hold.
Source: U.S. Air Force

Looking back over the history of strategic bombers, one thing leaps out. They have always been at the cutting edge of the technology available at the time. There was a world of difference between the sleek, heavily armed B-17s and the ungainly biplanes that preceded them. Yet, within a few years, the B-29 had arrived, bringing with it a level of size and firepower that made the Flying Fortress seem an ungainly anachronism. Yet, the B-29 itself was to reign for only a short time before it, too, was relegated to the ranks of obsolescence by the much larger and more capable B-36. This pattern was to continue, with each new generation of bomber being an improvement on the last. This progression was inevitable, since the strategic bomber was in competition with air defense systems from the moment of its inception.

Cost-effectiveness

The question of whether the investment made in the strategic bomber fleets prior to the introduction of nuclear weapons was justified by the results they achieved is the subject of prolonged and vigorous debate. There is little doubt that the claims made for the strategy of strategic bombing prior to World War Two were massively overstated. In the early part of World War Two, bombers were only just barely capable of penetrating air defenses in daylight, and when they tried, their casualties were appalling. They had to retreat to bombing under cover of darkness, a shift that brought problems all of their own. Simply finding targets at night was hard enough; hitting them with the bomb loads in use at the time was virtually impossible. When German propaganda broadcasts described the efforts of Bomber Command in 1940-42 as "scattering bombs at random over northwest Germany," they were (for once) telling the truth. Hitting the wrong city was commonplace; bombing the wrong country was not unknown.

As experience grew this situation changed, and both the British Bomber Command and the U.S. Army Air Force became proficient at finding their targets and destroying them. The question was whether the effort expended in doing so was justified by the results achieved. The cost of the strategic bomber fleets was undoubtedly high. In the case of the United States, the creation of the bomber fleet made the difference between the 200-division Army projected in mobilization plans from 1935 and the 95-division Army actually built in 1941-45. In Britain, Bomber Command cost the British taxpayer the enormous sum of £2.8 billion to £3.5 billion – out of a total defense expenditure of £23.1 billion and total government expenditure of £28.7 billion. Thus, about 10 percent of the British war effort was invested in the strategic bombing of Germany.

The other side of the ledger is harder to assess. Opponents of the World War Two bombing campaign are fond of pointing out that German war production actually increased while the bombing campaign was at its height. This is true but misses the obvious point: by how much more would it have increased if German cities had not been reduced to burned-out rubble? The bombing also forced the Germans to divert much of their war production into an eventually futile effort to defend their cities and their war production base. For example, the Germans ringed their cities with 20,000 heavy anti-aircraft guns. Those guns were the same "88s" that were very effective anti-tank guns. They were desperately needed on the Russian Front, and the German Army suffered greatly from their absence. In the final analysis, while the costs of strategic bombing in World War Two can be measured with a high degree of accuracy, its achievements cannot.

Typical Damage To Cities in Germany by 1945
Source: RAF Bomber Command

Nuclear weapons changed everything. World War Two had proved that targets were much more difficult to destroy than had been believed and that large numbers of aircraft carrying heavy bomb loads had to make repeated visits to such targets in order to ensure their destruction. When the U.S. dropped atomic devices on Hiroshima and Nagasaki, it demonstrated that a single bomber making one mission could destroy such targets. The cost-effectiveness measurement had swung decisively and finally in favor of strategic bombardment – provided nuclear weapons were used.

Air Defenses

Nuclear weapons had a more subtle effect than just allowing massive destruction on a much compressed time scale. They also presented air defense systems with challenges that dwarfed those of earlier years.

From the earliest days of the strategic bomber, those who expounded its virtues had faced opposition from those who proclaimed it to be obsolete. The basis behind these claims was always that some new development in air defense technology had rendered the bombers so vulnerable that they could not penetrate defenses based around this development. The technical developments in question included new engines for fighters that increased their top speed and rate of climb so that they had a better chance of intercepting the inbound bombers, new types of fire control for anti-aircraft guns that gave them better chances of hitting the bombers, sound detectors that gave improved warning of the bomber's approach, and so on. Throughout the 1920s and 1930s, the arguments were entirely theoretical, with claims that "the bomber is obsolete" being matched by equally unsupported claims that "the bomber will always get through." The development of radar in the late 1930s only added to the controversy. The outbreak of World War Two therefore was the first time that the opposing claims were subjected to practical verification.

It quickly became apparent that neither claim was absolutely correct. The technology developments that had taken place had affected both the offense and the defense, improving the capabilities of both. The fighters might be faster and climb more rapidly, but the bombers flew higher and were more heavily armed. The guns may be more accurate, but the bombers' improved performance made them more difficult targets. In the eternal battle between offense and defense, practical experience showed that the advantage lay with the offense, but only by a tiny margin. The bomber would always get through; during the whole of World War Two, no bomber raid was ever turned back by the defenses. But the cost was sometimes frightful. Over Schweinfurt, 60 B-17s out of 291 were shot down, representing 20.6 percent of the attackers. At Ploesti, 53 out of 177 B-24s were lost, a casualty rate of 29.99 percent. Schweinfurt in particular was a crucial case because it represented a perfect example for the defense. The B-17s were deep in hostile territory, flying to a known target that was ringed by anti-aircraft guns, and were subjected to waves of fighter attacks by top-of-the-line aircraft that had plenty of time to return to base, rearm and refuel, and then rejoin the battle. The casualty rate of 20 percent quickly became the "Schweinfurt Number," or the level of casualties that a competent air defense system could expect to inflict on a competent bomber force under near-ideal circumstances.

Air Defenses At Work
Source: U.S. Army Air Force

The Schweinfurt Number was alarming since it implied that a bomber could be expected to make only five missions before it and its crew were lost. Combined with the realization that destroying industrial targets meant repeated missions by large numbers of aircraft, this analysis suggested that the cost of a strategic air warfare campaign against a competent opponent might be more costly than any nation could be expected to endure. The bomber might always get through, but it would not be able to do so often enough to achieve the desired strategic aim. In effect, the Schweinfurt Number represented a victory for the defense.

Once again, it was the atomic bomb that made the difference. It only needed one aircraft to penetrate the defenses and reach its target and that target would be destroyed. This realization turned the Schweinfurt Number on its head. Against bombers armed with conventional weapons, achieving the Schweinfurt Number was a disaster for the offense; it meant that the bombers could not survive to attain their objective. Faced with nuclear-armed aircraft, the Schweinfurt Number was a disaster for the defense; it meant that 80 percent of the bombers would get through to destroy their targets, and that meant devastation on an unparalleled scale.

Furthermore, the atomic weapons were relatively light. Aircraft carrying them were able to fly faster and higher than they would when loaded down with large conventional bomb loads. In the late 1940s and early 1950s, air defenses were almost completely ineffective against high-flying B-36s armed with nuclear weapons.

Enter SAMS

Once again, the battle between air defenses and the bombers became one of claim and counter-claim. This time, the protagonists were the designers of surface-to-air missiles and the fully integrated air defense systems that combined them with missile-armed interceptors. This renewed debate was complicated by the need to consider the likely development of the systems in question during their service life. Aircraft were taking longer to develop and, when in service, they were likely to remain in the front line for much longer. This meant they had to be capable of facing both current and future threats. The 1950s debate was largely dominated by just how extensive those developments were likely to be.

Missile Threat 1960: SA-2 Guideline
Source: U.S. Army

This debate reached a crisis point over the period 1957-1959. Encouraged by the rapid rate of missile development in the early to mid-1950s, the missile design teams saw no reason why that development rate should not continue. Their projections for the performance of missile systems in 10 and 20 years' time were, therefore, extremely ambitious. If fulfilled, they would succeed in driving aircraft off the battlefield completely. Therefore, the case was made that there was no point in developing manned aircraft at all. In Britain, this argument was taken at face value. In Duncan Sandys' 1957 Defense White Paper, it was stated that guided missiles would replace both high-flying bombers carrying nuclear weapons and fast interceptor fighter aircraft trying to stop them. As a result, virtually all major manned aircraft programs were canceled and the British military aviation industry never recovered.

The largely theoretical debates of the late 1950s and early 1960s were put to practical test during the Vietnam War, three Arab-Israeli wars, and a number of other conflicts. These reiterated the lessons that had been learned a quarter of a century earlier. Air defense systems were far less effective than had been suggested; the same technical developments that had increased their lethality also enhanced the ability of aircraft to penetrate those defenses. Electronic technology had made surface-to-air guided missiles possible, but had also created the electronic warfare equipment needed to defend against them. Air-to-air guided missiles proved much less lethal than had been feared (or hoped, according to whether one was firing them or dodging them). Where kill rates in the 80 and 90 percent range had been expected, actual achievements were in the area of 2 to 10 percent. Despite the new technologies being deployed, the Schweinfurt Number remained the yardstick by which the efficiency of defense systems was judged, and it was a target that was seldom reached.

Once again, actual experience turned out to be a learning curve that was sometimes costly but winnowed out many false assumptions. For example, low-altitude penetration was found not to be the panacea that had been assumed. Short-range automatic gunfire proved to be as lethal to low-altitude aircraft as it had been in World War Two, but there was a lot more of it. Soldiers had been directed to fire blindly into the sky at the approach of hostile aircraft, trying to fill the area of sky an aircraft had to fly through with bullets. That didn't often work, but it did bring down the odd aircraft. By the end of the 1960s, the shoulder-fired anti-aircraft missile was commonplace, and it was making low-altitude operations over the battlefield increasingly dangerous. The key to evading missiles was spotting them and the more time there was to achieve that, the better. Thus, it began to appear that medium or high altitude offered better protection than low altitude. Low down, everything could shoot at the intruding aircraft. As altitude increased, the number of systems that could do so was progressively reduced until only the cream of the crop remained effective.

Integrated Air Defense Systems

Once the wars of the late 1960s and early 1970s were over and their lessons absorbed, the cycle started again. New technologies including data fusion, and multiple-redundant air defense networks were being introduced. Combined with a new generation of anti-aircraft missiles, these were, once again, promoted as spelling the end of the manned attack aircraft.

Developing these integrated air defense systems and the new anti-aircraft missiles proved to be much harder than the designers had anticipated. The air defense systems showed all the problems of systems integration that were commonplace in programs of that nature during the last years of the 20th century. They worked reasonably well on a small scale, but when they were expanded to include larger numbers of systems and cover a greater area, the computers and data transmission networks overloaded and crashed. Missiles also proved much harder to develop than had been anticipated, which was ironic since their projected performance levels were still much lower than the designers of the 1950s had projected for the late 1960s. In fact, the surface-to-air missile performance projected in the 1950s remains a distant target.

Missile Threat 2012: S-400 Triumf
Source: U.S. Army

Once again, when put to the test of combat in the real world, the new integrated air defense systems and their missiles and fighters proved incapable of producing the leak-proof defense that had been promised. By the time they had been designed and tested, their faults corrected, and their operators trained, the air forces they opposed had already developed the tactics needed to overcome them. A combination of stealth technology, precision-guided munitions, and finely honed offensive tactics took the integrated air defense systems down. This was easy to say, not so easy to achieve, but it was doable with the correct training and equipment. What those air defense systems did achieve was to ensure that the primary effort of the first couple of days and nights would be directed against those air defense systems. However, once suppression had been achieved, the aircraft they had been intended to defend against were free to operate at will.

Looking back over the history of the strategic bomber, the battle for supremacy between bomber and air defense system has been hard-fought. However, the bombers maintained their strategic supremacy over the defense even if the margins were, at times, desperately close. The bomber did always get through, as its proponents in the 1920s had predicted; it was just that sometimes not many of them came back.

Offensive Missiles

During the latter stages of the long, drawn-out battle against air defense systems, the manned strategic bomber had to fight another battle. This one was against a rival offensive system also intended to attack the heartland of the enemy and destroy his military industries and production infrastructure. That rival was the intercontinental ballistic missile, or ICBM. While the bomber has continued to defeat air defense systems, the conflict with the ICBM has essentially been lost. Today, in most strategic arsenals, the ICBM (along with its submarine-launched analog, the SLBM) is the primary means of strategic attack, with the manned bombers taking a secondary and supporting role.

LGM-118 Peacekeeper Fired From Hardened Silo
Source: U.S. Air Force

Ballistic missiles were claimed to have several advantages over manned bombers in the strategic attack role. These included being significantly less expensive than bombers, being impossible to shoot down, and providing a much faster response time to target. Missiles installed in hardened silos were also claimed to be more difficult to pre-empt, whereas bombers, it was alleged, could be caught on the ground by a surprise attack. It was these arguments that were used to justify the cancellation of the B-70 Valkyrie and the cut-back of the USAF bomber fleet.

In fact, all of these assertions were arguable and some were flat-out wrong. On the issue of cost, a single Minuteman I missile cost $1.315 million ($9.8 million in 2010 dollars), equating to 22 percent of the cost of a B-52E. However, the missile carried one warhead; the B-52 usually carried six (four gravity devices and two stand-off missiles). Thus, on a per-warhead delivered basis, the B-52 was actually around a third less expensive. Although the adoption of Multiple Independently targeted Re-entry vehicles (MIRVs) increased the number of warheads per missile, this was matched by increases in bomber load-out and the basic equation remained unchanged. In addition, the hardened silos required for the missiles cost between $14 million and $16 million. Thus, the cost of missile and silo was around $16-$17 million, and that did not include the other infrastructure needed for missile operation. This was virtually the same as the cost of a B-70 and more than double the cost of a B-52. In contrast, the bombers could be operated from any large airfield.

As we have discussed, the vulnerability of the bombers was also overstated, and the ability of defensive systems to shoot down inbound missiles was drastically underestimated. A moment's thought should have suggested that if it was easy to hit high-flying, high-speed bombers that could maneuver to avoid inbound missiles and shoot back at the defensive systems while using sophisticated electronic warfare techniques, shooting down a missile re-entry vehicle that was coming in on a mathematically predictable straight line course without any ability to maneuver, defend itself, or jam the defenses should have been much easier still. In fact, the ability to shoot down inbound missiles was demonstrated in 1959, and by 1964 the Zeus missile system was scoring kills with a high degree of probability. Ballistic missile defense was a demonstrated practical reality by 1965 and was only prevented from deployment by political decisions.

In contrast to the cost and vulnerability arguments, the danger that the bombers would be caught on the ground was a real one that was of significant concern to SAC. A partial answer was the Minimum Interval Take Off, or MITO. This could clear an airfield in 15 minutes, while 20 minutes' warning of an attack could be expected. Thus, the safety margin was tight but doable. However, the bombers had the advantage that they were recallable. They could take off, make their way to their assembly points (popularly known as fail-safe points), and wait there in comparative safety until they were either recalled or ordered to make their attacks. Typically, those assembly points were two hours' flying time, roughly 1,200 miles, from their targets. In contrast, missiles could not be recalled. Contrary to popular belief, ICBMs had neither abort nor self-destruct systems. Once launched, they were on their way to their targets and no change of mind was possible. It became apparent that this irreversibility was a serious problem and the launch order could only be given once positive proof of an enemy attack was received. Essentially this meant nuclear warheads initiating on or over U.S. territory. The lesson was that the bombers *might* be caught on the ground but the missiles *would* be and would have to rely on their silos to protect them until they could be launched.

The time to target argument was also much better founded than the cost and vulnerability issues. The bombers would take hours to reach their targets – two hours from their assembly points – while the flight time for the missiles from their launch silos was around 30-45 minutes. The B-70 would have solved this problem – from their assembly points the B-70s were 25 minutes from their targets and would get there 20 minutes before the ICBMs arrived. The critical point, though, was that the bombers could be recalled any time up to the point where they finally released their nuclear weapons. This gave the governments a final chance to avert the impending holocaust. Once the missiles were fired they were on their way, and no last-minute decisions could stop them. The time to target issue had another aspect. Bombers could be contacted and retargeted so that targets that would be missed because the bomber assigned to them had been lost could be reassigned to another aircraft. Missiles could not be, so losses inflicted by a defense system could not be compensated.

In retrospect, it appears that the decisions made in the 1950s were correct and the bomber and ICBM were complementary systems. This suggests that the reliance on ICBMs from the 1960s onward was an error. Perhaps with a new generation of strategic bombers in development, this error can be remedied.

APPENDIX ONE

AIRCRAFT COST BREAKDOWN
($ thousands)

Aircraft	Year	Airframe	Engines	Weapons	Electronics	Misc.	Total Then-year $	Total 2010 $
B-29	1945	399.541	109.194	3.977	34.738	91.738	639.188	7,659.224
B-36B	1949	1,384.418	388.498	30.241	55.974	640.869	2,500.000	22,390.567
B-36D	1951	2,530.112	774.117	30.241	55.974	747.681	4,138.125	34,348.460
B-36H	1953	2,077.785	1,088.712	30.241	80.272	872.436	4,149.446	33,433.540
B-36J	1954	1,969.271	853.837	32.036	77.691	707.379	3,640.214	29,301.760
B-47B	1952	1,767.094	283.082	5.336	43.835	350.109	2,449.456	19,894.010
B-47E	1953	1,293.420	262.805	6.298	53.733	253.411	1,869.667	15,064.560
B-50A	1946	684.894	258.999	5.524	71.369	123.060	1,143.846	12,632.640
B-52A	1952	26,433.518	2,848.120	9.193	50.761	47.874	29,389.466	238,695.620
B-52B	1953	11,328.398	2,547.472	11.520	61.198	482.284	14,430.872	116,274.580
B-52C	1954	5,359.017	1,513.220	10.983	71.397	293.346	7,247.963	58,108.830
B-52D	1955	4,654.494	1,291.415	17.928	68.613	548.353	6,580.803	52,971.920
B-52E	1956	3,700.750	1,256.516	4.626	54.933	931.665	5,948.490	43,605.800
B-52F	1957	3,772.247	1,787.191	3.016	60.111	862.839	6,485.404	49,645.290
B-52G	1959	5,351.819	1,427.611	6.809	66.374	840.000	7,692.613	56,883.190
B-52H	1960	6,076.157	1,640.373	6.804	61.020	1,501.422	9,285.776	67,582.540
B-58A	1960	6,447.702	1,117.120	26.674	1,294.791	3,555.573	12,441.860	90,552.750
B-70B	1963	6,006.000	4,500.000	0	2,589.582	4,977.802	18,073.384	127,292.486
FB-111A	1970						15,789.473	87,652.740
B-1B	1984						283,000.000	586,064.080
B-2A	1990						737,000.000	1,213,611.000
LRS-B	2010						550,000.000	550,000.000

Source: Post-World War II Bombers, by Marcelle Size Knaack

The above table shows the procurement costs of the bombers covered in this book. The last two columns show the full flyaway cost of the bombers complete with warload. One is for the years in which the aircraft was procured, the other adjusted for inflation to show the cost in 2010 dollars. What is immediately apparent from this table is the importance of mass production. This is critically important in unit-cost terms, as the small production runs of the B-1 and (especially) the B-2 had an overwhelming effect on unit costs. The importance of mass production can be gauged from the examples of the B-29 and B-50. The unit flyaway cost of the B-50 was 80 percent greater than that of the B-29 a year earlier, despite the similarity of the two aircraft. The difference between the two was in numbers built: almost 5,000 B-29s, but only 250 B-50s. The B-52s show a similar pattern, with astronomical costs for the first B-52As (which also carried the development costs), but a rapid decline in unit flyaway costs as production ramped up. This table also dispels the myth that the B-70 was an especially expensive aircraft. It cost 50 percent more than the B-58 and twice as much as a B-52H, but it brought unprecedented capability. The suggestion that it was exceptionally expensive stemmed from the circulation of cost figures for the pair of XB-70s that carried the research and development costs originally intended to be spread across a dozen prototypes.

APPENDIX TWO
SOURCES

As primary source material, this book extracted from two sets of official documents issued by the United States Air Force. One set is the Characteristics Summary (CS), and the other is the Standard Aircraft Characteristics (SAC). These are held by the United States Air Force Museum at Wright-Patterson Air Force Base, and both are in the public domain. PDF scans of these documents are available at two known online locations. One of these is the Hyperwar electronic document archive at http://www.ibiblio.org/hyperwar/USN/SAC/ and the other is the Alternate Wars resource center at http://www.alternatewars.com/SAC/SAC.htm. These sites contain a wealth of information that resolves many debates and casts light upon the issues in question. However, being online, both sites might suffer the Internet fate of vanishing or being hacked to destruction. (All too many valuable online resources have suffered such fates.) One of the motives behind preparing this book and the following volumes in the series was to preserve these documents in a more permanent form. The Characteristics Summary and Standard Aircraft Characteristics are also available in hard copy from the Air Force Historical Research Agency at Maxwell Air Force Base.

It is probably not surprising to learn that the content of both the Characteristics Summary and Standard Aircraft Characteristics is based upon a detailed and exhaustive specification that is 43 pages long. It is obvious from reading this document that the CS and SAC represent efforts to present the performance details of the aircraft they describe as fairly and accurately as possible. These are not public relations documents; they were classified information for many years and their equivalents for the latest types still are. As far as is possible, they have been faithfully reproduced in this book. Due to their age and haphazard use, and because they were printed on poor-quality paper, they had deteriorated badly. We have cleaned them up by removing dirt, tears and extraneous markings. We have neatened up straight lines that were distorted or damaged during the reproduction process. Sadly, some of the original pencil artwork dating from the 1940s had deteriorated beyond repair and had to be replaced by photographs. However, the data in these documents has not been changed. It is still the product of the exacting standards laid down by the USAF more than 60 years ago.

In preparing the text sections of this book, much reliance was placed on the following books.

American Combat Planes, Third Enlarged Edition, Ray Wagner, Doubleday, 1982

The B-1 Bomber, Aero Series Volume 32, William G. Holder

B-29 Superfortress, John Pimlott, Gallery Books, 1980

The Boeing B-47, Peter Bowers, Aircraft in Profile, Doubleday, 1968

Boeing Aircraft Since 1916, Peter M. Bowers, Naval Institute Press, 1989

Boeing B-52 - A Documentary History, Walter Boyne, Smithsonian Institution Press, 1981

Boeing's Cold War Warrior - B-52 Stratofortress, Robert F. Dorr and Lindsay Peacock, Osprey Aerospace, 1995

Convair B-36: A Comprehensive History of America's "Big Stick," Meyers K. Jacobsen, Schiffer Military History, 1997

Convair B-58 Hustler: The World's First Supersonic Bomber, Jay Miller, Aerofax, 1997

Decisions of Robert S. McNamara, James M. Roherty, University of Maryland Libraries, 1970

F-111 Aardvark - USAF's Ultimate Strike Aircraft, Tony Thornborough, Osprey Aerospace, 1993

F-111 Aardvark, Hans Halberstadt, Specialty Press, 1992

Fifty-Year War: Conflict and Strategy in the Cold War, Norman Friedman, Naval Institute Press, 2007

General Dynamics Aircraft and their Predecessors, John Wegg, Naval Institute Press, 1990

LeMay: The Life and Wars of General Curtis LeMay, Warren Kozak, Regnery History, 2011

Mission with LeMay, General Curtis E. LeMay, Doubleday, 1965

North American Aircraft 1934-1999, Volume 2, Kevin Thompson, Narkiewicz//Thompson, 1999

Northrop Flying Wings, Edward T. Maloney, World War II Publications, 1988

Post-World War II Bombers, Marcelle Size Knaack, Office of Air Force History, 1988

Post-World War II Fighters: 1945-1973, Marcelle Size Knaack, Office of Air Force History, 1986

Superfortress: The Boeing B-29 and American Airpower in World War II, General Curtis LeMay, Westholme Publishing

Terrorism, Afghanistan, and America's New Way of War, Norman Friedman, Naval Institute Press, 2003

The Price of Vigilance: Attacks on American Surveillance Flights, Larry Tart and Robert Keefe, Ballantine Books, 2002

United States Military Aircraft Since 1909, Gordon Swanborough and Peter M. Bowers, Smithsonian, 1989

Valkyrie: North American's Mach 3 Superbomber, Dennis R. Jenkins & Tony R. Landis, Specialty Press Publishers

Valkyrie: The North American XB-70: The USA's Ill-Fated Supersonic Heavy Bomber, Graham M. Simons, Pen and Sword Publishers, 2012

We Were Crewdogs, Tommy Towery, Amazon Digital Services, 2005

www.ingramcontent.com/pod-product-compliance
Lightning Source LLC
Chambersburg PA
CBHW080543230426
43663CB00015B/2690